Lecture Notes of the Institute for Computer Sciences, Social Informatics and Telecommunications Engineering 252

More information about this series at http://www.springer.com/series/8197

Imed Romdhani · Lei Shu
Hara Takahiro · Zhangbing Zhou
Timothy Gordon · Deze Zeng (Eds.)

Collaborative Computing: Networking, Applications and Worksharing

13th International Conference, CollaborateCom 2017
Edinburgh, UK, December 11–13, 2017
Proceedings

 Springer

Editors
Imed Romdhani
Edinburgh Napier University
Edinburgh
UK

Lei Shu
Guangdong University of Petrochemical
  Technology
Maoming
China

Hara Takahiro
Osaka University
Osaka
Japan

Zhangbing Zhou
China University of Geosciences
Beijing
China

Timothy Gordon
University of Nebraska–Lincoln
Lincoln
UK

Deze Zeng
School of Computer Science
China University of Geosciences
Wuhan, Hubei
China

ISSN 1867-8211   ISSN 1867-822X (electronic)
Lecture Notes of the Institute for Computer Sciences, Social Informatics
and Telecommunications Engineering
ISBN 978-3-030-00915-1   ISBN 978-3-030-00916-8 (eBook)
https://doi.org/10.1007/978-3-030-00916-8

Library of Congress Control Number: 2018954768

This Springer imprint is published by the registered company Springer Nature Switzerland AG
The registered company address is: Gewerbestrasse 11, 6330 Cham, Switzerland

Preface

We are delighted to introduce the proceedings of the 13th edition of the 2017 European Alliance for Innovation (EAI) International Conference on Collaborative Computing: Networking, Applications and Worksharing (CollaborateCom). This conference has brought together researchers, developers, and practitioners from around the world who are leveraging and developing collaboration between distributed teams of humans, computer applications, and/or autonomous robots to achieve higher productivity and produce joint products that would have been impossible to develop without the contributions of multiple collaborators.

The technical program of CollaborateCom 2017 consisted of 65 papers, in oral presentation sessions during the main conference tracks. The three-day conference included ten sessions. Aside from the high-quality technical paper presentations, the technical program also featured one keynote speech titled "Converged Technology for Intelligent Airport Services." The keynote speaker was Prof. Henry Wang from the University of West London, UK.

Coordination between the Steering Committee and the Organizing Committee was essential for the success of the conference. We sincerely appreciate the support and guidance of the general chairs: Prof. Takahiro Hara, Lei Shu and Imed Romdhani. We would like to thank the program chairs: Zhangbing Zhou, Timothy Gordon, and Takahiro Hara, who supervised the review process of the technical papers and compiled a high-quality technical program. We greatly appreciate the excellent support and hard work of the local chair, Prof. Imed Romdhani. We are also grateful to the conference manager, Dominika Belisova, for her support, and all the authors who submitted their papers to the CollaborateCom 2017 conference.

We strongly believe that the CollaborateCom conference provides a good forum for all researchers, developers, and practitioners to discuss all science and technology aspects that are relevant to collaborative computing. We also expect that the future CollaborateCom conference will be as successful and stimulating as indicated by the contributions presented in this volume.

August 2018

Imed Romdhani
Lei Shu
Hara Takahiro
Zhangbing Zhou
Timothy Gordon
Deze Zeng

Organization

Steering Committee

Imrich Chlamtac	EAI/Create-Net, Italy
Song Guo	University of Aizu, Japan
Bo Li	The Hong Kong University of Science and Technology, SAR China
Xiaofei Liao	Huazhong University of Science and Technology, China

Organizing Committee

Honorable Chair

Qinghua Zhang (President)	Guangdong University of Petrochemical Technology, China

General Co-chairs

Lei Shu	Guangdong University of Petrochemical Technology, China/University of Lincoln, UK
Takahiro Hara	Osaka University, Japan
Imed Romdhani	Edinburgh Napier University, UK

TPC Co-chairs

Timothy Gordon	University of Lincoln, UK
Zhangbing Zhou	China University of Geosciences, Beijing, China/TELECOM SudParis, France

General Track Co-chairs

Liehuang Zhu	Beijing Institute of Technology, China
Jianwei Niu	Beihang University, China

Track 1 Co-chairs

Jianwu Wang	University of Maryland, Baltimore County, USA
Zhuofeng Zhao	North China University of Technology, China

Track 2 Co-chairs

Yucong Duan	Hainan University, China
Antonella Longo	University of Salento, Italy

Track 3 Co-chairs

Shigang Yue	University of Lincoln, UK
Farshad Arvin	University of Manchester, UK

Track 4 Co-chairs

Helge Janicke	De Montfort University, UK
Leandros Maglaras	De Montfort University, UK/ABMS Open University, Switzerland

Local Co-chairs

Jiafu Wan	South China University of Technology, Guangzhou, China
Jianfeng Huang	Guangdong University of Petrochemical Technology, China

Workshops Co-chairs

Peng Li	University of Aizu, Japan
Chunsheng Zhu	The University of British Columbia, Canada

Publicity Co-chairs

Oli Mival	Edinburgh Napier University, UK
Weipeng Jing	Northeast Forestry University, China
Daichi Amagata	Osaka University, Japan

Posters and PhD Track Chair

Mithun Mukherjee	Guangdong University of Petrochemical Technology, China

Publication Co-chairs

Fei Lei	Beijing University of Technology, China
Deze Zeng	China University of Geosciences, Wuhan, China

Demo Chair

Amjad Mehmood	Guangdong University of Petrochemical Technology, China

Poster/Demo Co-chair

Sanjay Madria	Missouri University of Science and Technology, USA

Sponsorship Co-chairs

Li Yan	Guangdong University of Petrochemical Technology, China
Guangjie Han	Hohai University, China

Web Chair

Zhiqiang Huo   University of Lincoln, UK

Special Sessions

Special Session: Internet of Things

Special Session Chair
Ahmed Al-Dubai   Edinburgh Napier University, UK

Special Session: Collaborative Next Generation Networking

Special Session Co-chairs
Deze Zeng   China University of Geosciences, Wuhan, China
Heng Qi   Dalian University of Technology, China

Special Session: Collaboration Techniques in Data-Intensive Cloud Computing

Special Session Co-chairs
Shaojie Qiao   Chengdu University of Information Technology, China
Cheqing Jin   East China Normal University, China
Hongzhi Wang   Harbin Institute of Technology, China

Special Session: Collaborative Manufacturing System and Machinery Fault Diagnosis

Special Session Co-chairs
Ailin Yu   Guangdong University of Technology, China
Chilou Zhou   South China University of Technology, China
Jianfeng Huang   Guangdong University of Petrochemical Technology,
                                China

Workshop: Vehicular Telematics over Heterogeneous Wireless Networks

Workshop Chair
Daxin Tian   Beihang University, China

Conference Manager
Dominika Belisova   European Alliance for Innovation

Technical Program Committee

Ali Emre Turgut	Middle East Technical University, Turkey
Abdelrahman Osman Elfaki	University of Tabuk, Saudi Arabia
Alex Norta	Tallinn University of Technology, Estonia
Antonella Longo	University of Salento, Italy
Anna Lisa Ferrara	University of Surrey, UK
Athanasios Giannetsos	University of Surrey, UK
Aggeliki Tsohou	Ionian University, Greece
Antonis Tzounis	University of Thessaly, Greece
Artemios Voyiatzis	TU Wien, Austria
Bin Li	Guangzhou Maritime University, China
Christos Xenakis	University of Piraues, Greece
Chao Tong	Beihang University, China
Dayang Sun	The University of British Columbia, Canada
Francois Siewe	De Montfort University, UK
Fekade Getahun	Addis Ababa University, Ethiopia
Guolin He	South China University of Technology, China
Guangquan Xu	Tianjin University, China
Georgios V. Lioudakis	National Technological University of Athens, Greece
Georgios Karopoulos	National and Kapodistrian University of Athens, Greece
Honghao Gao	Shanghai University, China
Helge Janicke	De Montfort University, UK
Haoming Li	Freescale Semiconductors, Inc., USA
Haipeng Dai	Nanjing University, China
Iryna Yevseyeva	De Montfort University, UK
Jianlong Xu	Shantou University, China
Jianqiang Wang	Tsinghua University, China
Jian Wang	Inria, France
Jin Liu	Wuhan University, China
Jin Li	Guangzhou University, China
Joe Tekli	Lebanese American University (LAU), Lebanon
Joel Rodrigues	University of Beira Interior, Portugal
Kutluk Bilge Arikan	Atilim University, Turkey
Mengxuan Li	China Ship Development and Design Center, China
Maria Karyda	University of the Aegean, Greece
Marco Comerio	University of Milano-Bicocca, Italy
Mohamed Amine Ferrag	Guelma University, Algeria
Meikang Qiu	Pace University, USA
Mingliang Xu	Zhengzhou University, China
Man Hon Cheung	The Chinese University of Hong Kong, SAR China
Nanjangud C. Narendra	MS Ramaiah University of Applied Sciences, India
Nianjun Joe Zhou	IBM T. J. Watson Research Center, USA
Nikos Tziritas	Chinese Academy of Sciences, China
Ouyang Zhenchao	Beihang University, China

Payam Zahadat	University of Graz, Austria
Panagiotis Andriotis	University of the West of England, UK
Pavlina Fragkou	Technological Institute of Athens, Greece
Qiang Duan	Pennsylvania State University, USA
Shuichang Liu	Hunan University of Technology, China
Shangguan Wei	Beijing Jiaotong University, China
Shangguang Wang	Beijing University of Posts and Telecommunications, China
Shizhan Chen	Tianjin University, China
Stephan Reiff-Marganiec	University of Leicester, UK
Simon Watson	University of Manchester, UK
Shasha Mo	Beihang University, China
Sotiris Moschoyiannis	University of Surrey, UK
Song Guo	Hong Kong Polytechnic University, SAR China
Tomas Krajnik	Czech Technical University, Czech Republic
Tiago Cruz	University of Coimbra, Portugal
Vasilis Sourlas	University College London, UK
Wentao Wang	Guangzhou City Polytechnic, China
Wencan Zhang	Foshan University, China
Weiwei Fang	Beijing Jiaotong University, China
Yingchun Long	Shaoguan University, China
Yingjun Chen	Guangdong University of Petrochemical Technology, China
Yucong Duan	Hainan University, China
Yunchuan Sun	Beijing Normal University, China
Ying He	De Montfort University, UK
Ying Li	Beihang University, China
Yu Shui	Deakin University, Australia
Liangyong Qi	Qufu Normal University, China
Limin Sun	Chinese Academy of Sciences, China
Long Cheng	Virginia Tech, USA
Lu Liu	University of Derby, UK
Le Dong	University of Electronic Science and Technology of China (UESTC), China
Xiujuan Liang	Guangdong Ocean University, China
Xiaolei Ma	University of Washington, USA
Xiaobing Sun	Yangzhou University, China
Xiong Li	Hunan University of Science and Technology, China
Xinkai Wu	Cal Poly Pomona, USA
Zhipeng Cai	Georgia State University, USA
Zheli Liu	Nankai University, China

Contents

Internet of Things (IoT) and Collaboration

Collaborative Data and Workflow Management

Collaboration with Artificial Intelligence

Security and Trustworthy

Collaboration Techniques in Data-intensive Cloud Computing

Collaborative Next Generation Networking

Collaborative Manufacturing System and Machinery Fault Diagnosis

Main Track

Sentiment Analysis of Chinese Words Using Word Embedding and Sentiment Morpheme Matching

Jianwei Niu$^{(\boxtimes)}$, Mingsheng Sun, and Shasha Mo

State Key Laboratory of Virtual Reality Technology and Systems,
School of Computer Science and Engineering, Beihang University,
Beijing 100191, China
niujianwei@buaa.edu.cn

Abstract. Sentiment analysis has become significantly important with the increasing demand of Natural Language Processing (NLP). A novel Chinese Sentiment Words Polarity (CSWP) analyzing method, which is based on sentiment morpheme matching method and word embedding method, is proposed in this paper. In the CSWP, the sentiment morpheme matching method is creatively combined with existing word embedding method, it not only successfully retained the advantages of flexibility and timeliness of the unsupervised methods, but also improved the performance of the original word embedding method. Firstly, the CSWP uses word embedding method to calculate the polarity score for candidate sentiment words, then the sentiment morpheme matching method is applied to make further analysis for the polarity of words. Finally, to deal with the low recognition ratio in the sentiment morpheme matching method, a synonym expanding step is added into the morpheme matching method, which can significantly improve the recognition ratio of the sentiment morpheme matching method. The performance of CSWP is evaluated through extensive experiments on 20000 users' comments. Experimental results show that the proposed CSWP method has achieved a desirable performance when compared with other two baseline methods.

Keywords: Sentiment polarity analysis · Word formation rule
Sentiment morpheme matching · Word embedding
Synonym expanding

1 Introduction

Recent years has witnessed the rapid development of the Internet. With the explosive growth in the online comment number, the value of massive information has emerged gradually. Mining the valuable information from comments often relies on extracting the sentimental polarity of texts. In much previous work, the sentiment analysis is done at document level. However, the sentiment

© ICST Institute for Computer Sciences, Social Informatics and Telecommunications Engineering 2018
I. Romdhani et al. (Eds.): CollaborateCom 2017, LNICST 252, pp. 3–12, 2018.
https://doi.org/10.1007/978-3-030-00916-8_1

analyzing of comments often requires sentence-level or even word-level sentiment analysis. What's more, the word-level sentiment analysis is the basics of all other sentiment analyzing works.

One promising sentiment analysis method is to combine the manual tagged corpora with the supervised learning method. In this sentiment analysis method, a supervised learning model will be trained with tagged dataset, and then use the trained model to execute analyzing work. For training the machine learning models, [1] manually collected and tagged 177 negative tweets and 182 positive tweets and, [2] manually tagged 900 sentences and 2519 words. As can be seen that before the analysis work, lots of corpora must be manually collected and tagged for training the supervised machine learning models. However, collecting and tagging the massive corpora is time costly and boring. Additionally, the training set in [1] is collected in period time, and the training set in [2] only content limited sentiences and words. The limited size will lead these datasets cannot include enough sentiment expression form, thereby leading the bad adaptive capacity in different situations.

The other promising sentiment analysis method is to use massive untagged corpora to train unsupervised method. A typical practice of these methods is to use the statistical methods on massive corpora to calculate the probability of a word's sentiment polarity. [3] exploited the PMI to calculate the polarity score for the candidate sentiment words. However, the PMI is sensitive to frequency. It means that two low frequency words can also have a high PMI value. Additionally, [4] utilized word embedding method to convert words into word vectors and use word vectors to calculate the similarity between candidate words and sentiment seed sets. Word2vec tool can generate the real vectors for words according to the context of them. However, two words which have opposite sentiment polarity also can have similar context in sometimes.

In this paper, A novel Chinese Sentiment Words Polarity (CSWP) analyzing method is proposed. The design of the CSWP is to exploit the word embedding method and the sentiment morpheme matching method. The CSWP retains the advantages about flexibility and timeliness of the unsupervised methods. These features can lead to better practicality in real life. The performance of CSWP is evaluated through extensive experiments on 20000 online comments. The experimental results showed that the proposed CSWP method achieved a desirable performance compared with other methods.

The rest paper is organized as follows. Section 2 reviews related research about word-level sentiment analysis. Section 3 overviews the architecture of CSWP and describes the implement of CSWP in detail. Section 4 reports a series of experiments to evaluate the performance of CSWP, and the results are shown in the end of this section. Finally, conclusions are driven in Sect. 5.

2   Related Work

This section will review the related work in the field of word-level sentiment analysis. Up to now, there are two kinds of methods have been proposed for sentiment words analysis: the supervised based method and the unsupervised based method.

The methods based on supervised method always use some trained mathematical models and some manual tagged corpora to predict the sentiment polarity of words. For example, [5] considered the polarity judging question as a binary classification problem, and used SVM models to analyze the sentiment polarity. Moreover, [6,7] used conjunctions as the training features of machine learning models to judge the sentiment polarity of sentiment words. In addition, morphology information and syntactic information also have been exploited in sentiment polarity analysis [8]. What's more, with the huge growth in the use of microblogs [9,10], [11,12] implemented SVM model to extract the emoticons and as these emoticons as the judging gists for analyzing the sentiment polarity of text. They considered that emoticons can accurately reflect the real emotion of microblogs.

As for methods based on the unsupervised method, they usually utilize massive untagged corpora and statistical methods. [13] directly used the similarity of words to judge their sentiment polarity. [14] also used the value of similarity, but the authors considered the similarity as the features of clustering method. Additionally, the statistical variables such as Point Mutual Information, Coincident Entropy and PageRank also have been used in sentiment analysis [3,15]. These statistical variables are exploited to calculate the sentiment polarity score for candidate sentiment words. Because the unsupervised methods are based on untagged corpora and statistical methods, they generally have relative low precision ratio. However, the advance of do not need manual tagged corpora leads these methods always have strong timeliness and can adapt variable situations.

3 Methodology

This section will describe the detailed flow of the CSWP and the rationale behind the design of the CSWP. Firstly, the overview of the CSWP will be introduced, and then the detail of the CSWP will be described step by step. Finally, the pseudo code will be shown in the end of this section.

3.1 System Overview

The architecture of the proposed CSWP method is shown in Fig. 1. The CSWP method mainly contains three phases: the preprocessing phase, the initial judge phase and the further judge phase. In the preprocessing phase, a large collection of online comments is segmented into independent Chinese words. The segment step is implemented by using the HanLP Chinese segment tool[1] —a useful Chinese text processing tool. After finished the segment step, all the adjectives are picked out to build up candidate sentiment words set. In the initial judge phase, the candidate sentiment words are given. The initial judge phase is responsible to calculate polarity score for every candidate sentiment words. In the end, candidate words are sent into further judge phase. The further judge phase exploits

---

[1] https://github.com/hankcs/HanLP.

sentiment morpheme matching method to make further judge for the polarity of the candidate sentiment words, and the final judging results will be output by this phase.

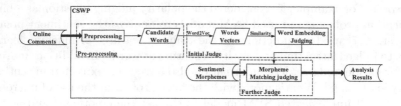

Fig. 1. Architecture of CSWP method

3.2 Preprocessing Phase

Unlike English, there are not separators between Chinese words, so the word segmentation is a necessary step in Chinese natural language processing. The preprocessing phase is responsible to segment the dataset and pick out all the candidate sentiment words by using the HanLP Chinese segment tool. During segmenting the dataset into independent words, the HanLP also tags the part-of-speech for every candidate sentiment words. The HanLP Chinese segment tool utilize "ad" to tag the adjectives. Then in the step of picking out the candidate sentiment words, the preprocessing phase picks out all the adjectives as the candidate words. The examples of Chinese words segmentation results are shown in Table 1.

Table 1. The example of word segmentation results

Original Sentence	Segment Result
今天天气很好 (The weather today is good)	今天/t 天气/n 很好/ad
欢迎来到中国! (Welcome to China!)	欢迎/v 来到/v 中国/ns ！/w

3.3 Initial Judge Phase

The initial judge phase is used to calculate the polarity score for every candidate sentiment words. The specific process of this phase can be divided into the following two steps:

- **Step 1. Generate Word Vectors**
  Firstly, all the words are sorted according to their frequency in the dataset, and then twenty obvious positive candidate words and twenty obvious negative candidate words are picked out to build up positive negative seed sets. These two seed sets will be used in step 2 to assist with calculating the polarity

score. Next, all the candidate sentiment words are converted into 200 dimensional vectors by exploiting word2vec tool. The word2vec tool can convert the words into continuous space vectors and while retain the context features for the words.

– **Step 2. Calculate the Polarity Score**
Firstly, the value of similarity between candidate sentiment words and sentiment seed sets (including the positive seed set and the negative seed set) is calculated. Then the similarity between candidate word and the positive seed set is defined as the word's positive similarity, and the similarity between a candidate word and negative seed set is defined as the word's negative seed set. After getting the similarity, the polarity score of a word is calculated by utilizing the word's positive similarity to minus it's negative similarity. The positive and negative of the score implies the positive and negative of the sentiment polarity of the word. The formula of computing similarity and polarity score are shown in 1 and 2, respectively.

$$sim(A_i|B) = \sum_{j=1}^{m} \frac{\sum_{l=1}^{k} A_{il} \times B_{jl}}{\sqrt{\sum_{l=1}^{k}(A_{il})^2} \times \sqrt{\sum_{l=1}^{k}(B_{jl})^2} \times m} \tag{1}$$

$$score(A_i) = sim(A_i|C) - sim(A_i|D) \tag{2}$$

where A donates the set of candidate words, and B donates the set of sentiment seeds (positive seeds or negative seeds). $A_i(i = 1, 2, \ldots, n)$ and $B_j(j = 1, 2, \ldots, m)$ donate the vector of the word. Vector A_i is composed by $A_{i1}, A_{i2}, \ldots, A_{ik}$, and vector B_j is composed by $B_{j1}, B_{j2}, \ldots, B_{jk}$. The subscript k is the dimension of the word vector. What's more, C donates the positive sentiment seed set, and D donates the negative sentiment seed set. C_j and D_j donate the vector of word, they have same structure as B_j.

3.4 Further Judge Phase

Although word embedding method can judge the polarity of sentiment words independently, the frequency of words and the context of words can influence the analyzing results. Moreover, the size and the content of text also will influence the results. All above factors may lead to a reduction in performance. To mitigate the influence of these issues, a sentiment word formation rule matching method is proposed to assist with the word embedding method. Through utilizing the formation rule matching method, the CSWP can correct some errors caused by previous factors. But if you want to use formation rules to judge the polarity of sentiment words independently, you may also get a bad result, because formation rules always hard to be summarized, and it is impossible to collect all rules. Therefore, an independent rule matching method cannot adapt complex real situations.

The sentiment word formation rules which the CSWP exploits is based on sentiment morpheme matching method and synonym expanding method. Existing work mentioned that some sentiment words express their sentiment through their interior morphemes, so exploiting some sentiment morpheme matching rules can also analyze the sentiment polarity of Chinese words. For example, "很好 |very good" only contains the positive morpheme "好 |good", so this word will be judged as positive sentiment word. But "不好 |not good" contains the privative morpheme "不 |not" and positive "好 |good", furthermore, the privative morpheme has more front position than positive morpheme in "不好|not good", so "不好 |not good" will be judged as negative sentiment word. The specific steps of this phase can be divided into following 3 steps:

- **Step1. Sentiment Morpheme Matching**
  After using cosine similarity to calculate the polarity score, CSWP scans every candidate word for checking whether it contains positive morpheme, negative morpheme and privative morpheme. In course of scanning morphemes, CSWP will utilize the morpheme matching rules to judge the sentiment polarity of the candidate words. If a candidate word cannot match any rule, then CSWP will jump to step 2. If all the candidate words have finished the sentiment morpheme matching, then CSWP will jump to step 3. The sentiment morpheme matching problem can be described as follows: given a candidate sentiment Chinese word $W = w_1w_2 \ldots w_n$, where w_i is the morpheme in the Chinese word W, and subscript i is the position indicator of w_i. The goal of the method is to determine the position of w_i in W. Before giving the specific rules description, we have several conventions about symbol expression, they are shown as follows:
  1. if w_i is a positive morpheme, then use p_i to replace it.
  2. if w_i is a negative morpheme, then use e_i to replace it.
  3. if w_i is a privative morpheme, then use r_i to replace it.
  So, the specific rules can be described as follows:
    - **Rule1:** given a W, if $p_i \in W$, $e_j \notin W$, $r_k \notin W$; then $score = 1$.
    - **Rule2:** given a W, if $p_i \in W$, $e_j \notin W$, $r_k \in W$ and $i < k$; then $score = 0$.
    - **Rule3:** given a W, if $p_i \in W$, $e_j \notin W$, $r_k \in W$ and $k < i$; then $score = -1$.
    - **Rule4:** given a W, if $p_i \notin W$, $e_j \in W$, $r_k \notin W$; then $score = -1$.
    - **Rule5:** given a W, if $p_i \notin W$, $e_j \in W$, $r_k \in W$ and $k < j$; then $score = 1$.
    - **Rule6:** given a W, if $p_i \notin W$, $e_j \in W$, $r_k \in W$ and $j < k$; then $score = 0$.
    - **Rule7:** given a W, if $p_i \in W$, $e_j \in W$, $r_k \notin W$ and $j < i$; then $score = -1$.
    - **Rule8:** given a W, if $p_i \in W$, $e_j \in W$, $r_k \in W$ and $k < j < i$; then $score = 1$.
- **Step 2. Synonyms Expanding**
  If a candidate word can't match any rule, then the process will jump to this step. The candidate word sent to this step will be expanded to some synonyms by searching synonym dictionary. Then, the CSWP will use this word's synonyms continue to execute step 1. And if one of the synonyms can match a rule, the polarity score of this candidate word also will be changed.
- **Step 3. Output Final Results**
  Finally, after step 1 has finished the sentiment morpheme matching process,

the final results have come into being. The candidate words which have positive score will be marked as positive sentiment words, and the candidate words which have negative score will be marked as negative sentiment words. Moreover, the words which have zero score will be given up.

3.5   Pseudo Code of CSWP

Algorithm 1 explains how CSWP works. Line 2–7 corresponds the word embedding judging phase. Line 8–14 corresponds the sentiment morpheme matching phase.

Algorithm 1. Sentiment polarity judging

Input: SDP dataset, sentiment morphemes, synonym dictionary.
Output: positive sentiment word set, negative sentiment word set.
  1: Let A donates the candidate word set, C donates the positive seed set, D donate the negative seed set.
  2: convert all A_i into word vectors.
  3: build up C and D /*C and D are picked from A*/.
  4: **for** all A_i **do**
  5:     use equation(1) to calculate the $sim(A_i|C)$ and $sim(A_i|D)$
  6:     $score(A_i) = sim(A_i|C) - sim(A_i|D)$
  7: **end for**
  8: **for** all A_i **do**
  9:     **if** A_i can match a rule of morpheme matching **then**
 10:         update $score(A_i)$ according to the rule.
 11:     **else**
 12:         utilize synonym expanding to expand synonyms and jump back to Line 9.
 13:     **end if**
 14: **end for**

---

4   Experiments and Results

In this section, we firstly introduce the preparing of the experimental dataset, and then we introduced a series of comparative experiments. The purpose of these experiments is to evaluate whether the CSWP method has a desirable performance in word-level Chinese sentiment analysis compared with two baseline method.

4.1   Dataset

To validate the proposed method, 20000 online comments were extracted from Star Data Platform[2], a text data supply platform. For the sake of convenience, the collection of these comments is named as SDP dataset. The source of SDP

---

[2] https://www.istarshine.com/index.php/Data/dataSurvey#platform.

dataset including microblogs, news and post bar. Then, through summarizing from the NTUSD Chinese sentiment words dictionary[3], three sentiment morpheme sets were build up: a positive sentiment morpheme set, a negative sentiment morpheme set and a privative morpheme set. As for the synonym dictionary utilized in CSWP, the HIT-CIR synonym dictionary[4] was downloaded, this dictionary was developed by HIT Center for Information Retrieval Lab. The sample of sentiment morphemes are shown in Table 2.

Table 2. The sample of the Sentiment Morphemes

Po-Morpheme	善 |kind、好 |good、美 |beauty、优 |good、喜 |happy、妙 |wonderful
Ne-Morpheme	丑 |ugly、妙 |evil、愤 |angry、乱 |disorder、悲 |sad、笨 |stupid
Pr-Morpheme	不 |no、无 |nothing、不曾 |never、没 |no、没有 |no、永不 |never

4.2 Experimental Results

In this subsection, the performance of the proposed CSWP system is evaluated with SDP dataset. To illustrate the advantages of CSWP, we also implement and evaluate an unsupervised baseline method [4] and a supervised method [2] for comparison.

For illustrating the performance of the CSWP method. The 10-fold cross-validation is performed to the three methods. In each time of experiments, 2000 comments of SDP dataset are randomly selected as the training data and the rest are the testing data. The training dataset is used to train supervised baseline method, and the testing dataset is used to evaluate the performance of three methods. The final comparative results are divided into positive sentiment words extracting results and negative sentiment words extracting results. The results are shown in Figs. 2 and 3.

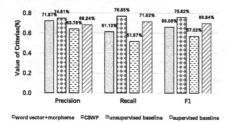

Fig. 2. Positive results

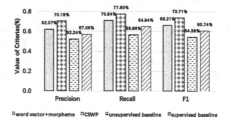

Fig. 3. Negative results

---

[3] http://www.datatang.com/data/44317.
[4] http://www.ltp-cloud.com/download/.

As can be seen from Figs. 2 and 3, the CSWP achieves the best F1 value, which is average 19.075% higher than unsupervised baseline and average 9.475% higher than supervised baseline. Additionally, we can see through the comparison of the first method and the CSWP that the synonym expanding step has average improved the accuracy of CSWP by 5.53% and average improved the recall ratio by 11.195%. It has brought significant improvement to the CSWP. The reason of the improvement is that the step of synonym expanding can improve the recognition ratio of the sentiment morpheme matching method. Therefore, there are more wrong results can be corrected by this phase, and thereby the performance of the CSWP is improved.

5   Conclusion

This paper proposed a novel Chinese Sentiment Words Polarity (CSWP) analyzing method that exploits the word embedding method and the sentiment morpheme matching method. Compared with the existing word embedding method, the performance of the CSWP method has achieved the significant improvement in analyzing the sentiment polarity of Chinese words. To illustrate the performance of the CSWP, two baseline methods were implemented, and then the three methods were evaluated on SDP dataset. The experimental results show that the CSWP method leads to a desirable performance compared with the unsupervised baseline method which only based on word embedding method, and it also can be seen from results that the performance of the CSWP also better than the supervised baseline method which based on maximum entropy model. The advantages of the CSWP method are that it only needs little manpower in preparing work, and it retains the advantages of flexibility and timeliness which belong to unsupervised method, so it will be more competent than supervised baseline method in different harsh work situation.

Acknowledgment. This work was supported by the National Natural Science Foundation of China (61572060, U1536107, 61472024), and CERNET Innovation Project (NGII20151104, NGII20160316).

References

1. Go, A., Bhayani, R., Huang, L.: Twitter sentiment classification using distant supervision. CS224N Project Report, Stanford, 1(2009):12 (2009)
2. Fei, X., Wang, H., Zhu, J.: Sentiment word identification using the maximum entropy model. In: 2010 International Conference on Natural Language Processing and Knowledge Engineering (NLP-KE), pp. 1–4. IEEE (2010)
3. Turney, P.D.: Thumbs up or thumbs down?: semantic orientation applied to unsupervised classification of reviews. In: Proceedings of the 40th Annual Meeting on Association For Computational Linguistics, pp. 417–424. Association for Computational Linguistics (2002)
4. Fan, X., Li, X., Du, F., Li, X., Wei, M.: Apply word vectors for sentiment analysis of app reviews. In: 2016 3rd International Conference on Systems and Informatics (ICSAI), pp. 1062–1066. IEEE (2016)

5. Pang, B., Lee, L., Vaithyanathan, S.: Thumbs up?: sentiment classification using machine learning techniques. In: Proceedings of the ACL-2002 Conference on Empirical Methods in Natural Language Processing, vol. 10, pp. 79–86. Association for Computational Linguistics (2002)
6. Hatzivassiloglou, V., McKeown, K.R.: Predicting the semantic orientation of adjectives. In: Proceedings of the Eighth Conference on European Chapter of the Association for Computational Linguistics, pp. 174–181. Association for Computational Linguistics (1997)
7. Kanayama, H., Nasukawa, T.: Fully automatic lexicon expansion for domain-oriented sentiment analysis. In: Proceedings of the 2006 Conference on Empirical Methods in Natural Language Processing, pp. 355–363. Association for Computational Linguistics (2006)
8. Ku, L.-W., Liang, Y.-T., Chen, H.-H.: Opinion extraction, summarization and tracking in news and blog corpora. In: Proceedings of AAAI, pp. 100–107 (2006)
9. Jansen, B.J., Zhang, M., Sobel, K., Chowdury, A.: Twitter power: Tweets as electronic word of mouth. J. Assoc. Inf. Sci. Technol. 60(11), 2169–2188 (2009)
10. Pak, A., Paroubek, P.: Twitter as a corpus for sentiment analysis and opinion mining. In: LREc, vol. 10 (2010)
11. Kouloumpis, E., Wilson, T., Moore, J.D.: Twitter sentiment analysis: the good the bad and the omg! Icwsm, 11(538-541), 164 (2011)
12. Huang, S., Han, W., Que, X., Wang, W.: Polarity identification of sentiment words based on emoticons. In: 2013 9th International Conference on Computational Intelligence and Security (CIS), pp. 134–138. IEEE (2013)
13. Gauch, S., Wang, J.: Corpus analysis for TREC 5 query expansion. In: TREC (1996)
14. Wiebe, J.: Learning subjective adjectives from corpora. AAAI/IAAI 20 (2000)
15. Geng, H.T., Cai, Q.S., Kun, Y., Zhao, P.: A kind of automatic text keyphrase extraction method based on word co-occurrence. J. Nanjing Univ. 42(2), 156–162 (2006)

Collaborative and Green Resource Allocation in 5G HetNet with Renewable Energy

Yi Liu[1,2](✉), Yue Gao[3], Shengli Xie[1,2], and Yan Zhang[4]

[1] School of Automation, Guangdong University of Technology, Guangzhou, China
yi.liu@gdut.edu.cn
[2] Guangdong Province Key Laboratory of IoT Information Technology,
Guangzhou, China
[3] Queen Mary University of London, London, UK
yue.gao@qmul.ac.uk
[4] University of Oslo, Oslo, Norway
yanzhang@ieee.org

Abstract. By deploying dense renewable-connected small-cells, heterogeneous networks (HetNets) are able to provide spectral and energy efficiencies for 5G system. However, the small-cell base stations (BSs) may suffer the intra-cell interferences and variabilities of renewable energy. In this paper, we firstly introduce a collaborative architecture to deal with intra-cell interferences and renewable uncertainty for different-tier of users in HetNets. A stochastic optimization problem is formulated to maximize the energy efficiency of collaborative HetNet. To solve the problem, a centralized resources allocation algorithm is proposed based on random variabilities of spectrum and renewable resources. Finally, the extensive numerical results are provided to verify the effectiveness of the proposed collaborative resources allocation method.

Keywords: Collaborative HetNet · Resource allocation
Renewable uncertainty

1 Introduction

Heterogeneous network (HetNet) is treated as a promising solution to support tremendous number of diverse terminals and wireless services in 5G system. However, the dense deployment of small-cell BSs and terminals in HetNet will lead to two important issues: spectrum efficiency and energy efficiency. To address these two issues, some technologies have been intensively studied. Massive multiple-input multiple-output (MIMO) technology have been proven to its potential of significantly improving the spectral efficiency about 10–20 times in the same frequency bandwidth [1]. Cognitive radio (CR) technology has been proposed to effectively utilize the spectrum [2,3]. The CR users/devices are allowed to opportunistically operate in the frequency bands originally allocated to the primary

© ICST Institute for Computer Sciences, Social Informatics and Telecommunications Engineering 2018
I. Romdhani et al. (Eds.): CollaborateCom 2017, LNICST 252, pp. 13–26, 2018.
https://doi.org/10.1007/978-3-030-00916-8_2

users/devices when these bands are not occupied by primary users. Along with the spectral efficiency, energy efficiency also attract intensive research interests. Recent research activities mainly focus on renewable connected BSs and devices, energy efficient communication techniques, energy-driven software defined radio and energy-efficient beamforming technologies for MIMO systems, etc.

To evaluate different spectrum and energy efficient technologies, an unified framework is expected for maximizing the spectrum efficiency while reduce the energy consumption. A widely accepted framework is defining the energy efficiency as the ratio of the transmitted traffic loads to the consumed energy for transmitting such loads [5–9]. Based on this definition, many literatures devoted to maximize the energy efficiency under different wireless network scenarios. In [7], the energy efficiency performance is improved in the heterogeneous cloud radio access network. An energy-efficient optimization problem with the resource assignment and power allocation is formulated to characterize user association with remote radio head or high power node. The authors in [8] propose a resource allocation algorithm to achieve maximum energy efficiency for a given spectrum efficiency for heterogeneous network by using coordinated multi-point transmissions. In [5], four green transmission technologies are introduced to balance the tradeoff between energy and spectrum efficiency for 5G wireless networks. An energy efficient and spectrum efficient wireless heterogeneous network framework for 5G systems is introduced in [6]. The system framework is based on cooperative radios, which aims at balancing and optimizing spectrum and energy efficiency. However, the small-cell base stations (BSs) may suffer the variabilities of renewable resources, which will drastically degrade the coverage and capacity of the heterogeneous networks.

In this paper, we dedicate to investigate the collaborative spectrum and power allocation method of macro-cell Bs and small-cell BSs by maximizing the energy efficiency. Taking into account of the uncertain renewable resources, we formulate a stochastic optimization problem to maximize the energy efficiency for collaborative HetNet. Three key parameters are obtained to characterize the proposed collaborative method: the optimal spectrum assignment of small-cell BSs, the optimal power levels of both small-cell and macro-cell users. To solve the stochastic optimization problem, we reformulate the original nonlinear fractional optimization problem as an equivalent convex feasibility problem. Then, A centralized algorithm based on sample average approximation (SAA) is proposed to solve the stochastic reformulated problem. Finally, the numerical results show the effectiveness of the proposed collaborative resource allocation method.

The remainder of this paper is organized as follows. In Sect. 2, the system model is introduced. The formulation of the stochastic optimization problem is formulated in Sect. 3. Meanwhile, a centralized algorithm based on SAA method is proposed. Section 4 presents the numerical results to assess the performance of the proposed schemes. Finally, the paper is concluded in Sect. 5.

2 System Model

2.1 Network Infrastructure

We consider a heterogeneous network consists of several macro-cells, which is overlaid by N number of small-cells, as shown in Fig. 1. Each macro-cell BS serves C number of user equipments (UEs) while each small-cell BS serves U number of nodes (UEs or devices). The macro-cell BS can be the traditional cellular network BS which has the fixed location and operation. The intra-backhaul (fiber or microwave backhaul) is used to connect the small-cell BSs to the macro-cell BS in each cell-site. In addition, the UEs and devices are uniformly distributed over the coverage areas of macro-cell and small-cell BSs.

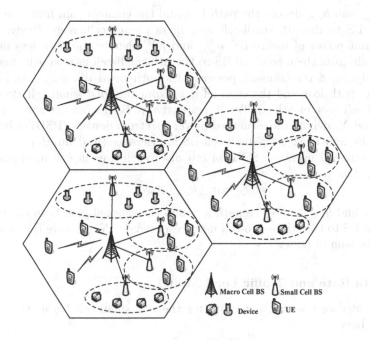

Fig. 1. System model of Hetnet.

2.2 Interference Mitigation Model with Collaboration

Two types of interferences should be carefully considered in Hetnets: Inter-cell interference and Intra-cell interference.

For macro-cell users, the inter-cell interference is coming from other macro BSs in adjacent cells. Meanwhile, the intra-cell interference is also caused by the macro BS transmits signal to other macro-cell users in the same cell. For small-cell users, the inter-cell interference is coming from other macro-cell BSs and small-cell BSs in adjacent cells. Meanwhile, the intra-cell interface is caused by the macro-cell BS and small-cell BSs in the same cell.

To mitigate the inter-cell interferences, collaboration between the macro BSs are critical. Using the backhaul, macro-cell BSs are able to exchange data, control information with each other. Consequently, the inter-cell interferences of macro-cell users and small-cell users can be coordinated. Also, in this paper, we assume that each macro-cell BS has the knowledge of the information of the channel from the BS to its overlaid small-cell users. Then, such channel information is used by macro BS to manage the interference to the small-cell users.

Hence, the signal-to-interference-plus-noise ratio (SINR) for the uth small-cell user in nth small-cell is given by

$$\gamma_{u,n} = \frac{\sigma_{u,n} h_{u,n}}{(P^M \sigma_{u,n}^M h_{u,n}^M + \sum_{m \neq n} p_m \sigma_{m,u,n} h_{m,u,n})} + B_0 N_0 \tag{1}$$

where $\sigma_{u,n}$ and $h_{u,n}$ denote the path loss and the channel gain from the served small-cell BS to the uth small-cell user in nth small-cell, respectively. P^M is the transmit power of macro-BS. $\sigma_{u,n}^M$ and $h_{u,n}^M$ denote the path loss and the channel gain from the macro-cell BS to the uth small-cell user in nth small-cell, respectively. p_m is the transmit power of the mth small BS. $\sigma_{m,u,n}$ and $h_{m,u,n}$ denote the path loss and the channel gain from the mth small cell BS to the uth small-cell user in nth small-cell, respectively. B_0 denote the spectrum of a channel and N_0 denote the estimated power spectrum density (PSD) of both the sum of noise and weak inter-small-cell BS interference (in dBm/Hz).

For macro-cell user, the SINR of cth macro-cell user in kth macro-cell can be obtained as

$$\gamma_{c,k} = \sigma_{c,k} h_{c,k} / B_0 N_M \tag{2}$$

where $\sigma_{c,k}$ and $h_{c,k}$ denote the path loss and the channel gain from the the kth macro-cell BS to the cth macro-cell user, respectively. N_M denote the estimated PSD of the sum of noise.

2.3   Data Rate and Traffic Load Model

Let $R_n(t)$ denote the sum data rate for the nth small-cell BS at time slot t. Then, we have

$$R_n(t) = \sum_{u=1}^{U} B_{u,n}(t) \log_2(1 + \gamma_{u,n} p_{u,n}(t)) \tag{3}$$

where $B_{u,n}(t)$ and $p_{u,n}(t)$ are the spectrum (spectrum resource) and the transmit power allocated to the uth small-cell user in the nth small-cell at time slot t, respectively.

Let $R_k^M(t)$ denote the sum data rate for the kth macro BS at time slot t. Then, we have

$$R_k^M(t) = \sum_{c=1}^{C} B_0 \log_2(1 + \gamma_{c,k} p_{c,k}(t)) \tag{4}$$

where $p_{c,k}$ is the transmit power allocated to the cth macro-cell user in nth small-cell.

Therefore, the sum data rate of the kth macro-cell at time slot t can be written as

$$R_k(t) = \sum_{n=1}^{N} R_n(t) + R_k^M(t). \tag{5}$$

In our model, we assume that the traffic load of each cell-site is different and use random variable $d_n(t)$ to indicate the traffic load of the nth cell-cite at time slot t. Let d_n^{max} denote the maximum value of the traffic load in nth cell-site. We have

$$0 \leq d_n(t) \leq d_n^{max}, \forall n, t. \tag{6}$$

To guarantee the QoS requirement of each cell, we set a minimum threshold for how much traffic load must be served. In this paper, we assume that for the entire time horizon, there is at least $1 - \delta$ probability that the total traffic load will be served. Then, we have the following relationship

$$Pr\left(\sum_{t=0}^{T-1}\sum_{n=1}^{N} d_n(t) - \sum_{t=0}^{T-1}\sum_{n=1}^{N} R_n(t) \leq 0\right) \geq 1 - \delta. \tag{7}$$

2.4 Energy Consumption Model

The total power consumption P_k for kth cell mainly depends on the power consumption of N number of small-cells and the macro-cell BS. The power consumption per small-cell is written

$$P_n(t) = a \sum_{u=1}^{U} p_{u,n}(t) + P_{circuit} + P_{basic} \tag{8}$$

where $p_{u,n}$ is the transmit power allocated to uth small-cell user in nth small-cell. a, P_{cir} and P_{bas} are the efficiency of the power amplifier, circuit power and basic power consumed by small-cell BS, respectively.

The power consumption per macro-cell is written

$$P_k^M = a^M \sum_{c=1}^{C} p_c + P_{circuit}^M + P_{basic}^M \tag{9}$$

where p_c is the transmit power allocated to cth macro-cell user in a macro-cell. a^M, P_{cir}^M and P_{bas}^M are the efficiency of the power amplifier, circuit power and basic power consumed by macro-cell BS, respectively.

Therefore, the total power consumption of kth cell is

$$P_k(t) = \sum_{n=1}^{N} P_n(t) + P_k^M. \tag{10}$$

3   Optimal Resource Allocation for Small-Cells

3.1   Problem Formulation

The energy efficiency is defined as the ratio of the sum data rate and the energy consumption.

$$\Theta(t) = \frac{\sum_{k=1}^{K} R_k(t)}{\sum_{k=1}^{K} P_k(t)} \tag{11}$$

The main objective of this paper is to maximize the energy efficiency by allocating the power and spectrum. In addition, it considers the power and spectrum variabilities of the renewable-connected small-cell BSs. Then, we have the stochastic optimization problem as follows

$$\textbf{(P1)} \quad \max_{p_{c,k}, B_{u,n}(t), p_{u,n}(t),} \quad \lim_{T \to \infty} \frac{1}{T} \sum_{t=1}^{T} \Theta(t) \tag{12}$$

$$s.t. \quad \sum_{u=1}^{U} p_{u,n}(t) \sigma_{sm} h_{sm} \leq \eta_s, \tag{13}$$

$$\sum_{c=1}^{C} p_{c,k} \sigma_{ms} h_{ms} \leq \eta_m, \tag{14}$$

$$\sum_{c=1}^{C} p_{c,k} \leq P_{k,max}, \tag{15}$$

$$\sum_{u=1}^{U} p_{u,n}(t) \leq \tilde{P}_n(t), \tag{16}$$

$$\sum_{u=1}^{U} B_{u,n}(t) \leq \tilde{B}_n(t), \tag{17}$$

$$Pr\Big(\beta \sum_{t=1}^{T} \sum_{n=1}^{N} d_n(t) - \sum_{t=1}^{T} \sum_{n=1}^{N} R_n(t) \leq 0\Big) \geq 1 - \delta, \tag{18}$$

where η_s and η_m denote the maximum interference that the small-cell BS allows to generate to the macro-cell users and the macro BS allows to generate to the small-cell users, respectively. σ_{sm} and h_{sm} denote the corresponding path loss and channel gain from the small-cell BS to the interfering macro-cell users, respectively. σ_{ms} and h_{ms} denote the corresponding path loss and channel gain from the macro BS to the interfering small-cell users, respectively. $P_{k,max}$ denote the maximum transmit power of the kth macro-cell BS. $\tilde{P}_n(t)$ and $\tilde{B}_n(t)$ denote the maximum transmit power and spectrum can be obtained in the nth renewable connected small-cell BS at time slot t, respectively. Constraint (18) ensures that for the entire time horizon, there is at least $1 - \delta$ probability that the served traffic loads is larger than or equal to the minimum level β, $0 < \beta < 100\%$.

3.2   Problem Transformation

The problem (**P1**) is a stochastic problem due to the uncertainty of the transmit power $\tilde{P}_n(t)$, available spectrum $\tilde{B}_n(t)$ and traffic loads $d_n(t)$ of small cell n at time slot t, respectively. In this paper, we use the Sample Average Approximation (SAA) method in which the true distributions of the transmit power, available spectrum and traffic load are replaced by empirical distributions by using the Monte Carlo simulation.

Specifically, to estimate the transmit power $\tilde{P}_n(t)$, the Monte Carlo simulation generates I number of scenarios, each with the same probability $1/I$. After the scenarios are generated, the expected value function of the transmit power can be estimated by the sample average functions as follows:

$$\tilde{P}_n(t) \sim I^{-1} \sum_{i=1}^{I} P_n(t, \varphi_i),$$

where $\varphi_i, i = 1, \cdots, I$, are independent and identically distributed (i.i.d.) samples of I realizations of the transmit power $\tilde{P}_n(t)$. Similarly, the expected value function of the available spectrum $\tilde{B}_n(t)$ and traffic load $d_n(t)$ can be estimated by the sample average functions as follows, respectively:

$$\tilde{B}_n(t) \sim I^{-1} \sum_{i=1}^{I} B_n(t, \omega_i), \quad d_n(t) \sim \frac{1}{I} \sum_{i=1}^{I} d_n(t, \xi_i),$$

where $\{\omega_i, \xi_i, i = 1, \cdots, I\}$ are independent and identically distributed (i.i.d.) samples of I realizations of the available spectrum and traffic load, respectively. Hence, the constraints (16) and (17) can be rewritten as follows:

$$I \sum_{u=1}^{U} p_{u,n}(t) \leq \sum_{i=1}^{I} P_n(t, \varphi_i) \tag{19}$$

$$I \sum_{u=1}^{U} B_{u,n}(t) \leq \sum_{i=1}^{I} B_n(t, \omega_i) \tag{20}$$

Moreover, let $G(\xi_i) \triangleq \beta \sum_{t=0}^{T-1} \sum_{n=1}^{N} d_n(t, \xi_i) - \sum_{t=0}^{T-1} \sum_{n=1}^{N} R_n(t)$. Accordingly, the constraint (18) can be estimated by an indicator function

$$I^{-1} \sum_{i=1}^{I} \mathbf{1}_{(0,\infty)}(G(\xi_i)) \leq \delta \tag{21}$$

where the value of the indicator function $\mathbf{1}_{(0,\infty)}(G(\xi_i))$ is equal to one when $G(\xi_i) \in (0, \infty)$ and zero when $G(\xi_i) \leq 0$.

In addition, the fractional objective function (12) of the optimization problem (**P1**) makes the problem to be a non-linear fractional programming problem. According to [7], the fractional objective can be converted to the subtractive form and the fractional programming problem (**P1**) can be transformed as

$$(\textbf{P2}) \quad \max_{P_{c,k}, B_{u,n}(t), P_{u,n}(t)} \sum_{k=1}^{K} \bar{R}_k - \Theta^* \sum_{k=1}^{K} \bar{P}_k$$

$$\text{s.t.} \quad (13)-(15), (19)-(21).$$

where $\bar{x} = \lim_{T \to \infty} \frac{1}{T} \sum_{t=1}^{T} x(t)$ and Θ^* is the optimal value of $\bar{\Theta}$. The problem (**P2**) is equivalent to problem (**P1**) by the following theorem.

Theorem 1. Θ^* *is an optimal solution for (**P1**) if and only if Θ^* is an optimal solution for (**P2**) to satisfy the constraints (13)–(15) and (19)–(21).*

Proof: We prove the Theorem 1 with two steps: sufficient condition proof and necessary condition proof.

(1) Sufficient condition proof: we define $\Theta^* = \frac{\bar{R}(\textbf{B}^*, \textbf{p}^*)}{\bar{P}(\textbf{B}^*, \textbf{p}^*)}$, where $\textbf{B}^*$ and $\textbf{p}^*$ are the optimal spectrum and power allocation policies of the *small-cell users*, respectively. It is easy to obtain the following expression:

$$\Theta^* = \frac{\bar{R}(\textbf{B}^*, \textbf{p}^*)}{\bar{P}(\textbf{B}^*, \textbf{p}^*)} \geq \frac{\bar{R}(\textbf{B}, \textbf{p})}{\bar{P}(\textbf{B}, \textbf{p})}, \tag{22}$$

where $\textbf{B}$ and $\textbf{p}$ are the feasible spectrum and power results by solving problem (**P1**). Then, we have

$$\begin{cases} \bar{R}(\textbf{B}, \textbf{p}) - \Theta^* \bar{P}(\textbf{B}, \textbf{p}) \leq 0 \\ \bar{R}(\textbf{B}^*, \textbf{p}^*) - \Theta^* \bar{P}(\textbf{B}^*, \textbf{p}^*) = 0 \end{cases}$$

It is obvious that $\max_{\{\textbf{B}, \textbf{p}\}} \bar{R}(\textbf{B}, \textbf{p}) - \Theta^* \bar{P}(\textbf{B}, \textbf{p}) = 0$ and the maximum value is obtained by the optimal spectrum and power allocation policies $\textbf{B}^*$ and $\textbf{p}^*$. The sufficient condition is proved.

(2) Necessary condition proof: we assume that $\hat{\textbf{B}}^*$ and $\hat{\textbf{p}}^*$ are the optimal spectrum and power allocation policies of the objective function of problem (**P2**), respectively. Then, we can obtain $\bar{R}(\hat{\textbf{B}}^*, \hat{\textbf{p}}^*) - \Theta^* \bar{P}(\hat{\textbf{B}}^*, \hat{\textbf{p}}^*) = 0$. For any feasible spectrum and power allocation policies $\textbf{B}$ and $\textbf{p}$, we have the following expression:

$$\bar{R}(\textbf{B}, \textbf{p}) - \Theta^* \bar{P}(\textbf{B}, \textbf{p}) \leq \bar{R}(\hat{\textbf{B}}^*, \hat{\textbf{p}}^*) - \Theta^* \bar{P}(\hat{\textbf{B}}^*, \hat{\textbf{p}}^*) = 0. \tag{23}$$

The above inequality can be derived as:

$$\frac{\bar{R}(\textbf{B}, \textbf{p})}{\bar{P}(\textbf{B}, \textbf{p})} \leq \Theta^* \quad \text{and} \quad \frac{\bar{R}(\hat{\textbf{B}}^*, \hat{\textbf{p}}^*)}{\bar{P}(\hat{\textbf{B}}^*, \hat{\textbf{p}}^*)} = \Theta^* \tag{24}$$

Hence, the optimal resource allocation policies $\hat{\textbf{B}}^*$ and $\hat{\textbf{p}}^*$ of the objective function of problem (**P2**) are also the optimal policies of problem (**P1**). The necessary condition is proved. ∎

Based on Theorem 1, the objective function of problem (**P1**) is transformed into the subtractive form in problem (**P2**). In the following subsection, we will propose an iterative algorithm (Algorithm 1) to solve problem (**P2**). In the Algorithm 1, the value of Θ is updated while ensuring the corresponding solution $\{\mathbf{B}, \mathbf{p}\}$ remains feasible in each iteration. The convergence proof is also provided.

3.3   Solution

To solve the problem (**P2**), we first define $F(\Theta) = \max\limits_{\{\mathbf{B}, \mathbf{p}\}} \bar{R}(\mathbf{B}, \mathbf{p}) - \Theta \bar{P}(\mathbf{B}, \mathbf{p})$
and have the following Lemma.

Lemma 1. *For all feasible $\mathbf{B}$, $\mathbf{p}$ and Θ, $F(\Theta)$ is a strictly monotonic decreasing function in Θ and $F(\Theta) \geq 0$.*

Proof: Let Θ_1 and Θ_2 denote the optimal value of the $F(\Theta)$ with optimal solution $\{\mathbf{B}_1, \mathbf{p}_1\}$ and $\{\mathbf{B}_2, \mathbf{p}_2\}$. Assume that $\Theta_1 > \Theta_2$, we have following expression:

$$
\begin{aligned}
F(\Theta_2) &= \bar{R}(\mathbf{B}_2, \mathbf{p}_2) - \Theta_2 \bar{P}(\mathbf{B}_2, \mathbf{p}_2) \\
&> \bar{R}(\mathbf{B}_1, \mathbf{p}_1) - \Theta_2 \bar{P}(\mathbf{B}_1, \mathbf{p}_1) \\
&> \bar{R}(\mathbf{B}_1, \mathbf{p}_1) - \Theta_1 \bar{P}(\mathbf{B}_1, \mathbf{p}_1) = F(\Theta_1)
\end{aligned}
\tag{25}
$$

Hence, $F(\Theta)$ is a strictly monotonic decreasing function in terms of Θ.

Moreover, let $\mathbf{B}_j$ and $\mathbf{p}_j$ be any feasible spectrum and power allocation policies, respectively. Let $\Theta_j = \frac{\bar{R}(\mathbf{B}_j, \mathbf{p}_j)}{\bar{P}(\mathbf{B}_j, \mathbf{p}_j)}$, then

$$
\begin{aligned}
F(\Theta_j) &= \max\limits_{\{\mathbf{B}, \mathbf{p}\}} \bar{R}(\mathbf{B}, \mathbf{p}) - \Theta_j \bar{P}(\mathbf{B}, \mathbf{p}) \\
&\geq \bar{R}(\mathbf{B}_j, \mathbf{p}_j) - \Theta_j \bar{P}(\mathbf{B}_j, \mathbf{p}_j) = 0.
\end{aligned}
\tag{26}
$$

Therefore, $F(\Theta) \geq 0$.   ∎

Then, we propose Algorithm 1 to solve problem (**P2**). The proposed algorithm is operated in two steps: initialization and iteration. In initialization step, the initial value of Θ, maximum number of iterations I_{max} and the convergence condition ε are given, respectively. In the iteration step, the optimal problem $F(\Theta_i)$ is solved to achieve the optimal value of $\mathbf{B}_i$ and $\mathbf{p}_i$ with Θ_i. Then, under the convergence condition ε, the value of Θ_{i+1} is updated with the $\bar{R}(\mathbf{B}_i, \mathbf{p}_i)$ and $\bar{P}(\mathbf{B}_i, \mathbf{p}_i)$ obtained in the last iteration. Further, we provide the convergence proof of Algorithm 1 by the following theorem.

Theorem 2. *The Algorithm 1 converges to the global optimal solution of $F(\Theta)$.*

Proof: Let Θ_i and Θ_{i+1} denote the energy efficiency of the heterogeneous network in the ith and $(i + 1)$th iteration, respectively. Note that in Algorithm 1, Θ_{i+1} is set by $\Theta_{i+1} = \frac{\bar{R}(\mathbf{B}_i, \mathbf{p}_i)}{\bar{P}(\mathbf{B}_i, \mathbf{p}_i)}$. Meanwhile, $F(\Theta) > 0$ as shown in Lemma 1, thus we can obtain

$$
\begin{aligned}
F(\Theta_i) &= \bar{R}(\mathbf{B}_i, \mathbf{p}_i) - \Theta_i \bar{P}(\mathbf{B}_i, \mathbf{p}_i) \\
&= \bar{P}(\mathbf{B}_i, \mathbf{p}_i)(\Theta_{i+1} - \Theta_i) > 0.
\end{aligned}
\tag{28}
$$

Algorithm 1. Spectrum and Energy Allocation.

Initialization:
1: Set the initial value $\Theta_i = 0$;
2: Give the maximum number of iterations I_{max};
3: Give the convergence condition ε;
Iteration:
4: Let the iteration index $i = 1$;
5: **for** $1 \leq i \leq I_{max}$
6:   Solve the following problem

$$F(\Theta_i) = \max_{\{\mathbf{B}_i, \mathbf{p}_i\}} \bar{R}(\mathbf{B}_i, \mathbf{p}_i) - \Theta_i \bar{P}(\mathbf{B}_i, \mathbf{p}_i)$$

$$\text{s.t.} \quad (13)-(15), (19)-(21); \qquad\qquad (27)$$

7:   Obtain $\mathbf{B}_i, \mathbf{p}_i, \bar{R}(\mathbf{B}_i, \mathbf{p}_i)$ and $\bar{P}(\mathbf{B}_i, \mathbf{p}_i)$;
8:   **If** $\bar{R}(\mathbf{B}_i, \mathbf{p}_i) - \Theta_i \bar{P}(\mathbf{B}_i, \mathbf{p}_i) < \varepsilon$, **then**
9:     Set $\{\mathbf{B}^*, \mathbf{p}^*\} = \{\mathbf{B}_i, \mathbf{p}_i\}$ and $\Theta^* = \Theta_i$;
10:     **break;**
11:   **else**
12:     Calculate $\Theta_{i+1} = \frac{\bar{R}(\mathbf{B}_i, \mathbf{p}_i)}{\bar{P}(\mathbf{B}_i, \mathbf{p}_i)}$ and $i = i + 1$;
13:   **end if**
14: **end for**

The above expression indicates that $\Theta_{i+1} > \Theta_i$ due to $\bar{P}(\mathbf{B}_i, \mathbf{p}_i) > 0$, which suggests that Θ increases in each iteration Algorithm 1. Thereby, the Algorithm 1 ensures Θ increases monotonically.

According to the definition of Θ presented in Sect. 2, it is easy to obtain that $\Theta_i > 0$ and $\Theta_{i+1} > 0$ and neither of them is the optimal value Θ^*. Since Θ^* is the maximum energy efficiency for all feasible $\{\mathbf{B}, \mathbf{p}\}$, we have $\Theta^* \geq \Theta_{i+1}$. When the updated Θ increases to Θ^*, we can obtain the value of Θ^* and $F(\Theta^*) = 0$. If the number of iteration in Algorithm 1 is sufficiently large and the optimal conditions as stated in Theorem 1 is satisfied, the problem $F(\Theta)$ converges to zero. Therefore, the global convergence of Algorithm 1 is proved.   ∎

4 Numerical Results

In this section, numerical simulations are performed to evaluate the performance of the proposed collaborative resource allocation method (denoted by "Proposed Collaborative Method") in a HetNet with renewable penetration. The fixed power allocation method (denoted by Fixed Power Method), is presented as the baseline. In the Fixed Power Method, the same and fixed transmit power is set for different small-cells without considering the uncertainty of renewable, and the optimal spectrum and power allocation derived in our paper is not utilized. The evaluation parameters are listed in Table 1.

Table 1. The simulation parameters

N	10	The number of small-cells
C	20	The number of macro-cell users
U	40	The number of small-cell users
B_0	5 MHz	The bandwidth of a spectrum channel
N_0	1 dBm/Hz	The estimated power spectrum density of noise
P_{cir}/P_{cir}^M	0.1W/10W	The circuit power of small-cell/macro-cell BS
P_{bas}/P_{bas}^M	0.1W/0.2W	The basic power of small-cell/macro-cell BS
a/a^M	2/4	The power amplifer of small-cell/macro-cell BS
$P_{k,max}$	100 W	The maximum transmit power of macro-cell BS
$1-\delta$	1/0.8	The probability of serving load

4.1   Energy Efficiency Comparison

Figure 2 shows the comparison of the energy efficiency of the proposed collaborative method and the fixed power method. The energy efficiency increases with the increment of the value of SINR because higher SINR leads to less power consumption by which the small-cell users can meet with their QoS requirements. It is noted that the proposed collaborative method is able to achieve better energy efficiency than that in the fixed power method. This is because the proposed method schedule the power usage of all small-cell users in collaborative way. Meanwhile, the optimal resource allocation solution in the proposed method guarantees the uncertainty of using renewable power can be greatly reduced.

In Fig. 2, we also compare the energy efficiency under two different QoS requirement cases: $1-\delta = 0.8$ and $1-\delta = 1$, respectively. The second case

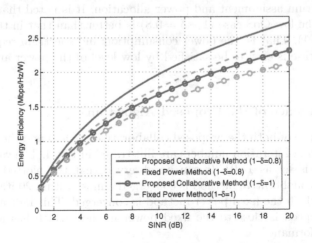

Fig. 2. Energy efficiency comparison in terms of SINR.

indicate that the QoS requirement of each small-cell should be 100% satisfied. It is observed that the energy efficiency in case $1 - \delta = 0.8$ is better than that in case $1 - \delta = 1$. That is, more powers are consumed to make users meet with the QoS requirements.

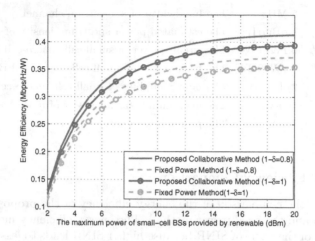

Fig. 3. Energy efficiency comparison in terms of the maximum power of renewable.

Figure 3 shows the energy efficiency comparison between the proposed collaborative method and the fixed power method under different value of the maximum power generated by renewable. In this case, the SINR is set as 1 dB. We can observe that the energy efficiency of the proposed collaborative method is often better than that of the fixed power method. This is because the proposed method can achieve the best energy efficiency performance due to gains of optimal spectrum assignment and power allocation. It is noted that the energy efficiency in the low QoS case $(1 - \delta = 0.8)$ is better than that in the high QoS case $(1 - \delta = 1)$. That is, the power consumption and spectrum requirement in the low QoS case is easy to be satisfied by low level of the power and spectrum allocation.

4.2   Convergence of the Proposed Algorithm

The convergence of both the proposed collaborative method and the fixed power method in term of iteration numbers are illustrated in Fig. 4. The value of SINR of small-cells is set as 1 dB. It can be observed that the plotted energy efficiency of the collaborative method is converged almost within 20 iteration numbers during which the fixed power method is converged. This indicates that the convergence speed is close to the fixed power method which has lower energy efficiency performance.

As shown in simulation results, the proposed collaborative method can achieve better performance than other scheme in HetNet. This is because the

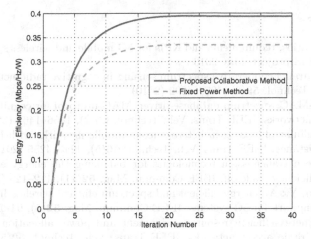

Fig. 4. Convergence of the proposed collaborative method and the fixed power method.

main concern of HetNet is how to provide various applications, by using only one universal device, and satisfy the diverse resources (i.e. spectrum, energy) requirement over multi-tier networks in an optimal way. The proposed collaborative method, imbedded in central controller of the HetNet, collects information of spectrum and renewable resources through the network, intelligently determines current operating settings, and controls the operation of all devices to gain optimal network performance. Hence, the collaborative capability of our method benefits for HetNet.

5 Conclusion

In this paper, we study the energy-efficient resource allocation problem for collaborative macro-cell and small-cell BSs in HetNet with renewable resources. Through stochastic optimization, we develop effective collaborative power and spectrum allocation mechanism for HetNet and show how to optimally schedule the power usage with corresponding allocation mechanism to maximize the energy efficiency. It is expected that this paper provides a collaborative modeling and optimization approach to effectively integrating renewable resource into HetNet.

Acknowledgment. The work is supported in part by programs of NSFC under grant nos. 61403086, 61773126.

References

1. Metis, "Scenarios, requirements and KPIs for 5G mobile and wireless system," ICT-317669 METIS project, May 2013
2. Liu, Y.: A parallel cooperative spectrum sensing in cognitive radio networks. IEEE Trans. Veh. Technol. **59**(8), 4079–4092 (2010)
3. Liu, Y.: SD-MAC: spectrum database-driven MAC protocol for cognitive machine-to-machine networks. IEEE Trans. Veh. Technol. **66**(2), 1456–1467 (2017)
4. Cao, W.: Cellular offloading in heterogeneous mobile networks with D2D communication assistance. IEEE Trans. Veh. Technol. **66**(5), 4245–4255 (2017)
5. Wu, Y.: Green transmission technologies for balancing the energy efficiency and spectrum efficiency trade-off. IEEE Commun. Mag. **52**(11), 112–120 (2014)
6. Hu, R., Qian, Y.: An energy efficient and spectrum efficient wireless heterogeneous network framework for 5G systems. IEEE Commun. Mag. **52**(5), 94–101 (2014)
7. Peng, M.: Energy-efficient resource assignment and power allocation in heterogeneous cloud radio access networks. IEEE Trans. Veh. Technol. **52**(5), 5275–5287 (2015)
8. Huq, K.M.S., et al.: Green HetNet CoMP: energy efficiency analysis and optimization. IEEE Trans. Veh. Technol. **64**(10), 4670–4683 (2015)
9. Liu, C.-H., Fong, K.L.: Fundamentals of the downlink green coverage and energy efficiency in heterogeneous networks. IEEE J. Sel. Areas Commun. **34**(12), 3271–3287 (2016)

On Cost Efficient Dataflow Computing Program Deployment in SDN Managed Distributed Computing Environment

Yating Zhang[1], Yuepeng Li[2], Long Zheng[3](✉), and Deze Zeng[2]

[1] Department of Computer Science and Engineering, Shanghai Jiao Tong University,
Shanghai, China
[2] School of Computer Science, China University of Geosciences, Wuhan, China
[3] College of Computer Science and Software Engineering, Shenzhen University,
Shenzhen, China
`lzheng.aizu@gmail.com`

Abstract. Dataflow computing has been regarded one of the most promising computing paradigms in the big data era. With the vast distribution of data sources, it is significant to deploy the dataflow based applications in distributed environment to digest these data. In dataflow computing, the data flows shall be transferred between different processing units to the accomplish the predefined semantics. Software-defined networking (SDN) has emerged as an effective network management technology to orchestrate the data flows among these processing units. For each data flow, a forwarding rule shall be inserted into the forwarding table of each switch on the routing path. However, the number of rules that can be inserted in one forwarding table is limited. We are motivated to take such constraints into the consideration of dataflow applications deployment in distributed computing environment managed by SDN. An efficient deployment algrotithm is proposed and evaluated in this paper.

1 Introduction

Dataflow computing, thanks to its charming characteristics in dealing with the large and stream data, has raised lots of attention for embracing the upcoming big data era. Specially, with the fast development of cloud computing, it has been widely regarded that it is ideal to deploy the dataflow computing programs in distributed environments to explore the vast cloud computing resources. As a result, many distributed dataflow computing based frameworks, e.g., GraphX [10], CIEL [6], TensorFlow [1], etc., have been proposed. These frameworks all share the same design principle that the program can be described as a directed graph where the data flows between the processes according to the predefined semantics. This raises one natural question on how to deploy these processes in the distributed computing environment, as illustrated in Fig. 1. This is generally referred as virtual network embedding (VNE), which has attracted much attention in the literature, as surveyed in [4]. However, we notice that existing network embedding studies usually consider traditional network architecture.

© ICST Institute for Computer Sciences, Social Informatics and Telecommunications Engineering 2018
I. Romdhani et al. (Eds.): CollaborateCom 2017, LNICST 252, pp. 27–36, 2018.
https://doi.org/10.1007/978-3-030-00916-8_3

Software-defined networking (SDN) [9] has been regarded as one of the essential technologies in the next-generation networks by allowing centralized management of the data flows in the network. Although it is promising to apply SDN to orchestrate the data flows between different processes, a new challenging problem due to the inherent characteristics of SDN is introduced. That is, SDN relies on the forwarding rules written in the SDN switches to manage forwarding behaviors for different flows passing through the switches. The rules are usually written in Ternary Content Addressable Memory (TCAM) such that the rules can be read in parallel for fast entry matching and corresponding processing. However, TCAM is expensive and power hungry. This limits the size of the forwarding table, or rule space.

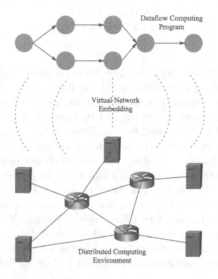

Fig. 1. Illustration of embedding a dataflow computing program into an SDN managed distributed computing environment

Therefore, it is significant to re-investigate the network embedding problem in SDN managed distributed environment, especially with the consideration of the inherent characteristics of SDN itself, e.g., the forwarding table size limitations. In this paper, we are motivated to investigate the cost-efficient dataflow application deployment problem in SDN managed distributed computing environment. The main contributions of this paper exist in the following folds:

- To our best knowledge, we are the first to take the SDN characteristics in the consideration of VNE. In particular, we consider the problem of cost-efficient dataflow application deployment in SDN managed distributed computing environment.
- We formulate the cost-efficient network embedding problem into a mixed integer linear programing (MILP) form and further propose a relaxation-based polynomial heuristic algorithm.

– Through extensive simulation based studies, the high efficiency of our proposed heuristic algorithm is proved by the fact that it performs much close to the optimal solution.

The rest of the paper is organized as follows: existing related work is summarized in Sect. 2. The system model is given in Sect. 3. Section 4 presents our MILP problem formulation. Section 5 proposes the heuristic algorithm. Performance evaluation results are reported in Sect. 6. Finally, Sect. 7 concludes this paper.

2   Related Work

To explore the vast distributed cloud computing resources, much effort has been devoted to study of how to deploy a dataflow computing program in distributed computing environment with different goal. For example, Chowdhury et al. [3] address the efficient mapping of virtual nodes and virtual links onto the substrate network resources to increase revenue and decrease cost of the infrastructure provider in the long run, in addition to balancing load of the substrate network resources. Sun et al. [11] consider the case that the user demands and the corresponding virtual network requests change dynamically, and study on how to reconfigure an existing embedding to minimize the reconfiguration cost. Botero et al. [2] consider an energy aware VNE with the goal of providing optimal energy efficient embeddings. After comprehensive survey on existing studies on VNE in the literature, we noticed that all existing studies consider traditional network architecture and none of them takes SDN into consideration.

The functionality of SDN deeply relies on the forwarding rule deployed in the SDN switches. While, as we have known, the forwarding rule space on the SDN switches is usually size-limited due to the expensive and power-hungry TCAM. As a result, pioneering researchers have widely discussed how to efficiently manage the SDN rules in the size-limited rule spaces. For example, Giroire et al. [5] focus on applying SDN for energy aware routing with respecting capacity constraints on links and rule space constraints on SDN routers on backbone networks. Kang et al. [8] present efficient rule-placement algorithms to deploy predefined forwarding policies in general SDN switches while preserving the rule-space constraints. Although the rule space constraints have already been widely discussed in the literature, it can be noticed that existing studies usually assume end-to-end traffic model. When it comes to dataflow computing paradigm, there are a number of dependent communication nodes. Existing modeling and optimization algorithms cannot be applied directly.

3   System Model

We consider a substrate network consisting of a number of geographically distributed servers interconnected by SDN switches. Hence, we can denote the substrate network as an undirected weighted graph $G^s = (N, S, L)$, where N

and S denote the set of servers and the set of SDN switches, respectively, and L is the set of communication links between the servers and the switches, as well as the ones between the switches. For each substrate server $n \in N$, the amount of available resource capacity is denoted as C_n. For each SDN switch $s \in S$, the forwarding table capacity (i.e., rule space size) is denoted as C_s. For each substrate network link $l \in L$, the amount of available communication resource capacity is denoted as C_l.

A dataflow computing program to be deployed can be abstracted as a virtual network request. As a result, we similarly model a dataflow program as a weighted directed acyclic graph (DAG) $G^v = (P, E)$, where P is the set of constituent processes of the dataflow computing program and E denotes the data dependency relationships between these processes. If there is an edge e_{uv} from process $u \in P$ to process $v \in P$, it indicates that the output flow of u shall flow to v as input flow. In other words, u is the parent process of v and v is the child process of u. A process may generate multiple output flows to different child processes. Different output flows may have different flow volume expansion relationship, either increase or decease. We therefore define $\alpha_{uv}, u, v \in P$ to denote the ratio of stream volume on edge $e_{uv} \in E$ to the total input stream volume to u. For each process $v \in V$, certain units of resources are needed. We denote the resource requirement of process $p \in P$ as R_p. Without loss of generality, we specially define p_0 as the first process as the front-end proxy that each computing request shall visit. Similarly, we define p_1 as the child process of p_0. The proxy process p_0 has been deployed on all the servers such that each can receive the computing requests from the clients. We view each request as a flow with different rates that shall traverse all the constituent processes in the dataflow computing program. We denote the set of flows as F.

4   Problem Formulation

Extended Dataflow Computing Graph Construction: We notice Gu et al. [7] invents an extended graph for VNE, with the joint consideration of substrate network and virtual network. Following their work, we extend our dataflow computing DAG into an extended dataflow computing graph $G^e = (V^e, S, E^e)$ by integrating the substrate network architecture as follows. For each vertex $v \in V$, we replicate it into $|N|$ copies in G^e such that each vertex $v \in V^e$ represents one possible process placement. As a result, V^e has $|V| \cdot |N|$ vertices, i.e., $|V^e| = |V| \cdot |N|$. The set S is inherited from substrate network graph G^s. Next, we construct the edge set E^e between the vertices in V^e and the switches in S. Let us first define $h(v)$ and $t(v)$ denote its hosting server and corresponding process for vertex $v \in V^e$, respectively. Specially, for tractability, we define $h(s) = s, \forall s \in S$. Then, for any vertex $v \in V^e$, if there is a link from $h(v_1) \in V^s$ to $s \in S$ in G^s, we create an edge from v to s in G^e, i.e., adding an edge e_{vs} to E^e, whose unit cost is inherited from G^s as $C_{h(v)s}$. Such process repeated until all vertices in the extended dataflow computing graph G^e.

After constructing the extended graph G^e, we start to build a formal optimization model to describe the problem to be studied as follows.

Process Placement Constraints: To ensure the functionality of the dataflow computing program, the first requirement is that all the processes must be completed placed in the substrate network. To this end, we first define a binary x_v to indicate whether virtual vertex v is chosen ($x_v = 1$) or not ($x_v = 0$). According to our extended graph construction process, it can be seen that $x_v = 1$ indicates that process $t(v)$ is placed on server $h(v)$. For each process, there must be one instance in the substrate network. This is equivalent to

$$\sum_{v \in V^e, t(v) = p} x_v = 1, \forall p \in P. \tag{1}$$

From the perspective of the substrate server, the processes that can be placed on it is limited by its resource capacity, i.e.,

$$\sum_{v \in V, h(v) = n} x_v R_{t(v)} \leq C_n, n \in N. \tag{2}$$

Flow Distribution Constraints: Let $\lambda_{uv}^{f_{p'p}}$ denote the flow rate between any two vertices u, v for flow $f \in F$ going from process p' to p, if there exists an edge $e_{uv}, e_{uv} \in E^e$ in graph G^e. If the rate of a flow going through v is larger than 0, it indicates that process $t(v)$ must be placed in server $n(v)$, i.e., $x_v = 1$. Therefore, we have

$$\frac{\sum_{f \in F} \sum_{e_{uv} \in E^e} \lambda_{uv}^{f_{p't(v)}}}{A} \leq x_v \leq A \sum_{f \in F} \sum_{e_{uv} \in E^e} \lambda_{uv}^{f_{p't(v)}}, \forall v \in V^e, e_{p't(v)} \in E, \tag{3}$$

where A is an arbitrary large number.

For each process $p \in P$, it receives one or several flows from its parent processes p' and generates one or several output flows, according to the predefined dataflow computing semantics. Such relationship can be described using the flow conservation constraints on the vertices in the extended graph as

$$\alpha_{pp''} \sum_{\substack{t(v) = p \\ e_{uv} \in E^e}} \lambda_{uv}^{f_{p'p}} = \sum_{\substack{t(v) = p \\ e_{vw} \in E^e}} \lambda_{vw}^{f_{pp''}}, \forall f \in F, e_{p'p}, e_{pp''} \in E. \tag{4}$$

Note that we treat the front portal as the first process that each flow shall visit. Therefore, the input flow rate of each front portal process, i.e., p_0, has already been determined. That is,

$$\Lambda_v^f = \sum_{\substack{t(v) = p_0 \\ e_{vw} \in E^e}} \lambda_{vw}^{f_{p_0 p_1}}, \forall f \in F, v \in V^e. \tag{5}$$

For each switch $s \in V^e$ in the extended graph, unlike the process which may make some data processing, it simply forward the flow to either another switch or a server deployed with wanted process. Therefore, we have:

$$\sum_{e_{us} \in E^e} \lambda_{us}^{f_{pp'}} = \sum_{\substack{e_{sw} \in E^e \\ t(w)=p' \text{ or } w \in S}} \lambda_{sw}^{f_{pp'}}, \forall s \in S, e_{pp'} \in E. \tag{6}$$

As each link is with certain communication capacity, the total stream volume shall not exceed its capacity. That is,

$$\sum_{e_{pp'} \in E} \sum_{\substack{e_{uv} \in E^e \\ h(u)=x \\ h(v)=y}} \lambda_{uv}^{f_{pp'}} \le C_{l_{xy}}, \forall l_{xy} \in L. \tag{7}$$

Rule Space Constraints: As all the servers are inter-connected by SDN switches, the flows between the dependent processes deployed on different servers shall go through the corresponding switches. Each flow shall occupy one rule on each switch along the routing path. Therefore, for each flow $f \in F$, whenever there is a non-zero flow going through a switch $s \in S$, it indicates that there is one rule in the forwarding table of switch s. To this end, we first define binary variable to describe whether flow f going through s ($x_s^f = 1$) or not ($x_s^f = 0$), which can be equivalently described as a linear function of the flow as

$$\frac{\sum_{e_{us} \in E^e} \lambda_{us}^{f_{pp'}}}{A} \le x_s^f \le A \sum_{e_{us} \in E^e} \lambda_{us}^{f_{pp'}}, \forall s \in S, f \in F, e_{pp'} \in E, \tag{8}$$

where A is an arbitrary large number.

For all the flows, the total rule space needed in each switch shall not exceed its rule space capacity. That is,

$$\sum_{f \in F} x_s^f \le C_s, \forall s \in S. \tag{9}$$

A Joint MILP Formulation: We are interested in minimizing the total communication cost for all the dataflow computing requests as

$$Cost_{com} = \sum_{f \in F} \sum_{e_{uv} \in E^e} \lambda_{uv}^{f_{t(u)t(v)}} \cdot P_{h(u)h(v)}. \tag{10}$$

By summing up all above, we get the following **Com-Min** problem:

Com-Min: $\min: \sum_{f \in F} \sum_{e_{uv} \in E^e} \lambda_{uv}^{f_{t(u)t(v)}} \cdot P_{h(u)h(v)},$

$\text{s.t.} : (1)-(9)$

$x_v \in \{0,1\}, \forall v \in V^e, x_s^f \in \{0,1\}, \forall f \in F, s \in S.$

Note that it is computationally prohibitive to solve this MILP problem due to the involvement of integer variables x_v, especially in large-scale network cases. To tackle this problem, we design a low-complexity heuristic algorithm in the next section.

5   Heuristic Algorithm Design

Relaxation has been widely regarded as an efficient way to address the MILP problem. Therefore, we are motivated to propose a relaxation-based heuristic algorithm by relaxing all the binary variables. Following such principle, we design our relaxation-based algorithm shown in Algorithm 1.

As shown in line 1 of Algorithm 1, we first relax all the binary variables into real ones ranging in $[0,1]$ to obtain a linear programing (LP) model **Com-Min-LP**, which can be solved in polynomial time. Once the values of $x_v, \forall v \in V^e$ are determined, the only thing left is to schedule the flows towards minimal cost under the constraints of SDN switches' rule space size limitations. In line 14, we first take the values of $x_v, \forall v \in V^e$ into **Com-Min-LP** ans solve the resulted in LP formulation to obtain an initial flow scheduling. Note that, we as relax the variables x_s^f into real number variables, the rule space constraints may be violated. Therefore, starting from 15, we try to take the rule space constraints into consideration until all flows are scheduled. We first convert all the non-zero x_s^f into 1 to indicate that one rule shall be embedded in $s \in S$ for flow $f \in F$ (line 16). After that, we initialize the unscheduled flow set $newFlowSet$ as empty set and start to check the flows that incur rule space constraints in lines 18–25. For each switch $s \in S$, we check whether converting all the non-zero x_s^s into 1 violates the rule space constraint or not. If there is enough space, we set the residual rule space as the space of the switch for next-round optimization (line 20); otherwise, we remove the flows with the least values of x_s^f and put f into $newFlowSet$ until s have enough space to accommodate the rest flows (lines 22–23). Accordingly, as s does not have enough space to accommodate more flows any more, we shall remove it from S for the next-round optimization. After we update the rule space for all switches and obtain the unscheduled flow set, we can re-solve **Com-Min-LP** with the updated system parameters to obtain new flow schedule solutions. Such routine proceeds until all flows get completed scheduled.

6   Performance Evaluation

In this section, we report our simulation based performance evaluation for our proposed relaxation heuristic algorithm ("Relax"), which is compared against the optimal solution ("Opt") and a greedy algorithm ("Greedy"). Commercial solver Gurobi[1] is used to solve our **Com-Min** and **Com-Min-LP** problems. In default, we consider a substrate network with $|N| = 5$ servers interconnected by

---

[1] http://www.gurobi.com.

$|S| = 3$ switches, where each switch is with $C_s = 5, \forall s \in S$. We then investigate how our algorithm performs under different scenarios with different settings and also how various system parameters affect the overall communication cost.

Algorithm 1. Relaxation-based Algorithm

1: Relax the binary variables x_v, solve the **Com-Min-LP** problem
2: Sort $x_v, \forall v \in V^e$ decreasingly into Π_v
3: **for all** Process $p \in P$ **do**
4: 　　**while** True **do**
5: 　　　　Find the first $x_v \in \Pi_v$ with $t(v) = p$
6: 　　　　Set the found out x_v as 1 and the others with $t(v) = p$ as 0
7: 　　　　**if** The host server $h(v)$ has enough resource to accommodate process $t(v)$
　　　　then
8: 　　　　　　break
9: 　　　　**else**
10: 　　　　　　Set the found out x_v as 0 and remove it from Π_v
11: 　　　　**end if**
12: 　　**end while**
13: **end for**
14: Take the values of $x_v, \forall v \in V^e$ as known into

$$\textbf{Com-Min-LP:} \quad \min : \sum_{f \in F} \sum_{e_{uv} \in E^e} \lambda_{uv}^{f_{t(u)t(v)}} \cdot P_{n(u)n(v)},$$

$$\text{s.t.} : (1) - (9)$$

$$0 \leq x_s^f \leq 1, \forall f \in F, s \in S.$$

　　and solve it to obtain the flow scheduling decisions
15: **while** Not all flows have been scheduled **do**
16: 　　Convert all the non-zero $x_s^f, \forall s \in S, f \in F$ to 1
17: 　　$newFlowSet \leftarrow \emptyset$
18: 　　**for all** $s \in S$ **do**
19: 　　　　**if** The switch $s \in S$ has enough rule space to accommodate the rules **then**
20: 　　　　　　Set the residual rule space as the rule space capacity of s
21: 　　　　**else**
22: 　　　　　　Remove the flows with the least values of x_s^f until s can accommodate all the flows, and put f into $newFlowSet$
23: 　　　　　　Remove s from S
24: 　　　　**end if**
25: 　　**end for**
26: 　　Resolve the **Com-Min-LP** with the updated rule space capacity constraints and updated flow set $newFlowSet$
27: **end while**

6.1　On the Effect of Rule Space

As our work intends to investigate how the rule space affects the dataflow computing program deployment and the corresponding communication cost, we first

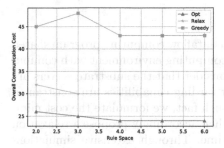 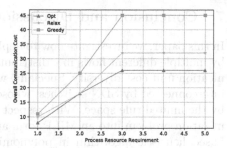

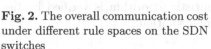

Fig. 2. The overall communication cost under different rule spaces on the SDN switches

Fig. 3. The overall communication cost under different process resource requirements

conduct a series of experiments by varying the number of rule space in each switches from 2−6 and plot the experiments in Fig. 2. We can first notice that the overall communication cost achieved by our algorithm is much close the optimal solution, under any values of rule space. This validates the correctness and efficiency of our algorithm. We also further notice that the communication cost shows as a decreasing function of the rule space. This is because with more rule space, more flows can go through the switches with lower unit communication cost and hence the communication cost decreases. However, when the rule space is large enough, most flows already can go though the switches with lower unit communication cost, the overall communication cost becomes convergent. Such phenomenon proves that the rule space indeed has deep influence on the dataflow computing program deployment and hence the communication cost, especially when the rule space is severely limited.

6.2 On the Effect of Process Resource Requirement

Next, we check how our algorithm performs under different process resource requirements by varying the resource requirement of each process. The experiment results are reported in Fig. 3. Once again, we notice that our algorithm performs much close to the optimal solution. This verifies that our algorithm can well adapt to the changes of process resource requirement and always obtain sub-optimal solution. We also notice that the overall communication cost also increases with the process resource requirement. This is because, when the process resource requirement increases, the number of processes that can be hosted by one server decreases. This makes more processes go through the switches, inevitably incurring comparatively higher communication cost. Considering an extreme case when all processes can be accommodated in one server. In this case, no communication cost is incurred as all communications can go through intra-server communication.

7   Conclusion and Discussion

In this paper, we investigate how to deploy a dataflow computing program shared by multiple different flows in a distributed computing environment with communication unit cost diversity. Specially, we consider that the substrate servers are interconnected by SDN switches, whose forwarding capabilities are constrained by the limited rule space. With respect to such fact, we formulate the cost minimization problem into an MILP form and then accordingly propose a relaxation based heuristic algorithm in polynomial time. Through extensive simulation-based studies, the high efficiency of our heuristic algorithm is verified by the fact that it performs much close to the optimal solution.

Acknowledgment. This work was partially sponsored by the National Basic Research 973 Program of China under grant 2015CB352403, the National Natural Science Foundation of China (NSFC) (61602301, 61402425).

References

1. Abadi, M., et al.: TensorFlow: a system for large-scale machine learning. In: Proceedings of OSDI, vol. 16, pp. 265–283 (2016)
2. Botero, J.F., Hesselbach, X., Duelli, M., Schlosser, D., Fischer, A., De Meer, H.: Energy efficient virtual network embedding. IEEE Commun. Lett. **16**(5), 756–759 (2012)
3. Chowdhury, N.M.K., Rahman, M.R., Boutaba, R.: Virtual network embedding with coordinated node and link mapping. In: INFOCOM 2009, pp. 783–791. IEEE (2009)
4. Fischer, A., Botero, J.F., Beck, M.T., de Meer, H., Hesselbach, X.: Virtual network embedding: a survey. IEEE Commun. Surv. Tutor. **15**(4), 1888–1906 (2013)
5. Giroire, F., Moulierac, J., Phan, T.K.: Optimizing rule placement in software-defined networks for energy-aware routing. In: 2014 IEEE Global Communications Conference (GLOBECOM), pp. 2523–2529. IEEE (2014)
6. Gonzalez, J.E., Xin, R.S., Dave, A., Crankshaw, D., Franklin, M.J., Stoica, I.: Graphx: graph processing in a distributed dataflow framework. In: Proceedings of OSDI, pp. 599–613. USENIX, Broomfield (2014)
7. Gu, L., Zeng, D., Guo, S., Xiang, Y., Hu, J.: A general communication cost optimization framework for big data stream processing in geo-distributed data centers. IEEE Trans. Comput. **65**(1), 19–29 (2016)
8. Kang, N., Liu, Z., Rexford, J., Walker, D.: Optimizing the one big switch abstraction in software-defined networks. In: Proceedings of the Ninth ACM Conference on Emerging Networking Experiments and Technologies, pp. 13–24. ACM (2013)
9. Kreutz, D., Ramos, F.M., Verissimo, P.E., Rothenberg, C.E., Azodolmolky, S., Uhlig, S.: Software-defined networking: a comprehensive survey. Proc. IEEE **103**(1), 14–76 (2015)
10. Murray, D.G., Schwarzkopf, M., Smowton, C., Smith, S., Madhavapeddy, A., Hand, S.: CIEL: a universal execution engine for distributed data-flow computing. In: Proceedings of ACM/USENIX NSDI, pp. 113–126 (2011)
11. Sun, G., Yu, H., Anand, V., Li, L.: A cost efficient framework and algorithm for embedding dynamic virtual network requests. Futur. Gener. Comput. Syst. **29**(5), 1265–1277 (2013)

A Short Review of Constructing Noise Map Using Crowdsensing Technology

Xuhui Zhang[1], Lei Shu[1,2(✉)], Zhiqiang Huo[1,2], Mithun Mukherjee[1], and Yu Zhang[2]

[1] Guangdong Provincial Key Laboratory
on Petrochemical Equipment Fault Diagnosis,
Guangdong University of Petrochemical Technology, Maoming, China
xuhui.zhang.sophia@outlook.com, mithun.mukherjee@outlook.com
[2] School of Engineering, University of Lincoln, Lincoln, UK
{lshu,zhuo,yzhang}@lincoln.ac.uk

Abstract. The advent of crowdsensing technology has provided a promising possibility for monitoring noise pollution in large-scale areas. Constructing noise map by using mobile smart phones in a cost-effective manner is being widely used in the city and industrial plants. In this short paper, the state-of-the-art crowdsensing-based noise map applications are first summarized. Furthermore, open research challenges associated with building up noise map are highlighted.

Keywords: Crowdsensing · Noise map · Mobile phone

1 Introduction

In the past decades, the increasing development of mobile smartphones has greatly evolved the crowdsensing technology, which allows citizens having smart phones and common goals to participate in measuring, uploading, and reporting events of interests with the help of enriched sensors embedded in smart phones, such as microphones, cameras, and the Global Positioning System (GPS) [1,2]. Particularly, the use of microphone and the GPS in smart phones has the capabilities of measuring precise sound level and geographical locations in ambient environment, and finally providing a solution to noise pollution monitoring [3] and constructing noise map as an alternative to traditional methods. In the smart cities, noise map is capable of providing sound level information for authorities and residents related to noise pollution distribution in regions of interest, such as streets, markets, and communities [4]. Traditionally, noise map methods include simulation-based maps, sensor networks, and grassroots campaigns; however, most of them require professional devices and human resources with an expensive way in both financial and time consumption [5]. In recent decades, crowdsensing-based noise map applications have been successfully applied in monitoring noise pollution in the filed of transport, community, and industrial

© ICST Institute for Computer Sciences, Social Informatics and Telecommunications Engineering 2018
I. Romdhani et al. (Eds.): CollaborateCom 2017, LNICST 252, pp. 37–43, 2018.
https://doi.org/10.1007/978-3-030-00916-8_4

plants in modern cities [6]. For instance, some urban noise map applications have been implemented, such as industrial noise map [7], traffic road noise maps of the city of Split, Croatia [8], and noise maps of New York City [9].

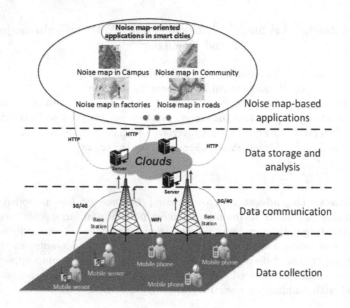

Fig. 1. Noise map based on crowdsensing in smart cities.

2 Crowdsensing-Based Noise Map in Smart Cities

In contrast with the use of professional devices to monitor noise pollution on-site, the application of crowdsensing-based noise map enjoys the advantage of widely used population participated in measuring and reporting noise pollution with the use of cost-effective smart phones. In general, the crowdsensing-based model for constructing noise map can be briefly divided into four levels: (1) data collection: amounts of sound level data is measured and uploaded by using mobile devices which can be not only smart phones, but also mobile devices having the capability of measuring sound level and communication functionalities [10]; (2) data communication: participators upload and report noise pollution by means of various networks, such as 3rd Generation and 4th Generation (3G/4G), WiFi, and even nearest base station supporting wireless communication (e.g., bluetooth and wireless sensor networks) [11]; (3) data storage and analysis: spatial-temporal data is persistently saved and analyzed related to applications of interest [1]; (4) noise map-based applications: urban applications are applicable to not only monitor noise pollution but also provide services associated with alleviating noise pollution [12]. The big picture of noise map based on crowdsensing in smart cities is shown in Fig. 1.

Table 1. A summary of state-of-the-art for noise map.

	Authors	Year	Objectives	Contributions	Data sources
Crowdsensing-based noise map	Maisonneuve et al. [13]	2009	Measuring and map noise pollution	Data calibration, community exposure, standards/interoperability	A mobile application named NoiseTube
	Kanjo et al. [14]	2010	Urban noise monitoring and map	Data calibration, community exposure, standards, unobtrusiveness, context awareness	A mobile application named NoiseSPY
	Rena et al. [15]	2010	Participatory urban noise map system	Data calibration, community exposure, unobtrusiveness, context awareness	A mobile application named Ear-Phone
	Schweizer et al. [16]	2011	Real-time participatory noise maps	1. Design an open urban sensing platform da_sense, which can also monitors toxic gases 2. Data calibration, community exposure, participatory	A mobile application named NoiseMap
	D'Hondt et al. [17]	2013	Verify the official noise map	Construct purely measurement-based noise maps with error margins	A mobile application named NoiseTube
	Liu et al. [9,10,18]	2014	Diagnose the noise pollution in NYC	1. A three dimension tensor for data analyzing [18] 2. Location ranking and noise composition analysis [9] 3. Compute the average of the top 10% big measurements as the real noise level [10]	311 complaint data, social media, road network data, Points of Interests (POIs)
	Hachem et al. [19]	2015	Customize the urban civics middleware for monitoring noise pollution	Apply data assimilation techniques to noise with mobile unplanned sensing	Microphone devices
	Poslončec-Petrić et al. [8]	2016	Dynamic noise map	Design web platform based on 3D urban information model	A mobile application named NoiseTube
	Zhu et al. [20]	2016	Accurate noise level measurements	Present a system iCal based on calibrating smartphones, consisting node-based calibration and crowdsourcing-based calibration	Microphone devices
	Kumar et al. [21]	2017	Monitor road traffic noise	1. A fuzzy inference system 2. Visualize the noise level and endanger degree on Google Maps by overlaying colors	Microphone devices
	Bozkurt et al. [7]	2017	Numerical simulation of industrial noise map	1. Numerical simulation on the basis of the prevailing sound propagation conditions 2. Designe noise barriers	B&K 2260 Sound and Frequency Analyser and microphone devices
Others	Rosão et al. [22]	2015	Recreational activities in strategic noise map	Main methods for noise characterization and modeling	N/A
	Wei et al. [23]	2016	Dynamic interpolation methods for accurately updating a noise map	Correction terms for sources path and propagation paths	Sensor nodes
	Cai et al. [24,25]	2016 2017	Update noise map in Guangzhou	1. Calculate noise pressure level deviation, then some roads can be directly updated by adding [24] 2. Only the S-R noise attenuation items update by a speed-density model [25]	Geographic Information System (GIS) & GPS & Videos

In practice, the microphones are widely used to measure acoustic data samples and simulate the frequency response of human hearing by an A-weighting filter [5]. Usually, sound level, timestamp, and GPS information as well as annotations can be collected from participators related to where, when, and what kinds of data sources of noise pollution. However, due to these heterogeneities introduced by devices made by different companies, deviation exists in crowd-sensing data contributed by participators, such as sound level and GPS data. Moreover, the purposes of contributing data using personal cost are also different. Taking this into account, in the recent decade, researchers have conducted a series of studies to improve the feasibility and accuracy of noise map. The typical techniques and applications related to noise map are summarised in Table 1.

For instance, Maisonneuve et al. [13] proposed a platform in 2009, Noise-Tube, which provides the functionality of GPS calibration and noise distribution visualization. The detail capabilities of NoiseTube were evaluated in [17]. Afterwards, Kanjo et al. [14] proposed a mobile platform, NoiseSPY, to monitor noise pollution using smartphones. Meanwhile, Rana et al. [15] presented the design, implementation and performance evaluation of an end-to-end participatory urban noise map system called Ear-Phone. Furthermore, a participatory sensing prototype, called NoiseMap [16], was proposed for providing an open urban sensing platform, aiming at collecting noise levels by using smartphones and gas information in ambient environment by using wireless sensor nodes. In addition, to avoid the data sparsity of noise levels, a three dimension tensor was modeled in [18], which presents regions, time slots, and noise categories, using a context-aware tensor decomposition method to fill in the missing entries. Liu et al. [10] proposed a method for calculating the average of the 10% maximum measurements as the noise level for which can actually reflect people's tolerance to noise. Moreover, Zhu et al. [20] presented a system, called iCal, for accurate noise level measurements based on calibrating smartphones. And researches in [8] created a real-time dynamic noise map based on 3D Urban Information Model. Recently, a data assimilation method was utilized by Hachem et al. [19], for the purpose of generating more accurate noise maps that combine simulated and measured noise levels. Kumar et al. [21] made use of a fuzzy inference system to classify the impact of noise pollution on human health and visualized the noise level on Google Maps by overlaying colors corresponding to the impact on health. Bozkurt et al. [7] studied the numerical simulation-based industrial noise map and designed noise barriers for reducing excessive noise.

In purpose of further enhancing the performance of constructing noise map, a number of published literatures dedicated to providing reliable and robust data services. Giving an example, for noise map system update, Wei et al. [23] proposed an updating method for dynamic noise map based on interpolation. Additionally, Cai et al. [24,25] further investigated a large-scale three dimension system for rapidly updating road traffic noise map. To justify the need of inclusion of entertainment noise, recreational activities in strategic noise map is classified and modeled in [22].

3   Open Research Challenges in Crowdsensing-Based Noise Map

There are still many limitations and open research challenges in crowdsensing-based noise map since noise propagation can be easily influenced by objects in the travel path. In urban regions, traffic is the main source of outdoor noise and usually difficult to predict due to the feature of continuous movement. To sum up, several factors may have effects on noise map performance, such as:

1. The microphones have different deviation for noise measurement (e.g., linearity and noise reduction techniques).
2. Unexpected sound level interference generated from objects and ambient environment (e.g., the weather and user movements).
3. Noise sources in some regions have multiple types (e.g., human activities, industrial noise, traffic noise, construction noise).
4. Users' private issues during participatory activities (e.g., GPS, acoustic file).
5. Stability of the connectivity between devices for full coverage of targeted areas of interest.
6. The key technical issues associated with spatial-temporal data towards noise map, such as sparse data storage, data calibration, and data reconstruction.

4   Conclusions

In this short paper, the typical crowdsensing-based applications for the noise map applied in smart cities are briefly presented and summarized. Furthermore, the general implementation and systems of crowdsensing-based noise map applications are summarised. Finally, open research challenges are discussed to further investigate the feasibility and effectiveness of noise map in smart cities.

Acknowledgement. This work is partially supported by Science and Technology Planning Project of Guangdong Province (No. 2017A050506057), China Maoming Engineering Research Center on Industrial Internet of Things (No. 517018), International and Hong Kong, Macao & Taiwan collaborative innovation platform and major international cooperation projects of colleges in Guangdong Province (No. 2015KGJHZ026).

References

1. Guo, B., et al.: Mobile crowd sensing and computing: the review of an emerging human-powered sensing paradigm. ACM Comput. Surv. (CSUR) 48(1), 1–31 (2015)
2. Shu, L., Chen, Y., Huo, Z., Bergmann, N., Wang, L.: When mobile crowd sensing meets traditional industry. IEEE Access 5(99), 15300–15307 (2017)
3. Anon: Future noise policy: European commission green paper. Noise News International, vol. 5, pp. 74–94(21), June 1997

4. Miller, L., Springthorpe, C., Murphy, E., King, E.A., et al.: Environmental noise mapping with smartphone applications: a participatory noise map of West Hartford, CT. In: INTER-NOISE and NOISE-CON Congress and Conference Proceedings, vol. 252, pp. 445–451, June 2016
5. Maisonneuve, N., Stevens, M., Ochab, B.: Participatory noise pollution monitoring using mobile phones. **15**(1, 2), 51–71 (2010)
6. Leao, S., Zhou, W.: Monitoring exposure to traffic noise with mobile phones in China: a review of context. Int. J. Inf. Comput. Sci. (IJICS) **3**, 52–63 (2014)
7. Bozkurt, T.S., Demirkale, S.Y.: The field study and numerical simulation of industrial noise mapping. J. Build. Eng. **9**(Supplement C), 60–75 (2017)
8. Poslončec-Petrić, V., Vuković, V., Frangeš, S., Bačić, Ž.: Voluntary noise mapping for smart city. In: ISPRS Annals of Photogrammetry, Remote Sensing and Spatial Information Sciences, vol. III-4/W1, pp. 131–137, August 2016
9. Wang, Y., Zheng, Y., Liu, T.: A noise map of New York city. In: Proceedings of the 2014 ACM International Joint Conference on Pervasive and Ubiquitous Computing: Adjunct Publication, pp. 275–278, September 2014
10. Liu, T., Zheng, Y., Liu, L., Liu, Y., Zhu, Y.: Methods for sensing urban noises. Technical report MSR-TR-2014-66, May 2014
11. Ganti, R.K., Ye, F., Lei, H.: Mobile crowdsensing: current state and future challenges. IEEE Commun. Mag. **49**(11), 32–39 (2011)
12. Guillaume, G., et al.: Noise mapping based on participative measurements. Noise Mapp **3**, 140–156 (2016)
13. Maisonneuve, N., Stevens, M., Niessen, M.E., Steels, L.: NoiseTube: measuring and mapping noise pollution with mobile phones. Inf. Technol. Environ. Eng. **2**(6), 215–228 (2009)
14. Kanjo, E.: NoiseSPY: a real-time mobile phone platform for urban noise monitoring and mapping. Mob. Netw. Appl. **15**(4), 562–574 (2010)
15. Rana, R.K., Chou, C.T., Kanhere, S.S., Bulusu, N., Hu, W.: Ear-Phone: an end-to-end participatory urban noise mapping system. In: Proceedings of the 9th ACM/IEEE International Conference on Information Processing in Sensor Networks, IPSN 2010, pp. 105–116, January 2010
16. Schweizer, I., Bärtl, R., Schulz, A., Probst, F., Mühläuser, M.: NoiseMap-real-time participatory noise maps. In: Second International Workshop on Sensing Applications on Mobile Phones, November 2011
17. D'Hondt, E., Stevens, M., Jacobs, A.: Participatory noise mapping works! An evaluation of participatory sensing as an alternative to standard techniques for environmental monitoring. Pervasive Mob. Comput. **9**(5), 681–694 (2013)
18. Zheng, Y., Liu, T., Wang, Y., Zhu, Y., Liu, Y., Chang, E.: Diagnosing New York city's noises with ubiquitous data. In: Proceedings of the 2014 ACM International Joint Conference on Pervasive and Ubiquitous Computing, pp. 715–725, September 2014
19. Hachem, S., Mallet, V., Pathak, A., Raverdy, P.G., Bhatia, R.: Monitoring noise pollution using the urban civics middleware. In: IEEE First International Conference on Big Data Computing Service and Applications, pp. 52–61, March 2015
20. Zhu, Y., Li, J., Liu, L., Tham, C.K.: iCal: intervention-free calibration for measuring noise with smartphones. In: IEEE 21st International Conference on Parallel and Distributed Systems (ICPADS), pp. 85–91, December 2015
21. Kumar, R., Mukherjee, A., Singh, V.: Traffic noise mapping of Indian roads through smartphone user community participation. Environ. Monit. Assess. **189**(1), 17 (2017)

22. Rosão, V., Grilo, Á.: The inclusion of recreational activities in strategic noise maps. In: Euronoise, January 2015
23. Wei, W., Van Renterghem, T., De Coensel, B., Botteldooren, D.: Dynamic noise mapping: a map-based interpolation between noise measurements with high temporal resolution. Appl. Acoust. **101**, 127–140 (2016)
24. Cai, M., Yao, Y., Wang, H.: A traffic-noise-map update method based on monitoring data. J. Acoust. Soc. Am. **141**(4), 2604–2610 (2017)
25. Cai, M., Zhang, Z., Ma, X., Li, F.: Rapid updating if 3D road traffic noise maps in large cities. Noise Control. Eng. J. **64**(3), 335–341 (2016)

Research of Positioning Tracking on Dynamic Target Based on the Integral Complementing Algorithm

Jianrong Xu[1], Guiping Lu[1], Jingsheng Lin[1], and Jianfeng Huang[2(✉)]

[1] Beijing Institute of Technology, Zhuhai, Zhuhai, China
380393916@qq.com, lgpcan@163.com, 742219569@qq.com,
[2] Guangdong University of Petrochemical Technology, Maoming, China
45214083@qq.com

Abstract. Aiming at the problem of single target object detection and tracking in unknown environment, we propose a dynamic target tracking and positioning method based on integral compensation algorithm. The discrete digital quantity is quantized and transformed into a continuous analog quantity, and the tracking direction is controlled by the angular rate control function. In the process of tracking, if the motion state of the target changes, the control function is directly integrated with the compensation algorithm to get a new tracking direction. Through the mathematical modeling analysis and experimental tests, experiments showed that in the single dynamic target object tracking, for the general object dynamic tracking, has a good dynamic, real-time. It has a certain application prospect in single target detection and multi-target tracking accuracy correction.

Keywords: Target location · Dynamic real-time tracking
Integral compensation

1 Introduction

Location is one of the key technologies of many intelligent applications, which is one of the most important problems in the realization of intelligent robots. It is also the basis of intelligent robot autonomous navigation and path planning. According to the presence or absence of the environmental model, the location method can be divided into the environment based on the model which can be divided into relative positioning, absolute positioning and combination of three types of positioning, no environment model positioning, and the establishment of simultaneous environmental modeling and simultaneous localization and mapping, [1, 2, 14]. The study method is carried out in the context of relative positioning. The current robot positioning algorithm is basically based on high-performance processor, with high detection accuracy of the radar, camera, ranging and other detection sensors. For robots with less processor performance and with limited hardware interface resources, however, it is less applicable. To solve this problem, this paper presents a simple digital sensor to achieve the goal of positioning and tracking.

© ICST Institute for Computer Sciences, Social Informatics and Telecommunications Engineering 2018
I. Romdhani et al. (Eds.): CollaborateCom 2017, LNICST 252, pp. 44–52, 2018.
https://doi.org/10.1007/978-3-030-00916-8_5

In order to solve this problem, this paper proposes a robot target tracking and positioning method based on integral compensation algorithm [6]. Robot in the unknown location of the limited environment uses its own relatively simple IO sensor for all-round detection, measures the relative direction of the target object [3, 5]. Through the processing of the integral compensation algorithm, the detected discrete digital quantity is quantized and transformed into continuous analog quantity to realize the tracking of the dynamic target object. For the detection of a single target object tracking, it avoids the use of complex sensors and high hardware processor. The sensor in its detection range gets the target mobile position information so that it can realize detection and tracking.

2 Integral Compensation Algorithm

2.1 Track Analysis

Robot detected the surrounding target object and achieved the target object positioning and tracking. If the target object was stationary, it could directly detect the angle θ of the target object relative to it, and perform the tracking target after the rotation angle θ. If the machine was moving and the target object was static or moving, the error in this way was very large, might not find the target object. At this time, the introduction of integral compensation algorithm could solve this problem. The machine was in the process of tracking the target object, and constantly corrected the direction with feedback relative to the robot. The walking path was shown in Figs. 1 and 2 (the green: robot; The yellow: target object).

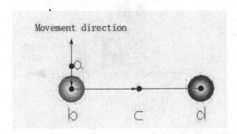
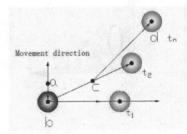

Fig. 1. Tracking path for fixed-point detection (Color figure online)

Fig. 2. Mobile detection walking path (Color figure online)

2.2 Integral Algorithm Principle

The angular rate control function required to make the robot needed to be rotated satisfies f(x). Assume that the target B was detected on the side at time t_1 (Fig. 3a).

At this time, it needed to adjust their own posture and to achieve tracking, and the angle required static point rotation was $\theta_1 = 90°$; If both robots were moving system, status change, t_2 moment, the robot ended its rotation and began to track when objects located, The rotation angle required for execution at this time was θ_2, $0 < \theta_2 < 180°$ (Fig. 3b).

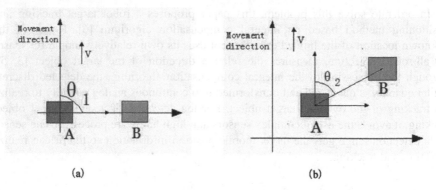

Fig. 3. Position analysis before and after rotation

In the figure, v was the direction of normal advance, A was our robot, and B was the opposite robot.

In the course of the process, we had integral process for ω to get the angle θ according to state diagram of Fig. 3, the state analysis before and after rotation positioning. The integral interval of function–f(x) was [t₁, t₂], the area surrounded by ω = 0, x = t₁, x = t₂, ω = f(x). As shown in Fig. 4.

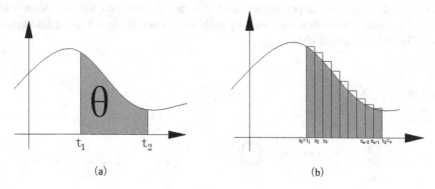

Fig. 4. Integral interval diagram

The interval [t₁, t₂] divided into n smaller interval [x₁, x₂], [x₂, x₃]......[x_{n-2}, x_{n-1}], [x_{n-1}, x_n], The intersection of the upper left corner and the function was parallel to the x-axis parallel to form a narrow square rectangle. It's length was:

$$\Delta x_1 = x_2 - x_1, \quad \Delta x_2 = x_3 - x_2, \ldots \Delta x_i = x_{i+1} - x_i \tag{1}$$

Take a little ε_i freely in each small interval $[x_i, x_{i+1}]$, $[x_i, x_{i+1}]$ as its end, $f(\varepsilon_i)$ as its high, the area of the narrow square rectangle was s_i, and the rectangles in the interval were summed:

$$\theta = \lim_{n \to \infty} \left(\left(\sum_{n=1}^{n} f(\xi_i) \right) \Delta x_i \right) = \lim_{n \to \infty} \sum_{n=1}^{n} s_i \tag{2}$$

If the longest length of the narrow square rectangle in these cells was λ, when $\lambda \to 0$ ($n \to \infty$), we could get a more accurate target angle of myopia, and it was,

$$\theta = \int_{t_1}^{t_2} f(x)dx = \int_{t_1}^{t_2} s_i dx \tag{3}$$

In practical applications, we made $t_1 = 0$, t_2 be the time to end the rotation ($t_2 \leq T_{max}$, T_{max} was the time required for the sensor to achieve $360°$ omni-directional scanning).

2.3 Algorithm Flow Chart

After the robot was powered on, all ports and peripherals were initialized, and the robot used a relatively simple IO sensor in a limited environment for unknown locations for omni-directional detection. The robot used the angular rate to control the movement direction of the robot after detecting the relative direction of the target object. When the target changed the movement state, the robot directly integrated the control function to correct the direction of the target relative to the robot, and kept the motion orientation detection of the target object at the same time as the tracking object. Through the processing of the integral compensation algorithm, the discrete digital quantity was processed and converted into continuous analog quantity to realize the tracking of the dynamic target object. The algorithm flow chart was as follows in Fig. 5.

3 Experiment and Result Analysis

3.1 Experimental Platform Introduction

The platform, used in the experiment, was composed of MultiFLEX™2 - AVR controller, digital sensor, motor-powered lithium battery, BDMC1203 motor drive, FAULHABER 2342 24CR geared motor and various robot hardware structure connected devices. As shown in Fig. 6.

3.2 Experimental Results

First, we simulated the static target tracking tests, as shown in Fig. 7. The green box at the center of the table represented the robot A and the yellow box B stood for the target. B was at (40 cm, 0) relative to A.

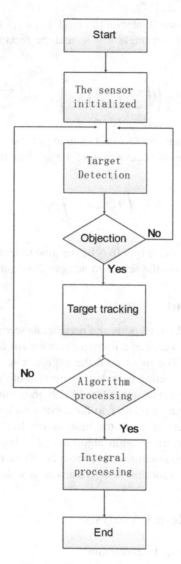

Fig. 5. Algorithm flow chart

In the test, we let B remain at (40 cm, 0), and the starting direction of the A robot was at an angle θ (0 ≤ θ ≤ 90°) from the horizontal axis. We made θ = 90° and reduce the angle of θ gradually until θ = 0°. At the same time, we recorded the time –T, required when A walked to B while the angle between A and B was 0°. Among them, three sets of static test data were recorded at table, as shown in Table 1.

We found that, due to the smoothness of the site, the roughness of the robot wheels, the battery provided for robot and other external factors [10], and relationship at angular rate function—f(x), when the angel was 0° between A and B, A might not immediately stop rotation and continued to move forward to find the target. It was

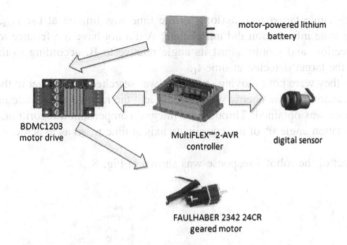

Fig. 6. Hardware structure diagram

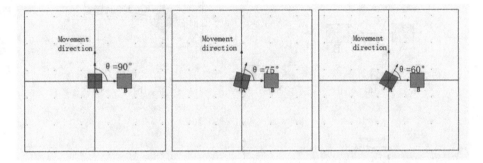

Fig. 7. Static test illustration (Color figure online)

Table 1. Test time-consuming (target was static)

Angle\Time consuming	T₁	T₂	T₃	T₄	T₅	T₆	T₇	T₈
90°	0	0	0	0	0	0	0	0
	1″30	1″46	1″23	1″14	1″23	1″48	1″27	1″09
75°	0	0	0	0	0	0	0	0
	1″56	2″86	2″44	3″24	2″83	2″78	2″75	3″26
60°	0	0	0	0	0	0	0	0
	3″41	2″92	2″90	2″83	3″43	2″89	3″17	3″18

necessary to perform the integral compensation process again and continued the reverse adjustment so that the A could find the specific direction of B and finally tracked B. The main solution to the reverse adjustment was to select the appropriate angular velocity–f(x) or to increase the roughness of the robot wheel. These factor, however, did not affect the actual effect for A and B that are the moving system.

In the dynamic target test, as long as the time was limited at $t < T_{max}$, and the surrounding state information did not change, A did not have a reference to B in the forward direction, and would adjust its angle relative to B, according to the relative position of the target detected at time t_1.

Because they were both moving system, A was searched for a target in the range of $0 \sim \theta^\circ_{max}$, as long as the enemy was detected and the relative coordinate angle θ° of the initial time was obtained. Through the integral compensation algorithm, A gained the actual rotation angle θ° of the coordinate axis at time t_1, so as to achieve the target tracking.

The effect of the robot's response was shown in Fig. 8.

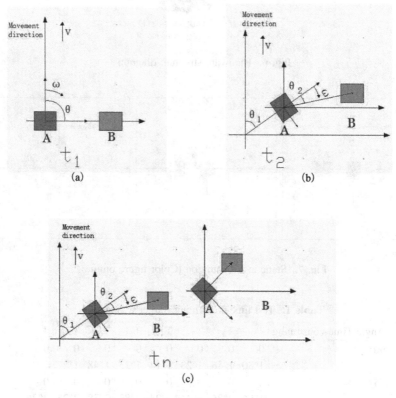

Fig. 8. State adjustment process

4   Conclusion

Based on the integral compensation algorithm, the robot target tracking and positioning method, by the digital sensor to detect the relative position of the target object direction, the robot converted the discrete digital signals detected and represented the enemy's direction into continuous analog by the integral algorithm. In the process of finding the target object, the robot performed integral compensation on the rotation function–$\omega = f(x)$, and quickly located the target object relative to its position. Through proper adjustment, the object was positioned and tracked. In the process of tracking, its system could still be aware of all the surrounding circumstances. When the surrounding situation changing, it would adjust its position to respond to this at any time, which verified that algorithm has real-time performance.

In the limited environment and limited resources of the controller IO port, the algorithm, to a certain extent, could solve the positioning and tracking of the target object within the effective range of the sensor detection, which had certain practical application significance.

Acknowledgements. This work is supported by Natural Science Foundation of Guangdong Province (No. 2016A030307029) and Maoming Engineering Research Center on Industrial Internet of Things (No. 517018).

References

1. Cho, B., Moon, W., Seo, W., et al.: A dead reckoning localization system for mobile robots using inertial sensors and Whell revolution encoding. J. Mech. Sci. Technol. **25**(11), 2907–2917 (2011)
2. Desouza, G.N., Kak, A.C.: Vision for mobile robot navigation: a survey. IEEE Trans. Pattern Anal. Mach. Intell. **24**(2), 237–267 (2002)
3. Kuang, J.M., Liu, M., Lin, X.: Moving target tracking of omnidirectional robot with stereo cameras. In: InTech Book, pp. 197–220 (2008)
4. Jung, B., Sukhatme, G.S.: Cooperative Multi-robot Target Tracking. Minneapolis, Minnesota, pp. 81–90 (2006)
5. Kieffer, M., Jaulin, L., Walter, E., Meizel, D.: Guaranteed mobile robot tracking using interval analysis. In: MISC 1999, Workshop on Application of Interval Analysis to System and Control, February 1999, Girona, Spain, pp. 347–360 (1999)
6. Kanayama, Y., Kimura, Y., Miyazaki, F., Noguchi, T.: A Stable Tracking Control Method for an Autonomous
7. Rogge, J.A., Aeyels, D.: Multi-robot coverage to locate fixed and moving targets. In: 2009 IEEE Control Applications (CCA) & Intelligent Control (ISIC)
8. Rogge, J., Aeyels, D.: Multi-robot coverage to locate fixed targets using formation structures. Comput. Sci. 1–13 (2012)
9. Burgard, W., Moors, M., Stachniss, C., Schneider, F.: Coordinated multi-robot exploration. IEEE Trans. Rob. **21**, 376–386 (2005)
10. Williams, R.L., Carter, B.E., Gallina, P., Rosati, G.: Dynamic model with slip for wheeled omnidirectional robots. IEEE Trans. Robot. Automat. **18**, 285–293 (2002)
11. Kobilarov, M., Sukhatme, G., Hyams, J., Batavia, P.: People tracking and following with mobile robot using an omnidirectional camera and a laser. In: IEEE International Conference on Robotics and Automation (2006)
12. Marković, I., Chaumette, F., Petrovic, I.: Moving object detection, tracking and following using an omnidirectional camera on a mobile robot. In: IEEE International Conference on Robotics & Automation, pp. 5630–5635 (2014)
13. Blackman, S.S., Popoli, R.: Design and Analysis of Modern Tracking Systems. Artech House, Norwood (1999)

14. Yu, Q.: Research on Mobile Localization Techniques for Wheeled Restaurant Service Robots. Sanghai Jiao Tong University, Sanghai (2013)
15. Hu, J., Liu, Y., Liu, Z.: The research of dynamic obstacle avoidance on simulation robot soccer. Artif. Intell. Robot. Res. **03**, 6–10 (2014)
16. Don, Y., Wangm, A., et al: Research on novel self-location method for indoor robot based on RFID. In: Application Research of Computers, pp. 749–753 (2016)
17. Gao, W., Wang, H., et al.: Research on the calibration for a modular robot. J. Mech. Eng. **50**(3), 33–40 (2014)
18. Gao, W., Zhou, L., et al.: Research overview of indoor localization methods for autonomous mobile robots. Transducer Microsyst. Technol. **32**(12), 1–5 (2013)
19. Bao, Q., Li, S., et al.: Survey of local path planning of autonomous. Transducer Microsyst. Technol. **28**(9), 1–4 (2009)
20. Li, Z., Can, Z., et al.: Target search strategy of no-difference between the groups of robots in martial arts contest. Microprocessors **34**(6), 63–65 (2013)
21. Wang, D.: Autonomous Localization Technology of Mobile Robot. China Machine Press (2016)
22. Yan, Y., Wang, X., Liu, C.: Indoor moving target tracking method based on collaborative information fusion in Internet of Things. Chin. J. Sci. Instrum. **34**(2), 352–358 (2013)
23. Liu, X., Zhou, J.: The research and practice of martial arts challenge robot. China Water Transp. **12**(10), 89–90 (2012)
24. Liang, S., Wang, J., Wu, Y.: Fuzzy algorithm of target tracking control for multiple mobile robots. Process Autom. Instrum. **29**(2), 5–7 (2014)
25. Yu, Q.: Research on mobile localization techniques for wheeled restaurant service robots. Shanghai Jiao Tong University, Shanghai (2013)
26. Zhao, Y., Chen, W.: State-of-the art in map based localization of mobile robot. J. Shang Hai Jiao Tong Univ. **36**(10), 1435–1438 (2002)
27. Luo, R.-H., Hong, B.: The progress of simultaneous location and mapping for mobile robot. Robot **26**(2), 182–186 (2004)

LWTP: An Improved Automatic Image Annotation Method Based on Image Segmentation

Jianwei Niu[✉], Shijie Li, Shasha Mo, and Jun Ma

State Key Laboratory of Virtual Reality Technology and Systems,
School of Computer Science and Engineering, Beihang University,
Beijing 100191, China
niujianwei@buaa.edu.cn

Abstract. Automatic image annotation is a technique that can be used to quickly generate tags for a massive dataset based on the content of the images. Nearest-neighbor-based methods such as TagProp are successful methods which have been used for image annotation. However, these methods focus more on weights based on the distances between the images and their neighbors, and ignore the weights of the different labels which can co-occur in the same image. In this paper, an improved method is proposed for automatic semantic annotation of images, which tags rare labels more effectively by processing the label matrix of the training set. In addition, image segmentation and data-driven methods are adopted to provide differential weights to the tags in one image, to improve the accuracy of the predicted tags. Experimental results show that the proposed method outperforms many classical baseline methods and can generate better annotation results than state-of-the-art nearest-neighbor based methods.

Keywords: Image annotation · Tag propagation
Image segmentation · Local weights

1 Introduction

Automatic-annotation of images, a technology used to quickly generate information labels, has recently gained a lot of popularity in the domain of image processing. The annotation process aims to mainly elucidate the semantic information of the content of the image. The nearest-neighbor-based image annotation methods have shown to produce good results recently, and Tag Propagation (TagProp) [1] is one of them. The key component of the nearest-neighbor-based methods is transferring tags. The accuracy of this kind of methods heavily relies on the quality of the neighboring images. In TagProp, the authors used the Corel 5K [2] image dataset for the training and evaluation of the method. However, researchers [3] have noted that tags provided by users are imprecise. Besides, TagProp considers the weights of the labels only based on the distances between

© ICST Institute for Computer Sciences, Social Informatics and Telecommunications Engineering 2018
I. Romdhani et al. (Eds.): CollaborateCom 2017, LNICST 252, pp. 53–62, 2018.
https://doi.org/10.1007/978-3-030-00916-8_6

the images. In reality, the weights of the labels can even vary within an image based on the image content.

To address the problems above, an improved image tagging method called the Local-Weighted Tag Propagation (LWTP) method is proposed in this paper. The proposed method, which is an extension of the TagProp method, combines the nearest-neighbor-based method and information retrieval for tag prediction. Frequency-tuned significant area detection and co-segmentation techniques are utilized to assign ranked weights to the tags of each image to improve the accuracy during the propagation process. Experimental results obtained by the LWTP outperform many baseline systems and reach the state-of-art systems, which shows the effectiveness of our method.

Specifically, the proposed method consists of the following steps: Firstly, search and crawling tools are used to supplement the image tags optionally. Secondly, the label dataset is preprocessed. Thirdly, a metric learning method is used to determine the weights of the labels based on their distances from the neighboring images. Fourthly, frequency-tuned significant area detection and co-segmentation techniques are utilized to assign ranking weights to the tags within one image. Finally, the labels of the target image are predicted based on transfer mechanism of nearest neighbor images.

The remainder of this paper is organized as follows. In the next section, we briefly review the related work. Section 3 describes the details of our approach including the steps and formulas used. Experimental results are reported in Sect. 4. Finally, our conclusion and future work are given in Sect. 5.

2   Related Work

In recent years, several learning-based methods have been applied for image annotation. The most representative methods can be broadly grouped into three categories: generative methods, discriminative methods and nearest-neighbor-based methods [4]. Some influential generative methods are the Cross Media Relevance Method (CMRM) [5], the Continuous Relevance Method (CRM) [6]and the Multiple Bernoulli Relevance Method (MBRM) [7]. These methods generally work by computing the joint probability of the tags and the visual features. In contrast, discriminative methods such as [8,9] treat image annotation as a classification problem and learn a separate classifier for each label. Nearest-neighbor-based methods treat the automatic annotation as the task of propagating labels from the neighboring images, including Joint Equal Contribution (JEC) method [10] and TagProp. More recently, new learning-based methods based on deep learning have been developed. These methods use neutral networks for feature extraction and have been discussed in [11–13]. While deep-neural-network based methods are promising, they need a large amount of aligned corpus data to train the models, which may be difficult to obtain.

Additionally, model-free image annotation methods based on information retrieval [14,15] techniques provide an inspiring solution. They use novel automatic labeling algorithms for identifying the semantic content of images by combining search and data mining techniques.

3   The LWTP Method

In this section, the proposed LWTP method for image annotation is described. Here by "Local-Weighted" it means that we consider the different label weights within a single image based on the content of the image. The LWTP method can be broken down into two main steps: training the preprocessing label matrix and predicting the image tags based on the transfer mechanism. Figure 1 shows the framework of LWTP.

LWTP is a nearest-neighbor method based on TagProp. Under the assumption that visual neighbors can transfer labels to each other, the probability density function for the presence of a label w in image i is defined as equation:

$$p(y_{iw} = +1) = \sum_{j=1}^{K} \pi_{ij} p(y_{iw} = +1|j) \tag{1}$$

where K is the number of the nearest neighbors. $p(y_{iw} = +1|j)$ indicates the presence of the label w in the image j. π_{ij} is the weight between the images i and j. Generally, the weight π_{ij} is defined as:

$$\pi_{ij} = \frac{exp(-d_\theta(i,j))}{\sum_{j'} exp(-d_\theta(i,j'))} \tag{2}$$

where $d_\theta(i,j))$ is a distance-based parameter. $d_\theta(i,j))$ is learned using metric learning. It is clear that the larger the distance is, the smaller will be the contribution of the weight of the neighbor. Since the accuracy of the method strongly depends on quality of the label dataset, it is necessary to first preprocess the label matrix.

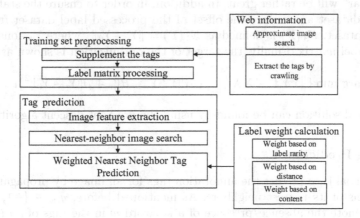

Fig. 1. Framework of the LWTP method.

3.1 Training Set Preprocessing

To tackle the deficiency in the labels, a similar image search engine[1] as well as a crawler is used to supplement the labels of the images. Then a method to balance the tag matrix is designed as following.

Let $\mathbf{L} = \{(x_1, y_1), (x_2, y_2), \ldots, (x_l, y_l)\}$ donate the training set and $\mathbf{C} = \{c_1, c_2, \ldots, c_q\}$ donate the label set, where x_i stands for the visual feature vector of each image and y_i stands for the image tag vector. $y_{iw} \in \{-1, +1\}$ denotes the absence/presence of a keyword c_w for an image i, to encode the image annotations. The correlation $(R_{i,j})$ between the labels i and j, which is used later, is defined as follows:

$$R_{i,j} = \frac{Col_{i,j}}{o_i + o_j - Col_{i,j}} \tag{3}$$

where o_i represents the frequency of the label c_i in the training set and $Col_{i,j}$ indicates the co-occurrence of the tags c_i and c_j. Here the label co-occurrence $Col_{i,j}$ refers to the situation where the labels c_i and c_j are both present at the same time in one image. The error function is defined as:

$$E(Y) = E_1(Y) + \alpha E_2(Y) + \beta E_3(Y) \tag{4}$$

where Y is the desired target label matrix to be processed. α and β are nonnegative integers to be solved. If the feature vectors of two images are similar, the probability of having the same labels in these two images is relatively large. So we define $E_1(Y) = \left\| YY^T - XX^T \right\|^2$ where Y is the tag matrix and X is the feature vector matrix. Besides, $E_2(Y) = \left\| Y^T Y - R \right\|^2$ is defined because of the assumption that there should be an association between the labels that appear together, where R stands for the correlation matrix. For example, if an image is tagged with the tags "ice", "snow", and "bear", then the probability of the label "polar" will be rather great. In addition, in order to ensure the stability of the label dataset and reduce the offset of the processed label dataset from the original dataset, $E_3(Y)$ is defined as $E_3(Y) = \left\| Y - Y_0 \right\|^2$ where Y_0 donates the original label matrix. Finally, the target of the optimization is shown as:

$$\arg \min_Y \{ \left\| YY^T - XX^T \right\|^2 + \alpha \left\| Y^T Y - R \right\|^2 + \beta \left\| Y - Y_0 \right\|^2 \}. \tag{5}$$

The optimal solution can be found by using the gradient descent algorithm.

3.2 Tag Prediction

The final goal is to predict the annotation tags for an image by propagating the annotations of its nearest neighbors. As mentioned before, $y_{iw} \in \{-1, +1\}$ is used to denote the absence/presence of a keyword w in the tags of an image i.

---

[1] http://image.baidu.com/?fr=shitu.

The prediction of the presence of the tag w in the image i is defined as Eq. (1). The calculation of $p(y_{iw} = +1|j)$ is given below:

$$p(y_{iw} = +1|j) = \begin{cases} 1 - \varepsilon & for\ y_{jw} = 1 \\ \varepsilon & for\ otherwise \end{cases} \qquad (6)$$

To avoid a prediction probability of zero, a very small factor $\varepsilon = 10^{-5}$ is used to replace any occurrence of zero. Then the objective function of the method becomes to maximize the equation:

$$L = \sum_{i,w} c_{iw} \ln p(y_{iw}) \qquad (7)$$

where c_{iw} is the cost for the imbalance between the presence of the keyword and its absence. This is defined as:

$$c_{iw} = \begin{cases} \dfrac{1}{n^+} & if\ y_{iw} = +1 \\ \dfrac{1}{n^-} & if\ y_{iw} = -1 \end{cases} \qquad (8)$$

where n^+ is the total number of the positive labels and n^- is the total number of the negative labels. As shown in Eq. (2), an approach similar to the one in [1] is used to define the weight between the image i and the image j by using the distance between them. In the whole training process, distance learning method is used to estimate the parameters. And the final logistic method uses weighted neighbor predictions as:

$$p(y_i = +1) = \sigma(\alpha \sum_j \pi_{ij} \times y_j + \beta) \qquad (9)$$

where $\sigma(z) = \frac{1}{1+e^{-z}}$ is used to boost the probability of the rare tags. α and β stand for the two parameters to estimate the weights based on the distance for each word. For Eq. (9), the calculation is based on the probability of the presence of the label y in the image i. As can be observed, the labels y_{ca} and y_{cb} in one picture c, have the same transfer probabilities for the target image. The previous nearest-neighbor method such as [1] does not distinguish the importance of different labels in an image. This paper proposes a novel method with a new and more sophisticated model which distinguishes between the label weights while taking into account the image segmentation in addition to distance-based weights. The prediction of this method is defined as:

$$p(y_i = +1) = \sigma(\alpha \sum_j \pi_{ij} \times v(j, y_j) + \beta) \qquad (10)$$

where $v(j, y_j)$ donates the weight of the label y in the image j based on the image segmentation. In order to extract local weights of labels, the "Frequency-tuned

Salient Region Detection (FSRD)" method [16], co-segmentation method [17] and Wordnet[2] are used to extract the area of each label. Algorithm 1 shows the whole algorithm for image annotation given by the LWTP method.

Algorithm 1. Image annotation

Input: Training set T with semantic annotation set V and unlabeled image I;
Output: Annotation results set $O = c1, c2, c3, c4, c5$
 1: **for** the training set **do**
 2:     use the metric learning to learn $\pi_{i,j}$ based on the distances
 3: **end for**
 4: **for** image I **do**
 5:     calculate the K nearest images
 6:     **for** image k from 1 to K **do**
 7:         **for** each word y_j of image k **do**
 8:             calculate $v(k, y_j)$of the image K based on segmentation
 9:         **end for**
10:     **end for**
11:     **for** each word c **do**
12:         calculate $p(y_{ic} = +1)$
13:     **end for**
14:     obtain c with 5 biggest $p(y_{ic} = +1)$
15: **end for**

---

4   Experiments and Results

4.1   Dataset and Evaluation Standards

In order to investigate the feasibility and the effectiveness of the proposed method, experiments are conducted on the Corel5K dataset. The Corel5K dataset contains 5,000 images from 50 Stock Photo CDs. Each CD includes 100 images and belongs to a particular theme. In the experiments, the visual feature set consists of global features Gist, RGB, LAB, HSV, local SIFT features, and Curvelet spectrum features. In order to evaluate the performance of the prediction annotation given by the LWTP method, each concept as a keyword is used to perform image retrieval operations on the dataset. The experiments take the average accuracy rate (Precision, P) and the average recall rate (Recall, R) over all concepts as evaluation metrics. At the same time, the number of annotation concepts with the positive recall value (N+) and the F1-measure (F1) are also considered in the experiments.

---

[2] http://wordnet.princeton.edu/.

4.2   Results and Analysis

Figure 2 shows the results of four examples. It includes four different types of pictures of the dataset where the left column shows the original labels of the image and right column shows the labels with probabilities given by the proposed method. It can be seen that the new results have more related tags. Table 1 shows the comparison results of the proposed LWTP method and other methods, including CRM, CMRM, etc. From Table 1, it can be observed that the LWTP method performs better than the traditional probabilistic methods such as CRM and CMRM in terms of precision, recall and F1-measure. The proposed method also performs better than the multi-class or multi-annotated image labeling algorithms such as SML. It also outperforms similar labeling methods, such as JEC, based on image feature extraction and label proximity propagation. Compared to the original TagProp method, the LWTP method obtains marked improvements of 2% for precision, 1% for recall, 2% for F1-measure and obtains 15 more words with positive recall.

Figures 3 and 4 show the retrieval P and the retrieval R for different values of nearest-neighbors (K). In these two figures, the blue curve represents the

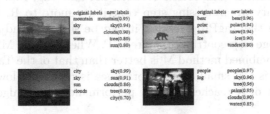

Fig. 2. Examples of the original and the new labels.

Table 1. Comparison of image auto-annotation effectiveness.

	P (%)	R (%)	F1-measure (%)	N+
CRM [6]	16	19	17.3	107
CMRM [5]	10	9	9.5	66
InfNet [18]	17	24	19.9	112
SML [8]	23	29	25.6	137
MBRM [7]	24	25	24.4	122
GS [19]	30	33	31.4	146
RF-optimize [20]	29	40	33.6	157
SVM-VT [9]	27	39	31.9	171
CNN-R [11]	32	41.3	37.2	166
JEC [10]	27	32	29.3	139
TagProp [1]	33	42	36.9	160
LWTP (our method)	**35**	**43**	**38.59**	**175**

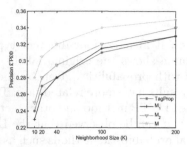

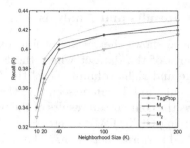

Fig. 3. Precision for different K.   **Fig. 4.** Recall for different K.

results of the original TagProp method, and the pink curve marked with M represents the results of our method. This includes the dataset preprocessing and adjustment of the local tag weights based on image segmentation. The black curve represented by M1 (Method 1) is the experimental result of the original TagProp method with our label matrix preprocessing method. The red curve, indicated by M2 (Method 2) is an improved version of the TagProp method which does not carry out preprocessing but only adjusts the weights based on image segmentation. From the comparison between M1 and TagProp, it can observed that the tag library preprocessing step contribute more to R. Comparing the curves of M2 and the TagProp results, it can be seen that adjusting only the weights of the image tags contributes more to P. When M1 and M2 are combined, the effect of the combined method M is better than that of the TagProp method. In addition, if K is too small, the performance is relatively low and unstable. When the number of K reaches 200, the performance of the algorithm achieves the desired effect.

Figure 5 compares the Mean Average Precision (MAP) of the TagProp method and the proposed method. This result is also in line with the expected improvement. In order to compare the algorithm and supplement the experimental results, the co-segmentation method is also tried for image segmentation and object extraction. Figure 6 shows the P-R value for different SNs, where SN represents the number of similar images used for collaborative segmentation.

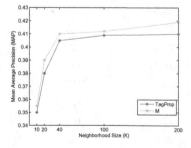

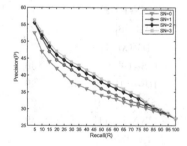

Fig. 5. Retrieval MAP for different K.   **Fig. 6.** Co-segmentation results.

As the value of SN increases, the P-R value also increases. However, the time complexity will also increase rapidly with increase in SN. Since there is no significant improvement in the P-R value for an increase of SN beyond 3, it is concluded that a value of SN less than 3 is preferable when using co-segmentation.

5 Conclusion and Future Work

In this paper, a novel method called LWTP was proposed for the automatic annotation of images. This method took into account both the content of images and the relations between an image and its neighboring images. By preprocessing the label matrix of the training set, this method balanced the differences in the distribution of the tags with low and high frequencies. Experimental results showed that the proposed method achieved an improved accuracy for image annotation, outperformed many baseline systems, and reached the state-of-art systems. In future works, we plan to adopt an optimization step to decrease the time complexity when preprocessing the label matrix. This study considers only the area when distinguishing the weights of labels based on image segmentation, and more factors will be investigated in future works.

Acknowledgement. This work was supported by the National Natural Science Foundation of China (61572060, 61772060) and CERNET Innovation Project (NGII20151004, NGII20160316).

References

1. Mensink, T., Verbeek, J., Schmid, C., Guillaumin, M.: TagProp: discriminative metric learning in nearest neighbor models for image auto-annotation. In: IEEE International Conference on Computer Vision, pp. 309–316 (2010)
2. Yang, J.Y., Liu, G.H.: Content-based image retrieval using color difference histogram. Pattern Recogn. **46**(1), 188–198 (2013)
3. Chang, S.F., Kozintsev, I.V., Kennedy, L.S.: To search or to label?: predicting the performance of search-based automatic image classifiers. In: ACM International Workshop on Multimedia, Information Retrieval, pp. 249–258 (2006)
4. Shimada, A., Nagahara, H., Taniguchi, R.I., Xu, X.: Learning multi-task local metrics for image annotation. Multimed. Tools Appl. **75**(4), 1–29 (2014)
5. Lavrenko, V., Manmatha, R., Jeon, J.: Automatic image annotation and retrieval using cross-media relevance models. In: International ACM SIGIR Conference on Research and Development in Informaion Retrieval, pp. 119–126 (2003)
6. Manmatha, R., Jeon, J., Lavrenko, V.: A model for learning the semantics of pictures. In: NIPS, pp. 553–560 (2003)
7. Manmatha, R., Lavrenko, V., Feng, S.L.: Multiple Bernoulli relevance models for image and video annotation. In: Proceedings of the 2004 IEEE Computer Society Conference on Computer Vision and Pattern Recognition, CVPR 2004, vol. 2, pp. II-1002–II-1009 (2004)
8. Chan, A.B., Moreno, P.J., Vasconcelos, N., Carneiro, G.: Supervised learning of semantic classes for image annotation and retrieval. IEEE Trans. Pattern Anal. Mach. Intell. **29**(3), 394–410 (2007)

9. Jawahar, C.V., Verma, Y.: Exploring SVM for image annotation in presence of confusing labels. In: British Machine Vision Conference, pp. 25.1–25.11 (2013)
10. Pavlovic, V., Kumar, S., Makadia, A.: Baselines for image annotation. Int. J. Comput. Vis. **90**(1), 88–105 (2010)
11. Maji, S., Manmatha, R., Murthy, V.N.: Automatic image annotation using deep learning representations. In: ACM on International Conference on Multimedia Retrieval, pp. 603–606 (2015)
12. Wang, Z., et al.: Weakly semi-supervised deep learning for multi-label image annotation. IEEE Trans. Big Data **1**(3), 109–122 (2015)
13. Chandra Sekhar, C., Sarangi, N.: Automatic image annotation using convex deep learning models. In: International Conference on Pattern Recognition Applications and Methods, pp. 92–99 (2015)
14. Wang, X.J., Zhang, L., Jing, F., Ma, W.Y.: AnnoSearch: image auto-annotation by search. In: IEEE Computer Society Conference on Computer Vision and Pattern Recognition, pp. 1483–1490 (2006)
15. Zhang, L., Wang, X.-J., Ma, W.-Y., Li, X.: Annotating images by mining image search results. IEEE Trans. Pattern Anal. Mach. Intell. **30**(11), 1919 (2008)
16. Hemami, S., Estrada, F., Susstrunk, S., Achanta, R.: Frequency-tuned salient region detection. In: IEEE Conference on Computer Vision and Pattern Recognition, CVPR 2009, pp. 1597–1604 (2009)
17. Irani, M., Faktor, A.: Co-segmentation by composition. In: IEEE International Conference on Computer Vision, pp. 1297–1304 (2014)
18. Metzler, D., Manmatha, R.: An inference network approach to image retrieval. In: Enser, P., Kompatsiaris, Y., O'Connor, N.E., Smeaton, A.F., Smeulders, A.W.M. (eds.) CIVR 2004. LNCS, vol. 3115, pp. 42–50. Springer, Heidelberg (2004). https://doi.org/10.1007/978-3-540-27814-6_9
19. Huang, J., Li, H., Metaxas, D.N., Zhang, S.: Automatic image annotation and retrieval using group sparsity. IEEE Trans. Syst. Man Cybern. Part B Cybern. Publ. IEEE Syst. Man Cybern. Soc. **42**(3), 838 (2012)
20. Fu, H., Zhang, Q., Qiu, G.: Random forest for image annotation. In: Fitzgibbon, A., Lazebnik, S., Perona, P., Sato, Y., Schmid, C. (eds.) ECCV 2012. LNCS, vol. 7577, pp. 86–99. Springer, Heidelberg (2012). https://doi.org/10.1007/978-3-642-33783-3_7

A Comparative Analysis of Content Delivery Capability for Collaborative Dual-Architecture Network

Xuan Liu[1,2], Peng Yang[1,2(✉)], Yongqiang Dong[1,2], and Syed Hassan Ahmed[3]

[1] School of Computer Science and Engineering, Southeast University, Nanjing, China
{yusuf,pengyang,dongyq}@seu.edu.cn
[2] Key Laboratory of Computer Network and Information Integration, Southeast University, Ministry of Education, Nanjing, China
[3] Department of Computer Science, Georgia Southern University, Statesboro, GA 30458, USA
sh.ahmed@ieee.org

Abstract. In order to deliver Internet content to people of the world for achieving the vision of "The Internet is for everyone", our group pioneered a collaborative dual-architecture network (DAN). For quantitative analysis of DAN's content delivery capability, in this paper we firstly propose a unified comparative model, in which network performance and user utility are taken into account. Then, by applying the model we conduct direct and indirect comparative analysis in detail. Numerical results shed light on that DAN outperforms TCP/IP, NDN (named data networking) and BSN (broadcast-storage network) in terms of delivery capability. Given this, we argue that DAN is favourable for content delivery.

Keywords: Dual-architecture · Content delivery
Comparative analysis · Network performance · User utility

1 Introduction

Along with the development of mobile networks and the widespread of intelligent terminals, urban residents can not only enjoy numerous contents through access to the Internet but also generate contents by themselves. As a significant driver the content is prompting the Internet evolving from an initial communication oriented network to content oriented one [1]. However, according to the latest survey released by Internet Society, currently, approximately 60 percent of the earth's population fails to access the Internet due to the factors of demographic, geographic and economic. Therefore, it's imperative to delivery Internet content to people of the world, especially for whom in the area with limited Internet infrastructure support, to eliminate the digital divide and achieve the vision of "The Internet is for everyone" envisaged by Vint Cerf.

© ICST Institute for Computer Sciences, Social Informatics and Telecommunications Engineering 2018
I. Romdhani et al. (Eds.): CollaborateCom 2017, LNICST 252, pp. 63–72, 2018.
https://doi.org/10.1007/978-3-030-00916-8_7

By its nature, the packet-oriented TCP/IP fails to be an ideal architecture for content delivery. To this end, there exist two types of approaches: (1) the dirty slate: constructing an overlay network above the packet-oriented network, e.g. content delivery network (CDN); (2) the clean slate: constructing a brand-new content-oriented architecture from scratch (e.g. NDN, content-centric networking (CCN)). Although the benefits of incremental deployment make the former become the overwhelming content delivery architecture currently, it's difficult for the parasitic architecture to deliver content in area with limited infrastructure. As to the latter, although the delivery efficiency could be significantly increased by in-network caching, the cost of reconstructing hinders the pace of deployment.

To solve the issue, our group led by Prof. Youping Li, the academician of Chinese Academy of Engineering, pioneered the big picture of DAN [2], which is composed of primary architecture (refers to TCP/IP) and secondary architecture (refers to BSN [3]), as shown in Fig. 1. From perspective of architecture, the relationship between the two architectures is symbiotic and complementary, which breaks the dependency of the overlay content-oriented network on TCP/IP. Furthermore, the secondary architecture, on one hand, adopts additional broadcasting transmission channels, such as digital cable, terrestrial, satellite and mobile broadcasting, to deliver content with less hop counts and more broad transmission range. The edge box, such as router/switch, set-top box, and Internet box, on the other hand, is used to store broadcasted contents locally in advance for reducing response delay of user's content request.

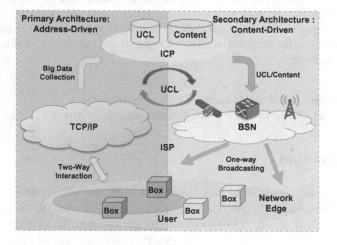

Fig. 1. The big picture of DAN

As an operational architecture involving stakeholders' interest (e.g. Internet Service Provider (ISP), Internet content provider (ICP) and user), even if DAN embracing many outstanding features especially in terms of architecture, in order to provide guidance for stakeholders' investment decision it's necessary to compare and analyse content delivery capability of DAN with the other architectures, such as TCP/IP and NDN. Thus, how to quantitatively analyse the capability is an urgent problem to be solved. Despite its importance, to the best of our knowledge, as of yet, no solutions have been presented. This paper addresses the problem for the first time and makes the following key contributions:

- *We proposed a unified comparative model of content delivery capability for network architecture from a high-level perspective, in which network performance and user utility are taken into account.*
- *We utilized the proposed model to quantitatively compare and analyse content delivery capability of DAN with TCP/IP, NDN and BSN to shed light on its superiority.*

The remainder of this paper is organized as follows: In Sect. 2 we introduce the related work. In Sect. 3 we present a multi-dimension methodology of comparing content delivery capability for architecture. In Sect. 4 we present a unified comparative model of the delivery capability, and followed by Sect. 5, we conduct direct comparative analysis on DAN with TCP/IP and NDN, and indirect comparative analysis on DAN with TCP/IP and BSN. Finally, concluding remarks are offered in Sect. 6.

2   Related Work

The related comparative work in area of network architecture can be divided into two major categories: qualitative and quantitative. For the qualitative comparative, the authors in [4,5] conducted comparing on the dirty slate architecture with the clean slate one, and the work [6] qualitatively analysed the evolution relationship between Internet architectural and biological. Although the qualitative studies can clearly illustrate the pros and cons of various architectures, the lack of rigorous mathematical proof makes those results difficult for stakeholders to make investment decision. For the quantitative comparative, the vast majority of work concentrate the comparative analysis on architecture in single aspect, such as transmission performance [7], scalability [8], deployment [9], evolution [10], and adaptability [11]. However, as of yet, no quantitative comparative analysis work on the content delivery capability for network architecture has been found.

In the closely related work, the authors in [12] proposed the 2ACT evaluation model. Our work is different in that their comparative model is used to compare application adaptation capability and takes network performance and economic factor into consideration while we respectively compare content delivery capability from bottom-up and top-down dimensions. Furthermore, although the authors in [13] adopted user utility to model convergence process of telecommunication network, TV broadcasting network and Internet, our work is different in that we conduct not only indirect comparison of content delivery capability by means of user utility but also direct comparison by means of network performance. Integrating advantages of the two models, we proposed a unified comparative model of content delivery capability for network architecture.

3   Methodology

In this section, we will present multi-dimension methodology of comparative analysis of content delivery capability for network architecture from a high-level perspective.

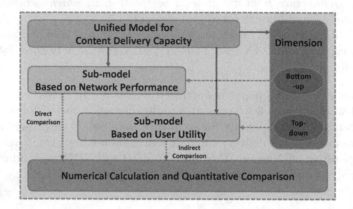

Fig. 2. A methodology of comparative study on content delivery capability

As user is ultimate consumer of content services it's more appropriate to evaluate content delivery capability from user's point of view. Therefore, we propose a methodology of comparative analysis as shown in Fig. 2. Above all, a unified comparative model including two dimensions, as shown in Fig. 2, needs to be constructed. The bottom-up dimension refers to directly compare according to network performance, while the top-down dimension refers to indirectly compare according to user utility. Then, based on the model various numerical calculation and quantitative comparison need to be conducted. Finally, the content delivery capability of architecture can be clearly obtained.

- *Bottom-Up Dimension*
  Starting from architecture itself, for user it's quality of content service that could be considered as the equivalent to content delivery capability. While the quality depends on network performance of architecture, for example, naming method, routing protocol and transmission mechanism. Therefore, the comparative model based on network performance is key to directly analyse.
- *Top-Down Dimension*
  Starting from external of architecture, for user utility generated by consumption of content service is capable of indirectly reflecting content delivery capability while the utility function depends on various factors. Therefore, the comparative model based on user utility is key to indirectly analyse.

4 Unified Comparative Analysis Model of Content Delivery Capability

In this section, we will detail a unified comparative analysis model. According to the methodology above it consists of sub-model based on network performance and sub-model based on user utility, as shown in Fig. 3.

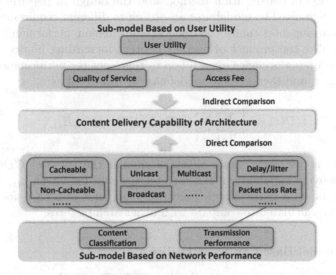

Fig. 3. A unified comparative analysis model of content delivery capability

In sub-model based on network performance, we model network performance as the product of content classification and transmission performance. As to content classification, there exist numerous content classifications, for instance, content can be divided into cacheable and non-cacheable on basis of reusability. As to transmission performance, it includes but not limited to the current network performance metrics, such as delay/jitter, error rate and loss rate.

In sub-model based on user utility, we take advantage of quality of content service and content access fee as primary parameters of utility function. The quality can reflect users' gain and the fee can reflect users' cost.

4.1 Sub-model Based on Network Performance

We denote A as an architecture to be compared and model the sub-model based on network performance as:

$$CDC_A = \frac{1}{m} \sum_{i=1}^{m} \sum_{j=1}^{n} p_{ij} T_{cont}(Perf)_{ij,A}$$

$$s.t. \sum_{j=1}^{n} p_{ij} = 1 \tag{1}$$

where m is the number of content classifications and n is the number of content types in particular classification. T_{cont} is the total amount of the content in the network and p_{ij} is the proportion of the content of the classification i and the type j. $(Perf)_{ij,A}$ is the transmission performance of the classification i and the type j in the architecture A, which is expressed as performance function with specific metric parameters.

The selection of classification method and the design of performance function can be customized by model user according to different requirements. Since content forwarding hop count can reflect transmission performance to some extent, we utilize the product of average content forwarding hop counts $H_{ij,A}$ and transmission performance in each hop to represent the performance denoted as $(HPerf)_{ij,A}$, and then the sub-model can be converted as:

$$CDC_A = \frac{1}{m} \sum_{i=1}^{m} \sum_{j=1}^{n} p_{ij} T_{cont} (HPerf)_{ij,A} H_{ij,A} \tag{2}$$

By Formula 2 we can obtain that the smaller the value of CDC_A is the better the delivery capability of the architecture will be. Given p_{ij}, $H_{ij,A}$ and $(HPerf)_{ij,A}$ under a particular classification, the value of CDC_A for an architecture can be calculated to compare with other architectures.

4.2   Sub-model Based on User Utility

Supposing that user is capable of selecting TCP/IP or BSN to access Internet content, we use $n \in \{1,2\}$ respectively to denote the two architectures, and use the status $s \in \{1,2,3\}$ respectively to denote the user's decision, that is one of architectures and both of them (that is DAN). The parameter $k_{s,n} = 1$ indicates whether to select the architecture n at the particular status s or not. Subsequently, we suppose the total number of user is T and denote P_s as the proportion of the number in the status s. Due to $\sum_{s=1}^{3} P_s = 1$, the number of user who select the architecture n is $T_n = \sum_{s=1}^{3} k_{s,n} P_s T$. Then we formulate the sub-model based on user utility under the status s as:

$$CDC_s = U_s = \alpha \sum_{t=1}^{3} \max_{1 \leq n \leq 2} q_{n,t} k_{s,n} R_t - \beta \sum_{n=1}^{2} k_{s,n} f_n T_n / T \tag{3}$$

The first half of Formula (3) indicates the gain user obtain through consuming content services while the second half represents the cost user spend, where t is content type provided by an architecture. We use $t \in \{1,2,3\}$ respectively represent non-sharing (such as voice, instant message, etc.), real-time sharing (such as live television, etc.) and non-realtime sharing (such as a document, image, etc.). The parameter R_t denotes user demand for the content of the type t, which is used for representing proportion of the content in the architecture n in the paper. The parameter $q_{n,t}$ is quality of content service supplied by the architecture n while f_n is access fee which is paid for using the architecture n

by user. In addition, the impact factor α indicating user's personal view to the quality, which reflects the differences among user in various social classes, while the impact factor β is used to balance the impact on user utility generated by user's benefit and expense.

By Formula 3 we can obtain that the bigger the value of CDC_s is the better the delivery capability of an architecture will be. Given specific parameter value, once the user utility from an architecture is calculated based on the sub-model, the value of CDC_s will be obtained.

5   Numerical Calculation and Comparative Analysis

In this section, we will conduct numerical calculation and comparative analysis of content delivery capability in direct and indirect ways by using the proposed unified comparative analysis model.

5.1   Direct Analysis

Because one of the biggest difference among TCP/IP, NDN and DAN is in-network caching, therefore we categorize the content into non-cacheable and cacheable. For example, real-time content, such as TV live and instance message, belongs to the non-cacheable type while non-realtime content such as video on demand is cacheable. Without loss of generality, we set average hop count of the non-cacheable in TCP/IP as $H = 16$. According to [11], hop count of the cacheable in NDN is $H' = 7$. In DAN, due to user's request hit in local on the benefit of storing content into edge devices in advance through broadcast channel we set hop count of the cacheable in DAN as $H' = 1$. Supposing that a piece of content is bigger than an IP packet, it's obvious that content transmission delay in a hop is higher than IP packet. Therefore we set forwarding performance in a hop in content-oriented network (refers to NDN and DAN) as r times higher than that in TCP/IP. Then, we denote the performance in a hop in TCP/IP as $(HPerf)_{TCP/IP}$ and the performance in content-oriented network is $r(HPerf)_{TCP/IP}$, $r \geq 1$. In addition, the proportion of the non-cacheable content is p_1 and the cacheable content is $p_2(p_1 + p_2 = 1)$. Hence, according to Formula 2 and the average hop count, we can get the value of content delivery capability in the three architectures as follows:

$$\begin{cases} CDC_{TCP/IP} = 16(HPerf)_{TCP/IP} \\ CDC_{NDN} = 7r(HPerf)_{TCP/IP} \\ CDC_{DAN} = (16P_1 + rp_2)(HPerf)_{TCP/IP} \end{cases} \tag{4}$$

As shown in Fig. 4, proportion of cacheable content doesn't affect the delivery capability of TCP/IP, as to DAN and NDN, the capability is bound to increase with the increase of the proportion. Comparing with NDN, the capability of DAN possesses a clear advantage no matter how the value of r changes and the advantage is inclined to increasing with the rising of the proportion of cacheable content. However, comparing with TCP/IP, DAN also possesses a clear advantage when $r = 1$, while with the rising of r, it will exceed TCP/IP when the proportion of cacheable content increases to a certain threshold. And according to the fact that the threshold in DAN is lower than that in NDN, it's proved that DAN can obtain the higher delivery capability with less content cache.

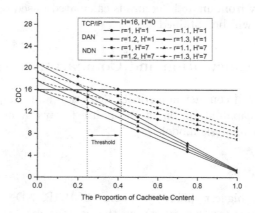

Fig. 4. The content delivery capability under the different architectures

5.2 Indirect Analysis

The quality of non-sharing content in TCP/IP, which is initially designed for end-to-end communication, is destined to surpass BSN. On the benefits of broadcasting mechanism, however, BSN is far ahead of TCP/IP in terms of content delivery. Therefore, we set the quality relationship among various content types as shown in Table 1.

Table 1. The quality relationship among various content types

Content type (t)	TCP/IP ($n = 1$) BSN ($n = 2$)	
Non-sharing ($t = 1$)	$q_{1,1} \geq q_{2,1}$	
Realtime sharing ($t = 2$)	$q_{1,2} \leq q_{2,2}$	
Non-realtime sharing ($t = 3$)	$q_{1,3} \leq q_{2,3}$	

In order to eliminate the difference between multi-dimensional parameters in the sub-model for making the value of Formula 3 comparable, we use the decimal scaling normalized method to standardize the specific values as follows. Quality of content is set as $q_{1,1} : q_{1,2} : q_{1,3} = 1 : 0.6 : 0.7$, $q_{2,1} : q_{2,2} : q_{2,3} = 0.2 : 1 : 0.9$. User demand is set as $R_1 : R_2 : R_3 = 0.2 : 0.3 : 0.5$ on basis of proportion of content types in network. Content access fee f_n is set as $f_1 : f_2 = 0.7 : 0.3$

according to the costs of architecture operation, such as equipment, maintenance and manpower. Supposing that the initial user follows a uniform distribution, we set $T_n/T = 1$ when the status is $s = 1$ and $s = 2$ and we set $T_n/T = 0.5$ when the status is $s = 3$.

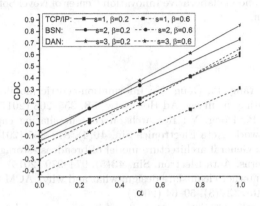

Fig. 5. The content delivery capability under different user evaluation factors and economic factors

As shown in Fig. 5, the delivery capability both BSN and DAN is better than TCP/IP no matter how the user evaluation factor α changes. Due to the higher the access fee on the ground of the costs in operation, the delivery capability of BSN is better than DAN in the initial stage. However, with the rising of the number of user, DAN is bound to exceed BSN as α increases to some certain threshold. Furthermore, although the delivery capability of the three architectures will decrease with the increase of economic factor β, DAN is also better than BSN and TCP/IP.

6   Conclusion

In this paper, we focused on the comparative analysis of content delivery capability of DAN with other architectures. Firstly, we proposed a unified comparative analysis model from a high-level view, in which network performance and user utility are taken into account. Further, we utilized the model to conduct direct comparative analysis of the delivery capability of DAN with TCP/IP and NDN, and the numerical results showed that DAN possesses a clear advantage that it will further increase with the rising of the proportion of cacheable content. Then we utilized the model to conduct indirect comparative analysis of the delivery capability of DAN with TCP/IP and BSN, and the numerical results revealed that DAN also outperforms them. Briefly, DAN is favourable for being an ideal content delivery architecture than other architectures.

Acknowledgment. We would like to express our heartfelt gratitude to Prof. Youping Li and the reviewers for their insightful suggestions. This work is supported by National Science Foundation of China under grants No. 61672155, No. 61472080, No. 61272532, Consulting Project of Chinese Academy of Engineering under grant No. 2018-XY-07, National High Technology Research and Development Program of China under grant No. 2013AA013503, and Collaborative Innovation Center of Novel Software Technology and Industrialization.

References

1. Liu, X., Li, Z., Yang, P., Dong, Y.: Information-centric mobile ad hoc networks and content routing: a survey. Ad Hoc Netw. **58**, 255–268 (2017)
2. Liu, X., Yang, P., Dong, Y.: Research on content sharing capability for dual-architecture network. Acta Electronica Sin. **46**(4), 849–855 (2018)
3. Yang, P., Li, Y.: General architecture model of broadcast-storage network and its realization patterns. Acta Electron. Sin. **43**(5), 974–979 (2015)
4. Feldmann, A.: Internet clean-slate design: what and why? ACM SIGCOMM Comput. Commun. Rev. **37**(3), 59–64 (2007)
5. Rexford, J., Dovrolis, C.: Future internet architecture: clean-slate versus evolutionary research. Commun. ACM **53**(9), 36–40 (2010)
6. Dovrolis, C., Streelman, J.T.: Evolvable network architectures: what can we learn from biology? ACM SIGCOMM Comput. Commun. Rev. **40**(2), 72–77 (2010)
7. Zaitsev, D.A., Shmeleva, T.R.: Parametric Petri net model for Ethernet performance and QoS evaluation. In: Proceedings of the 16th German Workshop on Algorithms and Tools for Petri Nets (AWPN 2009), Karlsruhe, Germany, vol. 501, pp. 15–28 (2009)
8. Lin, S., Wu, J., Xu, K.: Analysis and evaluation of internet resource distribution models. J. Tsinghua Univ. Sci. Technol. **50**(1), 58–62 (2010)
9. Gill, P., Schapira, M., Goldberg, S.: Let the market drive deployment: a strategy for transitioning to BGP security. ACM SIGCOMM Comput. Commun. Rev. **41**(4), 14–25 (2011)
10. Garlan, D., Schmerl, B.: Ævol: a tool for defining and planning architecture evolution. In: Proceedings of the 31st International Conference on Software Engineering, pp. 591–594 (2009)
11. Zhu, M., Xu, K., Lin, S.: The evaluation method towards the application adaptability of internet architecture. Chin. J. Comput. **36**(9), 1785–1798 (2013)
12. Xu, K., Zhu, M., Wang, N., Lin, S., Wang, H., Li, T.: The 2ACT model-based evaluation for in-network caching mechanism. In: IEEE Symposium on Computers and Communications (ISCC), pp. 636–641 (2013)
13. Xu, K., Lin, S., Wu, J.: A three-network convergence evolution model and analysis based on user utility. Chin. J. Comput. **36**(5), 903–914 (2013)

AXE: Objects Search in Mobile Volunteered Service

Yao Wu[1,2], Wenjuan Liang[1,2], Yuncheng Wu[1,2], Hong Chen[1,2(✉)], and Cuiping Li[1,2]

[1] Key Laboratory of Data Engineering and Knowledge Engineering of Ministry of Education, Beijing, China
[2] School of Information, Renmin University of China, Beijing, China
{ideamaxwu,wenjuanliang,yunchengwu,licuiping,chong}@ruc.edu.cn

Abstract. Proliferation of ubiquitous smartphones makes location based services prevalent. People carry these devices around everyday and everywhere, which makes mobile volunteered services emerging. As far as we know, little work has been done on the search for mobile spatial textual objects, even though considerable researches have been done on moving objects query and spatial keyword query. In this paper, we study the problem of searching for mobile spatial textual objects in mobile volunteered services: given a set of mobile object and a user query, find the most relevant objects considering both spatial locations and textual descriptions. We model each mobile object as probabilistic instances with time recency. A new hybrid index is proposed for mobile spatial textual objects, called BIG-tree. And we propose an improved threshold algorithm to efficiently process the top-k query based on the index. We evaluate the performance of our approaches on real and synthetic datasets. Experimental results show our solutions outperform the baselines.

1 Introduction

Popularity of mobile devices makes location based services a compelling paradigm, which bring unique location-aware experiences to users. Location-based services hasten the advent of mobile crowdsourcing, and the need of searching for qualified mobile users becomes urgent [1]. Sometimes we submit certain queries, but cannot get satisfied results from traditional search engines, such as *get me a cab*, *fix my computer*, and *I need a house cleaner*. From these queries, what we expect is someone who can provide specific services with domain skills. In reality, people with skills like taxi driving, computer fixing and house cleaning are just around us. Xie et al. [2] propose a Volunteered Geographic Service system, which enables mobile users to efficiently monitor nearby services. In the proposed scenarios, mobile users are able to volunteer as providers of specific location-based services, and they are also able to subscribe specific services. With the diffusion of online mobile users, it is necessary to provide efficient means of enabling such queries for mobile volunteers.

© ICST Institute for Computer Sciences, Social Informatics and Telecommunications Engineering 2018
I. Romdhani et al. (Eds.): CollaborateCom 2017, LNICST 252, pp. 73–87, 2018.
https://doi.org/10.1007/978-3-030-00916-8_8

Existing LBS systems employ a spatial keyword search approach to provide LBS services [3,4], in which, given a set of point of interests (POIs) or region of interests (ROIs) and a user query with a location and several keywords, all relevant POIs or ROIs are returned. Current researches mainly focus on query over static objects, such as restaurants, hotels or sights. Little research has been done on query for mobile objects with both spatial and textual information, for example, *"find the nearest people who can fix a computer"*. We name this evolved location based services as **mobile volunteered services** for its unique features.

In mobile volunteered services, both spatial and textual information should be concerned as well as the mobility of users. No existing techniques can be employed seamlessly to enable the query without appropriate modifications. To address these issues, we introduce mobile spAtial teXtual objects sEarch (AXE). Volunteered users are the objects with textual description and location information and they move stochastically. But the range they move around is generally in their routine hotspots (e.g., home, work place and malls). They change their locations without a high speed or lasting moving, such as taxi drivers. We focus more on the mobility rather than the motion perspective (e.g., direction and speed). Our contributions are four-folds:

- We study the problem of mobile spatial textual objects search, model the objects based on probabilistic instances and measure the spatial textual similarity with time recency.
- We propose BIG-tree, a hybrid index structure based on sorted lists of spatial linear quad-tree and textual inverted index. Two baselines are proposed based on modified classic indexes, i.e., IR-tree with bounding box (IRBB) and top-k aggregation with partial score (TAPS).
- We also propose an efficient improved threshold algorithm with lazy refinement and prior pause (NEWLP) based on the new index for top-k query.
- We have conducted extensive experiments on both real and synthetic datasets. Experimental results show that our methods outperform the baselines.

2   Related Work

Spatial keyword search and moving objects/query search have been well studied for years. **Spatial Keyword Search**: The R-tree based solution is arguably the dominant index for spatial keyword query. IR-tree [5] integrates each node of R-tree with a summary of the text content in the corresponding subtree. Several variants of IR-tree exist, which optimize the efficiency, including DIR-tree, CIR-tree, CDIR-tree [5], WIR-tree [6], KR*-tree [7], IR^2-tree [3] and SKI [8]. They integrate the textual information into R-tree with different data structures. Quad-tree is another choice in indexing the spatial textual objects. SFC-QUAD [9] is based on space filling curve. IQ-tree [10] is associated with an inverted file that organizes the keyword expression. I^3-tree [11] adopts the quad-tree structure to hierarchically partition the data space into cells. ILQ-tree [12] is proposed to keep the non-empty leaf node of the quad-tree in an auxiliary disk-based one dimensional structure. **Moving Objects/Query Search**: In moving query researches [13–15], the query moves continuously while the data objects (e.g., hotels, restaurants) are stationary. *Safe region* (e.g., MW Voronoi) is used to model the moving query. In moving objects search [16], the objects move continuously while the query is stationary. Most existing solutions for moving objects indexes can be divided into object partitioning (e.g., TPR-tree [17]) and space partitioning (e.g., B^x-tree [18]).

Few work has been done on the mobile spatial textual objects search, which is different from existing works and essential in mobile volunteered services. There are two main challenges: (1) both spatial and textual information should be concerned. (2) the mobility of objects makes it difficult to model and index the objects. In this paper, we propose probabilistic instance model to capture the mobility of users and an improved threshold algorithm is presented to process the query based on our hybrid index structure BIG-tree.

3   Model AXE

3.1   Object Model

In mobile object environments, it is infeasible for the system to track the movement of objects and store the exact locations of objects at all times [16,19]. In this situation, it is impossible for queries to produce correct results based upon old data. However, if the degree of uncertainty is controlled, then the error of the answers to certain queries can be reduced. The routine hotspots of mobile users can be augmented with probabilistic estimates of the confidence of the occurrence. Generally speaking, there are two ways to model an object's current location. One is based on the history routine data and the other is based on the latest updated location. We introduce time recency to take both history data and latest data into consideration.

Definition 1 (Mobile Spatial Textual Object). *A mobile spatial textual object is represented with a triple $o = \langle \psi, l, r \rangle$, where $o.\psi$ is the set of keywords, $o.l$ is the last latitude and longitude of the objects with timestamp and $o.r$ is the set of probabilistic instances.* Correspondingly, a query is $q = \langle \psi, l \rangle$, where $q.\psi$ is the set of query keywords and $q.l$ is the query location with time. The probabilistic instance set $o.r$ for each object is represented by instances with probability, i.e., $c_j(p_i)$. For an instance c_j of an object o_i, the probability is p_i^j. A probabilistic instance represents a routine hotspot of an object, e.g., home. Given a set of moving objects $\mathcal{O} = \{o_1, o_2, ..., o_n\}$, the instance set $\mathcal{C}$ contains all instances with positive probability, i.e., $\mathcal{C} = \{c_j | \exists i(p_i(c_j) > 0)\}$.

In this paper, we give a naive statistic method to get the instance and corresponding probability of each object. Given the history locations $\mathcal{L} = \{l_1, l_2, ..., l_m\}$ of an object o, the probability p of instance c is, $p(c) = \frac{|l \in c|}{|\mathcal{L}|}$, i.e., of all the history locations, the ratio of the locations fall in a certain range. The inference method introduces distribution information of the objects' history locations, which indicates the probability of instances, i.e., routine hotspots.

In our implementation, each certain range is divided by quad-tree, which will be illustrated in the next section. More sophisticated methods (e.g., cluster techniques) can be exploited.

3.2   Similarity Measure

Definition 2 (Spatial Similarity). *Given an object o and a query q, the spatial similarity (spatial proximity) of o and q is defined as:*

$$Sim_S(o,q) = 1 - \frac{D(o.l, q.l)}{D_{max}} \tag{1}$$

where D_{max} is the maximum distance in the location space. For a mobile object, the update of the location is undetermined, and neither the history nor the updated last location can precisely predict the current location. We introduce time recency to infer the current location with probabilistic instances aggregation and last updated location. The spatial similarity can be expressed by,

$$D(o.l, q.l) = \theta d_1(o.l, q.l) + (1 - \theta)d_2(o.r, q.l) \tag{2}$$

where $d_1()$ is the Euclidean distance and $\theta = \lambda^{-(t_q - t_u)}$ is the time recency [20]. λ is the base number that determines the rate of recency decay, t_q is the query time and θ is monotonically decreasing with $t_q - t_u$. The similarity between the query location and probabilistic instance set is

$$d_2(o.r, q.l) = \sum_j p_j d_0(o.c_j, q.l) \tag{3}$$

where $p_j, o.c_j \in o.r$ and $d_0()$ is the Euclidean distance between q.l and centroid of instance $o.c_j$. The spatial similarity is based on probabilistic instances set and last location with time recency. Time recency is a key factor in measuring the spatial similarity based on locations updated by mobile objects. It is introduced in [21] and is applied widely as the measurement of recency for stream data, in which, the exponential decay function has been shown to be effective [22]. In this paper, we use the time recency to measure the importance between probabilistic instances and latest location. The validity of a location decreases when it is not updated for a long time.

Definition 3 (Textual Similarity). *Given an object o and a query q, the textual similarity (textual relevancy) of o and q is defined as:*

$$Sim_T(o,q) = \frac{\sum_{t \in o.\psi \cap q.\psi} w(t)}{\sum_{t \in o.\psi \cup q.\psi} w(t)} \tag{4}$$

where $w(t)$ is the weight of keyword t in textual information. In this paper we use the inverted document frequency (denoted by idf) as keywords weight, i.e.,

$$w(t) = ln \frac{|\mathcal{O}|}{count(t, \mathcal{O})} \tag{5}$$

where count(t, $\mathcal{O}$) is the number of objects containing token t. Infrequent tokens have more weights for their rarity.

Definition 4 (Spatial Textual Similarity). *Given an object o and a query q, the spatial textual similarity between o and q is defined as:*

$$Sim(o, q) = \alpha Sim_S(o, q) + (1 - \alpha)Sim_T(o, q) \qquad (6)$$

where $Sim_S(o, q)$ is the spatial similarity and $Sim_T(o, q)$ is the textual similarity. $\alpha \in [0, 1]$ is a preference parameter that balances the importance between distance proximity and text relevance.

Our mobile spatial textual objects search problem is substantially different from the existing problems. (1) We focus on the mobility rather than movement. (2) The spatial model is a set of discrete probabilistic instances rather than ROI or POI. (3) We take the temporal information to spatial textual similarity measurement.

4   Handle AXE: Object Indexing

We first introduce two straightforward modified methods as baselines. Then, we present BIG-tree, a hybrid index based on sorted lists of spatial linear quad-tree and textual inverted index, which essentially consists of $\underline{B}^+$-tree and $\underline{I}$nverted file index based on $\underline{G}$rid partition.

4.1   Baseline Methods

Two types of classical indexes for spatial keyword objects are: the tree based integrated index and the sort lists based aggregation. The corresponding representatives are IR-tree [5] and RCA [23]. IR-tree integrates each node of R-tree with a summary of the text content of the objects in the corresponding subtree. Specifically, each node contains a pointer to an inverted file that describes the objects rooted at the node. RCA is a new approach based on modeling the spatial keyword query as a top-k aggregation problem [24]. Give a query with m keywords and a location, it constructs $m + 1$ sorted lists. RCA is a rank-aware combined algorithm by accessing the lists in a score-bounded manner, which is an improved TA. Experiments show RCA performs better than IR-tree when processing spatial keyword query [11, 23].

We modify the IR-tree and RCA to adapt our situation. The two baselines are IR-tree with Bounding Box (IRBB) and Top-k Aggregation with Partial Score (TAPS). In the mobile spatial textual object model, each object is a set of probabilistic instances in terms of the spatial aspect. To adapt IR-tree, we draw a bounding box for the set of probabilistic instances. In IR-tree, The spatial attribute of each entry is a point, i.e., location coordinates. In IRBB, the spatial attribute is a rectangle with several probabilistic instances as shown in Fig. 1(a), i.e., the minimum quad-tree region that covers all the probabilistic instances.

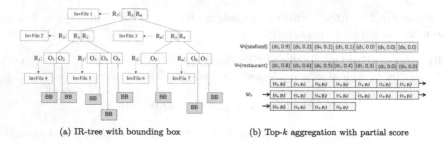

(a) IR-tree with bounding box   (b) Top-k aggregation with partial score

Fig. 1. Two baselines based on modified classical indexes.

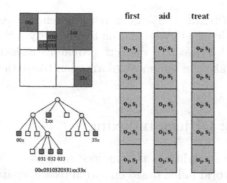

Fig. 2. Structure of BIG-tree. The left part is the linear encode based on extensive quad-tree and the right part is the sorted lists with score s_i based on keywords for object o_i.

To adapt RCA, each probabilistic instance in our model is an object in RCA model. And the similarity score of each mobile spatial textual object is the sum of all probabilistic instances. The differences of index structures between RCA and TAPS are shown as in Fig. 1(b). As we can see, the spatial list is far longer than the textual lists due to the several instances for each object. The query processing algorithms for IRBB and TAPS remain the same as in [5, 23].

However, IRBB inherits the disadvantages from IR-tree. First, the centralized R-tree mechanism requires a high update cost. Second, the processing cost to examine whether a node is relevant to the query keywords is not negligible. Besides, TAPS is also not efficient when processing mobile spatial objects due to its large number of probabilistic instances. Each object in RCA becomes several instances in TAPS. Therefore, it is difficult for both baselines to scale.

4.2 Our Methods

The key idea of our optimization is to sort the spatial attribute list offline based on an approximate spatial order-preserving encoding such that the two-dimensional location attribute values are encoded into one-dimensional values with the desirable property. A pair of encoded location values that are close together in the total order represents a pair of locations that are likely to be spatially close to each other. In this paper, we apply the well-known linear quad-tree [25] to obtain such a mapping. There are two useful properties of linear quad-tree encoding that we exploit in our algorithm. (1) A quad-tree is a space-partitioning tree data structure in which a d-dimensional space is recursively subdivided into 2^d regions, which shows simplicity and regularity in many applications. (2) As an efficient implementation of the disk-based quad-tree, the linear quad-tree is proposed to keep the non-empty leaf node of the quad-tree in an auxiliary disk-based one-dimensional structure (e.g., B^+ tree), where each node can be encoded by the space filling curve techniques.

In BIG-tree, the internal nodes are directory and the leaf nodes are the objects. The key in the tree is the one-dimensional space filling curve value, which mapped from the two-dimensional location coordinates. Each object at the leaf node is represented by a set of probabilistic instances with the last updated location. In the conventional quad-tree, the tree splits when the node is full. In our index structure, we map the bounding box into a **least quad cell**, i.e., the minimum quad-tree region that covers all the probabilistic instances. And the node splits not according to the number of items, but the size of bounding box. We call this **extensive quad-tree**. We make this modification because we only take quad-tree structure as the mapping method, and the data is stored in B^+-tree based on the one-dimensional value. The extensive quad-tree can hold a large number of objects under a quad cell, which facilitates the spatial search when we process the query.

In implementation, we encode the quad-tree nodes based on the Morton code (Z-order) because the Morton code of a node is encoded based on its split sequence, i.e., the path of the node in the quad-tree, and the code of a particular node (region) in the space is unique. This is essential because multiple quad-trees with different shapes are used in the paper. The way of how to derive the Morton code of a node based on its split sequence in two-dimensional space can be found in [25]. For the linear quad-tree, we only keep the solid leaf nodes on the disk by one-dimensional index structure (e.g., B^+-tree), which are ordered by their Morton codes. We apply a temporary buffer to solve the false positive problem as described in [23].

However, based on the properties of the linear quad-tree encoding, it is possible that some of the documents accessed in the searched spatial region (specified by some range of linear quad-tree values) could be false positives; i.e, the actual distance between the accessed document and query could be larger than the current search radius r_i at the ith iteration. To avoid processing these false positives too early, we maintain buffers to temporarily store these false positive documents: a false positive document that should have been processed later in the jth iteration (i.e., $j > i$) will be temporarily stored in the jth buffer. Thus, the documents in the jth buffer will be considered later during the jth iteration.

Based on the encoded linear quad-tree, our algorithm progressively accesses the documents (objects) in the spatial attribute list in iterations. The textual lists can be easily obtained. We index the mobile spatial textual objects by BIG-tree, shown in Fig. 2, which is a new hybrid index structure. The BIG-tree can be easily integrated into an existing relation database. We skip the BIG-tree manipulation (insertion and deletion) details due to the space limitation.

Existing geo-textual indexes are designed for processing spatial-keyword queries on static objects. They do not provide an efficient mechanism to maintain the index for the objects with mobile information. In **BIG-tree**, we encode the linear extensive quad-tree to construct the spatial sorted list and the textual lists with inverted files. To optimize the query processing, we apply quad-tree based spatial structure rather than R-tree for frequent updates. The reasons for using grid based structure are: (1) The grid based structure is update-friendly because the query region is indexed in mutually-exclusive cells. (2) We can use different indexing granularity for different queries by considering the spatial distribution and keyword distribution.

5   Wield AXE: Query Processing

5.1   Query Processing

In this paper, we focus on the top-k query. Given a query $q = \langle \psi, l, k \rangle$, retrieve k objects ranked according to the mobile spatial-textual similarity.

Definition 5 (Top-k Query). *Given a set of objects O and a query q, the answer set of a top-k mobile spatial textual objects search is a subset of O, A, such that*
(1) The size of A is k ,i.e., $|A| = k$, and (2) $\forall o^* \in A, \forall o \in O - A, Sim(q, o^*) \geq Sim(q, o)$
where Sim is the similarity function to evaluate the relevancy between a query and an object. According to the similarity measurement in Sect. 3, what differ us are the probabilistic instance set and time recency in measuring the similarity score between the query and each mobile spatial textual object.

Before the improved algorithm for TkQ, we present the threshold algorithm for top-k aggregation problem [24] in Algorithm 1, which consists of two main steps. First, perform a sorted access in parallel to each of sorted lists and compute the aggregated score of the object using the ranking function (Line 8). Then, update the threshold according to the aggregated score of the last seen object (Line 9–12). The algorithm terminates as soon as at least k objects have been seen whose score is at least equal to the threshold (Line 4–6).

Based on the threshold algorithm, we adapt our BIG-tree to the top-k query, specifically based on RCA [11], which is Rank-aware Combined Algorithm. We rank the spatial list based on quad-tree mapping rather than uniform grid in RCA. We name the modified RCA as mRCA. There are two main methods to optimize the threshold algorithm. One is to early terminate the iteration when accessing the sorted lists, as the RCA does. The other is to reduce the random access, which can reduce I/O cost. Based on these observations, to improve the efficiency, we propose optimized solution NEWLP for TkQ.

Algorithm 1. Threshold Algorithm

Input: $\mathcal{O}$: A set of objects
q: A query
$\mathcal{I}$: Inverted lists of spatial and textual attributes
Output: $\mathcal{R}$: Top-k results
1: $\mathcal{Q} \leftarrow$ an empty prior queue
2: $\theta_{ta} \leftarrow 1, \theta_q \leftarrow 0$
3: **while** true **do**
4:     **if** $\theta_{ta} < \theta_q$ **then**
5:         $\mathcal{R} \leftarrow$ Refinement($\mathcal{Q}$)
6:         **return** $\mathcal{R}$
7:     **end if**
8:     candidate   set $\{o_i\}$ $\leftarrow$
    SequentialAccess($q, \mathcal{I}$)
9:     **if** $|\mathcal{Q}| < k$ or $Sim(o_i, q) > \theta_q$ **then**
10:         add object o_i to queue $\mathcal{Q}$
11:         update threshold θ_q
12:     **end if**
13:     $\mathcal{R} \leftarrow$ Refinement($\mathcal{Q}$)
14:     $\theta_{ta} \leftarrow Sim(o_i, q)$
15: **end while**

Algorithm 2. NEWLP Improvements

1: **SequentialAccess**($q, \mathcal{I}$)

2: **if** o_i.score$< \theta_{score}$ OR
    o_i.num$> \theta_{num}$ **then**
3:     update $\theta_{score}, \theta_{num}$
4:     **break**   sequential
    access
5: **end if**
6:
7: **Refinement**($\mathcal{Q}$)
8: **if** o_i.score$> \theta_{ran}$ **then**
9:     RandomAccess(o_i)
10: **end if**

5.2 Lazy Refinement

In conventional threshold algorithms, the refinement of top-k results is carried out in every iteration. The access of the index increases the disk I/O, which incurs time latency. In NEWLP, we proceed random access until the score of the top-k results reach the threshold. We set a threshold to stop the unnecessary random access. The refinement of the top-k results is processed once they exceed the threshold, otherwise, they will be refined later with the other candidates. The modification takes place in Line 13 in Algorithm 1.

5.3 Prior Pause

We terminate each iteration when the score-bounded or number-bounded conditions satisfy in the sequential access. There are two core factors affecting the efficiency of TA: termination conditions and the number of random access times. In contrast to the RCA algorithm, which accesses only a score-bounded documents in each iteration, the documents accessed by Prior Pause is determined by a score interval and a fixed number of documents corresponding to each iteration. This difference between RCA and Prior Pause is motivated by two reasons. First, the upper-bound score for the ranking function relies on the minimum distance of all the unseen objects to the query location. The upper bound score could decrease very slowly if a fixed number of documents is accessed per iteration. Second, The drawback of score bounded method is that it may lead too

Table 1. Dataset statistics.

Dataset	# of objs	# of locs	# of terms	Region	Size
Twitter	61413	9.6556	90.4253	(24.54, −134.54, 58.41, −67.45)	138M
Foursquare	4163	64.6002	138.8080	(−54.80, −175.19, 83.97, 178.59)	78M
Syndata	194466	6.5	9.5	(−54.80, −175.19, 83.97, 178.59)	100M

Table 2. Parameters and their settings.

Parameters	Settings
Different datasets	Twitter FS **Syndata**
# of syn objects	40K 60K 100K 150K **200K**
# of query kwds	2 3 4 5 6
# of tok-k results	1 5 **10** 20 50
Parameter α	0.1 0.3 **0.5** 0.7 0.9
Skewness ratio	5.18 3.58 2.88 1.28 0.58 **0**

much unnecessary access if there is a large amount of objects in a certain score interval. Prior Pause wield the power of these two tricks. The modification lies in Line 8 in Algorithm 1.

The overall improvement for TA is explained in Algorithm 2, which gives the outlines of SequentialAccess($q, \mathcal{I}$) and Refinement($\mathcal{Q}$). Details can refer to [11]. In the improvements, $\theta_{score}, \theta_{num}, \theta_{ran}$ indicate score-bounded threshold, fixed number threshold and random access threshold, respectively.

6   Performance Evaluation

We modify and extend two classical methods as baselines to handle our problem, i.e., IRBB based on IR-tree and TAPS based on top-k aggregation. We compare our proposed mRCA and improved version NEWLP with the two baselines. We conduct our experiments on two real data sets and one synthetic data set from different evaluation metrics. All the algorithms are implemented in Java and run on a Linux server machine with an Intel(R) Xeon(R) CPU E5-2670 0 @ 2.60 GHz and 256 GB memory. We run each experiment three times and report the average results.

6.1   Data Sets

To the best of our knowledge, no available dataset targeting the envisioned mobile volunteered service exists. We use two real datasets[1] and one synthetic dataset to evaluate the performance. The first one is a real Twitter dataset. It provides check-ins data with content information across USA. The second real dataset is Foursquare. This dataset contains check-in records with check-in venues. These two datasets all contains check-in locations, check-in time, text content and user ID. We aggregate the locations and text content of each user as one mobile spatial object. Each location acts as an instance with occurrence probability. As there are too many instances and keywords for one object, which

---

[1] https://sites.google.com/site/dbhongzhi/.

is far more to describe the object, we generate a synthetic dataset based on the two real datasets. We split one "fat" object from aggregated real datasets into several virtual objects in the synthetic dataset. This can preserve the spatial proximity and text relevance from each user and generate reasonable data with average 6.5 instances and 9.5 keywords for each user. It is enough to describe the service skills of a user by 10 keywords (instead of a long web-page document) and to represent the routine hotspots by 7 instances. Table 1 summarizes details of the three datasets.

6.2 Evaluation Metrics

In the following experiments, we evaluate the performance of different indexes and algorithms from several aspects. We study the metrics including: (1) index building time; (2) index disk storage; (3) query processing time. The different aspects are: (1) different datasets; (2) varying size of datasets; (3) varying number of query keywords; (4) varying number of return results; (5) varying α in similarity measure and (6) skewness of query keywords. Table 2 summarizes the settings, where values in bold represent the defaults.

Index Construction. (1) Index Construction Time Index construction cost is used to measure the elapsed time when building the index. The time is affected by various factors, such as cache size and code optimization. It is difficult to provide a thoroughly fair comparison and we report the average time. **(2) Index Storage Cost** We use the size of index on disk to evaluate the space efficiency. The index storage includes the spatial and textual attribute.

Query Processing. The query parameters include number of keywords, query skewness, size of k and preference parameter α. To make the queries resemble what users would likely use, we generate the query sets randomly from the provided datasets. For each round of experiments, we generate query sets on each dataset, in which the number of query keywords is from 1 to 7 with an average 4. Each set consists of 30 queries. For evaluating the query performance free from cache impact, we generate 1,000 queries for experiments to warm up the experiment system.

6.3 Experiment Results

Different Datasets. We evaluate the index building time, index disk storage and query processing time on three different datasets as shown in Table 1. The two baseline methods IRBB, TAPS and our proposed algorithm mRCA and NEWLP are compared. The experiments results are shown in Fig. 3. TAPS shows high building time due to the possible massive probabilistic instances. In terms of index disk storage, the sorted lists based methods (i.e., TAPS, mRCA and NEWLP) on the real data sets (i.e., Twitter and Foursquare) incur higher costs. This is because for each object in the real datasets, the merged object has too many instances and keywords, which leads to duplicates in the storage. When the instances and keywords decrease as shown in Fig. 3(b) - Syndata, the storage costs are similar for all indexes. In fact, the Syndata more resembles the real data format from mobile volunteered service if it exists. As for the query processing time, NEWLP performs best of all, which is about five times better than IRBB. To be noted, mRCA and NEWLP share the same index structure (BIG-tree), which makes the index building time and index storage quite the same.

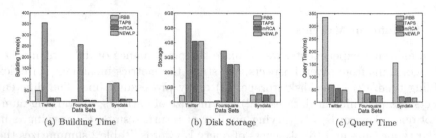

(a) Building Time   (b) Disk Storage   (c) Query Time

Fig. 3. Different datasets.

Varying Size of Datasets. In this experiment, we examine the scalability in terms of increasing size of datasets. We vary the size of synthetic data from 40K to 200K. As shown in Fig. 4, when the size of datasets increases, the efficiency of four indexes and processing algorithms decrease. However, the three aspects of building index time, index disk storage and query processing, our proposed BIG-tree and NEWLP perform best of all. As we have mentioned, mRCA and NEWLP share the same index as BIG-tree but NEWLP is an improved version in terms of query processing. BIG-tree maps the bounding box of set of probabilistic instances from quad-tree to one-dimensional value, which reduces the duplicates of storage. NEWLP optimize the threshold algorithm in two aspects, i.e., early iteration termination and reduced random access. Results show that these two optimizations work.

Varying Number of Query Keywords. We vary the number of query keywords from 2 to 6 to evaluate the query processing algorithms on the synthetic dataset. Since an object is considered relevant if it contains at least one query keyword, results in Fig. 5 show the query time increases as the number of query keywords increases especially for IRBB. However, the sorted lists based methods scale smoothly because the pruning techniques that take into account both spatial and textual relevance are more effective.

Varying Number of Query Results. The number of query results, i.e., the value of k is set from 1 to 50 to evaluate all the algorithms. The IRBB query time increases quickly while the sorted lists based methods work well without much fluctuation. The query processing latency for TAPS, mRCA and NEWLP

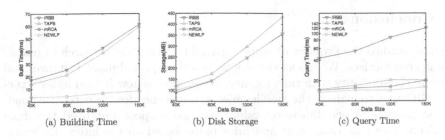

Fig. 4. Varying size of datasets.

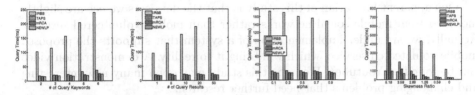

Fig. 5. Number of   **Fig. 6.** Number of   **Fig. 7.** Varying α in   **Fig. 8.** Skewness of
query keywords.   query results.   ranking function.   query keywords.

is mainly affected by the sorting of spatial lists, sequential access and random access of the sorted lists. As k increases, the overhead of sorting is fixed and the running time increases due to the sequential/random access. NEWLP performs better than mRCA due to its lazy refinement and prior pause that can reduce random access and terminate the iteration earlier (Fig. 6).

Varying α in Ranking Function Preference parameter α indicates the importance of spatial and textual attributes in the similarity measurement. As α increases, the spatial relevance plays a more important role in determining the final results. IRBB is more sensitive to α because it examines the spatial attribute first. When α is larger, the spatial relevance dominates the results and this reduces the running time. On the contrary, the other three algorithms are not sensitive to α because the spatial and textual sorted lists are accessed in parallel (Fig. 7).

Skewness of Query Keywords. We evaluate the impact of query term frequency skewness. The skewness ratio is defined as term frequency compared to average frequency of all keywords. For each keyword, the frequency is n and the average frequency is m. The skewness ratio for each keyword is $ln(n/m)$. Results in Fig. 8 show that, the frequent query keyword incurs high query time for sorted lists based methods. The reason is that when the query keyword frequency is high, the sorted lists for keywords become long, which incurs time latency to access the lists. But NEWLP still shows advantages over others. Notice that IRBB performs better for both high frequency and low frequency query keywords. One reasonable explanation is that, the spatial pruning power generates and dominates to terminate the iteration early.

7 Conclusions

We have studied the problem of mobile spatial textual objects search in mobile volunteered services. We model the objects based on probabilistic instances and measure the similarity with time recency. We propose a new hybrid index structure, BIG-tree, to manage the mobile objects, which encodes the extensive quadtree mapping into one-dimension value. We also propose improved threshold algorithm with lazy refinement and prior pause based on the index. Extensive experimental results show that our methods outperform the two proposed baselines and achieve better performance.

One apparent limitation of this study is that the data sets we use are slightly modified from mobile social networks rather than mobile volunteered services. Actually, we are under implementation of a system that supports the proposed mobile volunteered service, which will bring it to reality. A demonstration video can be found at Youtube[2]. We hope this study may open many new interesting and challenging problems that need further research.

Acknowledgment. This work is supported by National Science Foundation of China (No. 61532021), National Basic Research Program of China (973) (No. 2014CB340403), and National High Technology Research and Development Program of China (863) (No. 2014AA015204).

References

1. Cen Chen, S.-F.C., Hoong Chuin Lau, A.M.: Towards city-scale mobile crowdsourcing: task recommendations under trajectory uncertainties. In: IJCAI, pp. 1113–1119 (2015)
2. Xie, X., Jin, P., Yiu, M.L., Du, J., Yuan, M., Jensen, C.S.: Enabling scalable geographic service sharing with weighted imprecise voronoi cells. TKDE **28**(2), 439–453 (2016)
3. De Felipe, I., Hristidis, V., Rishe, N.: Keyword search on spatial databases. In: ICDE, pp. 656–665 (2008)
4. Cao, X., et al.: Spatial keyword querying. In: Atzeni, P., Cheung, D., Ram, S. (eds.) ER 2012. LNCS, vol. 7532, pp. 16–29. Springer, Heidelberg (2012). https://doi.org/10.1007/978-3-642-34002-4_2
5. Cong, G., Jensen, C.S., Dingming, W.: Efficient retrieval of the top-k most relevant spatial web objects. PVLDB **2**(1), 337–348 (2009)
6. Wu, D., Yiu, M.L., Cong, G., Jensen, C.S.: Joint top-k spatial keyword query processing. TKDE **24**(10), 1889–1903 (2012)
7. Hariharan, R., Hore, B., Li, C., Mehrotra, S.: Processing spatial-keyword (SK) queries in geographic information retrieval (GIR) systems. In: SSDBM, p. 16 (2007)
8. Cary, A., Wolfson, O., Rishe, N.: Efficient and scalable method for processing top-k spatial boolean queries. In: Gertz, M., Ludäscher, B. (eds.) SSDBM 2010. LNCS, vol. 6187, pp. 87–95. Springer, Heidelberg (2010). https://doi.org/10.1007/978-3-642-13818-8_8

---

[2] https://www.youtube.com/watch?v=8LtMZ3AqVTc.

9. Christoforaki, M., He, J., Dimopoulos, C., Markowetz, A., Suel, T.: Text vs. space: efficient geo-search query processing. In: CIKM, pp. 423–432 (2011)
10. Chen, L., Cong, G., Cao, X.: An efficient query indexing mechanism for filtering geo-textual data. In: SIGMOD, pp. 749–760 (2013)
11. Zhang, D., Tan, K.-L., Tung, A.K.H.: Scalable top-k spatial keyword search. In: EDBT/ICDT, pp. 359–370 (2013)
12. Zhang, C., Zhang, Y., Zhang, W., Lin, X.: Inverted linear quadtree: efficient top k spatial keyword search. In: ICDE, pp. 901–912 (2013)
13. Wu, D., Yiu, M.L., Jensen, C.S., Cong, G.: Efficient continuously moving top-k spatial keyword query processing. In: ICDE, pp. 541–552 (2011)
14. Huang, W., Li, G., Tan, K.-L., Feng, J.: Efficient safe-region construction for moving top-k spatial keyword queries. In: CIKM, pp. 932–941 (2012)
15. Wu, D., Yiu, M.L., Jensen, C.S.: Moving spatial keyword queries: formulation, methods, and analysis. ACM Trans. Database Syst. **38**(1), 7 (2013)
16. Zhang, M., Chen, S., Jensen, C.S., Ooi, B.C., Zhang, Z.: Effectively indexing uncertain moving objects for predictive queries. PVLDB **2**(1), 1198–1209 (2009)
17. Saltenis, S., Jensen, C.S., Leutenegger, S.T., López, M.A.: Indexing the positions of continuously moving objects. In: SIGMOD, pp. 331–342 (2000)
18. Jensen, C.S., Lin, D., Ooi, B.C.: Query and update efficient B+-tree based indexing of moving objects. In: VLDB, pp. 768–779 (2004)
19. Cheng, R., Prabhakar, S., Kalashnikov, D.V.: Querying imprecise data in moving object environments. In: ICDE, pp. 723–725 (2003)
20. Chen, L., Cong, G., Cao, X., Tan, K.-L.: Temporal spatial-keyword top-k publish/subscribe. In: ICDE, pp. 255–266 (2015)
21. Li, X., Croft, W.B.: Time-based language models. In: CIKM, pp. 469–475 (2003)
22. Efron, M., Golovchinsky, G.: Estimation methods for ranking recent information. In: SIGIR, pp. 495–504 (2011)
23. Zhang, D., Chan, C.-Y., Tan, K.-L.: Processing spatial keyword query as a top-k aggregation query. In: SIGIR, pp. 355–364 (2014)
24. Fagin, R., Lotem, A., Naor, M.: Optimal aggregation algorithms for middleware. J. Comput. Syst. Sci. **66**(4), 614–656 (2003)
25. Gargantini, I.: An effective way to represent quadtrees. Commun. ACM **25**(12), 905–910 (1982)

Modeling the Impacts of WiFi Signals on Energy Consumption of Smartphones

Yuxia Sun[1], Junxian Chen[1], and Yong Tang[2(✉)]

[1] Department of Computer Science, Jinan University, Guangzhou, China
tyxsun@jnu.edu.cn, junxianchen001@gmail.com
[2] College of Computing, South China Normal University, Guangzhou, China
ytang@scnu.edu.cn

Abstract. In this paper, we explore the impacts of the WiFi signal strengths under normal signal conditions on the energy consumption of smartphones. Controlled experiments are conducted to quantitatively study the phone energy impacts by normal WiFi signals. As the experimental results show, the weaker the signal strength is, the faster the phone energy dissipates. To quantitatively describe such impacts, we construct a time-based signal strength-aware energy model. The energy modeling methods proposed in the paper enable ordinary developers to conveniently compute phone energy draw by utilizing cheap power meters as measurement tools. The modeling methods are general and able to be used for phones of any type and platform.

Keywords: WiFi environment · Phone energy consumption · Signal strength
Modeling method

1 Introduction

With the incredible popularity of smartphones all over the world, the energy consumption problem of smartphones has gained growing attentions. Constrained battery capacity of smartphones is a pain spot that users have to face while enjoying various energy-consuming applications. Thus, it is significantly important to understand and then optimize the energy consumption of smartphones.

WiFi connection, being the prime way for smartphone users to access the Internet, is a major source of smartphone energy consumption [1, 2]. With the WiFi switch being on, it is experienced by many smartphone users that a phone's energy drains in various rates under different WiFi environments, even if the phone keeps the same application state (e.g. running no applications) and with the same hardware settings in all the environments. As reported by prior works, WiFi environments have notable impacts on smartphones' energy draw [3]. For instance, poor signal condition obviously inflates energy drain [4–6].

This work is supported by the National Natural Science Funds of China under Grant #61402197, Guangdong Province Science and Technology Plan Project #2017A040405030, Guangdong Province Natural Science Funds Team Project #S2012030006242, and Tianhe District Science and Technology Plan Project #201702YH108 in Guangzhou City of China.

© ICST Institute for Computer Sciences, Social Informatics and Telecommunications Engineering 2018
I. Romdhani et al. (Eds.): CollaborateCom 2017, LNICST 252, pp. 88–97, 2018.
https://doi.org/10.1007/978-3-030-00916-8_9

This paper is concerned with the impacts of normal WiFi environments on smartphone energy consumption. We conduct a couple of experiments to investigate the impacts of normal rather than weak signal strengths on phone energy draw, and construct a time-based energy model to describe the impacts. We empirically investigate the impacts of WiFi signal strengths on the energy dissipation of smart phones, and propose energy models to depict these impacts. It is noteworthy that although the model created in this paper is phone-type dependent, however, the method to create the models could be applied to any phone. Our modeling methods require a cheap power meter as a measurement tool and the model parameters are also easily available, thus enabling ordinary developers to analyze phone energy draw in a convenient manner.

This work primarily has the following two contributions:

(1) Empirically study the quantitative relationship between the signal strength and the phone energy consumption under normal WiFi signal environments.
(2) Propose a novel time-based phone energy model considering the WiFi signal impacts, and facilitate ordinary developers to compute mobile energy consumption in a simple way.

The rest of the paper is organized as follows. Section 2 presents our research questions and methodology, and details our method of measuring the phone energy consumption. Section 3 elaborates how WiFi signal strengths impact phone energy draw using some experiments, and proposes a time-based energy model. Section 4 discusses the causes of the impacts observed in the experiments. We discuss the related works in Sect. 5 and conclude in the last section.

2 Methodology

2.1 Research Questions

In this paper, we investigate the impacts of WiFi signal strengths on energy consumption of smart phones while maintaining basic network communications. To exclude the energy consumption interference of various applications and non-WiFi radios, we only study the phone in basic state – a state in which Bluetooth/GSM/3G radios are disabled, the screen is off, the phone runs no applications while keeping the WiFi switch on. To exclude the interference from other WiFi hotspots or devices, we perform the experiments with only one WiFi AP during the night hours, when

Fig. 1. Power meter

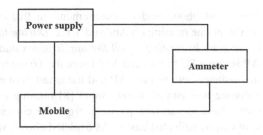

Fig. 2. Power measurement

interference is minimum. *In our experiments, we measure the total energy consumption of the smartphone in the basic state.* The energy draw is not only due to the WiFi NIC but also other phone components including CPU, screen and so on.

By performing experiments, we explore the following research questions:

Q1:   How does WiFi signal strength impact the energy consumption of a smart phone?

Q2:   What energy model can be constructed to indicate this impact?

2.2   Measurement of Energy Consumption

Figure 1 shows the power meter used in our experiment, which consists of a power supply with adjustable stabilized voltage and a current meter. The sampling rate of the power meter is 2 current samples per second. Its resolution is 10 mV/1 mA which enables sample collection with a very fine granularity, 10 mW, as required in [7].

To measure the overall system power of a smart phone, we unload the battery of the phone and connect the phone to the power meter as illustrated in Fig. 2. During all these measurements, the voltage value U is adjusted to a constant. By reading the current value I, we can get the power drain value P, i.e. U * I, of the phone.

To measure the overall energy consumption of a smart phone during any t seconds, we collect all the current samplings using the above power meter. Because the sampling rate is 2 samples per second, the sampling duration t consists of $2t$ sampling periods and each period is 0.5 s. The overall energy consumption of the smart phone within t seconds is calculated as follows:

$$E(t) = \Sigma_{i=1}^{2t} UI_i * 0.5 = 0.5U\Sigma_{i=1}^{2t} I_i. \tag{1}$$

3   Impact of WiFi Signal Strength

In this section, we conduct experiments to investigate the impact of WiFi signal strength on phone energy, so as to get answers to research questions Q1 and Q2. The signal strength is measured in RSSI (Received Signal Strength Indicator) level.

3.1   Energy Data Collection

The smart phone under measurement, in this experiment, is Samsung Galaxy GT-S7898 phone running on Android 4.1.2. *During the measurement, we keep the phone in basic state by turning off all the applications and keep the WiFi switch on.* We use an AP set on a PC to transmit WiFi signals. To control the WiFi signal strength, we adjust the distance between the AP and the smart phone. The RSSI level is measured using a software tool named *Wirelessmon* [8] running on a laptop. The laptop is placed at a spot where to measure phone energy, the corresponding WiFi signal strength at that spot can be collected easily. As depicted above, while collecting the phone energy data in different spots, we use the same experimental settings except for the phone-AP distance, so as to exclude the impacts of external factor as much as possible.

We adjust the phone-AP distance, ranging from 0.5 m to 4 m with the interval 0.5, by placing the phone at eight different spots. At each spot, we monitor the total energy consumption of the phone for a period of time (for instance, 30 s). Table 1 lists the results acquired at the end of 30 s. The first column shows the eight phone-AP distances measured in meters. The second column denotes the signal strengths, measured in RSSI levels, at each spot. The last column represents the total energy consumption (Joule) of the phone within 30 s under each RSSI level.

Table 1. Distance, RSSI and energy consumption in 30 s

Distance (m)	RSSI (dBm)	Energy consumption (J)
0.5	−38	36
1	−40	40
1.5	−42	44
2	−44	48
2.5	−46	51
3	−47	55
3.5	−48	62
4	−49	70

To visualize the above results, we use Fig. 3 to demonstrate the total energy consumption of the phone within 30 s under eight RSSI levels. We make the following observation from the graph in Fig. 3: with the signal strength increased (e.g., from −49 dBm to −38 dBm), that is, with the phone-AP distance decreased (e.g., from 4 m to 0.5 m), the energy consumption of the phone can be reduced obviously (e.g., from 70 J to almost half, namely 36 J).

At each measurement spot, we measure the energy consumption of the smart phone during 30 s by utilizing the methodology described in part B of Sect. 2. The stabilized voltage U of the power meter is set to a constant of 4.2 V. With the power meter, we can log 60 current values within 30 s. And then, we can calculate the corresponding energy values along the time according to Eq. (1).

Figure 4 plots the phone energy consumption (Joule) sampled along 30 s under four RSSI levels mentioned above. Eight types of scatterplots are made by different point types and point colors. *For example, under the RSSI level of −40 dBm, the scatterplot consists of 60 black and square sampling points.* We can make the following observation from the graph in Fig. 4:

(1) Under a given signal strength (i.e., RSSI level), the total energy draw of the phone increases with the time in a near-linear trend.
(2) During each sampling period, under a higher signal strength (i.e. higher RSSI value), the total energy draw of the phone is lower.

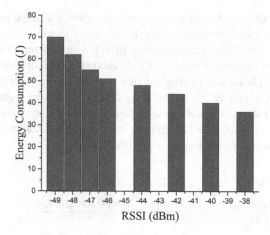

Fig. 3. Energy consumption in 30 s vs RSSI.

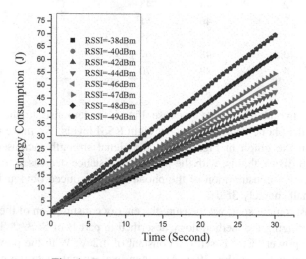

Fig. 4. Energy consumed along with time

3.2   Energy Model

This subsection aims at introducing a simple measurement-time based model for estimating the energy consumption of smart phones as a function of the WiFi signal strength. We use three curve fitting approaches compared with each other to develop a model that is able to match well the energy consumption with RSSI and time values exhibited in Fig. 4, and the detailed steps are as follows:

(1)   Create linear regression models of energy consumption vs time under given RSSI levels: For each given RSSI level, Fig. 4 illustrates a curve fitting process of the energy consumption with the time, and the corresponding linear regression equation is in accordance with the following formula.

$$E(t) = \beta_1 t + \beta_0 \tag{2}$$

where $E(t)$ is the total energy consumption of the phone within the time period t; β_0 and β_1 being two model parameters.

(a) Determine β_0 value: Under the RSSI level of -38 dBm, we set up a linear regression model for energy draw vs time, shown in Column 2 Row 2 in Table 2, by utilizing the statistical values of the 60 black points plotted in Fig. 4. As the model demonstrates, the parameter β_0 is fitted to 1.76.

(b) Determine β_1 value: For the other RSSI levels of -40 dBm to 49 dBm, we use the energy values vs time plotted in Fig. 4, together with β_0 value of 1.76, to create seven linear regression models, as shown from Row 3 to Row 9 of Column 2 in Table 2.

(c) Validate models: To evaluate the model predicted data deviation from the experimental data, we perform three GoF (Goodness of Fit) tests, namely SSE (Sum of Squared Errors), R-square value and RMSE (Root Mean Squared Error). The SSE and RMSE tests are based on affinity to zero, while the R-square value should approximate to one. Suppose that y_i, $\hat{y}_i$ and $\bar{y}$ $(0 \leqslant i \leqslant 60)$ represent experimental data, model predicted data and average experimental data, respectively, and v denotes the difference between the number of experimental data and the number of adjustable parameters, then the three test methods are formulated as the following formulas 3–5 [9].

$$SSE = \sum_{i=1}^{n} (y_i - \hat{y}_i)^2. \tag{3}$$

$$R - square = 1 - \frac{SSE}{\sum_{i=1}^{n}(y_i - \bar{y})^2}. \tag{4}$$

$$RMSE = \sqrt{\frac{SSE}{v}}. \tag{5}$$

Table 2 shows the three GoF test results from Column 3 to 5: RMSE values are close to zero, R-square values are close to one, and the results from the three tests are consistent with each other. It is observed that our models are able to predict

Table 2. RSSI, energy model and GoF test results

RSSI	Energy model	SSE	R-square	RMSE
-38 dBm	$E_1(t) = 1.173t + 1.76$	0.56	0.99	0.21
-40 dBm	$E_2(t) = 1.311t + 1.76$	8.78	0.98	0.56
-42 dBm	$E_3(t) = 1.421t + 1.76$	8.36	0.99	0.52
-44 dBm	$E_4(t) = 1.532t + 1.76$	5.54	0.99	0.30
-46 dBm	$E_5(t) = 1.629t + 1.76$	8.75	0.98	0.55
-47 dBm	$E_6(t) = 1.735t + 1.76$	8.86	0.98	0.58
-48 dBm	$E_7(t) = 1.995t + 1.76$	6.75	0.99	0.42
-49 dBm	$E_8(t) = 2.291t + 1.76$	6.94	0.99	0.48

experimental data very well using the error analysis methods SSE, R-square value, and RMSE. Therefore, under a given RSSI level, the following model of energy consumption with time is reliable:

$$E(t) = \beta_1 t + 1.76. \tag{6}$$

In (6), the value of depends on the value of RSSI level, as shown at the Column 1 and 2 in Table 2.

(2) Create regression model of $|RSSI|$ vs β_1: Fig. 5 illustrates three curve fitting methods of the absolute value, $|RSSI|$, with the parameter β_1, where the eight $|RSSI|$ values (namely 38, 40, 42, 44, 46, 47, 48 and 49) are derived from Column 2 in Table 1, and the eight β_1 values (from 1.173 to 2.291) are derived from Column 2 in Table 2. Accordingly, we set up the linear regression, quadratic linear regression and logarithmic linear regression models for β_1 with $|RSSI|$, and Fig. 6 compares the GoF tests of the three models to select the best one for explaining the relationship between the $|RSSI|$ and β_1. From Fig. 6 we can see that the quadratic linear regression model has the largest value of R-Square, and the SSE and RMSE values are smaller than the other two methods. Thus, we can get the quadratic relation as follows:

$$\beta_1 = 0.009|RSSI|^2 - 0.7|RSSI| + 14.87. \tag{7}$$

(3) Create the target energy model: By substituting the value of β_1 from (7) into (6), we can get the energy model with time and RSSI levels as follows:

$$E(RSSI, t) = \left(0.009|RSSI|^2 - 0.7|RSSI| + 14.87\right)t + 1.76. \tag{8}$$

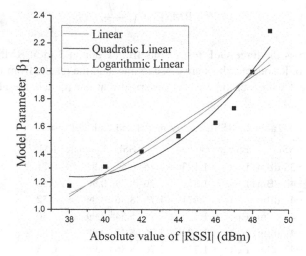

Fig. 5. $|RSSI|$ vs energy model parameter β_1

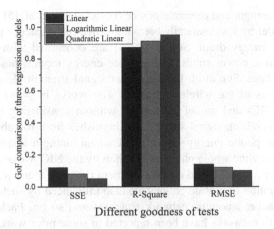

Fig. 6. Different goodness of tests for three models

The energy model (8) is a function of WiFi RSSI level and time. The model can simply but reliably estimate the impact of WiFi signal strength on phone energy at real time. We can set the part concerned RSSI in (8) to zero, and |RSSI| equals 78. It reviews that when the RSSI level is below −78 dBm the phone energy draws quickly while above −78 dBm the impact decreases but still exists, which proves the conclusion drew in (5). Further, Eq. (8) can be transformed to:

$$E(RSSI, t) = [0.009(|RSSI| - 38)^2 + 1.26]t + 1.76 \tag{9}$$

The formula (9) illustrates that in the normal WiFi environment, i.e. when the RSSI level ranges from −78 dBm to −38 dBm, the energy consumption decreases as the WiFi signal strength gets improved.

4 Discussions

When exploring the impact of WiFi signals on phone energy, we focus on good signals, whose RSSIs are over −50 dBm, rather than weak signals. We observed that the phone energy draw goes up with the decline of the signal strength under good signal conditions. The increment of energy drain could be caused by the rate adaptation at the physical layer with the changed signal strength, even if neither data re-transmission nor re-association with AP is triggered by the good signals.

5 Related Work

A major fraction of the energy consumption in smartphones comes from the WiFi radio [6]. The impact of WiFi signal strength on phone energy consumption has been studied in some previous works. For example, Gupta et al. [4] measure the phone energy draw under poor signal strength and dynamic power control. Ding et al. [5] propose a signal strength-aware model by systematically breaking down the impact of poor WiFi signal strength on phone energy drain. Sun et al. [6] are concerned with phones' energy consumption in active power states, and propose energy models based on the application layer throughput. Sun et al. [6] claim that signal strength alone cannot always capture the dynamics of the wireless channel. The works in [4–6] focus on phone energy drawn by NICs and model the energy without considering time as an input parameter. Our research on signal strength distinguishes from the above ones as follows: we study the phone energy under good signal strength condition, where the energy is consumed by the whole phone rather than by the NIC; we construct the signal strength-aware energy model based on measurement time together with signal strength.

Energy consumption of mobile phones are also influenced by such network factors as packet types, packet amounts, network channels and so on. Packet-driven phone energy draw in WiFi networks have been reported in some prior works. For instances, Sun et al. [6] and Zhang et al. [10] study the impact of TCP and UDP packets on phone energy consumption. Khan et al. [11] and Xu et al. [12] investigate the impact of packet size and amount on phone energy draw. Prasad and Balaji [3] create a phone energy model considering network channels.

6 Conclusions and Future Work

We investigated, in this paper, the impacts of normal WiFi signals on the energy consumption of smartphones by a detailed measurement. Experiments were conducted on the phone in basic state at night to minimize interferences. We empirically studied the impact of good signal strength on the phone energy draw, and created a signal-strength aware model based on measurement time to depict the impact, by comparing three regression methods. Our research results confirm the following experience of many phone users: higher signal strength implies lower energy drain even under normal WiFi signal conditions. The modeling method proposed in this paper enable developers to conveniently analyze the phone energy draw in WiFi environments, because the method only requires cheap power meter as a measurement tool and the model parameters are also easily available.

Although the models proposed in this paper is phone-type dependent, the method to create the models could be applied to any type of phones. In order to improve our model methods, we plan to collect more experimental data on more types of phones. We look forward to study the impacts of other WiFi environmental factors on the phone energy, and then create energy models with the most prominent influencing factors.

References

1. Li, D., Hao, S., Gui, J., Halfond, W.G.: An empirical study of the energy consumption of android applications. In: Proceedings of 2014 IEEE International Conference on Software Maintenance and Evolution (ICSME), pp. 121–130, September 2014
2. Pathak, A., Hu, Y.C., Zhang, M.: Where is the energy spent inside my app? Fine grained energy accounting on smartphones with Eprof. In: Proceedings of the 7th ACM European Conference on Computer Systems, pp. 29–42, April 2012
3. Prasad, S., Balaji, S.: Real-time energy dissipation model for mobile devices. In: Shetty, N. R., Prasad, N.H., Nalini, N. (eds.) Emerging Research in Computing, Information, Communication and Applications, pp. 281–288. Springer, New Delhi (2015). https://doi.org/10.1007/978-81-322-2550-8_27
4. Gupta, A., Mohapatra, P.: Energy consumption and conservation in WiFi based phones: a measurement-based study. In: Proceedings of 4th Annual IEEE Communications Society Conference on Sensor, Mesh and Ad Hoc Communications and Networks (SECON 2007), pp. 122–131, June 2007
5. Ding, N., Wagner, D., Chen, X., Pathak, A., Hu, Y.C., Rice, A.: Characterizing and modeling the impact of wireless signal strength on smartphone battery drain. ACM SIGMETRICS Perform. Eval. Rev. **41**, 29–40 (2013)
6. Sun, L., Deng, H., Sheshadri, R.K., Zheng, W., Koutsonikolas, D.: Experimental evaluation of WiFi active power/energy consumption models for smartphones. IEEE Trans. Mob. Comput. **16**(1), 115–129 (2017)
7. Gomez Chavez, K.M.: Energy efficiency in wireless access networks: measurements, models and algorithms. Dissertation, University of Trento (2013)
8. WirelessMon tool, PassMark Software Inc. http://www.passmark.com/products/wirelessmonitor.htm
9. Help Documentation on Evaluating Goodness of Fit, the MathWorks, Inc. https://www.mathworks.com/help/curvefit/evaluating-goodness-of-fit.html
10. Zhang, L., et al.: Accurate online power estimation and automatic battery behavior based power model generation for smartphones. In: Proceedings of 2010 IEEE/ACM/IFIP International Conference on Hardware/Software Codesign and System Synthesis (CODES +ISSS), pp. 105–114, October 2010
11. Khan, M.O., et al.: Model-driven energy-aware rate adaptation. In: Proceedings of the Fourteenth ACM International Symposium on Mobile Ad Hoc Networking and Computing, pp. 217–226, July 2013
12. Xu, F., Liu, Y., Li, Q., Zhang, Y.: V-edge: fast self-constructive power modeling of smartphones based on battery voltage dynamics. In: Proceedings of USENIX NSDI, vol. 13, pp. 43–56, April 2013

Constrained Route Planning Based on the Regular Expression

Jing Wang, Huiping Liu, and Zhao Zhang$^{(\boxtimes)}$

School of Computer Science and Software Engineering,
East China Normal University, Shanghai, China
{jingwang,hpliu}@stu.ecnu.edu.cn, zhzhang@sei.ecnu.edu.cn

Abstract. Traditional route planning algorithms, which mainly focus on common metrics to find the optimal route from source to destination, are not enough to solve route planning requirements with location constraints like sequence, alternative and avoidance. For example, finding the shortest path passing the whole or a part of user-defined locations or location categories in order or disorder, or not passing some specified locations or categories. Mainly focusing on these scenarios, this paper formalizes the constrained route planning problem based on the regular expression generated by user requirements and gives a general framework for the exact solution. By using different shortest path algorithms, we show how the framework works efficiently with shortest path algorithms. Finally, extensive experiments on real road network datasets demonstrate the efficiency of our proposal.

Keywords: Constrained route planning · The regular expression
The shortest path · Dijkstra's algorithm · A* search algorithm

1 Introduction

Route planning based on metrics such as distance, time, cost, etc. [1–3], has been rapidly developed in recent decades. However, there are some route planning requirements constrained by locations which are common in daily life but cannot be solved by traditional route planning algorithms. Consider a road network in Fig. 1 where each node indicates a Point of Interest (POI), each directed edge represents a one-way route between POIs with an associated number indicating its length. Suppose after working at A, Tom prefers to go to a restaurant to have a meal first and then choose a cinema or bar to relax (he can only visit one of them because of insufficient time), after that he should go home at I, but along the way home he would like to avoid mall F due to traffic jams. Tom wants an ideal route which not only satisfies above location requirements but also has the minimum total length.

Similar problems have received significant attentions. Optimal route queries [4–13] search the shortest route that starts from the query point and passes

© ICST Institute for Computer Sciences, Social Informatics and Telecommunications Engineering 2018
I. Romdhani et al. (Eds.): CollaborateCom 2017, LNICST 252, pp. 98–108, 2018.
https://doi.org/10.1007/978-3-030-00916-8_10

through a user-defined category or keyword set in order, partial order or disorder. In spite of the significant contributions made by previous works, they are limited to solve route planning problems like the example in Fig. 1.

Therefore, in this paper, we study the problem of finding the optimal route for a fixed source and destination pair with given multiple location constraints like sequence, alternative and avoidance. Considering such route planning requirements always cover rich semantics, the regular expression, a character sequence to represent matching patterns that strings should be in accordance with, is adopted to express route planning queries. By taking advantages of existing operator definitions, the user-defined constraints can be expressed completely and precisely. First, we formalize the Constrained Route Planning Problem (CRPP) based on the regular expression. Then we devise a general framework, which supports shortest path algorithms such as the Dijkstra's algorithm and A* search algorithm, to solve the CRPP.

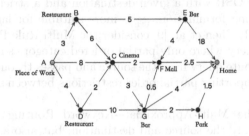

Fig. 1. An example of the constrained route planning problem.

The main contributions of this paper can be summarized as follows:

- We propose and formalize the CRPP based on the regular expression, that is to find the shortest path from the source to destination in accordance with customized location constraints like passing sequence, alternative and avoidance of locations or location categories.
- We devise a general framework to solve the CRPP with the exact solution, and implement it by using the Dijkstra's algorithm and A* search algorithm.
- Extensive experimental evaluations performed on real datasets show the efficiency of the proposed approaches.

The remainder of this paper is organized as follows. In Sect. 2, we briefly review related works. Section 3 gives necessary notations and a formal problem definition of this paper. Section 4 describes the general framework of our solutions, following two implementations: the Dijkstra-based CRPP algorithm and the A* search-based CRPP algorithm. Section 5 reports our extensive experiments. Finally Sect. 6 concludes the paper.

2   Related Work

The optimal route query with multiple constraints has been extensively investigated. Li et al. [4] propose the Trip Planning Query (TPQ) in spatial databases where each spatial object has a location and a category. The aim of the TPQ is to find the shortest path from the source to the destination that passes through at least one object from each category in a defined set of categories. In the TPQ, users cannot specify the passing order of categories, and [4] only gives approximate solutions. Sharifzadeh et al. [5] study an Optimal Sequenced Route (OSR) query which strives to find the shortest path from a fixed source that passes through at least one node from given category sets in a specified order. [5] gives solutions in Euclidean space - the LORD and R-LORD algorithms as well as in metric space - the PNE algorithm. By preprocessing given category sequences, a series of Additively Weighted Voronoi Diagrams (AWVD) are constructed to solve OSR queries effectively [6,7]. The Generalized Shortest Path (GSP) query [8] is essentially the OSR with a given destination and a strict order. By using dynamic programming formulation, [8] is more suitable for larger graphs. Different from the OSR, Chen et al. [9] consider the Multi-Rule Partial Sequenced Route (MRPSR) query where only partial ordered categories are specified. [10] solves the optimal route query from the source and passes through a user-defined set of categories, supporting partial order restrictions between some specific categories of the set.

[11] proposes the Multi-Approximate-Keyword Routing (MAKR) query, which defines not only the source and destination, but also a set of (keyword, threshold) pairs to find the shortest path that passes through at least one matching object per keyword with the matching degree higher than the corresponding threshold. Keyword-aware Optimal Route (KOR) query [12,13] gives approximate solutions to find a path from the source to the destination, covering a set of user-specified keywords, satisfying the travel budget and optimizing the route popularity. However, MAKR and KOR don't take keyword sequences into consideration, and adding keyword matching degree, path popularity, etc. is only suitable for specific scenarios that contain these information.

Also using the regular expression to define constrained route problems, main concerns of the formal-language-constrained shortest path problem [14] are edges where labels of edges on the route should satisfy the regular expression.

To the best of our knowledge, existing works mainly focus on constraints of location categories, while some do not allow the sequence constraints, some just give approximate solutions, some take additional consideration into factors such as the route popularity which only applies to specific scenarios, none of them solve the alternative and avoidance constraints. For more general constrained route planning problems, this paper takes a comprehensive consideration of sequence, alternative and avoidance constraints as well as gives the exact solution.

3 Preliminary

Definition 1 (Graph). A directed weighted graph $G(V, E)$ consists of a set of nodes V and a set of edges E. $v \in V$ represents a location with a category $v.c$. $e = (v_i, v_j)$ denotes a directed edge from $v_i \in V$ to $v_j \in V$ with an nonnegative weight $w(e)$. We define G as a general graph, it can be a road network where V is the set of POIs and E is the set of shortest paths between POIs.

Definition 2 (Constrained Route Query). The constrained route query, denoted as q, is a regular expression that makes up of five kinds of elements: the source s, the destination t, a set of locations in V, a set of location categories in V and six operators $\cdot$, $|$, $^\wedge$, $*$, $+$, $(\ )$ (see Table 1.).

Table 1. Operators in the Constrained Route Query

Operator	Meaning
Join $\cdot$ (can be omitted)	Indicates concatenation between locations or categories.
Alternative $|$	Separates alternative locations or categories.
Non-operator $^\wedge$	Connects avoidance locations or categories.
Kleene closure $*$	Indicates zero or more occurrences of locations or categories.
Positive closure $+$	Indicates at least one occurrences of locations or categories.
Brackets $(\ )$	Defines the range of operators.

Generated by the combination of above elements, q can cover almost all kinds of route planning requirements constrained by locations. Thus the constrained route query of Tom can be represented as $q = work \cdot Restaurant \cdot (Cinema|Bar) \cdot (^\wedge mall) \cdot home$, where $work$, $home$ and $mall$ are specific locations while $Restaurant$, $Cinema$ and Bar are categories. Since a location can be regarded as a single category, locations can be solved by transferring them into categories. So following sections only discuss the processing of categories.

However, closure operators $*$ and $+$ can be simplified: (1) a certain category appearing zero or more times has no influence on route planning results and can be removed from q; (2) passing a certain category one or more times can be simplified as once according to properties of the shortest path. Therefore, we mainly focus on other four operators.

In traditional regular expression theory, a string (can be seen as a route of characters) is accorded with a regular expression only if they have a complete matching. For example, only 'ACFI' and 'ACGI' are satisfied for $AC(F|G)I$, one more or one less character are all unacceptable. But in CRPP, q only contains categories that users care about, also it is insignificant to define all passed categories in q. It is a key issue when applying the regular expression to the CRPP and the solution will be stated in 4.2.

Definition 3 (Constrained Route Planning Problem). Given a directed weighted graph $G(V, E)$ and a constrained route query q, constrained route planning problem based on the regular expression $CRPP(G, q)$ intends to find the shortest path that satisfies q in G.

So the CRPP of Tom is: to find the shortest path that satisfies $q = work \cdot Restaurant \cdot (Cinema|Bar) \cdot (^\wedge mall) \cdot home$ in the graph illustrated in Fig. 1. Actually, his ideal result is $A \rightarrow D \rightarrow C \rightarrow G \rightarrow H \rightarrow I$ with the length of 12.5.

4   Solutions

4.1   The Framework

In order to solve the CRPP, a general processing framework is proposed by taking the shortest path algorithm as the main line while the constrained route planning query assists in filtering routes which don't meet location constraints.

First of all, q is parsed to a Deterministic Finite Automaton (DFA) represented by the transition table T, which is recorded as $(state, location/category) \rightarrow nextstate$. See an example in Figs. 2 and 3 for q of Tom. Particularly, different from traditional regular expression that $^\wedge$ only constrains the next character of a string, in CRPP one can't pass operand categories of $^\wedge$ until arriving at the next constrained categories in q. For example, Tom wants to avoid passing $mall$ along his way from $Cinema$ or Bar until getting $home$. Above definition of avoidance constraints needs a special processing: first the non-operator and its operands are stored together as a transition condition, for example, $(state_4, ^\wedge mall) \rightarrow state_6$; then add into T a new transition from the added transfer result state to itself with the non-condition, for example, $(state_6, ^\wedge mall) \rightarrow state_6$ (showed in dashed boxes in Figs. 2 and 3). Now there are two transitions of $state_6$ whose conditions have a overlap that $home$ is satisfied both for $home$ and $^\wedge mall$. In order to get the shortest qualified route as soon as possible, that is, to forward the route as much as possible, we give a lower priority to the non-condition so that every time facing transitions like $(state_6, home)$, it will first move to $state_7$, thus keep the determinacy of DFA. As a result, we can check the qualification of a route through T: a route is qualified if and only if the start state can be led to an accepting state in the order of nodes of this route.

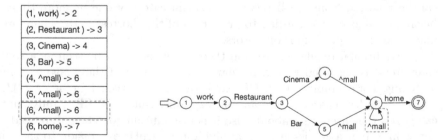

Fig. 2. The state transition table.   **Fig. 3.** The state transition diagram.

In this paper, we use two classical shortest path algorithm - Dijkstra's algorithm and A* search algorithm to show the implementation of our framework.

Because Dijkstra's algorithm is the basis of many shortest path algorithms and can be easily extended to them, while A* search algorithm is one of the most popular and effective target-directed methods by using a heuristic estimation.

4.2   The Dijkstra-Based CRPP Algorithm

Instead of the original Dijkstra's algorithm [15], we use a variant of it because its result is sure the shortest route but may be unqualified for location constraints. When updating the distance from s to v, we keep all partial routes not merely the shortest one, so that all possible qualified routes are taken into consideration. Particularly, a route will be discarded if some nodes on it are avoidance locations or belong to avoidance categories for the current state in T.

As stated in Definition 2, traditional regular expressions are limited in CRPP for they are a complete matching. To solve this, we define an arbitrary state arb to represent states not in T, $nowstate$ and $paststate$ to indicate the current state and its last non-arbitrary state, respectively. If a node satisfies transition conditions, it will be transferred directly; otherwise, since its subsequent nodes are likely to meet transition conditions, we mark its $nowstate$ as arb and expand it according to $paststate$. A local priority queue LQ_v is used to store candidate routes from s to v, denoted as $rt(path, dist, nowstate, paststate)$ where $path$ is the shortest path while $dist$ is its length. Routes in LQ_v are sorted by $rt.dist$ in an ascending order. Then a global priority queue GQ is used to preserve nodes during processing ordered incrementally by the minimal $rt.dist$ in their LQs.

Algorithm 1. CRPP(G, T)

Input: graph G, transition table T
Output: the shortest path in G satisfied q and its length
1 Get the $startState$ and $endState$ in T;
2 Create $rt_s(rt_s.path.add(s)$, 0, $T(startState, s)$, $startState)$;
3 LQ_s.enqueue(rt_s); GQ.enqueue(s);
4 **while** GQ *is not empty* **do**
5 $\quad$ $nd_i \leftarrow GQ$.dequeue(); $rt_i \leftarrow LQ_{nd_i}$.dequeue();
6 $\quad$ **if** $rt_i.nowstate = endState$ **then**
7 $\quad\quad$ **return** rt_i;
8 $\quad$ **else**
9 $\quad\quad$ **if** LQ_{nd_i} *is not empty* **then**
10 $\quad\quad\quad$ GQ.enqueue(nd_i);
11 $\quad\quad$ GetLinks(G, T, GQ, nd_i, rt_i);

However, above process will produce a lot of redundant routes, which surely cannot be the shortest qualified route. It is a waste of memory and computation resources to consider redundant routes, more importantly, they may be expanded in later steps, which will result in continuous unnecessary calculations. Based on above observations, we design two pruning rules to filter redundant routes.

Pruning Rules. When considering two candidate routes rt_i and rt_j of v:

(1) if $rt_i.nowstate = rt_j.nowstate \neq arb$, the longer route should be pruned;
(2) if $rt_i.nowstate = rt_j.nowstate = arb$ and $rt_i.paststate = rt_j.paststate$, the longer route should be pruned.

Proof. Suppose $rt_i.dist < rt_j.dist$, the shortest qualified path from s to t is $rt_j.path + p(v, t)$ where $p(v, t)$ is the path from v to t (+ means to concatenate two routes). That is, $endState$ can be reached from $rt_j.nowstate$ (if $rt_j.nowstate \neq arb$) or $rt_j.paststate$ (if $rt_j.paststate = arb$) through $p(v, t)$. As rt_i and rt_j share the same state ($nowstate$ if $nowstate \neq arb$, otherwise $paststate$), rt_i can reach $endState$ through $p(v, t)$ too. Because $rt_i.dist < rt_j.dist$, then $rt_i.path + p(v, t) < rt_j.path + p(v, t)$, which is a contradiction. If $rt_i.path + p(v, t)$ is not qualified, neither can $rt_j.path + p(v, t)$. So rt_i is always better than rt_j and we can safely discard rt_j without changing the correctness of algorithms. □

Algorithm 1 shows the details of Dijkstra-based CRPP (G, T) algorithm. It starts expanding nodes from s, then continuously takes the shortest path until its $nowstate$ reaches $endState$. If GQ is empty, there is no qualified result at all. Otherwise the route will be expanded by invoking Algorithm 2 Getlinks(G, T, GQ, nd_i, rt_i) and during expanding, attributes of expanded routes will be set using aforementioned transition rules. Before adding to the priority queue, pruning rules are employed to check if it is a redundant route.

Algorithm 2. GetLinks(G, T, GQ, nd_i, rt_i)

Input: graph G, transition table T, global priority queue GQ, current node
      nd_i, the optimal candidate route to be extended rt_i

1 **foreach** *directly linked node u of nd_i in G* **do**
2   Create $rt_k(rt_i.path.add(u), rt_i.dist + w(nd_i, u), nowstate, paststate)$;
3   **if** *u isn't in GQ* **then**
4   LQ_u.enqueue(rt_k); GQ.enqueue(u);
5   **else if** *there exists a rt_j in LQ_u s.t. $rt_j.nowstate = rt_k.nowstate$* **then**
6   Pruning rules are used to decide which one should be held in LQ_u;
7   **else**
8   LQ_u.enqueue(rt_k);

Since above algorithm is equivalent to continually find the next shortest path from s to t and check whether it is qualified for constraints, its validity is obvious. Also, the use of pruning rules only reduces the search space and improves the efficiency of the algorithm without deteriorating the correctness, so the validity of Dijkstra-based CRPP algorithm is proved.

4.3   The A* Search-Based CRPP Algorithm

In essence, A* search algorithm [16] works like Dijkstra's except that at each step it expands a node v with the minimal evaluation length $\hat{f}(v) = g(v) + \hat{h}(v)$, where $g(v)$ is the actual shortest length of the route from s to v and $\hat{h}(v)$ represents the estimated length from v to t. Hence, the process of A* search-based CRPP algorithm is nearly the same as Dijkstra-based only to add a new attribute $esdist$ representing $\hat{f}(v)$, and redefine the priority of LQ as an ascending order of $esdist$. Intuitively, the correctness of A* search-based CRPP algorithm is proved.

5   Experimental Evaluation

5.1   Experimental Settings

All algorithms are written in Java and run on an Intel Core i5-4460 3.20 GHz CPU PC with 16 GB memory and a Windows platform.

Datasets. We use a real road network of California [4] with 68,345 nodes of 64 different categories and 137,980 edges. In order to investigate the impact of different graph sizes and graph structures on our solutions, we randomly choose a proportion of nodes and their relevant edges from the original graph to generate different sizes of subgraphs. The ratio of selected nodes is represented as the parameter num.

Queries. In order to ensure the generality of q, we set the normalized form of q as $s(c_1|c_2|...|c_k)_1()_2...()_j(^\wedge(c_1|c_2|...|c_l))t$. Assuming that each query has j categories that need to be connected sequentially, k choices for each of these categories, and after the current route there are l categories that cannot be passed (j, k, and l are all positive integers), generally, all constrained route queries can be expressed as this normalized form. So for each experiment, we generate 100 basic query instances with randomly chosen s, t and categories.

Parameter settings of the experiment are presented in Table 2.

Table 2. Parameter settings

Parameter	Range	Default value
num	25%, 50%, 75%, 100%	50%
j	1, 2, 3	2
k	1, 2, 3	2
l	0, 1, 2	0

5.2   Performance

We mainly focus on the response time and the number of expanded nodes which indicate the processing efficiency and the size of the search space, respectively.

In particular, we observe the number of nodes which are reduced to be extended by non-operators. To the best of our knowledge, there's no previous works that solve the same constrained route planning problem as ours, so we only compare Dijkstra-based CRPP algorithm and A* search-based CRPP algorithm, focusing on their performance differences. Note that below 'D-CRPP' and 'A-CRPP' both represent algorithms with pruning rules.

Effect of the Graph. We study the influence of G's scale and structure on our algorithms by varying num. Figures 4(a) and 5(a) show that the more number of nodes in a graph, the more search space and processing time the algorithm needs. It is because the average number of nodes of the shortest path in large graphs is often more than that in small graphs.

Effect of the Constrained Route Query. Figures 4(b) and 5(b) plot the performance when varying j. It can be seen that with the increase of j, the algorithm performance has a decline, that is because the more sequenced categories in q, the more calculations algorithm needs to check constraints.

In Figs. 4(c) and 5(c), the performance of algorithms falls with the increase of k. The reason is that when $k = 1$, there is a fixed category should be passed so it's equivalent to narrow search scope for algorithms; then when k increases, algorithms can only choose one among categories separated by |, which will accelerate the processing. Consider an extreme case that all categories in G are added as an alternative in each bracket of q, that is, $k = 64$, then every possible route is qualified.

Another important concern is l. See Fig. 6, with no surprise, more nodes are reduced to be extended because more candidate routes are excluded when l increases. It is interesting to note that there is a performance difference between D-CRPP and A-CRPP. With the increase of l, D-CRPP needs less processing time as well as less expanded nodes while A-CRPP needs more. This is because Dijkstra's algorithm only expands routes with the minimum length based on the current route, but A* search algorithm takes future conditions into account to expand routes with the shortest evaluation length from s to t. While we assume that the avoidance constraints appear at the end of the normalized form of q, many unqualified routes are used to estimate the shortest route in A*. And if a node on an expanded route belongs to the avoidance categories, this route will be discarded instead of transferred to an indeterminate state, that's why this phenomenon only appears when varying l rather than other parameters.

Effect of Pruning Rules. Assume the response time more than 3 min is unacceptable, in the process of experiment, we find that unacceptable query rates of both Dijkstra-based and A* search-based CRPP algorithms without pruning rules are nearly 100%, which indicates the good efficiency of pruning rules.

Comparison of Dijkstra-Based and A*-Search Based Algorithms. As shown in above diagrams, clearly A-CRPP outperforms D-CRPP in all cases. For the same kind of query, the performance of A-CRPP can be one order of magnitude better than D-CRPP. Also, as the size of G or constraints in q varies, the performance change of D-CRPP is faster than A-CRPP. However, since the

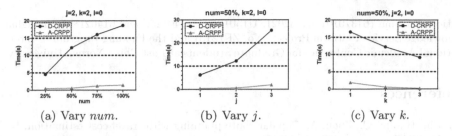

(a) Vary *num*.   (b) Vary *j*.   (c) Vary *k*.

Fig. 4. Average response time when varying *num*, *j*, *k*.

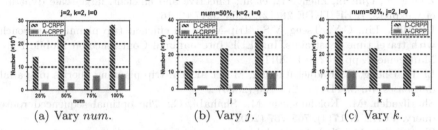

(a) Vary *num*.   (b) Vary *j*.   (c) Vary *k*.

Fig. 5. Average number of expanded nodes when varying *num*, *j*, *k*.

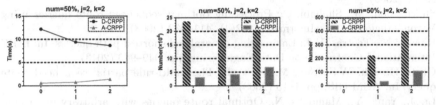

(a) Average response time. (b) Average number of ex- (c) Average number of re-
panded nodes.   duced expanded nodes.

Fig. 6. Performance when varying *l*.

estimated length in A* search may base on routes which are in conflict with
avoidance constraints, A-CRPP tends to get lower performance while D-CRPP
gets better when avoidance constraints increase.

6   Conclusion

This paper investigates the constrained route planning problem, which is first
formalized by defining the constrained route query as the regular expression,
then gives a general framework for exact solutions. Subsequently, a Dijkstra-
based CRPP algorithm and an A* search-based CRPP algorithm are proposed
while utilizes pruning rules to prune redundant routes. Finally, we demonstrate
the efficiency of our approaches through an extensive experimental evaluation.

Acknowledgements. Our research is supported by the National Key Research and
Development Program of China (2016YFB1000905), National Natural Science Foun-

dation of China (61370101, 61532021, U1501252, U1401256 and 61402180), Shanghai Knowledge Service Platform Project (No. ZF1213) and the Funding Program of International Academic Conference for Graduate Students at East China Normal University.

References

1. Liu, H., Jin, C., Zhou, A.: Popular route planning with travel cost estimation. In: DASFAA, (2), pp. 403–418 (2016)
2. Zhang, S., Qin, L., Zheng, Y., et al.: Effective and efficient: large-scale dynamic city express. IEEE TKDE **28**(12), 3203–3217 (2016)
3. Lu, H.C., Lin, C.Y., Tseng, V.S.: Trip-Mine: an efficient trip planning approach with travel time constraints. In: IEEE International Conference on Mobile Data Management, pp. 152–161 (2011)
4. Li, F., Cheng, D., Hadjieleftheriou, M., et al.: On trip planning queries in spatial databases. In: SSTD, pp. 273–290 (2005)
5. Sharifzadeh, M., Kolahdouzan, M., Shahabi, C.: The optimal sequenced route query. VLDB J. **17**(4), 765–787 (2008)
6. Sharifzadeh, M., Shahabi, C.: Additively weighted Voronoi diagrams for optimal sequenced route queries. In: Workshop on Spatio-Temporal Database Management. ACM (2009)
7. Sharifzadeh, M., Shahabi, C.: Processing optimal sequenced route queries using Voronoi diagrams. GeoInformatica **12**(4), 411–433 (2008)
8. Rice, M.N., Tsotras, V.J.: Engineering generalized shortest path queries. In: IEEE International Conference on Data Engineering, pp. 949–960 (2013)
9. Chen, H., Ku, W.S., Sun, M.T., et al.: The multi-rule partial sequenced route query. In: ACM GIS, pp. 1–10 (2008)
10. Li, J., Yang, Y., Mamoulis, N.: Optimal route queries with arbitrary order constraints. IEEE TKDE **25**(5), 1097–1110 (2013)
11. Yao, B., Tang, M., Li, F.: Multi-approximate-keyword routing in GIS data. In: ACM SIGSPATIAL International Conference on Advances in Geographic Information Systems, pp. 201–210 (2011)
12. Cao, X., Chen, L., Cong, G.: Keyword-aware optimal route search. PVLDB **5**(11), 1136–1147 (2012)
13. Cao, X., Chen, L., Cong, G., et al.: KORS: keyword-aware optimal route search system. In: IEEE International Conference on Data Engineering, pp. 1340–1343 (2013)
14. Barrett, C., Jacob, R., Marathe, M.: Formal language constrained path problems. Computing **30**(3), 234–245 (1998)
15. Dijkstra, E.W.: A note on two problems in connexion with graphs. Numerische Mathematik **1**(1), 269–271 (1959)
16. Hart, P.E., Nilsson, N.J., Raphael, B.: A formal basis for heuristic determination of minimum path cost. IEEE Trans. Syst. Sci. Cybern. SSC4 **4**(2), 100–107 (1968)

A Human-Machine Collaborative Detection Model for Identifying Web Attacks

Yong Hu[1,2], Bo Li[1,2(✉)], Weijing Ye[2], and Guiqin Yuan[1,2]

[1] School of Computing Science and Engineering, Beihang University, Beijing, China
libo@act.buaa.edu.cn
[2] State Grid Zhejiang Electric Power Company,
Information and Telecommunication Branch, Hangzhou, China

Abstract. Machine learning plays an important part in detecting web attacks. However, it exhibits high false alarm rate due to the lacking of labeled data. Humans perform better than machines in attack recognition, while suffer from low bandwidth. In this paper, we adopt a collaborative detection model, based on machine learning augmented with human interaction to detect web attacks. We leverage human knowledge to continuously optimize the detection model and make machines smarter against fast-changing web attacks. To eliminate the bottleneck of humans, we design an selection mechanism which could recommend most suspicious anomaly behaviors for humans to correct the false decision of machines. In addition, we also define a human involvement ratio, k, to represent how much efforts that human contributes to the collaborative detection model. By tuning k, the model accuracy and human workloads could be effectively balanced. We conduct several comprehensive experiments to evaluate the effectiveness of our model using reallife datasets. The results demonstrate that our approach could significantly improve the detection accuracy compared with traditional machine learning approaches.

Keywords: Web attacks · Collaborative detection · Machine learning

1 Introduction

With the rejuvenation of Artificial Intelligence, researchers tend to use machine learning approaches to detect web attacks. Machine learning approaches could handle network traffic at a high speed without human intervention, and has been applied into some web security systems such as Web Application Firewall (WAF). Anomaly detection is a kind of unsupervised machine learning techniques and has been widely used to web attack detection. Similar to other unsupervised approaches, it also suffers from low accuracy due to the lacking of labeled data. In machine learning domain, it is also referred to as "cold-start" problem which greatly affects the feasibility of applying anomaly detection techniques into production environments.

© ICST Institute for Computer Sciences, Social Informatics and Telecommunications Engineering 2018
I. Romdhani et al. (Eds.): CollaborateCom 2017, LNICST 252, pp. 109–119, 2018.
https://doi.org/10.1007/978-3-030-00916-8_11

On the contrary, humans perform much better than machines in identifying web anomalies and attacks. Current security products are still highly dependent on humans to find anomalies and create the corresponding signatures and rules so as to detect similar attacks. The advantage is high accuracy with high detection speed since only known signatures are matched during the detection phase. The bandwidth of human is limited, thus it is impossible for security experts to keep up with the emerging and continuously changing web attacks.

Naturally we adopt a machine-human collaborative detection model to improve the detection performance without sacrificing the detection speed. In this model, human intelligence is crucial to improve detection accuracy of machines. Our main contributions are summarized as follows:

- We introduce a collaborative detection model to identify web attacks from web logs. The model is a continuously updating loop. First, machines identify anomalies and ranking mechanism recommend most suspicious behaviors for human decision. The results are feedback to the model and make the model smarter.
- We carefully analyze the web log datasets and design a feature extraction method to ensure relative high detection accuracy. We design some rules to control how humans are involved, and find a suitable k value, which is used to represent the ratio of human participation in the collaborative model.
- We conduct several experiments to evaluate the effectiveness of our model. The results show that our model can effectively improve the accuracy rate in the case of limited human collaboration. The model performance and human workloads could be well balanced.

Section 3 describes the structure of the model. Section 4 describes the data analyzed by our system. Section 5 accounts for the steps of human participation in the model. Section 6 includes experimental settings, model details and results with analysis. Section 7 sums up conclusions.

2   Related Work

In this paper, our model comes from the active detection model [1] combining the human intuition with machine learning technology. We follow it and make some differences. We simplified the process of unsupervised learning algorithms. Secondly, we provide artificial intuition two opportunities to participate in the detection and pay more attention to the single web logs' information mining with proper data quantization and feature extraction features methods

In terms of machine learning and anomaly detection. [2] focused on the query parameters in the web request and proposed several mathematical models used to detect anomalies; [3] proposed an unsupervised learning method used to detection network anomalies online; [4] proposed a enhanced SVM method used to implement network intrusion detection. Statistics-based methods are primary to discovery distribution information counting on statistical techniques. For the statistical analysis of URI, G.V. [2,14] applied the Gaussian distribution and

Markov model to analyze attribute length, attribute character distribution structural inference, token finder, attribute presence or absence and attribute order.

3   Model

The schematic diagram of this collaborative detection model (CDM) is shown in Fig. 1. CDM is divided into three main stages:

1. The model classifies the data using the unsupervised learning algorithm.
2. Select minor part of the classified data and submit it to the security expert. Investigate and label it with the help of knowledge of analyst.
3. Transport the labeled data back to the model to train the supervised learning algorithm which outputs the final detection result.

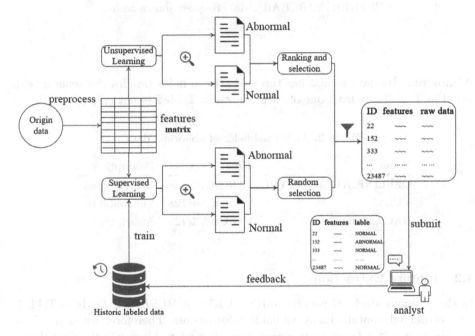

Fig. 1. The schematic diagram of this collaborative detection model

To start with CDM can identify part of the most threatening and false detection positives data, which will be presented to the security experts. Manual analysis can improve the system reliability and recognition rate, and timely detect the latest security threats. Therefore, the CMD owns both a computer's efficient computing power and some capacity the machine temporary lacks.

4   Data Preprocessing

This chapter mainly corresponds to the data preprocessing process in the model.

4.1 Data Characteristic

Our model processes web logs. In this paper, the source data provided by data center comes from the enterprise website. The data is only divided into two categories of normal and abnormal, instead of further classified attack type.

Normal. Most of the source data is normal, its data format follows the generic weblogs' format. The two key fields we adopt are shown in Table 1

Table 1. Some fields of normal data

Name	Type	Description
REQ_URI	VARCHAR(2048)	Request URI
REFERER	VARCHAR(2048)	Request source address
...	...	... ...

Abnormal. Its data format has three additional fields besides the general field listed in Table 1. At least one of them shown in Table 2 is not empty.

Table 2. Additional fields of abnormal data

Name	Type	Description
OFFLINE_ATTACK_TYPE	VARCHAR(128)	Attack type
VUL	VARCHAR(128)	Vulnerabilities
HACK_TOOL	VARCHAR(128)	Attack tool

4.2 Feature Extraction

In the previous study of peers, the REQ_URI and REFERER fields in Table 1 are considered contain many valuable information. Therefore, we decided to use these two key fields to quantize the collected weblogs as our algorithms' input. Get the union of the REQ_URI and REFERER fields as UR to remove the redundant information, and extract the features shown in Table 3. Here are detailed explanations of some fields:

ID 4 Num_token. If a URI path is shown as follow:
www.example.com/login.php?login_attempt=1&l=110

For easier analysis, pure digital and single letter are ignored. Then we get the token set of an URI string:
[www, example, com, login, php, attempt]

So the number of token is 6. Statistical analysis of tokens frequency contributes to anomaly detection.

ID 5 Num_Count_Keyword. We will list a set of key words. Each occurrence of a word in this set lead the statistic plus one.

[select, union, from, and, then, else, count, print, alter, md5, script, php, ini, config, log, mdb, passwd, /etc/passwd]

ID 6 Num_Count_Keychar. We will list a set of key character. Each occurrence of a character in this set lead the statistic plus one.

[Space , { , } , [,] , (,)]

ID 11 Relative Entropy. Related Entropy represents the degree of string confusion. It is calculated:

$$e = -\sum_{i=1}^{m} p_i \log p_i, \quad pi = \frac{n_i}{n}. \tag{1}$$

m is the number of different characters of URI, N is the total number of characters. n_i is the number of ith characters whose frequency is p_i.

Table 3. Extracted features

ID	Name	Type	Description
1	Num_Digit	Integer	Number of Digit in UR String
2	Num_Letter	Integer	Number of Letter in UR string
3	Num_Punctuation	Integer	Number of Punctuation in UR string
4	Num_token	Integer	Number of token in UR string
5	Num_Count_Keyword	Integer	Number of key words count in UR string
6	Num_Count_Keychar	Integer	Number of key character count in UR string
7	Length_UR	Integer	Length of UR
8	Length_Max_Par	Integer	The max length of parameter
9	Length_Min_Par	Integer	The min length of parameter
10	Depth	Integer	The UR path depth
11	Relative Entropy	Float	Relative entropy of UR string

5 Detection Process

5.1 Unsupervised Learning Process

Its main function is coarse particle size anomaly detection, by which the model can select minor data for artificial analysis. This provide the first participatory position of human. Using k-means algorithm, the web logs are divided into two categories. It is impossible for analyst to observe all the data every day, so how to select the data effectively is of great importance. We adopt the key parameter k of the model to represent the human selection ratio.

The normal clustering center point $c^{(n)}$ and anomaly clustering center point $c^{(a)}$ are obtained. And the rank of each web log is calculated based on the vector distance between the single feature vector from its related center point.

Assume that the ith data is marked as normal whose features vector is $v_i^{(n)}$, its rank $r_i^{(n)}$ is calculated:

$$r_i^{(n)} = \|v_i^{(n)} - c^{(n)}\|. \tag{2}$$

Assume that the jth data is marked as abnormal whose features vector is $v_j^{(a)}$, its rank $r_j^{(a)}$ is calculated:

$$r_j^{(a)} = \frac{1}{\|v_j^{(a)} - c^{(a)}\|}. \tag{3}$$

We pick up part of the data from raw data that is marked as normal and abnormal. The choice principle is based on rank values but for different reasons. Assume that the input data size is z, there are n entries marked as normal, with a entries marked as abnormal, our filter ratio is $k(0 < k < 1)$.

For the data marked as abnormal, the model needs to select the top $a \cdot k$ items that have the shortest distance from the abnormal center point. The closer to the center, the greater the threat it may be. Security experts should analysis it carefully. For the data marked as normal, the system needs to select the top $a \cdot k$ items which have the longest distance from the abnormal center point. This part of the data has the greatest probability of mis-detection and some new types of attacks may be missed. The selected data will be analyzed by the security personnel, marked with the corresponding label and added to historical label data set, which is used to train a supervised learning model.

5.2 Supervised Learning Process

In this collaborative detection model, the final detection results of the input raw data are given by this step. In addition to that, a second collaborative detection will be conducted after a supervised learning analysis. Using random forest algorithm, the system can reclassify the raw data and get the final results. The analysts will also conduct a review of supervised learning's result.

Assume that the input data size is z, there are n entries marked as normal, with a entries marked as abnormal, our filter ratio is $k(0 < k < 1)$. This time we randomly selected $a \cdot k$ items from each kind of result (total $2 \cdot a \cdot k$ items) and submit them to the experts to analysis again. According to such a random method, the model can rule out the effects of some accidental factors.

An Accurate Description of k. The humans workload W means how many web logs human need to analyse every day. It is determined by k and the quantity of abnormal results: $N_{a(u)} and N_{a(s)}$ that come from unsupervised learning module and the supervised learning module. Though k is a fixed value, the system can still dynamically determine the actual workload based on the traffic size and threatening situation.

$$W = 2 \cdot N_{a(u)} \cdot k + 2 \cdot N_{a(s)} \cdot k. \tag{4}$$

6   Experiment

6.1   Experiment Settings

We test total 810,000 normal and 90,000 abnormal web logs. It will be divided into 30 groups, each group has 3,000 items of abnormal data and 27,000 items of normal data, its ratio is 1:9. Each set of data is considered daily web traffic. Our experiment is divided into two parts:

Model Verification. To start with, we only use k-means algorithm to detect the daily data. Then we use CDM to analyze the same data set to verify the feasibility and effectiveness of the model. It is worth noting that the attributes of this set of data (abnormal or normal) are known. The real label of the data is used to simulate the process of experts' detection and to test the validity of the experimental results.

Example of tth day:

1. Preprocess the raw data. Get the features matrix F_t
2. Use the unsupervised model U_t and matrix F_t to mark the input data Get the normal data and abnormal data table with rank score: N_t, A_t. Based on the ratio k, a set of data P_t are selected from N_t and A_t
3. Use the supervised model S_t and matrix F_t to mark the input data. Get the labeled data R_t. Based on the ratio k, a set of data Q_t are selected from R_t
4. Get the union of P_t and Q_t: D_t. The security personnel analysis the data set D_t. Generates a set of data with labels L_t
5. Add L_t to the historical database Z_{t-1}. to get the new database Z_t. Based on the data set Z_t, the new supervised learning model S_{t+1} is trained
6. The final results are R_t

Suitable Selection of k. After verifying the CDM model, we repeatedly modify the k to find a reasonable value, expecting to get a reasonable k value, while ensuring the accuracy of the model and maintaining a reasonable manual cooperation workload.

6.2   Results Related to Model Verification

We combine the results of pure unsupervised learning algorithm (UL) and CDM with the form shown in Fig. 2.

For UL: it is not difficult to notice that TPr has always fluctuated between 55% and 70%. The FPr amplitude is greater with big variance value.

Here are such a few points from the results of CDM ($k = 0.1$):

- TPr is maintained at more than 86.5% level, indicating that the model owns excellent exception detection capabilities.
- FPr is maintained at a very low level, up to a maximum of 0.07 except the 2nd day, which indicates the reliability of this model.

– TPr has a spiral upward trend with the development of time. Ultimately, it is maintained at 93% level. While the FPr spiral drops and eventually remains at an ideal level.

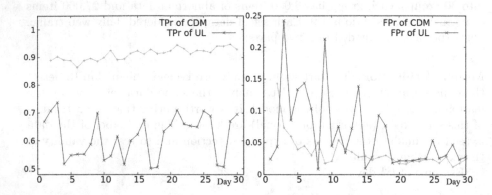

Fig. 2. Comparison of two methods' trends

6.3   Results Related to Selection of k

After setting different k values $(0.06, 0.08, 0.09, 0.10, 0.11, 0.12, 0.14, 0.16)$ for the model, we calculated the mathematical mean of the corresponding values of TPr, FPr, and human collaborative detection workload, as shown in Table 4 and Fig. 3. There are several intuitive results and our observation:

– When k ranges from 0.06 to 0.08, TPr and FPr have several significant changes. This is related to the working principle of the model and the random forest algorithm. Due to the small value of k, the lack of sufficient training samples to separate the two types of data.
– When k is greater than 0.09, TPr is on the rise, but there is still fluctuation. The 2nd round of human participation introduced in Sect. 5 lead to it. In this step, the data is randomly selected. Even if the same k value, each time there will be subtle differences.
– The change of FPr is not obvious while $k > 0.09$.
– The workload increases as k increases. This conforms to our algorithmic design.

We consider that k value around 0.12, able to meet the needs of this model performance. The human collaborative workload data accounts for only 3.3% of the overall test data.

Table 4. Experimental results of different k values for cooperative detection model. The 'Items' column means the number of the weblogs people need to analyze

Day	TPr	FPr	Items	TPr	FPr	Items	TPr	FPr	Items	TPr	FPr	Items
k	0.06			0.09			0.12			0.16		
1	-	-	244	-	-	368	-	-	490	-	-	654
2	0.696	0.058	552	0.853	0.129	904	0.846	0.102	1188	0.855	0.112	1578
3	0.824	0.038	1326	0.897	0.086	2001	0.915	0.099	2678	0.892	0.097	3537
6	0.834	0.026	959	0.862	0.048	1434	0.876	0.047	1907	0.893	0.068	2544
9	0.842	0.010	1222	0.886	0.018	1852	0.898	0.020	2451	0.904	0.019	3230
12	0.847	0.020	542	0.893	0.043	837	0.902	0.041	1119	0.901	0.039	1476
15	0.894	0.016	482	0.934	0.029	746	0.928	0.039	985	0.925	0.032	1291
18	0.884	0.013	739	0.913	0.031	1107	0.922	0.038	1456	0.917	0.023	1928
21	0.920	0.008	556	0.944	0.014	840	0.956	0.014	1117	0.949	0.013	1477
24	0.886	0.010	536	0.928	0.026	818	0.927	0.019	1079	0.927	0.016	1419
27	0.910	0.015	597	0.938	0.025	905	0.943	0.024	1192	0.945	0.023	1567
30	0.903	0.014	573	0.930	0.023	875	0.935	0.023	1156	0.934	0.022	1529
Avg	0.867	0.016	687	0.912	0.034	1047	0.917	0.035	1390	0.918	0.034	1838

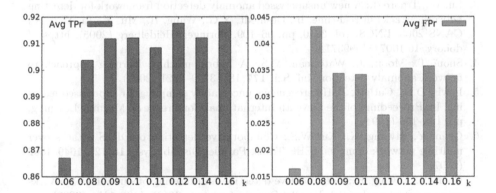

Fig. 3. The average TPr, FPr and workload of different k values

7   Conclusion

Our supporting feature extraction method is useful. Whether in the unsupervised learning model or in the collaborative detection model, this feature extraction method can extract the information in the raw data and detect some of the anomalies within the allowable range of FPr. This collaborative detection model can greatly improve the accuracy of detecting abnormal data with limited human workload. And with the accumulation of data, performance continues to increase and reach a stable state. In this model, there is an appropriate k value around 0.12 while ensuring the accuracy of the model and maintain a reasonable collaborative workload.

Both to optimize the machine learning algorithm and to propose deeper feature extraction methods are good ideas to improve this detection model. These are part of our future work.

Acknowledgement. The authors gratefully acknowledge the anonymous reviewers for their helpful suggestions. This work is supported by supported by China 863 program (No. 2015AA01A202) and project of Telecommunication Company of State Grid Zhejiang Electric Power Company (5211XT16000A).

References

1. Veeramachaneni, K., Arnaldo, I., Korrapati, V., Bassias, C., Li, K.: AI^2: training a big data machine to defend. In: 2016 IEEE 2nd International Conference on Big Data Security on Cloud (BigDataSecurity), IEEE International Conference on High Performance and Smart Computing (HPSC), and IEEE International Conference on Intelligent Data and Security (IDS), pp. 49–54. IEEE (2016)
2. Kruegel, C., Vigna, G.: Anomaly detection of web-based attacks. In: Proceedings of the 10th ACM Conference on Computer and Communications Security, pp. 251–261. ACM (2003)
3. Lu, W., Traore, I.: A new unsupervised anomaly detection framework for detecting network attacks in real-time. In: Desmedt, Y.G., Wang, H., Mu, Y., Li, Y. (eds.) CANS 2005. LNCS, vol. 3810, pp. 96–109. Springer, Heidelberg (2005). https://doi.org/10.1007/11599371_9
4. Shon, T., Moon, J., Waterman, M.S.: A hybrid machine learning approach to network anomaly detection. Inf. Sci. **177**(18), 3799–3821 (2007)
5. Lewis, D.D., Catlett, J.: Heterogeneous uncertainty sampling for supervised learning. In: Proceedings of the Eleventh International Conference on Machine Learning, pp. 148–156 (1994)
6. Chen, Y., Hwang, K., Ku, W.S.: Collaborative detection of DDoS attacks over multiple network domains. IEEE Trans. Parallel Distrib. Syst. **18**(12), 1649–1662 (2007)
7. Chen, Y., Hwang, K.: Collaborative detection and filtering of shrew DDoS attacks using spectral analysis. J. Parallel Distrib. Comput. **66**(9), 1137–1151 (2006)
8. Yao, D., Yin, M., Luo, J., Zhang, S.: Network anomaly detection using random forests and entropy of traffic features. In: 2012 Fourth International Conference on Multimedia Information Networking and Security, pp. 926–929. IEEE (2012)
9. Zhang, J., Chen, C., Xiang, Y., Zhou, W.: Robust network traffic identification with unknown applications. In: Proceedings of the 8th ACM SIGSAC symposium on Information, Computer and Communications Security, pp. 405–414. ACM (2012)
10. Nadiammai, G., Hemalatha, M.: Effective approach toward intrusion detection system using data mining techniques. Egypt. Inform. Journal. **15**(1), 37–57 (2014)
11. Hodge, V., Austin, J.: A survey of outlier detection methodologies. Artif. Intell. Rev. **22**(2), 85–126 (2004)
12. Bhuyan, M.H., Bhattacharyya, D.K., Kalita, J.K.: Network anomaly detection: methods, systems and tools. IEEE Commun. Surv. Tutorials **16**(1), 303–336 (2014)

13. Ektefa, M., Memar, S., Sidi, F., Affendey, L.S.: Intrusion detection using data mining techniques. In: 2010 International Conference on Information Retrieval and Knowledge Management (CAMP), pp. 200–203. IEEE (2010)
14. Threepak, T., Watcharapupong, A., Assent, I. Web attack detection using entropy-based analysis. In: The International Conference on Information Networking 2014 (ICOIN 2014), pp. 244–247. IEEE (2014)

A Reinforcement Learning Based Workflow Application Scheduling Approach in Dynamic Cloud Environment

Yi Wei[1(✉)], Daniel Kudenko[2,3], Shijun Liu[1], Li Pan[1], Lei Wu[1], and Xiangxu Meng[1]

[1] School of Computer Science and Technology,
Shandong University, Jinan, China
weiyi9008@hotmail.com,
{lsj,panli,i_lily,mxx}@sdu.edu.cn
[2] Department of Computer Science, University of York, York, UK
daniel.kudenko@york.ac.uk
[3] Saint Petersburg National Research Academic University of the Russian
Academy of Sciences, St Petersburg, Russia

Abstract. Workflow technology is an efficient means for constructing complex applications which involve multiple applications with different functions. In recent years, with the rapid development of cloud computing, deploying such workflow applications in cloud environment is becoming increasingly popular in many fields, such as scientific computing, big data analysis, collaborative design and manufacturing. In this context, how to schedule cloud-based workflow applications using heterogeneous and changing cloud resources is a formidable challenge. In this paper, we regard the service composition problem as a sequential decision making process and solve it by means of reinforcement learning. The experimental results demonstrate that our approach can find near-optimal solutions through continuous learning in the dynamic cloud market.

Keywords: Cloud computing · Infrastructure as a service
Service composition · Markov decision process · Q-learning

1 Introduction

With the rapid development of cloud computing technologies, a large number of cloud-based applications are delivered across the internet. Cloud workflow applications are typical ones which can be used to handle complex and combinatorial tasks in academia and industry. For example, Cloud-based design and manufacturing (CBDM) [1] is a popular collaborative working pattern which utilizes cloud resources to execute applications to achieve cooperation across multiple enterprises. Scheduling workflow applications in clouds means using compositional cloud services to execute tasks contained in workflows. In the cloud market, IaaS providers provides various on-demand computing resources in the form of virtual machines (VMs). SaaS providers can use them to run their applications cost-effectively. However, how to choose appropriate VM instances to execute workflow tasks is not easy. Relationships among

© ICST Institute for Computer Sciences, Social Informatics and Telecommunications Engineering 2018
I. Romdhani et al. (Eds.): CollaborateCom 2017, LNICST 252, pp. 120–131, 2018.
https://doi.org/10.1007/978-3-030-00916-8_12

tasks need to be considered and there are multiple alternative VM instances with various configurations and prices provided by different IaaS providers.

Several works have been proposed to address workflow scheduling problems in the literature [2, 3]. Most studies are based on the assumption that the execution time of each task on different types of VM instances has been known in advance and it will not change. However, this assumption is not reasonable because SaaS providers hardly know the real performance of VMs in a dynamic cloud environment. In addition, some factors such as task parallelization and data transmission are seldom considered. Our main contribution of this paper is taking into account all these features in our model and proposing an effective workflow scheduling approach based on reinforcement learning. Compared with existing methods, our approach can learn the dynamic performance of the cloud market and generate near-optimal workflow application scheduling without any prior knowledge.

The rest of this paper is structured as follows. Section 2 gives an overview of relevant related work. In Sect. 3, we describe the three-tier cloud market model and then present the problem formulation in this context. Section 4 introduces the basic theories of reinforcement learning and details our approach. Experimental results and conclusion are given in Sects. 5 and 6 respectively.

2 Related Work

In recent years, the research on scheduling cloud based workflow applications has been studied intensively [2, 3]. Generally, monetary cost and makespan are two optimization objectives in this field. In our work, we focus on minimizing the workflow cost to help SaaS providers get more profits. There have been some existing approaches [4, 5] regarding this topic, but their considerations of workflow constraints and operating environment are inadequate. Most of them only consider some basic constraints (e.g. budget and deadline) and ignore the uncertain and dynamic characteristics of cloud markets.

In contrast, selecting services for workflow scheduling in the unknown and changing cloud environment can be viewed as Markov Decision Processes (MDPs), which can be solved by reinforcement learning approaches naturally. Some researches [6, 7] have applied Q-learning algorithm to achieve service composition. However, their problem models are very general and of course does not take into account the features of workflow applications. Similar to our objective, [8, 9] try to help SaaS providers to optimize resource allocation to their applications. But their application model is not a workflow thus it is different from our workload-based model.

3 Problem Statement

3.1 System Model

As shown in Fig. 1, there are three parties in the three-tier cloud marketplace: application users, SaaS providers and IaaS providers. Application users can get access to applications provided by SaaS providers. SaaS providers rent cloud resources from IaaS providers to run their applications and serve their customers. We assume that there are some SaaS providers who deliver workflow applications to their customers. That means these SaaS providers need to lease a collection of cloud resources to execute all tasks contained in workflows. In an open public cloud environment, the cloud market is diverse and full of uncertainty. Specifically, there are lots of different types of computing resources in the form of VM instances offered by IaaS providers with varying prices and configurations. Also the performance of VMs is always fluctuant because of the change of time and workloads. Furthermore, from the perspective of SaaS providers, their workflow applications normally have some constraints, such as deadline, task dependencies and hardware configuration. In order to maximize their profits in the long run, SaaS providers need to select the appropriate IaaS service for each task to execute their workflow applications profitably.

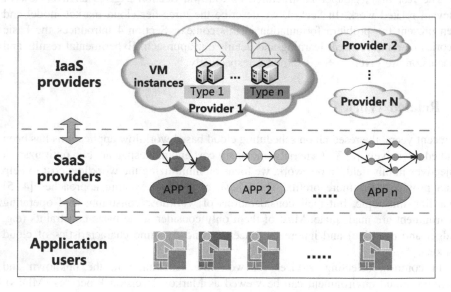

Fig. 1. Three-tire cloud marketplace

3.2   Problem Formulation

Workflow Model. In general, a workflow application is represented as a directed acyclic graph (DAG) $WA = (T, E)$. The finite set $T = \{T_1, \ldots, T_N\}$ denotes N tasks in the workflow. $E = \{E_{i,j} | 1 \leq i, j \leq N, i, j \in N^+\}$ is the set of directed edges which describes the precedence constraints between tasks. An edge $E_{i,j} = (T_i, T_j)$ states that T_j is the child task of T_i and it cannot be executed until all of its parent tasks have been completed. In a given workflow, the task without any parent tasks is called a start task T_{start} and the task without any successors is called an end task T_{end}. We assume that there is only one T_{start} and T_{end} in our model. *Data* is a $N \times N$ matrix where

$Data(T_i, T_j)$ is the amount of data that required to be transmitted from T_i to T_j. Each task is expected to be executed on one or more VM instances.

A Workflow application WA generally has some constraint $Constraint(WA) = \{GC, TC\}$. The former set $GC = \{deadline, budget\}$ defines the maximum makespan and cost of the whole workflow that users would like to accept. The later set $TC = \{TC_1, ..., TC_N\}$ contains N subsets which describe the restrictions of tasks. $TC_i = \{parallelism_i, CPU_i, memory_i\}$ denotes the maximum parallelism degree and the minimum configuration requirements of VM for task T_i.

Cloud Resources Model. The cloud market has M IaaS services $Resources = \{VM_1, ..., VM_M\}$. Each of them defines one type of VM instances $VM_i = \{DataCenter_i, eP_i, inP_i, outP_i, CPU_i, memory_i, bandwidth_i\}$, where $DataCenter_i$ identifies the location of VM_i, eP_i is the hourly execution cost, inP_i and $outP_i$ are the cost of transferring and receiving per unit of data from other VMs, and other attributes denote the VM capacity. Due to the task features and VM configurations, task runtime on different types of VMs is varying. Moreover, for one task, its runtime is not constant even though it is executed on the same VM. This is because the VM performance is also affected by its data center's workloads. There are K workload conditions $W = \{W_1, ..., W_K\}$ and the probability matrix for $DataCenter_i$ is $WP_i = \{P_i^1, ..., P_i^K\}$, where $\sum_{j=1}^{K} P_i^j = 1$. Supposing $VM(T_i)$ and $VMnum(T_i)$ represent the VM type and number that is scheduled to T_i, and $W(VM_j)$ is the current workload condition of $DataCenter_j$.

Task Execution Time and Cost. Let $basicET(T_i, VM_j, W_k)$ denote the execution time of task T_i on one VM_j instance when the data center condition is W_k. As some tasks can be executed concurrently on the same type of VMs, the actual execution time is:

$$ET(T_i, VM(T_i), W(VM(T_i))) = basicET(T_i, VM(T_i), W(VM(T_i)))/VMnum(T_i) \quad (1)$$

Generally, it is assumed that VM instances are charged hourly, thus the task execution cost can be calculated by:

$$\begin{aligned} &EC(T_i, VM(T_i), W(VM(T_i))) \\ &= VM(T_i).eP * [ET(T_i, VM(T_i), W(VM(T_i)))] * VMnum(T_i) \end{aligned} \quad (2)$$

Data Transfer Time and Cost. Let $Bandwidth$ is a $M \times M$ matrix, in which $Bandwidth(VM_i, VM_j)$ is the bandwidth between VM_i and VM_j. For a pair of consecutive tasks, the data transfer time and cost between them are defined by (3) and (4) respectively.

$$TT(T_i, T_j) = \frac{Data(T_i, T_j)}{Bandwidth(VM(T_i), VM(T_j))} \quad (3)$$

$$TC(VM(T_i), VM(T_j)) = Data(T_i, T_j) * (VM(T_i).outPrice + VM(T_j).inPrice) \quad (4)$$

Workflow Application Cost. The whole workflow cost is the total expense for all tasks execution, which contains the tasks' execution cost and data transfer cost. The computational formula for each task's cost is:

$$\text{Task\_cost}_i = EC(T_i, VM(T_i), W(VM(T_i))) + \sum_{j \in children(T_i)} TC(VM(T_i), VM(T_j)) \quad (5)$$

Thus the total cost of workflow application is $WA_{cost} = \sum_{i=1}^{N} \text{Task\_cost}_i$.

Workflow Makespan. Let $ST(T_i)$ and $ET(T_i)$ are the earliest start time and finish time of task T_i. For the start task T_{start}, we have:

$$ST(T_{start}) = 0 \quad (6)$$

$$ET(T_{start}) = ST(T_{start}) + ET(T_{start}, VM(T_{start}), W(VM(T_{start}))) \quad (7)$$

For the other tasks, their ST and ET values can be computed recursively:

$$ST(T_i) = \max_{T_j \in parents(T_i)} \left\{ ET(T_j) + TT(T_j, T_i) \right\} \quad (8)$$

$$ET(T_i) = ST(T_i) + ET(T_i, VM(T_i), W(VM(T_i))) \quad (9)$$

Therefore, the total workflow execution time is $WA_{makespan} = ET(T_{end})$.

Cost-optimal Scheduling Problem. SaaS providers derive their profits from the margin between the revenue obtained from customers and the expense of renting cloud resources from IaaS providers. In order to maximize profits, the best policy is reducing the workflow application cost at the most and guaranteeing the makespan within customers' deadline constraints. Therefore, this problem can be formally defined as follows:

$$\begin{cases} min & WA_{cost} \\ s.t. & WA_{makespan} \leq deadline \\ & VMnum(T_i) \leq TC_i.parallelism_i \\ & VM(T_i).CPU \geq TC_i.CPU_i \\ & VM(T_i).memory \geq TC_i.memory_i \end{cases} \quad (10)$$

4   Workflow Scheduling Approach Using Q-Learning

4.1   Theoretical Foundations

Reinforcement learning (RL) [10] is a widely used method in the field of machine learning. Faced with an unknown environment, an agent without prior knowledge can improve its behavior based on the interactions with its environment. In general, reinforcement learning problems can be modeled as Markov Decision Processes (MDPs)

$\mathcal{M} = \langle \mathcal{S}, \mathcal{A}, \mathcal{P}, \mathcal{R}, \gamma \rangle$. $\mathcal{S}$ is a set of environment states and $\mathcal{A}$ is a set of actions that an agent can take. $\mathcal{P}$ defines the probability of the state transition, where $\mathcal{P}_a(s, s') = \mathbb{P}(s_{t+1} = s' | s_t = s, a_t = a)$ represents the possibility of action a in state s at time t will move to a new state s' at time $t + 1$. $\mathcal{R}$ is a reward function which yields a reward for each state transition. $\gamma \in [0, 1]$ is a discount factor which is used to balance the influence of present reward and future rewards. The goal of RL agents is to find the optimal behavior for each state to maximize the accumulated discounted rewards in the long-term.

Q-learning [11] as a model-free reinforcement learning algorithm which can be used to find optimal policies by learning from previous decision-making experiences. It uses Q function to approximate the long-term benefit of each state-action pair <s, a> by updating Q values during learning processes. The update rule is defined in (11), where $\alpha \in [0, 1]$ is the learning rate and $\gamma \in [0, 1]$ is the discount factor. It will be updated based on the next state s' and obtained reward $R(s, a, s')$.

$$Q(s, a) = Q(s, a) + \alpha[R(s, a, s') + \gamma max_{a'} Q(s', a') - Q(s, a)] \qquad (11)$$

4.2 Level-Based Workflow Scheduling Approach

In general, the workflow scheduling problem is a multidimensional, multi-choice, multi-constraint optimization problem (MMMO), which is NP-hard to solve. On this basis, in the dynamic cloud market, performance of IaaS services is always filled with uncertainty. For SaaS providers, it is hard to predict the task execution time on different VMs at a certain time in advance. Therefore, traditional heuristic approaches such as genetic algorithms do not perform well. By contrast, we can model the IaaS service composition problem as a MDP and solved it by Q-learning algorithm. Our level based scheduling approach involves two phases: initialization phase and decision-making phase. We will describe them respectively.

4.2.1 Initialization Phase

In this phase, workflow application tasks will be classified into different execution levels. Execution level EL represents the task scheduling sequence in this workflow. All tasks belonging to the same level will be scheduled at the same time during the decision-making phase. As we mentioned before, for any task T_i, only when all its parent tasks have been finished, it can be executed. According to this principle, the execution level allocation algorithm is shown below:

Algorithm 1:　Execution level allocation algorithm

```
1.    T_start.EL ← 1
2.    add T_start to FinishTasks
3.    T_current ← T_start
4.    while T_current ! = T_end
5.        for ∀ T_i ∈ children(T_current)
6.            if T_j ∈ FinishTasks, where ∀ T_j ∈ parent(T_i) then
7.                T_i.EL ← T_current.EL + 1
8.                add T_i to ExecuteTasks
9.            end if
10.        end for
11.        add ExecuteTasks to FinishTasks
12.        T_current ← FinishTasks(T_current).next
13.    end while
```

4.2.2　Decision-Making Phase

During this phase, task scheduling plans will be decided and executed according to the sequence of *EL*. When the whole workflow application has been scheduled, it means one decision-making process has been completed. Such a learning process will be repeated many times until the near-optimal scheduling plan has been found. In this part, we will first describe the key elements of this Q-learning problem and then present the algorithm in decision-making phase.

A. State Space and Actions

The state space S contains all possible states that SaaS providers can experience. We define each state as a 3-tuple: $s = (EL, datacenter, time)$, where:

- *EL* is the current execution level that will be scheduled;
- *datacenter* is a set which records the VM locations for all tasks in the last *EL* level;
- *time* is the total execution time of the uncompleted workflow until now.

Given a state $s \in S$, the corresponding action set $A(s)$ includes all available actions that can be taken. Supposing there are C tasks in current *EL* level, each action at state s is expressed as a collection shown in (12), where $VMid_c$ and $VMnum_c$ are the VM type and number allocated to task T_c.

$$a = \{(VMid_1, VMnum_1), \ldots, (VMid_C, VMnum_C)\} \tag{12}$$

B. Reward Function

Because the goal of application scheduling algorithm is to find the cost-optimal choices for the whole workflow, the reward function. $R(s, a, s')$ at state s is given by the following equations:

$$\begin{cases} R_{success} - \sum_{T_i.EL=S.EL} \text{Task\_cost}_i, \text{ if } s.EL = EL_{final} \text{ and } s'.time \leq deadline \\ R_{fail} - \sum_{T_i.EL=S.EL} \text{Task\_cost}_i, \text{ if } s.EL = EL_{final} \text{ and } s'.time > deadline \\ - \sum_{T_i.EL=s.EL} \text{Task\_cost}_i, else \end{cases} \quad (13)$$

C. Action Selection and State Transition

At a decision time T_i, we adopt the ε-Greedy policy to choose an action for current state s. It means that the optimal action based on current knowledge will be chosen with a high probability $(1 - ε)$, while a random action instead of the best one be taken with a low probability ε, where $ε \in [0, 1]$. Once SaaS performs a specific action a, its state will change from s to s'. The corresponding transitions can be described as follows:

$$\begin{cases} s'.EL = s.EL + 1 \\ s'.datacenter = \{a.VMid_c.DataCenter | c = 1, \ldots, C\} \\ s'.time = s.time + \max_{T_i.EL=s.EL} ET(T_i) \end{cases} \quad (14)$$

where $s'.EL$, $s'.datacenter$ and $s'.time$ are elements of new state s'. Meanwhile, the Q value of state-action pair $<s, a>$ will be updated based on (11).

D. Q-learning based IaaS service composition algorithm

Algorithm 2: Q-learning based IaaS service composition algorithm

---
```
1.  Loop (for each scheduling decision-making process)
2.     Choose action a from A(s) using ε-Greedy policy
3.     Rent appointed VMs to execute tasks according to
       action a
4.     Move to the new state s' according to (14)
5.     if s' is a new state then
6.        add s' into state set S
7.        For ∀a' ∈ A(s'), initialize Q-values Q(s',a')
8.     end if
9.     calculate reward r ← R(s,a,s') using (13)
10.    update Q(s,a) using (11)
11.    s ← s'
12. end Loop
```
---

5 Experiment Results and Analysis

In this section, we evaluate our level based workflow scheduling approach through a series of experiments. We first describe the basic experiment settings and then present the relevant results and analysis.

5.1 Experimental Setup

Attributes of Cloud Resources. We simulate a dynamic cloud environment which involves two IaaS providers. Each of them has one data center and offers three kinds of VM types with different configurations and prices. Data transfer speeds and costs between different data centers are varying. In terms of the performance of data centers, we define two kinds of workload conditions: normal condition (NC) and busy condition (BC). For a task, its execution time under the busy condition is 1.5 times of that under the normal condition on the same VM instance. The probability of each condition in different data centers is different. Let $p = (p_1, p_2)$ denote the probability of BC in two data centers. We test 5 cases $\{(0, 0), (0.2, 0.4), (0.3, 0.7), (0.7, 0.9), (1, 1)\}$ in our experiments, which implies the data centers' conditions are both normal, both a little busy, one a little busy and one busy, both busy, both very busy respectively.

Workflow Application Settings. In our experiment, we test 8 cases with different number of tasks in the workflow. The number of tasks is varied from 3 to 10. Each task excepting T_{end} has at least one child task. The average number of child tasks for tasks is set to 2. Task execution time on different VMs and the amount of transmitted data are randomly generated in [10 min, 100 min] and [5 GB, 20 GB] respectively. The deadline and budget constraints are set dynamically based on the value bounds of workflow makespan and monetary cost.

Q-Learning Parameters. We set the the values of learning rate α and discount factor γ to 0.6 and 0.8 respectively. The initial value of parameter ε is 0.2. We decrease its value gradually so as to reduce explorations and obtain the best renting decisions with a high probability. As for the reward function, we set $R_{success} = 1$ and $R_{fail} = -5$.

Baseline Algorithms. We compare our algorithm (QA) with alternative five service selection strategies: optimal strategy (OS), random strategy (RS), conservative strategy (CS), adventurous strategy (AS) and guess strategy (GS). OS strategy is an ideal baseline, which assumes that all information about the cloud market (e.g. task execution time and data center conditions at a given time) is known in advance. RS is a simple strategy in which a random workflow scheduling plan is chosen. Both CS and AS give constant workflow scheduling plans each time. The difference is that they are based on different data center conditions. Specifically, CS gives the plan that is the optimal one under data centers' busy condition (i.e. $p = (1,1)$), while AS gives the plan that is the optimal one under data centers' normal condition (i.e. $p = (0,0)$). GS strategy assumes that SaaS providers guess the market condition is $p = (0.3, 0.7)$.

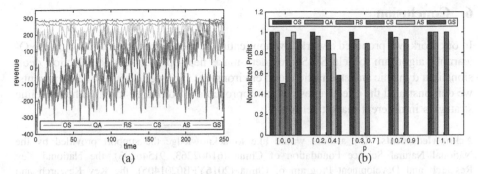

(a)

(b)

Fig. 2. (a) Performance comparison of six strategies. The profit of each time slot equals the sum profits of 20 consecutive service composition decision-making rounds. (b) Profits comparison under different data center conditions. If the real normalized value is less than 0, we set it to 0 in this figure.

5.2   Experiments and Results

In our experiments, there are 5 cases with respect to data center conditions and 8 cases regarding the number of tasks. We test our workflow scheduling approach and other 5 baselines under these scenarios. For each scenario, we do experiments 10 times with different stochastic workflows. Because reducing workflow application cost to maximize profits is the ultimate goal of SaaS providers, we focus on the service composition profits obtained by applying different scheduling strategies in each round. Figure 2a shows the comparison results of 6 strategies for one experiment. In this scenario, the number of workflow tasks is 6 and the data center's condition is $p = (0.2, 0.4)$. It is clear that the workflow scheduling plans generated by QA gain low profits at the early stage of decision-making rounds. However, the profit curve grows gradually and then reaches a high and relatively stable level which is close to the maximum profit curve produced by OS strategy. By contrast, workflow scheduling plans generated by RS strategy and GS strategy always get low profits during the whole period. Furthermore, we also compare QA with other 5 strategies when its final near-optional scheduling plans have been obtained. We calculate the total profits in last 100 rounds of our QA and other baselines respectively. And then we normalize results based on the profit obtained by OS. Figure 2b gives the profit comparisons under different conditions of data centers. It can be seen that no matter what the condition is, QA is able to generate high profits which are close to the maximum profits. In terms of the experiments in other scenarios, we can get similar results as shown in Fig. 2. Due to the space limitation, they are not included in this paper.

6 Conclusion

In our work, we proposed a workflow application scheduling approach based on the Q-learning algorithm to help SaaS providers make near-optimal service selection decisions in a dynamic and stochastic cloud environment. Through a series of experiments, we demonstrated the effectiveness of our approach and compared it with other baseline strategies in different market settings.

Acknowledgments. The authors would like to acknowledge the support provided by the National Natural Science Foundation of China (61402263, 91546203), the National Key Research and Development Program of China (2016YFB0201405), the Key Research and Development Program of Shandong Province of China (2017CXGC0605), the Shandong Provincial Science and Technology Development Program (2016GGX106001, 2016GGX101008, 2016ZDJS01A09), the Natural Science Foundation of Shandong Province (ZR2014FQ031), the Fundamental Research Funds of Shandong University (2016JC011), the special funds of Taishan scholar construction project, and China Scholarship Council (201606220190).

References

1. Wu, D., Rosen, D.W., Wang, L., Schaefer, D.: Cloud-based design and manufacturing: a new paradigm in digital manufacturing and design innovation. Comput. Aided Des. **59**, 1–14 (2015)
2. Smanchat, S., Viriyapant, K.: Taxonomies of workflow scheduling problem and techniques in the cloud. Future Gener. Comput. Syst. **52**, 1–12 (2015)
3. Masdari, M., ValiKardan, S., Shahi, Z., Azar, S.I.: Towards workflow scheduling in cloud computing: a comprehensive analysis. J. Netw. Comput. Appl. **66**, 64–82 (2016)
4. Fakhfakh, F., Kacem, H.H., Kacem, A.H.: A provisioning approach of cloud resources for dynamic workflows. In: 8th IEEE International Conference on Cloud Computing, pp. 469–476. IEEE (2015)
5. Wei, Y., Pan, L., Yuan, D., Liu, S., Wu, L., Meng, X.: A cost-optimal service selection approach for collaborative workflow execution in clouds. In: 20th IEEE International Conference on Computer Supported Cooperative Work in Design, pp. 351–356 (2016)
6. Wang, H., Zhou, X., Zhou, X., Liu, W., Li, W., Bouguettaya, A.: Adaptive service composition based on reinforcement learning. In: Maglio, P.P., Weske, M., Yang, J., Fantinato, M. (eds.) ICSOC 2010. LNCS, vol. 6470, pp. 92–107. Springer, Heidelberg (2010). https://doi.org/10.1007/978-3-642-17358-5_7
7. Jungmann, A., Kleinjohann, B.: Learning recommendation system for automated service composition. In: 2013 IEEE International Conference on Services Computing, pp. 97–104 (2013)
8. Yan, Y., Zhang, B., Guo, J.: An adaptive decision making approach based on reinforcement learning for self-managed cloud applications. In: 2016 IEEE International Conference on Web Services, pp. 720–723 (2016)

9. Barrett, E., Howley, E., Duggan, J.: Applying reinforcement learning towards automating resource allocation and application scalability in the cloud. Concur. Comput. Pract. Exp. **25**(12), 1656–1674 (2013)

10. Kaelbling, L.P., Littman, M.L., Moore, A.W.: Reinforcement learning: a survey. J. Artif. Intell. Res. **4**, 237–285 (1996)

11. Watkins, C.J., Dayan, P.: Q-learning. Mach. Learn. **8**(3–4), 279–292 (1992)

p-Faster R-CNN Algorithm for Food Detection

Yanchen Wan[1(✉)], Yu Liu[1], Yuan Li[2], and Puhong Zhang[2]

[1] State Key Laboratory of Software Development Environment,
Beihang University, Beijing, China
wyc491946376@163.com, buaa_liuyu@buaa.edu.cn
[2] The George Institute for Global Health at Peking University
Health Science Center, Beijing 100191, China

Abstract. Eating healthily helps prevent disease, and it can be achieved by identifying the kinds and ingredients of the food to determine whether the diet is healthy. In this paper, we innovatively propose p-Faster R-CNN algorithm for healthy diet detection, which is based on Faster R-CNN with Zeiler and Fergus model (ZF-net) and Caffe framework. Before the input layer, the Gauss Pyramid is applied to form a multi-resolution pyramid of images, which expands the number and the scale of the samples. In the training stage, the multi-scale Spatial Pyramid Pooling Layer is added after the convolution layer to extract multi-scale features. To evaluate the performance of p-Faster R-CNN, we compare it with Fast R-CNN and Faster R-CNN. The experiment results demonstrated that p-Faster R-CNN increases the AP value of each kind of food by more than 2% compared with Faster R-CNN, and p-Faster R-CNN, Faster R-CNN are superior to Fast R-CNN in accuracy and speed. At last, the total dataset we established is used to construct the application of judging the healthy diet by uploading intake photos.

Keywords: Food health · Object detection · Faster R-CNN · Pyramid Convolutional neural network

1 Introduction

Healthy diet plays a key role in the prevention of chronic diseases, such as hypertension, blood fat, obesity, etc. High intake of Na is a contributing factor to hypertension, fat intake has a direct effect on blood fat, and calorie intake is directly associated with obesity. So with rapid identification of the kind of food, food calories, fat and Na degree on the basis of food ingredients, we can determine whether food is healthy. Using this idea, "intelligent diet" smartphone application can be constructed for the realization of innovative service model of Internet plus health management.

As the mainstream of artificial intelligence, machine learning has concerned "diet" in the field of agricultural production. Steven Melendez introduces a Climate Corporation dedicated to establish an agricultural digital analysis center [1]. By interpreting soil data, it guides growers to use seeds, water, pesticides, fertilizers more precisely. At the same time, machine learning also takes interest in "health" in the aspects of

© ICST Institute for Computer Sciences, Social Informatics and Telecommunications Engineering 2018
I. Romdhani et al. (Eds.): CollaborateCom 2017, LNICST 252, pp. 132–142, 2018.
https://doi.org/10.1007/978-3-030-00916-8_13

medical. A variety of diseases can be measured and diagnosed by the related medical data. In 2016, a biosensor company called Sentrian has developed medical diagnosis system based on the data [2]. This system owns the information of patients, and makes early diagnosis by observing subtle associations. However, the above applications only regard diet or health alone. There is no relevant machine learning combing diet with health.

In this paper, we put forward the research target of healthy diet detection based on deep learning. We make the following major contributions through this paper:

1. We use Gaussian Pyramid to get multi-scale pictures.
2. We use multi-scale Spatial Pyramid Pooling Layer to increase feature diversity.
3. Object detection is applied in food and health fields.

This paper is divided into five sections, the third, fourth sections are the point. Section 1 is the research background and objectives. Section 2 presents object detection algorithm. Section 3 is a detailed description of the p-Faster R-CNN. Section 4 shows the experimental results, and Sect. 5 concludes the paper.

2 Related Work

Object detection began to integrate the neural network algorithm in 2012. Until 2014, Ross Girshick published [3] in CVPR2014, which marks the beginning of object detection in the deep learning. To avoid mapping for each proposal, Kaiming He published [4] in ECCV2014, and put forward the "spatial pyramid pooling" concept. Then, Ross Girshick's [5] is a combination of R-CNN and SPP-net. In 2015, Faster R-CNN first proposed "Region Proposal Network (RPN)", which incorporates the proposal extraction into convolution network. In order to realize the real-time detection, J Redmon published [6] in 2016. YOLO integrates proposal prediction and classification into a single neural network model. After that, the SSD algorithm based on YOLO was introduced, and the object detection technology is developing rapidly.

Image processing commonly uses the method of pyramid. There are two types of pyramid: low-pass, bandpass. Low-pass Pyramid is smoothed by a suitable smoothing filter and sampled smooth image. Bandpass Pyramid is formed by interpolation algorithms between adjacent images [7]. Pyramid can produce image features of different resolutions in scale space. Image pyramid is the foundation, and feature pyramid is expansion. Multiscale feature extracted by SIFT show that multi scales can be very useful.

Faster R-CNN has made a perfect detection effect, but the training and testing are in a single scale image without considering the multi-scale feature extraction [8]. To solve this problem, this paper proposes p-Faster R-CNN algorithm for food detection, which implements multi-scale pyramid at the stage of image preprocessing and feature extraction.

3   p-Faster R-CNN

In [3], Ross Girshick uses two different scales of image (180 * 180, 224 * 224) to train the network. In the same network structure, the same fixed length feature is extracted in the SPP layer and tested in the ImageNet 2012 dataset, and the results are as follows:

From Table 1, compared SPP single-size trained with no SPP, the top-5 error is reduced by 0.62%, 0.38%, 0.72%, 0.85%, which shows that the SPP layer can improve the detection accuracy; and compared SPP single-size trained with SPP multi-scale trained, the top-5 error is reduced by 0.50%, 0.44%, 0.61%, 0.68%, which indicates that multi-scale images can improve the result of object detection.

Table 1. No SPP, single scale SPP, multi-scale SPP error contrast table

Model	SPP Type					
	No SPP		SPP single-size trained		SPP multi-size trained	
	Top-1 (error %)	Top-5	Top-1	Top-5	Top-1	Top-5
ZF-5	35.99	14.76	34.98	14.14	34.60	13.64
Convnet-5	34.93	13.92	34.38	13.54	33.94	13.33
Overfeat-5	34.13	13.52	32.87	12.80	32.26	12.33
Overfeat-7	32.01	11.97	30.36	11.12	29.68	10.95

In Faster R-CNN algorithm proposed by [8], the input image scale is single, and according to the real-time demand, SPP layer only using a scale feature extraction. So inspired by [4], we improved Faster R-CNN in consideration of the multi-scale characteristics and images, and proposed a p-Faster R-CNN algorithm. The improvement is mainly manifested in two aspects: Gauss Pyramid Layer for the input images; Multi-scale SPP Layer for feature extraction.

3.1   Gaussian Pyramid Layer

Training the network with different sizes of images can increase the scale invariance and reduce overfitting. The pyramid algorithm in computer vision can generate different scales images to achieve this goal. Here, we adapt the widely-used Gaussian Pyramid.

Gaussian Pyramid is a multiscale description of a graph. It usually consists of 2 steps: smoothing through a low-pass filter; sampling or interpolating a smoothing image to obtain a series of reduced or enlarged images [9].

For each input image in the network, we use 5 * 5 convolution filter and interlaced drop sampling.

$$G_k(x, y) = \sum_{i=-2}^{2} \sum_{j=-2}^{2} w(i,j) G_{k-1}(2x+i, 2y+j) \tag{1}$$

$$w(i,j) = \hat{w}(i) \times \hat{w}(j) \tag{2}$$

Here $G_k(x,y)$ is the layer k of image pyramid, $w(i,j)$ is convolution filter, $\hat{w}(i)$ is Gauss density distribution function. After Gaussian pyramid G_0 forms a N layer image pyramid $G_1, G_2, ..., G_n$. Each input picture is processed into 5 scales images in p-Faster R-CNN.

3.2 The Spatial Pyramid Pooling Layer

The Spatial Pyramid Pooling Layer can not only accept input images of any size, but also generate fixed-length feature representation.

Feature Mapping
In object detection, the SPP layer can map the features only once compared to the R-CNN without extracting features for each proposal. We use spatial mapping to find the location of the representation in the feature map corresponding to the proposal of the original image. Suppose that (x', y') is the coordinate point on the feature map. (x, y) is the point on the original picture. Then there is the following conversion relationship between them:

$$(x,y) = (S * x', S * y') \tag{3}$$

S is the product of all strides in CNN. In turn, from (x, y) to (x', y'):

$$x' = \lfloor x/S \rfloor + 1 \tag{4}$$

$$y' = \lfloor y/S \rfloor + 1 \tag{5}$$

Multi-scale Feature Extraction
Adding a multi-scale Spatial Pyramid Pooling Layer after the last convolution layer in Faster R-CNN can generate multi-scale representation in the feature map. In [4], the network allows arbitrarily sized images through the SPP layer which normalizes uniformly.

There is no multiscale pooling in Faster R-CNN, and the image can be divided into the length of 16 * 256-d with single scale. In order to improve the accuracy, we learn from the multi-scale pyramid pooling in [4]. At the end of the pooling layer, a multi-scale SPP layer is added to extract the features in four scales, which emphasizes both local and whole image information.

As shown in Fig. 1, regardless of size, the input pictures are divided into 16 blocks, 9 blocks, 4 blocks, 1 blocks, a total of $16 + 9 + 4 + 1 = 30$ bin, which means the representation is the fixed 30 * 256-d. Then they are handled by the full connection layer and the classification layer.

In a word, a feature map is obtained by the convolution layer at the front, then features are extracted from the entire image by mapping. At last, we apply the spatial pyramid to each candidate window to gain the fixed length representation.

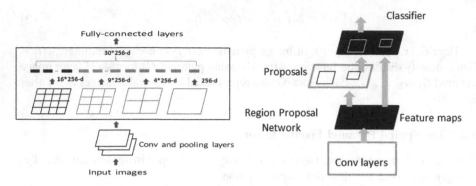

Fig. 1. Schematic diagram of the multi-scale SPP.

Fig. 2. Schematic diagram of Faster R-CNN.

3.3   p-Faster R-CNN

p-Faster R-CNN is an improved Faster R-CNN with pyramid algorithm.

Faster R-CNN
Faster R-CNN has two networks, RPN (Region Proposal Networks) and Fast R-CNN (detection network). As shown in Fig. 2, the RPN network accepts an input picture and outputs a series of proposals with the object's score. In order to generate accurate proposals, we slide a n * n window on the feature map to get a low dimensional feature vector. Then the feature vectors are fed into the classification network (Fast R-CNN).

Zeiler and Fergus Model (ZF-net)
The p-Faster R-CNN uses ZF-net [10] which has 5 conv layers and 3 fc layers. It takes 224 * 224 images (3 channels color planes) as input, and is convolved with 96 different filters whose size is 7 * 7 with a stride of 2. The feature maps are then passed through a linear function, pooled (3 × 3 regions, stride 2) and contrast normalized across feature maps. Similar operations are repeated in layer 2, 3, 4, 5. The last two layers are fully connected, and the final layer is a k-way softmax function [8].

p-Faster R-CNN
The p-Faster R-CNN adds the Gauss Pyramid Layer before the input of Faster R-CNN, and the multi-scale SPP layer before the full connection layer. As shown in Fig. 3, each input picture is sampled into 5 scales by the Gauss Pyramid Layer. The representation are extracted by dividing input pictures into 16 blocks, 9 blocks, 4 blocks, 1 blocks to form the fixed 30 * 256-d in the multi-scale SPP layer. The loss function, the training process, and the parameters are same with the Faster R-CNN.

This network is optimized using the loss function of multiple tasks (regression function and classification function):

$$L(\{p_i\}, \{t_i\}) = \frac{1}{N_{cls}} \sum_i L_{cls}(p_i, p_i^*) + \lambda \frac{1}{N_{reg}} \sum_i p_i^* L_{reg}(t_i, t_i^*) \qquad (6)$$

p-Faster R-CNN

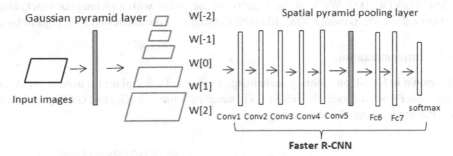

Fig. 3. The architecture of p-Faster R-CNN.

i is the index of anchor in the mini-batch, p_i is the predicted probability of anchor i being an object. p_i^* is the ground-truth label. t_i^* is a 4 dimensional vector representing the coordinate of the proposal. t_i^* is the coordinate of positive anchor. The classification loss L_{cls} is log loss over two classes (object vs. not object). The regression loss L_{reg} can be represented as:

$$L_{reg}(t_i, t_i^*) = R(t_i - t_i^*) \qquad (7)$$

R is the robust loss function. The term $p_i^* L_{reg}$ means L_{reg} is activated when $p_i^* = 1$ and disabled otherwise ($p_i^* = 0$). The above two terms are normalized with N_{cls} and N_{reg}, and λ is a balancing weight.

4 Experiment

4.1 Software and Hardware

Deep learning framework of this project is Caffe with python interface. We need to configure Caffe and pycaffe. Due to the long training time, we equip GPU and CUDA computing architecture assisted GPU complex calculation. The graphics card is GeForce GTX TITAN X, and the corresponding driver is nvidia-375.39.

4.2 Datasets

The database includes 400 kinds of single food which refers to the original ecological food, not mixed with other foods, such as fruits, vegetables, steamed bread, etc. The food is divided into western food and Chinese food.

For western food, we download the Food-101 from the Computer Vision Lab (CVL). It includes 101 kinds of western food, and each kind has 1000 pictures sized 40–100k. For Chinese food, 300 kinds are listed according to the national standards of food classification system first of all. Then they are collected from Baidu and Google by crawler. And each class contains about 500 pictures.

For object detection, the input image must be tagged imitating the data format of PASCAL VOC2007. We mark the location of the object with a rectangular block, and generate the corresponding XML file with the frame's coordinates and the object class.

4.3   Implementation

As shown in Fig. 4, an arbitrary scale image (3 channel color plane) is used as input. In Gaussian Pyramid Layer, the image G_0 is sampled 4 times as G_1, G_2, G_3, G_4, and they are the input of the ZF-net.

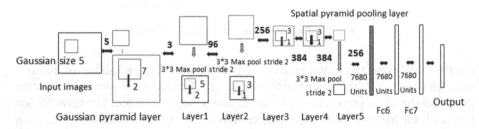

Fig. 4. Details of the network architecture of p-Faster R-CNN.

Then through 5 layers of convolution and pooling: the first layer has 96 different convolution filters whose kernel size is 7 * 7 with stride 2 and pooling window is 3 * 3 with stride 2; the second layer owns 256 different 5 * 5 filters and 3 * 3 pooling window with both stride 2; the third layer consists of 384 different 3 * 3 filters with stride 1, not pooling; The fourth layer is the same as the third one. There are 256 different 1 * 1 filters with stride 1 and 3 * 3 pooling window with stride 2 in the fifth layer. Then the multi-scale Spatial Pyramid Pooling Layer is connected.

In the SPP layer, 4 layers of spatial pyramid (1×1, 2×2, 3×3, 4×4, a total of 30 bins) are used to extract features. Each window generates the representations of 7680 (30×256) in length. These features are sent to the full connection layer.

There are 50% of the positive samples, 50% of the negative samples. We use a learning rate of 0.001 for 60k mini-batches, and 0.0001 for the next 20k mini-batches. The threshold of NMS is set to 0.7.

4.4   Experimental Result

We select the food pictures that are not trained to test and get good visualization results (Fig. 5). We test the some of the food dataset, calculate the accuracy of detection. The AP of each type remains above 0.7, as shown above (Table 2).

Fig. 5. Visualization results of p-Faster R-CNN

Table 2. The AP of part of food using p-Faster R-CNN.

Category	AP
apple-pie	0.7401
almond	0.8689
bread	0.7454
cheesecake	0.8077
chicken_wings	0.8884
hamburger	0.8944
hot_dog	0.9021
ice-creams	0.8699
macadamia	0.8748
peanut	0.7471
pine_nut	0.8741
raisin	0.8964
soup	0.9976
spaghetti_carbonara	0.9454
sesame	0.8403

4.5   Experimental Contrast

Experimental Dataset
We select 20 kinds of food in food-101 and mark them as VOC2007 data format for experimental comparisons. They are apple-pie, bread, cheesecake, baby bac ribs, baklava, beef carpaccio, beef tartare, chicken wings, club sandwich, donuts, egg, french fries, hamburger, hot dog, ice-cream, onion ring, pizza, steak, soup, spaghetti.

Contrast Between p-Faster R-CNN and Fast R-CNN
We use VOC 2007 and VOC 2012 dataset for Fast R-CNN and p-Faster R-CNN, and obtain their mAP and running speed. As Region Proposal Network (RPN) shares full-image convolutional features with the detection network in p-Faster R-CNN, thus enabling nearly cost-free region proposals [8]. It shows the framework of p-Faster R-CNN algorithm is better. As shown in Table 3, "method" represents algorithm; "prop" represents the algorithm and number of proposals; "*val*" is the validation set; and "*test*" is the test set. "07": VOC 2007 trainval, "07 + 12": union set of VOC 2007 trainval and VOC 2012 trainval.

Table 3. mAP Comparison between Fast R-CNN and p-Faster R-CNN

Method	Prop	Training data	Val (mAP)	Test (mAP)	Time (ms)
Fast RCNN	SS,2000	VOC 07	66.2%	63.9%	1830
Fast RCNN	SS,2000	VOC 07+12	68.5%	67.7%	1830
p-Faster RCNN	RPN,300	VOC 07	69.1%	68.0%	342
p-Faster RCNN	RPN,300	VOC 07+12	72.3%	70.7%	342

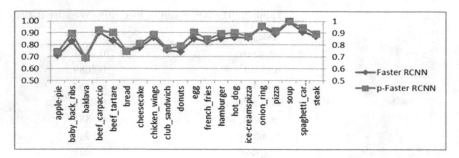

Fig. 6. The AP of Faster RCNN and p-Faster RCNN in each class (Color figure online)

Contrast Between Faster R-CNN and p-Faster R-CNN

We test the above experimental dataset, respectively using Faster RCNN and p-Faster RCNN. And the AP results are shown in Fig. 6. The abscissa is the name of each kind of food, a total of 20; the ordinate represents the AP value (the Maximum is 1, the interval is 0.1). The blue line represents the AP of each food for Faster RCNN, and the red line is that for p-Faster RCNN. As can be seen, for baby_back_ribs, beef_tartare, egg, p-Faster RCNN results improved significantly that AP value increased by about 5%. For cheesecake, donuts, hamburger, hot_dog, the results of p-Faster RCNN slightly improved that the AP value increased by about 2%. By contrast, the red line has been always above the blue line, which means that the detection accuracy of p-Faster R-CNN is slightly higher than that of Faster R-CNN for each kind.

Table 4 shows the AP value of Faster R-CNN and p-Faster RCNN. The mAP for Faster RCNN is 0.8360, and p-Faster RCNN is 0.8741. Compare both AP and mAP, p-Faster RCNN algorithm is more superior without considering the running speed.

4.6   Application

300 types of Chinese food and 100 kinds of food in food-101 are used as the dataset of the application.

As shown in Fig. 7, the food health application is divided into three layers. The client layer is the user interface. The business logic layer can calculate calories and other contents of food after detecting its type, and judge whether it's healthy by criteria. The data storage layer mainly manages and transfers the food information.

Table 4. The AP of food using Faster R-CNN and p-Faster R-CNN

Category	Faster R-CNN	p-Faster R-CNN
apple-pie	0.7099	0.7401
baby_back_ribs	0.8282	0.8955
baklava	0.6828	0.6902
beef_carpaccio	0.9024	0.9225
beef_tartare	0.8342	0.9033
bread	0.7454	0.7454
cheesecake	0.7776	0.8077
chicken_wings	0.8634	0.8884
club_sandwich	0.7541	0.7674
donuts	0.7408	0.7900
egg	0.8533	0.9043
french_fries	0.8264	0.8467
hamburger	0.8527	0.8944
hot_dog	0.8639	0.9021
ice_cream	0.8597	0.8699
onion_ring	0.9494	0.9591
pizza	0.8916	0.9150
soup	0.9932	0.9976
spaghetti_carbonara	0.9091	0.9454
steak	0.8718	0.8918
mAP	**0.8360**	**0.8741**

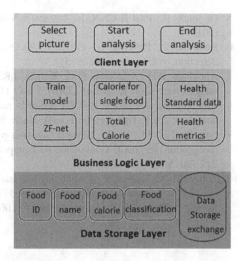

Fig. 7. The Application system architecture diagram.

5   Conclusion

This paper introduces the process of food data acquisition, the improvement process of p-Faster R-CNN algorithm, the network model, and the whole process of network configuration, training and testing. The correlation algorithms are compared and analyzed by the AP and mAP of each kind of food, which shows the superiority of the p-Faster R-CNN in a full range.

Acknowledgements. This research is supported by The National Key Research and Development Program of China (2016YFC1300205).

References

1. Melendez, S.: How machine learning will change what you eat. Mind and Machine (2016)
2. Siva, N.: Machine learning will keep us healthy. Lancet (2016)
3. Girshick, R., Donahue, J., Darrell, T., Malik, J.: Rich feature hierarchies for accurate object detection and semantic segmentation. In: Proceedings of the IEEE Conference on Computer Vision and Pattern Recognition, vol. 10, pp. 2–6 (2014)
4. He, K., Zhang, X.: Spatial pyramid pooling in deep convolutional networks for visual recognition. IEEE Trans. Pattern Anal. Mach. Intell. **37**(9), 1904–1916 (2014)

5. Girshick, R.: Fast R-CNN. In: Computer Vision and Pattern Recognition, vol. 9, pp. 3–10 (2015)
6. Redmon, J., Divvala, S., Girshick, R.: You only look once: unified, real-time object detection, vol. 6, pp. 1–4 (2015)
7. Andelson, E.H., Anderson, C.H., Bergen, J.R., Burt, P.J., Ogden, J.M.: Pyramid methods in image processing. RCA Eng. **29**(6), 33–41 (1984)
8. Ren, S., He, K.: Faster R-CNN: towards real-time object detection with region proposal networks. IEEE Trans. Pattern Anal. Mach. Intell. **6**, 1137–1149 (2015)
9. Lan, Z., Lin, M., Li, X.: Beyond Gaussian pyramid: multi-skip feature stacking for action recognition. In: IEEE Conference on Computer Vision and Pattern Recognition, pp. 204–212 (2015)
10. Zeiler, M.D., Fergus, R.: Visualizing and understanding convolutional networks. In: Fleet, D., Pajdla, T., Schiele, B., Tuytelaars, T. (eds.) ECCV 2014. LNCS, vol. 8689, pp. 818–833. Springer, Cham (2014). https://doi.org/10.1007/978-3-319-10590-1_53

PUED: A Social Spammer Detection Method Based on PU Learning and Ensemble Learning

Yuqi Song[1,2], Min Gao[1,2(✉)], Junliang Yu[1,2], Wentao Li[3], Lulan Yu[1,2], and Xinyu Xiao[1,2]

[1] Key Laboratory of Dependable Service Computing in Cyber Physical Society (Chongqing University), Ministry of Education, Chongqing, China
{songyq,gaomin,yu.jl,lulanyu,xiaoxy}@cqu.edu.cn
[2] School of Software Engineering, Chongqing University, Chongqing, China
[3] Centre for Artificial Intelligence, School of Software, Faculty of Engineering and Information Technology, University of Technology Sydney, Ultimo, Australia
wentao.li@student.uts.edu.au

Abstract. In social network, people generally tend to share information with others, thus, those who have frequent access to the social network are more likely to be affected by the interest and opinions of other people. This characteristic is exploited by spammers, who spread spam information in network to disturb normal users for interest motives seriously. Numerous notable studies have been done to detect social spammers, and these methods can be categorized into three types: unsupervised, supervised and semi-supervised methods. While the performance of supervised and semi-supervised methods is superior in terms of detection accuracy, these methods usually suffer from the dilemma of imbalanced data since the number of unlabeled normal users is far more than spammers' in real situations. To address the problem, we propose a novel method only relying on normal users to detect spammers exactly. We present two steps: one picks out reliable spammers from unlabeled samples which is imposed on a voting classifier; while the other trains a random forest detector from the normal users and reliable spammers. We conduct experiments on two real-world social datasets and show that our method outperforms other supervised methods.

Keywords: Spammer detection · Social network · PU Learning
Ensemble Learning

1 Introduction

With the rapid development of internet, social network has become an excellent medium for both sharing information and delivering products and services. It is hardly a surprise that online users of social network are growing exponentially every year, and people incline to make their commercial decisions after checking

© ICST Institute for Computer Sciences, Social Informatics and Telecommunications Engineering 2018
I. Romdhani et al. (Eds.): CollaborateCom 2017, LNICST 252, pp. 143–152, 2018.
https://doi.org/10.1007/978-3-030-00916-8_14

the online reviews. For example, users of YouTube tend to choose something to watch according to others' ratings and comments. However, in normal cases, social network is vulnerable to malicious information propagated by some users with special purpose [1,2]. Spammers as they were called, plan to benefit from advertising, posting nonsenses and spreading fake information. The existence of such spammers breaks down the ecological environment of network and affect the user experience of genuine users. Moreover, a diverse array of security risks might be caused as well, for instance, users' privacy information may be filched by phishing links and the recommended lists may be contaminated by spam. Hence, spammer detection has become a much-needed task in social service.

To the best of our knowledge, social spammer detection has attracted extensive attention from both academia and industry. As has been studied in previous literatures, spammer detections are categorized into unsupervised methods, supervised methods, and semi-supervised methods, etc. Unsupervised spammer detection methods [3–5] do not need the labeled samples, which can cut down the cost of labeling. But the absence of labels may lead to the low accuracy of the detection result. In contrast, supervised methods [6–8] and semi-supervised [9–11] methods perform better than unsupervised methods with the supervision of the labels. However, they might be exposed to a highly-risky situation where only one class label is available, because these methods highly rely on both positive and negative labels. In addition, it is time-consuming to label numerous spammers in real situations. In this work, we propose a novel spammer detection method based on Positive and Unlabeled Learning (PU Learning) [12] and Ensemble Learning [13], named PUED. The procedure of PUED contains two phases: first, a voting classifier is trained to pick out reliable negative samples (RN) from unlabeled samples; second, the detection classifier is constructed from positive and reliable negative samples. The main contributions of this paper are as follows:

- Propose a novel method PUED to detect spammers in social network;
- Evaluate and compare the performance of the PUED on two real-world datasets with supervised methods;
- Discuss the effect of the proportion of positive samples in our method, and demonstrate that PUED is capable of discriminating spammer effectively through merely a few positive samples.

The remainder of this paper is organized as follows. Section 2 provides related work. The problem statement and the illustration of PUED method are shown in Sect. 3. In Sect. 4, we conduct experiments on two real-world datasets. Finally, Sect. 5 concludes this research with potential direction for future work.

2   Related Work

2.1   Social Spammer Detection Methods

Generally speaking, the notable social spammer detection methods can be classified into three methods on the basis of labeled data as follows.

Unsupervised Detection methods mainly utilize the social network topology to identify the abnormal nodes. Gao et al. [3] exploited similarities of text content and URLs to cluster users in Facebook. The method of combining social relation graphs and user link diagrams was proposed in [4]. Zhang et al. [5] adopted 12 types of topological features in ego network to detect spammers.

Supervised Detection methods usually extract relevant characteristics of users. Benevenuto et al. [6] extracted the user behavior characteristics and tweet content characteristics to detect spammers. Wei et al. [7] explored characteristics of spammers and network stability on Twitter. A group modeling framework was proposed in [8], which adaptively characterizes social interactions of spammers.

Semi-supervised Detection methods leverage labeled samples and massive unlabeled samples. A hybrid method that aimed to detect multiple spammers from user characteristics and user relationships was proposed in [9]. In [10], the trust propagation which utilized PageRank to propagate labels was used to recognize spammers. Li et al. [11] used the Laplace method to extract features.

Among these methods, supervised methods outperform the unsupervised methods, but they are limited by abundant labeled data while unsupervised methods suffer from low accuracy. Semi-supervised methods also need a part of labeled data. Either supervised or semi-supervised methods depend on both positive and negative samples. In our work, only a few positive labeled data and plenty of unlabeled data are exploited in particular.

2.2   PU Learning

The approach merely utilizing positive and unlabeled data is called Positive and Unlabeled Learning or PU Learning. In the initial research, PU Learning mainly aimed at the text classification [12], then researchers applied this method to other field, such as the web page classification, the disease gene identification, and the Multi-graph learning.

PU Learning mainly consists of two steps [12]. Step 1: Identify the reliable negative samples (RN) from the unlabeled samples (U) according to the positive samples (P). Step 2: Construct the binary classifier by positive samples and reliable negative samples.

In real-world situation, despite that there are enormous unlabeled users and a large scale of the labeled normal users, the number of labeled spammers is still quite small. In addition, the expense of manually marking spammer is exceedingly higher than labeling normal user. Compared with the traditional methods, PU Learning has definite advantage whether in labeling time, labor force or the amount of labeled samples.

2.3   Ensemble Learning

Ensemble Learning [13,14], which integrates multiple learning algorithms, is a powerful method to obtain better performance than one learning classifier. Currently, it is almost being used in every latest research, from text mining to image processing. Commonly-used Ensemble Learning techniques include Bagging and Boosting [15].

Bagging tries to implement similar learners on small sample populations and then takes the mean value of all the predictions. In generalized bagging, we can use different learners on different populations to reduce the variance error. As a most common example, the Random Forest (RF) algorithm integrates bagging with random decision trees to make great progress in accuracy.

Boosting is an iterative method which adjusts the weight of an observation based on the last classification. If a sample was discriminated wrong, the method would increase the weight of the sample and vice versa. In general, Boosting decreases the bias error and builds strong predictive models, however, they may sometimes over fit on the training data. During the many typical algorithm of Boosting, Adaboost is a frequently-used one and Gradient Boosting Decision Tree (GDBT) is a novel one which achieve better performance.

3   PUED Method

3.1   Problem Statement

Let $\mathbf{X} \in \mathbb{R}^{n \times t}$ be the t features of n users in a social network, and $\mathbf{Y} \in \{0, 1\}^n$ are corresponding labels of those users. $y_i = 0$ indicates that the ith user account is a spammer and $y_i = 1$ otherwise. U, P, RN represent the unlabeled samples, positive samples and reliable negative samples, respectively. Meanwhile μ, l, r represent the number of users in the corresponding samples. Since only a few positive samples and plenty of unlabeled samples are used, we assume that $l \ll \mu$. In order to balance the scale of P with RN, we set $r \approx l$.

The task of the spammer detection can be summarized as follows: Given the features of all n instances and some positive labels, learning a model PUED with well performance, and then classifying the unknown user account.

3.2   PUED Framework

The framework of our proposed method consists of two steps, as described in Fig. 1, and each step will be illustrated in detail.

Step1: Pick out Reliable Negative Samples Recursively. Picking out reliable negative samples well and truth is a critical stage in PU Learning. Theoretically, after maximizing the confidence of the negative samples and ensuring the positive samples are correctly classified, we can get a superior classifier. It is vital to find as many reliable accurately-classified negative samples as possible from the unlabeled dataset. So we utilize Ensemble Learning to construct a multi-classifier. The common combination strategy of bagging for classification task is voting. More specifically, the trained classifier h_i predict a tag from the label set $\{C_1, C_2, ...C_N\}$ or the unlabeled sample $\mathbf{x}_i$. And then the predictive output on the sample $\mathbf{x}_i$ is expressed as an N dimensional vector $(h_i^1(x), h_i^2(x), ..., h_i^N(x))$, where $h_i^j(x)$ is the output of h_i on the label C_j. The absolute-majority-voting

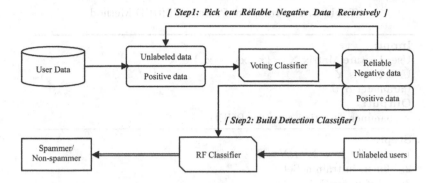

Fig. 1. The framework of PUED

accepts the predicted label whose occupancy is more than half, otherwise it rejects the prediction, as is shown in Eq. (1).

$$f(n) = \begin{cases} c_j, & if \sum_{i=1}^{T} h_i^j(x) > 0.5\sum_{k=1}^{N}\sum_{i=1}^{T} h_i^k(x); \\ reject, otherwise \end{cases} \quad (1)$$

In this work, five sub-classifiers predict the 1 or 0 label of unlabeled samples, and then vote for spammer label. The accepted threshold of spammer increases to 0.75 for higher precision, in Eq. (2). The five sub-classifiers include Logistic Regression classifier, Naive Bayes classifier, Decision Tree classifier, Random Forest Classifier and Gradient Boosting Decision Tree classifier. The powerful effect of the ensemble method will be presented in our experiment.

$$f(n) = \begin{cases} 0, if \sum_{i=1}^{5} h_i^0(x) > 0.75\sum_{k=0}^{1}\sum_{i=1}^{5} h_i^0(x); \\ 1, otherwise \end{cases} \quad (2)$$

Note that, each new predicted spammer would be added into the training set and these spammers form the reliable negative group.

Step2: Build Detection Classifier. A binary classifier is built in step 2, which differentiates between normal users and spammers by Random Forest algorithm. Random Forest is an ensemble algorithm which constructs a multitude of many decision trees at training time and outputs the class and it has a slight advantage in the individual tress. It can fill the gap in unbalanced data and maintain accuracy.

The procedures are as follows: firstly, the classifier is trained by the reliable negative samples and positive samples. Then the detection classifier can be utilized to distinguish the labels of samples: the user is a spammer if the predicted label is negative, otherwise the user is legitimate.

The whole process of PUED method which combines step 1 and step 2 is shown in Table 1. The parameter α determines the quantity of positive samples, and we will analyze it in the experiment part. The parameter β means the proportion of unlabeled samples in training stage, it is set to 0.5 in our work.

Table 1. The complete Process of PUED Method

Input:
User Feature Matrix $\mathbf{X} = \{\mathbf{x}_1, \mathbf{x}_2, \cdots \mathbf{x}_n\} \in \mathbb{R}^{t \times n}$
User Labels $\mathbf{Y}$
Parameter α, β
Output:
A spammer detection classifier PUED

Step:
1:   $P = \emptyset, \quad U = \emptyset, \quad RN = \emptyset$
2:   for $\mathbf{x}_i$ in trainingSet
3:       if $\mathbf{y}_i == 1$
4:           $P = P \cup \mathbf{x}_i$
5:       else
6:           $U = U \cup \mathbf{x}_i$
7:   Vote $\leftarrow mulclf.learn(\alpha P, \beta U)$
8:   for $\mathbf{x}_i$ in $(1 - \beta)U$
9:       if Vote.predict$(\mathbf{x}_i) == 0$
10:          $\beta U = \beta U \cup \mathbf{x}_i$
11:          Vote $\leftarrow mulclf.learn(\alpha P, \beta U)$
12:          $RN = RN \cup \mathbf{x}_i$
13: PUED $\leftarrow rfclf.learn(P, RN)$
14: for $\mathbf{x}_i$ in testSet
15:      userLabel $=$ PUED.predict $(\mathbf{x}_i)$

---

4   Experiments

4.1   Datasets and Metrics

Two real datasets provided by Benevenuto [6,16] were used for evaluation. The one is from Twitter [6] which contains 1650 labeled users, and 355 spammers in those labeled users. Each user has 62 features which are derived from tweet content and user social behavior. The other one is from YouTube [16], which includes 188 spammers and 641 legitimate users. Each user has 60 features which are derived from video attributes, individual characteristics of user behavior, and node attributes.

The experiments were conducted by 5-fold cross validation 10 times, where an average values of each set of trials were generated to represent the final results. We adopt the three frequently-used evaluation metrics, i.e., *Precision*, *Recall* and *F-measure* for performance evaluation.

4.2   Experimental Results

Credibility of Reliable Negative Samples. To draw statistical valid conclusions, we implemented several traditional methods to carry out the voting in PUED, and otherwise compare its results with each of them.

Such traditional methods include Naive Bayes (NB), Logistic Regression (LR), Decision tree (DT), Random Forest (RF) and Gradient Boosting Decision Tree (GBDT). Precision, Recall and F-measure should all be taken into consideration when judging the credibility of classifying work. And the parameter is set as 0.5, which will be explained later. Table 2 reports the credibility of reliable negative samples on both datasets. The best values are bolded in each dataset. In Twitter dataset, the precision reached 0.876 and F-measure achieved 0.826 of PUED method while sacrificing a little recall. Similarly, in YouTube dataset, precision and F-measure of our method were higher than those generated by any other single classifier. Generally, the experimental results verify the validity of Ensemble Learning. In addition, the obtained higher credibility guarantee the accuracy in the next step of our experiment to a certain extent.

Table 2. Credibility of Reliable Negative Samples

	Metrice	LR	NB	DT	RF	GBDT	PUED
Twitter	Precision	0.722	0.612	0.654	0.662	0.864	**0.876**
	Recall	0.352	0.45	0.79	**0.864**	0.746	0.792
	F-measure	0.46	0.384	0.716	0.75	0.792	**0.826**
YouTube	Precision	0.702	0.686	0.516	0.53	0.81	**0.862**
	Recall	0.756	0.624	0.74	**0.87**	0.689	0.688
	F-measure	0.722	0.618	0.608	0.75	0.75	**0.76**

Compare PUED with Other Methods. To further demonstrate that our proposed method has competitive performance, we especially compared the F-measure results of PUED with the same five traditional supervised methods we used in the last experiment, which exploit various proportion of labeled spammers in training. Similarly, two sets of trials on two datasets are conducted. In each sets of trials, we set the spammer ratio as 0%, 1%, 2%, 5%, 10%, 20%, and 30% respectively. The results of different methods are described in Table 3, with the best value in each dataset bolded as well. Note that, the results of PUED did not change at all, due to the fact that no labeled spammer was used in our method.

According to the experimental results, we could make several conclusions. First of all, in comparison with tradition methods, the F-measure of PUED, reaching 0.795, outperformed any other ones in Twitter dataset; likewise, increasing at least by 6.2% (compared with the best performer RF) in YouTube. Secondly, since the performance of supervised classifiers highly depended on labeled spammers, when the proportion of labeled spammers was low, they almost did not work. Thirdly, PUED, who only utilized positive samples, significantly outperforms other traditional methods whose labeled spammers are less than 30% in both datasets. Therefore, facing with the dilemma of imbalanced data in supervised learning, our proposed method can effectively address the problem.

Table 3. F-measure comparison between PUED and other methods

	Spammer ratio	LR	NB	DT	RF	GBDT	PUED
Twitter	0%	0	0	0	0	0	**0.795**
	1%	0.214	0.14	0.376	0.24	0.38	0.795
	2%	0.296	0.21	0.558	0.45	0.548	0.795
	5%	0.35	0.426	0.644	0.612	0.586	0.795
	10%	0.36	0.49	0.69	0.706	0.654	0.795
	20%	0.38	0.51	0.71	0.736	0.72	0.795
	30%	0.45	0.542	0.716	0.776	0.78	0.795
YouTube	0%	0	0	0	0	0	**0.72**
	1%	0.232	0.269	0.218	0.27	0.25	0.72
	2%	0.262	0.314	0.246	0.276	0.262	0.72
	5%	0.39	0.418	0.422	0.53	0.37	0.72
	10%	0.416	0.432	0.538	0.624	0.478	0.72
	20%	0.542	0.434	0.618	0.65	0.562	0.72
	30%	0.644	0.44	0.646	0.678	0.674	0.72

4.3 Parametric Sensitivity Analysis

In this subsection, we will discuss the sensitivity of the parameter α which determines the proportion of positive samples chosen. The experimental results on both datasets are shown in Fig. 2.

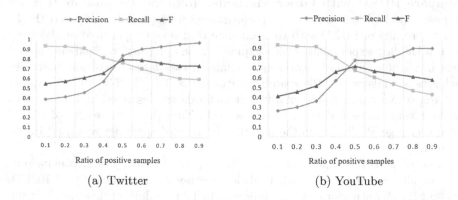

(a) Twitter   (b) YouTube

Fig. 2. Performance of PUED with varying α on datasets

Figure 2(a) shows the fluctuant performance of PUED with the different values of α in the Twitter dataset. Note that, with the increasing of α, the number of positive samples became large. It can be observed that the precision increases while the recall reduces as a result of existing imbalanced data. In order to balance the performance, we took $\alpha = 0.5$ in experiment, where F-measure can reach the optimal state. Figure 2(b) shows the performance in YouTube, and thus, α was set as 0.5 to make the precision and recall balance in experiment as well.

In summary, our proposed method PUED significantly outperforms several state-of-the-art supervised methods in credibility and F-measure. To the best of our knowledge, it can achieve competitive performance without sufficient labeled spammers. In addition, we studied the performance tradeoffs in various schemes of parameter, and an optimization was obtained. Experimental studies indicate that PUED can obtain favorable result merely using a few positive samples, significantly reducing the cost of labeling.

5 Conclusion and Future Work

In this paper, we propose a novel method PUED which integrates PU Learning and Ensemble Learning. It aims to construct a detection classifier under the circumstances of a few positive samples and sufficient unlabeled data. In general, PUED is consist of two steps: (1) picking out reliable negative samples from unlabeled users with the voting strategy; (2) utilizing the Random Forest classifier which is trained from positive and reliable negative samples to distinguish spammer. Experimental results on the two real-world datasets demonstrate that our approach, as a general and base method, has highly competitive performance. Furthermore, PUED shows its computational merits in detecting spammers. Thus, the proposed method has a reasonable overhead in recognizing spammers in social networks. This provides the foundation for further enhancement in terms of improving its accuracy, combining PUED with various state-of-the-art supervised methods, and detecting spurious comments.

Acknowledgments. The work is supported by the Basic and Advanced Research Projects in Chongqing under Grant No. cstc2015jcyjA40049, the National Key Basic Research Program of China (973) under Grant No. 2013CB328903, the Guangxi Science and Technology Major Project under Grant No. GKAA17129002, and the Graduate Scientific Research and Innovation Foundation of Chongqing, China under Grant No. CYS17035.

References

1. Hu, X., Tang, J., Zhang, Y., Liu, H.: Social spammer detection in microblogging. In: IJCAI, vol. 13, pp. 2633–2639 (2013). Citeseer
2. Fei, G., Mukherjee, A., Liu, B., Hsu, M., Castellanos, M., Ghosh, R.: Exploiting burstiness in reviews for review spammer detection. In: Proceedings of the Seventh International AAAI Conference on Weblogs and Social Media, pp. 175–184. AAAI (2013)
3. Gao, H., Hu, J., Wilson, C., Li, Z., Chen, Y., Zhao, B.Y.: Detecting and characterizing social spam campaigns. In: Proceedings of the 10th ACM SIGCOMM Conference on Internet Measurement, pp. 35–47. ACM (2010)

4. Tan, E., Guo, L., Chen, S., Zhang, X., Zhao, Y.: UNIK: unsupervised social network spam detection. In: Proceedings of the 22nd ACM International Conference on Information & Knowledge Management, pp. 479–488. ACM (2013)
5. Zhang, B., Qian, T., Chen, Y., You, Z.: Social spammer detection via structural properties in ego network. In: Li, Y., Xiang, G., Lin, H., Wang, M. (eds.) SMP 2016. CCIS, vol. 669, pp. 245–256. Springer, Singapore (2016). https://doi.org/10.1007/978-981-10-2993-6_21
6. Benevenuto, F., Magno, G., Rodrigues, T., Almeida, V.: Detecting spammers on twitter. In: Collaboration, Electronic Messaging, Anti-abuse and Spam Conference (CEAS), vol. 6, p. 12 (2010)
7. Wei, W., Joseph, K., Liu, H., Carley, K.M.: Exploring characteristics of suspended users and network stability on twitter. Soc. Netw. Anal. Mining **6**(1), 51 (2016)
8. Wu, L., Hu, X., Morstatter, F., Liu, H.: Adaptive spammer detection with sparse group modeling (2017)
9. Wu, Z., Wang, Y., Wang, Y., Wu, J., Cao, J., Zhang, L.: Spammers detection from product reviews: a hybrid model. In: 2015 IEEE International Conference on Data Mining (ICDM), pp. 1039–1044. IEEE (2015)
10. Li, Z., Zhang, X., Shen, H., Liang, W., He, Z.: A semi-supervised framework for social spammer detection. In: Cao, T., Lim, E.-P., Zhou, Z.-H., Ho, T.-B., Cheung, D., Motoda, H. (eds.) PAKDD 2015. LNCS (LNAI), vol. 9078, pp. 177–188. Springer, Cham (2015). https://doi.org/10.1007/978-3-319-18032-8_14
11. Li, W., Gao, M., Rong, W., Wen, J., Xiong, Q., Ling, B.: LSSL-SSD: social spammer detection with Laplacian score and semi-supervised learning. In: Lehner, F., Fteimi, N. (eds.) KSEM 2016. LNCS (LNAI), vol. 9983, pp. 439–450. Springer, Cham (2016). https://doi.org/10.1007/978-3-319-47650-6_35
12. Liu, B., Dai, Y., Li, X., Lee, W.S., Yu, P.S.: Building text classifiers using positive and unlabeled examples. In: Third IEEE International Conference on Data Mining, ICDM 2003, pp. 179–186. IEEE (2003)
13. Polikar, R.: Ensemble learning. In: Zhang, C., Ma, Y. (eds.) Ensemble Machine Learning, pp. 1–34. Springer, Heidelberg (2012)
14. Sun, Y., Tang, K., Minku, L.L., Wang, S., Yao, X.: Online ensemble learning of data streams with gradually evolved classes. IEEE Trans. Knowl. Data Eng. **28**(6), 1532–1545 (2016)
15. Bühlman, P.: Bagging, boosting and ensemble methods. In: Gentle, J., Härdle, W., Mori, Y. (eds.) Handbook of Computational Statistics, pp. 985–1022. Springer, Heidelberg (2012). https://doi.org/10.1007/978-3-642-21551-3_33
16. Benevenuto, F., Rodrigues, T., Almeida, V., Almeida, J., Gonçalves, M.: Detecting spammers and content promoters in online video social networks. In: Proceedings of the 32nd International ACM SIGIR Conference on Research and Development in Information Retrieval, pp. 620–627. ACM (2009)

Position vs. Attitude: How Topological Factors Influence Our Difference in the Attitudes on Online Interrelationships? A Case Study with Language Use

Bo Wang[1,2(✉)], Yingjun Sun[1,2], Yuexian Hou[1,2],
Dawei Song[1,2], and Ruifang He[1]

[1] School of Computer Science and Technology,
Tianjin University, Tianjin, China
{bo_wang, sunyingjun1993, yxhou, dwsong, rfhe}@tju.edu.cn
[2] Tianjin Key Laboratory of Cognitive Computing and Application,
Tianjin, China

Abstract. Though current researches of online collaboration often study the social relationship from an objective view, individuals' subjective attitudes on their interrelationships are more important for collaboration. Inspired by sociolinguistic theories, the latest work indicates that individuals' different attitudes on interrelationships can be measured by interactive language. However, it is still an open problem that what kind of factors influences our different attitudes on interrelationships. In this work, we investigate how individuals' position i.e., the topological factors in social network influence the differences in our bidirectional attitudes on interrelationships. Measuring the attitudes with interactive language on Enron email dataset, we analyze the correlation between attitudes and the topological factors of email network. The results indicate that individuals' differences in attitudes on interrelationships are related to some typical topological factors. These results inspire us to measure individuals' attitude in online collaboration with their topological factors in social network.

Keywords: Attitude · Online collaboration · Social network topology
Interrelationship · Interactive language

1 Introduction

In online collaboration, it is an essential problem to understand the nature of social interrelationships. Most current studies [1] suppose that the properties of social relationships are independent from participants' attitudes, and topological features of social network are most widely used to understand the social relationship. However, when exploring the formation of collaboration, the role of individuals' subjective attitudes become critically important. In latest studies [2] individuals' interactive language is proved to be more capable to understand individuals' attitudes. However, the

© ICST Institute for Computer Sciences, Social Informatics and Telecommunications Engineering 2018
I. Romdhani et al. (Eds.): CollaborateCom 2017, LNICST 252, pp. 153–163, 2018.
https://doi.org/10.1007/978-3-030-00916-8_15

topological features may still be a latent cause which influences individuals' language on interrelationship, and can also be beneficial to understand and measure individuals' different attitudes on interrelationship indirectly. For example, whether two people are friends or lovers depends largely on their own attitudes, while a large number of common friends can also help to change their relationship.

1.1 Language Analysis in Signed Social Network Studies

Nowadays, researchers try to combine the language and network features to understand social relationship. Through measuring the ability of the feature sets of social behavioral and textual information, Adalı et al. [3] drew the conclusion that these two kinds of information were practically equivalent between pairs of individuals' interaction. Pang and Lee [4] extended the model of text based statistical learning approach proposed by Bramsen et al. [5]. Their improvement was inspired by an assumption of homophily, i.e., certain social relationships correlate with agreement on certain topics. Tan et al. [6] predicted attitudes about social events by utilizing Twitter follows and comments. West et al. [7] developed a model combining textual and social network information to predict the person-to-person evaluations in the signed social network.

1.2 Measurement of Bidirectional Difference in Social Interrelationship

There are also some latest studies analyzed social relationships directionally or asymmetrically. For directed relationships, Leskovec et al. [8] first considered an explicit formulation of the sign prediction problem. Their prediction methods are based on the theory of social balance and status. Bach et al. [9] and Huang et al. [10] framed sign prediction as a hinge-loss Markov random field, a type of probabilistic graphical model introduced by Broecheler et al. [11]. West et al. [7] developed a model that synthesizes textual and social network information to jointly predict the polarity of person-to-person evaluations. Wang et al. [2] investigated the subjective difference of interrelationship with interactive language features.

1.3 Our Approaches

Although current studies have proposed the measure of two individuals' different attitudes with interactive language features [2, 7], they do not explore the intrinsic causes of the difference in individuals' attitudes. If individuals' attitudes only depend on their own ideas, we can only measure their attitudes with subjective factors e.g., the interactive language. However, an individual's attitude on one of his social relationships is also affected by other relationships. Therefore, we try to examine whether social network topological factors can affect individuals' attitudes, and shall we introduce topology features into the measurement of individuals' attitudes.

2 Topological and Linguistic Features in Sociolinguistic Theories

Interactive language is a good resource to describe individuals' attitudes in social interaction. The theory of communicative action [12] reconstructs the concept of relationship with the communicative action instead of the objectivistic information. Thus we can utilize the linguistic structures to understand the social relationships. Sapir-Whorf hypothesis [13] also supposed that the semantic structure shapes the way in which a speaker formed conceptions of the world including social relationships. Therefore we can try to investigate the different attitudes with the interactive language.

How can we describe an individual's interactive language style in order to describe his attitude on his interrelationship? In sociolinguistics, Holmes [14] proposed four important dimensions to study the language used in social interrelationship:

(1) The solidarity-social distance scale: concentrate on the solidarity of the relationships in social interrelationship.
(2) The social status scale: concentrate on the relative status of the individuals in social relationship.
(3) The formality scale: concentrate on the formality of language that individuals use in different places, topics and relationships.
(4) The referential and affective scale: concentrate on referential and affective function of the language that individuals use in social interrelationship.

Among these four dimensions, the first two concern about the topological features of social relationship, and the last two aim at the features of interactive languages.

Inspired by Holmes' theory, firstly, we use four interactive language features to indicate individuals' attitudes, including frequency, length, fluency and sentiment polarity which indicate quantity, formality and affective scale of the interactive language. Second, we then investigate the correlation between topological and linguistic factors. The calculation of linguistic features will be introduced in Sect. 4.2.

3 Topological Factors on Social Network

In this section, we introduce three most widely studied topological factors on social network which can potentially affect individuals' different attitudes on interrelationship.

3.1 Degree and Clustering Coefficient of Individuals

As for a vertex A, the degree of A which can indicate an individual's range of social relationships is defined as the number of vertexes connected with A. The clustering coefficient indicates the probability of any two friends of A are also friends in social network. It is also known as an indicator to measure A's ability to gather friends into a cluster. If the degree of A is n and the number of edges between these n vertexes is k, the clustering coefficient $C(A)$ of A can be calculated with Formula (1):

$$C(A) = \frac{k}{C_n^2} \tag{1}$$

Why degree and clustering coefficient are selected for this work? In intuition, the range of one's social relationships and the clustering degree of one's friends may affect individuals' different attitudes on social interrelationships.

3.2 Embeddedness of Interrelationships

In social network, the embeddedness of an interrelationship indicates the number of common friends of two individuals engaged in an interrelationship. Embeddedness is believed to indicate the strength of social relationship. We suppose that embeddedness is also related to the degree of attitudes' difference. This assumption is based on the similar idea of the strength measurement of social relationship: it is widely believed that more common friends make two individuals connected to each other more tightly. In this work, we will investigate whether more common friends can also make two persons' attitudes on their interrelationship more consistent.

3.3 The Balance of Triadic Closure

The Traditional Balance Theory. A triadic closure consists of any three persons and the interrelationships between them. In traditional balance theory, each relationship is singed with binary tag '+' or '−', which indicates positive or negative relationship. With binary signs, there are four different signs combinations. As shown in Fig. 1, the balance theory claims that two of them are balanced while the other two are unbalanced. The balanced triadic closures are stable while the unbalanced ones tend to become balanced.

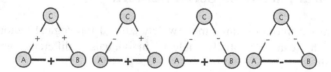

Fig. 1. All schematic diagrams of the triadic closure in the balance theory. The first and third are balanced triangles, while the other two are unbalanced.

The Extension of the Balance Theory. The traditional balance theory can be explained with the concept of homogeneity, i.e., in a triadic closure, the more consistent of the two individuals' views on the third one, the more positive their attitudes on their interrelationship are, or vice versa. The homogeneity-based explanation can help to extend the traditional balance theory from binary signs to continuous value, and from undirected relationship to directed relationship, because it describes the balance with individual's attitude instead of objective signs. This extension makes it possible to investigate the correlation between triangle balance and attitudes' difference.

In latest work [15], the traditional balance theory is extended to a directed version based on homogeneity explanation. In this extension, a person A's attitude on person B is presented as a continuous value $|AB|$ on a directed edge (A, B), and vice versa. Since our aim is to investigate the bidirectional attitudes' difference between A and B, we build an extended triadic closure with four directed edges include (A, B), (B, A), (A, C) and (B, C) as shown in Fig. 2. Instead of the binary sign, we label each directed edge with a real-value in [0, 1] to indicate the attitude of the participant on the start point, e.g., $|AB|$ indicates the value of A's attitude on his relationship with B.

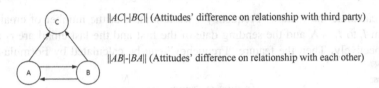

$\||AC|-|BC|\|$ (Attitudes' difference on relationship with third party)

$\||AB|-|BA|\|$ (Attitudes' difference on relationship with each other)

Fig. 2. Extension of the balance theory: determine the balance by comparing the difference between A and B's attitudes on each other and the difference between A and B's attitudes on C.

In this extended triadic closure, we measure the balance of the triadic closure by comparing two differences: firstly, when the difference between $|AC|$ and $|BC|$, i.e., $\||AC| - |BC|\|$, is smaller than a threshold, we recognize the 'third party difference' between A and B's attitudes on C as '−', which means A and B have similar attitudes on their interrelationships with C. Otherwise we recognize the 'third party difference' as '+', which means A and B have different attitudes on their interrelationships with C.

Secondly, when the difference between $|AB|$ and $|BA|$, i.e., $\||AB| - |BA|\|$, is smaller than the same threshold, we recognize 'bidirectional difference' as '−' which means A and B have similar attitudes on their interrelationship. Otherwise, we recognize 'bidirectional difference' as '+' which means A and B have different attitudes. The threshold here is determined by the average of all bidirectional differences on every interrelationship. If the 'third party difference' and 'bidirectional difference' have same signs, we identify the directed triadic closure as balanced, otherwise, it is unbalanced.

4   Experiments

In the experiments, we investigate the correlation between the three topological factors and individuals' bidirectional difference in attitudes. The individuals' attitudes on relationships are characterized with four language features inspired by Holmes' theory.

4.1 Dataset

We utilized the Enron email dataset which contains 0.5M emails exchanged between 151 Enron employees. We choose this dataset because it contains both the interactive language pieces (email content) and social network topology (send and receive relationships). To make the investigation more reliable, we only selected the interrelationships where at least 15 emails were sent in each direction. The filtered dataset contains 1078 interrelationships between 647 individuals.

4.2 Attitudes (Language Features) Calculation

For each ordered pair of individuals I_i and I_j, I_i's attitude on his relationship with I_j is calculated by the value of four language features using emails sent from I_i to I_j:

(1) To calculate the feature "Frequency", we assume that the number of emails sent from I_i to I_j is N and the sending date of the first and the last email are t_1 and t_2, respectively. Then the feature "Frequency" can be calculated by Formula (2):

$$frequency\_score_{i,j} = \frac{N}{t_2 - t_1} \qquad (2)$$

(2) To calculate the feature "Length", we assume that the number of emails sent from I_i to I_j is N and the total number of words in these emails is w, then the feature "Length" can be calculated by Formula (3):

$$length\_score_{i,j} = \frac{w}{N} \qquad (3)$$

(3) To calculate the feature "Quality", we utilize the SRI language modeling toolkit (SRILM)[1] with Formula (4) to measure the perplexity score which has a negative correlation with the quality of a sentence. In this formula, $prob$ is the generating probability of a sentence. '$words$' and '$oovs$' are the count of the words and out of vocabulary words in the sentence, respectively.

$$perplexity\_score_{i,j} = 10^{(-\log prob/(words - oovs + 1))} \qquad (4)$$

(4) To calculate the feature "Sentiment", we utilize a sentiment dictionary[2] to count the sentiment words. Each positive or negative word is valued 1 or -1, respectively. Assume there are S sentences in the emails sent from I_i to I_j, and the sum of all scores of sentiment words is W, then the feature "Sentiment" is calculated by Formula (5):

$$Sentiment\_score_{i,j} = \frac{W}{S} \qquad (5)$$

---

[1] http://www.speech.sri.com/projects/srilm/
[2] http://www.keenage.com/download/sentiment.rar.

4.3   Attitudes' Bidirectional Difference vs. Degree and Clustering Coefficient

Degree vs. Attitudes' Difference. In the first experiment, for each individual I, we calculate $\bar{D}_{I,k}$, which is the average of the attitudes' bidirectional differences on I's all interrelationships. In formula (6), $f_k(I, I_i)$ is I's attitude to his friend I_i of language feature k. C is the set of I's all friends. Then $\bar{D}_{I,k}$ is calculated with formula (6).

$$\bar{D}_{I,k} = \frac{1}{|C|}\sum_{I_i \in C} |f(I, I_i) - f(I_i, I)| \tag{6}$$

Then, for each language feature k, we calculated the Pearson Correlation Coefficient between individuals' degree and the attitudes' average difference on their social relationships, i.e., $\bar{D}_{I,k}$. The results are shown in the first column in Table 1.

Table 1. Pearson Correlation Coefficient between topological factors of individuals and the average bidirectional difference in the attitudes on their social relationships.

Attitudes measured by language features	Pearson Correlation Coefficient	
	Degree	Clustering coefficient
Frequency	0.085	−0.044
Length	−0.650	−0.378
Quality	−0.109	0.189
Sentiment	−0.438	0.200

Clustering Coefficient vs. Attitudes' Difference. In the second experiment, for each individual I, we calculated the clustering coefficient with Formula (1), as well as the average of attitudes' bidirectional difference $\bar{D}_{I,k}$ of I. Then, we calculated the Pearson Correlation Coefficient between individuals' clustering coefficient and the attitudes' average difference, i.e. $\bar{D}_{I,k}$. The results are shown in the second column in Table 1.

Observations. According to results in Table 1, attitudes' difference measured by 'Length' and 'Sentiment' have relatively more significant negative correlation with the degree, and the other two features have no significant correlation. This indicates that a person with more friends may be more active to cater to the partners' attitudes, i.e., have less difference in attitudes, especially reflected on the length and sentiment score.

Though 'Length' and 'Sentiment' have relatively higher correlation with clustering coefficient, the absolute values are too small, which indicates that there is no significant correlation between the clustering coefficient and the attitudes' difference in this case.

Furthermore, the correlation of frequency is the lowest. One possible explanation is that the send/replay relationships between the emails can always lead to similar bidirectional email sending frequency between two individuals, which is independent with the attitudes or social topological factors of the individuals.

In general, in this set of experiments, we find that the number of friends of the individuals may have influence on their different attitudes on their interrelationships.

4.4 Attitudes' Bidirectional Difference vs. Embeddedness

In the third experiment, we investigate the correlation between their embeddedness and the bidirectional difference in the attitudes on them, which is also measured by four language features, respectively. The results are shown in Table 2.

Table 2. Pearson Correlation Coefficient between embeddedness and the average bidirectional difference in the attitudes on social relationships

Language features	Pearson Correlation Coefficient
Frequency	−0.823
Length	−0.979
Quality	−0.678
Sentiment	−0.696

In Table 2, the embeddedness of interrelationship has significant negative correlation with the attitudes' difference. This indicates that if two individuals have more common friends, they will have more similar attitudes on their interrelationship.

The traditional triadic closure theory states that the strength of a social interrelationship has a positive correlation with the number of common friends. Our results extend the theory to the positive correlation among the number of two individuals' common friends, the strength of their interrelationship and the consistency of their attitudes on their interrelationship.

4.5 Attitudes' Bidirectional Difference vs. Balance Theory

In this experiment, based on extended balance theory and bidirectional attitudes measuring, we investigate whether unbalanced triangles tend to become balanced in social network evolution.

In this experiment, we divided emails into seven time intervals. From Jan, 1999 to Jun, 2002, every six months is divided as an interval. We firstly calculated the number of balanced and unbalanced triangles on each time interval, according to traditional and extended balance theory. Secondly, for each two adjacent time intervals pair, we calculated two transformation percentages: (1) The percentage of the balanced triangles in previous interval which become unbalanced in next interval; (2) The percentage of the unbalanced triangles in previous interval which become balanced in next interval. The two percentages on all six adjacent time intervals pairs are shown in Fig. 3. In Fig. 4, we calculated the average transformation percentages between balanced and unbalanced triangles on all six adjacent time intervals pairs.

As we can see from Fig. 3, the percentage of unbalanced triangles changed to balanced triangles (green bars) is larger than balanced triangles changed to unbalanced (blue bars) in all cases in. In Fig. 4, we also find that in average the triangles tend to become balanced on both traditional and extended balance theory.

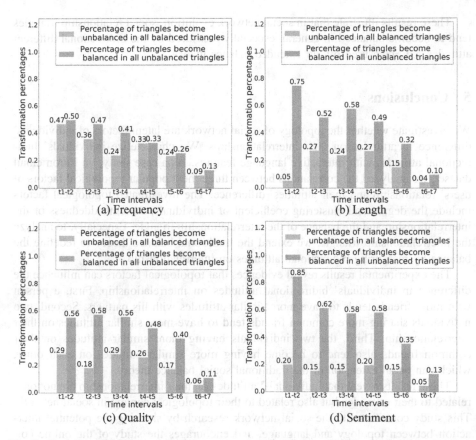

Fig. 3. Transformation percentages between extended balanced and unbalanced triangles measured by four language features on adjacent time intervals pairs.

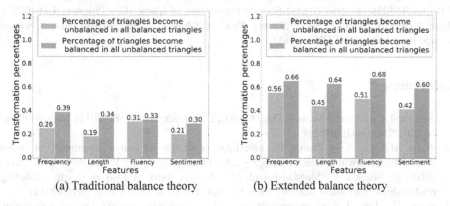

Fig. 4. Average transformation percentages between balanced and unbalanced triangles measured by four language features on all six adjacent time intervals pairs.

These results illustrate that in social network evolution, social relationship triangles tend to become balanced in general, especially measured by the bidirectional different attitudes, i.e., measured by our extended balance theory.

5 Conclusions

We investigate whether the topology of social network are latent factors of individuals' difference in attitudes on their interrelationships. We characterize individuals' bidirectional attitudes with interactive language features. As a case study, on Enron email dataset, we analyzed the correlations between three most popular topological factors of users' relationship and their attitudes' difference. The investigated topological factors include the degree and clustering coefficient of individuals, the embeddedness of the interrelationship and the balance of the interrelationship triangle. Especially, to analyze the interrelationship triangle, we extend the traditional balance theory to redefine the balance by measuring bidirectional attitudes on interrelationship.

The experimental results reveal evidences that topological factors can influence the difference in individuals' bidirectional attitudes on interrelationship. First, a person with more friends tends to have more similar attitudes with his partners. Second, two individuals sharing more common friends tend to have more similar attitudes on their interrelationship. Third, the two individuals having more similar attitudes on their common friends also tend to become having more similar attitudes on each other, which can be an extension of the traditional social balance theory.

These results reveal that individuals' attitudes on their interrelationship are not only related to their own idea but also related to their topological context in social network. This study contributes to the social network research by showing the potential interaction between topology and language, and encourages the study of the online collaboration on social relationship synthesizing the objective and subjective features.

Acknowledgments. This work is supported by National High-tech R&D Program of China (2015AA015403), National Natural Science Foundation of China (Key Program, U1636203), Major Project of National Social Science Fund of China (14ZDB153) and Tianjin Natural Science Foundation (14JCQNJC00400).

References

1. Aggarwal, C.C.: Social Network Data Analytics. Springer, New York (2011). https://doi.org/10.1007/978-1-4419-8462-3
2. Wang, B., Yu, Y.S., Zhang, P.: Investigation of the subjective asymmetry of social interrelationship with interactive language. In: Proceedings of the World Wide Web (2016)
3. Adalı, S., Sisenda, F., Magdon-Ismail, M.: Actions speak as loud as words: predicting relationships from social behavior data. In: Proceedings of World Wide Web (2012)
4. Pang, B., Lee, L.: A sentimental education: sentiment analysis using subjectivity summarization based on minimum cuts. In: Proceedings of Association for Computational Linguistics (2004)

5. Bramsen, P., Escobar-Molano, M., Patel, A., Alonso, R.: Extracting social power relationships from natural language. In: Proceedings of Association for Computational Linguistics (2011)
6. Tan, C.H., Lee, L., Tang, J., Jiang, L., Zhou, M., Li, P.: User-level sentiment analysis incorporating social networks. In: Proceedings of ACM Special Interest Group on Knowledge Discovery and Data Mining (2011)
7. West, R., Paskov, H.S., Leskovec, J., Potts, C.: Exploiting social network structure for person-to-person sentiment analysis. Trans. Assoc. Comput. Linguist. (2014)
8. Leskovec, J., Huttenlocher, D., Kleinberg, J.: Predicting positive and negative links in online social networks. In: Proceedings of World Wide Web (2010)
9. Bach, S., Huang, B., London, B., Getoor, L.: Hinge-loss Markov random fields: convex inference for structured prediction. In: Proceedings of Uncertainty in Artificial Intelligence (2013)
10. Huang, B., Kimmig, A., Getoor, L., Golbeck, J.: A flexible framework for probabilistic models of social trust. In: Proceedings of International Social Computing, Behavioral-Cultural Modeling and Prediction Conference (2013)
11. Broecheler, M., Mihalkova, L., Getoor, L.: Probabilistic similarity logic. In: Proceedings of Uncertainty in Artificial Intelligence (2010)
12. Habermas, J.: The Theory of Communicative Action. Beacon Press, Boston (1981)
13. Sapir, E.: The status of linguistics as a science. Linguistic Society of America (1929)
14. Holmes, J.: An Introduction to Sociolinguistics. Routledge, London (2013)
15. Wang, B., Sun, Y.J., Han, B., Hou, Y.X., Song, D.W.: Extending the balance theory by measuring bidirectional opinions with interactive language. In: Proceedings of the World Wide Web (2017)

Route-Oriented Participants Recruitment in Collaborative Crowdsensing

Shu Yang, Jinglin Li$^{(\boxtimes)}$, Quan Yuan, and Zhihan Liu

State Key Laboratory of Networking and Switching Technology,
Beijing University of Posts and Telecommunications, Beijing, China
jlli@bupt.edu.cn

Abstract. Route-oriented participants recruitment is a critical problem in collaborative crowdsensing, where task publisher uses monetary reward to motivate private cars collecting data along their routes. For map producers, route-oriented crowdsensing scheme helps them achieve maximum roads coverage with a limited budget, by selecting appropriate participants from a group of candidates.

Focused on route-oriented participants recruitment problem, this paper first formalizes the road network and vehicle route model. Each vehicle's route is mapped to a coverage rate on the road set. The recruitment problem therefore transforms to a combinatorial optimization problem, which has proved to be NP-hard. To find a solution, we proposed an approximation algorithm, which leverages submodularity to reduce computation complexity and has a worst performance guarantee. Finally we evaluate the performance of proposed algorithm on real road and trajectory data in Beijing, China.

Keywords: Participants recruitment · Collaborative crowdsensing
Vehicle trajectory · Approximate algorithm

1 Introduction

The rise of big data, the method of collecting data is of great importance. Being intellectualized and networked, smart vehicles are able to sense and communicate in urban area. Their intrinsic mobility can be leveraged to dynamically collect urban data in different time and areas [1]. A promising data service is collecting data for HD (High Definition) map [2], which built from environmental data of multiple sensors. The map producers, such as Here, TomTom and Baidu, need lidar/camera/IMU data to build a live map for autonomous driving [3]. The huge volume of information, as well as fast updating frequency to build a "live" map, challenges map producers because their own devices undoubtedly could

This work is supported by the National Science and Technology Major Project of China under Grant No. 2016ZX03001025-003 and Special found for Beijing Common Construction Project.

© ICST Institute for Computer Sciences, Social Informatics and Telecommunications Engineering 2018
I. Romdhani et al. (Eds.): CollaborateCom 2017, LNICST 252, pp. 164–175, 2018.
https://doi.org/10.1007/978-3-030-00916-8_16

not meet these requirements. Some researchers therefore proposed crowdsensing in which private cars are incentivized to accomplish a sensing task and upload data to map producer. The incentives could be either real or virtual money.

In real scenario, each private car has its own short-term route which includes a sequence of road segments and sensing cost. For a budget-constrained task publisher, participants recruitment turns into a combinatorial optimization problem. Hence, how to select appropriate participants to maximize road coverage with limited budget is a critical problem for HD map crowdsensing. Concentrated on this problem, this paper has following three contributions.

Problem Formalization of Route-Oriented Participants Recruitment. The problem is route-oriented because road coverage rate is considered as a major indicator in this paper. We first formalize urban road networks as a graph, the road segments are represented by edges in the graph. Then fine-grained trajectory of vehicle is simplified into route, a sequence of edges in graph. With each route has its unique coverage rate on graph, the task publisher selects participants that maximize road coverage within a given budget.

Approximation Algorithm Using Submodularity. The formalized problem is NP-hard, which has no polynomial solution unless $NP = P$. We look for a greedy algorithm guaranteeing lower bound with a ratio of $(1 - 1/e)$. Specifically, we observe and prove that the coverage rate function is submodular, which enables us to employ the property in submodular optimization.

Performance Evaluation by Real Data. To validate effectiveness of proposed algorithm, real road networks and vehicle trajectories in Beijing are used. Selected major roads in Beijing urban area are extracted. Taxi trajectories are partitioned into sequence of road segments. Preprocessed data are fed into our proposed algorithm and two other algorithms, including *naive selection* and *pureGreedy selection*. The results are compared and analyzed to demonstrate effectiveness of approximation algorithm.

The rest of this paper is organized as follows: Sect. 2 describes basic scenario and definitions of participants recruitment. Section 3 presents our proposed approximation algorithm. Section 4 presents simulation results and analysis. We delay our discussion of related work until Sect. 5, in order not to interrupt reader's mind. The paper ends, in Sect. 6, with some conclusions and future works on route-oriented crowdsensing problem.

2 Preliminaries

This section describes the scenario of participants recruitment and frequently used notations.

2.1 Scenario Description

The task publisher on the cloud publishes task among candidate vehicles. Then candidate vehicles report their short-term route to task publisher, who decides to choose appropriate participants at last. The communication between task publisher and vehicles is supported by cellular network. Figure 1 is a description of route-oriented participants recruitment.

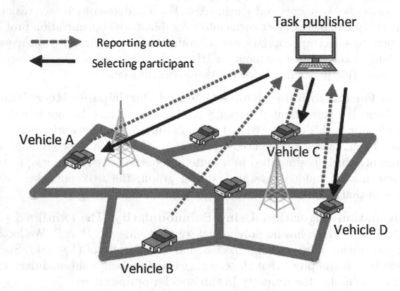

Fig. 1. A description of route-oriented participants recruitment. Task publisher and vehicles communicates by cellular network.

2.2   Models and Measurement

We consider the scenario where task publisher distributes the sensing task to candidate vehicles on the urban road networks.

Definition 1-Road Networks: The road network is modeled as a graph $G = (V, E)$, where the intersections are denoted as vertex V and road segments are denoted as edge E. The set of roads is denoted by $E = \{e_1, e_2, ..., e_m\}$, where m is the number of road segments need to sense.

Definition 2-Participant's Route: A participant p_i's route r_i is a sequence of segments pertaining to one trip. Each segment in r_i is an edge $e \in E$, with an arriving time stamp $e.t_1$ and a leaving time stamp $e.t_2$, i.e. $r : e_1 \rightarrow e_2 \rightarrow ... \rightarrow e_k$, where $0 < e_k.t_2 - e_1.t_1 \leq \triangle T$. $\triangle T$ defines the maximum prediction time of participant's route. Participants need to report short-term route prediction to task publisher, larger $\triangle T$ renders lower prediction accuracy due to uncertainty in real transport environment.

Definition 3-Dependent Coverage: A dependent coverage of p_i on road networks E is $C_{p_i}^{dep(P_{i-1})}(E) = \{r_i \cap (E - C_{p_{i-1}}^{dep(P_{i-2})}(E))\}$, when $P_{i-1} = \{p_1, p_2, ..., p_{i-1}\}$ has sequentially made their coverage. As the name suggested,

$C_{p_i}^{dep(P_{i-1})}(E)$ is not only related to the length of r_i, but also depending on $C_{p_{i-1}}^{dep(P_{i-2})}(E)$ which is resulted from $i-1$ previously selected participants.

By definition, for any p_i, if $P_1 \subseteq P_2 \subseteq P$, below equation always stands:

$$C_{p_i}^{dep(P_2)}(E) = C_{p_i}^{dep(P_1)}(E) \cap C_{p_i}^{dep(P_2 \setminus P_1)}(E) \tag{1}$$

Thus,

$$\|C_{p_i}^{dep(P_2)}(E)\| \leq \|C_{p_i}^{dep(P_1)}(E)\| \tag{2}$$

Definition 4-Global Coverage Rate: Given a road networks' edge set E and a group of participants P, with each participant's r_i is consisted of a series of edges, the global coverage rate is $\|C_P^{global}(E)\|$, i.e. the ratio of all covered edges' length to the total E's length. For example, if there are 2 candidate participants $P = \{p_1, p_2\}$, with $r_1 = \{e_1, e_2\}$ and $r_2 = \{e_2, e_3\}$ respectively. We also assume $E = \{e_1, e_2, e_3, e_4\}$. The global coverage rate of p on E is $\|C_P^{global}(E)\| = (|e_1| + |e_2| + |e_3|)/(|e_1| + |e_2| + |e_3| + |e_4|)$.

3 Participants Recruitment with Budget Constraint

In this section, we describe the maximum global coverage with the budget constraint and present the corresponding algorithm to address it.

3.1 Problem Formalization

In practical scenarios, the budget of task publisher for rewarding participants is limited. Additionally, each participant has unique cost and coverage conditions, making it difficult for participants selection. Considering the set of candidate participants $P = \{p_1, p_2, ..., p_n\}$ is associated with cost set $D = \{d_1, d_2, ..., d_n\}$. That is, each p_i has a cost d_i. The total cost of selecting participants should not exceed a given budget B.

Definition 5-Maximum Coverage Rate with Budget Constraint: Given an edge set $E = \{e_1, e_2, ..., e_m\}$ and a potential participant set $P = \{p_1, p_2, ..., p_n\}$, with the corresponding cost set $D = \{d_1, d_2, ...d_n\}$. Costs are additive and illustrated by $d(P) = \sum d(p_i) = \sum_{i=1}^n d_i$. The maximum global coverage rate under budget constraint B asks for a subset $P' \subseteq P$, such that the total cost of P' is no more than B, i.e., $d(P') = \sum_{p_j \in P'} d_j \leq B$, and the global coverage rate $\|C_{P'}^{global}(E)\|$ is maximized.

Formally, this optimizing problem is given by:

$$\max_{P' \subseteq P} C_{P'}^{global}(E) \quad s.t. \quad d(P') \leq B \tag{3}$$

3.2   Leveraging Submodularity

To solve the given problem, we prove that the set function of the global coverage rate is nondecreasing submodular, so that we could employ the property in submodular optimization.

Definition 6-Submodularity: Given a finite set E, a real-valued function $f(\cdot)$ on the subsets of E is submodular if:

$$f(A) + f(B) \geq f(A \cap B) + f(A \cup B) \ \forall A, B \subseteq E \tag{4}$$

It is convenient to use an incremental style of above inequality. If the function satisfied the *diminish returns* rule for all element x and all pairs $A \subseteq B$, denoted as:

$$f(A \cup \{x\}) - f(A) \geq f(B \cup \{x\}) - f(B) \tag{5}$$

Then, $f(\cdot)$ is said to be nondecreasing if $f(A) \leq f(B)$ for all $A \subseteq B \subseteq E$. Based on the given preliminaries, we obtained the following lemma and further give its proof.

Lemma 1: Given edge set E and a participants set $P'(P' \subseteq P)$, the set function of the global coverage rate $\|C_{P'}^{global}(E)\|$ is nondecreasing submodular.

Proof: It is straight forward that $\|C_{\emptyset}^{global}(E)\| = 0$ because not a single participant has been selected to cover. Consider P''s two arbitrary subsets P_1'' and P_2'', $P_1'' \subseteq P_2'' \subseteq P'$, we have $\|C_{P_1''}^{global}(E)\| \leq \|C_{P_2''}^{global}(E)\|$ since a route set $r_{P_1''}$ always has bigger(at least equal when $P_1'' = P_2''$) global coverage rate than $r_{P_2''}$.

Then we consider any candidate participant $p_x \in P - P'$ and edge set E, when P_1'', P_2'' has been selected. Note that $P_1'' \subseteq P_2'' \subset P$. By Eq. (3), it holds:

$$\|C_{p_x}^{dep(P_2'')}(E)\| \leq \|C_{p_x}^{dep(P_1'')}(E)\| \tag{6}$$

It also holds that:

$$\|C_{P_1'' \cup \{p_x\}}^{global}(E)\| - \|C_{P_1''}^{global}(E)\| = \|C_{p_x}^{dep(P_1'')}(E)\| \tag{7}$$

$$\|C_{P_2'' \cup \{p_x\}}^{global}(E)\| - \|C_{P_2''}^{global}(E)\| = \|C_{p_x}^{dep(P_2'')}(E)\| \tag{8}$$

Combining (6), (7), (8) we have:

$$\|C_{P_1'' \cup \{x\}}^{global}(E)\| - \|C_{P_1''}^{global}(E)\| \geq$$
$$\|C_{P_2'' \cup \{x\}}^{global}(E)\| - \|C_{P_2''}^{global}(E)\| \tag{9}$$

It is satisfied with the *diminish returns* rule (6) in which the difference from adding an new element to a set P'' is at least as large as that from adding the same element to a superset P' of P'', therefore $\|C_P^{global}(E)\|$ is nondecreasing submodular with $\|C_{\emptyset}^{global}(E)\| = 0$.

3.3 Approximation Algorithm

Motivated by the submodular property of coverage [4], we proposed an approximation algorithm to address the global coverage rate with guaranteed performance. As shown in Algorithm 1, the algorithm partially uses an enumeration technique, and then employs greedy heuristic to get selection results for maximum global coverage rate with budget constraint.

Algorithm 1 is mainly composed by two components. The first component is in line 2–line 3, which enumerates all subsets S_1 whose cardinality is smaller than k, and has cost less than B. The enumerated subset who has the most global coverage rate is set as H_1, the candidate subset of the first component. Another candidate is generated from the second component from line 4–line 12. This component first enumerates some subsets S_2 whose cardinality $Card(S_2) = k$, and complements these subsets using the greedy algorithm (line 6–line 11).

Algorithm 1. Approximation Algorithm for Maximum Coverage Rate with Budget Constraint Problem

---

Input: Edge set $E = \{e_1, e_2, ..., e_m\}$, potential participants set
$\quad\quad P = \{p_1, p_2, ..., p_n\}$ and corresponding cost set $D = \{d_1, d_2, ..., d_n\}$,
$\quad\quad$ budget B, a predefined integer k.
Output: Participants set $P' \subseteq P$.

1 $H_1 \leftarrow \emptyset,\ H_2 \leftarrow \emptyset$
2 **for** all $S_1 \subseteq P$, such that $|S_1| < k$, and $d(S_1) \leq B$ **do**
3 $\quad$ if $\|C_{S_1}^{global}(E)\| > \|C_{H_1}^{global}(E)\|$ then $H_1 \leftarrow S_1$
4 **for** all $S_2 \subseteq P$, such that $|S_2| = k$, and $d(S_2) \leq B$ **do**
5 $\quad$ $T \leftarrow P \backslash S_2$
6 $\quad$ **Repeat**
7 $\quad\quad$ find p_j that maximize $\|C_{p_j}^{dep(S_2)}(E)\|/d(p_j)$
8 $\quad\quad$ if $d(S_2) + d(p_j) \leq B$ then
9 $\quad\quad\quad$ $S_2 \leftarrow S \cup p_j$
10 $\quad\quad$ $T \leftarrow T \backslash p_j$
11 $\quad$ **Until** $T = \emptyset$
12 $\quad$ if $\|C_{S_2}^{global}(E)\| > \|C_{H_2}^{global}(E)\|$ then $H_2 \leftarrow S_2$
13 if $\|C_{H_1}^{global}(E)\| > \|C_{H_2}^{global}(E)\|$, $P' \leftarrow H_1$, else $P' \leftarrow H_2$.
14 return P'

Theorem 1: For $k \geq 3$, Algorithm 1 has an approximation ratio of $(1 - 1/e)$ for the maximum global coverage rate with budget constraint problem. That is:

$$C_{P'}^{global} \geq \underbrace{(1 - 1/e)}_{\approx 0.632} C_{optimal}^{global}, \quad \text{for } k \geq 3 \quad\quad\quad (10)$$

where $C_{optimal}^{global}$ is the optimal value of the total global coverage rate that can be achieved by any participants set $P' \subseteq P$. See Khuller's work [5] for a detail proof.

The time complexity of Algorithm 1 is $O(l^{k+2})$, where k is an integer that is bigger or equals to 3. This algorithm is polynomial and achieves an approxima- tion guarantee of $(1-1/e)$. Since the complexity of proposed algorithm increases with k, we recommend to set $k = 3$ as usual. To get better performance in cov- erage rate, a larger k could be set with a price of larger time complexity.

4   Real Data Based Simulation

We evaluate the performance of the proposed algorithm using real road networks and trajectory data from Beijing, China. Then we make a comparison between proposed algorithm and other two algorithms, and finally make an analysis on these results.

4.1   Simulation Data and Settings

Road Networks in Beijing. The road network (V, E) is built from Beijing map [6]. The detailed information of map is trivial, therefore only main roads are solicited in our experiment. Each road has its direction and length, which are important for building road set E.

Taxi Trajectory Data. We extract route from real taxi trajectory data col- lected by MSRA [7]. The data package includes over 10000 taxicabs' trajectories on several days in November 2013. For each day the data package contains a full-scale GPS during 24 h. Since trajectory is too detailed for use, we simplified the GPS trajectory into route by trajectory-map-matching [8], i.e. transforming GPS trajectory into series of road segments, and tag each segment with arriv- ing/leaving time. Considering the scenario of participants recruitment for HD map sensing, a vehicle could predict its short-term route in $\triangle T$. After defining an initial time t_{init}, we randomly choose a batch of taxi, whose trajectory is in the range of selected urban area and within time $[t_{init}, t_{init} + \triangle T]$.

Figure 2 is a sketch map of road networks, which is located in a prosperous block in Haidian district, Beijing. Selected roads are in blue and three road exam- ples are presented in Fig. 2(a) and (b). Additionally, three routes/trajectories are

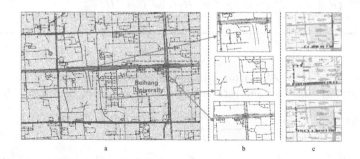

Fig. 2. A sketch map of road networks and routes. a: selected roads are in blue; b: examples of road segment; c: examples of route. (Color figure online)

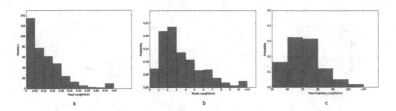

Fig. 3. Statistics of roads and route data.

also presented in Fig. 2(c). To give an insight of simulation configuration, Fig. 3 shows some statistics of road and route data. Note that total trajectory length in Fig. 3(c) is the whole length of all candidates' trajectories.

Participants Cost. Unfortunately, there is no real cost data of participants. As a rule of thumb, each driver has different preference and driving cost. Therefore we generate a cost d_i for each candidate participant with uniform distribution, i.e. $D \sim U[a, b]$. Hence, costs and routes are synthesized to support our simulation.

Overall, simulation settings are illustrated in Table 1.

Table 1. Simulation settings

$[t_{init}, t_{init} + \triangle T]$	$[16, 16.5]$ (30 min)
Road segments number	362
Candidate participants number	$\{5, 10, 15, 20, 25, 30\}$
U(a, b)	$[1, 0]$
Budget	$\{40, 60, 80, 100\}$

4.2 Simulation Results

Our proposed approximation algorithm is named after **boundedGreedy selection** to indicate its bounded performance guarantee. Besides our proposed algorithm, two other algorithms are arranged to make comparison. **Naive selection**. Task publisher randomly chooses participants when participants arrive, until the total cost exceeds budget B. **PureGreedy Selection**. PureGreedy algorithm repeatedly picks participant p_i that has the maximum $\triangle C/d_i$ until the total cost exceeds budget B. It is easy to applied pureGreedy with high efficiency. PureGreedy works fine most time but it could not guarantee the worst performance. This will inevitably deteriorate coverage on urban sensing, where task publisher needs stable and balanced coverage performance. Figure 4 illustrates the comparison of three algorithms. The simulation runs 100 times and results are averaged.

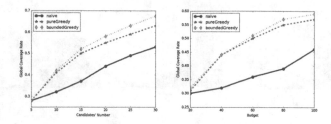

Fig. 4. Comparison of three algorithms on coverage rate. left: impact of candidates' number, budget = 100; right: impact of budget, candidates' number = 20.

Impact of Participants Number. Figure 4(left) shows *Candidates' number-Global Coverage Rate plot* under a fixed budget $B = 100$. The curves generally show that the global coverage rate increases with the candidates' number. The reason is two-fold: First, when candidates' number n is relatively small ($n \leq 20$) and budget is enough, hiring a new candidate is always feasible and beneficial to coverage rate. Second, when n is big, the budget is not enough to hire all candidates. However, more candidates could lead to more combinations of routes, making it more likely to find a combination with higher coverage rate. Moreover, this figure demonstrates that boundedGreedy outperforms naive and pureGreedy selection. It could be prudently speculated that the performance gain of boundedGreedy is also increasing with candidates' number.

Impact of Participants Budget. Figure 4(right) shows *Budget-Global Coverage Rate plot* under a fixed candidate number $N = 20$. From this facet, boundedGreedy still outperforms other two algorithms. Intuitively, increasing budget is always good so that we could hire more participants. For example, hiring with $B = 60$ gets larger global coverage rate than that when $B = 80$, and hiring with $B = 100$ gets larger coverage rate than $B = 80$. Nonetheless, this effect conforms with *diminish returns* rule that the utility gain $\triangle rate / \triangle budget$ decreases as budget increases.

5   Related Work

Crowdsensing has been a hot topic recent years. The research on this field primarily focus on economic model where each participant is only associated with a cost value and no physical scenario is further considered. Lee [9] designed and evaluated RADP incentive mechanism, where users can sell their sensing data to a service provider with a bid price. The proposed mechanism focuses on minimizing and stabilizing incentive cost while maintaining enough participants. Yang [10] and Duan [11] both proposed a platform-centric model where platform provides a reward shared by participants using Stackelberg game. To protect participants' privacy, Dimitriou [12] and Krontiris presented an auction protocol guaranteeing anonymity of bidders.

Leveraging vehicles for crowdsensing as well as data processing have gained extensive attention. Zhu [13] proposed PUS (Pervasive Urban Sensing) framework and used probe cars to sense traffic density. The authors also designed a compressive sensing algorithm to tackle sparsity of data. Yuan [14] observed that the distribution of probe vehicles is uneven over space and time. He therefore proposed an adaptive and compressive data gathering scheme based on matrix completion theory. Beside data processing, there are some works focused on optimal participants recruitment of crowdsensing. Song [15] aims to select the most appropriate participants with different budget constraints, a multi-task-oriented QoI (Quality of Information) optimization problem is discussed and converted to a nonlinear knapsack problem. Zhang [16] proposed an event-driven QoI-aware participatory sensing framework with energy and budget constraints where the main method is boundary detection. The above works discuss participants recruitment in a grid-based approach, where urban area is partitioned into small squares. The grid-based approach gives researchers convenience to model some urban sensing requirements, such as traffic flow or air quality, but remains coarse and unappeasable if applied to fine-grained sensing tasks.

The fined-grained sensing task usually associates with participants' trajectories. For example, in a HD map sensing task, participant (smart vehicle) may collect 3D environmental data along his trajectories. Hence, HD map sensing task needs an accurate trajectory model, rather than coarse grid-based motion model of potential participants. To address this problem, Zhang [17] considered the optimal quality-aware coverage in mobile crowdsensing networks, where POIs are sensed by passing-by participants. TRACCS [18] is a trajectory-aware coordinated design for urban crowdsourcing. The authors formulated crowd-task scheduling as an optimization problem and developed computationally-efficient heuristic to tackle the problem. Hamid [19] proposed an efficient recruitment scheme for vehicles in urban sensing applications. They utilized trajectories of the candidate participants, and applied a minimal-cover greedy algorithm for recruitment.

6 Conclusion

This paper has discussed route-oriented participants recruitment of collaborative crowdsensing. Task publisher collects candidates' route and selects appropriate participants to sense data along their routes. Given a limited budget, our proposed approximation algorithm could achieve larger global coverage rate than other two algorithms on real data simulation.

In the future, we will consider a more complicated and realistic scenario where participants may drop out the sensing task during task execution. This needs a more vivid model to depict both vehicle's and driver's behavior. Moreover, a remedy algorithm should be considered to reduce the influence of dropping out.

References

1. Kanhere, S.S.: Participatory sensing: crowdsourcing data from mobile smartphones in urban spaces. In: 2011 IEEE 12th International Conference on Mobile Data Management, Lulea, pp. 3–6 (2011)
2. Gwon, G.-P., et al.: Generation of a precise and efficient lane-level road map for intelligent vehicle systems. IEEE Trans. Veh. Technol. **66**(6), 4517–4533 (2017)
3. Levinson, J., et al.: Towards fully autonomous driving: systems and algorithms. In: 2011 IEEE Intelligent Vehicles Symposium (IV), Baden-Baden, pp. 163–168 (2011)
4. Krause, A., Guestrin, C.: Near-optimal observation selection using submodular functions. In: AAAI, vol. 7 (2007)
5. Khuller, S., Moss, A., Naor, J.S.: The budgeted maximum coverage problem. Inf. Process. Lett. **70**(1), 39–45 (1999)
6. http://more.datatang.com/data/45422
7. Yuan, J., et al.: T-drive: driving directions based on taxi trajectories. In: Proceedings of the 18th SIGSPATIAL International Conference on Advances in Geographic Information Systems. ACM (2010)
8. Lou, Y., et al.: Map-matching for low-sampling-rate GPS trajectories. In: Proceedings of the 17th ACM SIGSPATIAL International Conference on Advances in Geographic Information Systems. ACM (2009)
9. Lee, J.-S., Hoh, B.: Sell your experiences: a market mechanism based incentive for participatory sensing. In: 2010 IEEE International Conference on Pervasive Computing and Communications (PerCom). IEEE (2010)
10. Yang, D., et al.: Crowdsourcing to smartphones: incentive mechanism design for mobile phone sensing. In: Proceedings of the 18th Annual International Conference on Mobile Computing and Networking. ACM (2012)
11. Duan, L., Kubo, T., Sugiyama, K., Huang, J., Hasegawa, T., Walrand, J.: Motivating smartphone collaboration in data acquisition and distributed computing. IEEE Trans. Mob. Comput. **13**(10), 2320–2333 (2014)
12. Dimitriou, T., Krontiris, I.: Privacy-respecting auctions as incentive mechanisms in mobile crowd sensing. In: Akram, R.N., Jajodia, S. (eds.) WISTP 2015. LNCS, vol. 9311, pp. 20–35. Springer, Cham (2015). https://doi.org/10.1007/978-3-319-24018-3_2
13. Zhu, Y.M., Liu, X., Wang, Y., Liu, Wu, J.: Pervasive urban sensing with large-scale mobile probe vehicles. Int. J. Distrib. Sens. Netw. **57**(6), 177–182 (2013)
14. Yuan, Q., Liu, Z.H., Li, J.L., Yang, F.C.: An adaptive and compressive data gathering scheme in vehicular sensor networks. In: International Conference on Parallel and Distributed Systems IEEE, Melbourne, pp. 207–215. IEEE (2015)
15. Song, Z., Liu, C.H., Wu, J., Ma, J., Wang, W.: QoI-aware multitask-oriented dynamic participant selection with budget constraints. IEEE Trans. Veh. Technol. **63**(9), 4618–4632 (2014)
16. Zhang, B., Song, Z., Liu, C.H., Ma, J., Wang, W.D.: An event-driven QoI-aware participatory sensing framework with energy and budget constraints. ACM Trans. Intell. Syst. Technol. **6**(3), 1–19 (2015)
17. Zhang, M., et al.: Quality-aware sensing coverage in budget-constrained mobile crowdsensing networks. IEEE Trans. Veh. Technol. **65**(9), 7698–7707 (2016)

18. Chen, C., et al.: TRACCS: a framework for trajectory-aware coordinated urban crowd-sourcing. In: Second AAAI Conference on Human Computation and Crowd-sourcing (2014)
19. Hamid, S.A., Takahara, G., Hassanein, H.S.: On the recruitment of smart vehicles for urban sensing. In: 2013 IEEE Global Communications Conference (GLOBE-COM). IEEE (2013)

Management Node Selection Based on Cloud Model in a Distributed Network

Hanyi Tang[1,2(✉)], Qibo Sun[1], and Jinglin Li[1]

[1] State Key Laboratory of Networking and Switching Technology,
Beijing University of Posts and Telecommunications, Beijing, China
thyideyx@gmail.com, {qbsun, jlli}@bupt.edu.cn
[2] CETC Key Laboratory of Aerospace Information Applications, Beijing, China

Abstract. Network has become an indispensable part of people's lives. However, network insecurity still has negative impact on the development of network. Trust evaluation is becoming the core of network security enhancement. In distributed network, the node with the highest trust value is often selected as the subnet management node. The traditional distributed trust evaluation frameworks cannot achieve the best effect because of the ignorance of trust value stability of each node. To address this problem, this paper proposes a management node selection method based on cloud model. This method employs the cloud model to analyze the stability of network nodes, and selects the optimal node based on the three numerical features of cloud model. The experiment results show the effectiveness of our method.

Keywords: Trust evaluation · Network security · Cloud model

1 Introduction

With the development of network technology, distributed network is wildly used in reality. A lot of fraud problems appear for malicious node behavior. Network trust evaluation becomes a key technology in the field of network security.

In the distributed network environment, there is no centralized trust management node to calculate the trust of other nodes in the network. In traditional trust evaluation management system, the network are divided into clusters and the node with highest trust currently is selected as the trust management node. However, the behavior of nodes in a distributed environment is dynamic, and the trust of nodes changes over time. Therefore, dynamic trust evaluation node selection is an important method in a trust evaluation management system. A new trust evaluation node is selected when the trust of current trust evaluation node descends. However, the trust management node may change continually. Therefore, it is better to select a more stable node as the trust evaluation management node. We will tackle the problem by considering the node trust and stability of node trust in evaluation management node.

The paper presents a trust evaluation management node in distributed computing. Cloud model is extensively employed in this paper to solve the problem [12–14]. Firstly, backward cloud model is employed to evaluate the stability of each node. Then, an algorithm based on forward cloud model is proposed to select the trust evaluation

I. Romdhani et al. (Eds.): CollaborateCom 2017, LNICST 252, pp. 176–185, 2018.
https://doi.org/10.1007/978-3-030-00916-8_17

management node. Experiment results illustrate that our method is more accurate than other method.

The remainder of the article is organized as follows. We summarize the previous work in Sect. 2. Our management node selected method is described in detail in Sect. 3. We evaluate our method in Sect. 4. Conclusions are finally drawn in Sect. 5.

2   Related Work

The research in [3] proposes a trust evaluation model in cloud computing environment. The feedback factor and feedback density factor are introduced into the model to evaluate the trust of feedback. A trust computing model which based on experience and probabilistic statistical explanation is proposed in [4]. The concept of experience which is used to measure trust is introduced in the model. The derivation of credibility and comprehensive calculation formulation which are derived from empirical recommendations is presented. It is crude that use arithmetic mean of trust value can't prevent malicious network nodes from attacking reputation system. Based on Bayesian, a trust model which uses prior knowledge to obtain estimation parameters and posterior probabilities is proposed in [5]. However, the trust model did not consider the dynamically change of trust. Subjective trust management model based on fuzzy set theory is proposed in [6]. The concept of membership degree in fuzzy set theory is introduced to describe the fuzziness of trust.

All the above methods focus on the trust evaluation. However, for a large scale distributed network, it is unable to authorize a centralized trust management node to calculate the trust of other nodes in the network. We need to divide the network into clusters and select a trust evaluation management node for each cluster. We will address the problem in this paper.

Based on probability theory and fuzzy set theory, cloud model is proposed by [9] to qualitatively evaluate the uncertainty transformation model. Cloud model have widely used in many fields such as intelligent control, fuzzy evaluation, and evolutionary computation. In this paper, we propose a trust evaluation management node selection method based on cloud model.

3   Management Node Selection Based on Cloud Model

Our management node selection framework is shown in Fig. 1. Our management node selection method consists of three modules. Firstly, the trust value of the candidate nodes is obtained (Sect. 3.1). Secondly, the backward cloud model is extensively employed to evaluate the stability of the candidate nodes (Sect. 3.2). Finally, based on forward cloud model, a management node selection algorithm is proposed (Sect. 3.3).

3.1   Node Trust Calculation Based on Historical Behavior Data

Our paper focus on how to select the optimal management node rather than node trust evaluation. Therefore, this paper will use the trust evaluation method proposed in [10].

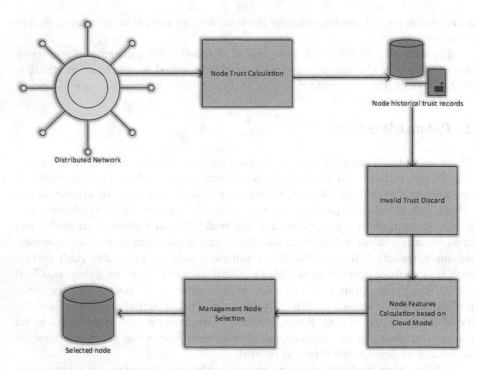

Fig. 1. Management node selection framework based on cloud model

Suppose $CN = \{cn_1, \ldots cn_i \ldots cn_{\max}\}$ denotes all the candidate nodes. Suppose that the behavior properties are $I = \{I_1, I_2, \ldots, I_m\}$. The trust value of the node of node cn_i in time t is calculated as follows:

$$NT_i^t = \sum_{p=1}^{m} w_p \times \tau_t \left(I_p(cn_i) \right) \tag{1}$$

where w_p represents the weight of behavior properties, $\tau_t \left(I_p(cn_i) \right)$ represents the value of the behavior property.

The replacement of node trust calculation method does not affect the performance of the management node selection method.

3.2   Node Stability Evaluation Based on Cloud Model

Cloud model [11] is a famous model to describe the transition between the qualitative concept and the quantitative values. Based on probability theory and fuzzy set theory, cloud model is developed with serious considering of the relation between randomness and fuzziness.

Definition 1 cloud and droplet. Suppose that U is a quantitative domain, and C is the qualitative concept of U. If quantitative value $x \in U$ and x is a stochastic implementation of the qualitative concept C, $\mu(x) \in [0, 1]$, which denotes the certainty from x to C, is a random number with a stable tendency:

$$\mu : U \rightarrow [0, 1], \forall x \in U, x \rightarrow \mu(x) \tag{2}$$

Then the distribution of X in the domain U is called cloud, which is denoted by $C(X)$. Each x in X is called a droplet.

In cloud model, the features of the droplets are expressed three numerical value of the cloud. Cloud model employs three numerical features expectation (*Ex*), entropy (*En*), and hyper-entropy (*He*) to represent the stability of a node, as $C(Ex, En, He)$. *Ex* is the expectation of the distribution of the droplets. *En* represents the uncertainty of *Ex*. *He* is used to measure the uncertainty of entropy, which is determined by the randomness and fuzziness of entropy.

In this paper, all historical trust values of a specified node cn_i comprise a trust cloud as follows:

$$TC_{cn_i}(Ex^{cn_i}, En^{cn_i}, He^{cn_i})(0 \leq Ex \leq 1, 0 \leq He \leq 1) \tag{3}$$

Each trust value NT_i^t is a droplet. *Ex* is the expectation of all historical trust values as the basic trust. *En* is the entropy of trust, which reflect the uncertainty of trust relationship. *He* is the hyper entropy of trust, which reflect the uncertainty of *En*.

This paper extensively employ the backward cloud in [11] to evaluate the stability of trust values. Because the recent historical trust is more important than the old historical trust, we add a time-aware expectation, entropy, and hyper-entropy calculation method in backward cloud generator. In time-aware expectation, entropy, and hyper-entropy calculation, weights are assigned to the historical trusts. The weight of a trust is higher when the trust evaluation time is more near to current time. In our extended backward cloud, the features of the historical trust values is calculated as follows:

(1) The average value of historical trust values and the variance of historical trust values is calculated as follows:

$$\overline{T} = \frac{1}{n} \sum_{t=t_1}^{t_n} \frac{(t - t_1)}{\sum_j (t_j - t_1)} NT_i^t \tag{4}$$

$$A = \frac{1}{n} \sum_{t=t_1}^{t_n} \frac{(t - t_1)}{\sum_j (t_j - t_1)} |NT_i^t - \overline{T}| \tag{5}$$

$$B^2 = \frac{1}{n-1} \sum_{t=t_1}^{t_n} \frac{(t - t_1)}{\sum_j (t_j - t_1)} (NT_i^t - \overline{T})^2 \tag{6}$$

(2) *Ex* is calculated as follows:

$$Ex = \overline{T} \tag{7}$$

(3) *En* is calculated as follows:

$$En = \sqrt{\frac{\pi}{2}} \times A \tag{8}$$

(4) *He* is calculated as follows:

$$He = \sqrt{B^2 - En^2} \tag{9}$$

$C(Ex, En, He)$ can be used to measure the uncertainty and stability of node trust. In the cloud model, *Ex* is the expectation of historical trust values, *En* is the uncertainty of trust, and *He* is the uncertainty of *En*. A node with smaller values of *En* and *He* is more stable in trust.

In addition, we will discard outdated historical trust values based on time window. As shown in Fig. 2, we keep a window with the size of T_w. If a trust value time is beyond the window, the trust is discarded in our method.

We will show how to select the optimal management node in the next section.

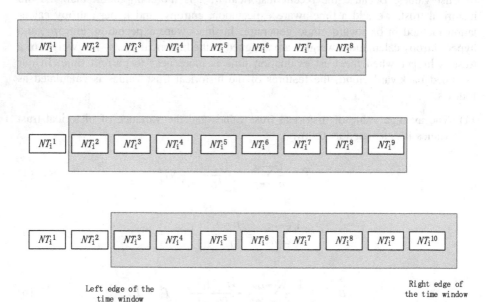

Fig. 2. Time window for invalid trust value discard

3.3   Management Node Selection

We will employ forward cloud to select the management node.

Firstly, we construct a benchmark cloud. The three features of the benchmark cloud are determined by the user, and are the largest values the user can accepted. We will select the management node by analyzing the distance between the trust cloud of candidate node and the trust benchmark cloud. This paper compares two trust cloud by the distance between the droplets. In this paper, the Euclidean distance is used to calculate the distance between two clouds.

Secondly, we use forward cloud generator to generate the normal cloud droplets of the benchmark cloud and the cloud of node cn_i. The normal cloud droplet is generated as follows:

(1) A normal random number En' with the expectation value En and the variance He is generated;
(2) A normal random number x_k with the expectation value Ex and the variance En' is generated;
(3) Calculate $y_k = e^{\frac{(x_k-Ex)^2}{2(En')^2}}$ as degree of certainty
(4) Add Drop (x_k, y_k) as a droplet for node cn_i

The cloud distance calculation algorithm based on the forward cloud is shown in Algorithm 1.

Algorithm 1: The distance calculation of cloud
Input: $TC_b(Ex, En, He)$ of Benchmark trust cloud features, $TC_{cn_i}(Ex, En, He)$ of candidate nodes, the Number of cloud droplet N.
Output: The distance between two clouds *Distance*
1)   Generate the normal cloud droplets by using forward cloud generator for the benchmark cloud $TC_b(Ex^b, En^b, He^b)$. Suppose the generated N droplets are denoted by $Drop(x_b^j, y_b^j)(1 \le j \le N)$.
2)   Generate the normal cloud droplets by using forward cloud generator for the cloud of cn_i . Suppose the generated N droplets are denoted by $Drop(x_{cn_i}^j, y_{cn_i}^j)(1 \le j \le N)$.
3)   Sort ($Drop(x_b^j, y_b^j)(1 \le j \le N)$) and $Drop(x_{cn_i}^j, y_{cn_i}^j)(1 \le j \le N)$ by x
4)   for $j = 1$ to N do
5) $dis_{bi} = dis_{bi} + \sqrt{(x_b^j - x_{cn_i}^j)^2 + (y_b^j - y_{cn_i}^j)^2}$
6)   return dis_{bi}

A smaller distance between the trust cloud of cn_i and the benchmark trust cloud means that the stability of cn_i is closer to the predefined ideal state. The higher the stability of the candidate node cn_i is, the better is it to be selected as a management node. On the contrary, a larger distance between the trust cloud of cn_i and the benchmark trust cloud indicates that the stability of the node bad and the node is excluded from the candidate nodes. We will select the node with the smallest distance as the management node.

4   Experiment and Analysis

The experiments conduct on the OMNET++ simulation software, and OMNET++ generates the historical interaction data of nodes and obtains the trusted value between nodes. We compare our dynamic trust evaluation management node selection method (DTE) with the static trust evaluation (STE) method which select the management node based on current node trust.

For visually show the sensitivity of the cloud model to the dynamic change of trust value, we illustrate the cloud model of nodes with varies behaviors. We will gradually add malicious behavior for a node with high trust. The experiment results are shown in Figs. 3, 4, 5, and 6. As shown in Figs. 3, 4, 5, and 6, the cloud model is very sensitive to the dynamic change of trust values. Cloud model will change a lot when each time to add the malicious behavior by 10% in this experiment.

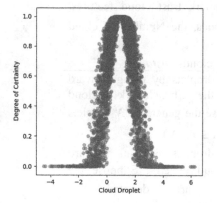 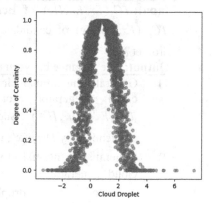

Fig. 3. Cloud drop distribution of node with high trust stability

Fig. 4. Cloud drop distribution of node with general trust stability

In order to verify the validity of the cloud distance calculation based on Euclidean distance, we set the cloud generated by non-malicious node as the benchmark cloud. Then, we generate different clouds by adding different percent of malicious behaviors to destroy the stability of the non-malicious node. We calculate the distance between the generated clouds and the benchmark cloud. The results are shown in Fig. 7.

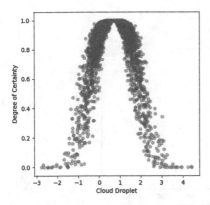

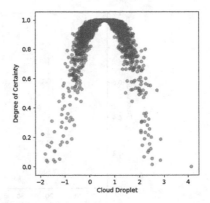

Fig. 5. Cloud drop distribution of node with low trust stability   **Fig. 6.** Cloud drop distribution of extremely unstable node

From Fig. 7, we can clearly see that the distance increases when the behavior of a node become more unstable.

In experiment 3, we evaluate DTE and STE that a fixed node is chosen as the evaluation node by comparing the two methods in management node selection. Suppose there is a none-malicious node cn_j. The methods need to select a node cn_i to evaluate the trust value of cn_j. The experiment results are shown in Fig. 8. As shown in Fig. 8, the x-axis represents the ratio of malicious nodes, and the y-axis represents the evaluation result of cn_j.

We can see clearly through Fig. 8 that the trust of cn_j drops rapidly in STE with the increase of the proportion of malicious nodes in the network. However, the trust of cn_j in DTE is relatively stable. The experiment results show the effectiveness of our proposed management node selection approach.

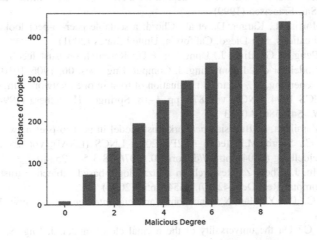

Fig. 7. Distance between benchmark cloud and trust cloud with different stability

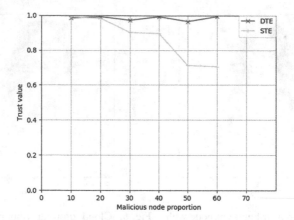

Fig. 8. Experiment results of STE and DTE

5 Conclusion

We propose a trust evaluation management node selection method in this paper. The core idea of the proposed method is to analyze the stability of nodes based on the historical behavior data and cloud model. The experiment results in simulated network illustrate the effectiveness of our method.

Acknowledgment. The work is supported by NSFC (61571066), and CETC key laboratory of aerospace information applications open project fund.

References

1. Foster, I., Kesselman, C.: The Grid: Blueprint for a New Computing Infrastructure. Morgan Kaufmann, San Francisco (1999)
2. Stoica, I., Morris, R., Karger, D., et al.: Chord: a scalable peer-to-peer lookup service for internet applications. San Diego, California, United States (2001)
3. Wang, Y., Peng, X.G., Bian, J., Dong-Lai, F.U.: Research on trust feedbacks credibility evaluation model for cloud computing. J. Comput. Eng. Des. **06**, 1906–1910 (2014)
4. Beth, T., Borcherding, M., Klein, B.: Valuation of trust in open networks. In: Gollmann, D. (ed.) ESORICS 1994. LNCS, vol. 875, pp. 1–18. Springer, Heidelberg (1994). https://doi.org/10.1007/3-540-58618-0_53
5. Wang, Y., Vassileva, J.: Bayesian network trust model in peer-to-peer networks. In: Moro, G., Sartori, C., Singh, M.P. (eds.) AP2PC 2003. LNCS (LNAI), vol. 2872, pp. 23–34. Springer, Heidelberg (2004). https://doi.org/10.1007/978-3-540-25840-7_3
6. Tang, W., Hu, J., Chen, Z.: Research on a fuzzy logic-based subjective trust management model. J. Comput. Res. Dev. **42**(10), 1654–1659 (2005)
7. Li, D., Liu, C., Du, Y., Han, X.: Uncertainty artificial intelligence. J. Softw. **15**(11), 1583–1594 (2004)
8. Li, D., Liu, C.: On the universality of the normal cloud model. J. Eng. Sci. **6**(8), 28–34 (2004)

9. Li, D.: Uncertainty Artificial Intelligence. National Defend Industry Press, Beijing (2005)
10. Yang, G., Sun, Q., Zhou, A., Li, J., Yuan, X., Tang, H.: A context-aware trust prediction method based on behavioral data analysis in distributed network environments. In: IEEE, International Conference on Dependable, Autonomic and Secure Computing, International Conference on Pervasive Intelligence and Computing, International Conference on Big Data Intelligence and Computing and Cyber Science and Technology Congress, pp. 674–680. IEEE Press (2016)
11. Yuan, L., He, Z., Zeng, G.: A resource trade model based on trust evaluation for grid computing. In: Network and Parallel Computing Workshops, 2007. NPC Workshops. IFIP International Conference, pp. 506–510. IEEE Press (2007)
12. Chen, J.J., Zhang, S.B.: Study on trust evaluation model based on cloud model and trust chain. Appl. Res. Comput. **32**, 249–253 (2015)
13. Zhang, T., Yan, L., Yang, Y.: Trust evaluation method for clustered wireless sensor networks based on cloud model. Wirel. Netw. 1–21 (2016)
14. Ayadi, O., Halouani, N., Masmoudi, F.: A fuzzy collaborative assessment methodology for partner trust evaluation. Int. J. Intell. Syst. **31**(5), 488–501 (2016)

CNTE: A Node Centrality-Based Network Trust Evaluation Method

Xiang Yuan[1,2(✉)], Qibo Sun[1], and Jinglin Li[1]

[1] State Key Laboratory of Networking and Switching Technology,
Beijing University of Posts and Telecommunications, Beijing, China
{yuanxiangsky, qbsun, jlli}@bupt.edu.cn
[2] CETC-Key-Laboratory-of-Aerospace Information Applications,
Beijing, China

Abstract. Network trust evaluation is an important mechanism in improving network security. Network trust is determined by the node trust and the topology of the network. To improve the evaluation accuracy and efficiency, we propose a node centrality-based network trust evaluation method. Firstly, the node trust is calculated by employing the node behavior analysis. Secondly, node centrality in the network is calculated based on coefficient variation. Finally, the network trust is calculated based on the above-mentioned steps. Experiment results show that our proposed method can improve the evaluation accuracy.

Keywords: Network trust · Trust evaluation · Node behavior
Node centrality

1 Introduction

The scale of network is now growing continuously. On the one hand, because of the complexity of the network, the network confronts various internal security threats. On the other hand, due to the improper operation of the users, the malicious attacks from hackers expose the network to serious external security threats. However, the traditional identity-based network security mechanism is unable to solve this problem effectively. Therefore, network trust evaluation based on the node behavior has attracted the attentions from the researchers [1].

The traditional trust model evaluates the trust of the network node by constructing the trust relationship among the entities of the network and quantifying the interactive information between the network nodes. There is a trust relationship between people in sociology, and the trust of each of them will affect the trust of the groups of these people. Compared to groups in social relations, where the trust of each node constituting the subnet is known, the trust value of the entire subnet can be evaluated and quantified. When the information in the network needs to go through a subnet, we can assess the trust value of the network to determine whether the information is transmitted through this network. The ambiguity of trust relationships and the uncertainty of node behaviors are the greatest challenge of current trust evaluation research. At present, the researchers put forward a variety of evaluation models [3–12], including the Bayesian theory-based model, Fuzzy set theory-based model, DS evidence

© ICST Institute for Computer Sciences, Social Informatics and Telecommunications Engineering 2018
I. Romdhani et al. (Eds.): CollaborateCom 2017, LNICST 252, pp. 186–196, 2018.
https://doi.org/10.1007/978-3-030-00916-8_18

theory-based model and so on. These models can effectively promote the development of network trust evaluation and improve the network security. However, the existing model also has some of the following problems:

(1) Most of the trust evaluation methods focus on the node trust evaluation, and the solution for the trust evaluation of the entire network is lacking.
(2) The existing network trust evaluation methods that combine the node trust based on average trust of all node do not consider the characteristics of the entities in the network and the location of the entity itself.

To solve the above problems, a trust evaluation method based on node centrality is proposed on the basis of previous ideas. The proposed method makes the trust evaluation objective and fair by taking into account the topological position of the network nodes. The experiment results show the effectiveness of our method.

The remainder of the article is organized as follows. The Sect. 2 gives a brief review of related work. Section 3 gives definitions of relevant problems. In Sect. 4, the experiment results are given. Section 5 gives a summary of the article.

2 Related Work

Trust evaluation is the key technology to support the construction of network trust system. Many scholars and experts have studied the evaluation of trust. As early as 1996, Blaze [1] and others put forward the concept of trust management in order to solve the problem of service security in Internet. Trust is considered as an important information that helps the user to make a judgment about a network entity or a network. Then, the Chinese scholar Lin Chuang et al. [2] put forward the concept of trusted network. The basic properties of trusted network and the problems to be solved are discussed.

In recent years, many scholars try to quantify the dynamic trust relationships in the network. In the paper [3], a Bayesian network-based approach is proposed to compute the trust value of network entities. The method considers the impact of authentication and network interaction behavior on trusted metrics. Time window and time factor are introduced to improve the timeliness and dynamic adaptability of the model. The method in paper [4] is proposed based on fuzzy decision analysis. Multiple user behaviors evidence is considered, and ordered binary comparison theory is employed to get the optimal weights. A trust evaluation method based on cloud model is proposed in paper [8]. By introducing penalty mechanism and attenuation function, the method can make up the deficiency of dynamic change of cloud model in pervasive trust environment. The method based on cloud model takes full account of the diversity and uncertainty of trust objects, and the results are more accurate than traditional methods.

These trust evaluation models focus on the trust evaluation of a single network entity, but there is not much discussion about the relationship between entities and the overall topology of the network. We will address the problem in this paper (Fig. 1).

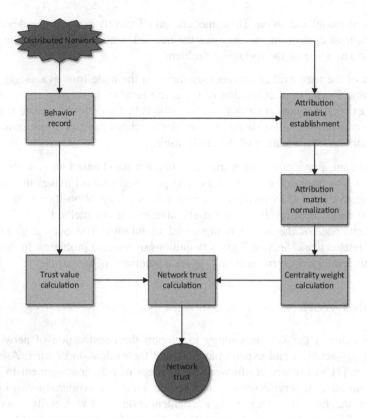

Fig. 1. Framework of network trust evaluation method

3 Proposed Network Trust Evaluation Method

3.1 Node Trust Calculation

Let $v_1, v_2, v_3, \ldots v_n$ represent network entities (nodes or resources) in a network, $\alpha_1, \alpha_2, \alpha_3, \ldots \alpha_n$ represent the trust values of corresponding node in the network. The network trust is determined by the trust of all nodes in the network. Therefore, we firstly need calculate node trust. In this paper, we focus on network trust calculation. For the generality of the scheme, the node trust calculation method is replaceable, and the effectiveness of our method is not influenced. Therefore, this paper employs the method in [15] to calculate the node trust value.

3.2 Attribution Matrix Establishment

The contribution of different node to network trust varies. We employ centrality to evaluate the different contribution. In order to guarantee the completeness, we select two global centrality attributes and two local centrality attributes to evaluate the node centrality. These four centrality attributes are closeness centrality, betweenness centrality, semi centrality, and interaction centrality. The closeness centrality describes the average minimum distance of a node to other nodes. The betweenness centrality describes the number of shortest paths through the node. These two properties reflect the global centrality of the node. The semi local centrality reflects the number of the first and the second nearest neighbors in the network. The more number of neighbors of a node, the greater the influence of the node is. The interaction centrality reflects the interaction times of the network nodes. These two properties reflect the local centrality of the node. The proximity centrality, betweenness centrality, and semi local centrality are defined in the paper [14]. The interaction centrality is defined as follows.

Definition 1 Interaction centrality. Entities in the network interact with each other to transfer data. Interaction centrality is defined as follows:

$$C = C_t + \sum_k C_k d(k) \tag{1}$$

Because the node interaction is a continuous process, the attenuation factor δ is introduced. δ is a time decay function. The closer the interaction time to the current time is, the more important the interaction is to the evaluation. The attenuation function is defined as follows:

$$\delta(k) = \frac{k}{t-1} \tag{2}$$

where k is the timestamp, and the $t-1$ is the longest time interval considered in the current system.

Definition 2 Semi centrality. For a node n_i, the $Nei(n_i)$ is defined as the number of all neighbors that can be reached within 2 steps from the n_i, and then we defined

$$Q(n_j) = \sum_{n_i \in p(n_j)} Nei(n_i) \tag{3}$$

where $n_i \in p(n_j)$ represents the set of the number of all neighbors that can be reached within 1 step from n_j. Thus, the semi centrality of the node n_i can be obtained

$$semi(n_i) = \sum_{w \in P(i)} Q(w) \tag{4}$$

The semi local centrality reflects the number of the first and two order neighbors of the corresponding node in the network. The more number of neighbors of a node is, represents the greater the influence of the node is.

Definition 3 Closeness centrality. We defined d_{ij} as the length of the shortest path between the node n_i and the node n_j. Then the average length of the shortest path from a node to other nodes is:

$$d_i = \frac{1}{n-1} \sum_{i \neq j} d_{ij} \tag{5}$$

A smaller d_i denotes that n_i is closer to other nodes in the network. The closeness centrality is defined as:

$$Closeness(n_i) = \frac{1}{d_i} = \frac{n-1}{\sum_{i \neq j} d_{ij}} \tag{6}$$

Definition 4 Betweenness centrality. Betweenness centrality is defined as the percent of shortest path that pass through n_i. The betweenness centrality is defined as

$$Betweenness(n_i) = \sum_{i \neq s, i \neq d, s \neq d} \frac{sp^i_{s,d}}{sps, d} \tag{7}$$

where sp_{sd} is the number of the shortest path from the source node n_s to the destination node n_d, and sp^i_{sd} is the number of the shortest path passing through ni from the source node n_s to the destination node n_d.

Suppose the number of centrality indicator is n. Then the centrality vector of the i-th node is $X_i = [x_{i1}, x_{i2}, \ldots \ldots, x_{in}]$. Where $x_{i1}, x_{i2}, \ldots x_{in}$ is the centrality indicator of the i-th node. Now we construct a matrix for node centrality evaluation. The centrality evaluation matrix of the network is as follows:

$$X = \begin{Bmatrix} x_{11} & x_{12} & \cdots & x_{1n} \\ x_{21} & x_{22} & \cdots & x_{2n} \\ \vdots & \vdots & \ddots & \cdots \\ x_{m1} & x_{m2} & \cdots & x_{mn} \end{Bmatrix} \tag{8}$$

where $x_{11}, x_{21} \ldots x_{n1}$ is the centrality vector of the first node, and there are m network nodes. In this paper, four centrality indicators are used to evaluate the node centrality. Among them, x_{i1} represents the semi centrality indicator of the i-th node, and x_{i2} represents the closeness centrality indicator of the i-th node; x_{i3} represents the betweenness centrality indicator of the i-th node, and x_{i4} represents the Interaction centrality indicator of the i-th node. The evaluation indicator vector of ith node is $X_i = [x_{i1}, x_{i2}, x_{i3}, x_{i4}]$.

3.3   Attribution Matrix Normalization

As for the centrality indicator in the matrix, the dimensions of the centrality indicators are different. Therefore, it is necessary to normalize the centrality evaluation matrix so that the dimensions of the centrality indicators are in the same level. The maximum-minimum method is used to normalize the data. The maximum-minimum method is as follows:

$$x_{ij} = \frac{x_{ij} - \{\min(x_{1j}, x_{2j}, \ldots, x_{mj})\}}{\{\max(x_{1j}, x_{2j}, \ldots, x_{mj})\} - \{\min(x_{1j}, x_{2j}, \ldots, x_{mj})\}} \tag{9}$$

3.4 Centrality Weight Calculation

We employ the coefficient variation method, which is an objective method, to calculate the weight of the centrality indicator. Firstly, the mean and variance are calculated by the following:

$$\overline{x}_i = \frac{1}{n} \sum_{j=1}^{j=m} x_{ji}, i = 1, 2 \ldots n \tag{10}$$

$$s_i = \frac{1}{n} \sqrt{\sum_{j=1}^{j=m} (x_{ji} - \overline{x}_i)^2}, i = 1, 2 \ldots n \tag{11}$$

Based on the mean and variance, the coefficient variation of each centrality indicator can be calculated by the following:

$$CV(i) = \frac{\overline{x}_i}{s_i}, i = 1, 2 .. n \tag{12}$$

After getting the coefficient variation of each centrality indicator, the centrality weight χ_i of each centrality indicator is calculated by the following:

$$\chi_i = \frac{CV(i)}{\sum_{k=1}^{n} CV(k)}, i = 1, 2 \ldots n \tag{13}$$

In this method, n equal to 4, which represents that there are 4 centrality indicators.

Node centrality calculation comprehensively consider the node position in the network, and current node statement. Based on the weight of the centrality indicator, the centrality of each node is calculated as follows:

$$p(i) = \sum_{j=1}^{j=n} x_{ij} * \chi_j = 1, 2 \ldots m \tag{14}$$

3.5   Network Trust Evaluation

Based on the node centrality, we now calculate the contribution weight of each node to the network trust. A node with higher node centrality contributes more to network trust. Therefore, the contribution weight of each node to the network trust is calculated as follows:

$$\varpi_i = \frac{p(i)}{\sum\limits_{k=1}^{k=m} P(k)}, i = 1, 2 \ldots m \tag{15}$$

Suppose $v_1, v_2, v_3, \ldots v_n$ is the nodes in the network. The overall network trust is calculated as follows:

$$\Gamma(v_1 \ldots v_n) = \sum_{i=1}^{N} \omega_i \alpha_i \tag{16}$$

4   Experiment and Analysis

We experiment on a discrete event simulation platform named OMNET++, which is an open source and multi-protocol network simulation software. It can simulate all kinds of network environment effectively. We experiment on two networks: (1) start network. Star network topology is shown in Fig. 2. (2) BUPT campus network. The BUPT campus network topology is shown in Fig. 3. For the two networks, the interaction between nodes is simulated and the interaction records between nodes are recorded. In the experiment, we compare CNTE (node centrality-based network trust evaluation method) with MBEM (mean-based evaluation method, the network trust is the average of the node trust).

The first experiment is conducted on the start network. Firstly, we want to see how the two methods act when the behavior of a central node changes. Therefore, we increase the number of successful interactions of node 1. The experiment results are shown in Fig. 4. Secondly, we want to see how the two methods act when the behavior of a non-central node changes. Therefore, we increase the number of successful interactions of node 2. The experimental results are shown in Fig. 5. As can be seen in Figs. 4 and 5, the accuracy of our method is higher than the compared method.

The second experiment is conducted on the BUPT campus network. Firstly, how the two methods act when the behavior of a central node changes is evaluated. We increase the number of successful interactions of node 1. The experiment result is shown in Fig. 6. Secondly, how the two methods act when the behavior of a non-central node changes is evaluated. We increase the number of successful interactions of node 31. The experimental results are shown in Fig. 7. Experiment results show that the network trust ascends quickly when the trust of a core node increases. Otherwise, the network trust changes slowly. Therefore, our approach has a good response to the impact of different network nodes on the overall network trust.

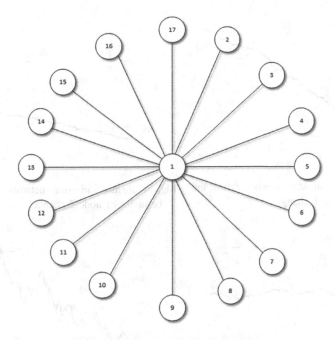

Fig. 2. Star network topology

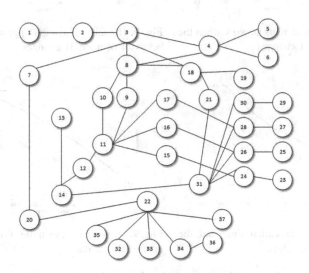

Fig. 3. BUPT campus network topology

In the experiment, the relationship between the performance of the algorithm and the network complexity is discussed. The network topology is abstracted as a graph, and the network complexity is described by the number of nodes N and the number of edges M in the network. In Fig. 8, the relationship between the efficiency of the

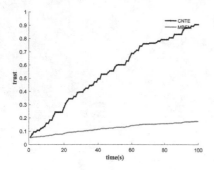

Fig. 4. Results in star network when the behavior of node 1 changes

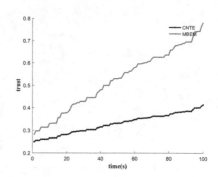

Fig. 5. Results in star network when the behavior of node 2 changes

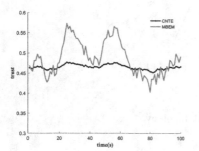

Fig. 6. Results in campus network when the behavior of node 1 changes

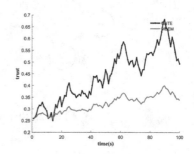

Fig. 7. Results in campus network when the behavior of node 31 changes

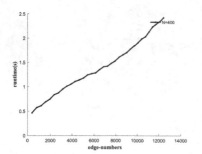

Fig. 8. Algorithm execution time and the number of different edges

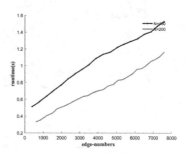

Fig. 9. Algorithm execution time under two quantitative nodes

algorithm and the edges of the network is given when N = 400 is used. With the increase of the number of edges, the execution time of the algorithm is increasing. Figure 9 compares the execution time in the N = 300 and N = 500 networks as the M continues to increase. From the experiment, we can see that the execution efficiency of the algorithm is less than 1 s in N < 400 and M < 4000. The experiment show that the execution time of the algorithm increases with the complexity of the network, but the algorithm has higher efficiency when the network size is small.

5 Conclusions and Future Work

In this paper, we propose a method of network trusted evaluation based on network centricity. This method is used to evaluate the trust value of subnets composed of network nodes. This approach solves the problem of evaluation of the entire subnet trust. The network trust is calculated based on the node trust and the network topology. Firstly, we calculate the trust value of each node in the network based on the node behavior. Then, based on the network topology, the node centrality is calculated by using the coefficient variation. Finally, based on the node centrality, our method combines the node trust to calculate the network trust. Experiments show that the proposed method has high performance and availability. The method has good performance in the case of small network size, but it is also worth optimizing for large networks.

Acknowledgment. The work is supported by NSFC (61571066), and CETC key laboratory of aerospace information applications open project fund.

References

1. Blaze, M., Feigenbaum, J., Lacy, J.: Decentralized trust management. IEEE Computer Society, p. 164 (1996)
2. Lin, C., Peng, X.: Research on trustworthy network. Proc. Chin. Soc. Comput. **28**(5), 751–758 (2005)
3. Liang, H., Wu, W.: Research on credible measurement model based on dynamic Bayesian networks. J. Commun. **9**, 68–76 (2013)
4. Melaye, D., Demazeau, Y.: Bayesian dynamic trust model. In: Pěchouček, M., Petta, P., Varga, L.Z. (eds.) CEEMAS 2005. LNCS (LNAI), vol. 3690, pp. 480–489. Springer, Heidelberg (2005). https://doi.org/10.1007/11559221_48
5. Gao, Y., Liu, W.: BeTrust: a dynamic trust model based on bayesian inference and Tsallis entropy for medical sensor networks. J. Sensors **2**, 1–10 (2014)
6. Liang, H.Q., Wu, W.: Research of trust evaluation model based on dynamic Bayesian network. J. Commun. **34**(9), 68–76 (2013)
7. Sun, Q.: Research on P2P network reputation model based on cloud model and trusted recommendation source. University of Science & Technology China (2010)
8. Wang, J., Yang, J., Yang, W., et al.: Research on trust mechanism based on cloud model in P2P networks. Comput. Eng. **40**(5), 124–128 (2014)
9. Ren, K., Li, T., Wan, Z., et al.: Highly reliable trust establishment scheme in ad hoc networks. Comput. Netw. Int. J. Comput. Telecommun. Netw. **45**(6), 687–699 (2004)
10. Ma, J., Zhao, Z., Ye, X.: Evaluation of user behavior in trustworthy networks based on fuzzy decision analysis. Comput. Eng. **37**(13), 125–127 (2011)
11. Feng, R., Xu, X., Zhou, X., et al.: A trust evaluation algorithm for wireless sensor networks based on node behaviors and D-S evidence theory. Sensors **11**(2), 1345–1360 (2011)
12. Ganeriwal, S., Srivastava, M.B.: Reputation-based framework for high integrity sensor networks. In: DBLP, pp. 66–77 (2004)

13. Ahmed, A., Bakar, K.A., Channa, M.I., et al.: A survey on trust based detection and isolation of malicious nodes in ad-hoc and sensor networks. Front. Comput. Sci. **9**(2), 280–296 (2015)
14. Ren, X., Linyuan, L.: A survey of network important node ranking methods. Sci. Bull. **13**, 1175–1197 (2014)
15. Lu, X.: Research on trust evaluation model of mobile ad hoc networks. Anhui University (2014)

Minimum Cost Load Migration
in Distributed Software Defined Networks

Kuangyu Qin[1,2], Chuanhe Huang[1,2(✉)], N. Ganesan[3], and Kewei Liu[1,2]

[1] Computer School of Wuhan University, Wuhan, China
huangch@whu.edu.cn
[2] Collaborative Innovation Center of Geospatial Technology, Wuhan, China
[3] Regional Institute of Co-operative Management, Bangalore, India

Abstract. Software defined networking is a network paradigm which separates the control plane and the data plane. In a large SDN network, multiple controllers are used for handling switches' requests. Because of the unbalanced requests, sometimes some controllers get overloaded. If switch's management can be shifted from the overloaded controller to idle controllers, network performance can be improved. But shifting the switches will bring cost to the system. In this paper, the isolation nodes problem is studied. A minimum cost load migration approach and a heuristic migration algorithm are proposed. The proposed load migration approach can avoid the isolation nodes. The simulation results show that the proposed approach enhances the system performance.

Keywords: SDN · Load migration · Isolation nodes

1 Introduction

Compare to traditional network, the software defined networking (SDN) has the advantage of flexibility, scalability and virtualization [1]. In SDN, for every new flow, the switches request the controller according to the openflow [2] protocol. If the size of the network is large enough, single controller is not sufficient for dealing with the requests from all switches. Although topology shared controllers cluster can manage larger size network than single controller, but when the network size is keep increasing, distributed multiple controller SDN gets better performance. In distributed multiple controllers environment, sometimes a controller gets overloaded, while other controllers do not get fully used. If the system supports the mechanism to migrate the load from the overload controller to the underload controllers, the network performance can be improved.

Researchers have proposed approaches about how to balance the loads between controllers. Those solutions are mostly based on game theory. There is little research or no research considers the isolation nodes problem in SDN load migration. The isolation nodes will cause extra overhead when switches request the controllers. On the other hand, the load of the controller is changing frequently. A very balanced load situation in this moment is not so necessary.

© ICST Institute for Computer Sciences, Social Informatics and Telecommunications Engineering 2018
I. Romdhani et al. (Eds.): CollaborateCom 2017, LNICST 252, pp. 197–207, 2018.
https://doi.org/10.1007/978-3-030-00916-8_19

Consider switches migration will cause topology change and the communication will be affected until routing system gets convergence. The cost of the migration is non-negligible. Thus a migration approach which has lower cost is more useful.

In this paper, we studied the isolation nodes problem and proposed a connected load migration approach which can decrease the controller's load to the safe level with the minimal cost.

2   Related Work

For solving the problem that maps switches to their master controller, the authors of [3] designed the elastic distributed control system ElasticCon and proposed a switch migration protocol. A load balancing algorithm based on lowest utilization policy is proposed in [4]. The literature [5] proposed a lightweight collaborative mechanism for SDN controllers. An architecture which includes super controller and regular controller is proposed in [6]. The network is arranged as clusters. The super controller sends the state vectors to regular controllers and implements the load allocation. The authors of [7] proposed the DALB. The overloaded controller will collect the information of other controllers temporary, it has the low time efficiency. To solve this problem, the literature [8] proposed a load notification mechanism. In the approach, every controller notifies its load to other controllers in regular intervals. The authors of [9] proposed a dynamically switches adjusting approach. The approach adjusts the number of activated controllers and sleeping controllers according to the real time flow situation. The authors used the greedy knapsack and simulated annealing to solve the problem. The literature [10] described a multiple controller hibernation model. The authors proposed a genetic algorithm to get the optimal solution. A pareto-based optimal controller placement approach is narrated in [11]. The authors considered the performance, fault tolerance and load balancing and also proposed a policy for switches migration when fault happened. The authors of [12] proposed the approach for maximum resource utilization on the constraints of processor, bandwidth and memory. By using the non-cooperative game theory, they proposed the switches migration algorithm to maximum the benefits of players. The authors of [13] modeled the dynamic controller allocation for the stable matching problem. With the game theory, they also proposed a layered two phase algorithm to get the Nash equilibrium solution.

3   System Framework and Problem Formulation

3.1   System Framework

The system architecture is shown as Fig. 1. The bottom part is the data accessing and forwarding layer. The middle part is the control layer. The controller receives the requests from the switches and sends the flow table item information back. To implement the load migration among controllers, the system has a service module which known as Load Migration Service (LMS). The LMS is on the top level of the SDN.

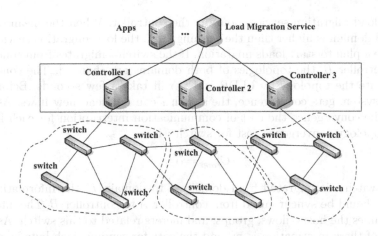

Fig. 1. The system view of the load migration for SDN

3.2 Problem Formulation

We define the network as a graph $G = (V, E)$. The V is the set of switches and the E is the set of links. Each link has latency. The network has k domains. Each domain has a controller to manage its switches. The set of controllers is denoted as $CV = \{c_1, c_2, ..., c_k\}$. Assume the controller $c1$ is the overloaded controller. The set of switches set in each domain is denoted as $S = \{s_1, s_2, ..., s_k\}$ where s_j is the switches set managed by the controller j. Let $S' = \{s_1', s_2', ..., s_k'\}$ be the switches set after migration, where s_j' is the switches set in new domain j. When switches send requests to controller, the controller can be modeled as an M/M/1 queuing model. Suppose packets arrive according to a Poisson process and the processing times of the packets are independent. Let λ_j denotes the total arrival rate of requests at the controller j, the f_i denotes the requests from switch i. Then λ_j can be calculated as follows

$$\lambda_j = \sum_{i \in S_j} f_i \tag{1}$$

Let controller's processing capacity as u. According to the queuing theory, the expected mean service time τ_j of controller j can be calculated as follows:

$$\tau_j = \frac{1}{u_j - \lambda_j} \tag{2}$$

Let p_{ij} denote the path from switch i to controller j. The latency of the path is the sum of latency for each link on this path. For each switch i, the response time includes the round trip latency for the path to controller and the processing time for the request. It can be denoted as

$$t_{ij} = 2d_{ij} + \tau_j, \; d_{ij} = \sum_{e \in p_{ij}} d_e \tag{3}$$

The load migration service monitors the controller. When the mean service time of a domain is higher than the warning level, the load migration service will calculate a plan to start loads migration. If the switch i migrates from controller A to controller B, the topologies of both domains are changed. The controller will update the topology by LLDP and it will take a few seconds. Before the routing system gets convergence, the switch i can not send new flows. Assume during the convergence the cost of communication interruption for each flow is α, the topology convergence cost for switch i is

$$C_{topo}^{i} = \alpha f_i \tag{4}$$

As the switch i is migrated from domain A to domain B, the information for switch i should be synchronized from controller A to controller B. The information includes the hosts, flows, groups, and meters related to this switch. Assume the size of these information is m_i and the cost for sending each byte is β. The cost of the synchronization is

$$C_{syn}^{i} = \beta m_i \tag{5}$$

The cost for migrating switch i is

$$C_i = C_{topo}^{i} + C_{syn}^{i} = \alpha f_i + \beta m_i \tag{6}$$

If a controller is overloaded, migrate many switches at once is easy to cause congestion. A better way to reduce the side effects is migrating switches one by one. As previous definition, the s_1 is the original switch set and the s_1' is the switch set after migration. The switches which need to be migrated is

$$q = s_1 - s_1' \tag{7}$$

The total cost for migration is

$$C = \sum_{i \in q} C_i \tag{8}$$

The goal of the approach is to find a minimum cost migration plan that after migration the mean service time for each domain will be lower than the safe value t_s.

$$\min \sum_{i \in q} C_i$$
$$s.t. \ \tau_j < t_s, j = 1, .., k \tag{9}$$

3.3   The Isolation Nodes Problem

The isolation nodes problem must be avoided during the load migration. The isolation nodes problem is the phenomenon that a domain is divided to two isolated parts because some key nodes in it are migrated to other domain. One example of the isolation nodes problem is shown as Fig. 2.

In the Fig. 2 there are two control domains managed by controller 1 and controller 2. In the Fig. 2(a) the load of control 2 is high. The migration plan decides to migrate the switch A from domain 2 to domain 1 in order to decrease the load of control 2. But this causes the isolation nodes problem. In the Fig. 2(b), The switch B can not connect to other domain 2's switches directly because the switch A is the key switch connects switch B. Assume that the host H1 needs to communicate with the host H2. Before migration, once the switch B requests the controller 2, the controller 2 will issue the flow rules for all switches along the path. But after migration, not only switch B needs to request the controller 2 for its flow table item, but also the switch A needs to request controller 1. It will cause burden to both controllers. Hence the performance decreases.

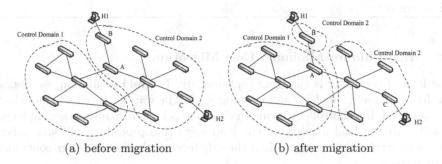

(a) before migration   (b) after migration

Fig. 2. The migration causes the isolation nodes.

If we decide to migrate switch A, the switch B should follow. The switch B is the migration dependent set of switch A. The migration algorithm needs to calculate the migration dependent set for each switch. If a switch is migrated, the switches in its migration dependent set need also be migrated.

4   Algorithm Designing

4.1   Algorithm for Calculating the Migration Dependent Set

For every node, we can identify a migration dependent set. If no other nodes depend on this node, the node's migration dependent set is empty. The main idea of the algorithm is dyeing to neighbors. The start node is the controller. The dyeing range is in the same domain. A queue is used in the algorithm. When there is no new nodes added to the queue, the algorithm ends. The detail of the algorithm is shown as Algorithm 1.

In the algorithm, each node enters the queue at most once. If the maximum degree of the graph is k, the time complexity of this algorithm is $O(kn)$.

Algorithm 1. Migration dependent set calculating algorithm

Input: graph G, the switch set S, node v to be migrated, controller $c1$

Output: migration dependent set H

1: $Q \leftarrow \phi$, $G' \leftarrow subGraph(G, S[1])$
2: all nodes colors in G' ← black
3: v 's color ← gray, $c1$'s color ← white
4: $addQueue(Q, c1)$
5: while $Q \neq \phi$
6:      $u \leftarrow outQueue(Q)$, $N \leftarrow getNeighbors(G', u)$
7:      for each node i in N
8:          if $getColor(i) ==$ black then $setColor(i,$ white$)$; $addQueue(Q, i)$
9: end while
10: $H \leftarrow$ remaining black nodes
11: return H

4.2 Algorithm for Minimum Cost Migration

The load of controller is changing continuously. To avoid oscillation, we define two levels, namely, safe level and warning level. The warning level is higher than the safe level. If a controller's mean service time is higher than the warning level, it will start the load migration. The load migration procedure will stop when the mean service time is lower than the safe level or there is no other controller to migrate.

Our algorithm uses a heuristic method to get the minimum cost solution. The migration includes many steps. In each step, there is only one switch gets migrated. Before we migrate each switch, the switch's migration dependent set is calculated. The switch and its migration dependent set will be considered as one big switch. Once a switch is migrated, a new switches-controller's mapping state is obtained. The algorithm constructs a states graph to trace the state transformation. For every new state there is a pointer indicates its old state. When a new state satisfies the goal, the reverse path from goal state to the initial state is a candidate plan. To get the minimum cost plan, we divide the cost of migration into two parts. One part is associated with the cost has been spent in current step. Another part is the cost to be spent for getting the goal. Let x denote a state. Define $f(x)$ as the total cost for the goal where x will be passed by. The $g(x)$ denotes the cost that has spent from initial state to current state x. The future cost need to spend is denoted by $h(x)$. Hence the cost $f(x)$ and the minimum cost $f^*(x)$ can be denoted as follow

$$f(x) = g(x) + h(x), \ f^*(x) = g^*(x) + h^*(x) \tag{10}$$

Because the future cost can not be measured, the heuristic function $h(x)$ is constructed to estimate the optimistic cost for the future steps. Assume that for a particular state x, the f_{min} is the new flows rate on switch which has the smallest new flows rate in remaining switches, f_{max} is the new flows rate for the switch which has the biggest new flows rate and m_{min} is the information size for the switch which has the least information. If we migrates each switch, the load of controller will decrease f_{max}, we can calculate the value n that migrate at most n switches from current state the controller will achieve the safe level. We use these parameters to estimate the optimistic future cost. The optimistic $h(x)$ can be expressed as

$$h(x) = n(\alpha f_{min} + \beta m_{min}) \tag{11}$$

It is easy to see that the optimistic function $h(x)$ is no more than the real minimum future cost function $h^*(x)$.

$$h(x) \leq h^*(x) \tag{12}$$

In the algorithm we use the queue $OPEN$ and $CLOSED$ to record the visited states. Searching starts from the initial state is. The function $calcTime$ calculates the mean service time for the state x. The function $getNeighborStates$ finds the neighbor states of x. It moves one border switch from current state and calculates the switch's migration dependent set. If the migration dependent set is not empty, the switches and its dependent set will be seen as one big switch and moved together. The move of the switch is towards the neighbor domain which has least service time. If the move causes the distance from switch to controller greater than the threshold, this move must be abandoned.

Let the initial state is s and the set of goal state candidates is denoted by Γ. Let $r \in \Gamma$. Let P_{i-j} stand for the set of all paths from state i to state j. And let $P_{i-\Gamma}$ denote the set of paths going from state i to the set Γ. The $p_{i-r} \in P_{i-\Gamma}$ stands for any path from i to r. The set of cheapest paths from i to j is denoted

---

Algorithm 2. Minimum cost migration algorithm (MCMA)

Input: graph G, the set of switch set S, safe level ts, controller position $c1$
Output: migration plan P
1: $is \leftarrow S$, $OPEN \leftarrow \{is\}$, $CLOSED \leftarrow \{\}$
2: generate the state graph $SG \leftarrow \{is\}$
3: while true
4:      $x \leftarrow out\_queue(OPEN)$, $CLOSED \leftarrow CLOSED + \{x\}$
5:      if $calcTime(x) \leq t_s$ then out while
6:      $NS \leftarrow getNeighborStates(G, x, c1)$
7:      for each y in NS do
8:          calculate $f(y) \leftarrow g(y) + h(y)$
9:          If y is a new state, then
10:             add y into SG, let y point to x, append y into $OPEN$
11:         else if $newf(y) < oldf(y)$ then
12:             update y point to x, if y in $CLOSED$ then move y to $OPEN$
13:         sort $OPEN$ by their f values
14: end while
15: $RP \leftarrow$ the path from x to is
16: $P \leftarrow$ reverse the RP
17: return P

---

by P^*_{i-j}. Let the C^* stands for the cheapest cost of paths from s to Γ and let the Γ^* stand for the set of optimal goals.

Lemma 1. *At any time before the MCMA terminates, there exists an OPEN state x' on p^*_{s-r} with $f(x') \leq C^*$*

Proof. Consider any optimal path $p^*_{s-r} \in P^*_{s-\Gamma}$, $p^*_{s-r} = s, x1, x2, ..., x', ..., r$. The MCMA finds neighbor states from initial state. There must be one state in p^*_{s-r} is in *OPEN*. Let x' be a *OPEN* state on p^*_{s-r}. Since all parents of x' are in *CLOSED* and the path $s, x1, x2, ..., x', ..., r$ is optimal, the pointers assigned to x' are along $p^*_{s-x'}$, hence, $g(x') = g^*(x')$. Since $h(x) \leq h^*(x)$, we obtain:

$$f(x') = g^*(x') + h(x') \leq g^*(x') + h^*(x') = f^*(x') \tag{13}$$

And also since $x' \in p^*_{s-r}$, we have $f^*(x') = C^*$ and

$$f(x') \leq C^* \tag{14}$$

Theorem 1. *The algorithm MCMA returns the minimum cost migration plan.*

Proof. Suppose algorithm MCMA terminates with a goal node $t \in \Gamma$ for which $f(t) = g(t) \geq C^*$. The MCMA will order the *OPEN* and set the smallest cost state at the first. Hence when t was chosen for expansion, it satisfied:

$$f(t) \leq f(x) \quad \forall x \in OPEN \tag{15}$$

This means that all states in *OPEN* satisfy $f(x) \geq C^*$. However, according to the Lemma 1 there was at least one OPEN state satisfies $f(x) \leq C^*$. Therefore the terminating t must have $g(t) = C^*$. Hence the algorithm MCMA returns the minimum cost migration plan.

5   Simulation

We perform numerical simulations to evaluate our approach. Our simulation program is developed in python. The python package NetworkX is used for modeling the networks. In the simulation we use two network topologies, one topology is AS-733 in 1st January, 1999, another topology is Oregon-1 in 31st March, 2001. Those topologies are collected from the Stanford Network Analysis Project (SNAP). The AS-733 has 531 nodes and the Oregon-1 has 10670 nodes. On these topologies, the high degree nodes are candidates to place controllers. We put 5 controllers on AS-733 and 30 controllers on Oregon-1. At the beginning, each controller manages almost equal number of switches.

We set the average number of new flows rate for each switch as $f_i \in [30, 80]$. For each switch the simulation program generates new flows that follows the Poisson distribution. Each flow includes the switch address pair (s, t). The program checks whether the path crosses domains. If it does, the extra request will be added to the controller in every related domain. In the AS-733 topology, we set the processing capacity of the controller as $u_j = 5000$ per second. In the Oregon-1 topology, the processing capacity of the controller is $u_j = 15000$ per second. The size of data for each switch in controller is $m_i \in [100, 5000]$ KB. On both topologies, the latency for every link is set as 1 ms.

To simulate the real environment, we random select some hot spots. If a switch is selected as a hot spot, its host's average new flow rate will become double. The hot spot will sustain for some time and then fade out. During the simulation, the percentage of the hot spots increases in the first 50 s, and then fade out in next 50 s, and then increases in next 50 s again. In the simulation, the warning level for the service time is set as 5 ms. The safe level is 0.5 ms. Once a switch is migrated, new flows on that switch will be suspended for one second, the response time of the new flow becomes 1000 ms and the average blocked data size for each flow is set as 500 KB.

We simulate the average response time for the switches while the request rate is changing. The static controllers (S-CNTL) scheme and the game playing algorithm (GPA) are used to compare with our approach. In S-CNTL scheme the controller-switch mapping is fixed. In GPA scheme, the overloaded controller select a most wanted switch to migrate and broadcast to other controllers. Those controllers discuss their difference of the average response time as the benefit. The controller which obtains the highest benefit will keep the switch. The response time is calculated according to the formula 3. The cost is calculated according to the formula 8. During the migration the allowed maximum path latency from switch to controller is 5 ms.

The Fig. 3 shows the average response time in AS-733 and Oregon-1. From the figures we can see when the load is increasing, the response time of S-CNTL scheme increases very fast as it does not support dynamic switch assignment. The GPA and MCMA support load migration, their performances are significant better than S-CNTL. As the MCMA chooses the plan which has less new flows be suspended and it supports isolation nodes avoidance. When the load is heavy, it has less response time than the GPA.

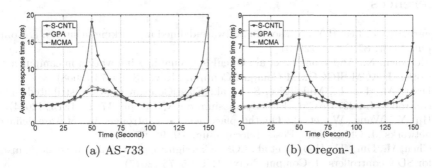

(a) AS-733   (b) Oregon-1

Fig. 3. Response time

The Fig. 4 show the cumulative costs of the load migration for GPA and MCMA. As the GPA migrates the switches according to maximizing the benefit while the MCMA selects the minimum cost switches to migrate, the MCMA uses less cost than the GPA.

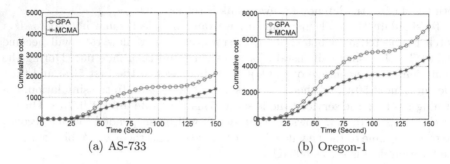

(a) AS-733   (b) Oregon-1

Fig. 4. Cost of migration

6   Conclusion

In large scale networks, multiple controllers are used for handling switches' requests. If the mapping between the controllers and switches is static, it is easy to cause controller overloaded. We studied the load migration of the controllers in SDN and introduced the isolation nodes problem. In this paper, a connected minimum cost heuristic algorithm is proposed for the load migration. The results of the simulation show that our approach can significant balance the loads between controllers with low cost. As the algorithm is still complicated, a more efficient load migration algorithm will be the future work.

Acknowledgments. This work is supported by the National Science Foundation of China (No. 61772385, No. 61373040, No. 61572370).

References

1. Farhady, H., Lee, H.Y., Nakao, A.: Software-defined networking: a survey. J. Comput. Netw. **81**, 79–95 (2015)
2. Mckeown, N., Anderson, T., et al.: OpenFlow: enabling innovation in campus networks. J. ACM SIGCOMM Comput. Commun. Rev. **38**, 69–74 (2008)
3. Dixit, A., Hao, F., Mukherjee, S., et al.: ElastiCon; an elastic distributed SDN controller. In: 2014 ACM/IEEE Symposium on ANCS, pp. 17–27. IEEE (2014)
4. Hu, Y., Wang, W., et al.: On the placement of controllers in software-defined networks. J. China Univ. Posts Telecommun. **19**, 92–97 (2012)
5. Chen, M., Ding, K., Hao, J., et al.: LCMSC: a lightweight collaborative mechanism for SDN controllers. J. Comput. Netw. **121**, 65–75 (2017)
6. Sufiev, H., Haddad, Y.: A dynamic load balancing architecture for SDN. In: Science of Electrical Engineering, pp. 1–3. IEEE (2016)
7. Zhou, Y., Zhu, M., Xiao, L., et al.: A load balancing strategy of SDN controller based on distributed decision. In: International Conference on Trust, Security and Privacy in Computing and Communications, pp. 851–856. IEEE (2014)

8. Yu, J., Wang, Y., Pei, K., et al.: A load balancing mechanism for multiple SDN controllers based on load informing strategy. In: Network Operations and Management Symposium, pp. 1–4. IEEE (2016)

9. Bari, M.F., Roy, A.R., Chowdhury, S.R., et al.: Dynamic controller provisioning in software defined networks. In: International Conference on Network and Service Management, pp. 18–25. IEEE (2013)

10. Fu, Y., Bi, J., Wu, J., Chen, Z., Wang, K., Luo, M.: A dormant multi-controller model for software defined networking. J. China Commun. **11**, 45–55 (2014)

11. Hock, D., Hartmann, M., Gebert, S., et al.: POCO-PLC: enabling dynamic pareto-optimal resilient controller placement in SDN networks. In: Computer Communications Workshops, pp. 115–116. IEEE (2014)

12. Cheng, G., Chen, H., Hu, H., et al.: Dynamic switch migration towards a scalable SDN control plane. Int. J. Commun. Syst. **29**, 1482–1499 (2016)

13. Wang, T., Liu, F., Guo, J., et al.: Dynamic SDN controller assignment in data center networks: stable matching with transfers. In: IEEE INFOCOM 2016, pp. 1–9. IEEE (2016)

Hybrid-Aware Collaborative Multipath Communications for Heterogeneous Vehicular Networks

Yana Liu[✉], Wei Quan, Jinjie Zeng, Gang Liu, and Hongke Zhang

School of Electronic and Information Engineering,
Beijing Jiaotong University, Beijing, China
{ynliu1993,weiquan}@bjtu.edu.cn

Abstract. With the large-scale deployment of wireless access technologies and infrastructures, heterogeneous vehicular networks have been widely studied in recent years. However, it produces unstable link reconstruction due to frequent switch among heterogeneous access networks. Multipath TCP (MPTCP) becomes a promising means to maintain link connectivity by using multiple access interfaces. How to efficiently collaborate multiple links is still a challenge. In this article, we propose Hybrid-Aware Collaborative Multipath Communications for Heterogeneous Vehicular Networks, named HCMC-V. First, we accurately evaluate the weights of different paths by real-time sensing the propagation delay, the packet drop rate, and the bottleneck link capacity. Then, we present a hybrid-aware multipath collaboration mechanism which considers path weights in its decision making process. HCMC-V provides transparent and effective vehicular services through multiple available wireless technologies. Finally, extensive simulations show that HCMC-V significantly reduces transmission delay and improves packet transmission reliability.

Keywords: Collaborative · Multipath · Heterogeneous vehicular networks

1 Introduction

Nowadays, vehicular networks have attracted extensive attention to improve traffic safety and efficiency. Traffic congestion and safety have become global issues. According to the research from the World Health Organization (WHO), more than 125 million people die in traffic accidents every year [1]. In vehicular networks, there are many wireless technologies and infrastructures have been deployed to support the vehicular applications. For instance, IEEE Dedicated Short-Range Communication (DSRC) enables efficient real-time information exchange among vehicles (V2V). Wireless Access for Vehicular Environment (WAVE) has been applied to the Vehicle-to-Infrastructure (V2I) communications. The Long Term Evolution (LTE) scheme has the ability to support vehicular applications [2].

Heterogeneous vehicular networks, which integrate the aforementioned wireless technologies, can completely satisfy unique requirements of the Intelligent Transport System (ITS). As mentioned above, DSRC, LTE, and WAVE are vital to support relevant applications for vehicular networks. However, with the explosive growth of

© ICST Institute for Computer Sciences, Social Informatics and Telecommunications Engineering 2018
I. Romdhani et al. (Eds.): CollaborateCom 2017, LNICST 252, pp. 208–218, 2018.
https://doi.org/10.1007/978-3-030-00916-8_20

vehicles, LTE networks are easily overloaded. Moreover, DSRC integrated with IEEE 802.11p presents poor performance in the wide coverage. Obviously, the single type of these access technologies is far from enough to satisfy all the requirements of vehicular services at the same time.

Currently, many research efforts have begun towards realize highly efficient heterogeneous vehicular communications in a cooperative manner. Zheng *et al.* presented a multi-layer and soft-defined HetVNET in detail, which enabled a far more flexible configuration capability [6]. Dong *et al.* analyzed and solved the issues of energy-efficient cluster management in heterogeneous vehicular networks [7]. However, the above newest researches concentrated on the global design of heterogeneous vehicular networks and failed to analyze its advanced execution mechanisms.

We investigated a new paradigm named Smart Identifier NETworking (SINET) and proposed a SINET customized solution enabling crowd collaborations for software defined Vehicular networks (SINET-V) [5]. Through the crowd sensing, network function slices are flexibly organized with a group of function-similar components. Different function slice(s) are further driven to serve various applications by using crowd collaborations. Extending SINET-V, a hybrid-aware multipath collaboration mechanism is proposed in this paper, named HCMC-V. We focus on the collaboration of heterogeneous vehicular networks at the transport layer. As a promising transport protocol, MPTCP is able to utilize multiple disjoint paths simultaneously and realize seamless vertical handover among multiple paths [6, 12]. The main contributions of this article are showed as follows:

(1) We make a comprehensive analysis of key challenges in heterogeneous vehicular communications and propose our considerations.
(2) We accurately evaluate the weights of different paths by real-time sensing the propagation delay, the packet drop rate, and the bottleneck link capacity.
(3) We present a hybrid-aware path collaboration mechanism according to the path weights, which provides transparent and effective vehicular services through multiple available wireless technologies.

The rest of this article is structured as follows. In the next section, we analyze the challenges in heterogeneous vehicular communications and propose our considerations. In Sect. 3, we describe the workflow of our proposal in detail. In Sect. 4, experimental results validate the benefits of the proposed HCMC-V. Finally, Sect. 5 makes a conclusion and proposes future work.

2 Our Considerations

A key challenge in heterogeneous vehicular networks is how to support a dynamic and instant composition of heterogeneous networks. Heterogeneous vehicular communications pose huge challenges in the deployment of vehicular networks, such as unbalanced link, inter-system handover, and big data processing. Here, we summarize the key challenges for the present limits of heterogeneous vehicular networking.

On the one hand, the hardware performances difference between the On-Board Unit (OBU) and the Roadside Unit (RSU) is great. Due to obviously different communication coverage, the unbalanced links arise. In particular, the reliable communication coverage of the RSU is about 1 km, nevertheless, that of the OBU is only 400 m. As a result, it may be too far for the OBU to receive information from RSU. Communication quality will deteriorate because of such unbalanced links.

On the other hand, there are a wide variety of services, such as real-time warning messages and various entertainment services. These services have different requirements, which require different vehicle-to-other connectivity, such as vehicle-to-vehicle (V2V), vehicle-to-Internet (V2I) and vehicle-to-road infrastructure (V2R) connectivity. Therefore, the collaboration among vehicles and others is challengeable.

As mentioned above, MPTCP efficiently pools the network resources and improves network throughput by enabling data transmission over multiple interfaces. Beyond that, MPTCP has the distinct advantages in heterogeneous vehicular networks [8, 10, 13]. MPTCP is a TCP extension being standardized by the IETF, and is backward compatible with TCP [9, 12]. Therefore, the aforementioned advantages can be obtained without modifying the applications and the existing network devices (*e.g.* firewall or middle box). Besides, MPTCP naturally implements make-before-break, so MPTCP can be incrementally deployed to support mobility.

However, enabling MPTCP in vehicular networks will not be feasible without resolving the above challenges. Kuhn *et al.* proposed Delay Aware Packet Scheduling (DAPS) which aims to reduce the receiver's buffer blocking time [3]. Zhu *et al.* proposed a mobility-aware multimedia data transfer mechanism using Multipath TCP in Vehicular Network [4]. However, they failed to sense the true link state. Based on the above analysis and considerations, we present our proposal HCMC-V in the following, which provides transparent and effective vehicular services through multiple available wireless technologies.

3 Solution: HCMC-V

HCMC-V is proposed to address multipath collaboration caused by heterogeneous wireless networks, as shown in Fig. 1. First, through crowd sensing, SINET-V controller can obtain the real link quality in real time. Then, through HCMC-V mechanism, the available paths are utilized according to the path weight ζ. As illustrated in Fig. 2, the main workflow of HCMC-V includes Hybrid Aware, Path Scheduling, and Packets Management. In the initial phase, the statuses of available paths are sensing through Hybrid Aware, and the key parameters mentioned earlier are recorded and passed to Path Scheduling model. In the path scheduling phase, the path weight will be calculated and used to schedule the available paths. It should be noted that the Hybrid Aware model will dynamically monitor the statuses of available paths and pass valid parameters to the Path Scheduling model. In the following, we described the model of Path Weight and the multipath collaboration policy in detail.

3.1 Model of Path Weight

To get a reasonable Path Weight, we redesign the definition of the weight. The path weight of each path relies on three link parameters: the propagation delay (RTT), the

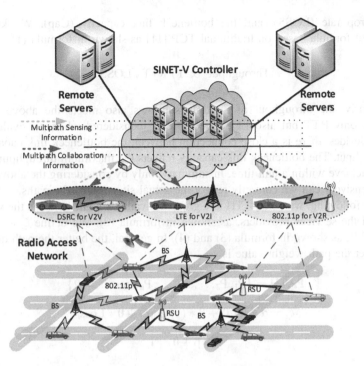

Fig. 1. This figure shows the architecture of SINET-V.

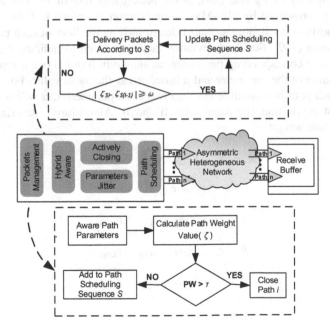

Fig. 2. This figure shows the workflow of HCMC-V.

packet drop rate (LOSS), and the bottleneck link capacity (Cap). We know the throughput formula based on traditional TCP [11] as shown in formula (1).

$$\text{Throughput} \propto 1 \big/ \text{RTT}\sqrt{\text{LOSS}} \tag{1}$$

Similarly, the throughput of multiple subflows also meets the above relationship. Not only RTT but also LOSS needs to be considered when we evaluate link quality. Besides, there is a close connection between the bottleneck link capacity and the throughput. The bottleneck link capacity reflects the maximum throughput that the link can achieve within a unit time. In summary, only by considering the above factors comprehensively can we correctly reflect the actual situation of the paths.

In the following, we take PATH as a group of available paths between the vehicular users and the services providers, as shown in formula (2). We define ζ_i as the path weight of P_i, as shown in formula (3) and (4). In general, the better the path quality is, the smaller the path weight value is.

$$\text{PATH} = \{P_1, P_2, \ldots, P_i, \ldots, P_n, \ n \ > \ = \ 2\} \tag{2}$$

$$\zeta_i = \alpha * \text{RTT}_i + \beta * (1/\text{Cap}_i) + \theta * \text{Loss}_i \tag{3}$$

$$\alpha + \beta + \theta = 1 \tag{4}$$

In the formula (3), RTT_i represents the Round Trip Time of P_i, Cap_i is the bottleneck link capacity of P_i, and Loss_i is the packet loss rate of P_i. The above three parameters are normalized by Min-Max Normalization as shown in formula (5). α, β and θ are all positive constants less than 1 determined by the jitter of each parameter as shown in formula (7–9). Standard deviation factor ε is used to indicate the degree of fluctuation among corresponding parameters as shown in formula (6). σ represents the standard deviation of the parameter and μ is defined as the mean value. For example, if the RTT of each path is more different than two extra parameters, α will be accounted for the largest proportion compared with β and θ. Algorithm 1 describes how to calculate the path weight.

$$\overline{X} = \ X - X_{\text{MIN}}/X_{\text{MAX}} - X_{\text{MIN}} \tag{5}$$

$$\varepsilon_X = \sigma_X/\mu_X \tag{6}$$

$$\alpha = \varepsilon_{RTT}\big/\varepsilon_{RTT} + \varepsilon_{Cap} + \varepsilon_{Loss} \tag{7}$$

$$\beta = \varepsilon_{Rate}\big/\varepsilon_{RTT} + \varepsilon_{Cap} + \varepsilon_{Loss} \tag{8}$$

$$\theta = \varepsilon_{Loss}\big/\varepsilon_{RTT} + \varepsilon_{Cap} + \varepsilon_{Loss} \tag{9}$$

HCMC-V will constantly monitor and update available radio interfaces. If there are packets needed to be sent, available paths will be scheduled according to the above Path Weight. In the following, the detailed scheduling policy will be presented.

Algorithm 1: Path weight calculation method

```
path weight (Output)
   {getSD is the function of calculating standard
deviation factor; getC is the function of calculating
weight coefficient α, β and θ; getPW is the function of
calculating path weight value ζ_i };
   for each Pi∈PATH do
   begin
       ε_RTT  := getSD(Pi);
       ε_Rate := getSD(Pi);
       ε_Loss := getSD(Pi);
   end.
   α := getC(ε_RTT);
   β := getC(ε_Rate);
   θ = getC(ε_Loss);
   for each Pi∈PATH do
   begin
       ζ_i = getPW(α,β,θ);
   end.
```

3.2   Multipath Collaboration Policy

The vehicle users select suitable paths according to the multipath control information from SINET-C controller. The above information includes the sequence of available paths and the path weights of these paths. The ζ_i of Pi is calculated based on Algorithm 1. According to the path weight value, available paths list S can be obtained. In the following, we take S = {S1, S2... Sj... Sm, $n \geq m \geq 2$} as a group of available paths. The ζ_i value of Si is smaller than S_{i+1}. Because the better the path quality is, the smaller the path weight value is. It should be noted that the poor paths will not be selected temporarily.

Algorithm 2: Multipath collaboration policy

```
the list of available pahts(Output)
```

{ Sort(PiP_i, ζ_i P_i,ζ_iP_i,ζ_i) is to sort P_iP_i based on ζ_i in ascending.};

```
    for each Pi∈PATH do
    begin
      if ζᵢ≤τ;
         S.append(Pi);
    end.
```
$S = Sort(\text{Pi}, \zeta_i);$

```
    for each Pi∈PATH do
    begin
```
        if $\left|\zeta_{S_i} - \zeta_{S_{i-1}}\right| \geq \omega$;

        $S = Sort(\text{Pi}, \zeta_i);$

```
    end.
    for each Si∈S do
    begin
      while unackᵢ<cwndᵢ do
        begin
           transmit packets on Si.
        end.
    end.
```

In HCMC-V, the parameter τ is proposed as path selection threshold. On the one hand, paths with $\zeta_i \leq \tau$ can be treated as available paths. In other words, Paths with $\zeta_i > \tau$ will be abandoned temporarily to ensure that packets are able to be sent quickly via good paths. On the other hand, ζ_{S_i} is dynamic with the links quality. But only when $\left|\zeta_{S_i} - \zeta_{S_{i-1}}\right| \geq \omega$, path scheduling list S will change. The parameter ω works as the switching threshold of path weight. If the link quality changes little ($\left|\zeta_{S_i} - \zeta_{S_{i-1}}\right| < \omega$), path scheduling sequence will not change which is able to minimize the number of link switching and ensure the stability of path scheduling. The specific algorithm to implement path scheduling is shown in Algorithm 2.

It should be noted that τ and ω can be obtained by a large number of experiments. Before the data sending, the multipath scheduling policy will select the paths according to the order of the array S. The first one in the array will be the best path. HCMC-V can select a 'fastest' path based on not only its RTT but also its real link quality, and avoid blind roll polling compared with Round Robin or Lowest RTT First [9].

4   Evaluation

We conducted a group of experiments to verify the feasibility and efficiency of HCMC-V. We performed the experiments under the NS-3 open source network simulator. In our experiments, we used the Routes Mobility Model in NS-3 to simulate the vehicular networks. The Routes Mobility Model can generate realistic mobility traces by querying the Google Maps Directions API. The information, obtained from the Google Maps services, allows the simulator to generate realistic mobility traces based on real-world locations and road networks. We analyzed the performance of HCMC-V from two aspects, the packet transmission reliability and transmission delay.

Obviously, the efficiency of HCMC-V relies on τ and ω. We usually set $\tau = 0.85$ to ensure using all of subflows as much as possible. We further evaluated the throughput according to the switching threshold ω. We can see that different thresholds will affect the performance of HCMC-V. On the one hand, if ω is too large, HCMC-V will become insensitive to severe fluctuation, and perform as well as traditional scheduling policies. On the other hand, if ω is too small, it will result in frequent path switching. We can set different threshold values according to path jitter. For example, we can set a larger threshold for the paths with frequency fluctuation and set a smaller threshold for the smooth paths.

We assessed the performance of the proposed paths scheduling policy by comparing with the state-of-the-art multipath scheduling mechanisms, including the Delay-Aware Packet Scheduling (DAPS) and mobility-aware MPTCP scheduling (MA-MPTCP). We set paths parameters according to Table 1. Figure 3 is a snapshot of the total throughput on all paths, and we can see that the throughput of HCMC-V is significantly better than those of other scheduling policy. The throughput of HCMC-V with $\omega = 0.3$ is 30% higher than that of MA-MPTCP. The throughput of DAPS is far lower than that of HCMC-V. The main reason is that MA-MPTCP is failed to sense the paths statuses, and DAPS only focus on the transmission delay. HCMC-V can dynamically sense and schedule the best path(s) using hybrid aware policy.

Table 1. Path characteristics

Path	RTT/ms	Rate/Mbps	Loss
Path 1	20	8	5%
Path 2	150	2	2%
Path 3	100	4	3%
Path 4	50	6	4%
Path 5	150	1	1%
Path 6	50	5	2%
Path 7	100	3	1%

We performed another set of experiments with varying the number of subflows, as shown in Table 1, and we also fixed $\tau = 0.85$. By comparing these results, we can see RTT based on HCMC-V has an obvious decreasing trend, compared with other strategies, as shown in Fig. 4. For example, when there are five subflows, the delay of HCMC-V is reduced by 20% compared with DASP, and it is reduced by 40% compared with MA-MPTCP. The main reason is that HCMC-V is able to dynamically sense and adjust multiple paths in real time. Hence, it can flexibly call up the better paths through multipath collaboration mechanism.

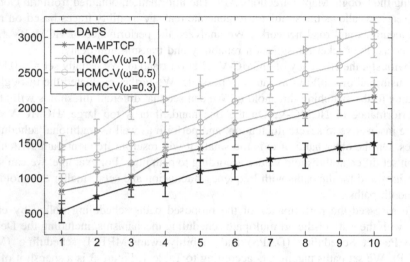

Fig. 3. This figure shows the total throughput with different policies during 10 s.

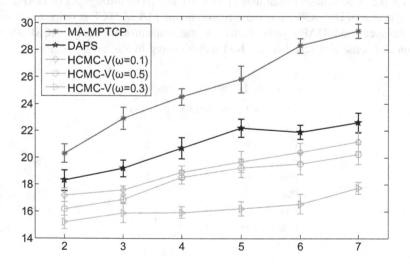

Fig. 4. This figure shows transmission delay of different subflows.

5 Conclusion and Future Work

This article presents a MPTCP communication architecture and proposes an innovative HCMC-V solution for heterogeneous vehicular networks. Specifically, we accurately evaluate the weights of different paths by real-time sensing the propagation delay, the packet drop rate, and the bottleneck link capacity. Then, we present a hybrid-aware path collaboration mechanism according to the path weight, which provides transparent and effective vehicular services through multiple available wireless technologies. Extensive simulations show that HCMC-V significantly reduces transmission delay and improves the packet transmission reliability. In our future work, we plan to implement HCMC-V in Linux implementation of MPTCP to evaluate the performance gain in realistic network conditions.

Acknowledgment. This work was supported by the National Natural Science Foundation of China (NSFC) under Grant No. 61602030 and 61232017, the National Key R&D Program under Grant No. 2016YFE0122900, the Fundamental Research Funds for the Central Universities under Grant No. 2016RC036 and 2015JBM009.

References

1. Zheng, K., et al.: Heterogeneous vehicular networking: a survey on architecture, challenges, and solutions. IEEE Commun. Surv. Tutor. **17**(4), 2377–2396 (2015)
2. Zhang, H., Dong, P., Quan, W., et al.: Promoting efficient communications for high-speed railway using smart collaborative networking. IEEE Wirel. Commun. **22**(6), 92–97 (2015)
3. Kuhn, N., et al.: DAPS: intelligent delay-aware packet scheduling for multipath transport. In: IEEE International Conference on Communications, June 2014, pp. 1222–1227 (2014)
4. Zhu, D., et al.: Mobility-aware multimedia data transfer using multipath TCP in vehicular network. In: International Wireless Communications and Mobile Computing Conference, June 2017, pp. 1041–1046 (2017)
5. Quan, W., et al.: Enhancing crowd collaborations for software defined vehicular networks. IEEE Netw. **30**(4), 10–15 (2016)
6. Zheng, K., et al.: Soft-defined heterogeneous vehicular network: architecture and challenges. IEEE Netw. **30**(4), 72–80 (2016)
7. Dong, P., et al.: Energy-efficient cluster management in heterogeneous vehicular networks. In: IEEE INFOCOM 2016 - IEEE Conference on Computer Communications Workshops, April 2016, pp. 644–649 (2016)
8. Paasch, C., et al.: Exploring Mobile/WiFi handover with multipath TCP. In: ACM SIGCOMM, August 2012
9. Ford, A., et al.: TCP extensions for multipath operation with multiple addresses. RFC6824, January 2013
10. Yang, L., et al.: Multi-copy data dissemination with probabilistic delay constraint in mobile opportunistic device-to-device networks. In: IEEE, International Symposium on IEEE Computer Society, June 2016, pp. 1–9 (2016)

11. Sarwar, G., et al.: Mitigating receiver's buffer blocking by delay aware packet scheduling in multipath data transfer. In: IEEE WAINA, March 2013
12. Paasch, C., et al.: Experimental evaluation of multipath TCP schedulers. In: ACM SIGCOMM, August 2014
13. Xu, C., et al.: Congestion control design for multipath transport protocols: a survey. IEEE Commun. Surv. Tutor. 18(4), 2948–2969 (2016)

Internet of Things (IoT) and Collaboration

RETaIL: A Machine Learning-Based Item-Level Localization System in Retail Environment

Xiaoyi Xu[1]([⊠]), Xiaoming Chen[1], Jiang Ji[1], Feng Chen[1], and Addicam V. Sanjay[2]

[1] Intel Asia-Pacific Research and Development Ltd.,
Shanghai, People's Republic of China
{xiaoyi.xu,xiaoming.chen,jiang.ji,
andy.chen}@intel.com
[2] Intel, Chandler, AZ, USA
addicam.v.sanjay@intel.com

Abstract. Radio-frequency identification (RFID) technology has become the key focus of indoor localization recently. The low cost and flexibility allow numbers of passive RFID-based algorithms been proposed for indoor localization. However, in a real-world environment including retail store and supermarket with large-scale item-level deployment of RFID tags and complex surroundings, these algorithms may not be available due to the collision and interference. Existing algorithms either require extra hardware or only take a small number of tags into consideration, facing difficulty in applying to these places. In this paper, we propose a novel machine learning-based REal-Time and Item-Level (RETaIL) indoor localization system, which is designed to tolerate various interference. RETaIL incorporates three machine learning algorithm, J48, SVM and cloth grouping, for indoor localization. Validations in both complex laboratory environment and real-world Levis outlet store demonstrate the accuracy and efficiency of RETaIL and its capability of dealing with interference in retail environment.

Keywords: Passive RFID · Machine learning · Item-level localization
Retail environment

1 Introduction

Embedded sensors are changing the way people live and retailers manage merchandise. As one of the sensor technologies, radio-frequency identification (RFID) technology is attracting growing interests in various applications [1], and its wider adoption defined the revolution of the Internet of Things. With the desirable features of cost-effective, contactless communications, high data rate and easy implementation, item-level deployment of RFID technology is applied in warehouse, supermarket, retail store and factories [2]. During the past decades, item-level RFID offered tangible benefits to both suppliers and retailers [3, 4] in product tracking, supply chain, anti-counterfeiting and stock estimation. However, there are still losses caused by unsolved problems including

© ICST Institute for Computer Sciences, Social Informatics and Telecommunications Engineering 2018
I. Romdhani et al. (Eds.): CollaborateCom 2017, LNICST 252, pp. 221–231, 2018.
https://doi.org/10.1007/978-3-030-00916-8_21

misplaced items, out-of-stock items and inventory shrinkage, which make RFID technology-based real-time item-level localization urgently needed in retail environment.

Compared with the relative simple environment that most indoor localization implemented in, including dense tag environment [5] and clutter environment [6], retail store or warehouse environment is much more complicate. The main challenges of applying indoor localization algorithm in retail environment lay in: (1) thousands of RFID tags may be densely deployed in a small area; (2) several RFID readers may be deployed within the range of backscattered signal that tags send back; (3) different materials of shelves, walls and other obstacles may exist; (4) costumers may cover or touch the tags or move around in the room all the time. Under such circumstances, the signals among RFID tags and readers can be greatly altered by interference of tag-tag collisions, reader-reader collision, signal reflections of different surfaces as well as other environment factor including human activities, temperature, noise and humidity.

In this paper, we propose a novel item-level localization system that focuses on retail environment by combining three efficient machine learning algorithms, Support Vector Machine, J48 and a novel algorithm named cloth grouping. The proposed system can make use of various information and its performance is robust to challenges from real-world store with thousands of items and crowded customers moving around. Based on Intel® Retail Sensor Platform we offer a simple way for retailers to locate products of interest efficiently and accurately, and eventually reduce losses from misplaced or out-of-stock items.

The rest of the paper is organized as follows: in Sect. 2, we present a brief review of related work in the field of RFID localization and machine learning algorithms that applied in RFID-based problems. Section 3 introduces the proposed localization system RETaIL, including the detailed feature description and algorithm description. In Sect. 4, after tested RETaIL in lab environment, we turn to practical application in Levis outlet store for further evaluation. Finally, we briefly conclude our work in Sect. 5.

2 Relation to Prior Work

A variety of indoor localization algorithms have been proposed in last decades using RFID technology including active RFID-based localization algorithms [7–9, 20] and passive RFID-based algorithms [2, 5, 10]. The cost-efficient nature of passive RDIF enabled large-scale deployment of embedded RFID tags and created many dense tag environments. Due to the fact that passive RFID tags are easily interfered by dense tags and dense readers, algorithms were proposed to solve the tag collision and reader collision problems [11] in dense RFID environments [5, 12–15, 20]. However, most of these algorithms are proposed and tested in a relatively simple environment. For example, in Zhang's work [2], the dense environment has only 16 tags/m^2. InPLaCE [6] system is proposed to deal with clutter environment, but there are less than 50 tags for testing. Performing item-level indoor localization in a complex environment is still a challenging task.

In terms of prediction approach, besides math-physics-based methods, machine learning algorithms were also applied in RFID-based problems. For example, Li [16] extracted read rate, phase and RSSI features to distinguish human-object interaction including still, translation, rotation, swipe and cover touch using several 2-class SVMs. Later, they also proposed a machine learning pipeline named PaperID [17] to distinguish multiple simultaneous gestures over RFID tag by incorporating SVM with similar features. Machine learning algorithms achieve good classification performance based on RFID parameters, which provide insights into RFID technology-based problem including indoor localization.

3   System Framework

In this paper, we developed a novel localization system with the purpose of locating the items with RFID tags in a retail environment. The deployment of the RFID system is as follow: a large number of clothes that are densely placed in different areas are embedded with RFID tags. Several RFID readers are deployed in the room, which will send energy to RFID tag, and read the received signal information, including RSSI, frequency and phase from tags. Based on these setting, localization system is developed by incorporating machine learning algorithms and the data collected from readers.

Figure 1 shows the framework of RETaIL, including data collection stage, feature extraction stage, prediction stage, voting stage to output the final location based on the results from multiple algorithms.

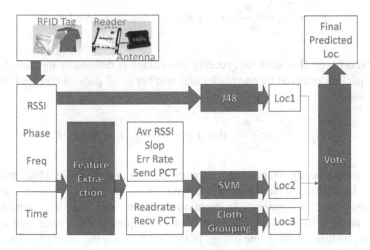

Fig. 1. Overview of system framework.

3.1   Feature Extraction

For the three algorithms we adopted in this system, different information is used with respect to the function of each algorithm. Here, RF channel parameter including frequency, RF phase, RSSI, as well as corresponding reader IDs are used to build model.

Besides, as each tag might get read by multiple readers more than once in a given period of time, a sliding window (window size = T) which slides every T/2 with 50% overlap is utilized to segment the RF channel parameters reported by each reader. For each segment, seven features are derived from RSSI, RF phase, frequency and time.

Average RSSI Value. Passive RFID tags operate by reflecting the RF signal transmitted to them from a reader and RSSI is a measurement of reflected signal. In the retail environment, RFID tags are densely deployed within limited area, in which the signals among tags and readers can be greatly altered by interference of RFID tag collisions, reader-reader collisions as well as the environment factor, making uncontrolled RSSI values can't reflect accurate information. However, by keeping the maximum power level, we can utilize the average RSSI values that each reader received from a tag within segments as features [17], which makes an n-dimension feature vector.

RFID tags can receive signals only in a short distance, so usually a tag can mainly receive signal from several readers around it. Besides, signal-sending rates of all readers are adjusted to be distinct from each other, which makes read rate information effective for classification. The definitions are as follow:

Tag Read Rate. The tag read rate is defined as the number of packets received from each tag by each reader per second.

Sent Percentage. For each RFID reader, sent percentage is defined as the ratio between number of packets received from one tag and number of all packets received by this reader (Eq. (1)).

$$SP_{i,j} = \frac{\sum_a \sum_b \theta_{ab}}{\sum_b \theta_b}, \theta = 1 \; if \; a \in tag_i, b \in reader_j. \tag{1}$$

Receive Percentage. For each tag, receive percentage is defined as the ratio between number of packets received by one reader and number of all packets received from this tag by all readers.

$$RP_{i,j} = \frac{\sum_a \sum_b \theta_{ab}}{\sum_a \theta_a}, \theta = 1 \; if \; a \in tag_i, b \in reader_j. \tag{2}$$

Phase and frequency wrap around between 0–3.14 and 902–928 MHz and repeat recurrently. Ideally, when having X axis as frequency and Y axis as phase, a series of parallel lines could be obtained. As mentioned above, with a sliding window of T minutes with 50% of overlap, we get the phase/frequency ratio over one of these parallel lines instead of doing line fitting. In the end we took the average of this sliding window period as feature. RF parameters phases and frequencies are utilized to compute slope and error rate as follow:

Slope. It's the slope of the graph when phase values were plotted against frequency.

$$slope = \frac{\left(\sum_{t=0}^{T} frequency \times \sum_{t=0}^{T} phase\right) - count \times \sum_{t=0}^{T} frequence \times phase}{\left(\sum_{t=0}^{T} frequency\right)^2 - count \times \sum_{t=0}^{T} frequency^2}. \quad (3)$$

Error Rate. Due to the interference, signals may vary from time to time and error rate is an estimation of the fluctuation of phase and frequency. In (4), t is between $(n - 1)T/2$ and $n * T/2$, denoting the nth slide window.

$$error\ rate = \frac{\max(phase_t)}{\min(frequency_t)} - \frac{\min(phase_t)}{\max(frequency_t)}. \quad (4)$$

Finally, for n readers, average RSSI value, tag read rate, sent percentage, receive percentage, slope and error rate are calculated and encoded into n-dimension features according which reader receives these signals, respectively.

3.2   Machine Learning Algorithms

The model we propose is a machine learning model instead of a math-physics based model because signal strength is not a directly indicative of distance in the case of retail environment with disorganized interference, obstruction and collision. Furthermore, our early stage experiments show that although count of reader reads are good indicative of distance, only using the read rate was not giving stable results. Therefore, we took a slightly different approach by using a voting mechanism between two supervised machine learning models and one unsupervised machine learning model

J48. For each tag, more than one signals are received by different readers within a period, each signal reflects the characteristics of the tag. As a powerful approaches to discover useful patterns from large and complex bulk of data, J48 [18] is used to make full use of all these signals. Reader information, RSSI, frequency and phase are used as independent features and each signal is treated as a sample to perform multi-label classification. Pre-trained model are used to predict locations for each sample of a tag. Finally, the location with highest voting score is selected.

SVM. We implement optimized LIBSVM [19] with RBF kernel and tuned parameters and use SVM as a multi-class classifier in this project. To overcome the unbalanced numbers of samples in each location, weight parameter w is set to be inversely proportional to the number of samples for each class. Prior to location prediction, exhaustive feature selection algorithm is use to try every combinations of the six kinds of features described in Sect. 3.1. To ensure robustness of model, we use training datasets of different size to perform feature selection process and then validate the accuracy of the constructed model. Finally a feature subset that obtained the highest accuracies is selected to construct SVM model. At deployment stage, same feature set and scale range is used for query data.

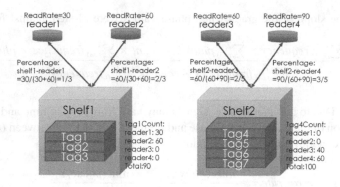

Fig. 2. Illustration of cloth grouping algorithm. Left panel matches criteria 1 and tight panel matches criteria 2.

Cloth Grouping. In this system, read rate of every reader is specially adjusted to be different from each other. System compares the read rate of every tag by every reader with pre-stored read rate of every shelf. A tag is predicted to be located in one shelf when it meets one of the following criteria: (1) read rate of a tag is close to read rate of a shelf; or (2) percentage of shelf-reader is close to percentage of tag-reader (as shown in Fig. 2).

Voting Strategy and Optimization. For J48 and SVM, multiple signals are received from one tag and each signal is used for prediction, a voting process is used to decided prediction result for each tag. After prediction results are obtained from each algorithms, a voting strategy is utilized to decide the final location of an item. Specially, if three different locations are predicted for an item by three algorithms, after validations and tests, we found that simply ignore cloth grouping result and compare the confidence of the J48 and SVM and take the result of the algorithm with higher prediction confidence as the final result gives good accuracies.

To implement real-time localization system, the following optimization approaches are utilized to improve efficiency while retaining high accuracy: (1): For the three supervised algorithms, parallelized computing is enabled; (2): Sliding window size $T = 2$ min is defined to have a better tradeoff between size of training data and efficiency; (3): For the most time consuming algorithm, SVM, a novel implementation is developed to compress model and multi-thread is used to decrease computing time, detailed engineering implementation of the speedup library is not described as it is less relevant to this study.

4   Experiments

This section outlines the details related to deployment of both the laboratory and real retail store and evaluate proposed approach towards attaining the end objective of determining item location inside a retail environment.

4.1   Experiment Results on Lab Environment

To evaluate how machine learning algorithms helps in dealing with interference for item-level localization, we setup a laboratory with dimensions of 27 foot * 27 foot to imitate retail environment. Considering that a real store would have a dense population of tags, we had brought in shelves and racks and populated them with of real clothing with respect to the lab deployment. The passive RFID deployment is based on Intel Retail Sensor Platform and the layout is shown in Fig. 3. In Fig. 3, the gray portions are either walls, desks, lab shelves, or areas where items cannot be placed. The light blue rectangles designate the shelves of our "store" with tagged jeans, which are the targets that will be used to evaluate their predict locations. Rectangles A/D designate the wooden furniture and H/I are metal racks that are deployed among shelves to imitate real store and to increase interference and multipath effect. The black squares represent the RFID readers, which are approximately 100 in. up from the floor. Totally 730 jeans are distributed in shelves with uneven numbers for evaluation and researchers movements are also included to imitate real store.

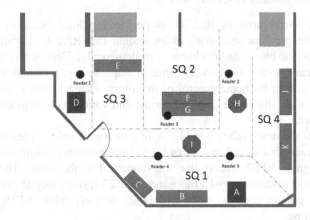

Fig. 3. Layout of the laboratory for experimental evaluation of RETaIL.

In a real store, instead of knowing the exactly position accurately within centimeters, the most important localization task is to obtain the real time information about which area is the query clothes locate at and whether the clothes were moved. To this end, firstly we divided room into four sub-quadrants (SQ), within which shelves are closely deployed. Numbers of tags in these sub-quadrants are 267, 90, 78 and 295, respectively. Secondly, we have the settings configured as "mobility" scan such that we get a high read rate, which makes it easier to see moving tags.

The readers collect tag IDs, frequency, phase and RSSI information for feature extraction. Models and parameters are trained offline before validation. For testing, we collect data from three different time periods in three days (10 min each time), within which about 2.6–3.1 million signals are received by five readers. These signals are sent to the system for localization and the prediction accuracies are shown in Table 1. From the table we can see that among the three algorithms, the highest accuracies are

Table 1. Prediction accuracies in laboratory

Accuracy	SVM	J48	Cloth group	Voting
Day 1	89.86%	88.62%	89.19%	93.74%
Day 2	93.39%	88.64%	88.78%	93.69%
Day 3	91.76%	88.86%	89.00%	93.18%
Average	91.67%	88.71%	88.99%	93.54%
Time	5.3 s	2.7 s	3.7 s	6.0 s

obtained by SVM. For three independent tests, the average accuracies for three algorithms are 91.67%, 88.71% and 88.99%, respectively. By combining all results to generate stable prediction location, accuracies of final result after voting process are 93.74%, 93.69% and 93.18%, increase consistently from highest accuracy that obtained from single algorithm. Moreover, it only takes 6 s to locate 730 clothes from ~ 3 million signal, indicating RETaIL can provide real-time localization on single cloth.

4.2   Experiment Results in Levis Store

One of the key innovations of RETaIL is performing localization in very clutter environment. The previous section gives an insight that RETaIL is capable of predicting locations for hundreds of clothes simultaneously. Here we further test the system in real retail store, a Levis outlet store in Napa Valley, which also adopts Intel Retail Sensor Platform for better control of inventory accuracy. Environment is more complicate in this test due to the crowded people and various collisions and reflections in the outlet store.

The layout of the store is shown in Fig. 4, in which each color represents one of the seven sub-quadrants that are taken care of by a shop assistants. White rectangles with four digits designate RFID readers that are dispersed in the room. The number of tagged clothes and readers are ~ 10 thousands and 25 respectively at our test period. All clothes are put on shelves, racks and tables densely while RDIF readers are deployed on ceiling.

The main purpose of item-level localization in store is to get real-time information about which sub-quadrant is the query clothes locate in and which assistant should be responsible for them if they are misplaced. As in real store they need to know item locations from time to time and readers need to keep collecting data all the time, the RFID settings used in store is slightly different from laboratory. Read rate is relative lower than in lab such that less storage space and less prediction time is needed.

Similarly, 10 min data is used for testing by comparing the predicted location with the manually collected ground truth data. The prediction process repeats three times on different testing data to ensure reliable results. About 0.89–0.94 million signals from ~ 600 clothes are extracted for feature extraction and prediction each time. Table 2 shows the prediction accuracies of three algorithms and final voting results. As expect, in a real outlet store with more complex environment, RETaIL still gives satisfying localization results with an overall accuracy of 90.79% and a 1.14% STD across test results for three days. For each day, different algorithms get best prediction performance. For Day 1, the highest accuracy of 90.02% is obtained by J48 while in

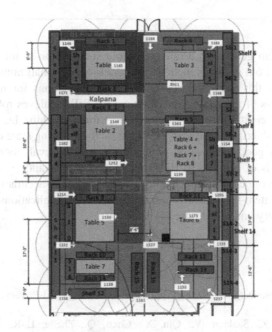

Fig. 4. Layout of Levis retail store in Napa valley.

Table 2. Prediction accuracies in Levis outlet store

Accuracy	SVM	J48	Cloth group	Voting
Day 1	90.02%	90.77%	84.64%	91.03%
Day 2	90.49%	89.60%	75.84%	89.55%
Day 3	91.79%	90.07%	80.75%	91.79%
Average	90.76%	90.15%	80.41%	90.79%
Time	1.3 s	1 s	1 s	1.6 s

Day 2 and Day 3, the highest accuracies of 90.49% and 91.79% are obtained by SVM. Overall, the average accuracies of voting result (90.79%) is better than that of using only SVM, J48 or cloth grouping, whose accuracy are 90.76%, 91.15% and 80.41%, respectively. Also, with lower read rate and less received signals, it takes only 1.6 s to perform localization for ~ 600 clothes, demonstrating the efficiency of our system.

It should be noticed that under such configuration, only part of tags are read in the evaluation process, making localization for unread clothes unavailable. Actually, with current configuration, a higher read rate is obtained as compared with deep scan mode and it's easier to get more signals from moved tags, making our system suitable for detecting misplaced clothes. For those tags that wasn't read by RFID reader, they may not be moved within 10 min. Localization for those clothes can be easily implemented by only extracting signal received from corresponding tags in a longer time range.

5   Conclusions

The proposed system guarantees a reliable indoor localization solution in retail environment. Different from previous methods in which only a small number of tags were taken into account, this work focuses on predicting locations for hundreds of tags accurately regardless of perplexing interference. RETaIL achieves robust localization results in complex environment by incorporating three machine learning algorithms that make use of both original and statistic features. By imitating store environment in a lab, RETaIL shows good localization performance. Further evaluation in Levis outlet store with thousands of clothes, 30 RFID readers, obstacles and crowded customers, demonstrates reliable localization accuracy of RETaIL. The accuracy and robustness make it suitable for item-level localization in various retail applications including store, supermarket, industry and warehouse.

References

1. Garfinkel, S., Rosenberg, B.: RFID: Applications, Security, and Privacy. Addison-Wesley, Boston (2005)
2. Zhang, Z., Lu, Z., Saakian, V., Qin, X., Chen, Q., Zheng, L.-R.: Item-level indoor localization with passive UHF RFID based on tag interaction analysis. IEEE Trans. Industr. Electron. **61**, 2122–2135 (2014)
3. Roussos, G.: Enabling RFID in retail. Computer **39**, 25–30 (2006)
4. Roussos, G., Kourouthanassis, P., Moussouri, T.: Appliance design for mobile commerce and retailteinment. Pers. Ubiquit. Comput. **7**, 203–209 (2003)
5. Yang, P., Wu, W.: Efficient particle filter localization algorithm in dense passive RFID tag environment. IEEE Trans. Industr. Electron. **61**, 5641–5651 (2014)
6. Chandrasekaran, V., Narayan, K., et al.: InPLaCE RFID: indoor path loss translation for object localization in cluttered environments. In: IEEE Tenth International Conference on Intelligent Sensors, Sensor Networks and Information Processing (ISSNIP 2015), pp. 1–6 (2015)
7. Ni, L.M., Liu, Y., Lau, Y.C., Patil, A.P.: LANDMARC: indoor location sensing using active RFID. Wirel. Netw. **10**, 701–710 (2004)
8. Madigan, D., Einahrawy, E., Martin, R.P., Ju, W.-H., Krishnan, P., Krishnakumar, A.: Bayesian indoor positioning systems. In: Proceedings of IEEE 24th Annual Joint Conference of the IEEE Computer and Communications Societies, pp. 1217–1227 (2005)
9. Öktem, R., Aydin, E.: An RFID based indoor tracking method for navigating visually impaired people. Turk. J. Electr. Eng. Comput. Sci. **18**, 185–198 (2010)
10. Yan, D., Zhao, Z., Ng, W.: Leveraging read rates of passive RFID tags for real-time indoor location tracking. In: Proceedings of the 21st ACM International Conference on Information and Knowledge Management, pp. 375–384 (2012)
11. Meguerditchian, C., Safa, H., El-Hajj, W.: New reader anti-collision algorithm for dense RFID environments. In: 18th IEEE International Conference on Electronics, Circuits and Systems (ICECS 2011), pp. 85–88 (2011)
12. Vorst, P., Schneegans, S., Yang, B., Zell, A.: Self-localization with RFID snapshots in densely tagged environments. In: 2008 IEEE/RSJ International Conference on Intelligent Robots and Systems, pp. 1353–1358 (2008)

13. Joshi, G.P., Mamun, K.M.A., Kim, S.W.: A reader anti-collision MAC protocol for dense reader RFID system. In: WRI International Conference on CMC 2009, pp. 313–316 (2009)
14. Bueno-Delgado, M.V., Ferrero, R., Gandino, F., Pavon-Marino, P., Rebaudengo, M.: A geometric distribution reader anti-collision protocol for RFID dense reader environments. IEEE Trans. Autom. Sci. Eng. **10**, 296–306 (2013)
15. Eom, J.-B., Yim, S.-B., Lee, T.-J.: An efficient reader anti-collision algorithm in dense RFID networks with mobile RFID readers. IEEE Trans. Industr. Electron. **56**, 2326–2336 (2009)
16. Li, H., Ye, C., Sample, A.P.: IDSense: a human object interaction detection system based on passive UHF RFID. In: Proceedings of the 33rd Annual ACM Conference on Human Factors in Computing Systems, pp. 2555–2564 (2015)
17. Li, H., et al.: PaperID: a technique for drawing functional battery-free wireless interfaces on paper. In: Proceedings of the 2016 CHI, pp. 5885–5896 (2016)
18. Neeraj, D.B., Girja, S., Ritu, D.B., Manisha, M.: Decision tree analysis on J48 algorithm for data mining. JARCSSE **3** (2013)
19. Chang, C.-C., Lin, C.-J.: LIBSVM: a library for support vector machines. ACM Trans. Intell. Syst. Technol. (TIST) **2**, 27 (2011)
20. Gao, Z., Ma, Y., Liu, K., Miao, X.: An indoor multi-tag cooperative localization algorithm based on NMDS for RFID. IEEE Sens. J. **17**(7), 2120–2128 (2017)

A Point of Interest Recommendation Approach by Fusing Geographical and Reputation Influence on Location Based Social Networks

Jun Zeng, Feng Li$^{(\boxtimes)}$, Junhao Wen, and Wei Zhou

Graduate School of Software Engineering,
Chongqing University, Chongqing, China
{zengjun,lifeng,jhwen,zhouwei}@cqu.edu.cn

Abstract. With the rapid development of location-based social networks (LBSNs), more and more people form the habit of sharing locations with their friends. Point of interest (POI) recommendation is aiming to recommend new places for users when they explore their surroundings. How to make proper recommendation has been a key point on the basis of existing information. In this paper, we propose a novel POI recommendation approach by fusing user preference, geographical influence and social reputation. TFIDF is used to represent user preference. Then, we further improve recommendation model by incorporating geographical distance and popularity. In the dataset, we find friends in LBSNs share low common visited POIs. Instead of directly getting recommendation from friends, users attain recommendation from others according to their reputation in the LBSNs. Finally, experimental results on real-world dataset demonstrate that the proposed method performs much better than other recommendation methods.

Keywords: POI recommendation · Collaborative filtering
Location-based social networks · Geographical influence

1 Introduction

As an extension of traditional social network, location-based social networks (LBSNs) has been booming, e.g., Foursquare and Brightkite [1–8]. Check-in has gradually become a new life style. More and more people form the habit of sharing location with their friends. Then, users generate lots of check-in records. In general, check-in data includes user information, time and location information and reviews [9, 10]. Point of interest (POI) recommendation is aiming to recommend new places which users have not visited before when they explore their surroundings.

POI recommendation recently has been a hot topic. Collaborative filtering (CF) is widely applied to POI recommendation because of simplicity and extendibility. There are much work about memory-based CF [1, 2, 9, 11] and model-based CF [3, 4, 6–8, 10, 13, 14]. For example, Ye et al. [11] incorporated social relationship into recommendation. Friend-based CF (FCF) [1] directly recommends POIs for users from those locations their friends visited before. Compared with traditional user-based CF (user-CF), this method has lower computational overhead. However, the method is limited

© ICST Institute for Computer Sciences, Social Informatics and Telecommunications Engineering 2018
I. Romdhani et al. (Eds.): CollaborateCom 2017, LNICST 252, pp. 232–242, 2018.
https://doi.org/10.1007/978-3-030-00916-8_22

because the tastes of one users' friends maybe vary greatly. Some matrix factorization (MF) based methods can easily fuse factors, such as geographical distance and social relation, but a common problem is how to tune the appropriate parameters.

In this paper, we propose a novel method to improve POI recommendation. The main contributions are as follows:

- TF-IDF way is adopted to describe user preference. As a supplement of traditional similarity, TF-IDF demonstrate user preference in a more personalized way.
- Different from existing work, K-medoids method is utilized to cluster user's visited locations to find check-in center for each user.
- Instead of directly generating recommendation from friends, every user generate different contribution degree according to their social reputation in social network.
- We incorporate improved user preference, geographical influence and social reputation into user-CF. Experimental result on the real world dataset show our model outperforms other evaluated methods.

The rest of the paper is organized as follows. Section 2 briefly reviews the related work about the POI recommendation. Section 3 elaborates the proposed method which fuses TF-IDF based user preference, geographical influence and social reputation. Section 4 conducts experiments on real dataset to evaluate the performance of the proposed method. Section 5 concludes this paper.

2 Related Work

The main task of POI recommendation is to recommend new POIs that users may be interested in for users by analyzing their historical behaviors. This section reviews existing POI recommendation techniques on how they employ some factors:

- Reviews & Category. Reviews and category information provide a better understanding about the POIs. However, there are only a few studies having utilized category and reviews information for POI recommendation. Gao et al. [3] studied content information including POI properties, user interest and sentiment indications from users' tips. They use the sentiment scores of tips to infer user interest. Bao et al. [2] modeled user preference with a weighted category hierarchy (WCH) like a tree, then selected local experts for each location category using HITS. Scores for candidate locations are predicted from the opinions of the selected local experts. Hu et al. [8] discovered that users' rating for a specific location is determined by the intrinsic characteristics of the location (review, category and popularity) and the extrinsic characteristics (geographical neighbors).
- Geographical information. Geographical information has a significant impact on human decision making. Yuan et al. [9] assumed human tend to visit nearby POIs to their previous locations and modeled the willingness of visiting a location with a power law distribution. Zhang et al. [18] utilized kernel estimation with an adaptive bandwidth to model the geographical correlation between POIs and estimate the relevance score for users on unvisited locations. Cheng et al. [12] modeled the probability of a user's check-in on a location as Multi-center Gaussian Model.

- Social Influence. Some existing work also considered social influence. Ye et al. [11] argued that friends tend to have similar behavior and friends might provide good recommendation for a given user due to their potential correlated check-in behavior. Cheng et al. [12] fused MF with social influence for POI recommendation. However, experimental results on [12] demonstrated social influence is not so important because of low common visited POIs between friends. In this paper, we adopt a new method to exploit the social reputation, not simple friend link.

Our study differentiates itself from these existing work in some aspects. First, TF-IDF technology is adopted to represent personalized user preference. Second, we use K-medoids method to cluster user's visited locations to find check-in centers for each user, not common center [12]. Then, geographical influences including distance and location popularity are not incorporated by naïve Bayes [9]. Finally, we use social reputation to measure users' contribution degree, not simple social link in [11, 16, 18].

3 Fused Method with User Preference, Geographical Information and Social Reputation

This section first defines the problem, and then presents a unified framework to perform POI recommendation.

3.1 Problem Definition

Let $U = \{u_1, u_2, u_3, ..., u_{|U|}\}$ and $L = \{l_1, l_2, l_3, ..., l_{|L|}\}$ be the user set and location set, where $|U|$ and $|L|$ denote the number of users and locations. Given users' check-in data (U and L) and the corresponding social relationship S, the task of POI recommendation is defined as in (1). We calculate score for locations that user never visited before, and return a ranked list of candidate POIs to users.

$$U \times L \times S \to Score \tag{1}$$

3.2 TF-IDF Based Similarity Between Users

User-CF finds similar users based on a similarity measure. Then scores on items are calculated by a weighted combination of historical ratings from similar users. We can easily get a $|U| \times |L|$ check-in matrix C from check-in records. $C_{u,l}$ means check-in frequency that user $u \in U$ has checked in $l \in L$. If $C_{u,l} = 0$, it means user u has never visited location l. The recommendation score that user u will check in a location l is denoted as $Score_{u,l}$ as in (2), where $Sim_{u,v}$ is the similarity between user u and user v.

There are many ways to measure similarity weight between users, such as cosine similarity and Pearson's correlation coefficient. We adopt the widely used cosine similarity $Sim_{u,v}$ between users u and user v as in (3).

$$Score_{u,l} = \frac{\sum_v Sim_{u,v}C_{v,l}}{\sum_v Sim_{u,v}} \tag{2}$$

$$Sim_{u,v} = \frac{\sum_{l\in L} C_{u,l}C_{v,l}}{\sqrt{\sum_{l\in L} C_{u,l}^2}\sqrt{\sum_{l\in L} C_{v,l}^2}} \tag{3}$$

Some works used visited/unvisited way [9, 11] or check-in frequency [2, 3, 7] to represent user preference. The former only shows whether users visited a location or not. The latter roughly indicates user preference. These methods can't really demonstrate user preference precisely. In this case, we use TF-IDF to describe user preference in a fine-grained way.

TF-IDF [19] is widely used in information retrieval, document classification and other related fields. It measures the importance of a word to a document, just like the importance of visited locations to users. On the one hand, the importance of the word is proportional to the frequency of the word (TF) in the document. Meanwhile, the importance of the word is inversely proportional to the frequency in the corpus (IDF). Similarly, the more frequently user u checks in location l, the more important the location l is to user u as in (4). If less people visit location l, but user u visits location l individually, it means user u prefers location l relatively as in (5). We assume TF-IDF can represent personalized preference as in (6), not in a generalized way.

$$TF_{u,l} = \frac{total_{u,l}}{total_u} \tag{4}$$

$$IDF_l = log\left(\frac{|U|}{total_l} + 1\right) \tag{5}$$

$$TFIDF_{u,l} = TF_{u,l}IDF_l \tag{6}$$

where $total_{u,l}$ is check-in frequency for user u in location l, $total_u$ is the total number of check-ins for user u. $total_l$ is the total check-in frequency in location l, $TFIDF_{u,l}$ is the importance of POI l to user u.

Cosine similarity between users is improved by TF-IDF as in (7). An interesting phenomenon is that $Sim_{u,v}$ is not equal to $Sim_{v,u}$, which is greatly different from traditional similarity. As mentioned above, we use TF-IDF to represent the importance of locations for users. When measuring similarity of pairwise users, different locations generate different contribution according to their importance for users, not always the same. If location l is more important for user u, location l should be endowed with a larger weight when measuring similarity between others and u. In fact, this is a more personalized way, because we consider user real preference.

$$Sim_{u,v} = \frac{\sum\limits_{l \in L} C_{u,l} C_{v,l} TFIDF_{u,l}}{\sqrt{\sum\limits_{l \in L} C_{u,l}^2} \sqrt{\sum\limits_{l \in L} C_{v,l}^2}} \tag{7}$$

3.3 Social Reputation Influence for Recommendation

In Brightkite dataset [14], we find the average ration of common visited locations between friends is only 0.45%. It implies that less than 1% locations are commonly visited by friends and friends' preference about POIs may vary greatly. Therefore, we think it is unreasonable that some researchers directly generate recommendation for users from limited friends [1], or require target users' user-specific latent vector are closed to their friends [16, 17].

Empirical result demonstrates users tend to seek advice from people with high reputation. We assume users' reputation has an effect on recommendation result. Users with high reputation generate more contribution than those who have less reputation.

There are some link analysis approaches to measure weight of nodes in networks, such as PageRank, Hyperlink - Induced Topic Search (HITS) and TrustRank. Google Search uses PageRank to assign a numerical weighting to web pages to present their relationship and importance according to hyperlinks between them. We adopt widely used PageRank to calculate the weight level of user u, namely user reputation score $PageRank_u$. We normalize each reputation as in (8), where Rep_u is the social reputation of user u.

$$Rep_u = \frac{PageRank_u}{max(PageRank_{u \in U})} \tag{8}$$

3.4 Geographical Influence for Recommendation

When recommending locations to users in mobile environment, geographical distance is a very important factor. Meanwhile, popularity of locations should also be considered. In this section, the concerned geographical influence includes distance and popularity. For simplicity, the effect of geographical distance dis is denoted as $g(dis)$. Some researchers considered the relationship between check-in probability and geographical distance follow the power-law distribution [1, 9, 11] as in (9) where a and b are

$$g(dis) = a \times dis^b \tag{9}$$

parameters of a power-law distribution. Others think the relationship between probability of check-in and geographical distance follow inverse proportion [12] as in (10) or exponential function [15] as in (11). The common basic idea is almost consistent as follow: human tends to visit nearby POIs, and check-in probability of visiting a POI decreases as distance increases. Thus, we try to find the relatively appropriate method.

$$g(dis) = \frac{1}{dis} \qquad (10)$$

$$g(dis) = e^{-dis} \qquad (11)$$

Users always prefer visit nearby POIs close to some check-in centers like home or office [8, 11, 14]. In this case, an important work is to find check-in centers for each user. In order to avoid check-in outliers, we choose k-medoids method that is different from [12] to cluster locations user u visited and find the check-in centers for user u, like office and home. Nearby POIs closed to the center are good choices when recommending POIs for users.

Generally, the popularity of POIs also affects user decision making. A popular POI could provide better user experience in some aspects, so we adopt method in [6] to measure popularity of POI as in (12) where $p(l)$ is the popularity of location l, $totalCk_l$ is the total check-in frequency in location l, $totalPeo_l$ is the number of people who checked in location l.

$$p(l) = \frac{1}{2}\left\{\frac{totalCk_l}{max(totalCk_{l \in L}) - 1} + \frac{totalPeo_l}{max(totalPeo_{l \in L}) - 1}\right\} \qquad (12)$$

3.5   Unified Framework for POI Recommendation

Each factor mentioned above, such as TF-IDF based user preference, geographical information, social reputation, can be utilized to improve POI recommendation. Naturally, we proposed a unified framework named TSG to integrate these factors. Let $Score_{u,l}$ denotes the check-in score of user u at location l as in (13), where $dis_{u,l}$ is the nearest geographical distance between POI l and u's check-in center, such as user u's home or office.

It is worth mentioning that the product rule has been widely used to fuse different factors for POI recommendation in the previous work [6, 11, 12, 18] and has shown high robustness. In this framework, we calculate check-in score of unvisited locations and return a top-N POIs list for user u.

$$Score_{u,l} = \frac{\sum_{v} Sim_{u,v} C_{v,l} g(dis_{u,l}) p(l) Rep_v}{\sum_{v} Sim_{u,v}} \qquad (13)$$

4   Experimental Evaluation

In this section, we design and conduct several experiments to compare the recommendation qualities of the proposed method with other CF methods.

4.1   Dataset Analysis and Metric

We set a bounding box and extract 1422625 Brightkite check-ins from the dataset in [14]. The dataset is crawled from online LBSNs—Brightkite from Apr. 2008 to Oct. 2010. Check-in dataset includes user ID, location ID, longitude and latitude of POI, check-in timestamp and social relationship. To reduce noise data, we remove users who have fewer than 5 check-ins and locations which is less than 5 check-ins. The check-in density of the dataset is 1.36×10^{-3}. We randomly choose 70% as the training set and the remaining 30% as the testing set.

To evaluate the performance of the proposed method, we use precision Pre@N and recall Rec@N as the evaluation metric. Pre@N means the ratio of hit POIs to the recommendation list. Rec@N means the ratio of hit POIs to the ground truth. N is the length of the recommendation list. In our experiment, we set N = 5, 10, 20. To clearly compare with other methods, we focus on the relative improvements we achieved, instead of the absolute values.

4.2   Experimental Results

Performance Comparison Between TFIDF-Based Similarity and Cosine Similarity. In Sect. 3.2, we think the importance of POIs to users has an effect on similarity between users. Thus we use TF-IDF to enhance traditional user preference. In order to verify whether TF-IDF efficiently improves the performance of user-CF, we compare the recommendation results from traditional cosine similarity in (3) and TFIDF-based similarity in (7).

The precision and recall for them are plotted in Fig. 1 on top 5/10/20. In these figures, TF-IDF based way always exhibits the better performance under all values of N. It means TF-IDF based similarity can improve recommendation. And it describes user preference in a more accurate and personalized way.

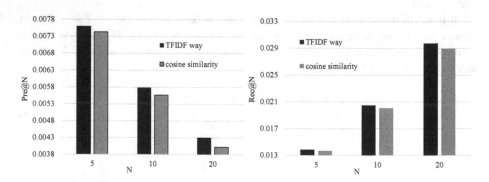

Fig. 1. Performance about different similarity

Performance on Different Methods Modeling Geographical Distance Influence. In Sect. 3.4, there are three methods to model geographical distance in POI recommendation as follow: power law distribution, exponential function and inverse proportion. We respectively incorporate these three methods into user-CF as in (14).

$$Score_{u,l} = \frac{\sum\limits_{v} Sim_{u,v} C_{v,l} g(dis)}{\sum\limits_{v} Sim_{u,v}} \tag{14}$$

Figure 2 shows the compared performance among different models on top 5/10/20 recommendation. We observe the inverse proportion is always perform better than other methods in terms of both Pre@N and Rec@N. It is reasonable since the probability of user checking in location to distance presents relatively slow descending tendency.

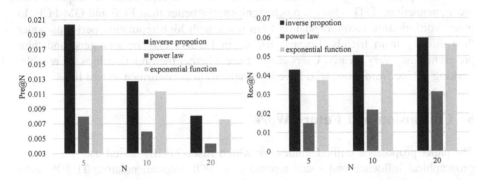

Fig. 2. Performance for different models of geographical distance

Comparison with Other POI Recommendation Approaches. Three factors, TF-IDF based user preference, geographical influence and social reputation, are incorporated into our unified models, denoted by TSG. We compare the proposed method with the following CF methods:

User-CF: the classical method is widely used in all kinds of applications.
FCF: In this way, users only get recommendation from their friends in LBSNs [1].
GM-FCF: this is the development of FCF. The method uses power law distribution to model geographical distance between friends [1].
USG: Three factors, namely user preference, social influence and geographical influence, are incorporated into unified CF [11].

Figure 3 reports the comparison results of top 5/10/20 recommendation with the baseline methods. TSG outperforms other methods significantly in all metrics. For example,

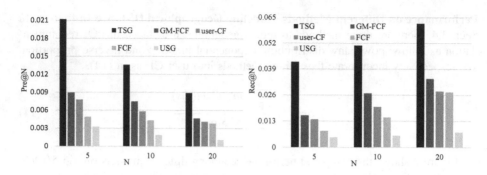

Fig. 3. Performance comparison

TSG attains 0.023 Pre@5, while user-CF achieves 0.0078. This implies that TFIDF-based user preference, geographical influence and social reputation can improve POI recommendation. TSG achieves much significantly better than FCF and GM-FCF. In other word, getting recommendation from users with high reputation performs better than directly from friends. Because friends in LBSNs may be strangers, and their preference may vary greatly. Users can't ensure whether their relationships are reliable. Seeking advice from those who have high reputation is confirmed in real life.

5 Conclusion and Future Work

The paper proposes a unified framework which fuses TF-IDF based user preference, geographical influence and social reputation in POI recommendation. TF-IDF technology is utilized to describe personalized user preference. Furthermore, we model geographical influence including geographical distance and popularity, then generate recommendation for users according to other's reputation in LBSNs. Experiment results on real dataset show that the proposed method performs better than other methods.

There are several directions to investigate in the future. First, information in LBSNs has not been fully utilized, such as user generated content (UGC), detailed POI information and social activities. Then, user influence should be determined by their activities on the social network rather than just friends. These information will be analyzed in our future work. We try to find and ensure the efficiency of temporal influence in POI recommendation.

Acknowledgement. This research is supported by the National Natural Science Foundation of China (Grant No. 61502062, Grant No. 61672117 and Grant No. 61602070), the China Post-doctoral Science Foundation under Grant 2014M560704, the Scientific Research Foundation for the Returned Overseas Chinese Scholars (State Education Ministry), and the Fundamental Research Funds for the Central Universities Project No. 2015CDJXY.

References

1. Ye, M., Yin, P., Lee, W.-C.: Location recommendation for location-based social networks. In: 18th SIGSPATIAL International Conference on Advances in Geographic Information Systems, pp. 458–461. ACM Press, New York (2010)
2. Bao, J., Zheng, Y., Mokbel, M.F.: Location-based and preference-aware recommendation using sparse geo-social networking data. In: 20th International Conference on Advances in Geographic Information Systems, pp. 199–208. ACM Press, New York (2012)
3. Gao, H., Tang, J., Hu, X., Liu, H.: Content-aware point of interest recommendation on location-based social networks. In: 29th AAAI Conference on Artificial Intelligence, pp. 1721–1727. AAAI Press, Menlo Park (2015)
4. Lian, D., Zhao, C., Xie, X., Sun, G., Chen, E., Rui, Y.: GeoMF: joint geographical modeling and matrix factorization for point-of-interest recommendation. In: 20th ACM SIGKDD International Conference on Knowledge Discovery and Data Mining, pp. 831–840. ACM Press, New York (2014)
5. Liu, Q., Ma, H., Chen, E., Xiong, H.: A survey of context-aware mobile recommendations. Int. J. Inf. Technol. Decis. Mak. **12**, 139–172 (2013)
6. Liu, B., Fu, Y., Yao, Z., Xiong, H.: Learning geographical preferences for point-of-interest recommendation. In: 19th ACM SIGKDD International Conference on Knowledge Discovery and Data Mining, pp. 1043–1051. ACM Press, New York (2013)
7. Gao, H., Tang, J., Hu, X., Liu, H.: Exploring temporal effects for location recommendation on location-based social networks. In: 7th ACM Conference on Recommender Systems, pp. 93–100. ACM Press, New York (2013)
8. Hu, L., Sun, A., Liu, Y.: Your neighbors affect your ratings: on geographical neighborhood influence to rating prediction. In: 37th International ACM SIGIR Conference on Research and Development in Information Retrieval, pp. 345–354. ACM Press, New York (2014)
9. Yuan, Q., Cong, G., Ma, Z., Sun, A., Thalmann, N.M.: Time-aware point-of-interest recommendation. In: 36th International ACM SIGIR Conference on Research and Development in Information Retrieval, pp. 363–372. ACM Press, New York (2013)
10. Yuan, Q., Cong, G., Sun, A.: Graph-based point-of-interest recommendation with geographical and temporal influences. In: 23rd ACM International Conference on Conference on Information and Knowledge Management, pp. 659–668. ACM Press, New York (2014)
11. Ye, M., Yin, P., Lee, W.-C., Lee, D.-L.: Exploiting geographical influence for collaborative point-of-interest recommendation. In: 34th International ACM SIGIR Conference on Research and Development in Information, pp. 325–334. ACM Press, New York (2011)
12. Cheng, C., Yang, H., King, I., Lyu, M.R.: Fused matrix factorization with geographical and social influence in location-based social networks. In: 26th Conference on Artificial Intelligence, pp. 17–23. AAAI Press, Menlo Park (2012)
13. Tang, J., Hu, X., Gao, H., Liu, H.: Exploiting local and global social context for recommendation. In: 23rd International Joint Conference on Artificial Intelligence, pp. 2712–2718. AAAI Press, Menlo Park (2013)
14. Cho, E., Myers, S.A., Leskovec, J.: Friendship and mobility: user movement in location-based social networks. In: 17th ACM SIGKDD International Conference on Knowledge Discovery and Data Mining, pp. 1082–1090. ACM Press, New York (2011)
15. Liu, S.D., Meng, X.W.: Approach to network services recommendation based on mobile users' location. J. Softw. **25**, 2556–2574 (2014). (in Chinese)
16. Feng, Y., Li, H., Chen, Z.: Improving recommendation accuracy and diversity via multiple social factors and social circles. Int. J. Web Serv. Res. **11**, 32–46 (2014)

17. Ma, H., Zhou, D., Liu, C., Lyu, M.R., King, I.: Recommender systems with social regularization. In: 4th ACM International Conference on Web Search and Data Mining, pp. 287–296. ACM Press, New York (2011)
18. Zhang, J.-D., Chow, C.-Y.: GeoSoCa: exploiting geographical, social and categorical correlations for point-of-interest recommendations. In: 38th International ACM SIGIR Conference on Research and Development in Information Retrieval, pp. 443–452. ACM Press, New York (2015)
19. Spertus, E., Sahami, M., Buyukkokten, O.: Evaluating similarity measures: a large-scale study in the orkut social network. In: 11th ACM SIGKDD International Conference on Knowledge Discovery in Data Mining, pp. 678–684. ACM Press, New York (2005)

An Electricity Power Collection Data Oriented Missing Data Imputation Solution

Jiangqi Chen[1], Han Li[2,3(✉)], Ting Zhao[1], and He Liu[1]

[1] Advanced Computing and Big Data Technology Laboratory of SGCC,
Global Energy Interconnection Research Institute, Beijing, China
{chenjiangqi,zhaoting,liuhe}@geiri.sgcc.com.cn
[2] College of Computer Science,
North China University of Technology, Beijing, China
lihan@ncut.edu.cn
[3] Beijing Key Laboratory on Integration and Analysis of Large-Scale
Stream Data, Beijing, China

Abstract. In Smart Grid, the incompleteness of electricity power collection data is gradually prominent. Thus, this paper presents an electricity power collection big data oriented missing data imputation solution, which comprises a big data processing framework and a missing data imputation method for power consumption data. Based on big data techniques, the given framework supports the large-scale electricity power collection data acquisition, storage and processing. To get a better result, the proposed method takes advantage of the correlation between the loss rate of power and the user power consumption. The feasibility and the effectiveness of the proposed method is evaluated. Experimental results show the proposed method is able to convert incomplete data set into complete data set, and has good imputation stability. Compared with the KNN algorithm, the proposed method has a lower imputation error, and is a positive attempt to combine domain-specific algorithms with traditional algorithms.

Keywords: Missing data imputation · Electricity power collection data
Big data · KNN · Data quality

1 Introduction

Being accompanied by the development of information techniques, communication techniques and IoT techniques, the total amount of data accumulated is rapidly increasing in nearly all fields. In order to make use of these data, more and more attentions have been paid to big data techniques [1] and data mining techniques in both academia and industry. Since data quality can have a significant effect on the conclusions that can be drawn from the data, it is necessary to preprocess the data [2].

Missing data occurs when no data value is stored for the variable in an observation [3]. Owing to the complexity of data accumulation, storage and processing, data missing is inevitable. Since data missing may reduce the data quality, it has become a challenging problem, and it is vital to replace missing data with substituted values.

© ICST Institute for Computer Sciences, Social Informatics and Telecommunications Engineering 2018
I. Romdhani et al. (Eds.): CollaborateCom 2017, LNICST 252, pp. 243–252, 2018.
https://doi.org/10.1007/978-3-030-00916-8_23

Missing data imputation is a kind of technique that can convert incomplete data set into complete data set using appropriate strategies [4]. Recent years, a number of literatures show that the missing data imputation methods have begun to be discussed and applied in industry, medicine and other fields [4]. In the field of statistics, many mature missing data imputation methods have been proposed, such as the mean value method, the regression method, the hot-deck method, the expectation maximization method and so on. Although missing data imputation methods have been applied in a certain number of fields, it is still a challenging problem in the electric power industry. Thus this paper focuses on the missing data imputation method for the electricity power collection data.

Additionally, massive electricity power collection data is continuously produced by smart meters in the power grid of China. As an example, more than 400 million smart meters have been installed by the end of 2016. That is, the amount of electricity power collection data is rapidly increasing day by day. Therefore, a data processing framework for the electricity power collection data is required.

In conclusion, to solve the problem in missing data imputation for electricity power collection data, the missing data imputation method and the data processing framework are investigated in this paper.

2 Related Work

Data missing is one of the most ubiquitous and realistic problems in nearly every field. In the late 1970s, researchers begin to pay their attentions to resolve the problem of data missing. Recently, researchers at home and abroad have proposed plenty of missing data imputation techniques. Since most imputation methods are restricted to one type of variable whether categorical or continuous, a multi-objective genetic algorithm for missing data imputation MOGAImp is proposed in 2015 [5]. MOGAImp is proved to be effective and flexible, and is expected to be adapted in different application domains. In 2016, three missing data imputation methods based on fuzzy-rough methods are given [6]. Experimental results show these methods are effective. However, the time complexity is a little high and could be reduced. In 2017, a multiple imputation method in the presence of nonignorable nonresponse is proposed [7]. The multiple imputation method is verified to be relatively robust in bias and coverage. However, its efficiency is required to be improved. In addition to the traditional missing data imputation methods, missing data imputation methods which make use of domain knowledge has begun to draw more attention. In 2015, a hybrid prediction model with missing value imputation for medical data is presented [8]. The proposed hybrid model is the first one to use combination of K-means clustering with multilayer perceptron. Experimental results show the proposed method is feasible, robust and efficient. In 2016, a data imputation method based on the manufacturing characteristics is proposed for resolving the data missing problem in steel industry [9]. In the method, a correlation analysis method called NGCC and its corresponding model are used. The experimental results indicate that the proposed method is feasible and exhibits a better performance on the accuracy [9]. In 2017, a missing data imputation method based on genetic algorithms is given for questionnaires. In the method, Bayesian and Akaike's information criterions are taken as the fitness functions [10]. Experimental results show that the proposed method is more effective than Multivariate Imputation by Chained Equations (MICE) algorithm [11]. As illustrated above, traditional missing data imputation methods are not universal, and making use of the domain knowledge is becoming a trend of the imputation of missing data. Thus, an electricity power collection data oriented missing data imputation method is proposed by combining the domain knowledge and the traditional missing data imputation method in this paper.

Furthermore, since the scale of electric power data rapidly increases, how to efficiently processing the electric power data has become a core issue in the construction of smart grid. In 2015, a Spark based unified cluster computing platform which is suitable for storing and performing big data analytics on smart grid data is proposed [12], and the feasibility of the platform is depicted. In 2017, a big data framework for analytics in smart grids is presented, which contains various big data techniques including Flume, HDFS, MapReduce, Hive, Tableau and so on [13]. By applying the framework on two scenarios to visualize the energy, the feasibility of the framework is verified. Since the electricity power collection data is a part of the electric power data, the scale of electricity power collection data is also large. Thus, this paper designs a big data processing framework to support the processing of electricity power collection data in the power grid in China.

3   The Proposed Big Data Processing Framework

In order to establish a proper big data processing framework for electricity power collection data, the characteristics of the power grid of China are summarized. (1) Large scale: In China, the size of the electric power grid is very large and is expanding year by year. Thus, the amount of the electricity power collection data rises rapidly. (2) Multilayer: There are multiple layers in the power grid of China, such as the headquarters, the provincial power grid and the prefectural power grid. From the perspective of the headquarters, the headquarters and the provincial power grid are two major layers. (3) Multiple data types: The electricity power collection data is divided into three main types, including the real-time data, the archive data and the historical data. The real-time data is continuously generated by smart meters. The archive data contains the information of users. The historical data is similar to the real-time data, but is generated during a period of time in the past. (4) Different performance requirements: According to the requirements of different electric power applications, the time to achieve an data processing varies from minute to hour.

As shown in Fig. 1, a big data processing framework for electricity power collection data is designed to accords with the above characteristics. In brief, the proposed framework is divided into two layers, can support large-scale data processing with MapReduce and Spark, and is able to accumulate and store the real-time data, the archive data and the historical data.

In the framework, the data acquisition subsystem focuses on accumulating data from intelligent meters, and transferring these data into data storage subsystem. In the data collection module, data are obtained by establishing long connections between the data collection module and the intelligent meters through socket. In the real-time data

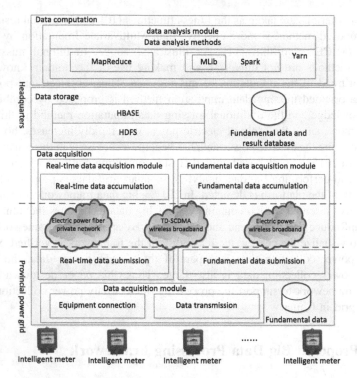

Fig. 1. The big data processing framework for electricity power collection data is divided into two layers including the provincial power gird and the headquarters, and is composed of three subsystems including the data storage subsystem, the data computation subsystem and the data acquisition subsystem.

acquisition module, Kafka is used for building real-time data pipelines. In order to transfer the fundamental data which refers to the history data and the archive data, an ftp service is applied in the fundamental data acquisition module. The data storage subsystem is an integrated storage environment, in which MySQL is used to save archive data, HDFS is applied to receive original electricity power collection data, and HBASE is used to save the parsed electricity power collection data. The data computation subsystem concentrates on the processing of electricity power collection data. Missing data imputation methods and a distributed computation environment based on MapReduce and Spark are the key components.

4 The Proposed Missing Data Imputation Method

In the electric power industry, power which is defined as the rate at which electrical energy is transferred by an electric circuit is a key indicator for user behavior analysis. Therefore, this paper takes the power consumption as the research object, and the data missing problem in this paper is defined as how to calculating the missing power consumption data.

4.1 Description of the Data Missing Problem

The description of the data missing problem in this paper is depicted as follows.

There are N users in a transformer area T. Every day, the smart meters record the power consumption of the transformer area for each user. Assuming the collection of power consumption occurs M times/day, $M \times D$ records are collected within D days. In this paper, (d, m) represents the mth time point in the dth day, P_{dmT} represents the output power of the transformer area T, P_{dm0} depicts the loss of power, the power consumptions of N users are respectively depicted by P_{dm1}, P_{dm2}, ..., P_{dmN}. Then P_{dm0} is set to $P_{dmT} - (P_{dm1} + P_{dm2} + \cdots + P_{dmN})$. As a result, the problem to be resolved in this paper is described as calculating the missing power consumption data for the ith user P_{dmi}.

4.2 Roadmap of the Proposed Method

In practical applications, any data entry whose power consumption is missing will be discarded. Due to the high missing rate of power consumption, the amount of data will be obviously reduced and the accuracy of further analysis will also decreased. Thus, it is necessary to calculate the missing power consumption. Since considering the domain knowledge during the imputation of missing data can get better result, a missing power consumption data imputation method is proposed by combing the KNN algorithm and the correlation between the loss rate of power and the user power consumption. In the proposed method, the KNN algorithm is used to construct a candidate set, while the domain knowledge is used to select a right candidate.

The technology roadmap of the proposed method is divided into three stages. In the first stage, the loss rate of power is calculated by estimating the state of transformer area T. In the second stage, the missing user power consumption is estimated according to the daily power curve. In the last stage, the result is adjusted based on the correlation between the loss rate of power and the user power consumption.

4.3 Estimation of the Loss Rate of Power

For the mth time point in the dth day, the ratio of the power consumption for user n to the total power consumption is represented by $r_{dmn} = P_{dmn}/P_{dmT}$, and the loss rate of power at a certain time is able to be estimated according to the ratio of the power consumption for each user to the total power consumption within the transformer area. The details are described as follows:

At time point (d, m), $[r_{dm1}, r_{dm2}, ..., r_{dmN}]$ is considered as a sample and is represented by R_{dm}. G is a set of time points with complete user power consumption. For $(d, m) \in G$, if all users' power consumption within the transformer area are known, R_{dm} is complete, the loss rate of power r_{dm0} can be calculated using formula (1), and $\{(R_{ij}, r_{ij0})|(i, j) \in G\}$ is used to represents a known sample set.

$$r_{dm0} = P_{dm0}/P_{dmT} = 1 - (r_{dm1} + r_{dm2} + \cdots + r_{dmN}) \tag{1}$$

For each time point $(d, m) \notin G$, R_{dm} is incomplete, and the loss rate of power is unknown. So the loss rate of power for R_{dm} is estimated as follows:

There are u users which are represented as $n_1, n_2, \ldots, n_u$. The time point is (d, m). R_{dm}^* which does not have any missing data is excerpted from R_{dm}, and is represented as $R_{dm}^* = [r_{dmn_1}, r_{dmn_2}, \ldots, r_{dmn_u}]$. R_{ij}^* is excerpted from R_{ij}, and can be depicted as $R_{ij}^* = [r_{ijn_1}, r_{ijn_2}, \ldots, r_{ijn_u}], (i, j) \in G$. Based on the KNN algorithm in which the city block distance is used, k_1 candidates $\{ R_{i_u j_u}^* \}_{u=1}^{k_1}$ are selected from $\{ R_{ij}^* | (i, j) \in G \}$, and the loss rate of power for R_{dm} is preliminarily estimated according to formula (2).

$$\widetilde{r_{dm0}} = \frac{1}{k_1} \sum_{u=1}^{k1} r_{i_u j_u 0} \tag{2}$$

4.4　Estimation of the Missing Power Consumption

Based on the known daily power curves, the missing data of power consumption in an incomplete daily curve is able to be estimated as follows:

The daily power curve of user n in the dth day is represented by $L_{dn} = [P_{d1n}, P_{d2n}, \ldots, P_{dMn}]$. Due to the missing of P_{dmq}, L_{dq} is incomplete. Therefore, L_{dq}^* which does not have any missing data is excerpted from L_{dq}, and is represented as $L_{dn}^* = [P_{dm_1 q}, P_{dm_2 q}, \ldots, P_{dm_l q}]$. Assuming H_{ij} is the aggregation of daily power curves where both $\{P_{im_u j}\}_{u=1}^l$ and P_{jmi} do not have any missing data, $L_{ij}^* = [P_{im_1 j}, P_{im_2 j}, \ldots, P_{im_l j}], (i, j) \in H_{ij}$ which does not have any missing data is excerpted from H_{ij}, and $\{(L_{ij}, P_{imj}) | (i, j) \in H_{ij}\}$ is used to represents a known sample set. Based on the KNN algorithm in which the correlation distance is used, k_2 most candidates $\{ L_{i_u j_u}^* \}_{u=1}^{k_1}$ are selected, and the missing power consumption is estimated according to formula (3).

$$P_{dmq}^{(u)} = P_{i_u m j_u} \times \left(\sum_{w=1}^l P_{dm_0 q} \right) / \left(\sum_{w=1}^l P_{i_u m_w j_u} \right), u = 1, 2, \ldots k_2 \tag{3}$$

4.5　Adjustment of the Missing Power Consumption

Assuming the power consumptions of v users are not complete, the sum of missing power consumption can be calculated on the basis of the known user power consumption and the loss rate of power according to formula (4).

$$\sum_{j=1}^v \widetilde{P_{dmq_j}} = (1 - \widetilde{r_{dm0}}) P_{dmT} - \sum_{i=1}^u P_{dmn_i} \tag{4}$$

Based on the correlation between the power consumption and the loss rate of power, the final power consumption will be adjusted as follows:

At the time point $(d, m) \notin G$, there are k_2 candidates $P_{dmq_j}^{(u)}, j = 1, 2, \ldots, v, u = 1, 2, \ldots, k_2$ for each absent user power consumption P_{dmq_j}. That is, there are k_2^v

candidates for v user power consumption. For each candidate, the difference between $\sum_{j=1}^{v} P_{dmq_j}^{u_j}$ and $\sum_{j=1}^{v} \widetilde{P_{dmq_j}}$ is calculated, and $\{P_{dmq_j}^0\}_{j=1}^{v}$ is used to represent the candidate that have the minimum difference.

Then, the corresponding loss rate of power is calculated according to formula (5).

$$r_{dm0}^0 = 1 - \left(\sum_{i=1}^{u} P_{dmn_i} + \sum_{j=1}^{v} P_{dmq_j}^0\right)/P_{dmT} \tag{5}$$

If $r_{dm0}^0 \in [max(r_1, \widetilde{r_{dm0}} - r_2), \widetilde{r_{dm0}} + r_2]$, the final candidate of the loss rate of power $\widehat{r_{dm0}}$ is set to r_{dm0}^0. If $r_{dm0}^0 < max(r_1, \widetilde{r_{dm0}} - r_2)$, $\widehat{r_{dm0}}$ is set to $max(r_1, \widetilde{r_{dm0}} - r_2)$. If $r_{dm0}^0 > \widetilde{r_{dm0}} + r_2$, $\widehat{r_{dm0}}$ is set to $\widetilde{r_{dm0}} + r_2$.

Next, based on $\widehat{r_{dm0}}$, the sum of the missing user power consumptions is calculated according to formula (6).

$$\sum_{j=1}^{v} \widehat{P_{dmq_j}} = (1 - \widehat{r_{dm0}})P_{dmT} - \sum_{i=1}^{u} P_{dmn_i} \tag{6}$$

Finally, the missing data is recalculated according to formula (7).

$$\widehat{P_{dmq_j}} = \left[(1 - \widehat{r_{dm0}})P_{dmT} - \sum_{i=1}^{u} P_{dmn_i}\right] \times P_{dmq_j}^0 / \left(\sum_{h=1}^{v} P_{dmq_h}^0\right) \tag{7}$$

5   Experiments and Results

The experiments are designed to evaluate the feasibility and effectiveness of the proposed missing data imputation method. In the experiments, a realistic data set obtained from the smart meters in a certain transformer area of China is applied. For the purpose of calculating the imputation error, a subset of the data set, which has no missing data, is considered as the fundamental data set. Based on the three-phase characteristics of electricity power collection data, the fundamental data set is divided into three data sets, including Tran1_PhaseA, Tran1_PhaseB and Tran1_PhaseC. PhaseA, PhaseB and PhaseC respectively refers to the three phases of three-phase electric power. The scales of these data sets are the same, and they have the same attributes. Taking data set Tran1_PhaseA as an example, the basic information of Tran1_PhaseA is given in Table 1.

Table 1. Basic information of Tran1_PhaseA.

Number of attributes	Time slot (days)	Number of users	Frequency per day
10	50	44	48

To accomplish the experiments, the data sets should contain a certain number of missing data. The rate of missing data is defined as the percentage between the amount of missing data and the total amount of all data. In this paper, a data construction method is used to produce data sets with different rates of missing data.

Except for the rate of missing data, four other parameters are defined, which are the percentage of missing data for each time point (Thr_era2), the percentage of missing data for each daily power curve (Thr_era3), the percentage of time points without missing data (Thr_era4) and the percentage between the amount of complete daily power curves and the total amount of all power curves (Thr_era5). According to the practical experience, a fix value is set to each of the above parameters, which is listed in Table 2.

Table 2. Values of parameters.

Parameter	Thr_era2	Thr_era3	Thr_era4	Thr_era5
Value	80%	80%	5%	5%

The imputation error is defined as the mean value of the absolute error between the data set processed by the proposed method and the original data set. Assuming the data set which is processed by the proposed method and the original data set are respectively $ds1$ and $ds2$, the imputation error is calculated according to formula (8).

$$err\_rate = mean(mean(abs(ds1 - ds2))) \tag{8}$$

In general, the procedure of the experiments comprises three main steps. In the first step, the data construction method generates an incomplete data set by randomly deleting a certain percentage of data from the data set. In the second step, the proposed missing data imputation method is applied to the data set. In the last step, the imputation error is calculated.

To verify the feasibility of the algorithm, the proposed method is applied to data sets Tran1_PhaseA, Tran1_PhaseB and Tran1_PhaseC, and the rate of missing data of each data set is respectively set to 10%, 20%, 30%, 40% and 50%. Figure 2 shows the imputation errors of the experiments.

Based on KNN algorithm, the proposed missing data imputation method takes the loss rate of power into account when the missing user power consumption is calculated. In order to verify the effectiveness of the algorithm, the missing data are calculated

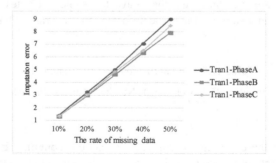

Fig. 2. The imputation errors of the experiments show that with the increasing of the rate of missing data, the imputation error tends to increase proportionally. That is, the proposed method is able to converts incomplete data to complete data, and is relatively stable.

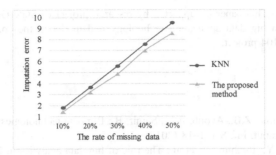

Fig. 3. The imputation errors of both the KNN algorithm and the proposed method shows that compared with the KNN algorithm, the proposed method has a lower imputation error. That is, it is able to get a data set with higher data quality.

using both the KNN algorithm and the proposed method. Figure 3 illustrates the imputation errors of both the KNN algorithm and the proposed method.

Due to the spatiotemporal correlation of the power consumption data,transformer area id, timestamp and user id are considered as the row key when storing data. Therefore, the proposed method is able to be supported by MapReduce or Spark. In addition, since the KNN algorithm is implemented on Mlib which is a machine leaning library provided by Spark, the efficiency of the proposed missing data imputation method is improved compared with that of a traditional serial program.

6 Conclusion

To solve the problem of missing data in the electric power industry, an electricity power collection big data oriented missing data imputation solution is investigated in this paper. The given solution consists of a big data processing framework for electricity power collection data and a missing data imputation method for power consumption data. The proposed framework accords with the characteristics of the power grid in China, and is able to support the acquisition, the storage and the computation of the electricity power collection data. Meanwhile, the proposed missing data imputation method calculate the missing values of user power consumption on the basis of KNN algorithm and the correlation between the loss rate of power and the user power consumption. Experimental results indicate the proposed missing data imputation method is a relatively stable method to converts incomplete data to complete data. Compared with the missing data imputation method which only bases on the KNN algorithm, the proposed method is able to generate more accurate values. Additionally, the proposed method has made a positive attempt to combine the traditional missing data imputation algorithm and the domain knowledge in the electric power industry. In the future, more professional knowledge is going to be applied to solve other data quality problems. The promotion and evaluation of the efficiency of the proposed solution is also the future work.

Acknowledgments. This paper is supported by research project of State Grid Corporation of China "Research on big data application technology and model in the company key areas" SGRIJSKJ(2016) 1104 project.

References

1. Ahmed, O., Fatima, Z.B., Ayoub, A.L., Samir, B.: Big data technologies: a survey. J. King Saud Univ. Comput. Inf. Sci. 1–18 (2017)
2. Ejaz, A., Ibrar, Y., Ibrahim, A., et al.: The role of big data analytics in Internet of Things. Comput. Netw. **129**, 1–13 (2017)
3. Song, Q., Shepperd, M.: A new imputation method for small software project data sets. J. Syst. Softw. **80**(1), 51–62 (2007)
4. Penny, K.I., Chesney, T.: Imputation methods to deal with missing values when data mining trauma injury data. In: The 28th International Conference on Information Technology Interfaces, pp. 213–218. IEEE Press, Cavtat (2006)
5. Fabio, L., Claudomiro, S., Igor, A., et al.: Multi-objective genetic algorithm for missing data imputation. Pattern Recognit. Lett. **68**, 126–131 (2015)
6. Mehran, A., Richard, J.: Missing data imputation using fuzzy-rough methods. Neurocomputing **205**, 152–164 (2016)
7. Im, J., Kim, S.: Multiple imputation for nonignorable missing data. J. Korean Stat. Soc. (2017, in press)
8. Archana, P., Sandeep, K.S.: Hybrid prediction model with missing value imputation for medical data. Expert Syst. Appl. **42**, 5621–5631 (2015)
9. Zheng, L., Jun, Z., Ying, L., Wei, W.: Data imputation for gas flow data in steel industry based on non-equal-length granules correlation coefficient. Inf. Sci. **367–368**, 311–323 (2016)
10. Celestino, O.G., Fernando, S.L., Francisco, J., et al.: Missing data imputation of questionnaires by means of genetic algorithms with different fitness functions. J. Comput. Appl. Math. **311**, 704–717 (2017)
11. Buuen, S., Groothuis, O.: MICE: multivariate imputation by chained equation in R. J. Stat. Softw. **45**, 1–67 (2011)
12. Shyam, R., Bharathi, G.H., Sachin, K.S., et al.: Apache spark a big data analytics platform for smart grid. Proc. Technol. **21**, 171–178 (2015)
13. Amr, A., Munshi, Y.A., Mohamed, R.I.: Big data framework for analytics in smart grid. Electr. Power Syst. Res. **151**, 369–380 (2017)

Curve-Registration-Based Feature Extraction for Predictive Maintenance of Industrial Equipment

Shouli Zhang[1(✉)], Xiaohong Li[1], Jianwu Wang[2], and Shen Su[3]

[1] Department of School of Computer Science and Technology,
Tianjin University, Tianjin 300072, China
zhangshoulia@163.com
[2] Department of Information Systems, University of Maryland,
Baltimore County, Baltimore, MD 21250, USA
[3] Beijing Key Laboratory on Integration and Analysis of Large-Scale
Stream Data, North China University of Technology, Beijing 100144, China

Abstract. With the growing adoption of Internet of Things (IoT), predictive maintenance is gaining momentum for ensuring the reliability of industrial equipment. A common practice of predictive maintenance is to conduct feature extraction on the original sensor data, then conduct deep learning to train predictive maintenance model with the extracted data and finally, conduct prediction by model. Because of the low value density of industrial sensor data stream, feature extraction is usually based on dimensionality reduction. However, traditional methods for dimensionality reduction seldom consider time-lagged correlations which are very common among industrial sensor data streams. More importantly, time-lagged correlations are less sensitive to the traditional dimensionality reduction methods, leading to poor effect of feature extraction. In this paper, we propose a feature extraction method based on curve registration to deal with the time-lagged correlation problem. Our experimental results indicate that our method can: (1) effectively improve the accuracy of prediction; and (2) improve the performance of the prediction model.

Keywords: Predictive maintenance · Time-lagged correlation
Curve registration · Feature extraction

1 Introduction

Predictive maintenance techniques are playing a critical role in a large variety of industries to help anticipate equipment failures to allow for advance scheduling of corrective maintenance. Predictive maintenance is performed based on an assessment of the health status of equipment [1]. Thanks to the rapid development of IoT, massive sensors are deployed on industrial equipment to monitor health status. Thus, a predictive maintenance model can be built by analyzing such sensor data to predict potential failures. With the considerable development of deep learning in recent years, deep-learning-based methods have become popular for predictive maintenance [2–4]. A common practice for predictive maintenance is to conduct deep learning, and feature

© ICST Institute for Computer Sciences, Social Informatics and Telecommunications Engineering 2018
I. Romdhani et al. (Eds.): CollaborateCom 2017, LNICST 252, pp. 253–263, 2018.
https://doi.org/10.1007/978-3-030-00916-8_24

extraction plays an important role. This is because the big volume of data streams will result in heavy cost to learning knowledge [2] so that cannot be directly imported into the learning model. And it is difficult to select effective sensors from the massive sensors by their names manually.

In recent years, a number of researchers have applied dimensionality reduction techniques to capture effective features from raw sensor data [5–8]. Feature extraction can be used to transform a set of observations of possibly correlated original data set into a set of values of uncorrelated features by calculating the eigenvectors of the covariance matrix of the original inputs. Thus, extraction effect depends on the correlation between different dimension data. When the correlation of different dimensions is strong, the extraction effect will be obvious and vice versa.

In practical industrial scenarios, there is a common phenomenon that sensor data are correlated with time lags (noted as time-lagged correlation in this paper). On one side, this is from the differences of the system clocks; on the other side, the working principles of the industrial equipment also result in time-lagged correlations among sensor data streams. The time-lagged correlations make the original correlation among sensors seem to be uncorrelated [9], and also decrease the effect of feature extraction. Unfortunately, the existing feature extraction methods [10–13] generally do not consider time-lagged correlation.

In order to improve the extraction effect, we propose a feature extraction method based on curve registration to solve the time-lagged correlation problem. Our challenge here is to figure out the time lags among sensors. To that end, we evaluate the correlations between each pair of sensors based on curve registration methods, and cluster such sensors according to the calculated correlations. With the appropriate time lag adjustment, we manage to map the high-dimensional sensor data to a low-dimension space with adequate original information. The extracted features are passed through an LSTM network, which can be viewed as a deep neural network, to perform predictive maintenance.

2 Related Works

2.1 Feature Extraction Technique for Predictive Maintenance

Feature extraction is one effective way to reduce dimensions and the most import step before training the predictive maintenance model for massive high-dimensional data. Susto [10] employ a supervised regression methodology, called Supervised Aggregative Feature Extraction [11, 12], which exploits a functional learning paradigm to model learning problems with time-series type inputs and scalar output, de facto bypassing the feature extraction phase. Zhang [2] present a log-driven failure prediction system for complex IT systems, which automatically extracts features from IT system logs and enables earlier failure predictions through the LSTM approach on discovering the long-range structure in history data. Kimura [13] adopt a supervised machine learning technique to develop an online template extraction method and a future extraction method that characterizes the abnormality of logs based on the generation patterns of logs. Kimura [14] propose a modeling and event extraction method on network log data using a tensor factorization approach.

Although the above researches are able to automatically extract features from the log files, but their log format is predefined so that it is relatively easy to extract features and template. However, the sensor data is unorganized. Besides, they do not care about the time warping which results in time-lagged correlation among different sensors.

2.2 Predictive Maintenance

Machine-learning approaches are the most popular methods for prognostics. Several quantitative models ranging from simple linear discriminant analysis, more complex logistic regression analysis, and neural networks have been proposed for prediction [15]. Susto develops a multiple classifier machine learning methodology to deal with the unbalanced datasets that arise in maintenance classification problems [16]. But it cannot deal with the high dimensionality of dataset. Baban [17] use a fuzzy logic approach to develop a decision-making system that allows determining the lifetime of the needle and plane predictive maintenance of the needle of a sewing machine. However, it requires expert knowledge and depends on datasets of small quantity. He [18] present an approach for pre-processes sensor signals using short time Fourier transform (STFT). Based on a simple spectrum matrix obtained by an optimized deep learning structure STFT, large memory storage retrieval neural network is built to diagnose the bearing faults. Liu [1] perform a vibration signal analysis to study and extract the behavioral pattern of the bearings. Then use a few machine learning models to classify the type of failure. Finally, they apply a Collaborative Recommendation Approach (CRA) to analyze the similarity of all the model results to suggest in advance.

The above literatures have solved the problem of predictive maintenance to a certain extent, but their method cannot be directly applied on predictive maintenance for large-scale industry because of 'high' and 'wide' sensor data set. In addition, the solution is still mainly dependent on the professional knowledge. However, different industry production environment is various and complex. It is difficult to understand professional knowledge for developers.

3 Problem Analysis

Feature extraction extracts information from the original data as an effective feature [8]. The goal of feature extraction is to find a lower-dimensional data space that will allow projecting the original high-dimensional data on it and form a new presentation of the original data. Herein, we give the formal definition about feature extraction in this paper as following.

Given a sample x_i (i = 1, ..., N) with H-dimensional vectors lying in a data space S (S $\in R^H$), we need to find a space F (F $\in R^L, L < H$) with L dimension, that makes $x \mapsto x' = F(x)$. In which, x' is the effective features with lower dimension and sufficient information extracted from the original sample data x.

Most feature extraction methods are based on the correlation between sensors. These methods convert the correlated sensor data into a new of linearly uncorrelated presentation (described as feature) by linear transformation. However, in a real production, there is a serious phenomenon that the time warp exists between different sensors which results in time-lagged correlation. This changes the correlation between sensors which can reduce the effect of feature extraction [19].

Next, we explain the time-lagged correlation with a real case in a power plant. There are over ten thousand of sensors deployed on hundreds of equipment in a power plant to monitor machine status at real-time. Figure 1 shows an original sensor data sample generated by a coal mill including 15 sensor data streams. In this paper, we consider Pearson correlation coefficient as the correlation between sensors which is a common used metric. Pearson correlation coefficient between A9 and A10 is 0.171, which indicates that A9 and A10 are irrelevant. But after alignment for A10 with time difference $\Delta t = -4$, Pearson correlation coefficient between A9 and A10 changes to 0.971, leading to the conclusion that A9 and A10 have strong correlation.

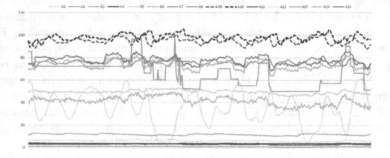

Fig. 1. Example of sensor data stream with time-lagged correlation

To extract feature from the sample data of coal mill, we apply PCA (Principal Component Analysis), which is a common feature extraction method, to the original data set. Without the time difference alignment, the data dimension is reduced from 15 to 7 with totally 98.8% original information. However, with the time difference alignment, the data dimension is reduced from 15 to 6 with the same amount of original information.

According to the above discussion, it is essential to solve time-lagged correlation before feature extraction. In this paper, we focus on the problem of feature extraction with time-lagged correlation and propose a curve-registration-based feature extraction method for predictive maintenance. Time lags for time-lagged correlation sensors are proofread by our method. Finally, we build a predictive maintenance model to predict the failures.

4 Time-Lagged Correlation Oriented Feature Extraction Method

4.1 Curve Registration for Time-Lagged Correlation Sensor Data

Curve registration is an effective way to solve time-lagged correlations. There are many researches on curve registration, the most common one is expectation maximization. The principle of feature extraction is based on correlation between different variables, our curve alignment is based on the correlation maximization. In this paper, we use Pearson correlation coefficient to measure the correlations between sequences. Work [19] presents a correlation-based curve registration method called S-GEM for double sequences. It aims to find a time difference function $d(t) = d^k(t)$ for two related sequential data TS_1 and TS_2. In which d is the order of function, k is the total number of iterations when computing $d(t)$. With the help of function $d(t)$, we can find a $\Delta t = d(t_i)$ to make Pearson correlation coefficient $\rho(TS_1(t), TS_2(t + \Delta t))$ maximized.

However, S-GEM is designed for two variables. For a big number of sensors deployed on equipment, such method is not practical if we need to conduct it on each pair of sensors. The first idea came to us is to find a variable as the baseline, then compare it with other remaining variables to find Δt in turn. However, this method brings up two problems: (1) which one should be selected as the baseline; (2) what should be done with the irrelevant variables compared to the baseline variable.

As a further thought, we cluster all variables into groups, and conduct curve registration within each pair of variables in the same group. To make the choice of the baseline variable that is not sensitive to the clustering result, we only cluster two variables into the same group when they are strongly correlated. And we manage to consider no curve registration problem in this way. It is the fundamental assumption of our method that sequences in the same cluster have the same correlation. Thus, every sequence in the same clusters can be selected as a reference curve, and we select the first one as curve registration. Other sequence can be aligned by S-GEM according with reference curve in turn.

Formally, our method works as following. Let $\{X_1, X_2, \ldots, X_h\}$ be h multivariate curves that can be considered as a waveform of observers for multi sensor data. Given at iteration $v = 1$, a K-means based clustering algorithm is applied on the original sensor data to cluster the wave curve into k groups $P^1 = \{G_1^1, G_2^1, \ldots, G_k^1\}$, and P refers to the partition. For every group, we select a random sequence as their reference curves as to form k references. Combined with S-GEM curve registration algorithm, we compared the other sequences with reference curves.

The procedure of alignment for sequences with time-lagged correlation is as following:

(1) *At the v-th iteration, compute the reference curves $R_1^v, R_2^v, \ldots, R_k^v$ for each group;*
(2) *For each curve X_i^v, $i = 1, \ldots, d$, compute the maximal Pearson correlation coefficient with the reference curve R_m^v of each group G_m^v of the current partition by S-GEM and get a Δt to compute the aligned curve $X_i^{\prime v} = X_i^v(t + \Delta t)$.*

(3) *Assign each curve X_i^{lv} to the group G_i^* which has the maximal Pearson correlation coefficient, then update the partition accordingly:* $P^{v+1} = \{G_1^{v+1}, G_2^{v+1}, \ldots, G_k^{v+1}\}$;

(4) *Update v and repeat from step (1) until no movement of elements among groups is observed in step (3).*

This method, structured as the k-means method, deals with the simultaneous optimal clustering and warping of curves, implemented by alternating Pearson correlation maximization steps. Every curve of sensor data has a maximize Pearson correlation coefficient with each other in the same group without time-lagged correlation.

4.2 Feature Extraction Using PCA

Principal component analysis (PCA) is a well-known feature extraction method. The basic principle of PCA is to collate the information from the interrelations of the variables. Then, PCA uses the orthogonal transforms to find the variable group with high correlation and realize the compression of the observed data to a lower dimension. After transformation with PCA, the greatest variance by any projection of the data comes to lie on the first principal component, the second greatest variance on the second coordinate, and so on.

Given a set of N observations, which is constructed with p-dimensional random variable $X = X_1, X_2, X_3 \ldots X_p$. The principle of PCA is to compute a new matrix $Y = A^T X$. $A = (A_1, A_2, \ldots A_m)$ is an orthogonal matrix.

The process of extracting the features from X is to find out A. The procedure works as following:

(1) *Normalization the data set with empirical mean;*
(2) *Calculate the covariance matrix for multi variables;*
(3) *Calculate the eigenvalue and eigenvectors for the covariance matrix;*
(4) *Sort the eigenvalues according to the contribution of each principal component. Select the first m eigenvalues and eigenvectors according an information threshold (noted as contribution) φ to form A.*
(5) *Calculate the final principal component Y by the transformation $Y = A^T X$.*

4.3 Predictive Maintenance Model

In this paper we take the failure prediction as a binary classification problem. By giving the input sequence and their labels, the output of prediction model is the probability of a forthcoming failure. The latter status of equipment depend on a long historical trend. Long Short Time Memory (LSTM) is a kind of Recurrent Neural Network (RNN), which can be viewed as a deep neural network. It is designed to improve storing and accessing information compared to classical RNNs. LSTM has recently been successfully applied in a variety of sequence modeling tasks [3]. Thus, we apply a LSTM-based network to build the predictive maintenance model.

The input feature vector sequence $x = (x_{t-L+1}, \ldots, x_t)$ is passed to a stack of multiple recurrently connected hidden layers through weighted connections to train the model. And the output is the sequence $y = (y_{t-L+1}, \ldots, y_t)$. The output y_t is a binary vector serving as a representation of the system status which can be used to parameterize the probability distributing $P\ (d_t|y_t)$ of the target d_t. The target d_t is a binary vector with 2 complementary classes.

$$P(d_t = k|y_t) = \hat{y}_t^k = \frac{\exp(y_t^k)}{\sum_{k'=1}^{K} \exp(y_t^{k'})}$$

where k is the number of classes and therefore, in our case $k = 2$. Given a threshold value $\mathcal{E}$, if the P is greater than $\mathcal{E}$, the predictive value can be regarded as an anomaly signal. On the contrast, it is a normal signal.

5   Experiments and Evaluation

5.1   Data Set and Environment

The experimental evaluation of our method is conducted on a cluster of 8 nodes, each node with 8-core Intel Xeon (E312xx) 8 GB processors and 32 GB of RAM, interconnected with 1 GBs Ethernet and each run in virtual machines with CentOS 6.4 and java 1.8.

The datasets used in our experiment is the real sensor data collected from a coal-fired power plant. We collect our experimental data from "primary air fan", "secondary air fan", "coal mill", "force draft fan" and "induced draft fan". The sensor number of them are respectively 45, 37, 49, 38 and 42. And the data recorder is 278400. The failure events in failure logs are regarded as some baselines to verify the predictive results.

5.2   Evaluation Metrics

For our evaluations, we consider the following performance metrics related to our prediction problem.

Precision: precision represents how many abnormities are accurate according to failure logs, which can be defined as following:

$$\text{Precision} = \frac{\text{True Positive}}{\text{True Positive} + \text{False Positive}}$$

Recall: Recall is a metric of the proportion of all possible correct results that our method actually discovers, which can be defined as following:

$$\text{Recall} = \frac{\text{True Positive}}{\text{All Positive}}$$

Contribution: Contribution presents the amount of information remained in extracted features compared to original data.

Dimension: Dimension means the dimension after dimension reduction of extracted features.

5.3 Experiment and Evaluation

Our predictive model aims at helping finding abnormity in advance, and has deployed in the real production. We compare our method with the following method to detect the abnormalities in Power Plant:

rule-based: Traditional rule-based methods to detect the abnormalities based on accumulative experience.

p-LSTM: We firstly extract features from original sensor data using PCA, the enter the features into LSTM neuro network to predict early failures.

dp-LSTM: Our proposed method, which firstly preprocess the original sensor data by cure registration, then extract features from curve registrated sensor data using PCA, finally enter the features into LSTM to predict early failures.

First, we conduct the feature extraction and compare the **Dimension** under the same contribution of 98.9%. The result is shown in Table 1. The average dimension reduction with dp-LSTM is 28.86% of the original dimensions, and the average dimension reduction with p-LSTM is 38.37% of the original dimensions. Table 2 shows the result of Contribution under the same dimension.

Table 1. Dimension reduction with same contribution

Device	Sensors	p-LSTM	dp-LSTM	Contribution
Primary air fan	45	20	16	98.9%
Secondary air fan	37	17	11	98.9%
Coal mill	49	13	10	98.9%
Force draft fan	38	14	11	98.9%
Induced draft fan	42	16	12	98.9%

Table 2. Contribution with same dimension

Device	Sensors	Extracted features	p-LSTM	dp-LSTM
Primary air fan	45	16	97.8%	99.51%
Secondary air fan	37	11	96.45%	99.62%
Coal mill	49	10	97.3%	98.71%
Force draft fan	38	11	97.76%	99.18%
Induced draft fan	42	12	97.8%	99.18%

Then we build a LSTM network with 4 hidden layers and 50 hidden units in each layer. We initialize all weight parameters uniformly in the range [−0.08, 0.08], while initializing the LSTM forget gate with a slightly higher bias (set bias value to 1.0) to encourage remembering at the beginning. We then train the network using mini-batch stochastic gradient descent with learning rate 0.001 and decay factor 0.95. We train each model for 50 epochs and decay the base learning rate after 10 epochs 6 by multiplying it with the decay factor 0.95 for each additional epoch. We select the first 80% as training data and the rest as testing data.

Figure 2 shows the precision and recall for different equipment with different methods. The average precision of rule-based method is 0.532. The average precision of p-LSTM is 0.714. The average precision of dp-LSTM is 0.78. The average recall of rule-based method is 0.474. While the average recall of *p-LSTM* is 0.78. The average recall of *dp-LSTM* is 0.856. It has virtually objectively proved that the deep learning-based predictive maintenance is more effective than the traditional rule-based method. Benefit from our curve registration for time-lagged correlation sensor data, it can be concluded that our method significantly contributes to the performance of the feature extraction and model applied.

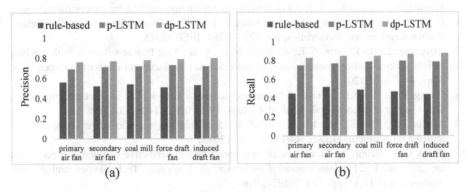

Fig. 2. Precision of different method for early failures prediction

6 Conclusion

The high-dimensional data for predictive maintenance and time-lagged correlation among sensors result in challenges to build predictive maintenance model. In order to extract effective features from massive high-dimensional sensor data with time-lagged correlation, this paper presents a time-lagged correlation based feature extraction method for predictive maintenance model. According to the experiments, we prove that: (1) our feature extraction method manages to improve the dimension reduction compared to the traditional feature extraction method while ensuring the contained original information; (2) our extracted features manage to reduce the training time of predictive maintenance resolution with assurance of predication accuracy.

Acknowledgments. This work was supported in part by a grant from the National Natural Science Foundation of China (Grant No. 61672042), the Program for Youth Backbone Individual, supported by Beijing Municipal Party Committee Organization Department (Grant No. 2015000020124G024).

References

1. Liu, Y.: Predictive modeling for intelligent maintenance in complex semiconductor manufacturing processes (2008)
2. Zhang, K., Xu, J., Min, M.R., et al.: Automated IT system failure prediction: a deep learning approach. In: 2016 IEEE International Conference on Big Data (Big Data), pp. 1291–1300. IEEE (2016)
3. Sipos, R., Fradkin, D., Moerchen, F., et al.: Log-based predictive maintenance. In: Proceedings of the 20th ACM SIGKDD International Conference on Knowledge Discovery and Data Mining, pp. 1867–1876. ACM (2014)
4. Rawat, S., Rawat, S.: Multi-sensor Data Fusion by a Hybrid Methodology—A Comparative Study. Elsevier, Amsterdam (2016)
5. Qiu, X., Fu, D., Fu, Z.: An efficient dimensionality reduction approach for small-sample size and high-dimensional data modeling. J. Comput. **9**(3), 576–580 (2014)
6. Sharma, N., Saroha, K.: A novel dimensionality reduction method for cancer dataset using PCA and feature ranking. In: International Conference on Advances in Computing, Communications and Informatics, pp. 2261–2264. IEEE (2015)
7. Abualigah, L.M., Khader, A.T., Al-Betar, M.A., et al.: Text feature selection with a robust weight scheme and dynamic dimension reduction to text document clustering. Expert Syst. Appl. **84**, 24–36 (2017)
8. Chang, P.C., Wu, J.L.: A critical feature extraction by kernel PCA in stock trading model. Soft Comput. Fusion Found. Methodol. Appl. **19**(5), 1393–1408 (2015)
9. Adelfio, G., Chiodi, M., Luzio, D., et al.: Simultaneous seismic wave clustering and registration. Comput. Geosci. **44**(13), 60–69 (2012)
10. Susto, G.A., Beghi, A.: Dealing with time-series data in predictive maintenance problems. In: 2016 IEEE 21st International Conference on Emerging Technologies and Factory Automation (ETFA), pp. 1–4. IEEE (2016)
11. Schirru, A., Susto, G.A., Pampuri, S., McLoone, S.: Learning from time series: supervised aggregative feature extraction. In: 2012 IEEE 51st Annual Conference on Decision and Control (CDC), pp. 5254–5259. IEEE (2012)
12. Susto, G.A., Schirru, A., Pampuri, S., McLoone, S.: Supervised aggregative feature extraction for big data time series regression. IEEE Trans. Industr. Inf. **12**(3), 1243–1252 (2016)
13. Kimura, T., Watanabe, A., Toyono, T., et al.: Proactive failure detection learning generation patterns of large-scale network logs. In: International Conference on Network and Service Management, pp. 8–14. IEEE Computer Society (2015)
14. Kimura, T., Ishibashi, K., Mori, T., et al.: Spatio-temporal factorization of log data for understanding network events. In: 2014 Proceedings IEEE INFOCOM, pp. 610–618. IEEE (2014)
15. Warriach, E.U., Tei, K.: Fault detection in wireless sensor networks: a machine learning approach. In: 16th International Conference on Computational Science and Engineering, pp. 758–765 (2013)

16. Susto, G.A., Schirru, A., Pampuri, S., et al.: Machine learning for predictive maintenance: a multiple classifier approach. IEEE Trans. Industr. Inf. **11**(3), 812–820 (2015)

17. Baban, C.F., Baban, M., Suteu, M.D.: Using a fuzzy logic approach for the predictive maintenance of textile machines. J. Intell. Fuzzy Syst. **30**(2), 999–1006 (2016)

18. He, M., He, D.: Deep learning based approach for bearing fault diagnosis. IEEE Trans. Ind. Appl. **53**(3), 3057–3065 (2017)

19. Jiang, G.X., Wang, W.J.: Correlation analysis in curve registration of time series. J. Softw. **9**, 2002–2017 (2014)

Predicting Next Points of Interests
Based on a Markov Model

Jie Xu$^{(\boxtimes)}$, Chunxiao Xing, and Yong Zhang

Department of Computer Science and Technology, Tsinghua University,
Beijing 100084, China
xuj15@mails.tsinghua.edu.cn,
{xingcx,zhangyong05}@tsinghua.edu.cn

Abstract. With the development of Global Position System (GPS) technology, the analysis of history trajectory becomes more and more important. The Location Based Service (LBS) can provide the user's location, the human movement location prediction from the history observations over some period have several potential applications and attract more and more attention. Predicting the user's next position usually includes finding the Points of Interests (POIs) from the historical trajectory and predicting the position with a certain statistical model. In this paper, we present a novel method based on Markov chain for prediction, our method include two contributions: the first one we use GEPETO variant algorithm to cluster for POIs to solve the former algorithm without considering the temporal factor, and the second one we present Mobility Markov Chain (MMC) model which exploits 3 previous states to infer the future location. Our experiments basing on the real Beijing trajectories dataset display that our algorithm can improve the prediction accuracy compared with the baseline algorithm.

Keywords: Next location prediction · Markov chain model · Cluster
GPS trajectory analysis

1 Introduction

With the modern geographic position technologies, more and more mobility locations are stored and shared [1]. The researches of the location through Global Positioning System (GPS) devices both from the industry and the research community with sensor, RFID or satellite, have been attracting lots of attention for its application in many different domains [2], such as using the complex sequential location data to observe the individual's activities motive or finding the POIs basing on the past trace, or judging someone whether are at home or at business sites currently [3]. It is important to provide location forecast services accurately, this makes moving object trajectory prediction an active research field [4, 5].

In this paper, we solve the problem of inferring the next location basing on the history mobility traces using the Markov model. This algorithm has two main steps, one is finding the POIs [6], the other is prediction using statistical model. Human historical location are first clustered with their temporal and spatial properties, and then

© ICST Institute for Computer Sciences, Social Informatics and Telecommunications Engineering 2018
I. Romdhani et al. (Eds.): CollaborateCom 2017, LNICST 252, pp. 264–274, 2018.
https://doi.org/10.1007/978-3-030-00916-8_25

the previous formed clusters are employed to train the Markov model. More accurately, in our method we present a different cluster method named GEPETO [7] variant taking into account the temporal factors before applying in the Mobility Markov Chain (MMC) [8]. The construct of our approach is present al Fig. 1. Furthermore, we assess the efficiency of our algorithm on a real location mobility dataset named Beijing taxi dataset, and the results demonstrate that our prediction under different configurations can achieve an accuracy for predicting the next location in the range of 60% to 70%.

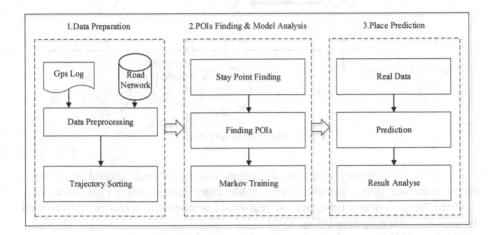

Fig. 1. Overview of system architecture

The rest of this paper is organized as follows: we propose a related important work in Sect. 2, and then discuss the methods of cluster among different scenery in Sect. 3, Afterwards, we describe how to infer the next place prediction with MMC in Sect. 4, experimental results are assessed in Sect. 5, and finally we summarize the paper in Sect. 6.

2 Related Work

Many previous work have been proposed to solve the location prediction. In this section, we introduce the related work and analyze the key technologies for different algorithms.

Ashbrook and Starner [3] proposed a method for predicting the next station by using the history POIs, they firstly clustered the location which are frequently visited by multi–user, secondly, they merged these POIs into a Markov model, the transition probability between different POIs represented the different Markov node transition probability. Our work is similar as the ideas [8], the differences lie in the cluster algorithm, the cluster algorithm is very important for prediction accuracy, POIs can be calculated by different methods, such as k-means, DBSCAN. We choose the GEPETO variant which not only considers the minimal threshold number of cluster, but also adds the temporal factors as input parameters.

Qiao [9] proposed a self-adaptive parameter selection algorithm called HMTP, in their approach, to avoid time-intensive distance computation between trajectory points,

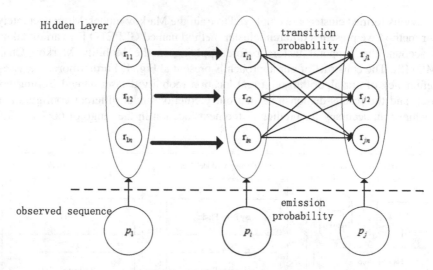

Fig. 2. Hidden Markov model

a density-based trajectory clustering algorithm was introduced. Second, they partitioned trajectory into segments to extract trajectory hidden states [10], third, they captured the parameters necessary for real-world scenarios in terms of objects with dynamically changing speed (Fig. 2).

Asahara [11] proposed an algorithm for predicting pedestrian movement on the basic of Mixed Markov chain mode (MMM), they took a pedestrian's personality and previous states as an unobservable parameter. Observable probability and the transition probability were simultaneously calculated, the user's next position was inferred by using the statistic model and the user's tracking data [12], by using the Expectation Maximization algorithm, the pedestrian's next location with the maximization likelihood was the most probable one.

Some other methods to predict the next position used the trajectories semantics. Krumm and Horvitz [13] presented a measure named predestination which made use of a history of a driver's destinations together with the driving behaviors to predict where the driver was going. They separated behaviors into four different probabilistic cues and then combined them to produce most likely cell destination, afterwards, they availed an open world modeling methodology by using the likelihood of visited unobserved locations based on the background properties of locations and on the trends in the data. The advantage lay in transferring the "out of the box" data into the fully trained data set more smoothly.

Chen [14] put forward an approach to predict both the future destination and the intended route of a person, rather than predicted each other separately. To find the POIs, they made use of a cluster algorithm named FBM (Forward–Backward Matching), and abstracted space partitioning and movement patterns by taking advantage of an extended CRPM (Continuous Route Pattern Mining). From these movement patterns, a pattern tree was built, and the tree was the core method for predicting the future destination and the intended route.

3 Cluster Algorithm

Our method include two steps. Firstly, for the sake of finding the POIs [20], a cluster algorithm is introduced, after that, the transition probability among POIs is calculated. During the second step, a prediction method for next place basing Markov mode is presented. In this section, we first discuss the methods of our cluster algorithm.

K-Means [15, 16]: the well known cluster algorithm is the K-Means which aims to partition n observations into k clusters, the K-Means algorithm takes advantage of the minimum squared distances error for each point to its cluster center, the error term is formal as follows:

$$Error = \sum_{i=1} \sum_{x \in C_i} d(x_i, y_i)$$

where the y_i indicates the center of each cluster C, the function d indicates the distance between the point x_i and the center. The algorithm firstly defines the number of k cluster, and then iterates computer distance between each candidate point and the center, decides the x_i point belongs to which cluster until the error is small enough.

Density-Based Clustering [16]: the K-Means has some disadvantage for assorting POIs, the biggest one lies on the algorithm in advance needs to know the number of cluster, this is much difficult for the user. To overcome the difficulty for forming arbitrary shape and reducing the influence of the point noise in the computation process, density-based clustering approach is introduced, this algorithm makes use of two parameters: Eps indicates the radius of a circle, MinPts indicates the minimum number of points in the circle. The algorithm first searches each point neighborhood through the database, if the neighborhood points contain sufficient MinPts, then creates a new cluster. If a point is a dense part of a cluster, and its neighborhoods are also part of that cluster, so iteratively adds all points which are found within the threshold ε until there are no new points can be added to any cluster.

Density-Time Cluster: (DT Cluster) [17] is an iterative clustering algorithm which is dependent on two scale parameters: for time threshold t and for spatial distance threshold d from a trail of mobility traces M. First, the algorithm constructs a cluster C, which includes all successive points within threshold distance d from each other. Second, the algorithm checks whether the accumulation time in the moving range is greater than the threshold t. If the condition is true, then creates a cluster to add to the POIs list. For a specific geographic delta scale, if two clusters centroids are within the delta scale, they will be merged.

In our paper, we use the GEPETO variant [7] to cluster the POIs from the trajectory. The GEPETO's inspiration stems from the Density-time cluster (DT Cluster), they are similar to each other. The methods takes in the radius r, the tolerance rate ι, the time window t, the distance threshold d and a trajectory point M as parameters. The algorithm first constructs an iterative cluster from trajectory M which is located in the time window t, then obtains the total number of points and if the distance between the point and the cluster centroids are less than the tolerance ι, adds the cluster to the list of L, otherwise simply discards. At last, the algorithm merges the clusters whose centroids are less than the threshold d value. In some cases, when within a specified radius, we may obscure prediction opportunities on a big radius area, for example, if we predict next location from small town, the accuracy definitely decrease from the city, so we narrow the radius down until the value is 0.1 km. The GEPETO [7] variant algorithm pseudocode is presented as follows:

Algorithm 1. GEPETO variant clustering algorithm

Parameters: trajectory T, time window t, radius r, tolerance rate ι , distance threshold d
1.discard the fast point whose speed is greater than 30Km/h
2: L put iu POIs; a empty cluster C
3: for i = 0 to S   do
4: totaltime = totaltime + (T[i + 1].time -T[i].time)
5: if totaltime <= t then
6:    put the trajectory T[i] to cluster C
7: else
8:    Compute the centroid of C
9. while(radius>0.1)   //find the sublocation from the fatherlocation
10.   cumulTime = cumulTime + (T[i + 1].time -T[i].time)
11:    if cumulTime <= t then
12:      Add the mobility trace T[i] to cluster C
13:    if C is not empty,
14:          C_sublocaion=C
15:    else   do nothing
16:    radius=radius/2;
17: C=C_sublocaion ; nOutlierradius = 0
18: for j = 0 to C.number do
19: if distance(C[j], C.centroid) > r then
20:   nOutlierradius = nOutlierradius + 1
21: end if
22: end for
23: if nOutlierradius /totalPointsNumber <ι then
24:    put the cluster C to L
25: end if
26:    totaltime= 0; Empty(C)
27: end if
28: end for
29: Merge clusters L if two clusters' centroids distance is less than distance threshold d
30: return

---

4 Next Place Prediction

In this section, we briefly discuss the notion of Mobility Markov Chain of several users' behavior which is treated as a discrete stochastic process. Once we get the POIs computed from GEPETO variant, we can define a set of states $P = \{...pi - 1, pi, pi + 1...\}$, each state pi means a frequent POIs and corresponds to a semantic geographical location, such as home, work, entertainment place, others place which sites are the people daily visit. We also can get the density of the clusters, the radius, and the stay time of mobility trace. A set of transitions, for instance, the phome -> pwork represents the transition probability from home to work. If the user never moves between two places, the transition probability is set to zero.

So as to predict the next place using the Markov mode, the transitions between different POIs can be represented as a transition matrix base on chronological statistical model, mention from [8], standard MMC forecasting future position depends only on the current location without considering the past states, however there is a semantic correlation between former state transitions, using a single current state means information losses and less accuracy. To solve this problem, we use 3 previous states in which the next state transition probability is dependent on the current state and the previous 2 states, which approach yields more precise predictions. More specially, the home, the work, the Entertainment place, others, if the probability from the 3 previous states to the predicting next location exists, the probability value is correspondingly assigned. The matrix is shown as follows:

From the Table 1, the second column stands for the current and two previous states, the reminder four columns for the prediction location represent the home, work,

Table 1. 3 previous states transition matrix

Order	Source/destination	H	W	E	O
1	WHE	1.00	0.00	0.00	0.00
2	WHO	0.90	0.00	0.10	0.00
3	WEH	0.00	0.86	0.10	0.04
4	WOH	0.00	0.76	0.24	0.00
5	HWE	0.39	0.00	0.00	0.61
6	HWO	0.38	0.10	0.52	0.00
7	HEO	0.91	0.00	0.09	0.00
8	HOW	1.00	0.00	0.00	0.00
9	HOE	0.80	0.00	0.00	0.20
10	EHO	0.00	0.00	0.00	0.00
11	EHW	0.90	0.00	0.00	0.10
12	EWH	0.00	0.90	0.00	0.10
13	EHW	0.92	0.00	0.00	0.08
14	EOH	0.00	1.00	0.00	0.00
15	OWH	0.07	0.93	0.00	0.00
16	OEH	0.00	1.00	0.00	0.00

entertainment, other location. The corresponding value is the transition probability. Take the 1st row for example, the transition probability from the WHE to the prediction H is 1.00, while to the remaining place is zero, meaning the probability is very small and can be nearly ignore. For some kinds of visited sequence, such as the WEO is rarely appear, so this kind of situation is discarded.

5 Experiment Result

In this section, we first introduce our experiments on real trajectory dataset, and second evaluate the accuracy of our prediction algorithm for different algorithm. We implement our experiment on Beijing trajectory dataset, this trajectory dataset contains 118 users' different trajectories over a period of 2 years, every sequence item includes longitude, latitude, direction, velocity, timestamp information, sampling frequency ranged from 10 s to about 5 min.

In order to evaluate the performance of algorithm, we make use of the 88 users' trajectory as labeled data for training the MMC model while the remainder as the test case. we select the HMM [18], MMM [11], MMC(2) [8] as the baseline algorithm, the MMC(2) means the MMC algorithm use two previous states.

Our experiments are implemented in python27 and performed with 16 GB RAM. We compare the precision, recall and F1 measure which are defined as follows [19]:

$$Precision = \frac{True\_positives}{True\_positives + False\_positives} \tag{1}$$

$$Recall = \frac{True\_positives}{True\_positives + False\_negatives} \tag{2}$$

$$F_1-measure = \frac{2 * Precision * Recall}{Precision + Recall} \tag{3}$$

The precision is the ratio between the number of correct predictions over the total number of predictions, the True_positives means the number of predicted as a positive sample, the False_positives is predicted as a positive class which is false, the False_negatives is forecasted as a false class which is true. In our experiment, POIs are deem to be true if predicted with the real location. According the definitions, the algorithm is "good" meaning the precision and the recall are both high.

The prediction precision of the different algorithms are displayed in Fig. 3, the HMM achieved 0.21, MMM achieved 0.37, MMC(2) achieved 0.57, our algorithm achieved 0.635.

As can be seen from Figs. 3 and 4, the HMM is not high, owing to the reason that the algorithm only deel with the transitions of unobserved states, and deems the user can go to anywhere if he want to, this situation is not realistic.

The MMM reach the 0.37, lower than the MMC, because the MMC don't take the temporal factor into consideration.

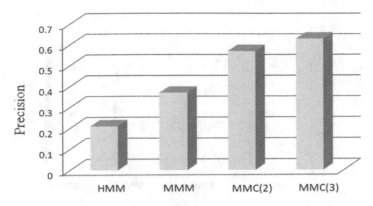

Fig. 3. Compare of precision between algorithms

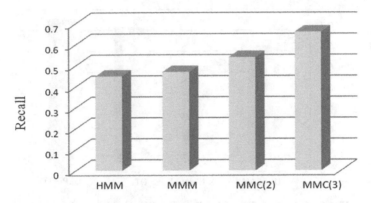

Fig. 4. Compare of recall between algorithms

The MMC(2) is lower than our algorithm, because we choose a GEPETO cluster for considering the temporal and the geographical factor, and for three previous states, we can take advantage of more historical information.

F1-measure: The F1 score is a measure to test the accuracy form both the precision score and the recall score, the F1 value can be interpreted as a weighted average of the precision rates and recall rate, where the F1 value achieves the optimal value at 1 and the worst at 0. From the Fig. 5, the MMC(3) gains the highest value at 0.64, this is in accordance with the precision rate and recall rate.

So as to explain the importance of the cluster algorithm, we also implement different cluster algorithm to find the POIs, we select the DBSCAN, K-Means, DJ, for the baselines, the accuracies are shown as the Fig. 6.

From the Fig. 6, we can see that DBSCAN, are lower than the DT and GEPETO variant, the K-Means is the lowest one, the reason lies in we can't give the suitable default number of cluster, if the k value is too big, the invalid POIs are included. The DT result is a little smaller than GEPETO variant, this can be explained that a tolerance rate ι which is used to control the centroids between clusters decides what

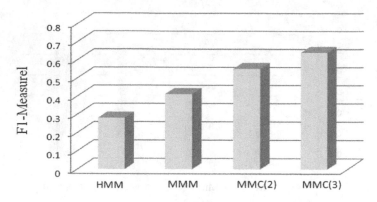

Fig. 5. Compare of F_1 measure between algorithms

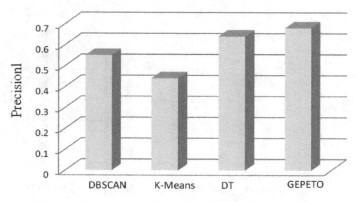

Fig. 6. Compare of precision between different cluster algorithms

kinds of cluster are discarded and merged, and the GEPETO variant cluster algorithm gains the higher accuracy rate in accordance with our expectations.

6   Conclusion

We have presented a novel prediction algorithm basing on Markov model chain which contain two steps, one is finding the POIs, and the other is training the MMC predicting model. First, to solve the previous cluster algorithm which don't consider the temporal factor, we select a GEPETO variant as our cluster algorithm. Second, for making better use of historical data, we exploit 3 previous states to infer the future location using the MMC algorithm.

For different implements on real trajectory, experiments results show that our approach can reach 0.635 accuracy rate than the baseline HMM, MMM, MMC(2) algorithm. In terms of our future work, we will apply our model to lane changing vehicle prediction, indeed, this is useful for the upcoming self-driving car area.

References

1. Zheng, Y., Li, Q., Chen, Y., et al.: Understanding mobility based on GPS data. In: Proceedings of the 10th International Conference on Ubiquitous Computing, pp. 312–321. ACM (2008)
2. Liu, P., Kurt, A.: Trajectory prediction of a lane changing vehicle based on driver behavior estimation and classification. In: 2014 IEEE 17th International Conference on Intelligent Transportation Systems (ITSC), pp. 942–947. IEEE (2014)
3. Ashbrook, D., Starner, T.: Using GPS to learn significant locations and predict movement across multiple users. Pers. Ubiquit. Comput. **7**(5), 275–286 (2003)
4. Lee, J.G., Han, J., Li, X., et al.: TraClass: trajectory classification using hierarchical region-based and trajectory-based clustering. VLDB Endow. **1**(1), 1081–1094 (2008)
5. Nascimento, J.C., Figueiredo, M.A.T., Marques, J.S.: Trajectory classification using switched dynamical hidden Markov models. IEEE Trans. Image Process. **19**(5), 1338–1348 (2010)
6. Liu, X., Liu, Y., Aberer, K., et al.: Personalized point-of-interest recommendation by mining users' preference transition. In: Proceedings of the 22nd ACM International Conference on Information and Knowledge Management, pp. 733–738. ACM (2013)
7. Gambs, S., Killijian, M.O., del Prado Cortez, M.N.: Show me how you move and I will tell you who you are. In: Proceedings of the 3rd ACM SIGSPATIAL International Workshop on Security and Privacy in GIS and LBS, pp. 34–41. ACM (2010)
8. Gambs, S., Killijian, M.O., del Prado Cortez, M.N.: Next place prediction using mobility markov chains. In: Proceedings of the First Workshop on Measurement, Privacy, and Mobility, p. 3. ACM (2012)
9. Qiao, S., Shen, D., Wang, X., et al.: A self-adaptive parameter selection trajectory prediction approach via hidden Markov models. IEEE Trans. Intell. Transp. Syst. **16**(1), 284–296 (2015)
10. Ling, Z.H., Richmond, K., Yamagishi, J.: An analysis of HMM-based prediction of articulatory movements. Speech Commun. **52**(10), 834–846 (2010)
11. Asahara, A., Maruyama, K., Sato, A., et al.: Pedestrian-movement prediction based on mixed Markov-chain model. In: Proceedings of the 19th ACM SIGSPATIAL International Conference on Advances in Geographic Information Systems, pp. 25–33. ACM (2011)
12. Govea, A.D.V.: Incremental Learning for Motion Prediction of Pedestrians and Vehicles. Springer, Berlin (2010). https://doi.org/10.1007/978-3-642-13642-9
13. Krumm, J., Horvitz, E.: Predestination: inferring destinations from partial trajectories. In: UbiComp 2006: Ubiquitous Computing, pp. 243–260 (2006)
14. Chen, L., Lv, M., Chen, G.: A system for destination and future route prediction based on trajectory mining. Pervasive Mob. Comput. **6**(6), 657–676 (2010)
15. Zhou, C., Frankowski, D., Ludford, P., et al.: Discovering personal gazetteers: an interactive clustering approach. In: Proceedings of the 12th Annual ACM International Workshop on Geographic Information Systems, pp. 266–273. ACM (2004)
16. Yuan, G., Sun, P., Zhao, J., et al.: A review of moving object trajectory clustering algorithms. Artif. Intell. Rev. **47**(1), 123–144 (2017)
17. Hariharan, R., Toyama, K.: Project Lachesis: parsing and modeling location histories. In: Egenhofer, M.J., Freksa, C., Miller, H.J. (eds.) GIScience 2004. LNCS, vol. 3234, pp. 106–124. Springer, Heidelberg (2004). https://doi.org/10.1007/978-3-540-30231-5_8
18. Mathew, W., Raposo, R., Martins, B.: Predicting future locations with hidden Markov models. In: Proceedings of the 2012 ACM Conference on Ubiquitous Computing, pp. 911–918. ACM (2012)

19. Yang, J., Xu, J., Xu, M., et al.: Predicting next location using a variable order Markov model. In: Proceedings of the 5th ACM SIGSPATIAL International Workshop on GeoStreaming, pp. 37–42. ACM (2014)
20. Zheng, Y., Zhang, L., Xie, X., et al.: Mining interesting locations and travel sequences from GPS trajectories. In: Proceedings of the 18th International Conference on World Wide Web, pp. 791–800. ACM (2009)

A Topology-Aware Reliable Broadcast Scheme for Multidimensional VANET Scenarios

Fengrui Liu[1,2], Chuanhe Huang[1,2(✉)], and Xiying Fan[1,2]

[1] State Key Lab of Software Engineering, Computer School,
Wuhan University, Wuhan, China
huangch@whu.edu.cn
[2] Collaborative Innovation Center of Geospatial Technology,
Wuhan University, Wuhan, China

Abstract. In Vehicular Ad-Hoc Network (VANET), fast and reliable emergency message dissemination among vehicles on the road has positive significance. Besides, the topology of VANET is dynamic and we need to consider the adaptability of message dissemination scheme to different scenarios. By studying the relation between reliable broadcast scheme and different effect factors, we improve the equation of contention window. To meet the needs of multidimensional scenarios, we propose a novel topology-aware broadcast scheme. Each node monitors its neighbors' state according to a FSM (finite-state machine) and transmits the information to proper nodes. The advantages of our scheme are that it enhances the transmission reliability in multidimensional scenarios and improves self-adaptability in dynamic VANET with low propagation latency. By evaluating the proposed solution, our scheme is implemented and simulation results are provided.

Keywords: VANET · Topology-aware · FSM · Self-adaption

1 Introduction

As a special type of Mobile Ad-hoc Network (MANET), VANET is a technology which uses moving cars as nodes. It helps us deliver emergency messages timely to reduce the probability of traffic accidents. However, due to the dynamic topology of the whole vehicle network, speedy movements of the nodes and high drop rates of the channel, new challenges raise in VANETs to broadcast messages reliably and rapidly. Aiming for overcoming these obstacles, we are supposed to design specialized schemes which can greatly improve the performance of VANET.

Vehicles in VANET can broadcast messages and communicate with other vehicles using IEEE 802.11p [1]. These vehicles always need to listen to their neighbors' state by exchanging short messages called beacons. Information inside a beacon may include vehicle's speed, location etc. As the beaconing load may saturate the capacity of the channel, channel congestion should be avoided as

© ICST Institute for Computer Sciences, Social Informatics and Telecommunications Engineering 2018
I. Romdhani et al. (Eds.): CollaborateCom 2017, LNICST 252, pp. 275–285, 2018.
https://doi.org/10.1007/978-3-030-00916-8_26

much as possible. In the broadcast scheme, the sender broadcasts an emergency message, other node who receives this message may be selected as forwarders.

What's more, in a real VANET scenario, the vehicles seldom move on a simple straight road, as there are always complex traffic routes, such as intersections (two-dimensional scenarios) [2] and flyovers (three-dimensional scenarios). A well-designed scheme should take full consideration of these scenarios.

The contributions of this paper are listed as follows:

- We design a FSM (finite-state machine) to help nodes monitor the states of each neighbor and they can make the corresponding decision based on the above information. This scheme improves the reliability of message dissemination in multidimensional VANET scenarios.
- We use a real-time prediction model to help vehicles dynamically optimize the rate of beacons. This scheme can minimize the channel occupancy time and reduce the messages collision.
- We take into full account the influence of node density, distance and channel quality in broadcasting process. The proposed scheme always selects an optimal node as the forwarder and it can fit to different scenarios.

The rest of this paper is organized as follows. In Sect. 2, we survey the related works. In Sect. 3, we point out the design of contention window model and beacon rate model. In Sect. 4, we elaborate the design of our proposed scheme. In Sect. 5, detailed theoretical analysis of the broadcasting scheme is presented. Section 6 describes the simulation environment and the results. Section 7 concludes the paper.

2   Related Work

Without considering the assistance of Road Side Units (RSUs) [3], the schemes in VANET can be categorized into two classes. One is based on senders' policy called sender-oriented approach, the other one is receiver-oriented approach which is based on receivers' policy.

The sender-oriented schemes make the sender decide which neighbor(s) would be chosen as forwarder(s) according to the network topology. This kind of schemes, proposed by Liu et al. [4] and Amoroso et al. [5], are able to rebroadcast message timely when the forwarders catch the rebroadcast instructions. The scheme proposed by Li et al. [6] selects the farthest node as forwarder for fast propagation, however, due to the high drop rate, packet collision and dynamic topology in VANET, the chosen nodes may not receive the message and lead to mistakes. In this case, the sender must modulate and rebroadcast the message until the forwarder sends ACK signals back. Besides, most sender-oriented approaches need to establish a steady connection with forwarders by handshaking. Take the scheme of Khan [7] as an example, which results in noticeable delay. This kind of schemes is highly dependent on beacons to exchange information, which requires the nodes broadcast their beacons frequently. Most of the researchers set a fixed beacon rate to make all the nodes maintain the same topology of the whole network, which may cause the channel collision. What's more, this method can't distinguish multidimensional scenarios, Spaho et al. [2] gives a performance comparison of OLSR and AODV protocols in a Crossroad Scenario, which shows unsatisfactory results. There must be supplementary schemes to cover the shortage.

The receiver-oriented schemes work differently. The sender broadcasts an emergency message to its neighbors firstly, if the neighbors receive the emergency messages successfully, they set up their own timers and broadcast the messages as soon as the timer expires. Based on the above method, the concept of contention window [8,9] is widely used and Reinders et al. [10] analyzes the performance of beacons in VANET. The Receiver-oriented schemes take full advantage of receivers' current position and it is unnecessary to consider network topology changes during the message broadcasting. Voicu et al. [11] propose ACK decoupling mechanism, which eliminates handshaking to realize fast propagation. Suzuki et al. [12] modifies AODV to get minimum end-to-end delay using primary user information and vehicle mobility information. Most of the receiver-oriented schemes don't need complex supplementary information, which reduce the probability of channel collision. However the sender doesn't know its neighbor nodes' state exactly, which leads to the poor performance in multidimensional scenarios.

3   System Model

3.1   Contention Window Model

Contention window (CW) is such as Signal to Noise Ratio (SNR), relative distance(D) [5,6] and vehicle-node density(ρ). Each node i within the transmission range of the sender should calculate its own contention window (CW_i) according to these factors.

SNR is used to quantify the quality of the channel in VANET. Larger SNR value means there are more signal than noise, so it's better to select the receivers with larger SNR as forwarders. We define impact factor of SNR (IF_{snr}) in Eq. (1), where SNR_{thresh} is the minimum threshold, SNR_i is the SNR value of node i and α is the exponential scaling factor.

$$IF_{snr} = \frac{(SNR_i - SNR_{thresh})}{\alpha} \tag{1}$$

In order to transmit the emergency message fast, most researchers [5,6] want to choose the furthest node from the sender as forwarder, which works well in some high-density node scenarios. As Fig. 1 shows, node D can act as an assistant by sending confirmation to prevent further dissemination at T_3 even though A moves out of the sender's broadcasting domain. However, Fig. 2 shows us the problem in low-density scenarios. Node A and B are far away from the sender at T_3, which causes the sender couldn't receive any confirmation. In this case, B is a better choice to forward the message though it's nearer to the sender.

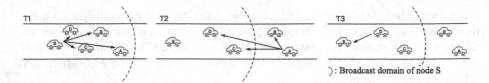

Fig. 1. A high-density nodes model

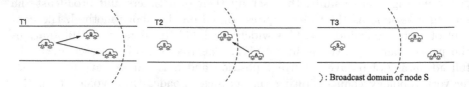

Fig. 2. A low-density nodes model

With regard to the high-density topology, we'd better give priority to the further nodes to make sure the rapid dissemination of messages. In the case of the low-density topology, the nearer node is a better choice to improve reliability in VANET. We define impact factor of position(IF_{pos}) in Eq. (2). In this equation, ρ is the practical density of the sender's neighbors, $\rho \in [0, 1]$. Here D_{max} is the maximum broadcast domain of the sender, D_i is the Euclidean distance between node i and sender and β is the scaling factor.

$$IF_{pos} = \beta(D_i - \rho D_{max})^2 \tag{2}$$

By combining with above factors, contention window of node i can be calculated by Eq. (3). CW_{base} is the minimum size of the size of contention window and k is a scaling factor to keep the contention window in a reasonable range.

$$CW_i = k\frac{IF_{pos}}{IF snr} + CW_{base} \tag{3}$$

3.2 Beacon Rate Model

We design a dynamic adjustment mechanism based on position prediction. The principle of triggering a new beacon is whether the vehicle's actual position via GPS is identical to the predicted position calculated by the motion model. In order to distinguish whether the prediction is valid, we define a threshold δ. If the difference between predicted and actual position is less than δ, we think it's an effective prediction and there is no need to broadcast a new beacon message. In contrast, a new beacon message will be scheduled to broadcast. As for the neighbors, they will continuously estimate the node's position before receiving an updated beacon.

A vehicle keeps an even speed or various speeds will respectively lead the beacon rate too high or too low. To avoid these problems, we'd better find an infimum and a supremum to limit the range of these beacons. The infimum is associated with the mathematical expectation of contention window ($E[CW]$) which is the expected time that a node have to wait on average before it can broadcast the message. As we focus on whether there are new nodes joining the network rather than the specific position of the neighbor nodes. $E[CW]$ can be calculated in Eq. (4), the infimum and the supreme is defined in (5).

$$E[CW] = \frac{\sum_{i=0}^{total\ nodes} E[CW_i]}{total\ nodes} \approx \frac{\sum_{i=0}^{total\ nodes} \frac{CW_{max,i}}{2}}{total\ nodes} \tag{4}$$

$$B_{inf} = E[CW], \ B_{sup} = 2E[CW] + T_{out} \tag{5}$$

If the time slot between the last beacon and the triggered beacon smaller than B_{inf}, it will schedule the beacon time at B_{inf}. If the time slot bigger than B_{inf} and smaller than B_{sup}, it will broadcast the beacon immediately. Otherwise, it'll schedule the beacon at B_{sup}.

4   Proposed Broadcast Scheme

4.1   Problem Statement

Both the sender-oriented scheme and receiver-oriented scheme have low reliability in multidimensional scenarios. In order to figure out the problem, refer to the model in Fig. 3, vehicle C who is the farthest neighbor of sender (S) is most likely to be chosen as the forwarder.

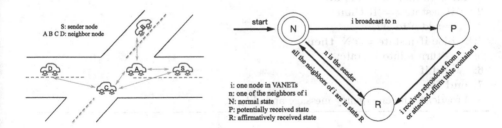

Fig. 3. An intersection scenario.   Fig. 4. FSM of node n.

In some contention-window-oriented scheme, C is chosen as the forwarder and broadcasts the message to node A, D and S. According to ACK decoupling mechanism, node S ensures its neighbors have received the message successfully, A cancels its broadcast scheme and B misses this message transmission forever.

4.2   Broadcast Scheme

In one broadcasting process, each node who receives the emergency message will choose a random time slot from the interval $[0, CW_{max}]$ and wait for that period of time. Obviously, the node with the smallest CW_{chosen} wins the chance to forward the emergency message. There is no need for the forwarder to send any extra ACK, because the rebroadcast message acts as an implicit ACK. As soon as the sender receives the same emergency message from others, it considers the emergency message has been forwarded successfully. Due to some accidental factors, the sender may miss the rebroadcast message, it will broadcast again after a timeout period (T_{out}). Upon receiving the same message twice from one sender, a node in the vicinity of both the source and the forwarder will broadcast to the original sender to cancel any further rebroadcasts.

To improve the reliability of broadcasting, in our scheme, each node should listen to beacons which helps to establish a neighbor table and the topology can also be estimated. The neighbor node is subject to a FSM, as Fig. 4 shows. We use node i and its neighbor node n as an example, normal state(N) means i deems n does not receive the emergency messages, potentially received state(P) means i doesn't promise n has received the emergency message and affirmatively received state(R) means i confirms that n has received the emergency message successfully. We conclude the process that node i broadcasts an emergency message in Algorithm 1 and the process that node i receives an emergency message from others in Algorithm 2.

Algorithm 1. Node i broadcasts an emergency message.

Input:
    The neighbor table of node i, NT_i;
Output:
    The affirm table of node i, AT_i;
1: **for** each node $n \in NT_i$ **do**
2:    **if** n.state == R **then**
3:        add n to AT_i;
4:    **else if** n.state == N **then**
5:        turn n into P state;
6:    **end if**
7: **end for**
8: broadcast the emergency message and AT_i;

---

5   Analysis

5.1   Average Per-hop Convergence Time

Average convergence time per-hop is a measure of how fast an emergency message is received by all the sender's neighbors. This performance indicator plays an important role in VANET, and it can speed up convergence.

In the emergency message forwarding process, nodes do not interfere with each other and emergency messages broadcasting is an independent event. According to a bi-dimensional Poisson process with the parameter $\hat{\lambda}$ ($\hat{\lambda} = \frac{\lambda}{E[CW]}$,

---

Algorithm 2. Node i receives an emergency message from node s.

Input:

   The affirm table of node s, AT_s; The neighbor table of node i, NT_i;

1: s.state = R;
2: **for** each node $n \in AT_s$ **do**
3:    **if** n $\in NT_i$ **then**
4:       n.state = R;
5:    **end if**
6: **end for**
7: **if** ever node in NT_i is in R state **then**
8:    turn them into N state;
9: **else**
10:    caculate the contention window CW_i;
11:    select a time slot CW_{select} randomly in $[0, CW_i]$;
12:    **while** $currenttime == CW_{select}$ **do**
13:       turn to algorithm 1;
14:    **end while**
15: **end if**

λ is the average number of nodes per hop), we are going to talk about the probability of collision based on Poisson distribution model. We define event S to be the successful broadcasting process, and the number(n) of messages at a particular time-slot (t) is one ($n = 1$), the probability of S can be expressed as Eq. (6). Similarly, the number of vehicles appearing at a certain place is subject to Poisson distribution. We define event F as having no forwarders in the sender's broadcast domain and the calculation method is given in Eq. (7).

$$P(S) = \frac{\hat{\lambda}^1 e^{-\hat{\lambda}}}{1!} = \hat{\lambda}^1 e^{-\hat{\lambda}} \tag{6}$$

$$P(F) = \frac{\hat{\lambda}^0 e^{-\hat{\lambda}}}{0!} = e^{-\hat{\lambda}} \tag{7}$$

Therefore, the average number of occurrences in the case of event S can be calculated by the mathematical expectation($E[S]$), and the details are given by Eq. (8).

$$E[S] = \sum_{i=1}^{\infty} [1 - P(S)]^{i-1} P(S)i = \frac{1}{P(S)} \tag{8}$$

Note that T_{out} is the time out value in a broadcasting process. Finally, the expression for mean per-hop rebroadcast latency is shown in Eq. (9)

$$T_{per} = P(F)T_{out} + [1 - P(F)][\frac{t}{P(S)}] \tag{9}$$

5.2 Average Per-hop Throughput

Average throughput per-hop reflects the payload size of the channel in a broadcasting process. In order to make our scheme work properly, the minimum bandwidth guarantee is required. We expect the scheme exchanges a small amount of data in the broadcasting process.

Assume that the certain payload size of an emergency message is S_{em}, the payload size of a beacon message is S_{bm}. Beacons have the characteristic of memoryless, and they are subject to exponential distribution ($B_{slot} \sim E(\lambda_b)$), as Eq. (10) shows,

$$f(B_{slot}) = \begin{cases} \lambda_b e^{-\lambda_b B_{slot}} & B_{slot} \geq 0 \\ 0 & B_{slot} < 0 \end{cases} \tag{10}$$

We limit the infimum and supremum of beacons in Eqs. (4) and (5) and we can calculate the interval between two adjacently beacons by using mathematical expectation of beacons in Eq. (11).

$$E(B_{slot}) = \int_0^\infty B_{slot} f(B_{slot}) \, dB_{slot}$$

$$= B_{inf} + \frac{e^{-\lambda_b B_{inf}} - e^{-\lambda_b B_{sup}}}{\lambda_b} \tag{11}$$

For one node in a broadcasting process, it receives $\frac{T_{per}}{E[B_{slot}]}$ times of beacons from one neighbor and finally, the expression for mean per-hop throughput is:

$$Throughput = \frac{\frac{\lambda T_{per}}{E(B_{slot})} S_{bm} + S_{em}}{T_{per}} \tag{12}$$

6   Performance Evaluation

We have set up a variety of scenarios to test the performance of the proposed broadcasting scheme. The simulation is performed in The Network Simulator (ns-3), version 3.26 and Simulation of Urban Mobility (sumo), version 0.30. Ns-3 is a discrete-event network simulator and we implement our broadcasting scheme with it. Sumo can simulate the real scene of VANET, we use it to generate 2D layout scenarios. In simulation, our scheme is compared with Abbasi's scheme [11] and Lu's scheme [13]. Table 1 lists the basic parameters used in our simulation.

Figure 5 shows the broadcast simulation results in a 2D scenario, the average per-hop delay reflects the performance of broadcasting speed. Note that for lower node density, the average per-hop delay is pretty high. The reason for this phenomenon is that these vehicles have to wait for a timeout slot before rebroadcast. Benefiting from the interactions between the density of the nodes and the size of the contention window, our proposed scheme can select the best message forwarder in a low node density scenario. In this way, our proposed scheme has a better performance in sparse scenarios and has a flat performance with others in dense scenarios.

In Fig. 6, we analyze the collision rate which indicates the percentage of the packet transmission failure. Due to the beacon messages in our proposed

Table 1. Simulation parameters

Attribute	Value
Data rate	1 Mbps
Transmission range	200 m
Total number of nodes	200 nodes
SNR_{thresh}	30 dB
Packet size	40 bytes
Vehicular speed	120 kmph
Propagation loss model	Nakagami propagation loss model
Mobility model	Sumo 0.30
Unit interval	1 ms

scheme, there are more messages to broadcast than other two scheme in a sparse scenario. In contrast to the dense scenarios, our scheme decreases the number of rebroadcasts and maintains the collision rate in an acceptable level. It represents that these messages have a greater possibility to be transmitted successfully.

In order to determine how many vehicles can receive the emergency message during one broadcasting process, we use reception ratio as a measurement. For 1-D scenario, we simulate in a highway model. For 2-D scenario, we use a grid model to simulate. What's more, we use the road model of New York City and Shanghai City to simulate realistic scenarios. Figure 7 shows the reliability of the proposed scheme in different scenarios. As we can see, our proposed scheme performs better in complex scenarios, which profits from the novel acknowledgement mechanism. Packet loss occurs frequently in the other two schemes because of the changing topology of vehicles. Hence our proposed scheme has a higher reliability in emergency messages broadcasting.

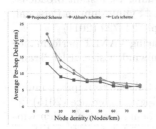
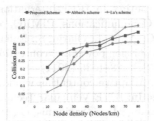
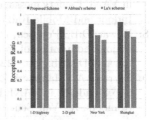

Fig. 5. Average per-hop delay under different vehicle densities

Fig. 6. Average collision rate under different vehicle densities

Fig. 7. Reception ratio of various scenarios

7 Conclusion

The proposed scheme gives full consideration to position, SNR and nodes density. The acknowledgement mechanism using neighbor table guarantees the scheme can achieve higher reliability. The simulation results indicate the performance of the proposed scheme is better than the compared schemes in multidimensional and complex VANET scenarios. In the future work, real world implementation to measure the performance of our proposed scheme in 3D VANET scenarios will be executed.

References

1. Ucar, S., Ergen, S.C., Ozkasap, O.: Multihop-cluster-based IEEE 802.11p and LTE hybrid architecture for VANET safety message dissemination. IEEE Trans. Veh. Technol. **65**(4), 2621–2636 (2016)
2. Spaho, E., Ikeda, M., Barolli, L., Xhafa, F.: Performance comparison of OLSR and AODV protocols in a VANET crossroad scenario. In: Park, J.J.J.H., Barolli, L., Xhafa, F., Jeong, H.Y. (eds.) Information Technology Convergence. LNEE, vol. 253, pp. 37–45. Springer, Dordrecht (2013). https://doi.org/10.1007/978-94-007-6996-0_5
3. Lin, C.-C., Chen, P.-C., Chang, L.-W.: On different-dimensional deployment problems of hybrid VANET-sensor networks with QoS considerations. Mob. Netw. Appl. **22**(1), 125–138 (2017)
4. Liu, J., Yang, Z., Stojmenovic, I.: Receiver consensus: on-time warning delivery for vehicular ad-hoc networks. IEEE Trans. Emerg. Top. Comput. **1**(1), 57–68 (2013)
5. Amoroso, A., Marfia, G., Roccetti, M.: Going realistic and optimal: a distributed multi-hop broadcast algorithm for vehicular safety. Comput. Netw. **55**(10), 25042519 (2011)
6. Li, M., Zeng, K., Lou, W.: Opportunistic broadcast of event-driven warning messages in Vehicular Ad Hoc Networks with lossy links. Comput. Netw. **55**(10), 24432464 (2011)
7. Khan, F., Chang, Y., Park, S.J., Copeland, J.: Handshaking vs. instant broadcast in VANET safety message routing. In: IEEE International Symposium on Personal, Indoor and Mobile Radio Communications, PIMRC, pp. 724–729 (2011)
8. Rawat, D.B., Popescu, D.C., Yan, G., Olariu, S.: Enhancing VANET performance by joint adaptation of transmission power and contention window size. IEEE Trans. Parallel Distrib. Syst. **22**(9), 1528–1535 (2011)
9. Berradj, A., Mammeri, Z.: Adaptive contention window scheme to improve multihop broadcast in VANETs. In: IEEE Vehicular Technology Conference (2015)
10. Reinders, R., Van Eenennaam, M., Karagiannis, G., Heijenk, G.: Contention window analysis for beaconing in VANETs. In: IWCMC 2011–7th International Wireless Communications and Mobile Computing Conference, pp. 1481–1487 (2011)
11. Abbasi, H.I., Voicu, R.C., Copeland, J.A., Chang, Y.: Performance optimization of a contention based broadcasting algorithm in VANETs. In: IEEE Global Communications Conference, GLOBECOM 2015 (2016)

12. Suzuki, T., Fujii, T.: Joint routing and spectrum allocation for multi-hop inter-vehicle communication in cognitive radio networks. Int. J. Intell. Transp. Syst. Res. **15**(1), 39–49 (2017)
13. Lu, Y., Ren, J., Qian, J., Han, M., Huo, Y., Jing, T.: Predictive contention window-based broadcast collision mitigation strategy for VANET. In: 2016 IEEE International Conferences on Big Data and Cloud Computing (BDCloud), Social Computing and Networking (SocialCom), Sustainable Computing and Communications (SustainCom) (BDCloud-SocialCom-SustainCom), pp. 209–215 (2016)

MAC-ILoc: Multiple Antennas Cooperation Based Indoor Localization Using Cylindrical Antenna Arrays

Wu Jie, Zhu Minghua$^{(\boxtimes)}$, and Xiao Bo

MOE Research Center for Software/Hardware Co-Design Engineering
and Application, East China Normal University, Shanghai 200062, China
52151500020@ecnu.cn, {mhzhu,bxiao}@sei.ecnu.edu.cn

Abstract. In this paper, a novel RSS (received signal strength) based indoor localization scheme is proposed based on multiple antennas cooperation with designed CAA (cylindrical antenna array). The CAA is composed of twelve directional antennas and could receive the signal of twelve dimensions for one tag at the same time. In the offline phase, the RBF (Radial Basis Function) neural network is trained to construct the relationship between received data of twelve dimensions and AOA (angle of arrival). The online positioning phase consists of two steps. In the first step, the AOA is obtained with the trained neural network and subarea is determined to which the unknown tag belongs. In the second step, the triangle localization algorithm is used in the determined subarea to get the accurate tag position. The experiment results show that the proposed approach not only reduces the miss hit rate for the subarea determination to 6.2%, but also provides comparable location accuracy to that of other two conventional RSS-based locating algorithms.

Keywords: RFID · RBF neural network · Indoor localization
Subarea determination · Directional antenna array

1 Introduction

The RFID (radio frequency identification) technology has attracted continuous attention in both academia and industries in recent years, such as logistics, health care, goods retail for low-cost, noncontact and non-line-of-sight. For example, RFID technology is used as a global localization system for an indoor autonomous vehicle for mobile robot localization and the system provides a really satisfactory performance even in the case that a very small density of tags [1].

Many indoor localization technologies with wireless non-contact radio frequency have been developed, such as indoor positioning based on UWB (ultra wide band), Bluetooth, Wi-Fi and RFID. The UWB [2] takes advantage of TOA (time of arrival) or TDOA (time difference of arrival) algorithm to achieve higher accuracy for the localization. At the same time, this method requires relative expensive hardware to achieve high synchronization accuracy which results into that UWB based indoor positioning technology is difficult to be promoted. The positioning study of Bluetooth and Wi-Fi is becoming more and more widely on account of the popularity of smart

© ICST Institute for Computer Sciences, Social Informatics and Telecommunications Engineering 2018
I. Romdhani et al. (Eds.): CollaborateCom 2017, LNICST 252, pp. 286–295, 2018.
https://doi.org/10.1007/978-3-030-00916-8_27

phones. However, Bluetooth [3] technology can only locate limited number of nodes. The big power consumption has confined promotion of Wi-Fi [4] technology. In comparison with other technologies in large-scale applications, RFID [5] is particularly suitable for indoor localization with the advantage of low power consumption, low price and easy to deploy.

In this study, we have designed the CAA (cylindrical antenna array) in composition of twelve directional antennas. For each tag position, the CAA receives twelve dimensions of tags data and corresponding RSS from twelve directional antennas. The proposed indoor localization method is divided into offline stage and online stage. In the offline stage, the model of RBF neural network is trained with the received information for CAA. In the online stage, the trained model is used to determine the subarea for unknown tags and the triangle localization algorithm are conducted to get the accurate location for unknown tags in the determined subarea.

The rest of the paper is organized as follows. Section 2 describes related work in the field of RSS and neural networks based RSS indoor localization. The overview of the system is given in Sect. 3. The detailed proposed algorithm is presented in Sect. 4. Experiments are conducted about the proposed method in Sect. 5. Conclusion and discussion are given in the final Section.

2 Related Work

In general, there are three kinds of methods for localization based on RSS: the trilateral localization, proximity algorithms and RSS fingerprint-based localization. The trilateral localization [6, 7] bases on the relationship between the RSS and distance. The distance is calculated by the radio signal channel transmission model between the RSS and distance. Then the position of tags is gotten by the trilateral technology with the calculated distances. Proximity algorithms [8] bases on the relative tags preset in the location area. The positioning accuracy is decided by the density of relative tags. RSS fingerprint-based localization [9] bases on the radio map composed of RSS vectors associated with corresponding tags locations.

In practical applications, indoor environment is so complex that it is difficult to be described with the specific equation. With the input of RSS data, the network tunes its inner coefficients to limit to a predefined minimal error. Then, the trained neural network is used to get the location of tags with the obtained RSS from the reader. The artificial neural networks based RSS indoor localization methods are divided into three categories: BPNN (back propagation neural networks) [11–13], FNN (fuzzy neural network) [14, 15] architecture and RBFNN (radial basis function neural network) [16, 17]. Compared with other two methods, the RBF neural network has ability of simple network structure, fast learning, and good approximation ability. So we choose the RBF neural network to construct the complex nonlinear relationship between received data of twelve dimensions and relative angle of arrival.

3 System Overview

The system is constituted by three parts: CAA readers, tags and server terminal. The CAA consists of twelve directional antennas. As shown in Fig. 1, twelve directional antennas are installed at two layers, and each layer includes six antennas. At the each layer, the angle between every two antennas is 120°. The angle between two adjacent antennas is 30° at different layers. Thus twelve antennas are distributed in the direction of 360°, which improves the resolution of angle of arrival. The twelve directional antennas adopt twelve independent radio frequency chips, and transmit to the MCU (micro control unit). The MCU receives and filters the data, and sends the processed data to the server terminal. In order to guarantee the stability of the system, the CAA is mounted in the area where the radius is less than 50 m.

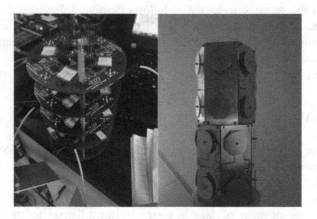

Fig. 1. The hardware of system and CAA.

With the aid of RBF neural network, the paper put forward an AOA based tags localization algorithm using cylindrical antenna arrays readers. The method is implemented in two phases. In the offline phase, RBF neural network is used to map the relationship between angle of arrival and twelve dimensions RSS data from twelve directional antennas. The tags localization is conducted with the two steps in the online phase. The first step is to implement the determination of subarea, and then triangulation positioning algorithm is conducted in the determined subarea.

4 Proposed Algorithm

4.1 Angle of Arrival Calculation

The received signal strength by CAA in the location area is not only determined by the relative angles, but also determined by relative distances between the tag and twelve antennas. Thus the relationship between RSS and AOA is nonlinear and very complicate. The three layers RBF neural network has strong nonlinear fitting ability and can map any complex nonlinear relationship [18]. So in this paper, we introduced the RBF neural network to fit complicate relationship between the twelve dimensions RSS by CAA and the angle of arrival.

RSS Preprocess. The distribution of RSS in the same distance between tag and reader is assumed as Gauss distribution in this paper. In the process of experiment, we find the nature of the signal strength is as following: (1) As the signal strength become weaker, the variance of RSS distribution is bigger. (2) According to the literature [18], the relationship between distance and RSS is logarithmic. When the RSS is lower than −90 dbm, the RSS has no significant change with the increase of distance. It would cause the measurement error increase. For the above two reasons, we limited the received signal strength range to greater than −85 dbm in order to improve the accuracy of positioning. The RSS below −85 dbm would be discarded.

Angle Calculation with RBF Neural Network. In this paper, RBF neural network is used to construct the nonlinear relationship between twelve dimensions RSS and angle of arrival. The three layer RBF neural network has strong nonlinear fitting ability and can map any complex nonlinear relationship.

As shown in Fig. 2, The RBF is composed of three layers: input layer, hidden layer and output layer. The input layer includes twelve nodes and the input vector X is $X = (RSS_{i\_1}, RSS_{i\_2}, RSS_{i\_3}, \ldots, RSS_{i\_10}, RSS_{i\_11}, RSS_{i\_12})$, where RSS_{i_j} refers to the tag signal strength received by j_{th} antenna. The hidden layer nodes include the activation equation and Gaussian radial basis function is used as the activation function in this paper. The output layer contains node A, and the A refers to linear combination of the hidden layer output. The relationship between twelve dimensions RSS and angle α can be described as following equation.

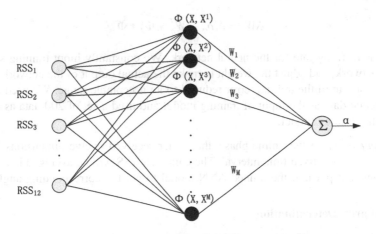

Fig. 2. The structure of RBF neural network.

$$\alpha = \sum_{i=1}^{N} W_i * \varphi_i(RSS_i) \tag{1}$$

where W refers to the output weights, the function φ refers to the activation function in the hidden layer.

Data Set Acquisition. In the offline phase, a series of reference points are set in the location area. Then records are made about the received signal strength and corresponding angle. The format of the collected data X for the j_{th} reference point is (RSS_{j_1}, RSS_{j_2}, RSS_{j_3}, ..., RSS_{j_12}, α_j). Then the vector X is taken as the RBF neural network input samples. The relative angle between reference point and reader is taken as the output of neural network.

The Weight Adjustment. In the process of neural network training, the difference between network expected output angle and actual output angle is used as the reference of weight adjustment. The error equation is defined as follows:

$$E = \frac{1}{2}e_q^2 = \sum_{i=1}^{N}\frac{1}{2}(o_i - \hat{o}_i)^2 = \sum_{i=1}^{N}\frac{1}{2}(\alpha_q - \hat{\alpha}_q)^2 \tag{2}$$

where e_q refers to the error when the q_{th} sample is input vector. The $\hat{o}_i$ refers to the network expected output, and the o_i refers to the actual output. The parameter a_q represents the actual angle of arrival and the $\hat{a}_q$ represents the angle derived from the RBF neural network. The parameter N refers to the number of test samples. We adopt LMS (least mean square) to adjust the corresponding weighs in the process of network training, as shown in Eq. 3.

$$\Delta W_i = \delta(o_q - W_q^T * \Phi) * \Phi \tag{3}$$

where δ is learning rate for the neural network. We constantly input training samples into the network, and adjust the weight to make the actual output of the network tend to expect output, until the training error reduced to an acceptable range. We used a set of 2000 original data as the input of training model and used a set of 200 data as the test data for the trained model.

AOA Acquisition. In the online phase, the reader received twelve dimensions RSS in the same time for a fixed time interval. The collected RSS will be averaged in the same dimensions and put into the trained ANN model to get the corresponding angle.

4.2 Subarea Determination

Due to multipath and NLOS (non-line of sight) interference in the indoor environment, the traditional RSS-based subarea determination caused a big bias and the hit rate for the right subarea is less than 85% [20]. Most of RF signals transmission is by the door or window and the rooms are not always separated by concrete, which would cause error by using the method of attenuation. Jiang [19] conducted the subarea determination with RSS order. The RSS is stronger in the subarea than the area out of the subarea. However, the assumption is invalid in the complex environment, which would cause the localization error.

Based on the calculated angle of arrival for the tags, the paper put forward a subareas determination method. As shown in figure, we deployed three CAA readers in the corner of the subarea. In order to eliminate the noise of the RSS, we use the redundancy design are designed and we use three readers instead of two readers to implement the subarea determination. If the AOA of tag calculated by three readers satisfies the conditions $\{3\pi/2 > \alpha_1 < 2\pi, 0 < \alpha_2 < \pi/2$ and $\pi/2 > \alpha_3 < \pi\}$, it is thought that tag is in corresponding subarea (Fig. 3).

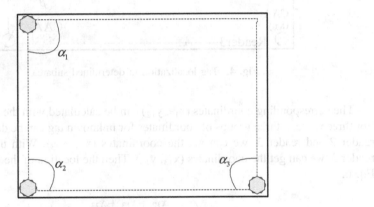

Fig. 3. The subarea determination graph

4.3 Tag Localization in Subarea

After the determination of subarea, the AOA based triangle positioning algorithm is conducted to get the location of unknown tags. As shown in Fig. 4, three CAA readers are prearranged in a subarea. However, if the relative angle of arrival equals zero, it is impossible for the two readers to get the tags position. The unknown tag position can be obtained with the Eq. 4.

$$\begin{cases} b^2 = a^2 + c^2 - 2ac\cos\alpha \\ a^2 = b^2 + c^2 - 2bc\cos\beta \end{cases} \tag{4}$$

where α, β refers to relative angles of arrival, the parameter a, b, c refers to the sides of the triangle. The triangle sides can be expressed as Eq. 5.

$$\begin{cases} a^2 = (x_1 - x_{12})^2 + (y_1 - y_{12})^2 \\ b^2 = (x_2 - x_{12})^2 + (y_2 - y_{12})^2 \\ c^2 = (x_1 - x_2)^2 + (y_1 - y_2)^2 \end{cases} \tag{5}$$

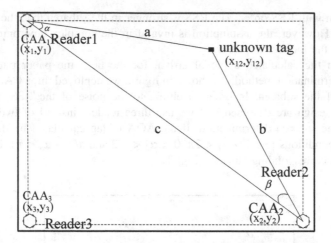

Fig. 4. Tag localization in determined subarea

The corresponding coordinates (x_{12}, y_{12}) can be calculated with the above equation. For three readers, three groups of coordinates for unknown tag can be derived. With the reader 2 and reader 3, we can get the coordinates (x_{23}, y_{23}). With the reader 1 and reader 3, we can get the coordinates (x_{13}, y_{13}). Then the location of the tag is derived in Eq. 6.

$$\begin{cases} x = \dfrac{x_{12} + x_{13} + x_{23}}{3} \\ y = \dfrac{y_{12} + y_{13} + y_{23}}{3} \end{cases} \tag{6}$$

where the parameter N refers to effective calculated coordinates. If the value of relative angle is zero, the calculated coordinates is thought to be ineffective.

5   Experiments

We conducted three experiments with the following designed system. The NRF52832 from Nordic company is adopted as MCU of 2.4 GHz RFID reader. The NRF24LE1 from Nordic company is adopted as MCU of RFID tags. The maximum send power of RFID tag is 4 dbm. The size of the directional antenna is 10 cm × 4 cm rectangular antenna. As shown in Fig. 1, twelve directional antennas are integrated into the CAA. In CAA, the main control chip is STM32F407. The server terminal configuration is Quad - Core Intel Core i5 and 8 GB RAM. The experiments were conducted in the area as shown in Fig. 5. The black lines and arrows show the walk paths and directions of tester. The black dots refer to place where received signal strengths are collected.

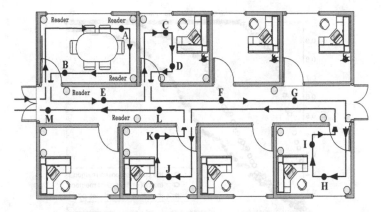

Fig. 5. The deployment of cylindrical antenna array and the system.

5.1 Subarea Determination Comparison

To verify the effectiveness of subarea determination method, we compared proposed method with other two kinds of relevant methods. In the first method, the fingerprint is used to determine the subarea. In the second method, we used the order of RSS in the paper [19] to conduct the subarea determination. We conducted experiments with three methods to determine the subarea in the same scenario. As is shown in Fig. 5, the path we walked is expressed as arrowed line. The RSS information was collected on the nine points (from the position A to the position I). We had conducted the experiments with three methods for five rounds and calculated the hit rates for the right subarea for these points. As it is shown in the Table 1, the proposed method provides highest hit rate for the subarea determination among three methods.

Table 1. The comparison of three different subarea determination methods

Methods	1st	2nd	3rd	4th	5th	Hit rates
Fingerprint based method	10	10	12	11	12	84.60%
RSS order based method	11	13	10	12	12	89.20%
Proposed method	13	11	12	12	13	93.80%

5.2 The Comparison of Three Different Localization Methods

In order to verify the effectiveness of the proposed localization method, we compared three methods: proposed method, the fingerprint-based method [21] and trilateral positioning method [10]. The three methods were conducted in the same subarea and used three readers in the same position. The CDF of three methods is depicted in Fig. 6. As it is shown in the figure, the accuracy of trilateral positioning method is lowest, and the positioning accuracy of proposed method is highest in three methods.

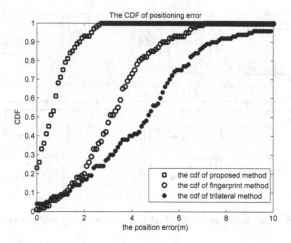

Fig. 6. The CDF of positioning error for three different methods.

6   Conclusion

The paper designed cylindrical antenna arrays and implemented AOA based indoor positioning system. The proposed method employs the RBF neural network to model the complex nonlinear relations between twelve dimensions RSS and corresponding AOA. Based on the calculated angle, we used the two steps solution to conduct the indoor localization. In the first step, a subarea is determined to which the unknown tag belongs. In the second step, the triangle localization algorithm is used in the determined subarea to get the accurate tag position. Through the experiment, it is proved that the proposed methods can improve the location accuracy with the help of CAA. In this paper, we conduct the proposed paper in the LOS condition. In the future research, the work will be focused on the use of CAA in the complex indoor environment.

Acknowledgments. This work has been supported by Science and Technology Commission of Shanghai Municipality [Grant No. 17511106902] and ECNU Postgraduate Student Scientific Research Innovation Projects [Grant No. ykc17076].

References

1. Digiampaolo, E., Martinelli, F.: Mobile robot localization using the phase of passive UHF RFID signals. IEEE Trans. Ind. Electron. **61**(1), 365–376 (2013)
2. Cazzorla, A., Angelis, G.D., Moschitta, A., et al.: A 5.6-GHz UWB position measurement system. IEEE Trans. Instrum. Meas. **62**(3), 675–683 (2013)
3. Zhao, X., Xiao, Z., Markham, A., et al.: Does BTLE measure up against WiFi? A comparison of indoor location performance. In: European Wireless 2014, Proceedings of European Wireless Conference, pp. 1–6. VDE (2014)
4. Wu, C., Yang, Z., Liu, Y., et al.: WILL: wireless indoor localization without site survey. In: 2012 Proceedings of IEEE INFOCOM, pp. 64–72. IEEE (2012)

5. Wang, J., Katabi, D.: Dude, where's my card? RFID positioning that works with multipath and non-line of sight. In: ACM SIGCOMM 2013 Conference on SIGCOMM, pp. 51–62. ACM (2013)

6. Shi, X., Ji, Z.: Indoor positioning system algorithm based on RFID. Univ. Psychol. **12**(3), 779–796 (2015)

7. He, T., Huang, C., Blum, B.M., Stankovic, J.A., Abdelzaher, T.: Range-free localization schemes for large scale sensor networks, pp. 81–95 (2003)

8. Shi, W., Han, X., Du, K., Li, J.: A novel solution for the optimal deployment of readers in passive RFID location system. In: Proceedings of the 2015 International Conference on Communications, Signal Processing, and Systems (2016)

9. Saab, S.S., Msheik, H.: Novel RFID-based pose estimation using single stationary antenna. IEEE Trans. Ind. Electron. **63**(3), 1842–1852 (2016)

10. Nowak, T., Hartmann, M., Zech, T., Thielecke, J.: A path loss and fading model for RSSI-based localization in forested areas. In: IEEE-APS Topical Conference on Antennas and Propagation in Wireless Communications, pp. 110–113. IEEE (2016)

11. Kuo, R.J., Shieh, M.C., Zhang, J.W., et al.: The application of an artificial immune system-based back-propagation neural network with feature selection to an RFID positioning system. Robot. Comput. Integr. Manuf. **29**(6), 431–438 (2013)

12. Miao, K., Chen, Y.D., Xiao, M.: An indoor positioning technology based on GA-BP neural network. In: International Conference on Computer Science & Education, pp. 305–309. IEEE (2011)

13. Gholami, M., Cai, N., Brennan, R.W.: An artificial neural network approach to the problem of wireless sensors network localization. Robot. Comput. Integr. Manuf. **29**(1), 96–109 (2013)

14. Kuo, R.J., Tseng, W.L., Tien, F.C., et al.: Application of an artificial immune system-based fuzzy neural network to a RFID-based positioning system. Comput. Ind. Eng. **63**(4), 943–956 (2012)

15. Huang, Y.J., Chen, C.Y., Hong, B.W., et al.: Fuzzy neural network based RFID indoor location sensing technique. In: International Joint Conference on Neural Networks, pp. 1–5. IEEE (2010)

16. Ding, H.L., Ng, W.W.Y., Chan, P.P.K., et al.: RFID indoor positioning using RBFNN with L-GEM. In: International Conference on Machine Learning and Cybernetics, pp. 1147–1152. IEEE (2010)

17. Moreno-Cano, M.V., Zamora-Izquierdo, M.A., Santa, J., et al.: An indoor localization system based on artificial neural networks and particle filters applied to intelligent buildings. Neurocomputing **122**, 116–125 (2013)

18. Jiménez, A.R., Seco, F., Prieto, J.C., Guevara, J.: Indoor pedestrian navigation using an INS/EKF framework for yaw drift reduction and a foot-mounted IMU. In: Positioning Navigation and Communication, pp. 135–143. IEEE (2010)

19. Jiang, Y., Xiang, Y., Pan, X., et al.: Hallway based automatic indoor floorplan construction using room fingerprints. In: ACM International Joint Conference on Pervasive and Ubiquitous Computing, pp. 315–324. ACM (2013)

20. Wang, B., Zhou, S., Liu, W., Mo, Y.: Indoor localization based on curve fitting and location search using received signal strength. IEEE Trans. Ind. Electron. **62**(1), 572–582 (2015)

21. Guzmánquirós, R., Martínezsala, A., Gómeztornero, J.L., Garcíaharo, J.: Integration of directional antennas in an RSS fingerprinting-based indoor localization system. Sensors **16**(1), 4 (2015)

Easing Traffic Congestion: An Improved Clustering Method for Sharing Bike Station Deployment

Jian Kang, Weipeng Jing$^{(\boxtimes)}$, and Chengfang Zhao

College of Information and Computer Engineering,
Northeast Forestry University, Harbin, China
{laurelkang,weipeng.Jing,chengfangzhao}@outlook.com

Abstract. An excessive number of cars cause serious traffic jams. Fortunately, a new kind of environmentally friendly transportation service, sharing bikes, came into being. In the cities with shared bikes, deploying shared bikes stations purposefully will make a contribution to reducing the pressure of the traffic. We aim to draw support from sharing bikes to improve the bad traffic. To find the real problems of the current traffic. We make full use of history taxi trajectories to analyze current traffic condition. We design a traffic jam detection framework in this paper. It is called CF framework for short. Derived from the density-based clustering algorithm of inspiration, we propose a new clustering method (CF-Dbscan). The new method has successfully been applied to the trajectories clustering. To deal with errors of devices, a road network matching algorithm (CF-Matching) helps match GPS points to real road network accurately. The first experiment proves that our clustering algorithm performs better than DBSCAN in the field of trajectory clustering. We design another experiment to verify the effectiveness of our CF framework in the real scene. The results of the experiments prove that we can achieve the purpose of reducing traffic jam with our framework.

Keywords: Sharing bikes · DBSCAN · Clustering · Road matching
Traffic congestion

1 Introduction

Recently, the urban traffic is getting worse. As the population of the cities grows, the number of private cars and public transport also increases. Although it satisfies people's travel needs to some extent, it has also caused great pressure to traffic. Fortunately, the bicycles came back to the sight of the public in the form of sharing. In the last few years, shared bikes have been springing up across many big cities of China. Commuters scan QR code on shared bikes with their mobile phones to borrow them from a station. They only have to pay a certain amount of money to ride the bike anywhere. In addition to environmental friendliness,

© ICST Institute for Computer Sciences, Social Informatics and Telecommunications Engineering 2018
I. Romdhani et al. (Eds.): CollaborateCom 2017, LNICST 252, pp. 296–308, 2018.
https://doi.org/10.1007/978-3-030-00916-8_28

the existence of sharing bikes can also improve traffic conditions by reasonably planning the station location.

By observing several cities with shared bicycles, it is not difficult to find that most of the shared bike stations [3] are deployed around personnel-intensive areas. There are some potential problems with such a deployment method. Firstly, bicycle resources are too much to be concentrated in personnel-intensive areas, people in other areas do not enjoy enough convenience so distribution is not balanced. Secondly, the environmentally friendly feature of sharing bicycles is not being used well. How to use shared bicycles to reduce traffic congestion is the core of this paper. With the development of location based service, GPS equipments are widely used by taxis [10]. We have collected a large number of taxi trajectory data. Information on traffic congestion of a city is hidden in the taxi trajectory data [11]. We apply the results of the analysis to shared bikes to find the most suitable station locations [5,13]. Our goal is to give pedestrians one more choice on traffic jams. This approach will reduce the number of vehicles on congested roads. As traffic congestion is mainly caused by motor vehicles. Bicycles travel on bike paths instead of occupying motor ways. This is a good way to divert pedestrians. The less vehicles in the motor ways, the more smooth the traffic will be.

Of course, it is not a compulsive act to choose a shared bike as a means of transportation. However, in the face of traffic congestion, shared bikes provide a new choice, which can guide people to choose other means of transportation to avoid the peak hours. There are always people who would rather ride a bike than wait for traffic jams in the car.

As we all know, there are always many trajectories generated by motor vehicles on the road at any time. In general, at certain intervals, the more trajectories on the road the more crowded the vehicles are. And we can identify traffic flow on a road as trajectories with similar temporal and spatial characteristics. We can find all the trajectories from the data set with similar temporal and spatial characteristics and treat them as on the same road segment. This conforms to the idea of clustering. Due to noise points in the data, we decided to use density-based clustering algorithm. We propose a framework (CF) to detect the traffic jam [2] in this paper. Trough taxi trajectory data mining to make traffic problems reveal. CF framework consists of two main phases, CF-Dbscan and CF-Matching. Compared with the traditional density-based clustering algorithm DBSCAN [1], the CF-DBSCAN is greatly improved. Traditional DBSCAN faces two potential problems in processing trajectory data. (1) The DBSCAN is an algorithm based on the location of points, it is too concerned about the location information of the point itself, so that the association between points and points is ignored. It may be well-suited for hashing irrelevant points, but it does not apply to trajectories that are closely related. Although a typical GPS trajectory consists of a series of points. Points belonging to the same trajectory are related to each other. The traditional DBSCAN will ignore some of the associations to make the clustering results unreasonable. (2) The traditional DBSCAN algorithm calculates the distance of every two points in the data set. There will be huge computational costs on a large number of data sets. After fully considering the limitations of the original method, the density clustering idea was redesigned in this paper to make it more suitable for the trajectories [8,12]. We take into account the interrelationships between the points. So the CF-DBSCAN algorithm considers each trajectory as a whole [7,9], capturing the common parts (if any) [4] of the two trajectories. We have eliminated a lot of distance comparisons between points and points. Instead, we compare the macro features of the trajectories. The CF-DBSCAN algorithm improves the computing performance and makes the clustering result clearer. CF-Matching is a road network matching algorithm that can map the trajectory points to the real road network even at a low sampling rate (e.g., the time between two sampling points exceeds 2 min), thereby solving the GPS error problem. In this paper, the spatial evaluation function [6] is introduced to analyze the correlation of each sampling point sequence. With this framework a traffic congestion map is generated. It represents the most suitable places for the deployment of shared bicycle stations.

The remaining parts of the paper are arranged as follows: Sects. 2 and 3 elaborates the methodology of CF framework. Section 4 introduces the experiments and evaluation. Finally, we sum up this paper in Sect. 5.

2   Mining Trajectories

We elaborate the core stage of our methodology, CF-Dbscan. In this section. We first use a clustering algorithm to mine the trajectory data. We will describe the two phases of the clustering algorithm in two subsections.

2.1   Clustering Trajectories

The clustering algorithm proposed in this paper has two core steps. For easy description, we define the taxi track sequence Tr as a series of time-sequential GPS spatial points, $Tr:p_1 \rightarrow p_2 \rightarrow \cdots \rightarrow p_n$. Each track has its unique identification code, Tr.id. Because the trajectory data is in the form of coordinate points on the two-dimensional plane in the data set. For trajectories, they have different shapes, lengths and geographical positions. So firstly, for any two trajectories to be compared, we need to standardize them as a preparation for formal clustering.

Get Public Parts. The task of CF-DBSCAN is to find congested roads within a specific period of time. In this paper, traffic congestion is defined in this way: if the number of trajectories on a road greater than the threshold during a fixed period of time, we regard this as a traffic jam. It is unscientific to use only the endpoints to calculate, because most of the trajectories do not strictly stop at a specific point from a specific point. For many taxis, the crowded road segments are not their entire journey, but only part of their whole trip. Figure 1 describes this situation.

For the situation shown in Fig. 1, we should not consider the overall trajectories, but should look at the trajectory split. For the trajectories, we should do

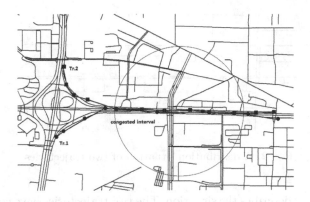

Fig. 1. The public parts of two tracks Tr.1, Tr.2

the following first. First of all, we need to know that the geographical coordinates are spherical coordinates. But for a city, for the convenience of computation, it can be abstracted as plane coordinates, and the error can be ignored. We regard longitude coordinates as X coordinates and latitude coordinates as Y coordinates. Then the trajectory is easily projected onto the X axis. We introduce four related variables $P1min, P1max, P2min, P2max$. They represent the endpoints of the projections (P1 and P2) above. To begin with, we have to figure out whether their projection has overlapping parts on the X axis. On X axis, if $P1max._x < P2min._x$ or $P2max._x < P1min._x$, obviously, their projections have no overlapping parts. We treat this situation as two trajectories without clustering conditions. So we do not need to do the remaining calculations. This judgment step can save a huge amount of calculation.

If the projection of the two tracks has an overlapping part, it means that two tracks have the initial condition of clustering, and only need further processing can we do cluster operation. In other words, they may have passed through the same road segments. We determine the common part of the original trajectory based on the projection boundary. The public section is used for a more thorough judgment.

CF-Dbscan. In this paper, the clustering algorithm is based on the public parts of two tracks. The traditional DBSCAN algorithm determines whether two candidates belong to the same cluster according to the spatial characteristics. But trajectory data contains more dimensions of information. The information needs to be considered as much as possible in order to achieve better clustering results. So DBSCAN is not suitable to directly use here. Therefore, we use the common parts of the trajectories to extend DBSCAN to an algorithm that is suitable for trajectory clustering.

We introduce a variable that represents spatial radius c_d. Variable c_t is used to represent temporal span. They represent the spatial-temporal feature of any two trajectories. But only the characteristics of spatial-temporal feature are not

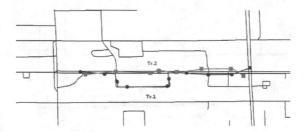

Fig. 2. A distribution situation of two trajectories

enough. Figure 2 describes the situation. The two trajectories have common parts and similar spatiotemporal characteristics. But in Fig. 2, they don't go through the same section of the road. Obviously, they should not be clustered into one cluster. To deal with this problem, we introduce a curvature index, which is represented by K. We define the curvature as the ratio of the actual distance from p_i to p_j and Euclidean distance between p_i and p_j. It is obvious that the actual driving distance is always greater than the Euclidean distance, so the curvature is always greater than or equal to 1.

The definition of curvature in this paper is shown as follow

$$K = \frac{L(p_i \to p_j)}{dist(p_i \to p_j)} \tag{1}$$

The more similar the shape of the two trajectories, the closer the result of the curvature will be. We set a threshold for the curvature gap ΔK. If the curvature difference satisfies the following formula, the result can be accepted.

$$|K_1 - K_2| \leq \Delta K \tag{2}$$

A set of neighborhood corresponding to a core trajectory is defined as $N_{c_d,c_t,k}(\mathrm{Tr}.i)$. The trajectories in this set are all trajectories that meet the clustering conditions with the core trajectories. For every common part, we call the left endpoint as the starting point, and the right endpoint is called the end point. This paper defines the clustering conditions according to the following rules. If a trajectory can be added to a neighbor, it needs to satisfy all conditions at the same time. (1) For the two cut public parts, the spatial distance between the starting points and the spatial distance between the end points should be within the threshold c_d. (2) For the two cut public parts, The temporal distance c_t between the two starting points should be within the threshold. (3) the absolute value of the curvature difference is within ΔK, i.e.,

$$N_{c_d,c_t,k}(Tr.i) = \{Tr.j \in \tau | dist(o_{T_i}, o_{T_j}) \leq c_d, dist(d_{T_i},$$
$$d_{T_j}) \leq c_d, |t_{T_i} - t_{T_j}| \leq c_t, |K_i - K_j| \leq \Delta K\} \tag{3}$$

where τ represents the set of tracks, $dist(\cdot, \cdot)$ denotes road net distance between two points. o_T and d_T denote starting point and end point, respectively. t_T

denotes the beginning timestamp of the public part, K is curvature while ΔK represents curvature threshold.

A capacity threshold named MinTrs is employed here to constrain the density of cluster. It denotes the lower bound of the number of trajectories in each cluster. If the number of trajectories belonging to a cluster exceeds MinTrs, i.e., $|N_{c_d,c_t,k}(Tr.i)| \geq$ MinTrs, then $Tr.i$ can be regarded as a core trajectory. Based on the number of existing shared bicycles we plan to deploy and the number of bicycle stations, we can flexibly adjust the above four thresholds, c_d, c_t, ΔK and MinTrs.

Considering the difference between one-way lanes and two-way lanes, we consider two-way lanes as two lanes and cluster them separately. Algorithm 1 gives a detailed description of the CF-Dbscan algorithm. Our CF-Dbscan algorithm required five parameters as input. A trajectories set τ and four threshold parameters, c_d, c_t, K and MinTrs. The procedure of GetNeighborhood (Line 5) helps find a neighborhood tracks set based on Eq. 3. The algorithm first randomly selects a trajectory from the set τ as the beginning. Then the procedure of GetNeighborhood can get the neighborhood set to the target trajectory. In the procedure of GetNeighborhood, to begin with, we cut two candidate trajectories on the basis of their projections on X axis (if any). If a track and multiple tracks have common parts, it will be cut many times. This will result in losing data. To avoid this phenomenon, in $N_{c_d,c_t,k}(Tr)$ original trajectories will be reserved instead of trajectories fragment. Although this approach will result in some redundancy, this is still a more comprehensive approach. Continue Algorithm 1. After obtaining the neighborhood set, it retrieves all unvisited trajectories within the neighborhood (line 12). In this way, the cluster is continuously expanded until it is saturated. Then one cluster is generated. In other words, we use open set M to reserve neighbor. The procedure will not stop until all trajectories of M are explored.

3   Clustering Result Matching

3.1   CF-Matching

After the execution of the CF-Dbscan, several clusters of trajectories are generated. To locate the location of the cluster accurately, first, find the core trajectory of the cluster. However, due to equipment errors and other external factors, they are not standardized. This error sometimes leads directly to wrong results and cannot be ignored. So in order to eliminate the error, we propose an algorithm to map the cores of these clusters to the real road network. We call our road network matching method as CF-Matching.

Get Candidates. The CF-Matching algorithm first traverses a trajectory and the road network around it, in order to determine the set of candidate points for each sampling point. Figure 3 describes the process. p_i denotes a sampling point of current trajectory, e represents road segments. c denotes the projection

---

Algorithm 1. CF-Dbscan for trajectories clustering

INPUT:
 A set of trajectories τ
 Four parameters introduced above c_d,c_t,K and MinTrs
OUTPUT:
 A cluster set C={C_1,C_2,C_3,...,$C_{|C|}$}

1: Set $c\_id = 1$
 Initialize all trajectories in τ as unvisited
2: **for** each $Tr \in \tau$ **do**
3: **if** Tr is unvisited **then**
4:   Mark T as visited
5:   GetNeighborhood(Tr)
6:   **if** $|N_{c_d,c_t,k}(Tr)| <$ MinTrs **then**
7:    Mark Tr as a non-core trajectory
8:   **else**
9:    Mark Tr as a core trajectory
10:    Put T into C_{c_id}
11:    Put trajectories of neighborhood set of Tr into M, i.e.,M $\leftarrow N_{c_d,c_t,k}$(Tr)-{Tr}
12:    **for** each $T_b \in$ M **do**
13:     **if** T_b is unvisited **then**
14:      Mark T_b as visited
15:      Put T_b into C_{cid}
16:      GetNeighborhood(T_b)
17:      **if** $|N_{c_d,c_t,k}(Tr)| \geq$ MinTrs **then**
18:       Insert $N_{c_d,c_t,k}$(Tr)-{Tr} into M
19:      **end if**
20:     **end if**
21:     **if** T_b is a non-core trajectory **then**
22:      Put T_b into C_{c_id}
23:     **end if**
     Remove T_b from M
24:    **end for**
    Increase c_id by 1
25:   **end if**
26: **end if**
27: **end for**

---

points of p_i on e satisfying $c = argmin_{\forall c_i \in e}$dist($c_i$, p), dist($c_i$, p) returns the distance between p_i and any point on e. To speed up the search for candidate points, we employ a window that follows the sampling point p_i to cut the whole network to reduce the search range. After executing this step, the algorithm will get a set sequence, the next question is how to choose one of the most suitable points from each candidates set so that P: $c_1^{j_1} \rightarrow c_2^{j_2} \rightarrow \cdots \rightarrow c_n^{j_n}$ best matches T:$p_1 \rightarrow p_2 \rightarrow \cdots \rightarrow p_n$.

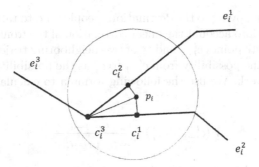

Fig. 3. Sampling point p_i and its candidate points

Correlation Analysis. Empirically, errors in GPS measurements can be reasonably described with a normal distribution $N(\mu, \sigma^2)$ of the distance between c_i^j and p_i. It indicates that, without considering the influence of other points, the probability that GPS observation p_i matches the candidate point c_i^j on the actual road network. We use a formula to describe the possibility $N(c_i^j)$ of c_i^j with regard to p_i:

$$N(c_i^j) = \frac{1}{\sqrt{2\pi}\sigma} e^{-\frac{(x_i^j - \mu)^2}{2\sigma^2}} \tag{4}$$

$x_i^j = \text{dist}(c_i^j, p_i)$, it denotes the distance between c_i^j and p_i. In order to make the number as uniform as possible. Empirically, we use a zero-mean normal distribution with a standard deviation of $0.002\,\text{km}$.

Road network matching can not be completed only on the basis of possibility. In practice, we can't ignore the impact from the front and back sampling points, otherwise it may result in a wrong matching result. Figure 4 describes an example. p_{i-1}, p_i, p_{i+1} are the sequence of sampling points that belong to the same trajectory. c_i^1 and c_i^2 are candidate points of p_i. We may match p_i to c_i^2 if we only consider the observation possibility. Because they are closer in geographical location. But in fact, as depicted in Fig. 4, if we match p_i to c_i^2 it will lead to a deviation from the right route.

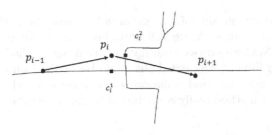

Fig. 4. An example that needs transmission probability

Actually, when moving to the destination, people tend to take a shorter route. This needs to take into account the linear correlation of the front and back points. Given two candidate points c_{i-1}^t and c_i^s of two neighboring trajectory points p_{i-1} and p_i, we define the possibility from c_{i-1}^t to c_i^s as the possibility of p_{i-1} to p_i on the real road network. We use the following formula to calculate the associated possibility.

$$V(c_{i-1}^t \rightarrow c_i^s) = \frac{d_{i-1 \rightarrow i}}{\omega_{(i-1,t) \rightarrow (i,s)}} \tag{5}$$

where $d_{i-1 \rightarrow i}$ is the Euclidean distance between p_{i-1} and p_i, $d_{i-1 \rightarrow i} = dist(p_i, p_{i-1})$. $\omega_{(i-1,t) \rightarrow (i,s)}$ returns the length of shortest path between c_{i-1}^t and c_i^s.

To calculate $\omega_{(i-1,t) \rightarrow (i,s)}$, we must first find shortest path. As the road network is a huge undirected map. Directly searching for the shortest path on it will bring exponentially increasing computational costs. So we employ a threshold to limit the search depth. In fact, if we can't find a path within this range, then the chance of the target point being the next candidate is very small. By combining Eqs. 4 and 5, we propose Eq. 6 for linear assessment.

$$F_s(c_{i-1}^t \rightarrow c_i^s) = N(c_i^s) * V(c_{i-1}^t \rightarrow c_i^s), 2 \leq i \leq n \tag{6}$$

where c_{i-1}^t and c_i^s are candidate points. They belong to sampling points p_{i-1}, p_i separately.

In all possible sequence of candidate points. We need to find a candidate point sequence with the highest total score according to Eq. 6. This candidate sequence is most likely the true path of this trajectory. The best match results follow the formula below:

$$P = argmax_{P_c} F(P_c), \forall P_c \in G'_T(V'_T, E'_T) \tag{7}$$

The result sequence of the calculated output is the sequence of candidate points with the greatest matching possibility. With CF-Matching, the core trajectory of each cluster can be accurately mapped to the real road network.

4   Experiments

We have prepared two groups of experiments to assess the performance of the CF framework. To begin with, we will describe a large-scale data set of actual taxi trajectories. Next we prove on our data set that our method is more suitable for the trajectory. Finally, we carried out field observations on the experimental results and made statistics and collation of the results, which proved that our station deployment method really contributed to improving the traffic condition.

4.1   Passenger Trajectories

The data set of taxi trajectory was collected in Beijing, China, in November 2011. A total of 12,000 taxis, a total of 230917631 GPS records. Each record contains nine fields. The fields associated with this study include the latitude, longitude, taxi ID, timestamp, and occupied status.

In this experiment, the travel pattern of pedestrians is fully taken into account. The way people travel on holidays is not like usual. For example, every working day has a similar peak. However, during the weekend, the peak hours in the morning may be somewhat later than usual, while the afternoon peaks last longer than usual. Compared to holidays, we tend to study regular working days. So we preprocess the data. In the use of shared bicycles to alleviate traffic congestion. We filter the data for the weekdays and the peak time data is extracted from the daily trajectories. Figure 5 shows the clustering result of CF-Dbscan. The dots in the figure indicate GPS points. From the diagram we can see that the shape of the crowded road is clearly shown in the result. Although there is still a little noise, it has little effect on the result.

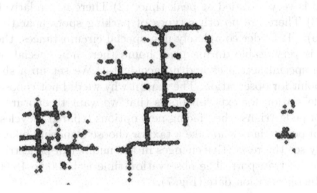

Fig. 5. Clustering effect shown in ArcGIS

We use the F-measure evaluation method to evaluate the performance of CF-Dbscan. We randomly select some roads, mark them to determine whether the tracks in the clustering result are the mark trajectories as the criterion. We randomly selected ten roads in Beijing to evaluate F-score of DBSCAN and CF-Dbscan. The contrast results are presented in Fig. 6. The higher the F-score value, the better the clustering effect. From Fig. 6, compared with DBSCAN, CF-Dbscan has an approximate 0.1 advantage over the average. This can prove that CF-Dbscan performs better than traditional DBSCAN on trajectory clustering.

4.2   CF Evaluation

To verify the actual effects of the CF framework. We need to do field observation and statistics. In order to allow pedestrians to travel in a regular and stable

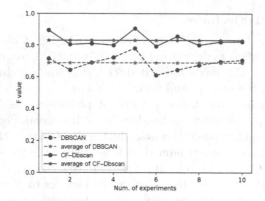

Fig. 6. Comparison of F values between original DBSCAN and CF-Dbscan

manner, we chose to conduct experiments for six consecutive days without holidays or special events. In order to control the influence of external factors, we chose a special experimental road, which has the following four characteristics. (1) This road is very crowded at peak time. (2) There is a relatively fixed taxi ride point. (3) There are no other types of parking spots near the taxi stand (e.g. bus stop). (4) Under completely non special circumstances, the number of moving cars is very stable during peak hours (here non special refers to non holidays, non special activities and no accidents). We set up a shared bicycle experiment point for observation. The reason why we did not choose an existing shared bicycle station for experiments is that we want to capture the changes in behavior of pedestrians when facing new options (shared bicycles). We count the number of pedestrians who take a taxi or choose a sharing bike. In this way, we can clearly see the respective changes in the number of pedestrians choosing the two modes of transport. The observation time is 17:00 to 18:00 points per day during the observation date (Fig. 7).

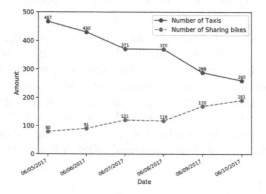

Fig. 7. Changes in the number of taxis and sharing bikes during the experiment

The solid line shows the number of taxis that change over time, and the lower dotted line shows the number of bicycles. From the chart we can easily see that there is a significant increase in the number of pedestrians choosing shared bicycles while the number of people taking taxis dropped obviously. The results can prove that the targeted placement of bicycles on traffic congested roads can relieve traffic pressure.

5   Conclusion

In this article, we propose a CF framework for the actual problems of traffic congestion. With the rise of shared bicycles, we hope to analyze the hidden congested sections from taxi trajectory data, and then use bicycles to solve the congestion problem. Reducing the number of vehicles on the road by allowing shared bikes to replace taxis to make traffic smoother. In order to find congestion, we use the improved clustering algorithm CF-Dbscan to cluster the trajectory data. Clustering results are mapped to real road network by road network matching algorithm, CF-Matching. We used two experiments to prove the performance of the framework itself and the effect in the actual scene.

Acknowledgement. The work described in this paper is supported by Guangdong Provincial Key Laboratory of Petrochemical Equipment Fault Diagnosis, Guangdong University of Petrochemical Technology (GDUPTKLAB201502) and Special Fund for Forest Scientific Research in the Public Welfare (201504307).

References

1. Bi, F.M., Wang, W.K., Chen, L.: Dbscan: density-based spatial clustering of applications with noise. J. Nanjing Univ. **48**(4), 491–498 (2012)
2. Ceder, A.: Public transit planning and operation: modeling, practice and behavior. Transport **30**(4), 448–450 (2015)
3. García-Palomares, J.C., Gutiérrez, J., Latorre, M.: Optimizing the location of stations in bike-sharing programs: a GIS approach. Appl. Geogr. **35**(1–2), 235–246 (2012)
4. Lee, J.G., Han, J., Whang, K.Y.: Trajectory clustering: a partition-and-group framework. In: ACM SIGMOD International Conference on Management of Data, pp. 593–604 (2007)
5. Li, Y., Luo, J., Chow, C.Y., Chan, K.L., Ding, Y., Zhang, F.: Growing the charging station network for electric vehicles with trajectory data analytics. In: IEEE International Conference on Data Engineering, pp. 1376–1387 (2015)
6. Lou, Y., Zhang, C., Zheng, Y., Xie, X., Wang, W., Huang, Y.: Map-matching for low-sampling-rate GPS trajectories. In: Proceedings of the ACM SIGSPATIAL International Symposium on Advances in Geographic Information Systems, ACM-GIS 2009, Seattle, Washington, USA, 4–6 November 2009, pp. 352–361 (2009)
7. Wang, W., Tao, L., Gao, C., Wang, B., Yang, H., Zhang, Z.: A C-DBSCAN algorithm for determining bus-stop locations based on taxi GPS data. In: Luo, X., Yu, J.X., Li, Z. (eds.) ADMA 2014. LNCS (LNAI), vol. 8933, pp. 293–304. Springer, Cham (2014). https://doi.org/10.1007/978-3-319-14717-8_23

8. Yan, L., Chow, C.Y., Lee, V.C.S., Li, Y., Zeng, J.: T2CBS: mining taxi trajectories for customized bus systems. In: Computer Communications Workshops, pp. 441–446 (2016)
9. Yuan, H., Qian, Y., Ma, B., Wei, Q.: From trajectories to path network: an endpoints-based GPS trajectory partition and clustering framework. In: Li, F., Li, G., Hwang, S., Yao, B., Zhang, Z. (eds.) WAIM 2014. LNCS, vol. 8485, pp. 740–743. Springer, Cham (2014). https://doi.org/10.1007/978-3-319-08010-9_80
10. Zhang, D., Li, N., Zhou, Z.H., Chen, C., Sun, L., Li, S.: iBAT: detecting anomalous taxi trajectories from GPS traces. In: International Conference on Ubiquitous Computing, pp. 99–108 (2011)
11. Zheng, Y., Liu, Y., Yuan, J., Xie, X.: Urban computing with taxicabs. In: International Conference on Ubiquitous Computing, pp. 89–98 (2011)
12. Zheng, Y., Yuan, N.J., Zheng, K., Shang, S.: On discovery of gathering patterns from trajectories. In: IEEE International Conference on Data Engineering, pp. 242–253 (2013)
13. Zhu, B., Xu, X.: Urban principal traffic flow analysis based on taxi trajectories mining. In: Tan, Y., Shi, Y., Buarque, F., Gelbukh, A., Das, S., Engelbrecht, A. (eds.) ICSI 2015. LNCS, vol. 9142, pp. 172–181. Springer, Cham (2015). https://doi.org/10.1007/978-3-319-20469-7_20

Sensor Data Classification for the Indication of Lameness in Sheep

Zainab Al-Rubaye[1,3]([✉]), Ali Al-Sherbaz[1], Wanda McCormick[2], and Scott Turner[1]

[1] Department of Computing and Immersive Technologies,
School of Art, Science and Technology, Northampton NN2 6JD, UK
{zainab.al-rubaye, ali.al-sherbaz,
scott.turner}@northampton.ac.uk,
zaynebraid@scbaghdad.edu.iq

[2] Department of Biology, Faculty of Science and Technology,
Anglia Ruskin University, Cambridge CB1 1PT, UK
wanda.mccormick@anglia.ac.uk

[3] Computer Science Department, College of Science,
University of Baghdad, Baghdad, Iraq

Abstract. Lameness is a vital welfare issue in most sheep farming countries, including the UK. The pre-detection at the farm level could prevent the disease from becoming chronic. The development of wearable sensor technologies enables the idea of remotely monitoring the changes in animal movements which relate to lameness. In this study, 3D-acceleration, 3D-orientation, and 3D-linear acceleration sensor data were recorded at ten samples per second via the sensor attached to sheep neck collar. This research aimed at determining the best accuracy among various supervised machine learning techniques which can predict the early signs of lameness while the sheep are walking on a flat field. The most influencing predictors for lameness indication were also addressed here. The experimental results revealed that the Decision Tree classifier has the highest accuracy of 75.46%, and the orientation sensor data (angles) around the neck are the strongest predictors to differentiate among severely lame, mildly lame and sound classes of sheep.

Keywords: Sensor data classification · Machine learning · Decision tree Lameness detection · Sheep

1 Introduction

Lameness is a painful impaired movement disorder, which relates to an animal's locomotion system and causes a deviation from normal gait or posture [1]. In sheep, footrot is the most common cause, resulting in 90% of the sheep lameness cases in the UK [2, 3]. Unfortunately, lameness has a negative impact on the sheep industry and overall farm productivity. Statistics from the Agriculture and Horticulture Development Board (AHDB) estimated the annual UK economic loss to be £10 for each ewe in 2016 [4]. The underlying reasons for the commercial loss in the UK sheep industry can be related to declines in various outcomes, including sheep body condition; lambing

© ICST Institute for Computer Sciences, Social Informatics and Telecommunications Engineering 2018
I. Romdhani et al. (Eds.): CollaborateCom 2017, LNICST 252, pp. 309–320, 2018.
https://doi.org/10.1007/978-3-030-00916-8_29

percentage; lamb birth weight; growth rate in lambs; wool growth; milk production and poor fertility in rams [5]. Hence, the lameness is listed as one of the main causes for sheep culling beside infertility and mastitis [6, 7].

Although lameness is endemic and cannot be eradicated entirely, the early detection of lameness will prevent the condition from spreading quickly within the flock. Thus, the advantages of early lameness detection can maximise the farm's income, enhancing sheep welfare to improving the entire flock performance and reducing the veterinary, medicine, and labour costs [5].

2 Lameness Detection

Since the indication for lameness correlates with changes in animal posture, gait, or behaviour, previous studies have utilised different types of data collection and data analysis methods which were applied in various ways for lameness detection in cattle. However, there is a paucity of research studies of sheep lameness detection.

2.1 Data Collection Methods

Initially, lameness was assessed by trained observers who scored the lameness level via a numerical rating system (NRS). Although the subjective method for scoring lameness can be implemented with no technical equipment and could suit on-farm assessment, it lacks the objective reliability [8].

Alternatively, surveillance cameras were used to record gait measurements which relate to lameness in the cows to be tested by computer vision techniques. For instance, back arch curvature was studied by [9–11], the body movements pattern was explored by [12], and the step overlap was investigated in cattle by [13, 14]. Despite the extraction of features that strongly relate to gait variables from computer vision techniques, as investigated by many authors, the implementation of computer vision techniques on the farm is still a challenging task [15].

Various sensor systems have been developed to evaluate animal movements using either leg mounted sensors or neck attached sensors. Most of the studies that have implemented data collection via sensors to detect lameness were undertaken with cattle rather than sheep. Mainly, the sensor devices that attached to the cow's leg, pedometers, were used [16] to calculate the mean number of steps per hour as an indicator for lameness in cattle, whereas in [6] the researcher depended on the measurement of the activity and lying behaviour for lameness indication.

Accelerometers have also been mounted to the leg to measure the gait features in relation to cow lameness. For example, the differences in the symmetry of variance for the forward acceleration of the hind legs of the cow were explored in [17]; the acceleration of legs and back of the cow was investigated in [18]; while the researcher in [19] measured the lying and standing time, the number of lying bouts, and step count to identify the characteristic of the lame limb. Statistically, the early signs of lameness were illustrated by [20] by performing the Principal Component Analysis (PCA).

Furthermore, a neck acceleration sensor was also explored in a pilot study that was conducted by [21] to investigate the relationship between the mobility score and the neck acceleration measurements which linked to the lame cow by using statistical kurtosis measurement.

2.2 Data Analysis Approaches

The resulting information from sensor-based data calls for more professional and precise approaches to analyse such relatively large data sets, in order to classify and infer animal behaviour. The concept of 'reality mining' has explored the idea of cross-collaboration between disciplines to produce more integrated approaches [22]. Therefore, Data Mining techniques, which are a confluence of many disciplines [23], have been used to analyse the sensor-based data to classify various behavioural types that could have played an important role to detect some illness concerns such as lameness.

Machine Learning (ML) is one set of techniques adopted within data mining which investigates how computers learn from the data set to enhance the performance of the tested algorithm automatically. Supervised ML algorithms (classification) can identify a complex pattern (class) of new test data, based on the attributes of previously known classes of training data sets, and predict an intelligent decision [21].

Apart from lameness detection, analysis methods and different classification approaches have mostly investigated different sensor-based data to identify a wide range of behaviour patterns for various species including cattle and sheep. The following two Tables 1 and 2 display the research studies which classify cattle and sheep behaviour by using ML with sensor-based data predictors.

Table 1. Cattle behaviour classification in research studies

Classification methods [reference]	Sensor type/position	Classify into
Decision tree [24]	2D accelerometers/neck	Active and inactive
Decision tree [25]	3D accelerometers/leg	Standing, lying, and walking
Decision tree [26]	3D accelerometers/neck	Foraging, ruminating, travelling, and resting
Ensemble [27]	3D accelerometers & manometer/neck	Grazing, ruminating, resting, and walking
CART [28]	GPS sensor/neck	Foraging, lying, standing and walking
HMM [29]	GPS, 3D accelerometer, 3D manometer/neck	Animal movements and transition behaviour
Multi-class SVM [30]	3D accelerometer/neck	Standing, lying, ruminating, and feeding
Decision tree [31]	3D Accelerometer/neck	Lying, standing, feeding

Table 2. Sheep behaviour classification in research studies

Classification methods [reference]	Sensor type/position	Classify into
LDA, classification tree, and developed decision tree [32]	Pitch & roll tilt sensor/neck	Active and inactive
LDA, QDA [33]	3D accelerometers/neck	Lying, standing, walking, running and grazing
Decision tree [34]	3D accelerometer/under the jaw	Grazing, lying, running, standing and walking
Statistical analysis methods [35]	3D accelerometer/under the jaw	Grazing, ruminating and resting

3 Research Method

Predominantly, the previous studies have investigated how to detect lameness in dairy cattle and how to classify their behaviour depending on ML techniques, while the undertaken research explored lameness detection in sheep via the classification of acceleration orientation and linear acceleration data that were retrieved from a mounted sensor within a neck collar.

3.1 Data Collection

The data were collected from Lodge Farm, Moulton College in Northamptonshire, UK, in January 2017 from seven sheep which were labelled as purple, green, and neutral by a trained shepherd to indicate 'severely lame', 'mildly lame', and 'sound' respectively. A Galaxy S4 Android 5.0 mobile device was attached to the sheep neck collar to record built in sensor data via a free Android sensor application called SensoDuino [36].

In the study, SensoDuino recorded three-dimensional acceleration, linear acceleration, and orientation sensor data into a log file in the SD card of the mobile device for later data analysis. The measurements were logged for 3–7 min while the sheep was walking on a flat field at ten samples per second. The video footages were also taken as ground truth recordings. Figure 1 shows the sensor position on the sheep neck at the farm.

Remark 1. The ethical approval and risk assessment request to visit the Lodge Farm and collect the data about the sheep movements via a sensor neck collar was authorised by the Moulton College research committee in April 2016.

3.2 Raw Data Interpretation

The accelerometer sensor calculates the changes in movements involving the gravity around three axes, while the linear acceleration measurements exclude it. Whereas, the orientation calculates the value of the angles around the neck (in degrees) for three dimensions.

Fig. 1. Sensor deployment on the Lodge Farm.

The initial plotting of the raw data and its class are shown in Fig. 2. It is visually interpreted that the sound class and non-sound class (severely and mildly lame) can be linearly separated in Fig. 2c. Therefore, the orientation group can be the best indicator for lameness in sheep. However, the severely lame and mildly lame class are overlapped and challenging to distinguish.

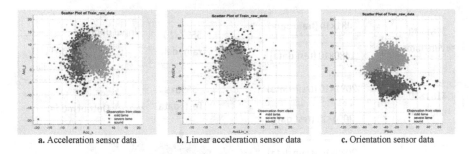

a. Acceleration sensor data   b. Linear acceleration sensor data   c. Orientation sensor data

Fig. 2. Sensor raw data plotting and its class.

On the other hand, the acceleration data group (Fig. 2a) has less impact than the orientation group, while the linear acceleration data (Fig. 2b) may not be as useful as a single predictor because of no gravity measurements here.

3.3 Raw Data Preparation for ML Classifier

In this pilot study, recordings from seven sheep were considered, their details are listed in Table 3. Each recording refers to the sheep that had been mounted with the SensoDuino sensor that retrieved ten10 readings per second. The lameness class for the participant sheep was either severely lame, mildly lame or sound.

Table 3. Details of the collected data

File name	Total samples (10 samples per second)	Sheep status
L1_severe	2961	Severely lame
L1_mild	4181	Mildly lame
S1	4050	Sound
L2_severe	4292	Severely lame
L2_mild	2211	Mildly lame
S2	2741	Sound
S7	1626	Sound

The input data to the classifier model, implemented in Matlab (Mathworks, USA) to be trained include acceleration data (Acc_x, Acc_y, Acc_z), linear acceleration data (AccLin_x, AccLin_y, AccLin_z), and orientation data (Azimuth, Pitch, Roll). Furthermore, another column was added to the previous nine input columns that indicated the status class of the sheep as either severely lame, mildly lame or sound. The *L1_severe* file (relating to a severely lame sheep) was divided into two files, one used to train the model and the other for testing the model. The same procedure was implemented to *L1_mild* and *S1* files that relate to mildly lame and sound sheep respectively. Figure 3 illustrates how the data files were prepared for Matlab learner classifier. It also shows how the model was built and tested.

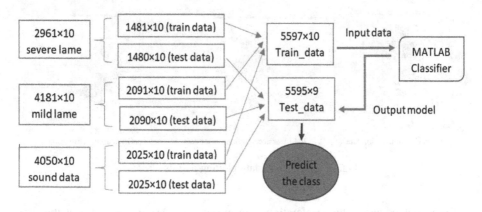

Fig. 3. Raw data preparation for ML classifier.

4   Initial Results and Discussion

A pilot study was applied to investigate the current supervised machine learning techniques which produced promising results regarding the best classifier performance, the strongest predictor group, and testing the prediction accuracy for the built models with new data set.

4.1   Investigation of the Best Classifier

The main experiment was conducted to evaluate the effective classifier for lameness detection when all nine predictors were used to train the model. The results in Fig. 4 show that the Simple Tree classifier (decision tree) has the highest test accuracy of 75.46% when it is tested with *Test_data* file (see Fig. 3).

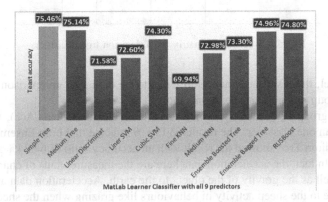

Fig. 4. MatLab classifier accuracy for (3 Acc, 3 AccLin, and 3 Angles) readings of SensoDuino.

The overall accuracy of the classifier performance and the sensitivity to predict each class separately are calculated by Eqs. (1) and (2) respectively as follows:

$$
\begin{aligned}
\text{Classifier accuracy} &= \frac{\text{Number of correct predictions}}{\text{Total number of predictions}} \\
&= \frac{(TP + TN)}{(TP + TN + FP + FN)}
\end{aligned}
\tag{1}
$$

$$
\text{The Sensitivity} = \frac{TP}{(TP + FN)}
\tag{2}
$$

The confusion matrix was used to measure the performance of a classifier learner on a set of known class data [37]. The diagonal line in the confusion matrix represents the overall of True Positive predictions (TP) and True Negative predictions (TN), which means that the actual classes match the predicted classes. Otherwise, the area above and under the diagonal are called False Negative (FN) and False Positive (FP) [38]. The confusion matrix for the Simple Tree classifier (decision tree) is presented in Fig. 5.

4.2   Investigation of the Strongest Predictor Group

For eliminating the number of lameness predictors, the attention was turned towards identifying the impact of each group among acceleration, linear acceleration, and orientation (angles). In general, when using the angle data as predictors to build the

Predicted Class / Actual Class	severerly lame	mildly lame	Sound		TPR / FNR
Severely lame	722	697	61		82.87 / 17.13
mildly lame	312	1732	46		48.78 / 51.22
Sound	159	98	1768		87.31 / 12.69

Fig. 5. A confusion matrix for a decision tree classifier.

training model, the result accuracy ratio tends to be higher in comparison to acceleration data group or linear acceleration group.

The first group of predictors, which are the acceleration data (Acc), were tested with more than one classifier. The results in Fig. 6 indicate that both Ensemble Bagged Tree and Medium Tree showed the result with an accuracy ratio of 64.24% and 64.06% respectively. In fact, the acceleration data here are the measurements of changing in the velocity as well as the gravity of the object to the earth. Acceleration data are expected to be sensitive to the sheep activity in behaviours like grazing when the sheep's head is down rather than being in a normal posture.

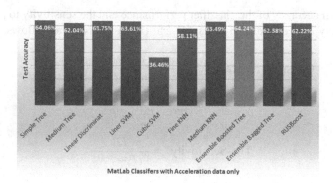

MatLab Classifers with Acceleration data only

Fig. 6. Accuracy results for Matlab classifiers when acceleration (include the gravity) is tested.

The second data group to be investigated was the linear acceleration (AccLin) which refers to acceleration only without gravity. These parameters show the changes in velocity as it is more helpful to know if the sheep are walking quickly, in a slow rhythm or not walking at all. In Fig. 7, the results show that the Ensemble Bagged Tree produced a higher rate of accuracy compared to the other classifiers. However, the overall accuracy of all classifiers is less than 44.52%. Consequently, the utilising of the linear acceleration sensor data as the only predictor are not quite as useful to indicate lameness.

The third and the most active group for lameness detection was the orientation data which indicated the value of the angle around x-axis (pitch), y-axis, (roll), and z-axis

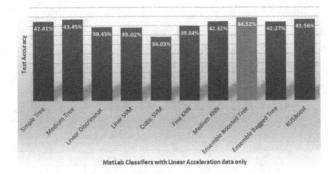

Fig. 7. Accuracy results for Matlab classifiers when the linear acceleration is tested.

(azimuth). The results in Fig. 8 reflect that the Simple Tree classifier can be used to produce a better prediction result among the other classifiers. Generally, when using the angle data as predictors to build the training model, the result accuracy ratio tends to be higher in comparison to the acceleration data group or linear acceleration group separately.

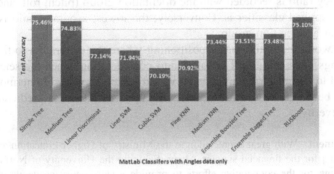

Fig. 8. Accuracy results for Matlab classifiers when azimuth, pitch, and roll are the only input predictors.

4.3 Testing the Models with Unseen Data Samples

The built models were tested with new unseen examples, which are listed in Table 3, to measure the reliability of the models with a new data set. In Fig. 9, the results show the sensitivity to predict the sound class (S7) is higher than 80% for all classifiers compared to the sensitivity to predict the mildly lame and severely lame classes (L2_mild and L2_severe), with the mean sensitivity of 60.93% and 60.18% respectively.

Furthermore, in Fig. 9, it was noticed that the accuracy ratio to predict lameness in sheep was affected by the initial placement of the mobile device. For instance, the movement of the sound sheep S2 during the experiment led the sensor to be shifted from its initial placement. As a result, the prediction accuracy of S2 was too low.

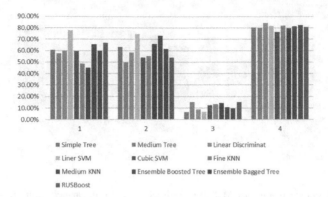

Fig. 9. The accuracy results for the trained models when new data set was tested (1 = *L2_severe*, 2 = *L2_mild*, 3 = *S2*, and 4 = *S7*)

5 Conclusion and Future Work

It is concluded from the current research that the Decision Tree is the best ML classifier for the sheep sensor-based data to predict the early signs of lameness. Moreover, the higher accuracy ratio is recorded with the orientation group (pitch, roll, and azimuth), whatever the applied classifier is. Conversely, the lowest accuracy ratio is registered with the linear acceleration group.

In future work, the initial sensor positioning where the calibration to the reference sensor readings is essential will be taken into consideration, since the sensor reading samples need to be reliable in a flat and a varied terrain as well. Furthermore, the raw data need to be pre-processed for the sake of improved lameness prediction and distinction in severity.

Acknowledgement. With great appreciation to the Ministry of Higher Education and Scientific Research in Iraq for the financial support. Many thanks to the University of Northampton and Moulton College for the cooperative efforts to provide a satisfactory academic environment. Many thanks for the Lodge Farm Shepherd 'Tim' who was very helpful in scheduling the observation time at Lodge Farm.

References

1. Van Nuffel, A., et al.: Lameness detection in dairy cows: part 1. How to distinguish between non-lame and lame cows based on differences in locomotion or behavior. Animals **5**(3), 838–860 (2015)
2. Groenevelt, M., Anzuino, K., Smith, S., Lee, M.R.F., Grogono-Thomas, R.: A case report of lameness in two dairy goat herds; a suspected combination of nutritional factors concurrent with treponeme infection. BMC Res. Notes **8**(1), 791 (2015)
3. Scott, P.D.: DipECBHM, CertCHP, DSHP, and FRCVS. In: Lameness Control in Sheep (2016). http://www.nadis.org.uk/bulletins/lameness-control-in-sheep.aspx. Accessed 13 Mar 2017

4. Brian, K.: Reducing Lameness for Better Returns (2016)
5. Defra: Lameness in Sheep (2003). http://adlib.everysite.co.uk/adlib/defra/content.aspx?id=000IL3890W.18B4NRK0LZK8LC. Accessed 14 Mar 2017
6. Alsaaod, M., et al.: Electronic detection of lameness in dairy cows through measuring pedometric activity and lying behavior. Appl. Anim. Behav. Sci. **142**(3–4), 134–141 (2012)
7. AHDB: Managing Cull Ewes (2016)
8. Flower, F.C., Weary, D.M.: Gait assessment in dairy cattle. Animal **3**(1), 87–95 (2009)
9. Poursaberi, A., Bahr, C., Pluk, A., Van Nuffel, A., Berckmans, D.: Real-time automatic lameness detection based on back posture extraction in dairy cattle: shape analysis of cow with image processing techniques. Comput. Electron. Agric. **74**(1), 110–119 (2010)
10. Viazzi, S., et al.: Analysis of individual classification of lameness using automatic measurement of back posture in dairy cattle. J. Dairy Sci. **96**(1), 257–266 (2013)
11. Viazzi, S., Bahr, C., Van Hertem, T., Schlageter-Tello, A., Romanini, C.E.B., Halachmi, I., Lokhorst, C., Berckmans, D.: Comparison of a three-dimensional and two-dimensional camera system for automated measurement of back posture in dairy cows. Comput. Electron. Agric. **100**, 139–147 (2014)
12. Poursaberi, A., et al.: Online lameness detection in dairy cattle using Body Movement Pattern (BMP). In: International Conference on Intelligent Systems Design and Applications, no. 1, pp. 732–736 (2011)
13. Song, X., Leroy, T., Vranken, E., Maertens, W., Sonck, B., Berckmans, D.: Automatic detection of lameness in dairy cattle-vision-based trackway analysis in cow's locomotion. Comput. Electron. Agric. **64**(1), 39–44 (2008)
14. Pluk, A., et al.: Evaluation of step overlap as an automatic measure in dairy cow locomotion. Am. Soc. Agric. Biol. Eng. **53**(4), 1305–1312 (2010)
15. Van Hertem, T., et al.: Improving a computer vision lameness detection system by adding behaviour and performance measures. In: Proceedings of International Conference on Agricultural Engineering, pp. 1–8 (2014)
16. Mazrier, H., Tal, S., Aizinbud, E., Bargai, U.: A field investigation of the use of the pedometer for the early detection of lameness in cattle. Can. Vet. J. **47**(9), 883–886 (2006)
17. Pastell, M., Tiusanen, J., Hakojärvi, M., Hänninen, L.: A wireless accelerometer system with wavelet analysis for assessing lameness in cattle. Biosyst. Eng. **104**(4), 545–551 (2009)
18. Chapinal, N., de Passillé, A.M., Pastell, M., Hänninen, L., Munksgaard, L., Rushen, J.: Measurement of acceleration while walking as an automated method for gait assessment in dairy cattle. J. Dairy Sci. **94**(6), 2895–2901 (2011)
19. Kokin, E., Praks, J., Veermäe, I., Poikalainen, V., Vallas, M.: IceTag3D^{TM} accelerometric device in cattle lameness detection. Agron. Res. **12**(1), 223–230 (2014)
20. Thorup, V.M., Munksgaard, L., Robert, P.E., Erhard, H.W., Thomsen, P.T., Friggens, N.C.: Lameness detection via leg-mounted accelerometers on dairy cows on four commercial farms. Animal **9**(10), 1704–1712 (2015)
21. Mottram, T.T., Bell, N.J.: A novel method of monitoring mobility in dairy cows. In: 1st North American Conference Precis. Dairy Management, pp. 2–3 (2010)
22. Krause, J., Krause, S., Arlinghaus, R., Psorakis, I., Roberts, S., Rutz, C.: Reality mining of animal social systems. Trends Ecol. Evol. **28**(9), 541–551 (2013)
23. Jiawei, H., Kamber, M., Pei, J.: Data Mining: Concepts and Techniques, 3rd edn. Elsevier, New York (2012)
24. Nadimi, E.S., Søgaard, H.T., Bak, T.: ZigBee-based wireless sensor networks for classifying the behaviour of a herd of animals using classification trees. Biosyst. Eng. **100**(2), 167–176 (2008)

25. Robert, B., White, B.J., Renter, D.G., Larson, R.L.: Evaluation of three-dimensional accelerometers to monitor and classify behavior patterns in cattle. Comput. Electron. Agric. **67**(1–2), 80–84 (2009)
26. González, L.A., Bishop-Hurley, G.J., Handcock, R.N., Crossman, C.: Behavioral classification of data from collars containing motion sensors in grazing cattle. Comput. Electron. Agric. **110**, 91–102 (2015)
27. Dutta, R., et al.: Dynamic cattle behavioural classification using supervised ensemble classifiers. Comput. Electron. Agric. **111**, 18–28 (2015)
28. de Weerd, N., et al.: Deriving animal behaviour from high-frequency GPS: tracking cows in open and forested habitat. PLoS ONE **10**(6), e0129030 (2015)
29. Guo, Y., Poulton, G., Corke, P., Bishop-Hurley, G.J., Wark, T., Swain, D.L.: Using accelerometer, high sample rate GPS and magnetometer data to develop a cattle movement and behaviour model. Ecol. Model. **220**(17), 2068–2075 (2009)
30. Martiskainen, P., Järvinen, M., Skön, J.-P., Tiirikainen, J., Kolehmainen, M., Mononen, J.: Cow behaviour pattern recognition using a three-dimensional accelerometer and support vector machines. Appl. Anim. Behav. Sci. **119**(1–2), 32–38 (2009)
31. Vázquez Diosdado, J.A., et al.: Classification of behaviour in housed dairy cows using an accelerometer-based activity monitoring system. Anim. Biotelem. **3**(1), 15 (2015)
32. Umstätter, C., Waterhouse, A., Holland, J.P.: An automated sensor-based method of simple behavioural classification of sheep in extensive systems. Comput. Electron. Agric. **64**(1), 19–26 (2008)
33. Marais, J., Le Roux, S.P., Wolhuter, R., Niesler, T.: Automatic classification of sheep behaviour using 3-axis accelerometer data. In: 25th Annual Symposium of the Pattern Recognition Association of South Africa (PRASA) (2014)
34. Alvarenga, F.A.P., Borges, I., Palkovič, L., Rodina, J., Oddy, V.H., Dobos, R.C.: Using a three-axis accelerometer to identify and classify sheep behaviour at pasture. Appl. Anim. Behav. Sci. **181**, 91–99 (2015)
35. Giovanetti, V., et al.: Automatic classification system for grazing, ruminating and resting behaviour of dairy sheep using a tri-axial accelerometer. Livest. Sci. **196**, 42–48 (2016)
36. Bitar, H.: SensoDuino: Log and Transmit Android Sensors to Arduino & PC via Bluetooth (2013)
37. Kevin, M.: Simple guide to confusion matrix terminology. Data School (2014). http://www.dataschool.io/simple-guide-to-confusion-matrix-terminology/. Accessed 28 Aug 2017
38. Tan, P., Steinbach, M., Kumar, V.: Introduction to Data Mining, 1st edn. Pearson Education India, Delhi (2006)

Collaborative Data and Workflow Management

Learning Planning and Recommendation Based on an Adaptive Architecture on Data Graph, Information Graph and Knowledge Graph

Lixu Shao[1], Yucong Duan[1(✉)], Zhangbing Zhou[2], Quan Zou[3],
and Honghao Gao[4]

[1] State Key Laboratory of Marine, Resource Utilization in the South China Sea,
College of Information and Technology, Hainan University, Haikou, China
751486692@qq.com, duanyucong@hotmail.com
[2] Department of Information Engineering, China University of Geosciences (Beijing),
Beijing, China
zbzhou@cugb.edu.cn
[3] College of Computer Science, Tianjin University, Tianjin, China
zouquan@tju.edu.com
[4] Computing Center, Shanghai University, Shanghai, China
gaohonghao@shu.edu.cn

Abstract. With massive learning resources that contain data, information and knowledge on Internet, users are easy to get lost and confused in processing of learning. Automatic processing, automatic synthesis, and automatic analysis of natural language, such as the original representation of the resources of these data, information and knowledge, have become a huge challenge. We propose a three-layer architecture composing Data Graph, Information Graph and Knowledge Graph which can automatically abstract and adjust resources. This architecture recursively supports integration of empirical knowledge and efficient automatic semantic analysis of resource elements through frequency focused profiling on Data Graph and optimal search through abstraction on Information Graph and Knowledge Graph. Our proposed architecture is supported by the 5W (Who/When/Where, What and How) to interface users' learning needs, learning processes, and learning objectives which can provide users with personalized learning service recommendation.

Keywords: Resource modeling · Knowledge Graph
Service recommendation · Semantic modeling

1 Introduction

Information overload and information confusion caused by exponential increase of Internet information restrict users' efficient use of resources. Knowledge Graph has become a powerful tool for expressing knowledge in the form of a marked

© ICST Institute for Computer Sciences, Social Informatics and Telecommunications Engineering 2018
I. Romdhani et al. (Eds.): CollaborateCom 2017, LNICST 252, pp. 323–332, 2018.
https://doi.org/10.1007/978-3-030-00916-8_30

directed graph and can endow text information with semantics. Knowledge base contains a set of concepts, examples and relationships [5]. The author of [10] took topic model as the basis for similarity calculation and obtained the entity catalog from Wikipedia. A large number of supervised learning methods, semi-supervised learning methods [2] based on eigenvectors appeared for achieving relation extraction. The authors proposed an information extraction framework for open domains and released an open information extraction prototype system which was based on self-supervised learning [1]. In [13] the author elaborated concepts of data, information, and knowledge. In [4] the authors divided the information extraction into three levels: entity, relation and attribute.

From the perspective of extending the concept of existing Knowledge Graph, we propose a three-layer architecture composing Data Graph, Information Graph and Knowledge Graph. Through modeling massive resources, users can quickly and accurately search the information they need in the resource processing architecture. With the help of classification of 5Ws (Who, When, Where, What and How) questions [3], it's easy to get the description of users' learning needs, learning processes and learning objectives. The 5Ws are questions whose answers are considered basic in information gathering or problem solving. They are often mentioned in journalism, research, and police investigations.

2   The Establishment of Resources Framework

We divide the expression of Knowledge Graph into three parts including $DataGraph_{DIK}$, $InformationGraph_{DIK}$ and $KnowledgeGraph_{DIK}$ based on the relationship among them. We define typed learning resource elements and the three-layer graph as follows:

Definition 1. *Resource elements. Resource elements include data, information and knowledge. We define resource elements as:*
$Elements_{DIK}: = <Data_{DIK}, Information_{DIK}, Knowledge_{DIK}>$.

Definition 2. *Graphs. We extend existing concept of Knowledge Graph and clarify expression of Knowledge Graph into Data Graph, Information Graph and Knowledge Graph.*
$Graph_{DIK}: = <(DataGraph_{DIK}), (InformationGraph_{DIK}), (Knowledge Graph_{DIK})>$.

Figure 1 shows the framework of resources processing based on Data Graph, Information Graph and Knowledge Graph. Table 1 shows the explanations of resource type and corresponding graphs.

Figure 2 shows the classification and transformation of 5W questions and relationships between the three-layer graphs. To be exactly, we calculate three frequencies of $Data_{DIK}$ in $DataGraph_{DIK}$. With the help of classification of 5W questions, it's easy to get the description of users' learning needs, learning processes and learning objectives and provide users with personalized learning recommendation service.

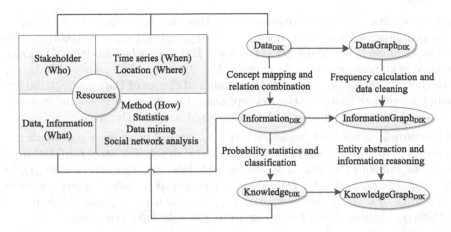

Fig. 1. Resources processing framework towards "5W" based on Graph$_{DIK}$

Table 1. Explanations of typed resources

	Data$_{DIK}$	Information$_{DIK}$	Knowledge$_{DIK}$
Semantic load	Not specified for stakeholders/machine	Settled for stakeholders/machine	Abstracting resources for revelation on unknown
Format	Discrete elements	Related elements	Probabilistic or categorization
Usage	Identification of existence after conceptualization	Communication	Reasoning and prediction
Answer	Who/When/Where	What	How
Graph	DataGraph$_{DIK}$	InformationGraph$_{DIK}$	KnowledgeGraph$_{DIK}$

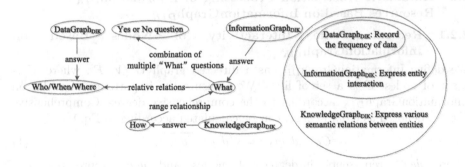

Fig. 2. Classification of "5W" questions and relationship between graphs

2.1 Statistics and Analysis of Data$_{DIK}$ Frequency Based on DataGraph$_{DIK}$

We use DataGraph$_{DIK}$ to record three kinds of frequencies of Data$_{DIK}$ including structural frequency, temporal frequency and spatial frequency. Structural frequency is defined as the number of times that Data$_{DIK}$ appears in different data structures. Temporal frequency is defined as the temporal trajectory of $Data_{DIK}$. Spatial frequency is defined as the spatial trajectory of $Data_{DIK}$. We give an example about frequency statistics of $Data_{DIK}$ when modeling $Data_{DIK}$ resource of knowledge points. As shown in Fig. 3, temporal frequency of $Data_{DIK}$ of the knowledge points represents the number of classes of $Data_{DIK}$. Spatial frequency represents times of $Data_{DIK}$ appeared in different professional systems. Structural frequency represents the educational mode of $Data_{DIK}$.

Definition 3. *Structural frequency (stru_f). stru_f represents the number of times of $Data_{DIK}$ appearing in different data structures. stru_f of $Data_{DIK}$ should be calculated according to the biggest data structure where $Data_{DIK}$ is appeared. For example, if a $Data_{DIK}$ is displayed as a node of a tree structure in a branch of a graph structure, stru_f of the $Data_{DIK}$ is 1 and the frequency of $Data_{DIK}$ displayed in a tree structure is not calculated repeatedly.*

Definition 4. *Spatial frequency (spat_f). spat_f is the occurring times of $Data_{DIK}$ appearing at different spatial locations describing the relative locations of multiple objects.*

Definition 5. *Temporal frequency (temp_f). temp_f represents times of $Data_{DIK}$ appearing in different time periods. For streaming $Data_{DIK}$ with timeliness, once we observe those $Data_{DIK}$ we should make responses in a timely manner because expired $Data_{DIK}$ will be meaningless.*

Definition 6. *$Data_{DIK}$ comprehensive frequency (DFreq). We define comprehensive frequency of a node as follows:*
   DFreq: = < stru_f, spat_f, temp_f >.

2.2   Automatic Abstraction Processing of Information$_{DIK}$ Resources Based on InformationGraph$_{DIK}$

2.2.1   Recording   the   Interactivity   of   Nodes   Based   on InformationGraph$_{DIK}$

We define InformationGraph$_{DIK}$ as a directed graph G (V, E), where V is a set of nodes. E is a set of lines. We measure the importance of nodes on InformationGraph$_{DIK}$ according to the comprehensive degree. Comprehensive degree, denoted as Com_degree, can be calculated according to Eq. 1:

$$Com\_degree = \sqrt{deg^+ * deg^-} \tag{1}$$

where deg^+ represents in-degree of nodes and deg^- represents out-degree of nodes. Therefore, further importance measurement of nodes on InformationGraph$_{DIK}$, denoted as "Impor", can be calculated according to Eq. 2:

$$Impor = \alpha DFreq * \beta Com\_degree \tag{2}$$

where α and β represent weight of comprehensive frequency of nodes on DataGraph$_{DIK}$ and comprehensive degree of interaction between nodes on InformationGraph$_{DIK}$ respectively. Both α and β can be obtained through data training.

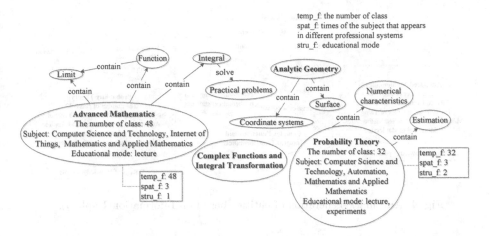

Fig. 3. Statistics about structural frequency, spatial frequency and temporal frequency based on DataGraph$_{DIK}$

2.2.2 Processing Data$_{DIK}$ Integration and Entity Abstraction Based on InformationGraph$_{DIK}$

InformationGraph$_{DIK}$ reflects communications and multiple interactions between entities. As shown in Fig. 4, new concept is generated by integrating Data$_{DIK}$ in Fig. 3. Different Data$_{DIK}$ resources are linked closely with each other in form of data structures including list, queue and tree. In order to improve the expression of resource architecture, we gather closely related Data$_{DIK}$ collection so as to analyze and abstract Information$_{DIK}$ resources. After gathering a certain number of entities as a group, we calculate the ratio of internal and external degree of interaction between entities according to Eq. 3:

$$cohesion = \frac{IFreq_{II}}{IFreq_{EI}} \tag{3}$$

where *cohesion* represents the ratio of internal degree of interaction and external degree of interaction. We restrict the related Data$_{DIK}$ collection must be connected to each other. *Cohesion* is an indicator of the degree of correlation between entities. *IFreq$_{EI}$* represents times of external interactions between entities and *IFreq$_{II}$* represents times of internal interactions between entities.

2.3 Analysis and Processing of Knowledge Based on KnowledgeGraph$_{DIK}$

2.3.1 Information Reasoning and Knowledge Forecasting on KnowledgeGraph$_{DIK}$

Path ranking algorithm uses each of different relational paths as a one-dimensional feature. Through constructing a large number of relational paths in KnowledgeGraph$_{DIK}$ to construct the eigenvector of relation classification

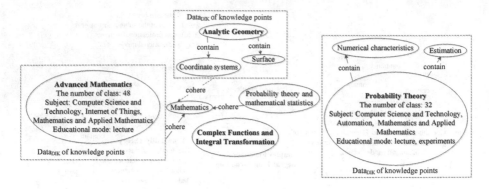

Fig. 4. Automatic generation of entities based on InformationGraph$_{DIK}$

and a relational classifier to extract the relationship between entities. Actual model abstractions should include abstractions from a set of existing relational entities and relationships to one or several new entities and new relationships. We create a truth table to indicate whether the information obtained through entity and relationship reasoning is true. We calculate the rate of correctness of a relationship, denoted as Cr (E1, R, E2), according to Eq. 4:

$$Cr(E1, R, E2) = \frac{\sum_{\pi \in Q} P(E_1 \rightarrow E_2)\theta(\pi)}{|Q|} \tag{4}$$

where $P(E1, E2)$ indicates one path between $E1$ and $E2$, Q indicates all paths starting from $E1$ and ending with $E2$, represents the weight obtained by training.

2.3.2 Importance Measurement of Nodes on KnowledgeGraph$_{DIK}$

Knowledge Graph have been widely adopted, in large part owing to their schema-less nature that enables Knowledge Graph to grow seamlessly and allows for adding new relationships and entities as needed. Each semantic relationship on KnowledgeGraph$_{DIK}$ has its own weight that is denoted as θ to represent the importance of the relationship. We evaluate the importance of nodes, denoted as *Final_impor* in KnowledgeGraph$_{DIK}$ according to Eq. 5 through marking and manipulating different types of semantic relationships between entities.

$$Final\_impor = \alpha DFreq * \beta Com\_degree * \gamma \frac{\sum_{i=1}^{n} \lambda_i * Rel_i}{n} \tag{5}$$

where λ_i represents the weight of relationship Rel_i and n represents the amount of relationship types.

3 Characteristics Analysis of Application of DIK Architecture

Through analyzing frequency statistics and calculating of Data$_{DIK}$ based on DataGraph$_{DIK}$, we filter Data$_{DIK}$ with lower integrated frequency and reduce appearance of false and useless $Data_{DIK}$. Unifying expressive forms of $Data_{DIK}$ based on $InformationGraph_{DIK}$, we eliminate redundant $Data_{DIK}$. Through integrating frequently-interactive $Data_{DIK}$ together, we can summarize general rules of $Information_{DIK}$. Relationship of $Data_{DIK}$ and $Information_{DIK}$ is lack of hierarchies and logicality. As a result, through classifying and statistically analyzing $Information_{DIK}$, taking empirical knowledge into consideration, we speculate unknown information and get probabilistic answers.

Because of restriction of relationships between $Data_{DIK}$, $Information_{DIK}$ and $Knowledge_{DIK}$, users cannot obtain $Information_{DIK}$ and $Knowledge_{DIK}$ directly based on $DataGraph_{DIK}$. They cannot obtain $Knowledge_{DIK}$ based on $InformationGraph_{DIK}$ as well. On cross-layer searching there are following cases including some resources cannot be searched, sometimes endless resources are searched or obtained resources don't match with users' information needs. We model these resources and search the integrated resources according to three-layer graphs. We use different resource architectures according to different cases.

4   Application of Learning Recommendation Service Based on DIK Method

Knowledge points are divided into three layers including $Data_{DIK}$, $Information_{DIK}$ and $Knowledge_{DIK}$. It is easy to get description of users' learning needs and learning processes based on architecture of $Graph_{DIK}$ with the introduction of "5W" questions. Through establishing learners' models and acquiring their current learning state, ability level and learning target, we provide users with an effective learning strategy. After getting learner's expected effort and learning objectives, we compute the learner's expected learning efficiency according to Eq. 6:

$$Expected\_effi = \frac{Total\_know}{Expected\_effort} \tag{6}$$

where $Total\_know$ represents total amounts of knowledge points that the learner has to study to achieve his/her target.

Figure 5 shows partial knowledge system of computer science. We assume that a user's learning objective is to master the course of principle of communication. Courses that he or she has been mastered and hasn't been mastered yet have been marked in the resource system. Each number marked with a course represents the average effort that users must put in order to master this course. If a user's expected effort is 90, then we can recommend the three learning programs as Fig. 5 shows.

According to the type of user's learning objectives, we choose the corresponding layer of resource processing architecture to traversal. Marking the knowledge points that the learner has learned and will learn on the resource processing architecture and traversing graphs, we can obtain all preorder nodes of target

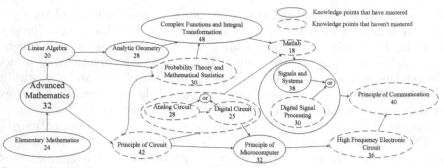

Recommend learning path:
1.Elementary Mathematics->Advanced Mathematics->Linear Algebra->Analytic Geometry->Complex
Functions and Integral Transformation->Matlab->Signals and Systems->Principle of Communication
2.Elementary Mathematics->Advanced Mathematics->Linear Algebra->Analytic Geometry->Complex
Functions and Integral Transformation->Matlab->Digital Signal Processing->Principle of Communication
3.Elementary Mathematics->Advanced Mathematics->Linear Algebra->Probability Theory and
Mathematical Statistics->Complex Functions and Integral Transformation->Matlab->Signals and Systems-
>Principle Of Communication

Fig. 5. An example of learning recommendation service based on Graph$_{DIK}$ resource processing architecture

knowledge points and recommend the complete learning path to users. We compute the actual learning efficiency of a user according to Eq. 7:

$$Actual\_effi = \frac{Got\_know}{Actual\_effort} \tag{7}$$

where Got_know represents the knowledge point that the learner has mastered and $Actual\_effort$ represents the learner's actual learning effort. Through analyzing changes of learner's ability, we can update learner model. According to the updated learner model and resource processing architecture, we re-acquire the learner's learning objectives and expected learning effort.

5   Related Work

Efficiency of search engines depends on a large number of labeled data. With the introduction of statistical machine learning methods, coreference resolution technology has entered a rapid development stage. Using the planned and extracted knowledge base, it extracted millions of rules from unlabeled question corpus and multiple knowledge bases to search a solution to problem analysis and query refactoring [8]. Development of software service system can be divided into stages of data sharing, information transfer, and knowledge creation in terms of data, information and knowledge [11]. In [12] the authors proposed a method to promote cross-language knowledge linking through concept annotations, which enriched cross-language knowledge links, and promoted knowledge sharing in different languages. Regional collaborative medical data centers are established to achieve integration among hospital information. Scientists have proposed numerous models for defining anything "as a service (aaS)", including discussions of products, processes, data and information management as a service [6]. In [9] the authors proposed a semantic-oriented cross-language ontology mapping (SOCOM) framework to enhance the interoperability of ontology-based systems involving multilingual knowledge base. In [7] the authors clarified the architecture of Knowledge Graph as a whole and extended the existing concept of Knowledge Graph into four aspects including Data Graph, Information Graph, Knowledge Graph and Wisdom Graph.

6 Conclusion

With the rapid development of Internet, it is a great challenge to quickly and accurately search resources that satisfy users' requirements. We propose a learning planning and recommendation approach based on an adaptive architecture composing Data Graph, Information Graph and Knowledge Graph. The architecture introduces empirical and theoretical rules to modelling $Data_{DIK}$, $Information_{DIK}$, $Knowledge_{DIK}$ and deals with inconsistency, redundancy and lack of resources effectively. We provide users with learning planning and recommendation service based on the adaptive architecture on $DataGraph_{DIK}$, $InformationGraph_{DIK}$ and $KnowledgeGraph_{DIK}$ aiming at improving the effectiveness and efficiency of learning. Through automatic abstraction and dynamic planning, the architecture will recommend optimized service to users after effective and adaptive resources search and self-organization. Currently we have interpreted our work with cases in all segments and in the next stage we will expand the scale of dataset to further verify the feasibility of our approach.

Acknowledgment. This paper is supported by NSFC under Grant (No. 61363007, No. 61662021), NSF of Hainan No. ZDYF2017128 and Hainan University Project (No. hdkytg201708).

References

1. Banko, M., Cafarella, M.J., Soderland, S., Broadhead, M., Etzioni, O.: Open information extraction from the web. In: IJCAI 2007, pp. 2670–2676 (2007)
2. Carlson, A., Betteridge, J., Wang, R.C., Hruschka Jr., E.R., Mitchell, T.M.: Coupled semi-supervised learning for information extraction. In: WSDM 2010, pp. 101–110 (2010)
3. Chatti, M.A., Dyckhoff, A.L., Schroeder, U., Ths, H.: A reference model for learning analytics. Int. J. Technol. Enhanc. Learn. **4**(5/6), 318–331 (2012)
4. Cowie, J.R., Lehnert, W.G.: Information extraction. Commun. ACM **39**(1), 80–91 (1996)
5. Deshpande, O., et al.: Building, maintaining, and using knowledge bases: a report from the trenches. In: ACM SIGMOD 2013, pp. 1209–1220 (2013)
6. Duan, Y., Fu, G., Zhou, N., Sun, X., Narendra, N.C., Hu, B.: Everything as a service (XaaS) on the cloud: origins, current and future trends. In: IEEE International Conference on Cloud Computing, pp. 621–628 (2015)

7. Duan, Y., Shao, L., Hu, G., Zhou, Z., Zou, Q., Lin, Z.: Specifying architecture of knowledge graph with data graph, information graph, knowledge graph and wisdom graph. In: 15th IEEE SERA 2017, pp. 327–332 (2017)
8. Fader, A., Zettlemoyer, L., Etzioni, O.: Open question answering over curated and extracted knowledge bases. In: 20th ACM SIGKDD 2014, pp. 1156–1165 (2014)
9. Fu, B., Brennan, R., O'Sullivan, D.: Cross-lingual ontology mapping and its use on the multilingual semantic web. In: International Workshop on the Multilingual Semantic Web, pp. 13–20 (2010)
10. Sen, P.: Collective context-aware topic models for entity disambiguation. In: International Conference on World Wide Web, pp. 729–738 (2012)
11. Shao, L., Duan, Y., Sun, X., Zou, Q., Jing, R., Lin, J.: Bidirectional value driven design between economical planning and technical implementation based on data graph, information graph and knowledge graph. In: 15th IEEE SERA 2017, pp. 339–344 (2017)
12. Wang, Z., Li, J., Tang, J.: Boosting cross-lingual knowledge linking via concept annotation. In: IJCAI 2013, pp. 2733–2739 (2013)
13. Zins, C.: Conceptual approaches for defining data, information, and knowledge. J. Assoc. Inf. Sci. Technol. 58(4), 479–493 (2007)

A 3D Registration Method Based on Indoor Positioning Through Networking

Haibo Li[1,3], Huahu Xu[1,3(✉)], Honghao Gao[1,2],
Minjie Bian[1,3], and Huaikou Miao[1,4]

[1] School of Computer Engineering and Science,
Shanghai University, Shanghai 200444, China
lihaibo_1990@163.com, huahuxu@163.com,
{gaohonghao, hkmiao}@shu.edu.cn
[2] Computing Center, Shanghai University, Shanghai 200444, China
[3] Shanghai Shang Da Hai Run Information System Co. Ltd.,
Shanghai 200444, China
[4] Shanghai Key Laboratory of Computer Software Testing
and Evaluating, Shanghai 201112, China

Abstract. The Augmented Reality (AR) technique has been widely used in the academic and industrial community, which integrates virtual data into the real-world environments. However, the key implementation to AR is the 3D registration method because it refers to effectively display object in virtual environment. Most of existing approaches are hard to ensure the quality of 3D registration. Thus, this paper proposes a 3D registration method based on indoor positioning, using gyroscopes, direction sensors and network communications. First, obtain user's line of sight by gyroscopes and direction sensors and send them to server through networking. Second, locate user position by indoor positioning. And then, using these data, calculate the conversion matrix between coordinate systems. Finally, Send data to the client over the network to integrate virtual data into the real-world environments. Our method can avoid the errors which may be impacted by the speed of movement and clearness of objects. Furthermore, experiments are carried out to show the feasibility, accuracy and validity of the proposed method.

Keywords: Network · Augmented Reality · 3D registration
Indoor positioning · Ultra wide-band

1 Introduction

Augmented Reality (AR) is a technique that uses additional graphics or textual information to dynamically enhance the surrounding natural scenes. AR systems allow users to interact with real and computer-generated objects by displaying 3D virtual objects registered in a user's natural environment [1]. 3D registration [2] is the process of positioning virtual object in 3D space, which is one of the most critical technique in AR systems.

At present, 3D registration method at home and abroad is divided into the following three kinds: recognition-based 3D registration, vision-based 3D registration [3] and

© ICST Institute for Computer Sciences, Social Informatics and Telecommunications Engineering 2018
I. Romdhani et al. (Eds.): CollaborateCom 2017, LNICST 252, pp. 333–343, 2018.
https://doi.org/10.1007/978-3-030-00916-8_31

self-tracing 3D registration [4]. Vision-based 3D registration is commonly used for its good overall performance in 3D registration [5, 6]. Though, this method still has a variety of shortcomings [7, 8]: (1) When the mark is blocked or partially blocked, the system cannot calculate 3D transformation matrix, and that will lead to the failure of 3D registration; (2) Marks are actually a kind of pollution to the real scene; (3) The identification of marks will reduce due to light, shadow, abrasion and other issues.

Consider to these shortcomings of existing 3D registration technique, this paper proposes a method to achieve 3D registration through indoor positioning. The application scenarios are mainly buildings, museums, tourist attractions and so on. In this type of application scenario, the disadvantages of current registration methods are particularly acute because of the harsh environment, and long term effective request. Because such scenes is not easy to change position, we can achieve 3D registration by position and direction of sight.

The rest of this paper is structured as follows. We introduce the indoor four-node spatial positioning model in Sect. 2. And Sect. 3 proposes a method using the indoor spatial positioning to complete 3D registration. Section 4 gives the architecture of AR system and analyzes the performance of this 3D registration method through our experiments. Section 5 is the conclusion of this paper.

2 Four-Node Spatial Positioning Model

Ultra wide-band (UWB) technology [9] is a short-range, high-bandwidth radio technology that was first used in military applications. The UWB signal has a bandwidth of gigahertz and a sub-millisecond pulse time width. Thus, its range resolution is extremely high, which even can reach the level of centimeters [10, 11]. In order to obtain the distance between positioning base station and locating tag, first measure the Time of arrival (TOA) [12] of the UWB signal, then multiply it by the known signal propagation speed, which is also mean speed of light. We select the UWB indoor positioning technology [13] for its good real-time performance, strong anti-interference ability and high positioning accuracy.

There are many algorithms based on three-node positioning algorithm in two dimensional plane, such as triangle centroid method [14]. If 2D space algorithm directly extends to 3D space, it will lead to increased time complexity and reduced positioning accuracy [15]. In this paper, we calculate the vertical position at first, and then transform 3D spatial positioning problem into 2D positioning problem.

For a start, place four UWB base stations indoors. To simplify the calculation, the base stations D_1 and D_4 are perpendicular to the horizontal plane, and the spatial coordinate system is established by setting the plane of D_1, D_4, and the unknown coordinate point D to the YOZ plane. The four-node spatial coordinate system is shown in Fig. 1.

The coordinates of point D_1, D_2, D_3 and D_4 are known while the coordinate of point D is unknown. And d1 represent the distance of D and D_1, so as to d_2, d_3 and d_4. Point D' is the projection of D in XOY plane.

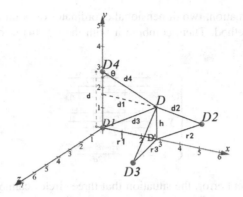

Fig. 1. Four-node spatial coordinate system

Known by Fig. 1:

$$h = d - d_4 \cos \theta \tag{1}$$

$$d_4^2 = d_1^2 - h^2 + (d - h)^2$$

$$= d_1^2 + d^2 - 2dd_1 \cos \theta \tag{2}$$

By Eq. (2):

$$\cos \theta = \frac{d_1^2 - d_4^2 + d^2}{2dd_1} \tag{3}$$

The vertical height of point D, which set as h, can be obtained from Eqs. (1) and (3):

$$h = d - d_4 \cos \theta = d - \frac{d_4^2 - d_1^2 + d^2}{2d} \tag{4}$$

Then the 3D spatial positioning problem is transformed into a 2D positioning problem by Eq. (5):

$$\begin{cases} r_1 = \sqrt{d_1^2 - h^2} \\ r_2 = \sqrt{d_2^2 - h^2} \\ r_3 = \sqrt{d_3^2 - h^2} \end{cases} \tag{5}$$

In the two dimensional plane XOY, the coordinates of points $D_1(x_1, y_1)$, $D_2(x_2, y_2)$ and $D_3(x_3, y_3)$, and the distances r_1, r_2, r_3 are known.

Using these information, two dimensional coordinates of point D' can be solved by triangular centroid method. Then, combine it with the Eq. (4) to complete 3D spatial positioning:

$$\begin{cases} x = \dfrac{\frac{x_1}{r_1+r_2}+\frac{x_2}{r_2+r_3}+\frac{x_3}{r_3+r_1}}{\frac{1}{r_1+r_2}+\frac{1}{r_2+r_3}+\frac{1}{r_3+r_1}} \\[2ex] y = \dfrac{\frac{y_1}{r_1+r_2}+\frac{y_2}{r_2+r_3}+\frac{y_3}{r_3+r_1}}{\frac{1}{r_1+r_2}+\frac{1}{r_2+r_3}+\frac{1}{r_3+r_1}} \\[2ex] z = d - \dfrac{d_4^2-d_1^2+d^2}{2d} \end{cases} \qquad (6)$$

Due to measurement error, the situation that three circles cannot intersect with one another might happen by using triangle centroid method. Under this situation, ignore the imaginary solution to solve it.

3   3D Registration

To accomplish registration, AR system involves the transformation of four coordinate systems [16] which are shown in Fig. 2.

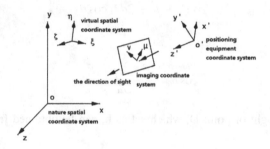

Fig. 2. 3D registered coordinate system

[x, y, z] represents the natural spatial coordinate system, which is the most basic and important one. Select one corner of the house as the origin, and stretch the axis along the intersection of the three planes of the corner. Set the floor plane as XOY plane, and Z axis perpendicular to the XOY plane.

[ξ, η, ζ] represents the virtual spatial coordinate system that is used to describe the virtual space.

[x', y', z'] indicates the positioning equipment coordinate system, whose origin is the center point of positioning equipment. Set the direction of sight as the Z axis. The positive direction of Z axis is the direction of sight.

[u, v] represents the imaging coordinate system. Its U, V axis are parallel to X, Y axis in the positioning equipment coordinate system and their positive directions are same.

3.1   Coordinate Transformation

In order to realize the accurate registration of the virtual object to natural scene, need to transform the coordinate of the virtual spatial coordinate system into the coordinate of the imaging coordinate system [17]. So must clarify the following coordinate transformation matrix: the transformation matrix O between the virtual spatial coordinate system and natural spatial coordinate system, the transformation matrix C between the natural spatial coordinate system and the positioning equipment coordinate system, and the transformation matrix P between the positioning equipment coordinate system and imaging coordinate system.

Since the relation between the virtual spatial coordinate system $[\xi, \eta, \zeta]$ and the natural spatial coordinate system $[x, y, z]$ is known, the geometric description $[\xi, \eta, \zeta]$ of 3D object can be transformed into the geometric description $[x, y, z]$. The homogeneous coordinate is shown as follows:

$$\begin{bmatrix} x \\ y \\ z \\ 1 \end{bmatrix} = O_{4 \times 4} \begin{bmatrix} \xi \\ \eta \\ \zeta \\ 1 \end{bmatrix} \tag{7}$$

In Eq. (7), $O_{4 \times 4}$ represents the transformation matrix between virtual spatial coordinate system and natural spatial coordinate system.

Similarly, the relation between the positioning equipment coordinate system and the imaging coordinate system is known because of the relative position of display device to the positioning equipment is fixed. Equation (8) shows the conversion relation, where matrix $P_{3 \times 4}$ represents the transformation matrix.

$$\begin{bmatrix} u \\ v \\ 1 \end{bmatrix} = P_{3 \times 4} \begin{bmatrix} x' \\ y' \\ z' \\ 1 \end{bmatrix} \tag{8}$$

The geometric description $[x', y', z']$ in the positioning equipment coordinate system is transformed into the geometric description $[x, y, z]$ in natural spatial coordinate system as follows:

$$\begin{bmatrix} x' \\ y' \\ z' \\ 1 \end{bmatrix} = C_{4 \times 4} \begin{bmatrix} x \\ y \\ z \\ 1 \end{bmatrix} \tag{9}$$

In Eq. (9), $C_{4 \times 4}$ shows the transformation matrix between the positioning equipment coordinate system and natural spatial coordinate system. Therefore, if the transformation matrix $C_{4 \times 4}$ can be obtained, the geometric description $[\xi, \eta, \zeta]$ in virtual spatial coordinate system is transformed into the geometric description $[u, v]$ in the imaging coordinate system. The equation is shown in Eq. (10).

$$\begin{bmatrix} u \\ v \\ 1 \end{bmatrix} = P_{3\times4}C_{4\times4}O_{4\times4} \begin{bmatrix} \xi \\ \eta \\ \zeta \\ 1 \end{bmatrix} \tag{10}$$

3.2   3D Registration Algorithm

To convert natural spatial coordinate system into positioning equipment coordinate system, matrix $C_{4\times4}$ must be achieved. For convenience, here, use Eq. (11) to express the transformation:

$$\begin{bmatrix} x' \\ y' \\ z' \end{bmatrix} = R \times \begin{bmatrix} x \\ y \\ z \end{bmatrix} + \begin{bmatrix} t_x \\ t_y \\ t_z \end{bmatrix} \tag{11}$$

The matrix R is a 3×3 matrix for the rotational transformation, and it reflects the rotation component that the positioning equipment relative to natural spatial coordinate system. The rotation component expresses the three basic rotation of the axis, which can be expressed as follows:

$$R = \begin{bmatrix} r_{xx} & r_{xy} & r_{xz} \\ r_{yx} & r_{yy} & r_{yz} \\ r_{zx} & r_{zy} & r_{zz} \end{bmatrix} \tag{12}$$

Use gyroscopes and direction sensors to attain direction of sight. As shown in Fig. 3, use Euler angle in rectangular coordinate system to describe space angle of the direction of sight. Angle θ is the angle rotated along X axis, and angle ψ is the angle rotated along Y axis while angle Φ for Z axis. The rotation direction is the counterclockwise rotation direction when viewed from the coordinate system origin in the positive direction of axis. The elements of matrix R are solved by these three angles, shown as follows:

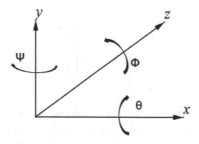

Fig. 3. Euler angles

$$\begin{cases} r_{xx} = \cos\psi\cos\Phi \\ r_{xy} = \sin\theta\sin\psi\cos\Phi - \cos\theta\sin\Phi \\ r_{xz} = \cos\theta\sin\psi\cos\psi + \cos\theta\sin\Phi \\ r_{yx} = \cos\psi\sin\Phi \\ r_{yy} = \sin\theta\sin\psi\sin\Phi + \cos\theta\cos\Phi \\ r_{yz} = \cos\theta\sin\psi\sin\Phi + \sin\theta\cos\Phi \\ r_{zx} = -\sin\psi \\ r_{zy} = \sin\theta\cos\psi \\ r_{zz} = \cos\theta\cos\psi \end{cases} \tag{13}$$

From Eq. (13), according to space angle obtained from positioning sensor, the matrix R is directly attained.

Vector $(t_x, t_y, t_z)^T$ represents translational transformation. And (t_x, t_y, t_z) is the coordinate of positioning equipment in natural spatial coordinate system, which is obtained from Eq. (6).

In summary, obtain the user's direction of sight by gyroscope and direction sensor at first. Then attain the user's positioning data through indoor spatial positioning technology. At last, calculate the conversion matrix $C_{4\times4}$ to achieve 3D registration by using these information. With the transformation relation of Eq. (10), 3D registration is completed.

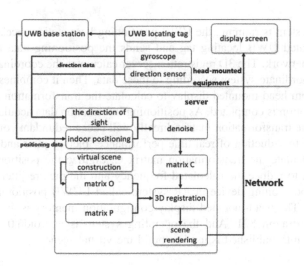

Fig. 4. AR system structure

4 Experiment

4.1 AR System Structure

As shown in Fig. 4, the entire AR system structure is divided into two parts: head-mounted display as the client and the remote 3D registration server. The head-mounted display integrates positioning equipment which includes UWB locating tag, gyroscope and direction sensor. The server collects the positioning data and the direction of sight data to complete the calculation of 3D registration.

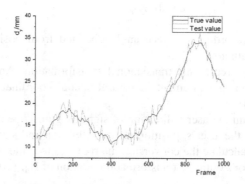

Fig. 5. Experimental error of 3D registration

When the system is running, the UWB positioning base station receives the signal from the integrated UWB locating tag and sends the positioning data to the remote server through network. The 3D registration server calculates the coordinate of the user in the natural coordinate system according to these data. Then it combines the direction of the signal from head-mounted display to calculate the transformation matrix. Since then, 3D registration is completed. As positioning information data acquisition speed is fast, calculate the transformation matrix directly will cause redundant computing. And it will also lead to reduction of real-time performance, picture jitter and other issues. Thus before calculate the transformation matrix C, digitize the positioning data and smooth the data to reduce the calculated frequency and the picture jitter.

The UWB positioning device in AR system called I-UWB positioning module in our experiment. The head-mounted display configuration memory is 4G. The CPU is Qualcomm snapdragon 821. And the operating system is android6.0. The WebGL interface that Html5 published is used to build the virtual scene.

4.2 Experimental Results and Analysis

The accuracy of 3D registration is the most important indicator, and the registration precision is analyzed by taking the d_y of the translation component in 3D registration (as the translation component of Y axis of imaging coordinate system). In experiment, set the moving speed to 1.1 m/s and the longest distance is no more than 6 m, which is

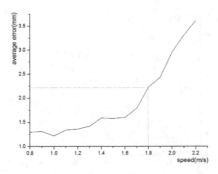

Fig. 6. Error of registration in moving

consistent with the general application environment. Test the accuracy of registration method. Figure 5 shows the change of d_y for 1000 consecutive frames.

In Fig. 5, the horizontal axis represents the frame sequence of virtual display in the experiment while the vertical axis represents the translation component d_y. The black solid line indicates the true value of d_y, and the red solid line represents the measured value of d_y. According to the result, the average difference between measured value and true value is 1.22 mm, and the error range is remained within 3 mm all the time. Because our experimental environment avoids the influence of wall reflection and object reflection, UWB can collect the high-precision positioning data. So the method based on indoor positioning meets high accuracy and small error fluctuation and stable registration precision.

Due to the special requirement of moving speed in large scene application environments, design a experiment to verify the effectiveness of the proposed method in the process of moving. The experiment set translation component d_y as evaluation criteria. The range of moving speed is 0.5 m/s–2.2 m/s, which is conform to reality. The result is shown in Fig. 6, where x axis represents moving speed and y axis represents average error of d_y.

From Fig. 6, with the increase of moving speed, the precision error of registration algorithm increases. When the moving speed is 1.8 m/s, the average error of AR system is less than 2.5 mm. When the moving speed exceeds 1.8 m/s, the error increases rapidly. Figure 7 shows the change of d_y for 300 consecutive frames when the moving speed is 2.2 m/s in experiment.

In Fig. 7, the black solid line indicates the true value of d_y, and the red solid line represents the measured value of d_y using the proposed method when the moving speed is 2.2 m/s. In these 300 consecutive frames, the average error of the measured value is 3.43 mm, where the maximum error is 8.9 mm. From the change curve, the trend of measured value coincides with true value, though it is lagging behind. It is caused by the lagging positioning information for the high-speed movement of users. At the same time, process of smooth positioning data to avoid picture jitter is the second reason for this lagging phenomenon. The blue solid line represents the measured data for vision-based registration method. In the moving speed of 2.2 m/s, this method is unstable to locate mark information, and the positioning matrix calculation fails frequently. The normal walking speed of users is 1.1 m/s–1.6 m/s. According to Fig. 7, the average

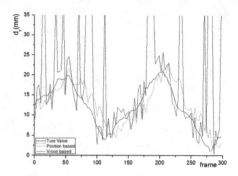

Fig. 7. Accuracy when the moving speed is 2.2 m/s (Color figure online)

error range is controlled below 1.5 mm. This experiment proves that under the moving situation, the proposed method maintain good positioning accuracy at normal pace. So that it is more suitable for large scene application than vision-based registration.

Above experiments prove that, at normal pace, the accuracy of registration method proposed in this paper meets the requirements of AR system. In the large scene, the system maintains good accuracy and stability with the normal pace of movement.

5   Conclusion

AR is gradually applied to all aspects of life, as one of the key techniques to AR, the effect of 3D registration directly affects the user experience. In this paper, a 3D registration method based on indoor positioning technology is proposed, which solves the shortcomings of traditional registration methods. In vision-based AR system, if the marks are not recognized, it will cause the failure of registration. Our method effectively avoids this situation for its no marks. But this method can only be applied to fixed scene. The next step, we will try to combine our method with vision-based registration method to complement each other.

References

1. Bajura, M., Neumann, U.: Dynamic registration correction in augmented-reality systems. In: Virtual Reality International Symposium, 1995. Proceedings, vol. 189 (1995)
2. Li, H., Hartley, R.: The 3D-3D registration problem revisited. In: IEEE, International Conference on Computer Vision, pp. 1–8. IEEE (2007)
3. Tamura, H., Yamamoto, H., Katayama, A.: Mixed reality: future dreams seen at the border between real and virtual worlds. Comput. Graph. Appl. IEEE **21**(6), 64–70 (2001)
4. Neumann, U., Cho, Y.: A Self-tracking augmented reality system. In: Virtual Reality Software and Technology (1996)
5. Dooley, M.J., Listick, B.E., Pirjanian, P.: Computer and vision-based augmented interaction in the use of printed media: US, US 7283983 B2 (2007)

A 3D Registration Method Based on Indoor Positioning Through Networking

6. Bohren, J., Papazov, C., Burschka, D., et al.: A pilot study in vision-based augmented telemanipulation for remote assembly over high-latency networks. In: IEEE International Conference on Robotics and Automation, pp. 3631–3638. IEEE (2013)
7. Klein, A., De Assis, G.A.: A markeless augmented reality tracking for enhancing the user interaction during virtual rehabilitation. In: Xv Symposium on Virtual and Augmented Reality, pp. 117–124. IEEE Computer Society (2013)
8. Simon, G., Berger, M.O.: Real time registration of known or recovered multi-planar structures: application to AR. In: British Machine Vision Conference 2002, BMVC 2002, Cardiff, UK, 2–5 September. DBLP (2002)
9. Headley, W.C., Da Silva, C.R.C.M., Buehrer, R.M.: Indoor positioning positioning of non-active objects using ultra-wideband radios. In: Radio and Wireless Symposium, pp. 105–108. IEEE (2007)
10. Gezici, S., Poor, H.V.: Position estimation via ultra-wide-band signals. Proc. IEEE **97**(2), 386–403 (2009)
11. Fontana, R.J.: Recent system applications of short-pulse ultra-wideband (UWB) technology. IEEE Trans. Microw. Theory Tech. **52**(9), 2087–2104 (2004)
12. Guvenc, I., Sahinoglu, Z.: Threshold-based TOA estimation for impulse radio UWB systems. In: IEEE International Conference on Ultra-Wideband, pp. 420–425. IEEE (2005)
13. Cassioli, D., Win, M.Z., Molisch, A.F.: The UWB indoor channel: from statistical model to simulations. IEEE J. Sel. Areas Commun. **20**(6), 1247–1257 (2002)
14. Zhang, C.W., Zhao, X.: The wireless sensor network (WSN) triangle centroid localization algorithm based on RSSI, vol. 63, p. 05008 (2016)
15. Shih, C.Y., Marrón, P.J.: COLA: Complexity-Reduced Trilateration Approach for 3D Localization in Wireless Sensor Networks. IEEE Computer Society, Washington (2010)
16. Yuan, M.L., Ong, S.K., Nee, A.Y.: Registration based on projective reconstruction technique for augmented reality systems. IEEE Trans. Vis. Comput. Graph. **11**(3), 254–264 (2005)
17. Yuan, M.L., Ong, S.K., Nee, A.Y.C.: Registration using natural features for augmented reality systems. IEEE Trans. Visual Comput. Graph. **12**(4), 569 (2006)

A Load Balancing Method Based on Node Features in a Heterogeneous Hadoop Cluster

Pengcheng Yang[1,3], Honghao Gao[1,2], Huahu Xu[1,3(✉)],
Minjie Bian[1,3], and Danqi Chu[4]

[1] School of Computer Engineering and Science,
Shanghai University, Shanghai 200444, China
huahuxu@163.com
[2] Computing Centre, Shanghai University, Shanghai 200444, China
[3] Shanghai Shang Da Hai Run Information System Co., Ltd.,
Shanghai 200444, China
[4] Equipment Office, Shanghai University, Shanghai, People's Republic of China

Abstract. In a heterogeneous cluster, how to handle load balancing is an urgent problem. This paper proposes a method of load balancing based on node features. The method first analyses the main indexes that determine node performance. Then, a formula is defined to describe the node performance based on the contributions of those indexes. We combine node performance with node busy status to calculate the relative load value. By analysing the relative load value of each node and the cluster storage utilization rate, the recommended value of the storage utilization rate for each node is calculated. Finally, the balancer threshold is generated dynamically based on the current cluster's disk load. The results of experiments show that the load balancing method proposed in this paper provides a more reasonable equilibrium for heterogeneous clusters, improves efficiency and substantially reduces the execution time.

Keywords: Cloud computing · Hadoop · Heterogeneous cluster
Load balancing · Relative load

1 Introduction

With the rapid development of the Internet and information technologies, increasing amounts of research and business data are produced. The amount of data has reached the PB level [1], and a single machine is unable to handle such large-scale data. This situation has led to the creation of cloud computing. Hadoop is an open source distributed processing system developed by the Apache Foundation [2]. In the field of big data, Hadoop has become an outstanding platform that can handle intensive computing tasks. The platform consists of many nodes, and data is stored in those nodes. After a job is submitted, Hadoop splits the job into several tasks, distributes it to the nodes, and returns the results. In data-intensive supercomputing, the cost of moving data is much higher than the cost of moving computing [3]. Moving the process of calculation to the data nodes saves large amounts of network bandwidth, effectively reduces the number of data transfers, and improves cluster efficiency. However, when new nodes are added

© ICST Institute for Computer Sciences, Social Informatics and Telecommunications Engineering 2018
I. Romdhani et al. (Eds.): CollaborateCom 2017, LNICST 252, pp. 344–354, 2018.
https://doi.org/10.1007/978-3-030-00916-8_32

or the number of files in the cluster change dynamically, the amount of data in each node can become unbalanced. When the data load among cluster nodes becomes unbalanced, many problems can arise. For example, the MapReduce program no longer makes good use of local computing, because the probability that the task must be assigned non-locally increases [4]. Thus, the node must copy the data from the other nodes, increasing the network load. The nodes cannot improve network bandwidth utilization and disk utilization. Consequently, the efficiency of the cluster is reduced and the execution time increases. Obviously, ensuring balanced data in the Hadoop cluster is very important. Data load balancing has gradually become an important research area in the field of distributed computing [5].

There are two solutions to this problem: static load balancing algorithms and dynamic load balancing algorithms. A static load balancing algorithm calculates the load of nodes using a pre-designed load balancing algorithm, which then allocates tasks [6]. However, this approach does not consider the node's resource load status. A static load balancing algorithm is simple to implement, but because it neglects the resource load, the final allocation scheme may not meet the requirements for load balancing and can lead to load imbalance. A dynamic load balancing algorithm considers the load information of the node to allocate tasks reasonably. However, because the load information must be calculated in real time, dynamic load balancing increases resource consumption [7]. Therefore, based on an analysis of the shortcomings of the two solutions, a data load balancing method based on node features for heterogeneous clusters is proposed.

The method proposed in this paper combines the static load balancing algorithm with the dynamic load balancing algorithm. First, the node performance is defined to calculate the node's data processing ability. Second, the node load status is evaluated by dynamically obtaining the current number of node connections. The node's relative load value is calculated by combining the node performance with the node load status. Then, node data is allocated considering the relative load value. Nodes with larger relative load values will be allocated more data.

The rest of this paper is organized as follows. Section 2 introduces load balancing and related works. Section 3 describes the construction of the load balancing method based on node features. The algorithm proposed in this paper is simulated and the simulation results are analysed in Sect. 4. Finally, Sect. 5 concludes and presents prospects for future work.

2 Related Works

As a framework for dealing with big data, Hadoop can fully utilize the advantages of large-scale clusters. The most important goals are to improve cluster efficiency and ensure full resource utilization. However, when the load in a cluster is unbalanced, problems will occur, such as low overall throughput of the cluster and resource underutilization. Many scholars have studied cluster load balancing through task scheduling, in which the load statuses and overall performance of clusters are analysed, and then, reasonable decisions are made. Gao et al. [8] conducted an in-depth study for implementing of MapReduce. The deviation of each node's running time in the Reduce phase is caused by differences in the performances of the nodes in the cluster. A load balancing algorithm based on node performance was proposed to solve this problem. First, the algorithm creates a pre-allocated list, named RPReduceNum, based on the performance of all nodes. Data is allocated to Reduce tasks based on the RPReduce-Num list, and high-performance nodes process more tasks in the Reduce phase. Therefore, this approach reduces the overall MapReduce running time and improves efficiency. However, it also causes large network consumption in the cluster. In the Reduce phase, the amount of received data for the Reducer is determined by a partitioning function. The Reducers with high input data become a performance bottleneck, which delays execution completion. To solve this problem, Fan et al. [9] proposed a method for storing the input data for a Reducer by creating a virtual partition. Each output of the Map task is assigned to a different virtual partition based on a hash function. All the virtual partitions are combined into the same number as the Reduce task by the LBVP algorithm, which ensures that the input data for each Reduce task is balanced. However, this approach ignores the problem of node heterogeneity. Zheng et al. [10] proposed a method of adaptive task scheduling method based on node capability. The tasks for nodes are distributed according to each node's history, current load status, performance, task characteristics and failure rate. Each node can adaptively adjust the number of running tasks, which decreases the time to completion for all tasks and improves node load balance. In HDFS, multiple copies of data blocks are placed on different DataNodes. Although this approach improves the fault tolerance of HDFS, the randomness of the default block may cause load imbalances between DataNodes. Lin et al. [11] proposed an improved load balancing algorithm to avoid adjusting data by using a balancer and minimizing block movement as much as possible to reduce the movement costs. This method mainly balances the loads of file blocks after addition or deletion, but it ignores the effects of dynamic addition or deletion in the cluster for load balancing. Wei et al. [12] proposed a new replica placement strategy to uniformly distribute the data, thus meeting the requirements of HDFS replica placement. This method does not need to run the balancer to make adjustments, but it still cannot avoid the problem of data imbalances after new nodes have been added or when node failures in clusters occur. Liu et al. [13] proposed an improved load balancing algorithm based on heterogeneous clusters that analysed four aspects of load imbalance: imbalance in input splits, imbalance in computation, imbalance in partition sizes, and imbalance in heterogeneous hardware. Xie et al. [14] proposed a strategy for storing data proportionally that involved distributing a large number of data sets to multiple nodes based on the computing ability of each node. In addition to the data redistribution algorithm for HDFS, a data reorganization algorithm was also implemented to solve the problem of data deviation caused by dynamic insertions or deletions. This strategy takes the heterogeneity of the nodes into account, but it ignores the impact of the heterogeneity of node storage on data storage.

First, this paper analyses the importance of default load balancing and the limitations exposed under heterogeneous clusters. Next, a method of load balancing for heterogeneous clusters is proposed. The method analyses the features of each node and then calculates a relative load value for each node. According to the relative load value, the data for clusters can be allocated more reasonably. A large number of conducted experiments show that the method reduces cluster imbalance, improves cluster efficiency and reduces execution time under certain environments.

3 Improved Load Balancing Method

In this paper, we propose a load balancing method based on node features in heterogeneous clusters. The heterogeneity of a heterogeneous cluster is reflected by high performance nodes handling the same work in less time and the different storage allocated by each node to the HDFS. When the data is allocated proportionally according to the performance of each node, due to the heterogeneity of the node's storage, the node's disk may not support the allocated amount of data. The scheme proposed in this paper is based on the performance of each node and on HDFS storage to calculate the theoretical value of data allocation and the threshold used to determine whether a node is at equilibrium status. Finally, the load balancing problem of heterogeneous clusters is processed in a method similar to homogeneous clusters. This approach simplifies the complexity of load balancing for heterogeneous clusters.

Storage of Node $(C_{conf}(i))$: Capacity is allocated to the HDFS by nodes and is not limited to the capacity of the node disk. $C_{conf}(i)$ represents the allocated capacity of the ith node.

Used capacity $(C_{used}(i))$: The used capacity of the HDFS by the node's storage. $C_{used}(i)$ represents the capacity used by the ith node.

CPU Performance of a Node $(P_{cpu}(i))$: As is known, it is impossible for dual-core performance to reach a full $1 + 1 = 2$ efficiency. By referring to the relevant information, in a multi-core CPU, the performance of each core is approximately only 0.8–0.9 times as much as that of a single-core CPU. Therefore, we set $\rho = 0.8$ and $\delta = 0.1$. The CPU Performance of a Node is defined as follows:

$$P_{cpu}(i) = \begin{cases} F_{cpu}(i), N_{core} = 1 \\ \left(\rho + \delta * e^{2-N_{core}(i)}\right) * F_{cpu}(i), N_{core} > 1 \end{cases} \tag{1}$$

where $N_{core}(i)$ represents the number of cores in the CPU, and $F_{cpu}(i)$ represents the CPU frequency of the ith node in GHz.

Memory Performance of Node $(P_{mem}(i))$: We use $P_{mem}(i) = N_{mem}(i) * F_{mem}(i)$ to measure the memory performance of nodes, where $N_{mem}(i)$ represents the memory size of the ith node in MBs. Here, $F_{mem}(i)$ denotes the memory frequency of the ith node in GHz.

Connection Number of Node $(Q(i))$: This value indicates the number of active connections established by a DataNode with the outside world. These connections are generally used to transmit or receive data, send control signals, etc. The larger the value, the busier the node and the greater its load. The sum of clustered connections is defined as:

$$Q = \sum_{i=1}^{n} Q(i) \tag{1}$$

Definition 1: Relative load value:

$$L(i) = \alpha \sin^2\left(\frac{P_{cpu}(i)}{\max(P_{cpu})} * \frac{\pi}{2}\right) + \beta \cos^2\left(\frac{P_{mem}(i)}{\max(P_{mem})} * \frac{\pi}{2}\right) + \gamma \cos^2\left(\frac{Q(i)}{\max(Q)} * \frac{\pi}{2}\right) \tag{2}$$

The relative load value describes the node's ability to carry its current load. Here, α, β and γ represent weight parameters of CPU performance, memory performance and number of connections, respectively, and $\alpha + \beta + \gamma = 1$. The upper bound of the relative load value is set to 1 and will be simplified in later calculations. By analysing the contributions of these parameters, we set $\alpha = 0.5$, $\beta = 0.3$, and $\gamma = 0.2$. The sum of the relative load value is defined as follows:

$$L = \sum_{i=1}^{n} L(i) \tag{3}$$

Definition 2: Cluster storage utilization rate:

$$R_{Avg} = \frac{C_{used}}{C_{conf}} * 100\% = \frac{\sum_{i=1}^{n} C_{used}(i)}{\sum_{i=1}^{n} C_{conf}(i)} * 100\% \tag{5}$$

where n is the total number of nodes in the cluster.

Definition 3: Relative load storage capacity:

$$C_{ideal}(i) = \frac{L(i)}{L} * C_{used}(i) \tag{4}$$

Definition 4: Relative load storage utilization rate:

$$R_{ideal}(i) = \frac{C_{ideal}(i)}{C_{conf}(i)} * 100\% \tag{5}$$

According to the ratio of a node's relative load value to its total relative load value, the data can be distributed proportionally. We obtain the storage capacity of nodes based on its relative load, which is relative to its load storage capacity. For one node, the ratio of storage capacity based on its relative load value to the storage capacity assigned to the HDFS is defined as its relative load storage utilization rate.

Definition 5: Maximum load value:

$$M = \left(0.8 + 0.2 * \sin^2\left(\frac{\pi}{2} * R_{Avg}\right)\right) \tag{6}$$

Due to heterogeneity of node disks, the storage capacity of each node will differ. When the node's relative load value is high, the node's storage is fairly limited. At this point, the allocated data size is greater than the available node storage. For this problem, this article defines the maximum load value for the node. The maximum load value is dynamically adjusted according to the cluster storage utilization rate. When the cluster storage utilization rate is larger, the maximum load value of the node will be increased accordingly. The value of M is between 80% and 100%.

We find nodes whose data ratios are greater than the maximum load value and calculate the total overflow capacity. The total overflow capacity of the nodes in the cluster is calculated as follows:

$$C_{supr}(i) = \sum_{i=1}^{n} (R_{ideal}(i) - M) * C_{conf}(i) \tag{7}$$

where n is the total number of nodes in the cluster, $i = 1, 2, \cdots, n$ and $R_{ideal}(i) > M$. Then, data is allocated to other nodes. This iteration runs until the cluster contains no overloaded nodes—those whose allocated data ratio is greater than the node's maximum load value.

Definition 6: Relative load threshold:

$$T(i) = t * R_{ideal}(i) \tag{8}$$

where the parameter t is a threshold entered by the user. This indicates the maximum value of the deviation between the node storage utilization rate and the cluster storage utilization rate. In the default load balancer, if the deviation is less than the threshold, we assume that the node is balanced. Due to the heterogeneity of node storage, the actual storage expressed by the same threshold will be different between nodes. Therefore, this paper recalculates the threshold of each node by referring to its relative load value.

The procedure of the algorithm is as follows.

By obtaining the hardware parameters of all nodes, the CPU performance and memory performance are calculated according to formulas (1) and (2). Then, combined with the number of current connections, the relative load value and the sum of the relative load values will be calculated according to formula (3). Next, analysing the proportion of the relative load value to the sum, the relative load storage capacity and utilization rates are calculated according to formulas (6) and (7). The maximum load value will be calculated according to formula (8). To ensure that all the relative load storage values are valid values, we compare the relative load storage utilization rate with the maximum load value; the relative load utilization rate is set to the maximum load value when the former is larger than the latter. Next, the overflow capacity is calculated by formula (9). Overflow will then be allocated to other nodes until, eventually no node whose relative load utilization rate is greater than the maximum load value will exist. After the threshold is entered, the relative load threshold is calculated for each node according to formula (10). All the nodes are divided into four groups as shown in Table 1.

Table 1. Node group

Groups	Conditions
overUtilizedDataNodes	$R(i) > R_{ideal}(i) + T(i)$
aboveAvgUtilizedDataNodes	$R_{ideal}(i) < R(i) < R_{ideal}(i) + T(i)$
belowAvgUtilizedDataNodes	$R_{ideal}(i) - T(i) < R(i) < R_{ideal}(i)$
underUtilizedDataNodes	$R(i) < R_{ideal}(i) - T(i)$

4 Experiments and Analysis

The following describes the simulation experiments conducted for this study. The experimental environment consists of three racks containing nine nodes. There are two nodes in rack 1, four in rack 2, and three in rack 3. The NameNode is located in rack 2, and its number is PC3. This node also acts as a DataNode. All the nodes are configured with the CentOS 7 operating system. The network topology is shown in Fig. 1. In the experiment, the load balancer is run on the NameNode. The hardware parameters of all the nodes are shown in Table 2.

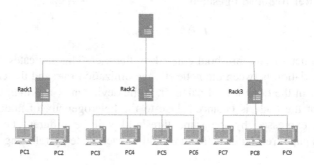

Fig. 1. Network topology

All the nodes are sorted in descending order by relative load value. PC1 is the node with the greatest relative load value and PC9 is the node with the lowest relative load value. The relative load values of all the nodes are shown in Fig. 2.

To compare the default load balancer with the improved load balancer in this heterogeneous cluster, the data block copies parameter is set to 3, and we delete some data to force the cluster to be unbalanced. We execute the instruction start-balancer.sh– threshold 10, which means that we set the threshold to 10% and execute the load balancer. Then, we run the balancer separately and observe the equilibrium effect. Finally, the WordCount program is executed to record the finish time for each balanced scheme. The cluster statuses are shown in Tables 3 and 4 (Fig. 3).

Table 2. Node hardware parameters

Number of node	CPU	Memory	Storage
PC1	3.5 GHz (4 CPUs)	4 GB (1.6 GHz)	80 GB
PC2	3.5 GHz (4 CPUs)	4 GB (1.6 GHz)	60 GB
PC3	3.5 GHz (4 CPUs)	4 GB (1.6 GHz)	40 GB
PC4	3.5 GHz (4 CPUs)	4 GB (1.6 GHz)	40 GB
PC5	2.1 GHz (2 CPUs)	3 GB (1.6 GHz)	70 GB
PC6	2.6 GHz (2 CPUs)	2 GB (1.333 GHz)	60 GB
PC7	2.6 GHz (2 CPUs)	2 GB (1.333 GHz)	30 GB
PC8	2.0 GHz (2 CPUs)	2 GB (1.333 GHz)	40 GB
PC9	2.2 GHz (2 CPUs)	1 GB (1.333 GHz)	50 GB

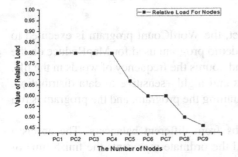

Fig. 2. Relative load value

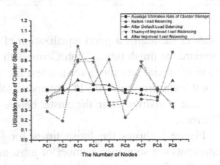

Fig. 3. Cluster storage utilization

Table 3. Cluster initial status

Number of node	Storage (GB)	Used (GB)	Used (%)	Relative load value
PC1	80	23.3	29.13	0.8
PC2	60	11.6	19.33	0.8
PC3	40	37.8	94.50	0.8
PC4	40	22.4	56.00	0.8
PC5	70	56.7	81.00	0.67
PC6	60	13.7	22.83	0.6
PC7	30	12.3	41.00	0.6
PC8	40	15.9	39.75	0.5
PC9	50	44.2	88.40	0.46

In Fig. 4, after running the improved load balancer, the data storage distribution is consistent with the trend in Fig. 2. This result shows that the improved load balancer works as expected.

The improved balancer will adjust the data distribution into an improved equalization status based on the relative load value. To verify that the improved load

Table 4. Cluster load status

Number of node	Default balancer					Improved balancer		
	Threshold T (%)	Balanced (%)	Balanced (GB)	Ideal storage (%)	Ideal storage (GB)	Threshold T (%)	Balanced (%)	Balanced (GB)
PC1	10	43.27	34.62	39.45	31.56	3.95	42.40	33.92
PC2	10	47.68	28.61	52.59	31.56	5.26	53.88	32.32
PC3	10	60.43	24.17	78.89	31.56	7.89	80.83	32.33
PC4	10	56.00	22.4	78.89	31.56	7.89	82.64	33.06
PC5	10	55.32	38.72	37.68	26.38	3.77	34.80	24.36
PC6	10	47.81	28.68	39.34	23.60	3.93	37.02	22.21
PC7	10	45.72	13.72	78.69	23.60	7.87	74.27	22.28
PC8	10	43.12	17.25	49.53	19.81	4.95	52.06	20.82
PC9	10	59.46	29.73	36.54	18.27	3.65	33.18	16.59

balancer maintains a good equalization effect, the WordCount program is executed to compare the finish times. WordCount is the demo program used for MapReduce on the Hadoop official website; it reads a text file and counts the frequency of words in the file. WordCount programs are I/O-intensive jobs and highly sensitive to data distribution. The data is distributed in the cluster before running the program, and the program is run 20 times.

Figure 5 shows the finish times for jobs from different balancers. The abscissa represents the sequence number of jobs, and the ordinate represents the finish time of jobs. The 20 groups of contrasting experiments show that there are still some uncontrollable factors in the experiment, and consequently, some deviation appears. However, the overall results are relatively stable, and the average completion time of the default balancer is longer than that of the improved balancer. These results verify that the improved balancer has a substantial effect on cluster performance.

In a data distribution-balanced cluster, the proposed balancer can effectively reduce the data migration problems of computing resources and data resources in different physical nodes caused by job scheduling. Thus, the network load is alleviated, the number of non-localized tasks decreases, and the execution time is reduced.

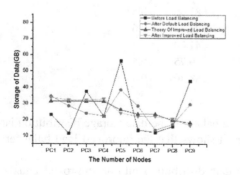

Fig. 4. Load balancer comparing experiment

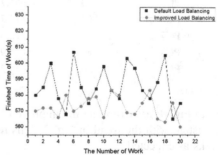

Fig. 5. Jobs running status

5 Conclusion

In this paper, we analysed the working principles of the default load balancer. However, in heterogeneous clusters, based on the performance differences, storage and current loads of each node, a load balancing method based on node features is proposed. This method provides a scheme for calculating a relative load value for each node. Then, the amount of data to be allocated and the appropriate threshold are calculated by considering the relative load value. Next, we move data and ensure that the deviations of the storage utilization rate are not greater than the threshold. Finally, through experimental analysis, the method is shown to cause the cluster to be more balanced, reduce the execution time of jobs, and improve the overall performance of the cluster.

Acknowledgements. This paper is supported by National Natural Science Foundation of China under Grant No. 61502294, Natural Science Foundation of Shanghai under Grant No. 15ZR1415200, CERNET Innovation Project under Grant No. NGII20160210, NGII20160614, NGII20160325, The Special Development Foundation of Key Project of Shanghai Zhangjiang National Innovation Demonstration Zone under Grant No. 201411-ZB-B204-012, and The Development Foundation for Cultural and Creative Industries of Shanghai under Grant No. 201610162.

References

1. Su, F., Peng, Y., Mao, X., et al.: The research of big data architecture on telecom industry. In: International Symposium on Communications and Information Technologies, pp. 280–284 (2016)
2. Apache Hadoop. http://hadoop.apache.org
3. Parsola, J., Gangodkar, D., Mittal, A.: Efficient storage and processing of video data for moving object detection using Hadoop/MapReduce. In: Lobiyal, D.K., Mohapatra, D.P., Nagar, A., Sahoo, M.N. (eds.) Proceedings of the International Conference on Signal, Networks, Computing, and Systems. LNEE, vol. 395, pp. 137–147. Springer, New Delhi (2017). https://doi.org/10.1007/978-81-322-3592-7_14
4. Bezerra, A., Hernandez, P., et al.: Job scheduling for optimizing data locality in Hadoop clusters. In: European MPI Users' Group Meeting, pp. 271–276 (2013)
5. Lin, W.W., Liu, B.: Hadoop data load balancing method based on dynamic bandwidth allocation. Huanan Ligong Daxue Xuebao/J. South China Univ. Technol. **40**(9), 42–47 (2012)
6. Fan, K., Zhang, D., Li, H., et al.: An adaptive feedback load balancing algorithm in HDFS. In: International Conference on Intelligent NETWORKING and Collaborative Systems, pp. 23–29 (2013)
7. Babu, B.G., Shabeera, T.P., Madhu Kumar, S.D.: Dynamic colocation algorithm for Hadoop. In: International Conference on Advances in Computing, Communications and Informatics, pp. 2643–2647 (2014)
8. Gao, Z., Liu, D., Yang, Y., et al.: A load balance algorithm based on nodes performance in Hadoop cluster. In: Network Operations and Management Symposium, pp. 1–4. IEEE (2014)

9. Fan, Y., Wu, W., Cao, H., et al.: LBVP: a load balance algorithm based on Virtual Partition in Hadoop cluster. In: IEEE Asia Pacific Cloud Computing Congress, pp. 37–41. IEEE (2012)

10. Zheng, X., Ming, X., Zhang, D., et al.: An adaptive tasks scheduling method based on the ability of node in Hadoop cluster. J. Comput. Res. Dev. **51**(3), 618–626 (2014)

11. Lin, C.Y., Lin, Y.C.: A load-balancing algorithm for Hadoop distributed file system. In: International Conference on Network-Based Information Systems, pp. 173–179. IEEE (2015)

12. Wei, D., Ibrahim, I., Bassiouni, M.: A new replica placement policy for Hadoop distributed file system. In: International Conference on Big Data Security on Cloud, pp. 262–267. IEEE (2016)

13. Liu, Y., Li, M., Alham, N.K., et al.: Load balancing in MapReduce environments for data intensive applications. In: Eighth International Conference on Fuzzy Systems and Knowledge Discovery, pp. 2675–2678. IEEE (2011)

14. Xie, J., Yin, S., Ruan, X., et al.: Improving MapReduce performance through data placement in heterogeneous Hadoop clusters. In: IEEE International Symposium on Parallel and Distributed Processing - Workshop Proceedings, IPDPS 2010, Atlanta, Georgia, USA, 19–23 April 2010, pp. 1–9. DBLP (2010)

Towards Collaborative Typed Resources Manipulation in Health-Care Environments

Lixu Shao[1], Yucong Duan[1(⊠)], Zhangbing Zhou[2], Antonella Longo[3], Donghai Zhu[1], and Honghao Gao[4]

[1] State Key Laboratory of Marine, Resource Utilization in the South China Sea, College of Information and Technology, Hainan University, Haikou, China
751486692@qq.com, duanyucong@hotmail.com, 466971642@qq.com

[2] Department of Information Engineering, China University of Geosciences (Beijing), Beijing, China
zhangbing.zhou@gmail.com

[3] Department of Engineering for Innovation, University del Salento, Lecce, Italy
antonella.longo@unisalento.it

[4] Computer Center, Shanghai University, Shanghai, China
gaohonghao@shu.edu.cn

Abstract. Web service is a popular solution to integrate components when building a software system, or to allow communication between a system and third-party users, providing a flexible and reusable mechanism to access its functionalities. Due to differences in medical level and extremely uneven distribution of medical resources, medical information technology lacks unified planning and is not supported by digital health care system. Thus diagnosis resources of patients cannot be shared by each medical institution. Inspections usually repeat which not only increases the burden of hospitalizing and physical injuries, but also leads to the waste of medical resources. We propose a framework towards constructing and searching typed health resources in terms of data, information and knowledge through a hierarchy composing Data Graph, Information Graph and Knowledge Graph in order to improve performance in accessing and processing resources. We use cases to illustrate the mechanism of the framework.

Keywords: Knowledge graph · Collaborative adaptation
Typed resources

1 Introduction

Most collaborative work takes place in environments with abundant information [7]. Medical information management systems are characterized by a high degree of collaborative work, mobility, and information access from many devices or artifacts [8]. Sharing medical resources such as patients' information and medical

© ICST Institute for Computer Sciences, Social Informatics and Telecommunications Engineering 2018
I. Romdhani et al. (Eds.): CollaborateCom 2017, LNICST 252, pp. 355–364, 2018.
https://doi.org/10.1007/978-3-030-00916-8_33

technology is conductive to achieve the bidirectional referral, remote consultation and other medical services between different medical institutions so as to provide patients with better medical conditions and reduce medical costs. In order to improve quality of medical health care services, we propose a typed medical resources sharing approach towards temporal and spatial optimization with collaborative storage and computation adaptation based on Data Graph, Information Graph and Knowledge Graph. [4] extended the existing concept of Knowledge Graph into four aspects including Data Graph, Information Graph, Knowledge Graph and Wisdom Graph. In [9] the authors proposed to answer the Five Ws problems through constructing the architecture of Data Graph, Information Graph and Knowledge Graph. We propose to clarify the expression of existing Knowledge Graph corresponding to the progressive manner of typed resources including $Data_{DIK}$, $Information_{DIK}$ and $Knowledge_{DIK}$. We specify the architecture of Knowledge Graph as the combination of $DataGraph_{DIK}$, $InformationGraph_{DIK}$ and $KnowledgeGraph_{DIK}$. In Fig. 1 we describe a framework of collaborative medical resource sharing system. Collaborating health care workers may include doctors, CDC, health bureau and so on. Persons and institutes with different expertise and access rights cooperate in mutually influencing contexts, for instance, clinical studies.

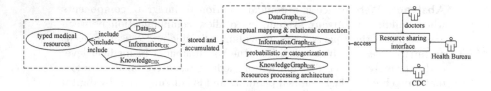

Fig. 1. A framework of collaborative medical resource sharing system

The rest of the paper is organized as follows. Section 2 introduces the construction of a collaborative medical information sharing service system. Section 3 elaborates the storage and computation adaptation towards sharing typed resources and Sect. 4 presents the results of our analytical and experimental evaluation of our proposed approach. Section 5 discusses the related work. And we summarize the conclusion of our work in Sect. 6.

2   Construction of Collaborative Medical Information Sharing Service System

Typed medical resources including $Data_{DIK}$, $Information_{DIK}$ and $Knowledge_{DIK}$ produced through medical activities are collected and accumulated into resource processing architecture. Definitions of typed resources and graphs are as follows.

Definition 1. *Typed resources. Typed resources including data, information and knowledge can be expressed as:*

$Resources_{DIK}: = <Data_{DIK}, Information_{DIK}, Knowledge_{DIK}>;$

D represents represent $Data_{DIK}$. I represents $Information_{DIK}$ and K represents $Knowledge_{DIK}$.

Definition 2. *Graphs. We propose to specify the existing concept of Knowledge Graph in three layers. Graphs can be expressed as:*

$Graph_{DIK}: = <(DataGraph_{DIK}), (InformationGraph_{DIK}), (Knowledge Graph_{DIK})>.$

With the extensive application of information technology, medical information systems are rapidly deployed and put into use in various medical institutions. Medical information systems integrate scattered medical resources and implement the centralized storage of medical resources to achieve the sharing of resources. Development of a service system can be divided into stages of data sharing, information transfer, and knowledge creation [10]. In the development of a medical information sharing service system, following situations will cause deficient design efficiency:

- Extra $Data_{DIK}$, $Information_{DIK}$ and $Knowledge_{DIK}$ which is not contained in original artifacts is introduced in resulting artifacts.
- Improper control of $Data_{DIK}$, $Information_{DIK}$ and $Knowledge_{DIK}$ flow.
- Redundant $Data_{DIK}$, $Information_{DIK}$ and $Knowledge_{DIK}$ that is produced and collected through performing activities repeatedly.

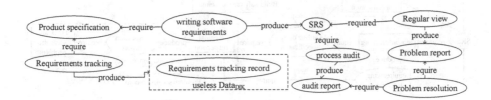

Fig. 2. Activities generating useless $Data_{DIK}$

2.1 Processing of Useless Resources$_{DIK}$

Useless $Data_{DIK}$, $Information_{DIK}$ and $Knowledge_{DIK}$ are modelled as resources that are generated during the participants' activities but are not useful for subsequent activities. Figure 2 shows the existence of useless $Data_{DIK}$ marked by a dashed box. The out degree of $Data_{DIK}$ "Requirements tracking record" is 0 which means that no activity requires the $Data_{DIK}$. The introduction of useless $Data_{DIK}$, $Information_{DIK}$ and $Knowledge_{DIK}$ requires additional human effort and improves the temporal complexity. We describe solution about useless $Data_{DIK}$, $Information_{DIK}$ and $Knowledge_{DIK}$ in Algorithm 1.

Algorithm 1.   Remedying useless Resources$_{DIK}$

Input: All activities act of software development
Output: software development activities after deleting use-
   less Resources$_{DIK}$
   If Resources$_{DIK}$ produced by act_i is not required act_j
      Deleting act_i;

2.2   Remedying Improper Data$_{DIK}$, Information$_{DIK}$ and Knowledge$_{DIK}$ Flow Control

Development activities of a service system should be performed according to a necessary execution sequence in order to improve the temporal efficiency and reduce costs of development. In actual development process, results of sequential implementation and parallel implementation of some activities are equivalent, but costs of parallel implementation are much lower. In Fig. 3 there is an execution dependency relationship between activity "regular inspection" and activity "track and solve problems". Activity "regular inspection" must be performed in advance because the execution of activity "track and solve problems" requires the Information$_{DIK}$ produced by activity "regular inspection". But implementation of activity "write test plan" does not depend on activity "write design specification". Thus these two activities can be executed in parallel. We elaborate method to remedy deficient Information$_{DIK}$ flow control in Algorithm 2.

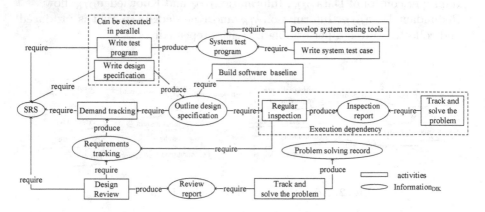

Fig. 3. A framework of collaborative medical resource sharing system

---

Algorithm 2.   Remedying deficient flow control of Information$_{DIK}$

Input: An improper execution order of activities
Output: An adjusted execution order of activities
   1. Find a topological order of activities that is deficient;
   2. Adjust pre-order activities to be effective;
   3. Computing a new topological order of deficient activities after remedying pre-order deficiencies;
   4. Repeat Step 2.

2.3   Processing of Redundant Data$_{DIK}$, Information$_{DIK}$ and Knowledge$_{DIK}$

Deficient design process of a service system comes from the situation that some development activities are not planned efficiently and the resulting product is not as effective as expected. Redundant Data$_{DIK}$, Information$_{DIK}$ and Knowledge$_{DIK}$ will cost more time and waste more storage space and redundant Data$_{DIK}$, Information$_{DIK}$ and Knowledge$_{DIK}$ will lead to inconsistency in the service system development. A redundancy occurs when a design artifact (perhaps partial) is represented multiple times, possibly in varying views. Redundancies can occur either in design or resource representation. We describe the processing approach to redundant Information$_{DIK}$ in Algorithm 3. We reserve the earliest activity that is the most feasible to produce a piece of Information$_{DIK}$ and minimize the occurrence of other repeated production to 1.

Algorithm 3.   Remedying Information$_{DIK}$ redundancy

Require: Collection of activities A and Information$_{DIK}$ I
Ensure: $activity \in A, info_{DIK} \in I$
 For : each $activity \in A$, info$_{DIK} \in I$ Do
   if   occurrence(activity,   info$_{DIK}$):   Amount(info$_{DIK}$) +=1;
     For info$_{DIK} \in I \wedge$ amount(info$_{DIK}$) ≥ 1 Do
       Adjust A, ensure amount (info$_{DIK}$) = 1
     End For
   End For

---

3   Collaborative Adaptation Towards Typed Resources Sharing

To enhance resources sharing between multi medical institutes and avoid repeated medical examination of patients, we propose a collaborative adaptation approach to reduce medical burden. We make the assumption that typed medical resources have been well organized on the hierarchy of DataGraph$_{DIK}$, InformationGraph$_{DIK}$ and KnowledgeGraph$_{DIK}$. We propose to measure searching efficiency according to computations related to transferring cost of resource types and scale of resources in order to determine which graph should be traversed preferentially. We define sharing medical resources and resources that have been organized on Graph$_{DIK}$ as follows:

Definition 3. *Sharing medical resources. Sharing medical resources are defined as a tuple SMR = <STY, SSC>, where STY is the type set of sharing resources represented by a triad < sty_D, sty_I, sty_K > and SSC is the scale of different kinds of sharing resources represented by a triad < ssc_D, ssc_I, ssc_K > where each scc denotes the scale of resource in the form of sty.*

Definition 4. *Resources on Graph$_{DIK}$. We define Resources on Graph$_{DIK}$ as a tuple RoG = <GTY, GSC>, where GTY is the type set of resources*

on $Graph_{DIK}$ represented by a triad $< gty_D, gty_I, gty_K >$ and GSC is the scale of different kinds of resources on $Graph_{DIK}$ represented by a triad $< gsc_D, gsc_I, gsc_K >$ where each gsc denotes the scale of resources in the form of gty.

3.1   Calculation of Resource Type Transferring Cost

We assign values from $Resources_{DIK}$ to each element in the type set STY of SMR to form combination case $STY' = \{sty'_D, sty'_I, sty'_K\}$ where sty'_D, sty'_I and sty'_K belong to $\{Data_{DIK}, Information_{DIK}, Knowledge_{DIK}\}$. The atomic type conversion cost of resources in SMR, denoted as $SCost$, is shown in Table 1. Transferring cost of all resources from SMR to STY', denoted as $CostTF_1$, can be calculated according to Eq. 1:

$$CostTF_1 = \sum_{D,I,K} SCost * ssc_i, i \in \{D, I, K\} \tag{1}$$

Table 1. Atomic type conversion cost of resource in SMR

	$Data_{DIK}$	$Information_{DIK}$	$Knowledge_{DIK}$
$Data_{DIK}$	$SCost_{D-D}$	$SCost_{D-I}$	$SCost_{D-K}$
$Information_{DIK}$	$SCost_{I-D}$	$SCost_{I-I}$	$SCost_{I-K}$
$Knowledge_{DIK}$	$SCost_{K-D}$	$SCost_{K-I}$	$SCost_{K-K}$

We assign values from $Resources_{DIK}$ to each resource in the type set GTY of RoG to form combination case $GTY' = \{gty'_D, gty'_I, gty'_K\}$ where gty'_D, gty'_I and gty'_K belong to $\{Data_{DIK}, Information_{DIK}, Knowledge_{DIK}\}$. The atomic type conversion cost of elements in RoG, denoted as $GCost$, is shown in Table 2. Transferring cost of all resources from GTY' to RoG, denoted as $CostTF_2$, can be calculated according to Eq. 2:

$$CostTF_2 = \sum_{D,I,K} GCost * gsc_i, i \in D, I, K \tag{2}$$

Table 2. Atomic type conversion cost of resource in RoG

	$Data_{DIK}$	$Information_{DIK}$	$Knowledge_{DIK}$
$Data_{DIK}$	$GCost_{D-D}$	$GCost_{D-I}$	$GCost_{D-K}$
$Information_{DIK}$	$GCost_{I-D}$	$GCost_{I-I}$	$GCost_{I-K}$
$Knowledge_{DIK}$	$GCost_{K-D}$	$GCost_{K-I}$	$GCost_{K-K}$

3.2   Cost of Searching SMR in RoG

Sharing medical resources including $Data_{DIK}$, $Information_{DIK}$, and $Knowledge_{DIK}$ are related to specific medical scene. The expansion of medical resources enable resource searching more inefficient which is called resource overload. In order to solve the problem we propose to adjust storage programs of sharing resources according to computation of searching cost. When resources are needed, health care workers can obtain resources through traversing $Graph_{DIK}$ directly rather than perform related medical activities to produce required resources. Table 3 shows the atomic type conversion cost of resource. Searching cost, denoted as $SECost$ can be calculated according to Eq. 3:

$$SECost = \sum_{D,I,K} (gsc + Cost * gsc') * ssc \tag{3}$$

where gsc' indicates the scale of medical resources that are found through traversing $Graph_{DIK}$ of the different type with initial resources of SMR.

Table 3. Atomic type conversion cost of resource

	$Data_{DIK}$	$Information_{DIK}$	$Knowledge_{DIK}$
$Data_{DIK}$	$Cost_{D-D}$	$Cost_{D-I}$	$Cost_{D-K}$
$Information_{DIK}$	$Cost_{I-D}$	$Cost_{I-I}$	$Cost_{I-K}$
$Knowledge_{DIK}$	$Cost_{K-D}$	$Cost_{K-I}$	$Cost_{K-K}$

3.3   Calculation of Benefit Ratio

The expected investment such as responding time of health care workers that is denoted as $Inve_0$ and the maximum total cost that is denoted as $Total\_cost_0$ are pre-set. After computing $CostTF_1$, $CostTF_2$ and $SECost$, we calculate the total cost of each program, denoted as $Total\_Cost$, according to Eq. 4:

$$Total\_Cost = CostTF_1 + SECost + CostTF_2 \tag{4}$$

The corresponding investment that is denoted as $Inve$ can be calculated according to Eq. 5 after computing the total cost of each resources searching program:

$$Inve = \mu * |Total\_Cost_0 - Total\_Cost| \tag{5}$$

where μ represents the required investment of reducing atomic $Total\_Cost$ that can be obtained through data training. And the ratio of investment and searching cost that is represented by $CostInv$ of each program can be calculated according to Eq. 6:

$$CostInv = \frac{Inve}{SECost} \tag{6}$$

Then we compare $CostInv$ and $Inve$ of each program with $CostInv_0$ and $Inve_0$ to determine whether the condition "$CostInv > CostInv_0 \& Inve < Inve_0$" is satisfied. When $CostInv$ is greater than $CostInv_0$, we make $CostInv_0$ equal to the current $CostInv$. If $CostInv$ is greater than $CostInv_0$, we perform the next step until the assignment towards STY and GTY are exhausted. We describe the specific process of investment driven searching sharing resources on resources of $Graph_{DIK}$ architecture composing $DataGraph_{DIK}$, $InformationGraph_{DIK}$ and $KnowledgeGraph_{DIK}$ in Algorithm 4.

Algorithm 4.   Calculating $CostInv$ of each resource type combination program

---
Input: SMR, RoG, $CostInv_0$
Output: The maximum $CostInv$
    For: each sty Do
        Assign value from Resources$_{DIK}$;
        Compute $CostTF_1$;
        For: each gty Do
            Assign value from Resources$_{DIK}$;
            Compute $CostTF_2$;
            Compute $SECost$;
            Compute $Total\_Cost$;
            If $(CostInv > CostInv_0 \& Inve < Inve_0)$
                $CostInv_0 = CostInv$;

---

4   Case Study

We give an example to illustrate the rationality verify the feasibility of our proposed approach. Here we have listed eight cases of SMR and RoG assignment and the corresponding calculations of $CostTF_1$, $CostTF_2$ and $SECost$. For convenience, we assign values to parameters in the equations. But the actual value

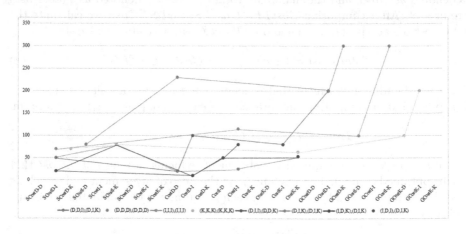

Fig. 4. Usage of indicators of $CostTF_1$, $SECost$ and $CostTF_2$

of each parameter should be obtained through data learning so as to compare the actual differences between results. Through comparing calculated results of $Total\_Cost$, we choose a program with the maximum $CostInv$ and the required investment should less than $Inve_0$. Figure 4 illustrates times of each indicator in $CostTF_1$, $SECost$ and $CostTF_2$ used in each program. In fact there are 27 * 27 programs because each element of SMR and RoG can be converted into one of the three types including $Data_{DIK}$, $Information_{DIK}$ and $Knowledge_{DIK}$.

5   Related Work

The growth of Internet has been accompanied by the growth of Web services such as e-commerce and e-health [12]. In [6] the authors elaborated an infrastructure enabling archetype-based semantic interoperability of Web Service messages exchanged in the health care domain. [2] presented a medical knowledge service system for cross-organizational healthcare collaboration such that all medical professionals and staff at different healthcare organizations could capture, store, manage, integrate and share medical knowledge. Scientists have proposed numerous models for defining anything "as a service (aaS)", including discussions of products, processes, data and information management as a service [3]. In [11] the authors proposed a multi-agent web service framework based on service-oriented architecture for the optimization of medical data quality in the e-healthcare information system. In [1] the authors introduced a new service-centric framework for data sharing and manipulation. A Web service oriented and process-centric framework for supporting collaborative engineering services was introduced in [5].

6   Conclusion

Collaboration among healthcare organizations depends on coordination, communication and control among healthcare organizations and effective sharing of medical resources. Typed resources including $Data_{DIK}$, $Information_{DIK}$ and $Knowledge_{DIK}$ should be integrated, managed and shared using the Internet and information technology. In order to optimize medical resource allocation and provide more efficient services, we elaborate solution for remedying deficient development activities of a collaborative medical resources sharing platform. Different healthcare practitioners may desire to access patient information or other information at various points in a healthcare workflow. We propose a resource processing approach towards temporal and spatial optimization with collaborative storage and computation adaptation for sharing typed medical resources so as to improve the quality of health service. In the next stage, we will expand the scale of dataset to verify the feasibility of our work.

Acknowledgment. This paper is supported by NSFC under Grant (No. 61363007, No. 61662021), NSF of Hainan No. ZDYF2017128 and Hainan University Project (No. hdkytg201708).

References

1. Alsboui, T., Hammoudeh, M., Abuarqoub, A.: A service-centric stack for collaborative data sharing and processing. Commun. Comput. Inf. Sci. **338**, 320–327 (2012)
2. Chen, Y.J.: A medical knowledge service system for cross-organizational healthcare collaboration. Int. J. Coop. Inf. Syst. **18**(01), 195–224 (2009)
3. Duan, Y., Fu, G., Zhou, N., Sun, X.: Everything as a service (XaaS) on the cloud: origins, current and future trends. In: IEEE International Conference on Cloud Computing, pp. 621–628 (2015)
4. Duan, Y., Shao, L., Hu, G., Zhou, Z., Zou, Q., Lin, Z.: Specifying architecture of knowledge graph with data graph, information graph, knowledge graph and wisdom graph. In: 2017 IEEE 15th International Conference on Software Engineering Research, Management and Applications (SERA), pp. 327–332 (2017)
5. Lee, J.Y., Lee, S., Kim, K., Kim, H., Kim, C.H.: Process-centric engineering web services in a distributed and collaborative environment. Comput. Ind. Eng. **51**(2), 297–308 (2006)
6. Mcilraith, S., Narayanan, S.: OWL-S: semantic markup for web services. In: Proceedings of the International Semantic Web Working Symposium (SWWS) (2001)
7. Reddy, M., Dourish, P.: A finger on the pulse: temporal rhythms and information seeking in medical work. In: ACM Conference on Computer Supported Cooperative Work, pp. 344–353 (2002)
8. Reddy, M.C., Spence, P.R.: Collaborative information seeking: a field study of a multidisciplinary patient care team. Inf. Process. Manag. **44**(1), 242–255 (2008)
9. Shao, L., Duan, Y., Sun, X., Gao, H.: Answering who/when, what, how, why through constructing data graph, information graph, knowledge graph and wisdom graph. In: Proceedings of the International Conference on Software Engineering and Knowledge Engineering (SEKE), pp. 1–7 (2017)
10. Shao, L., Duan, Y., Sun, X., Zou, Q., Jing, R., Lin, J.: Bidirectional value driven design between economical planning and technical implementation based on data graph, information graph and knowledge graph. In: 2017 IEEE 15th International Conference Software Engineering Research, Management and Applications (SERA), pp. 339–344 (2017)
11. Wu, C.S., Khoury, I., Shah, H.: Optimizing medical data quality based on multi-agent web service framework. IEEE Trans. Inf. Technol. Biomed. **16**(4), 745–757 (2012)
12. Yee, G.O.M., Zhang, L.J.: Estimating the privacy protection capability of a web service provider. Int. J. Web Serv. Res. **6**(2), 20–41 (2009)

Constructing Search as a Service Towards Non-deterministic and Not Validated Resource Environment with a Positive-Negative Strategy

Yucong Duan[1(✉)], Lixu Shao[1], Xiaobing Sun[2], Lizhen Cui[3], Donghai Zhu[1], and Zhengyang Song[1]

[1] State Key Laboratory of Marine, Resource Utilization in the South China Sea, College of Information and Technology, Hainan University, Haikou, China
duanyucong@hotmail.com, 751486692@qq.com, 466971642@qq.com, 1464626602@qq.com
[2] School of Information Engineering, Yangzhou University, Yangzhou, China
xbsun@yzu.edu.cn
[3] School of Information Science and Technology, Shandong University, Jinan, China
clz@sdu.edu.cn

Abstract. Internet resources are non-deterministic, non-guaranteed and ultra-complex. We provide a progressive search approach towards problems with positive and negative tendencies aiming at improving the credibility of resources through multi times progressive searching. Meanwhile, we introduce Knowledge Graph as a resource process architecture to organize resources on the network and analyze the tendency of searchers for retrieving information by semantic analysis. We calculate entropy of resources according to searching times and amount of items of each search to represent the reliability of resources with positive and negative tendencies. Resources with ambiguous tendency and false information will be eliminated during the process of progressive search and quality of searching results will be improved while avoiding dead loop of searching towards infinite and complex problems. We apply the searching strategy to a medical resource processing system that provides high precision medical resource retrieval service for medical workers to verify the feasibility of our approach.

Keywords: Bidirectional search · Knowledge graph
Resource modeling · Dynamic equilibrium

1 Introduction

Demand of accuracy for recommended searching results of users is greatly increased. Resources on Internet may be out of time, wrong and fictitious. We propose to improve the quality of resources through performing progressive searches towards problems covering positive and negative tendencies based

© ICST Institute for Computer Sciences, Social Informatics and Telecommunications Engineering 2018
I. Romdhani et al. (Eds.): CollaborateCom 2017, LNICST 252, pp. 365–373, 2018.
https://doi.org/10.1007/978-3-030-00916-8_34

in the resource processing architecture. Knowledge Graph is a knowledge base storing both unstructured and structured resources. Knowledge base contains a set of concepts, entities and relationships [4]. Knowledge Graph is a graph representing items, entities and users as nodes and linking nodes through edges. Based on the extension of existing concept of Knowledge Graph, in [9] the authors proposed to express Knowledge Graph in three levels including Data Graph, Information Graph and Knowledge Graph. In [2], the authors clarified the structure of Knowledge Graph according to the progressive relationships among data, information, knowledge and wisdom. In [8], the author proposed to answer 5W (Who/When, Where, What and How) problems by constructing Data Graph, Information Graph and Knowledge Graph. Chaim in [13] elaborated concepts of data, information and knowledge. Data is obtained by observing numbers or other basic individual projects. Information is conveyed through data and data combination. Knowledge is a general understanding and can be used to infer a new background. We introduce Knowledge Graph as a resource processing architecture to organize resources and apply our proposed searching service towards non-deterministic and not validated resource environment with a positive-negative strategy to medical resource management system to provide health care workers with efficient retrieval service.

2　Constructing Search as a Service with a Positive-Negative Strategy

When a user puts forward a noticeable or predisposing problem, there are many non-deterministic, non-fidelity and super-complex resources on the Internet. Faced with the situation, we propose to provide searching service towards non-deterministic and not validated resource environment with a positive-negative strategy. Meanwhile, we apply positive and negative search strategy to medical resource processing system to provide retrieving service for medical workers.

2.1　Investment Allocation of Positive-Negative Searching

According to the description of actual problem searched by searchers, we obtain related resources that satisfy users' information requirements and these resources can be divided into resources with positive and negative tendencies respectively. For example, when a user searches for "Whether changing contact address needs charging?". The positive tendency is that changing contact address needs charging and the negative tendency indicates that changing contact address doesn't need charging. Figure 1 shows progressive search results towards resources with positive and negative tendencies.

　　We propose to model users' requirements and count weight of searching resources with positive tendency and negative tendency respectively. Weight of resources with positive tendency, denoted as $Weight_p$ and weight of resources

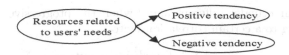

Fig. 1. Resources with positive and negative tendencies

with negative tendency, denoted as $Weight_N$ can be computed according to Eqs. 1 and 2:

$$Weight_P = \frac{Recource_P}{Recource_T} \qquad (1)$$

$$Weight_N = \frac{Recource_N}{Recource_T} \qquad (2)$$

where $Resource_P$ represents the amount of positive resources and $Resource_N$ represents the amount of negative resources. $Resource_T$ represents the total amount of all resources. We make the hypothesis that expected waiting time of users that denoted as T is already known. Items of each process of progressive search and searching times towards each item are fixed. According to the Eq. 3, we calculate the times of progressive search.

$$S\_times = \frac{T}{S\_items * Pert\_item} \qquad (3)$$

where S_times represents times of progressive search determined by users' investment. S_items represents amount of items per search. $Pert\_item$ represents searching time of each item.

2.2 Dynamically Balanced Bidirectional Search Service Provision

For questions proposed by searchers, we conduct dynamically balanced bidirectional search service strategy and traverse resource processing architecture to search relevant resources. According to obtained resources, we find the correlated factors with keywords in resources. We calculate $entropy_{T_K}$ of information which ranges from 0 to 1. The larger $entropy_{T_K}$ is, the lower confidence is. We calculate $entropy_{T_K}$ of resources according to Eq. 4 and total entropy of all resources with the same tendency that is denoted as $Entropy$ according to Eq. 5. Timeliness of resources is calculated according to Eq. 6. We use Eq. 7 to compute confidence of resources based on the entropy of resources obtained through progressive search process.

$$entropy_{T_K} = -\sum_{i=1}^{n} p_i log p_i \qquad (4)$$

where $entropy_{T_K}$ represents the entropy of resources obtained in time T_K in accordance with a certain factor in the progressive search, pi represents the probability of each type of answer, $Entropy$ represents the weighted average entropy of resource under different aging when the progressive search is performed according to a certain correlation factor.

$$Entropy = \frac{\sum_k^m Timeliness_{T_k} entropy_{T_k}}{m} \tag{5}$$

$$Timeliness = \frac{T_t - T_s}{T_c - T_s} \tag{6}$$

$$Confidence = S\_amount * Item\_amount * \int_1^n Entropy_{item_i} d(item_i) \tag{7}$$

According to calculated confidence of obtained resources, we make a judgement whether the ratio of positive and negative bidirectional resources confidence is greater than the threshold T or less than $1/T$. T can be obtained according to the learning algorithm. If the threshold condition is satisfied, return search results with high confidence to searchers. Otherwise we return to further allocation of users' investment to continue progressive search. Figure 2 shows the flowchart of constructing search as a service with positive and negative strategy.

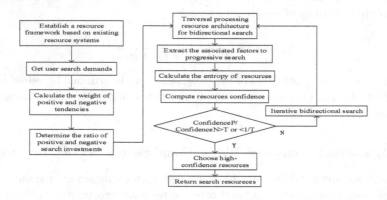

Fig. 2. Flowchart of constructing search with a positive-negative strategy

We clarify that correct resources are unique and divide search resources towards user's requirements into positive and negative tendencies in the non-deterministic, non-fidelity and super complex resource environment. We conduct progressive search strategy towards items related to resources and compute entropy of resources obtained through each progressive search process. Then we sort obtained resources according to their confidence from high to low and ultimately return ordered resources to users.

First of all, we establish a processing resource framework according to existing resource system and access to user search demands and compute weights of positive and negative resources. Secondly, we determine investment allocation according to weights of resources with positive tendency and negative tendency in each progressive search. Then we perform dynamically bidirectional search towards resources with different tendencies. Resources obtained through each progressive search are non-deterministic, not validated and with timeliness. We calculate entropy of resources indicating different tendencies so as to improve the reliability of resources. Resources with high entropy are unreliable. Finally, we determine whether *confidence* of recommended resources is greater than the threshold and recommend resources with higher confidence than the threshold to users.

3 Application of Dynamically Balanced Bidirectional Search Service Provision

3.1 Background of Application

In order to test the accuracy and reliability of recommended resources according to positive and negative bidirectional dynamic balanced search service, we take the background of medical workers' treatment of lung cancer as an example to show rationality of our approach. We apply the strategy to current medical resource processing system to improve the efficiency and accuracy of medical diagnosis and decision-making.

The search engine Bing has recommended 64300000 results when we search resources related to keywords including patients with lung cancer, treatment, chemotherapy. Sources of these resources are different including patients with lung cancer, relevant hospital and some academic institutions. Patients with lung cancer don't need to be responsible for their opinions about treatment of lung cancer released on the Internet which make the credibility of these resources limited. Resources released by relevant hospitals have an obvious tendency for their interests which makes current information more confusing. Information from academic papers is more credible. But because of the timeliness of information, previous information may not be suitable to new patients due to further deterioration of lung cancer. In such a complex resource environment, searchers still need to understand and analyze obtained resources to get reliable and accurate information.

3.2 Example of Dynamically Balanced Bidirectional Search

We obtain relevant resources that match to users' requirements from Bing and allocate investment to positive and negative search respectively. There are 64200000 results through searching keywords including patients with liver cancer, treatment and chemotherapy in Bing. According to statistical resources, there are 31200000 results with positive tendencies and 28800000 results with negative tendencies. We assume that expected waiting time (T) of users is 240 min and time spent on each search is 30 min. We assume that amount of items in each search is 20 and time spent on searching each item is 1.5 min. Table 1 shows the calculations of positive and negative bidirectional search investment and times of each progressive search process.

Table 1. Investment driven progressive search towards different tendencies

	Resource weight	Investments allocation	Search times
Progressive search according to "feasible"	0.48	116.6 min	4
Progressive search according to "infeasible"	0.44	108 min	3

We carry out progressive search covering positive and negative directions after getting resources. Taking progressive search towards positive tendency sources as an example, we make the assumption that item of the first positive progressive search is "patients with lung cancer, treatment, Chemotherapy, cost?". Through traversing processing resource architecture, we obtain resources illustrating that patients with lung canser need to pay $50,000, $100000 and $150000 of which amounts are 32900000, 35600000 and 29300000 respectively. Resources occurring at different times have timeliness and we can calculate the timeliness of corresponding positive resources. Results are shown in Table 2.

Table 2. Calculations of $entropy_{T_k}$ and *timeliness*

T_k	Resource	Failure resources	*Timeliness*	*entropy*
2015	689000 $50000	366000 (2012–2015)	0.40	0.11
	714000 $100000	194000 (2013–2015)	0.50	
	655000 $1500000	300300 (2013–2015)	0.50	
2016	734000 $50000	235000 (2013–2016)	0.75	0.09
	811000 $100000	220100 (2014–2016)	0.25	
	709000 $150000	403000 (2012–2016)	0.20	
2017	1610000 $50000	676000 (2014–2017)	1.00	0.21
	1850000 $100000	445000 (2016–2017)	1.00	
	1530000 $150000	219000 (2012–2017)	1.00	

Table 2 shows the entropy of resources at three different time. We calculate *Entropy* of three types of positive resources. It is obvious that the number of progressive search (*S_amount*) is 1 when we carry out the first positive progressive search. The total number of three types resources of progressive search (*Item_amount*) are 32900000, 35600000 and 29300000 respectively. We calculate confidence according to Eq. 7 and results we calculated are shown in Table 3.

We sort results according to confidence calculated and recommend results with high confidence degree to searchers, that is paid $50,000. We set the confidence threshold (T) that value is 11000000. The highest confidence of positive search results is 10577350 that it is less than the confidence T. Therefore, we

Table 3. Calculations of *Entropy* and *confidence*

Search results	$50000	$100000	$150000
Entropy	0.3215	0.1	0.283
confidence	10577350	3560000	829190

return a result that searchers should continue to enter the next progressive search to searchers. Search service will be end when carry out positive progressive search at the fourth time. Figure 3 shows the positive progressive search of various indicators of resources calculation. Similar to positive progressive search, we carry out negative progressive search for three times. If the confidence of resources obtained through each progressive search is greater than the threshold we set, we recommend these resources to searchers.

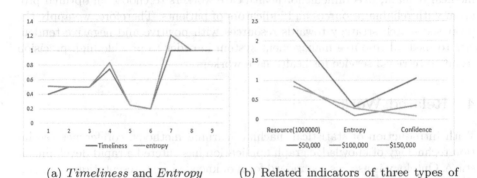

(a) *Timeliness* and *Entropy*   (b) Related indicators of three types of resources

Fig. 3. The calculation of indicators in positive progressive search resources

3.3 Comparison with Traditional Decision Method

Traditional decision-making programs have a low efficiency of resource processing, which make searchers still need to analyze and process constantly to screen some credible resources. For example, for the treatment of patients with lung cancer, searchers use respectively two types of methods to search. Table 4 gives comparison of the positive-negative directions dynamic balanced search strategy and traditional decision-making method for resources obtained on the Internet.

According to experimental results of above examples we provided, we can see that the dynamically balanced bidirectional search strategy towards problems with positive and negative tendencies can improve the confidence of resources through filtering out the ambiguous and unreliable resources. The significance of dynamically balanced bidirectional search strategy towards problems with positive and negative tendencies we proposed is to provide search

Table 4. Comparison of positive-negative search strategy and traditional methods

	Input	Direction	First search results (C: confidence)	Decision
Traditional program	360 min	Any	Chemotherapy (C = 42%) Radiation therapy (C = 51%)	Cannot make decisions
Bidirectional search program	120 min	Positive negative	"Radiation, Therapy, feasible" (C = 64%) "Radiation, Therapy, infeasible" (C = 17%)	Radiation therapy

and decision-making services toward non-deterministic, non-fidelity and super complex resource environment. Due to the massive resources with timeliness in medical domain, it is difficult for health care workers to choose an optimal program with reliable resources and indicators of patients. Therefore, we apply the proposed search strategy towards resources with positive and negative tendencies to medical resource management system in order to provide high-precision resource retrieval service for health care workers.

4   Related Work

With introduction of statistical machine learning methods, coreference resolution technology of knowledge graph application has entered a rapid development stage. Ontology is used as a standard form of knowledge representation in semantic networks [10]. Probase Microsoft used statistical machine learning algorithm to extract the concept of "IsA" [12]. For complex relationships between entities, TBox and ABox are used to simplify and implement relational reasoning based on the reasoning of descriptive logic for consistency checking [5]. For relationship extraction, there are a large number of semi-supervised learning methods [1]. Sen [7] used theme model as basis for similarity calculation and obtained the entity catalog from Wikipedia. Malin et al. in [6] proposed to use random walk model to carry out physical disambiguation of co-operative network data. Wu et al. in [11] chose Wikipedia as a data source to generate training corpus by automatic extraction. Fader et al. in [3] proposed a method of opening questioning and answering (OQA) system that used planned and extracted knowledge base to extract millions of rules from untagged question corpus.

5   Conclusion

Faced with the non-deterministic and not validated resource environment, we propose a dynamically balanced bidirectional search approach to construct search service provision. In the processing of progressive searching, we build a fuzzy vocabulary to filter out useless resources with ambiguous tendency.

Times of progressive searching and amount of items of each search are depended on users' investment. We propose to use entropy of resource sets to indicate the reliability of searching results. Computation of entropy are related to searching times and amount of items of each searching. We validated the rationality of positive-negative search strategy through applying the approach to medical resource processing system aiming at improving the quality of medical service and reducing medical burden of patients. In the future, we will expand the scale of dataset to further verify the feasibility of our proposed approach.

Acknowledgments. This paper is supported by NSFC under Grant (No.61363007, No. 61662021), NSF of Hainan No. ZDYF2017128 and Hainan University Project (No. hdkytg201708).

References

1. Carlson, A., Betteridge, J., Wang, R.C., Hruschka, E.R., Mitchell, T.M.: Coupled semi-supervised learning for information extraction. In: WSDM 2010, pp. 101–110 (2010)
2. Duan, Y., Shao, L., Hu, G., Zhou, Z., Zou, Q., Lin, Z.: Specifying architecture of knowledge graph with data graph, information graph, knowledge graph and wisdom graph. In: 15th IEEE SERA 2017, pp. 327–332 (2017)
3. Fader, A., Zettlemoyer, L., Etzioni, O.: Open question answering over curated and extracted knowledge bases. In: 20th ACM SIGKDD, pp. 1156–1165 (2014)
4. Lamba, D.S., et al.: Building, maintaining, and using knowledge bases: a report from the trenches. In: ACM SIGMOD, pp. 1209–1220 (2013)
5. Lee, T.W., Lewicki, M.S., Girolami, M., Sejnowski, T.J.: Blind source separation of more sources than mixtures using overcomplete representations. IEEE Signal Process. Lett. **6**(4), 87–90 (1999)
6. Malin, B., Airoldi, E., Carley, K.M.: A network analysis model for disambiguation of names in lists. Comput. Math. Organ. Theory **11**(2), 119–139 (2005)
7. Sen, P.: Collective context-aware topic models for entity disambiguation. In: 21st WWW 2012, pp. 729–738 (2012)
8. Shao, L., Duan, Y., Sun, X., Gao, H.: Answering who/when, what, how, why through constructing data graph, information graph, knowledge graph and wisdom graph. In: SEKE 2017, pp. 1–7 (2017)
9. Shao, L., Duan, Y., Sun, X., Zou, Q., Jing, R., Lin, J.: Bidirectional value driven design between economical planning and technical implementation based on data graph, information graph and knowledge graph. In: 15th IEEE SERA 2017, pp. 339–344 (2017)
10. Vol, N.: Ontology learning from text: methods, evaluation and applications. Comput. Linguist. **32**(4), 569–572 (2005)
11. Wu, F., Weld, D.S.: Autonomously semantifying Wikipedia. In: 16th ACM Conference on Conference on Information and Knowledge Management, pp. 41–50 (2007)
12. Wu, W., Li, H., Wang, H., Zhu, K.Q.: Probase: a probabilistic taxonomy for text understanding. In: ACM SIGMOD 2012, pp. 481–492 (2012)
13. Zins, C.: Conceptual approaches for defining data, information, and knowledge. J. Assoc. Inf. Sci. Technol. **58**(4), 479–493 (2007)

A Passenger Flow Analysis Method Through Ride Behaviors on Massive Smart Card Data

Weilong Ding[1,2(✉)], Zhuofeng Zhao[1,2], Han Li[1,2], Yaqi Cao[3], and Yang Xu[4]

[1] Data Engineering Institute, North China University of Technology,
Beijing 100144, China
dingweilong@ncut.edu.cn
[2] Beijing Key Laboratory on Integration and Analysis
of Large-Scale Stream Data, Beijing 100144, China
[3] Laboratory of Parallel Software and Computational Science,
Institute of Software, Chinese Academy of Sciences, Beijing 100080, China
[4] Beijing E-Hualu Information Technology Co., Ltd., Beijing 100043, China

Abstract. In transportation business, the *passenger flow* analysis counts the ridership of given bus stops on given time duration. On the smart card data from the card readers of buses, the calculation of passenger flow faces challenges: the accuracy or the latency is blamed, and the scalability is poor on large volume data. In this paper, we propose an effective method on massive smart card data, in which ride behaviors are modeled and the passenger flow can be achieved and efficiently. Our method is implemented by Hadoop MapReduce, and proves minute-level latencies on weekly historical data with nearly linear scalability.

Keywords: Smart card data · Passenger flow · Ride behavior
Urban computing

1 Introduction

In urban transportation, the *passenger flow* analysis counts the ridership of given bus stops on given time duration. It has been widely applied to find hot spots, improve bus scheduling and evaluate service quality, and is essential to build industrial intelligent system [1]. Accordingly, related research is always hot in academia. Traditionally, smart card data of buses is stored in data warehouse or relational database, and the passenger flow analysis is done by SQL composition or store procedure [2, 3] through statistic model on small samples. However, it still faces inherent limitations on massive data. First, the latency is intolerable when large data involved. To achieve the latest values, the database suffers long time because huge volume data should be loaded, scanned and sorted several times during query execution. Second, the accuracy is blamed due to complex ride behaviors of passengers. With simplified assumptions, traditional methods on small samples [4] could only count short-time passenger flow (e.g., five minutes duration) at limited bus stops. Third, the scalability is extremely poor when data or infrastructure grows.

© ICST Institute for Computer Sciences, Social Informatics and Telecommunications Engineering 2018
I. Romdhani et al. (Eds.): CollaborateCom 2017, LNICST 252, pp. 374–382, 2018.
https://doi.org/10.1007/978-3-030-00916-8_35

In this paper, we propose a novel analysis method for different types of passenger flow through ride behavior models. The contributions can be summarized as follows. (1) Ride behavior is modeled by business rules and statistics, and passenger flow would be achieved accordingly in an efficient way. (2) Passenger flow depicted as MapReduce jobs proves minute-level latencies on weekly data with nearly linear scalability in extensive conditions.

2 Motivation and Related Work

Our work was initiated by *Passenger Big Data Analysis Platform* in Beijing. We collaborated with *E-hualu*, one of the leader companies in China for intelligent transportation system (ITS). We had deployed a bus scheduling system for more than 30 new night-bus lines in late 2014, and were eager to improve the bus departure intervals and the passenger on-board time through Big Data technologies. A record as the data unit contains 13 attributes in Table 1 including three entities, two timestamps and two spatial attribute-groups. Currently, the smart card data was regularly processed through traditional databases, while the execution latency on massive data is too long to endure. It is urgent to find effective solutions, and that is our original motivation.

Table 1. A record structure of smart card data.

Attribute	Notation	Type
card_ID	Identity of smart card	Entity
line_ID	Identity of bus line	
bus_ID	Identity of bus	
begin_time	Timestamp of getting-on	Time
end_time	Timestamp of getting-off	
from_station_ID	Identity of getting-on station	Space
from_station_name	Name of getting-on station	
from_station_longitude	Longitude of getting-on station	
from_station_latitude	Latitude of getting-on station	
to_station_ID	Identity of getting-off station	
to_station_name	Name of getting-off station	
to_station_longitude	Longitude of getting-off station	
to_station_latitude	Latitude of getting-off station	

There is an assumption that the data has been cleaned to eliminate fallacious records. The low data quality obstructs the data analysis and user experience [5]. We employ data cleaning method previously proposed [6] on those massive spatio-temporal data to guarantee temporal consistency and semantic legality.

Database is the traditional technology for passenger flow analysis. Through persistent data storage, the smart card data is processed by SQL composition or store procedure [2]. On the card data in GTFS (General Transit Feed Specification) format, Tao et al. [7] demonstrate a multi-step methodology to examine the spatial-temporal dynamics of travel behaviors among bus passengers. But such technology suffers long latency, because holistic data ought to be scanned several times during execution [8].

To improve the latency, the statistic model is widely used on small samples to predict passenger flow in short-time. Ma et al. [2] build travel probability models on smart card data, and their DBSCAN joint algorithm could identify historical travel patterns and regularities. Zhang et al. [4] propose a Kalman filter method to forecast short-term passenger flow on heterogeneous data (including smart card data of buses). Their accuracy is high only on limited data, but cannot hold on large volume.

Big data technology is being adopted because traditional models cannot run well in continuous and scalable environment [9]. Through Hadoop, the intelligent transportation systems like SMARTBUS [10] and Xiong's work [1] integrate data in multiple layers and views. Through MapReduce on smart card data and bus GPS data, Zhang et al. [11] analyzed the passenger density to infer crowdedness and evaluate the vehicle scheduling, and Wang et al. [12] estimated boarding stop time and bus arrival time. All those works show their efficiency in specific business, but none of them has reported the passenger flow analysis yet, and we have to learn and start-up elaborately.

In brief, on massive smart card data of buses, it still lacks effective methods to analyze passenger flow.

3   Passenger Flow Analysis Through Ride Behaviors

3.1   Methodology

To take a bus at one stop, a passenger would have one of three behaviors: getting-on, getting-off and transfer. In this paper, we focus on the getting-on behavior and its passenger flow.

Definition 1. Getting-on (getting-off) passenger flow. For a bus stop s on any time duration δ_l by interval θ, the passenger flow of getting-on (getting-off) is the count of passengers who gets on (off) any bus b_i at s. $|l| = $ a day$/\theta$, $l > 0$.

The time durations are divided by the time *interval* θ which can be assigned as 30 min, 1 h or 1 day in practice. Therefore, the *passenger flow analysis* in this paper is the calculation to achieve the passenger flow defined above at all the bus stops on any duration. The getting-on and getting-off analyses are similar due to their symmetrical behaviors, so that only the former one would be discussed in details in the following parts.

The architecture of passenger flow includes three layers as a PaaS (platform as a service) fashion.

The bottom is data layer to maintain two kinds of data. The basic data is the dependent items for analysis, such as bus stop, bus line and vehicle id, which is preserved in relational database like MySQL. The smart card data would be uploaded daily from offline files to distributed file system HDFS after data cleaning. Compared with the basic data, the smart card data has much larger volume (1 TB vs. 100 MB) and updates in higher frequency (daily vs. weekly).

The middle is processing layer for analysis execution. Different types of passenger flow would be completed as respective MapReduce jobs. The time interval θ is 1 h by default, and could be adjusted on demand. Those jobs would be dispatched as parallel tasks. In fact, as an open layer, other jobs on those data rather than passenger flow analyses can be calculated here.

The top is the application layer to monitor jobs and get results. The *calculation console* is a web monitor for machines, services (e.g., jobtracker, tasktracker, namenode, datanode, zookeeper), and jobs (states, slot, task counter, load-balance). Some native commands like job submission and halt have been encapsulated as GUI (graphical user interface). The *map service* shows results in an online map, in which the bus stops, bus lines and vehicle trajectories are directly visualized. At selected bus stop, the analysis results can achieve intuitively in a pop-up table. The visual parameters like resolution and zoom can be also adjusted.

3.2 Getting-on Behavior and Its Passenger Flow

As the Definition 1, getting-on passenger flow ought to refer a location (i.e., bus stop) on given time (i.e., time durations).

There are three problems about time here. (1) One problem is to how discriminate a bus' different trips, when the records of the smart card data on the same bus were appended in sequential. A bus has high possibility to drive for service more than one round-trip in a day, and those different trips cannot be distinguished from each other directly. (2) The second problem is how to infer the stop and start time of a bus at one bus stop. The getting-on/off timestamp of passengers varies much due to the card tapping time of passengers. (3) The third problem is how to sensibly count passenger flow if the wait period $[t_m, t_n)$ of a bus overlaps two adjacent durations. For example, when $\theta = 1$ h, $t_m = 8{:}58$, $t_n = 9{:}01$; which is more rational reflections about the ridership during the period $[t_m, t_n)$: the duration $\delta_8 = [7{:}00\text{–}8{:}00)$ or $\delta_9 = [8{:}00\text{–}9{:}00)$?

To solve those problems, we observe the characteristics of data, and propose the following model with the symbols in Table 1.

Definition 2. Getting-on behavior model of passengers. For a bus stop s of bus b_j, the getting-on behavior in any record r conforms these characteristics:

(1) entity attribute $r.bus\_ID = b_j$;
(2) four spatial attributes of $r.from\_station\_*$ is related with bus stop s;
(3) all the long integers of temporal attribute $r.begin\_time$
   (a) can be clustered according to trips of bus service;
   (b) are smaller than the start time of b_j in high possibility;
   (c) are negative skewed because their mean is larger than their SD (standard deviation).

Here, the third one just reflects the facts of three problems above, and we would cope with them individually.

(a) To speed the clustering on those long integers to discriminate different trips, we include an auxiliary condition: for bus b_j, the successive records r_i and r_{i+1} belong to serial trips respectively if $(r_{i+1}.begin\_time - r_i.begin\_time) < \gamma$. We employ the empirical $\gamma = 420$ (i.e., 7 min), because we have learned from the official documents, a bus in Beijing spends at least 14 min for a round-trip.

(b) To infer the start time of bus b_j at stop s, we have to get rid of the skewness of original data. For the data in skewed distribution, logarithm transformation is feasible to find the normality, because it can turn multiplicative effects into additive ones. The calculation is the following procedure:

    i. for any $r_i.begin\_time$, transform it to its Natural Logarithm value g_i;

    ii. on all those logarithm values, calculate their mean m_g and SD sd_g;

    iii. the start time can be inferred as $t_m = $ EXP $(m_g + 2* sd_g)$, where EXP $(x) = e^x$.

(c) To count passenger flow in a time period overlapped two adjacent durations δ_i, δ_{i+1}, we refer the start time t_m got from (b): the getting-on ridership belongs to either δ_i if $t_m \in \delta_i$ or δ_{i+1} (i.e., $t_m \in \delta_{i+1}$). It is sound because the getting-on behavior depends on action of bus start.

Through the behavior model in Definition 2, the getting-on passenger flow analysis can be designed as two-step procedure in Fig. 1, and each step is implemented as a Hadoop MapReduce job. In this figure, the left part of either step is realized as a map task and the right one is a reduce task; each of which requires only one-pass to scan the data.

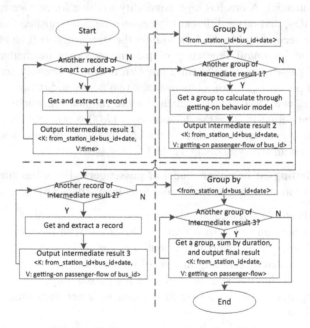

Fig. 1. Getting-on passenger flow analysis

The first step is to achieve the getting-on passenger flow of single bus. It is represented in the top part of the Fig. 1. Here, each record would be extracted by its attributes. The timestamp of getting-on (i.e., attribute $begin\_time$) is divided by two parts: $date$ and $time$. After grouping by the composition of station id, bus id and date, the calculation is done through the getting-on behavior model. The intermediate results could be sorted by time and then be outputted as the getting-on passenger flow of each bus. For example, if θ is set as 1 h, a output could be <3, 00028294, 20151208, 0, 0, 0, 0, 0, 0, 13, 0,0, 25, 0, 0, 0, 18, 0, 0, 0, 0, 0, 0, 0, 0, 0, 0>. It means the bus 0028294 at bus stop 3 on Dec. 8th 2015 has three trips when the ridership is 13 in [6:00, 7:00), 25 in [9:00, 10:00) and 18 in [13:00, 14:00).

The second step is to achieve the getting-on passenger flow of all the buses. It is expressed as the bottom part of Fig. 1. In this step, the output of the first step is read, and each record would be extracted by *from_station_id, bus_id, date* and vectors of *passenger flow* of single bus. After grouping by the composition of station id, bus id and date, the intermediate results could be sorted by time and then be outputted as the final getting-on passenger flow. For example, if θ is set as 1 h, a output could be <3, 20151208, 0, 0, 0, 0, 0, 64, 85, 105,128, 256, 204, 230, 242, 189, 205, 143, 145, 252, 286, 259, 235, 102, 82, 35>. It shows the getting-on passenger flow at bus stop 3 on any duration of Dec. 8th 2015 divided by one hour interval.

The **getting-off behavior model** for **the getting-off passenger flow analysis** could be defined analogously. In that model, the different attribute $r_i.end\_time$ and the bus stop time are focused. The inferred stop time $t_n = EXP (m_g - 2* sd_g)$ on logarithm values of getting-off attribute, because those timestamps are positive skewed and larger than stop time in high possibility.

4 Evaluations

4.1 Settings

The performance and effects are respectively evaluated as experiments and case studies in this section. Here, six virtual machines are used in our private Cloud to implement our method, each of which owns 4 cores CPU, 4 GB RAM and 1.2 TB storage with CentOS 6.6 x86_64 installed. Four Acer AR580 F2 rack servers via Citrix XenServer 6.2 were used for the virtualization, each of which own 8 processors (Intel Xeon E5-4607 2.20 GHz), 48 GB RAM and 80 TB storage.

We employ the smart card data of Beijing buses on eight days in 2013 which contains 24263142 records on 7349 buses of 233 lines involving 3581 bus stops. All the data was generated from the readers charging by distance, and each record contains 13 attributes as Table 1 in Sect. 2. The data has been cleaned in advance by our dedicated method [6]. To design the experiments on data in different volume, we have divided those 8-day data into eight parts by their dates.

Two different ways for the passenger flow analysis have been implemented for comparison. One is our method termed as BD (Big Data), in which passenger flow analysis are implemented as Hadoop MapReduce jobs. The counterpart is a statistical estimation method [13] termed as ODE (Origin-destination Estimation) in the current production environment.

4.2   Experiments

We compare and evaluate the performance through experiments below.

Experiment 1. The data of eight dates is used as the inputs of different volume. Run the two types of passenger flow analysis through both BD and ODE methods, and note their average executive times.

The result is showed as Fig. 2.

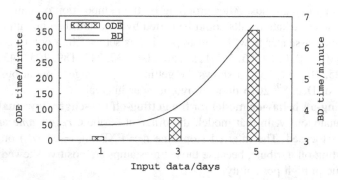

Fig. 2. The comparison of passenger flow analysis in different ways

As the input volume increases, the executive time through both methods rises, but through ODE it is longer than that of BD by two orders of magnitude in either analysis. The volume of three inputs is approximate 3 million, 5 million and 15 million respectively. The executive time through ODE grows sharply when the volume is bigger than 5 million, while that of BD rises almost linearly. On 3-day input, BD only consumes minute-level executive time, while the ODE requires more than 5 h. The low latency through BD comes from the parallel execution of two-step procedure for either analysis. But through ODE, the analysis requires multiple data scans to sort and query, and moreover it has to run on a single machine without parallelism.

We found the too long latencies through ODE, and only BD method is considered in the following experiments to evaluate the efficiency and scalability.

Experiment 2. The data of one day is appended to the input each test, and the executive times for getting-on analysis through BD are noted. For comparison, on each data volume, three different intervals, 10-min, 1-h and 4-h, are set respectively. The result is presented in Fig. 3(a). The average executive time on one million records in each test can be deduced as Fig. 3(b).

The getting-on analysis through BD method is proved scalable on data volumes. On the one hand, when input scales, the increment of executive time of getting-on analysis is better than linearity at any interval. In Fig. 3(a), the time is kept minute-level and not doubled even when the input grows eight folds. That trend can also be comprehended clearly from Fig. 3(b), where the average executive time on give size data declines to the steadiness about 10 s. It demonstrates that the processing capacity of BD method is stable and horizontally scalable. On the other hand, on the input of the same volume,

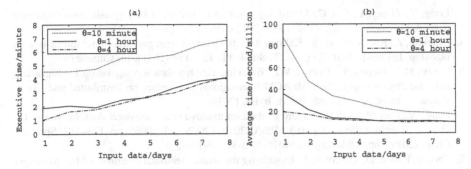

Fig. 3. The analysis under different intervals and inputs

the executive time varies by intervals. The larger interval has lower latencies, because either behavior model of BD method relies on the interval: smaller interval implies more time durations for calculation and requires more time to complete. It is interesting that when input scales, the capacity on given size data converges in any interval as Fig. 3(b), which also proves its scalability.

With the experiments above, our method proves minute-level latency on weekly data in a scalable fashion.

5 Conclusion

Through ride behavior model, we propose a method to analyze the passenger flow on massive smart card data. For any analysis on weekly historical data, our method can hold minute-level latency and keep nearly linear scalability in extensive conditions. It also efficiently shows practical results efficiently. Furthermore, we would research other rider behaviors, and would analyze their passenger flow through respective behavior models.

Acknowledgments. This work was supported by the Youth Program of National Natural Science Foundation of China (Nos. 61702014, 61602437), Beijing Natural Science Foundation (No. 4162021), R&D General Program of Beijing Education Commission (No. KM2015_1000 9007), the Key Young Scholars Foundation for the Excellent Talents of Beijing (No. 20140000 20124G011), Top Young Innovative Talents of North China University of Technology (Nos. XN018022, XN072-001) and Youth Innovation Foundation of North China University of Technology (No. 1473-1743028).

References

1. Xiong, G., Zhu, F., Dong, X., Fan, H., Hu, B., Kong, Q., Kang, W., Teng, T.: A kind of novel ITS based on space-air-ground big-data. IEEE Intell. Transp. Syst. Magn. **8**, 10–22 (2016)
2. Ma, X., Wu, Y.-J., Wang, Y., Chen, F., Liu, J.: Mining smart card data for transit riders' travel patterns. Transp. Res. C Emerg. Technol. **36**, 1–12 (2013)

3. Long, Y., Zhang, Y., Cui, C.: Identifying commuting pattern of Beijing using bus smart card data. Acta Geogr. Sin. **67**, 1339–1352 (2012). (in Chinese)
4. Chunhui, Z., Rui, S., Yang, S.: Kalman filter-based short-term passenger flow forecasting on bus stop. J. Transp. Syst. Eng. Inf. Technol. **11**, 154–159 (2011). (in Chinese)
5. Carey, M.J., Jacobs, S., Tsotras, V.J.: Breaking BAD: a data serving vision for big active data. In: Proceedings of the 10th ACM International Conference on Distributed and Event-Based Systems, pp. 181–186. ACM, Irvine (2016)
6. Ding, W., Cao, Y.: A data cleaning method on massive spatio-temporal data. In: Wang, G., Han, Y., Martínez Pérez, G. (eds.) APSCC 2016. LNCS, vol. 10065, pp. 173–182. Springer, Cham (2016). https://doi.org/10.1007/978-3-319-49178-3_13
7. Tao, S., Rohde, D., Corcoran, J.: Examining the spatial–temporal dynamics of bus passenger travel behaviour using smart card data and the flow-comap. J. Transp. Geogr. **41**, 21–36 (2014)
8. Dugane, R.A., Raut, A.: A survey on big data in real time. Int. J. Recent Innov. Trends Comput. Commun. **2**, 794–797 (2014)
9. Pelletier, M.-P., Trépanier, M., Morency, C.: Smart card data use in public transit: a literature review. Transp. Res. C Emerg. Technol. **19**, 557–568 (2011)
10. Ram, S., Wang, Y., Currim, F., Dong, F., Dantas, E., Saboia, L.A.: SMARTBUS: a web application for smart urban mobility and transportation. In: Proceedings of the 25th International Conference Companion on World Wide Web, pp. 363–368. International World Wide Web Conferences Steering Committee, Montreal (2016)
11. Zhang, J., Yu, X., Tian, C., Zhang, F., Tu, L., Xu, C.: Analyzing passenger density for public bus: inference of crowdedness and evaluation of scheduling choices. In: 17th International IEEE Conference on Intelligent Transportation Systems (ITSC 2014), pp. 2015–2022. IEEE (2014)
12. Wang, Y., Ram, S., Currim, F., Dantas, E., Saboia, L.A.: A big data approach for smart transportation management on bus network. In: 2016 IEEE International Smart Cities Conference (ISC2), pp. 1–6. IEEE (2016)
13. Xuemei, Z., Xiyu, Y., Xiaofei, W.: Origin-destination matrix estimation method of public transportation flow based on data from bus integrated-circuit cards. J. TongJi Univ. (Nat. Sci.), 1027–1030 (2012). (in Chinese)

Ranking the Influence of Micro-blog Users Based on Activation Forwarding Relationship

Yiwei Yang[1,2], Wenbin Yao[1,2(✉)], and Dongbin Wang[3]

[1] Beijing Key Laboratory of Intelligent Telecommunications Software
and Multimedia, Beijing University of Posts and Telecommunications,
Beijing, China
yiwei_yang@163.com, yaowenbin_cdc@163.com
[2] National Engineering Laboratory for Mobile Network Security,
Beijing University of Posts and Telecommunications, Beijing, China
[3] Key Laboratory of Ministry of Education for Trustworthy
Distributed Computing and Service,
Beijing University of Posts and Telecommunications, Beijing, China

Abstract. How to predict the influence of users in micro-blog is a challenging task. Although numerous attempts have been made for this topic, few of them analyze the influence of users from the perspective filtration mechanism. In this paper, we propose a novel Activation Forwarding Relationship Independent Cascade algorithm for analyzing the influence of users. The algorithm mainly consists of two parts: forwarding prediction and activation process. We predict the forwarding relationship by Random Forest (RF) and improve the Independent Cascade algorithm to construct an activation network. The algorithm can filter non influence users during the construction of the activation network, thus reducing the amount of ranking time. By calculating the user's activation capability, we rank user's influence. The experimental results show that our algorithm can achieve 95% accuracy in predicting forwarding relationships. Besides, our algorithm not only saves computing time, but also shows that the Top-10 users in the ranking list have better ability to spread information than the existing ranking algorithms.

Keywords: Activation forwarding · Random forest
Independent cascade model · Micro-blog

1 Introduction

As a large social network platform, Micro-blog has attracted the attention of many researchers on how to excavate the influential users. There are two problems in the mining process: how to define the influence and how to deal with a large number of user relationships.

At present, most of the research on the influence of user identification is based on the PageRank [1] or HITS algorithm [2]. The improvement of ranking algorithm can be divided into three categories. The first is user influence ranking in the different themes or different areas [3, 4]. Weng et al. proposed the Twitterrank algorithm [3] to measure the influence of users in Twitter. The algorithm takes both the topical similarity

© ICST Institute for Computer Sciences, Social Informatics and Telecommunications Engineering 2018
I. Romdhani et al. (Eds.): CollaborateCom 2017, LNICST 252, pp. 383–393, 2018.
https://doi.org/10.1007/978-3-030-00916-8_36

between users and the link structure into count when measure the influence of user. Besides, Ding et al. [4] also improved the PageRank algorithm from the view of topic. In addition, some other researches measure user influence by taking both user inter- action and network structure into consideration. One such work is TunkRank [5], a variant of PageRank. This approach reflects differences between users, more in line with the actual situation of network relations. However, complex interactions lead to high time complexity and space complexity. Finally, there is a way to improve the ranking algorithm is constantly updated the influence ranking according to the time [6, 7]. Hu et al. [6], consider three temporal factors that are BTF, FF and SF, and adopted them to PageRank algorithm. Then, they propose a novel algorithm T-PR. Ma et al. [7] focus on user behavioral characteristics and predict the probability that user will respond using logistic regression (*LR*). However, when the data dimension is high, the algorithm of *LR* is not very applicable.

These ranking algorithms have made some improvements from different aspects. However, they have the same problem that a large number of users without influence in the network to participate in the interactive ranking take up much computing time. So it is important to filter out the inactive users in the network. Compared with the above mentioned work, the main contribution of this paper is to filter the non influence users in the network by predicting the forwarding relationship between users, thus reducing the ranking time of the influential users.

The contributions of this paper can be summarized as follows:

- We focus on how to filter non influential users to reduce computation time. For this purpose, an algorithm is proposed, namely Activation Forwarding Relationship Independent Cascade (AFRIC) algorithm.
- We introduce the Random Forest (RF) algorithm to predict the forwarding rela- tionship between users according to the user's recent behavior and attribute data.
- In addition, we combine the results of activation into the improved Independent Cascade (IC) algorithm and construct an activation forwarding network for ranking the influence of users.

The rest of the paper is structured as follows. In Sect. 2, our approach is proposed. Section 3 shows the experimental results. Finally, Sect. 4 concludes this paper.

2   Our Approach

2.1   Factor Selection

Factor selection is the first step in predicting user activation relationships. In this section, ten factors that influence forwarding are explored, and the importance sequencing of these factors is trained. Then, several important factors are chosen as the influencing factors of forecasting information forwarding. Suppose that the user u is the superior user and the user v is the subordinate user. The ten factors in the Table 1 include the individual features of user u or user v and the interaction characteristics of the user pair (u, v). Besides, some factors are direct and some factors are recessive.

Table 1. Factors affecting forwarding

Factors	Means
F_F	Followers number of u/friends number of u
ST_ratio	Tweets number of v forward u/number of u tweets
ST_topic	jaccard of $v's$ topic set and $u's$ topic set
T_activity	Number of u tweets over a period of time
S_positive	Number of v forward over a period of time
T_created	Registration time of u
T_lists	Lists number of u involved in
S_friends	Friends number of v
T_forward	Average forwarding ratio of $u's$ tweets
T_time	Time period of u tweets (0–23)

2.2 Forwarding Prediction

Random Forest (RF) is a kind of classifier which is composed of multiple Classification and Regression Tree (CART). The training set used by each tree is sampled from the total training set. In the training of each node of the tree, the factors are derived from the random sampling of all factors in a certain proportion. The Random forest training process is as follows. Given a training set N, test set T, random sampling from N to form a new sub sample data. Each training sample $(F_{uv}, \sigma(u, v))$ contains two pats, which are the factors $F_{uv} = \{f_{m,uv} | m = 1, 2, \ldots M\}$ and the classes of the user pair $\sigma(u, v) = 0 :$ *No forwarding or* $\sigma(u, v) = 1 :$ *Forwarding*, where u and v are users. For all the factors, we randomly selected $m \leq M$ factors to construct a complete decision tree. Repeat the above steps and we can get k decision trees ($h_i(i = 1, 2, \ldots k)$). Finally, each decision tree is used to select the optimal classification. For a test sample $F_{u'v'} \in T$, the classification result is got by the way of vote. The formula is as follows.

$$\sigma(u', v') = majority \ vote\{(h_i(F_{u'v'}))\}_{i=1}^k \tag{1}$$

For each user pair $(u, v) \in E$, using the Random Forest model to train the factors of (u, v), we can predict whether the user v will forward the user $u's$ information. If $\sigma(u, v) = 1$, the user u can activate user v and $\sigma(v) = 1$, else $\sigma(u, v) = 0$ means the user u can't activate user v and $\sigma(v) = 0$.

The number of the decision trees and the number of factors selected in the node splitting is two important parameters of the Random Forest algorithm. The training set includes N user pairs and M factors. Each decision tree generates new training set by *Boostrap* sampling. When each tree node is split, m input factors are selected from the M factors, and then the best factor is selected to split from the m factors by *Gini*. Every tree splits all the way, until all the training examples of the node belong to the same class.

2.3   Independent Cascade Model

The Independent Cascade (IC) model is based on the theory of probability and the Interaction Particle System (IPS). Given the network $G(V,E)$, for each directed edge $e = (u,v) \in E$, we predict a value $\sigma(u,v)$. Here $\sigma(u,v) = 0$ or 1 is the state of the edge $e = (u,v)$. If $\sigma(u,v) = 1$, v will be activated by user u. In the IC model, once a user u is activated in step t, it will activate its neighbor user in the $t+1$ step. Besides, each active user has only one chance to activate its neighbor. The diffusion rules of the IC model are as follows. In the $t-1$ step, the active collection of nodes is defined as S_{t-1}. In the $t+1$ step, each active user $u \in d^i(v) \cap (S_t - S_{t-1})$ will activate it's out of the neighbor, where $d^i(v)$ denotes the input users of v. If successful, $v \in S_{t+1}$, otherwise user u will no longer attempt to activate the user v. Repeat the above steps until no user is activated in the network.

Influence is defined as the ability of users to drive other users to forward their information. This capability includes direct activation and indirect activation of the number of users. Suppose that the users activated by u are distributed in $layer_u$ layers, the number of users in the $1 \leq j \leq layer_u$ layer is marked as $Num(u,j)$. The influence of u is defined as the weight sum of users activated at different layers.

2.4   Activation Process

The main part of the AFRIC algorithm is the activation process. For $G(V,E)$, V is the set of user nodes, and E is the set of directed edges. The direction of the directed edge is the opposite direction of following. The output of the node u is represented by $d^o(u)$, and the input of the node u is represented by $d^i(u)$. As shown in formula (2), all nodes and edges are inactive at the beginning.

$$\begin{cases} \forall \sigma(v) = 0, & v \in V \\ \forall \sigma(u,v) = 0, & (u,v) \in E \end{cases} \tag{2}$$

In the graph, those whose $d^o(v) \neq 0$ are selected as seeds. As shown in Fig. 1, $S_0 = \{v_1, v_7, v_{10}, v_{16}\}$. For the seed $u \in S_0$, $\sigma(u) = 1$. Each seed will attempt to activate the users directly connected to it only once. According to the selected factors, if the Random Forest algorithm predicts that the connected user v will forward his

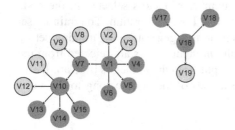

Fig. 1. The activation forwarding graph.

Table 2. Activate relationship and quantity.

Pre_v	v	Num_v
$Null$	v_1	4
v_1	v_7	1
v_7	v_{10}	3
$Null$	v_{16}	2

Algorithm 1. (AFRIC) Activate Forwarding Relationship Independent Cascade

---
Input: Social graph $G(V,E)$, F_{uv}, $(u,v) \in E$
Output: The forecast influential user list $L = (R,V)$
1: select seed $u \in S_0$, $d^o(u) \neq 0$
2: init each $Num_u = 0$
3: **for** every seed $u \in S_0$ **do**
4:   **for** every edge $(u,v) \in d^o(u)$ **do**
5:     $\sigma(u,v) = RF(F_{uv})$
6:     **if** $\sigma(u,v) = 1$ **then**
7:       $\sigma(v) = 1$
8:       $v \in S_1$
9:       $Num_u + 1$
10:      $Pre_v = u$
11:    **end if**
12:   **end for**
13: **end for**
14: **for** every $\sigma(v) = 1$ **do**
15:   link edge (pre_v, v)
16:   $layer_{pre_v} = layer_v + 1$
17: **end for**
18: **for** every $v \in S_0 \cup S_1$ **do**
19:   $Influence_v = \sum_{j=1}^{layer_v} e^{-(j-1)} \log(Num_{v,j})$, $Num_{v,j} \geq 1$
20: **end for**
21: $L = Rank(Influence_v)$
22: **return** L

---

information, the user can be activated by u, and $\sigma(v) = 1$. In the graph, the blue nodes are active users, and the gray nodes are not activated.

In the activation, we need to record each active connection and the number of direct activation per seed user. At the beginning, the precursors of the seeds are null. Once a seed is activated by another seed, we need to change its precursor. For example, v_7 can be activated by v_1, and $Pre_{v_7} = v_1$. After activation, the record table is shown in the Table 2.

2.5 Influence Calculation

The Table 2 records the users who activated more than zero, its precursors (Pre_v) and direct activation number (Num_v). Assuming that the directly activated users by v belong to the first layer, and the users activated by his followers belong to his second layer. If keep on going, we can then calculate the number of layers and the number of active users per layer. For example, the activation list of user v_1 is shown as follow.

$$List_{v_1} = \{(layer_1, 4), (layer_2, 1), (layer_3, 3)\} \tag{3}$$

The activation layer of user v is marked as $layer_v$, and the total number of layer $j(1 \leq j \leq layer_v)$ activations is marked as $Num_{v,j}$. However, the number of users in different layers contributes differently to the influence of user v_1. In fact, the greater of the layer, the smaller its contribution to user's influence. So we count the user's influence as the formula (4).

$$Influence_v = \sum_{j=1}^{j=layer_v} e^{-(j-1)} log(Num_{v,j}), \quad Num_{v,j} \geq 1 \tag{4}$$

3   Experiments

3.1   Experimental Setup

Our data set [8] contains four parts: user information, micro-blog information, user relation and micro-blog relation. In order to verify the changing trend of the running time of the algorithms with the increase of the amount of user data, we need to divide the whole data set. The main principle of segmentation is to make the relationship between users to focus as much as possible. So we divide the data according to the time sequence of user registration. The data sets are shown in Table 3. Set8 is the complete data set. The Set1 to Set7 is the segmentations of Set8 in accordance with the user registration time sequence. As time goes on, the amount of data increases gradually. The aim is to compare the running time of the AFRIC to the ranking algorithms in different data volumes.

Table 3. Data set list.

Datasets	#User	#Follow	#Tweet	#Retweet
Set1	935	21,813	1,659	458
Set2	5,212	110,041	8,802	2,371
Set3	10,934	219,478	17,425	4,979
Set4	20,205	431,241	31,756	9,713
Set5	30,957	658,147	49,014	14,857
Set6	40,137	875,945	64,970	19,987
Set7	50,925	1102,390	80,126	23,901
Set8	63,642	1,391,719	84,169	27,760

3.2   Forward Prediction

We use 70% user pairs from Set8 to train the Random forest algorithm and 30% user pairs to test the accuracy of the prediction. In the process of training, we mainly adjust and optimize the Random Forest algorithm from two aspects: the factors selection and the number of trees.

The ten factors listed in Table 1 are not all high impact factors, so in order to reduce the complexity of the algorithm we can choose several important factors to predict. In this paper, we use the *MeanDecreaseAccuracy* and *MeanDecreaseGini* as the basis for weighing the importance of the factors. *MeanDecreaseAccuracy* is the average accuracy reduction of the independent variables before and after the perturbation, and the *MeanDecreaseGini* is the reduction in the total number of nodes for all the tree variables. In the case of the two indicators, the importance ranking of the ten factors is shown in Fig. 2.

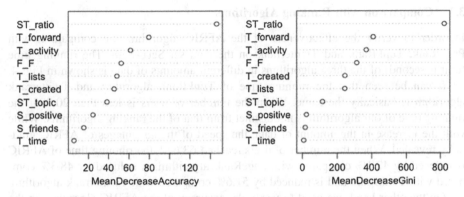

Fig. 2. Factors importance ranking, the horizontal axis is the index reduction quantity and the vertical axis is the factors' name.

As shown in Fig. 2, the importance rankings of factors in the two indicators are consistent and the influence of *T_time*, *S_friends* and *S_positive* are relatively weak. In the importance ranking chart of *MeanDecreaseGini*, it can be seen that the above three factors are close to zero. Therefore, taking the top seven factors can reduce the complexity of the algorithm on the basis of ensuring the accuracy of prediction. Besides, the number of trees in the Random Forest algorithm is an important factor

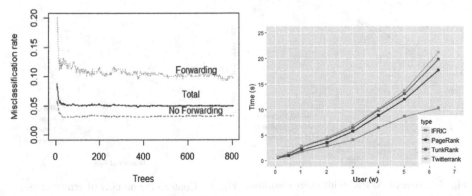

Fig. 3. The misclassification rate of prediction. **Fig. 4.** Time comparison of different algorithms.

affecting the accuracy. In the different number of trees, the misclassification rate is shown in Fig. 3.

As shown in Fig. 3, the green line represents the forwarding misclassification rate, the red line represents the no forwarding misclassification rate and the black line represents the total misclassification rate. With the increase of the tree number, the misclassification rate of Random Forest algorithm decreases. When the number of trees reaches 400, the misclassification rate is almost stable. Therefore, this paper constructs with 400 trees, and the accuracy rate can reach 95%.

3.3   Comparison with Ranking Algorithms

In order to verify the effectiveness of the AFRIC algorithm, we compare it with PageRank, TunkRank and Twitterrank on the data set Set1–Set8. The running time (unit is second) of the three algorithms in different amounts of data is shown in Fig. 4.

It can be seen that the running time of TunkRank algorithm and Twitterrank algorithm is basically the same. When the number of users is less than 20,205, the running time of our algorithm is not distinct from that of the ranking algorithms. While with the increase in the amount of data, the speed of the advantages of AFRIC gradually revealed. When the number of users reached 63,642, the running time of AFRIC is reduced by 42.1% compared with PageRank algorithm, is reduced by 48.3% compared with TunkRank and is reduced by 51.6% compared with Twitterrank algorithm.

On the other hand, we need to verify the accuracy of the AFRIC algorithm on the user influence ranking. We introduce from three aspects of the list's similarity, consistency and the ability of Top-10 users to spread.

We first verify the similarity of the Top-k users in list by the similarity index $Osim$. It determines the repeatability between the Top-k users of the two ranking lists. $Osim$ is defined as follows, where l_{k1} and l_{k2} are the Top-k user lists of L_1 and L_2. Here we choose Set8 as the data set and the experimental results are as shown in Fig. 5

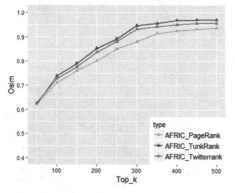 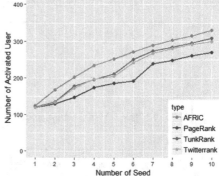

Fig. 5. *Osim* of AFRIC with other algorithm under different k.

Fig. 6. Contrast the number of activated users by different methods.

$$Osim(L_1, L_2)_k = \frac{|l_{k1} \cap l_{k2}|}{k} \tag{5}$$

As can be seen from Fig. 5, with the increase of k, the similarity increases gradually. When k grows to 500, the $Osim(L_{AFRIC}, L_{PageRank})$ reaches 93.6%, the $Osim(L_{AFRIC}, L_{TunkRank})$ reaches 97.2%, and the $Osim(L_{AFRIC}, L_{Twitterrank})$ reaches 95%. Therefore, the AFRIC algorithm has credibility in identifying high influence users.

To compare the consistency of the ranking lists, we propose index *Kendll tau*. It determines the rank consistency of two lists containing the same users. It is defined as follows.

$$Kendall\,tau(L_1, L_2) = \frac{1 - 2|(u', v') : u', v' \text{ is reverse order in } L_1, L_2|}{|L_1|(|L_1| - 1)} \tag{6}$$

where $|L_1|$ is the length of L_1, and L_2 has the same length with L_1. However, the AFRIC algorithm doesn't rank the inactive users. In order to ensure that the ranking lists contain the same users, we remove the inactive users from the PageRank list, TunkRank list and Twitterrank list. In addition, the contrast is implemented on the data Set8. The *Kendll tau* results of AFRIC contrast other three ranking algorithms are shown in Table 4. As can be seen from Table 4, when the number of users reached 63,642, the *Kendall tau* of AFRIC is 0.56 compared with PageRank algorithm, 0.65 compared with TunkRank algorithm and 0.62 compared with Twitterrank algorithm.

Table 4. *Kendall tau* ranking coefficient.

Pairs	Kendall tau
AFRIC vs PageRank	0.56
AFRIC vs TunkRank	0.65
AFRIC vs Twitterrank	0.62

In the last step, we compare the ability of Top-10 users to spread information in the ranking lists of the four algorithms on data Set8. Similar to influence maximization [9], we regard the Top-10 users as the seed set and simulate information spread in the network to get the number of finally activated users. Then we make a contrast on which method activates most users. The seed set size is from 1 to 10, according to the ranking lists of different algorithms. The Fig. 6 shows us that although all the trends are ascending, each time the number of activated users by AFRIC is greater than that by other three algorithms. From the overall activation trend, the number of activated users by AFRIC algorithm is more stable. It verifies the top users selected by our method are really most influential.

4 Conclusions and Future Work

We present an AFRIC algorithm to rank the influence of users in the micro-blog. It is better at running time and spreading information than existing ranking algorithms. The success of our algorithm is from (1) it filtered out inactive users in the network by activating forwarding and (2) it calculated the user's influence through the user's activation capability, which significantly improved the speed of ranking. The experiment results show that when the user amount reaches 63,642, the running time of AFRIC is reduced by 42.1% compared with PageRank algorithm, is reduced by 48.3% compared with TunkRank algorithm, and is reduced by 51.6% compared with Twitterrank algorithm. Besides, the similarity and consistency of AFRIC and ranking algorithms are credible. Finally, we verify the Top-10 users of our list are better at spreading information than that of other three lists. So when the greater the amount of data generated by micro-blog, the advantages of the AFRIC algorithm will be better displayed. In future work, we will take advantage of the user relationship to predict the information dissemination.

Acknowledgements. This work was partly supported by the NSFC-Guangdong Joint Found (U1501254) and the Co-construction Program with the Beijing Municipal Commission of Education and the Ministry of Science and Technology of China (2012BAH45B01) and National key research and development program (2016YFB0800302) the Director's Project Fund of Key Laboratory of Trustworthy Distributed Computing and Service (BUPT), Ministry of Education (Grant No. 2017ZR01) and the Fundamental Research Funds for the Central Universities (BUPT2011RCZJ16, 2014ZD03-03) and China Information Security Special Fund (NDRC).

References

1. Page, L., Brin, S., Motwani, R., Winograd, T.: The PageRank citation ranking: bringing order to the web. Technical report, Stanford InfoLab, November 1999. http://ilpubs.stanford.edu: 8090/422
2. Kleinberg, J.M.: Authoritative sources in a hyperlinked environment. J. ACM **46**(5), 604–632 (1999)
3. Weng, J., Lim, E.P., Jiang, J., He, Q.: Twitterrank: finding topic-sensitive influential twitterers. In: Third International Conference on Web Search and Data Mining, pp. 261–270. ACM (2010)
4. Ding, Z., Zhou, B., Jia, Y., et al.: Topical influence analysis based on the multi-relational network in microblogs. J. Comput. Res. Dev. **50**(10), 2155–2175 (2013)
5. Page, L.: The PageRank citation ranking: bringing order to the web. Stanf. Digit. Libr. Working Pap. **9**(1), 1–14 (1999)
6. Hu, W., Zou, H., Gong, Z.: Temporal PageRank on social networks. In: Wang, J., et al. (eds.) WISE 2015. LNCS, vol. 9418, pp. 262–276. Springer, Cham (2015). https://doi.org/10.1007/978-3-319-26190-4_18
7. Ma, X., Li, C., Bailey, J., Wijewickrema, S.: Finding influentials in Twitter: a temporal influence ranking model. arXiv preprint arXiv:1703.01468 (2017)

8. Data tang: 63641 sina micro-blog data set. http://www.datatang.com/data/46758. Accessed 20 Nov 2016

9. Kempe, D., Kleinberg, J., Tardos, É.: Maximizing the spread of influence through a social network. In: Proceedings of the Ninth ACM SIGKDD International Conference on Knowledge Discovery and Data Mining, pp. 137–146. ACM (2003)

UR Rank: Micro-blog User Influence Ranking Algorithm Based on User Relationship

Wenbin Yao[1,2], Yiwei Yang[1,2(✉)], and Dongbin Wang[3]

[1] Beijing Key Laboratory of Intelligent Telecommunications Software
and Multimedia, Beijing University of Posts and Telecommunications,
Beijing, China
yiwei_yang@163.com
[2] National Engineering Laboratory for Mobile Network Security,
Beijing University of Posts and Telecommunications, Beijing, China
[3] Key Laboratory of Ministry of Education for Trustworthy Distributed
Computing and Service, Beijing University of Posts
and Telecommunications, Beijing, China

Abstract. In this paper, a novel UR Rank (User Relationships based Ranking) algorithm is proposed for ranking the influence of the user. We first explore five factors that affect user relationship. They are following rate (*FR*) factor, activity (*ACT*) factor, authority (*ATR*) factor, interaction (*ITA*) factor and similarity (*SML*) factor. Then those factors are used in Support Vector Regression (SVR) model to predict the relationship between users. We assimilate such predicted relationship into a PageRank based transition probability to identify influential users. The experiments on a real micro-blog data set demonstrate that UR Rank algorithm has better performance and is more persuasive than the existing algorithms.

Keywords: Micro-blog · User influence · Support vector regression
PageRank

1 Introduction

User influence is defined as the interaction of an individual in ideas, feelings, attitudes, or behavior with other individuals or groups [1]. It is of great significance to identify influential users in the aspect of situation awareness, product promotion [2], expert recommendation [3] and public opinion guidance.

Most current user influence researches are based on the PageRank [4] algorithm. Some studies concentrate on incorporate temporal factors into PageRank algorithm [6, 7]. Bartoletti et al. [6] compute user reputation by using an arbitrary ranking algorithm in the most recent time window, and combine it with a summary of historical data. Hu et al. [7] studied temporal dimension in assessing the authority of nodes by adopting three temporal factors. However, they did not consider the difference between users, which has led to the weakness in practical application.

Recently, several researches such as [8–10] have applied interaction relationship of users to the ranking model. Ma et al. [8] focus on user behavioral characteristics and

© ICST Institute for Computer Sciences, Social Informatics and Telecommunications Engineering 2018
I. Romdhani et al. (Eds.): CollaborateCom 2017, LNICST 252, pp. 394–404, 2018.
https://doi.org/10.1007/978-3-030-00916-8_37

predict the probability that user will respond using logistic regression (*LR*). However, when the data dimension is high, the algorithm of *LR* is not very applicable. Weng et al. [9] measure the influence taking both the topical similarity between users and the link structure into account and proposed Twitterrank algorithm. However, they only consider the topic similarity between users, but ignore other factors that influence the user relationship. Ding et al. [10], consider the four relationships between users: repost, reply, copy and read between users and measure the influence of users by random walks of multi-relation data in micro-blog. However, the user relationship changes over time, so the pure formula definition of the user's four relations in this paper is unreasonable.

In this paper, we focus on the prediction of user relationships, which can be regarded as a preprocessing step for mining influential users. Then we apply the predicted relationship to the weight division of the PageRank algorithm to avoid the interference of inactive users to the ranking.

On analyzing the user influence, we organized our studies in tree questions: what factors are closely related to the relationship between users, how to predict the relationship between users and how to apply the user relationship to the influential user mining. The highlights of our work can be summarized as follows:

- We take the probability of comment and forward behavior as the index to measure the relationship between users and explore five factors. Besides, we describe the relationship between each factor and index by real data.
- Using the mining factors, we fit a regression model to predict the intensity of user relationship. We use a machine learning technique called support vector regression. Support vector machine are complex machine learning models which are better suited for data which has more complex patterns than linear regression can handle.
- By using the predicted user relationship as the basis of the weight distribution of the influence value, we improve the PageRank to avoid the interference of inactive user to the ranking.

The rest of this paper is organized as follows. In Sect. 2, we show the UR Rank algorithm. The experiment result is shown in Sect. 3. Finally, we make a conclusion and present some future researches in Sect. 4.

2 Influence Ranking Based on User Relationship

2.1 Factors Mining

The selection of factors is the basis of the prediction between users. The user relationship is affected by the superior user's attributes and the interactive behavior between users. In this section, we explore the impact of the following rate (*FR*) factor, activity (*ACT*) factor, authority (*ATR*) factor, interaction (*ITA*) factor, similarity (*SML*) factor on the user relationship. The user relationship (*UR*) is expressed as the average of the comment and forward probability. For users (v, u), user v followed u and the factors that affect their relationship are described below.

(1) *Following Rate (FR): FR* is defined as the popularity of user u, that is the ratio of the followers number ($FoNum_u$) to the friends number ($FrNum_u$), as shown in formula (1). The higher of the following rate, the higher the probability of other users to comment and forward the user's information.

$$FR = \frac{FoNum_u}{FrNum_u} \tag{1}$$

(2) *Activity (ACT): ACT* is defined as the tweet frequency of the u, that is the ratio of tweet number ($TNum_u$) to the time (ΔT), as shown in formula (2). The higher of the *ACT*, the greater the probability that the information will be read by his followers. Therefore, *ACT* gives us an idea of the likelihood of user's tweet being spread.

$$ACT = \frac{TNum_u}{\Delta T} \tag{2}$$

(3) *Authority (ATR): ART* is represented by user's level. Micro-blog user's level is divided into 48 levels, the higher the user's level, the greater of his authority. The authority degree of (v, u) is divided into 48 intervals from 1 to 48, and the average *UR* value is taken as the dependent variable.

(4) *Interaction (ITA): ITA* is defined as the ratio of number of v forwarded u (Fw_{uv}) to the total number of v forwarded (Fw_v), as shown in formula (3). The interaction intensity of (v, u) is divided into 20 intervals from 0 to 1, and the average *UR* value is taken as the dependent variable.

$$ITA = \frac{Fw_{uv}}{Fw_v} \tag{3}$$

(5) *Similarity (SML): SML* is defined as the *Jaccard* of the two user's tag, as shown in formula (4). $note_u$ is the tags set of u and $note_v$ is the tags set of v. The similarity degree of (v, u) is divided into 20 intervals from 0 to 1, and the average *UR* value is taken as the dependent variable.

$$SML = \frac{note_u \cap note_v}{note_u \cup note_v} \tag{4}$$

2.2   User Relationship Prediction Model

To evaluate the usefulness of the five mining factors, we first propose the support vector regression model. SVR (support vector regression) is a regression model based on SVM (support vector machine). The goal of SVR is to minimize the prediction error. It makes as many samples as possible on the optimal regression hyperplane, but it is not required to be absolute in the hyperplane but the distance from the hyperplane is small enough. Therefore, the loss function is introduced and the definition of the loss function is shown in formula (5).

$$Err\left(UR_{vu}, UR'_{vu}\right) = \begin{cases} 0, & \left|UR'_{vu} - w\phi(UR_{vu}) + b\right| \le \varepsilon \\ \left|UR'_{vu} - w\phi(UR_{vu}) + b\right| - \varepsilon, & \left|UR'_{vu} - w\phi(UR_{vu}) + b\right| > \varepsilon \end{cases}$$

(5)

where UR_{vu} is the value of the optimal hyperplane, and the value UR'_{vu} is the predicted user relationship of (v, u). The constant ε represents a sufficiently small loss value. It controls the fitting degree of the function and the training sample. If all the samples are in the pipeline with a diameter of 2ε, the error of the algorithm is 0.

In order to increase the fault tolerance of the algorithm, we need to set a soft edge. Therefore, we added penalty factor C and slack variable ξ. The final SVR model is shown in formula (6).

$$\min \frac{1}{2}\|w\|^2 + C\sum_{i=1}^{M} \xi_{vu} + \xi_{vu}^*$$
$$s.t. \begin{cases} UR'_{vu} - w \cdot UR_{vu} - b \le \varepsilon + \xi_{vu} \\ w \cdot UR_{vu} - UR'_{vu} + b \le \varepsilon + \xi_{vu}^* \\ \xi_{vu}, \xi_{vu}^* \ge 0 \end{cases}$$

(6)

2.3   UR Rank

Given a directed graph $G = (V, E)$, V is the set of users and E is the set of links. For each directed edge $e = (v, u) \in E$, the direction of the arrow indicates the direction of the following. Let PR_v be the PageRank value of v and $w(v, u)$ be the proportion of importance propagated from v to u. In PageRank algorithm, $w(v, u)$ is normally set to $1/d^o(v)$, where $d^o(v)$ is the friends number of v in G. If u has not follow any others, he will assimilate all the PageRank value of others. Therefore, to avoid the trap problem, it introduces the jump factor $1 - \alpha$. Besides, $d^i(u)$ is the follower number of u, and N is the number of users in G. In the $t + 1$ interaction, the PageRank value of u is shown in formula (7).

$$PR_u^{(t+1)} = \alpha \sum_{v \in d^i(u)} \frac{PR_v^t}{d^o(v)} + \frac{1-\alpha}{N}$$

(7)

In this section, we describe a new ranking function that incorporates the five factors into PageRank. In the PageRank $w(v, u)$ is weight for a transition form v to u, and is set to $1/|d^o(v)|$. In our UR Rank, the main purpose is to predict the user relationship by SVR model and investigate the contribution of user relationship to node ranking by weighting in node transitions. The UR Rank can be rewritten as follows, where R_v^t is the influence value of v in t interaction and UR_{vu} is the predicted relationship of (v, u).

$$R_u^{(t+1)} = \alpha \sum_{v \in d^i(u)} \frac{UR_{vu}}{\sum_{u' \in d^o(v)} UR_{vu'}} R_v^t + \frac{1-\alpha}{N} \tag{8}$$

According to the formula (8), the UR_{vu} is not only relevant to the degree of v but also related to the relationship degree of u and its directed neighbors. Given two users u and v, with u having posted a tweet, the task of UR_{vu} prediction is to predict the probability that v will comment and forward this tweet. Using the mining five factors we fit a SVR model, it is better suited for data which has more complex patterns. UR Rank is summarized in Algorithm 1, where F_{vu} is the factor set of v and u, ε is a small constant.

Algorithm 1. Influence Rank Based User Relationship (UR Rank)

Input: Social graph $G(V, E)$, F_{vu}, $(v, u) \in E$
Output: The influential user list $L = (R, V)$
1: init each $R_v = 1$, $t=1$, ε
2: **for** every user $u \in G$ **do**
3:   **for** every edge $(v, u) \in d^i(u)$ **do**
4:     $UR_{vu} = SVR(F_{vu})$
5:   **end for**
6: **end for**
7: **while**($\exists u$, $|R_u^t - R_u^{t-1}| > \varepsilon$)
8:   **for** every user $u \in G$ **do**
9:     $R^{(t+1)}{}_u = \alpha \sum_{v \in d^i(u)} \frac{UR_{vu}}{\sum_{u' \in d^o(v)} UR_{vu'}} R^t{}_v + \frac{1-\alpha}{N}$
10:   **end for**
11:   $t = t + 1$
12: **end while**
13:   $L = rank(R)$
13: **return** L

---

3   Experiments and Discussion

In the section, we conduct plentiful experimental work to compare our proposed algorithm UR Rank with existing ranking algorithms. We first describe the data set and data characteristics. Then we predict the UR (user relationships) and evaluate the performance of support vector regression. Finally, we propose the evaluation index and prove the effectiveness of our proposed algorithm.

3.1   Dataset

To evaluate the proposed approach, we collected micro-blog data from Sina Weibo [13]. It contains five parts: user information, following relation, tweet information, forward relation and comment relation. In order to verify the two aspects of user relationship prediction and influence ranking, we need to divide the whole data set.

The main principle of segmentation is to make the relationship between users to focus as much as possible. So we divide the data according to the time sequence of user registration. The amount of data is shown in Table 1, Set1 is the training set, Set2 is the test set, and the Set3 is the prediction and user ranking set.

Table 1. Data set list.

Datasets	#User	#Follow	#Tweet	#Forward	#comment
Set1	14605	320095	19358	86384	90157
Set2	7513	178571	9978	45465	48532
Set3	41524	893053	57234	230286	241578

3.2 User Relationship Prediction

Based on Set1, we apply scatter diagram and bar graph to show the influence of single factor on user relationship. The UR is defined as formula (9), where $P_{c,vu}$ is the probability of v comments u and $P_{f,vu}$ is the probability of v forwards u. The details are shown in Fig. 1.

$$UR = \frac{P_{c,vu} + P_{f,vu}}{2} \qquad (9)$$

As shown in Fig. 1, the five factor are positively related to UR. Although FR, ACT, and ATR are the attributes of u, they are also related to the relationship of (v, u). From Fig. 1(a), it is found that when $Log(FR) > 0$, the trend of scatter is quite consistent. In Fig. 1(b), the points are relatively scattered, and when $Log(ACT) > 5$ the correlation is obvious. Besides, the interaction factors ITA and SML are divided into 20 intervals from 0 to 1, they will directly affect the user relationship (UR). As shown in Fig. 1(d) and (e) they are also positively related to UR. However, we can see from (e), when the SML is close to zero, the UR is higher. The reason is that only a small number of labels appear on the platform several times, and the number of them is shown in the (f). In the process of computing the similarity, the labels of some users are not common, so the tendency of interest is not obtained. However, this unusual label may have some relevance. In other words, the computation of interest similarity is 0, and there may be some similarity between them.

When predicting user relationship (UR), we select logistic regression and support vector regression models. Figure 2 shows the relationship between the real values and the predicted values of the two models on the same data set (Set2). The (a) is the result of logistic regression and (b) is the result of support vector regression model Besides, the horizontal axis is the true UR and the vertical axis is the predict UR. The closer the regression forecast result is to the real value, the more accurate the prediction result is. From the comparison results we can see that the horizontal axis in the range of [0, 0.4], map (b) of the prediction points are closer to the real values than map (a). When the horizontal axis in the range of [0.4, 1], the prediction errors of the two models are greater. On the whole, the prediction error of the logistic regression model is 35.1%,

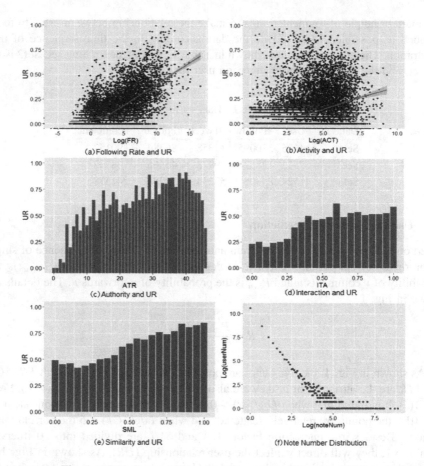

Fig. 1. The influence of five factors on user relationship (*UR*).

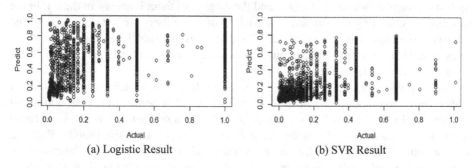

Fig. 2. Comparison of predicted and real values.

and the prediction error of support vector regression is 22.7%. The support vector regression model is more suitable for this problem.

3.3   Ranking Result

To better evaluate UR Rank, we conducted two different types of experimented on data Set3 to contrast it with existing PageRank and Twitterrank. First we compare their similarities in global ranking. Then we evaluate their performance in information dissemination.

(1) *Global Ranking:* The influence ranking list obtained from UR Rank is a relationship based influence. To compare the similarity of our algorithm with existing ranking algorithms, we calculate the commonly used Kendall τ [15] rank correlation coefficient. It determines the rank consistency of two lists containing the same users.

Our algorithm (UR Rank) was evaluated against PageRank and Twitterrank. As shown in Table 2, the UR Rank is more similar to Twitterank than to PageRank, because Twitterrank take topical similarities into consideration. This result shows that UR Rank has a certain fluctuation compared with the other two ranking algorithms, but the overall ranking list is credible.

Table 2. Kendall τ rank coefficient.

Pairs	τ
UR Rank and PageRank	0.52
UR Rank and Twitterrank	0.67

(2) *Information Dissemination:* We further investigate the performance of UR Rank, PageRank and Twitterrank with respect to information dissemination. In this section, we propose four indexes: forward number, comment number, approver number and topic number. For the top 10 users, the mean values of the 4 indexes involved in the tree algorithms are listed in Table 3.

From the statistical results of the four indexes in Table 3, it can be seen that the average numbers of the Top-10 users in UR Rank are higher than those of other two Top-10 users. More specifically, we compare the cumulative amount of the four indexes in three algorithms from Top-1 to Top-100. The results are shown in Fig. 3.

Table 3. Top-10 mean values of the four indexes.

Algorithm	Forward mean	Comment mean	Approver mean	Topic mean
UR Rank	77619.4	25713.4	31026	4.2
PageRank	43376.4	9057	17174.8	3
Twitterrank	45018.3	13224.1	17474.2	3.3

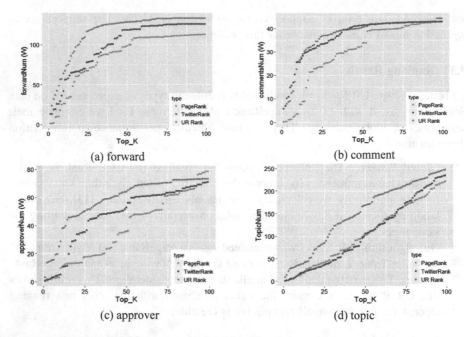

Fig. 3. The cumulative amount comparison of the four indexes in three algorithms from Top-1 to Top-100, ((a) forward cumulative number; (b) comment cumulative number; (c) approver cumulative number; (d) topic cumulative number).

It is obvious in Fig. 3 that (1) the cumulative values of the Top-k in UR Rank are higher than other two algorithms and this is because when calculating user relations, we use the probability of forwarding and comment as the indexes, and (2) when k is small, our proposed method is clearly superior to other two ranking algorithms. This shows that the top ranked users in our ranking list perform better in information dissemination, and (3) The result of our algorithm is much closer to the result of Twitterrank because Twitterrank considers the topic relevance between users. However, in figure (d) we can see that the total number of topics involved by Top-k users in our ranking list is significantly higher than that of the other two algorithms. Therefore, this proves that the influence of Top-k users in our list is not limited by the topic, and they can influence other users from more topics.

In summary, it is effective to consider the user relationship when ranking the influential users and using the support vector regression to predict the user relationship. In general, user relations changing over time, and are not satisfied with pure formula calculation. Therefore, it is reasonable to predict the user's relationship using the recent data of the user.

4   Conclusion and Future Work

This paper introduces user attributes into the influence ranking and proposes the relationship-based influence ranking algorithm. To predict the user relationship, we first mining the five influencing factors and analyze the correlation of them. Then we predict the user relationship using support vector regression model and calculate the weight of PageRank value transmission. Finally, the experiment results on three data set prove that the proposed UR Rank algorithm performs best in the influence spread and they are stable for Top-k users. In the future, we will future explore the factors importance analysis and temporal user relationship prediction.

Acknowledgements. This work was partly supported by the NSFC-Guangdong Joint Found (U1501254) and the Co-construction Program with the Beijing Municipal Commission of Education and the Ministry of Science and Technology of China (2012BAH45B01) and National key research and development program (2016YFB0800302) the Director's Project Fund of Key Laboratory of Trustworthy Distributed Computing and Service (BUPT), Ministry of Education (Grant No. 2017ZR01) and the Fundamental Research Funds for the Central Universities (BUPT2011RCZJ16, 2014ZD03-03) and China Information Security Special Fund (NDRC).

References

1. Rashotte, L.: In blackwell encyclopedia of sociology. J. Demogr. **16**(4), 208–210 (2007)
2. Kempe, D., Kleinberg, J.M., Tardos, E.: Maximizing the spread of influence through a social network. In: 9th International Conference on Knowledge Discovery and Data Mining, pp. 137–146. ACM (2003)
3. Song, X., Tseng, B.L., Lin, C.Y., et al.: Personalized recommendation driven by information flow. In: 29th International Conference of the ACM SIGIR on Research and Development in Information Retrieval, pp 509–516. ACM, New York (2006)
4. Page, L., Brin, S., Motwani, R., Winograd, T.: The PageRank citation ranking: bringing order to the web. Technical Report, Stanford InfoLab, November 1999. http://ilpubs. stanford.edu:8090/422
5. Kleinberg, J.M.: Authoritative sources in a hyperlinked environment. J. ACM **46**(5), 604–632 (1999)
6. Bartoletti, M., Lande, S., Massa, A.: Faderank: an incremental algorithm for ranking Twitter users. In: Cellary, W., Mokbel, M.F., Wang, J., Wang, H., Zhou, R., Zhang, Y. (eds.) WISE 2016. LNCS, vol. 10042, pp. 55–69. Springer, Cham (2016). https://doi.org/10.1007/978-3-319-48743-4_5
7. Hu, W., Zou, H., Gong, Z.: Temporal PageRank on social networks. In: Wang, J., et al. (eds.) WISE 2015. LNCS, vol. 9418, pp. 262–276. Springer, Cham (2015). https://doi.org/10.1007/978-3-319-26190-4_18
8. Ma, X., Li, C., Bailey, J., Wijewickrema, S.: Finding influentials in Twitter: a temporal influence ranking model. arXiv preprint arXiv:1703.01468 (2017)
9. Weng, J., Lim, E.P., Jiang, J., He, Q.: Twitterrank: finding topic-sensitive influential Twitterers. In: Third International Conference on Web Search and Data Mining, pp. 261–270. ACM (2010)
10. Ding, Z., Zhou, B., Jia, Y., et al.: Topical influence analysis based on the multi-relational network in microblogs. J. Comput. Res. Dev. **50**(10), 2155–2175 (2013)

11. Velissarios, Z., Andreas, K., Christos, M.: Real time analytics for measuring user influence on Twitter. In: 27th International Conference on Tools with Artificial Intelligence, pp. 591–597. IEEE (2015)

12. Zhang, J.X., Zhang, R.I., Sun, J.C., et al.: TrueTop: a sybil-resilient system for user influence measurement on Twitter. IEEE/ACM Trans. Netw. **24**(5), 2834–2846 (2016)

13. Data tang: 63641 sina micro-blog data set. http://www.datatang.com/data/46758. Accessed 20 Nov 2016

14. Ritterman, J., Osborne, M., Klein, E.: Using prediction markets and Twitter to predict a swine flu pandemic. In: First International Workshop on Mining Social Media, pp. 9–17. ACM (2009)

15. Knight, W.R.: A computer method for calculating Kendall's tau with ungrouped data. J. Am. Stat. Assoc. **61**(314), 436–439 (1966)

Using the MapReduce Approach
for the Spatio-Temporal Data Analytics
in Road Traffic Crowdsensing Application

Sandhya Armoogum[✉] and Shevam Munchetty-Chendriah

School of Innovative Technologies and Engineering,
University of Technology Mauritius,
La-Tour Koenig, Pointe-aux-Sables, Mauritius
asandya@umail.utm.ac.mu, shevam.mc@hotmail.com

Abstract. Crowdsensing applications are becoming more popular with time. In this work, we present a crowdsensing application for capturing road traffic information to help citizens to get real-time traffic condition. Such real-time information can be beneficial for citizens to plan their journeys. However, crowdsensing in this specific case, generates spatio-temporal data collected from numerous users; storing and processing such data in real-time can be quite challenging. The MapReduce programming approach has been proposed for processing data in this context. The MapReduce jobs used to process and analyze the data captured from the crowdsensing application are presented as well as the design of the crowdsensing application. Implementation of the MapReduce jobs proposed shows that data can be effectively processed and analyzed to present near real-time information about the road traffic flow while at the same time discarding used data which is no longer required.

Keywords: Crowdsensing · Big data · MapReduce · Spatio-temporal data
Data analysis

1 Introduction

In recent years, due to the affordable cost and availability of smart phones, the latter have become a ubiquitous part of everyday life, even in developing countries. Although, mobile phones are primarily used for communication, social networking, and web browsing; smart phones are also equipped with a plethora of sensors such as accelerometer, gyroscope, GPS, magnetometer, barometer, temperature sensor, humidity sensor, proximity sensor, digital compass, and ambient light sensor, as well as camera, and microphone. The sensing capabilities of smart phones allows the collection of a diverse range of data in the surrounding environment of the user. Given, that people almost always have their phones with them and are constantly interacting with them, they can thus capture real-time information (e.g. weather information, traffic information, street steepness, pavement type, noise levels, pollution) which can be aggregated and presented so as to be of use to other people [1, 2]. This people-centric sensing, commonly known as crowdsensing or mobile crowdsensing have opened up a world of opportunities for new applications that can have a huge societal impact [3].

© ICST Institute for Computer Sciences, Social Informatics and Telecommunications Engineering 2018
I. Romdhani et al. (Eds.): CollaborateCom 2017, LNICST 252, pp. 405–415, 2018.
https://doi.org/10.1007/978-3-030-00916-8_38

In [4], five categories of crowdsensing can be distinguished as shown in Table 1. The first two categories, namely participatory crowdsensing and opportunistic crowdsensing, is based on the involvement of the user in the crowdsensing process. Participatory crowdsensing is when users willingly interacting with the application to send data while in opportunistic crowdsensing data is captured and sent automatically with minimal user involvement. The remaining three categories is based on the type of data which is sensed: Environmental (e.g. temperature, air pollution), Infrastructure (e.g. traffic congestion), and Social (e.g. popular TV shows). To engage participation, the application needs to provide incentives for users to share data [5, 6, 7, 16]. In many cases, users participate so as to receive sophisticated services based on the collective statistical information mined from the data.

Table 1. Crowdsensing typology [4].

Involvement of the user in the crowdsensing process	Type of measured phenomenon
Participatory crowdsensing	Environmental crowdsensing
Opportunistic crowdsensing	Infrastructure crowdsensing
	Social crowdsensing

Eventually, with large amount of user participation, crowdsensing applications collect a large volume and variety of data in real-time continuously. The efficient data collection and storage, data processing, analytics, and security is non-trivial in such cases. This is no different from big data collected from various sensors in an IoT system. Data can be aggregated and processed using analytics to provide services and results of new dimensions. The crowdsensing paradigm has pushed analytic possibilities even further given the broad range of applications including traffic planning, weather monitoring, price-dispersion monitoring, and public safety [12]. The knowledge acquired can not only enhance people's day-to-day life but also help utility providers, healthcare providers and the social sphere [13]. In this work, a mobile crowdsensing based application is used for collection, aggregation, and analytics of real-time spatio-temporal data regarding road traffic flow. The mobile crowdsensing application allows users to push their location information as they travel. Such location information provided by commuting users, allows the system to capture average speed of flow of traffic along different routes which can be used to dynamically inform the population at large about the road congestion levels.

Spatial data (e.g. geographic data) is data pertaining to the location and geometry (space). Spatio-temporal data is spatial data which is time-varying in nature [8]. In [9], the authors define a spatio-temporal object as being one which has at least one spatial (e.g. location) and one temporal (e.g. timestamp) property. Typical examples of spatio-temporal objects include moving vehicles, spreading forest fire, earth quake, hurricane, and weather. With technological advances, large amount of spatio-temporal data is now available and it is becoming increasingly important to perform spatio-temporal data analysis and data mining in domains such as meteorology, biology, crop sciences, forestry, medicine, geophysics, ecology, and transportation management [10]. Moving objects (other than cars, trucks, buses, and train) are also more and more frequently connected such as drones, autonomous vehicles, and wireless sensors. However, representing, processing, analyzing, and mining of spatio-temporal datasets can be quite challenging due to the complex structure of spatiotemporal objects and the relationships among them in both spatial and temporal dimensions [11]. In this work, we investigate on the use of the MapReduce programming model to process and analyze spatio-temporal data captured by a crowdsensing application for traffic monitoring.

The paper is organized as follows. In Sect. 2, we present a mobile crowdsensing application for capturing spatio-temporal data from moving vehicles. In Sect. 3, we describe how the real-time continuous data is stored and processed using the MapReduce approach. Section 4 presents some results obtained and Sect. 5 concludes the paper and discusses the future work arising from this research.

2 Crowdsensing Application Design

There are two main architectures which are normally used for crowdsensing applications, namely, the client–server architecture, and the peer-to-peer architecture. Figure 1 below depicts the client–server architecture, where mobile users push information towards the server or requests information from the server. The server collects data from numerous users, perform processing, and responds to users' requests.

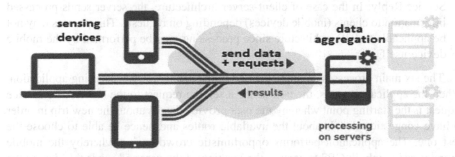

Fig. 1. Client-server crowdsensing architecture.

In the peer-to-peer architecture, sensing devices are inter-connected and share resources among themselves; there is no centralized server. Storage and computational functions are performed on the devices. An example of a sensing application using peer-to-peer architecture is vehicular application used to collect traffic information from all surrounding vehicles and determining the best route.

The client-server architecture has been adopted in this work for the mobile crowdsensing application. According to [14], mobile crowdsensing applications often involves the following six main processes:

1. User Registration: The user registration process is a one-time process enabling data providers (users) to register to the service and give details about themselves for identification. The process is usually performed during the first use of the

crowdsensing application. This process can be by-passed when acquiring the application using Play Store (Android) or App Store (iOS) since the latter has its own registration process which is inherited by the downloaded application.

2. Service Request: This process is performed by the end-user whereby the mobile phone requests a particular service from the service provider (or other mobile phones if using a peer-to-peer architecture). For instance, a request is sent to obtain road traffic details for the different routes available from a source location to a destination.

3. Data Collection: The mobile phones collect data using embedded sensors such as light sensor, temperature sensor, GPS, digital compass, camera, accelerometer, microphone, and Bluetooth as proximity sensor. The captured data is sent to a centralized server or other mobile phones depending on the application architecture for aggregation and processing. This process may be performed on periodically, continuously, on request, or when a certain condition is met.

4. Data Aggregation: The system, receiving the collected data, aggregates the latter with all the other data collected. The centralized approach is used for aggregation whereby all nodes send information to a single centralized server, or mobile phone requesting data. Data is usually aggregated in chronological order [15].

5. Data Processing: The aggregated data is processed using advanced analytic techniques to produce meaningful results and respond to queries. Raw data may require pre-processing tasks such as conversion, filtering, and cleaning.

6. Service Reply: In the case of client-server architecture, the server sends processed information to clients (mobile devices) depending on requests. This process may not be applicable to P2P architecture since processing may be performed by the mobile device itself.

The six main processes are implemented in the proposed crowdsensing application. When the application starts, the user sends a service request to the server. The service request is the starting point whereby the user provide details about the new trip in order to have congestion details about the available routes and hence be able to choose the best one. The application performs opportunistic crowdsensing whereby the mobile phone uses its' inbuilt GPS to capture the location of the user and sends this data to the server with minimal involvement of the user. Data collected from many other users in the same region is aggregated and processed to calculate the level of congestion of routes by calculating the average time taken to travel from one point to another. Such traffic information is the service reply sent in response to the service request. The mobile application was implemented using Android Studio, Google Maps, and Google Directions API on a smartphone with GPS. Figure 2 depicts the use case diagram of the application.

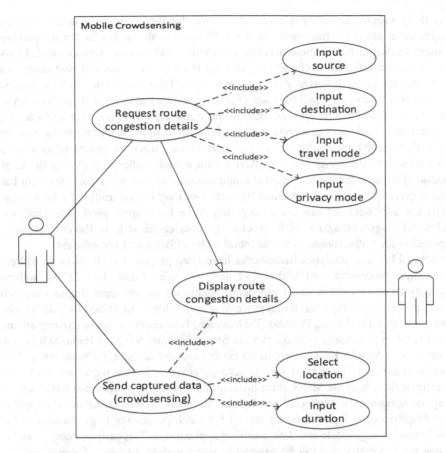

Fig. 2. Client-server crowdsensing architecture.

3   Data Collection, Processing, and Analytics

Depending on the number of users sending the data to the server, the server typically receives a large amount of data continuously. The crowdsensing mobile application may be programmed to send location information every 30 s or every few minutes. However, the crowdsensing application was designed to send data only when the user passes through a predefined point along the travel route specified by the user. This design choice is made such that the crowdsensing application uses less power and do not cause the battery of the smart phone to drain quickly. Moreover, for a higher adoption of the application, the mobile app is designed to send minimal amount of data to the server (identifier, location, time) as it passes predefined points along the route so as to reduce the data network cost for the transmission of data.

As such, there are predefined coordinates on the map along various routes and the user only send data to the server whenever the user reaches these points along the route. The data analytics part in this particular context is quite simple when considering the data provided by one user: by computing the time taken to travel from one point to the next along a route, the server is able to determine the average traffic flow and identify congestion zones (i.e. stretches where the traffic flow is slow). The higher the number of users feeding data, the more accurate the traffic condition can be estimated. However, it also becomes more challenging to keep track of data from different numerous users moving along different routes in real time. Data processing in this context involves real time or near real time analytics i.e. the data has to be analyzed as soon as it arrives so as to have an updated view of the traffic condition. In other applications, data may be stored and batch processed at a later time. But in applications such as the monitoring of road traffic, climate, seismic activity, data has to be processed as soon as it is received by the server [18, 19]. Another important challenge is storing the large volume of data. In the context of road traffic monitoring, we argue that once data has been aggregated, the data contributed by each user may not be useful at a later stage. Thus, the user data are discarded once they have been aggregated. Applying, the traditional programming model to process the data captured from the crowdsensing application for traffic monitoring was found to be difficult and not efficient.

Several big data analytics frameworks have been proposed in literature to address the storage, processing, and analytics of large volume of data. In [17], the authors distinguish between batch based processing technologies and technologies based on stream processing of big data. Batch processing technologies identified include Apache Hadoop, Jaspersoft, Dryad, Pentaho, Tableau, and Karmasphere. Some existing stream based big data processing technologies are Storm, Splunk, S4, SAP Hana, SQLstream s-Server, and Apache Kafka. Depending on the context at hand, different researchers have been using different tools for big data processing. In this work, we attempt to investigate the use of the MapReduce programming model to process the large volume of spatio-temporal data collected in real-time from the crowdsensing mobile application. MapReduce is a programming model for batch processing large datasets and is widely used in large-scale and data-intensive applications. This programming model is simple yet expressive and can be adapted to many real-world tasks. Through the two MapReduce functions, map () and reduce (), it is possible to perform many data analytical tasks e.g. data mining, and machine learning. Furthermore, the MapReduce programming model is capable of handling different types of data and is independent of the underlying storage system [20]. The map function typically processes key/value pairs to generate some intermediate data which can then be further processed by the reduce function which usually merges all intermediate values associated with a key. MapReduce has been specifically formulated such that the programs implementing the map and reduce functions can be executed in parallel on a large number computer for efficiency especially when processing big data. In this work, an Oracle database and the MapReduce programming model is proposed for processing the resulting spatio-temporal data from the crowdsensing application. MapReduce, despite being a batch processing framework, is deemed to be appropriate in this context, since it required to collect at least two readings regarding two points in a route to be able to calculate average speed of traffic thus it makes no sense to process each user data in a stream fashion. The Oracle database has been chosen for several reasons namely, its performance, stability, robustness in handling big data, and its ability to manage multiple databases within the same transaction. The database schema is shown in Fig. 3.

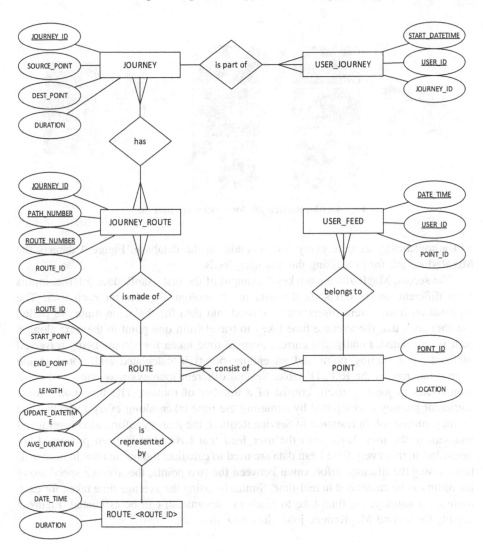

Fig. 3. Entity-Relationship Diagram (ERD) of the database.

Raw user_feeds when received are added as a new row in a table USER_FEED. The user_feeds involve both spatial (location) and temporal (date & time) data. To be able to determine the traffic flow, it is required to determine the time taken by users to travel from one point to the next in near real-time. Two MapReduce jobs are thus proposed to handle the task at hand. The first MapReduce job loops through every record in the table raw user_feeds (if any) and for each record, it converts the data into key/value pair, the key being the User ID and value being the Point ID concatenated with the date and time information. These key/value pairs are then sorted and merged so as to extract the data provided by different users (key User ID). The MapReduce job

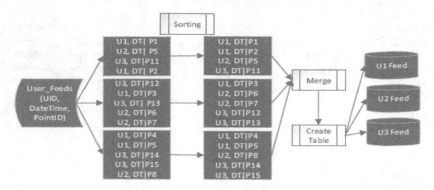

Fig. 4. MapReduce job for processing user_feed.

will automatically execute every few seconds on the database. Figure 4 depicts the MapReduce job for processing the raw user_feeds.

The second MapReduce job takes the output of the first MapReduce job (i.e. inputs from different users) and sorts the data in chronological order for each user. The information from several users are processed and data for the same route are pulled together such that the average time taken to travel from one point to the next along a path is calculated. Finally, the current average time taken for a route being traversed (defined by a starting point and an ending point) is calculated and stored in the appropriate row in the ROUTE table. Several different journeys may consist of common routes (a journey itself, consist of a number of routes). The time taken for a particular journey is computed by summing the time taken along every route that the journey consists of. In response to Service Request, the journey information is retrieved and sent to the user. Data from the user_feed that have already been processed are discarded so that every time fresh data are used to calculate the traffic flow in near real-time. Using the distance information between the two points, the average speed along the route can be calculated in real-time. Similarly, using the average time taken for each route on a journey, the time take to reach the destination can be estimated. Figure 5 depicts the second MapReduce jobs' data flow diagram.

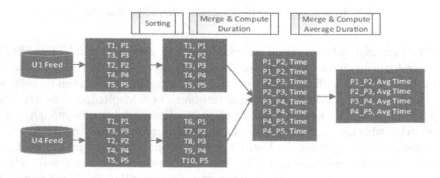

Fig. 5. MapReduce job for processing route duration.

4 Implementation and Results

A simple mobile application was developed to implement the crowdsensing for capturing road traffic information on the motorway M1 of Mauritius and gather some sample data that can be collected in real-time. However, since, it is beyond the scope of this work to deploy the mobile application on a large number of smart phones of users travelling at different points in time, a program (Data Generator) has been designed to simulate and generate input for a number of users. Figure 6 below shows the data processing top-down design on the server side. The processes to be performed by the server have been broken down into 5 sub-modules as shown in Fig. 6.

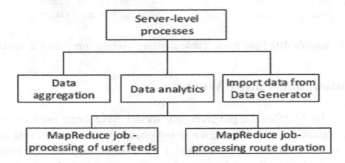

Fig. 6. Server top-down design.

The details for each sub-module are listed below:

- Data aggregation: This module is responsible in inserting new journeys (table user_journey) and crowdsensing data (table user_feeds) in their respective tables for processing.
- Import data from Data Generator: Retrieve data from the flat file created by the Crowdsensing Data Generator and insert the records in their respective tables for processing.
- MapReduce job – processing user feeds: All unprocessed records are arranged and placed in tables corresponding to each user.
- MapReduce job – processing route duration: The average duration for each route are calculated and stored/updated in the routes_duration field. For instance, all crowdsensing data for point AA2 to point AA5 are sorted and merged to compute the duration.

The data generator was designed to generate data from a random number of users (program takes as input a random number representing the number of users). The data generator also chooses a path randomly for each user and sets the start time to be different. The data feed generated for the users were output to a file for import to the database. However, the generator program was limited to generating data for a limited number of journeys for testing. Google Maps was used to display the traffic flow using color codes. A sample of the route table that was obtained is shown in Fig. 7.

Data Grid

ROUTE_ID	START_POINT	END_POINT	LENGTH_KM	UPDATE_DATETIME	AVG_DURATION
AJ2AE2	AJ2	AE2	7	06/05/2017 23:02:07.625000	10
AF1AJ2	AF1	AJ2	7	06/05/2017 23:02:07.625000	10
AA2AA5	AA2	AA5	7	06/05/2017 23:02:07.625000	7
AA5AC2	AA5	AC2	7	06/05/2017 23:02:07.627000	7
AC2AF1	AC2	AF1	7	06/05/2017 23:02:07.629000	7
AF1AG4	AF1	AG4	7	06/05/2017 23:02:07.631000	15
AG4AH3	AG4	AH3	7	06/05/2017 23:02:07.633000	8
AH3AI2	AH3	AI2	7	06/05/2017 23:02:07.634000	15
AI2AI3	AI2	AI3	7	06/05/2017 23:02:07.635000	15
AA5AD5	AA5	AD5	7	06/05/2017 23:02:07.637000	7
AD5AE2	AD5	AE2	7	06/05/2017 23:02:07.639000	7
AE2AI3	AE2	AI3	7	06/05/2017 23:02:07.641000	13

Fig. 7. Sample data from Route Table showing average time taken in minutes.

5 Conclusion and Future Work

In this work, the MapReduce programming model have been used to process and analyze data captured in real-time from moving objects via a crowdsensing application. Such real-time information can be beneficial for citizens to plan their journeys. The proposed data analytics effectively processes spatio-temporal data to determine the average traffic flow along a route in real-time. Used data are discarded so that the system does not end up with massive data tables after a few days. In this crowdsensing application, the data captured is only being processed to calculate the traffic flow, however such an application's data, when collected for a certain period of time, can be for predicting traffic flow and evaluating fuel efficient routes.

Future work includes implementing a web interface to capture other data about the journey e.g. rain, accident, working day, bank holiday and to extend the data analytics on the data captured to predict traffic flow in the long run as well as using currently captured data to find actual traffic flow. Moreover, for such crowdsensing applications to be successful, user participation is important. It is also being planned to investigate on possible incentives for such crowdsensing applications to ensure high adoption. Finally, when users provide traffic information, there are privacy concerns, unless the application is to be used for tracking vehicle movement by an organization. Further work to study and assess the privacy issues is also planned.

References

1. Rodrigues, J.G., Aguiar, A., Barros, J.: SenseMyCity: crowdsourcing an urban sensor. arXiv preprint arXiv:1412.2070 (2014)
2. Campbell, A.T., et al.: The rise of people-centric sensing. IEEE Internet Comput. **12**, 12–21 (2008)
3. Ganti, K., Ye, F., Lei, H.: Mobile crowdsensing: current state and future challenges. IEEE Commun. Mag. **49**, 32–39 (2011)

4. InfoSec Institute: Crowdsensing: state of the art and privacy aspects, July 2014. http://resources.infosecinstitute.com/crowdsensing-state-art-privacy-aspects/

5. Lee, J., Hoh, B.: Sell your experiences: a market mechanism based incentive for participatory sensing. In: Proceedings of IEEE PerCom 2012, Manheim, Germany (2010)

6. Tham, C., Luo, T.: Quality of contributed service and market equilibrium for participatory sensing. IEEE Trans. Mob. Comput. 14(4), 829–842 (2015)

7. Yang, D., Xue, G., Fang, X.: Crowdsourcing to smartphones: incentive mechanism design for mobile phone sensing. In: Proceedings of ACM MobiCom 2012, Istanbul, Turkey (2012)

8. Yang, H., Parthasarathy, S.: Mining spatial and spatio-temporal patterns in scientific data. In: Proceedings of the 22nd International Conference on Data Engineering Workshops (ICDEW 2006), p. 146 (2006)

9. Venkateswara Rao, K., Govardhan, A., Chalapati Rao, K.V.: Spatiotemporal data mining: issues, tasks and applications. Int. J. Comput. Sci. Eng. Surv. (IJCSES) 3(1), 39 (2012)

10. Shekhar, S., et al.: Spatiotemporal data mining: a computational perspective. ISPRS Int. J. Geo-Inf. 4, 2306–2338 (2015). https://doi.org/10.3390/ijgi4042306

11. Bogorny, V., Shekhar, S.: Spatial and spatio-temporal data mining. In: The Proceedings of the IEEE 10th International Conference on Data Mining (ICDM), Sydney, NSW, Australia (2010)

12. Pallavi, A.R., Annapurna, V.K.: Enforcing security for smartphone user by crowdsourcing model using internet of things. Int. J. Adv. Res. Comput. Sci. Technol. (IJARCST 2016) 4(2), 1217 (2016)

13. Gilbert, P., Cox, L.P., Jung, J., Wetherall, D.: Toward trustworthy mobile sensing. In: Proceedings of the Eleventh Workshop on Mobile Computing Systems, HotMobile 2010, Annapolis, Maryland, pp. 31–36 (2010)

14. Talasila, M., Curtmola, R., Borcea, C.: Handbook of Sensor Networking: Advanced Technologies and Applications. CRC Press, Boca Raton (2015)

15. Bhatlavande, A.S., Phatak, A.A.: Data aggregation techniques in wireless sensor networks: literature survey. Int. J. Comput. Appl. 115(10), 4 (2015)

16. Tham, C.-K., Sun, W.: A Spatio-temporal incentive scheme with consumer demand awareness for participatory sensing. J. Comput. Netw. 108, 148–159 (2016)

17. Yaqooba, I., et al.: Big data: from beginning to future. Int. J. Inf. Manag. 36, 1231–1247 (2016)

18. Marz, N., Warren, J.: Big Data: Principles and Best Practices of Scalable Real-Time Data Systems. Manning Publications Co., Shelter Island (2015)

19. Gill, A.Q., Phennel, N., Lane, D., Phung, V.L.: IoT-enabled emergency information supply chain architecture for elderly people: the Australian context. Inf. Syst. 58, 75–86 (2016)

20. Jiang, D., Ooi, B.C., Shi, L., Wu, S.: The performance of MapReduce: an in-depth study. J. Proc. VLDB Endow. 3(1–2), 472–483 (2010)

An Efficient Critical Incident Propagation Model for Social Networks Based on Trust Factor

XiaoMing Li[1,2], Limengzi Yuan[1], ChaoChao Liu[1], Wei Yu[1], Xue Chen[1], and Guangquan Xu[1(✉)]

[1] School of Computer Science and Technology,
Tianjin University, Tianjin, China
lxm696@163.com, {ylmz, chaochaoliu, weiyu,
xuechen, losin}@tju.edu.cn
[2] School of Information Science and Engineering,
Zaozhuang University, Shandong, China

Abstract. Studying patterns of social behavior among users based on micro blogs, QQ posts, and comments is essential to understanding the information propagation process during critical incidents. A common problem of information propagation models based on epidemic dynamics is that they regard the probability of information being propagated successfully across different nodes as a constant. But in real-world scenarios, infection probability varies depending on the trust relationship between people. In this paper, a novel information propagation model for critical incidents is proposed that takes into account the trust factor based on information propagation theory.

Keywords: Trust factor · Cps · Social networks · Incident propagation

1 Introduction

Trust models are classified according to different classification dimensions. For example, the authors in [1] classified existing trust models into six categories. The authors in [2] performed fine-grained classification of trust models, and the categories included BeliefmM [3, 4], a straightforward mathematical formula model [5], a fuzzy theory-based model [6], a Bayesian model [7], and recommendation algorithms based on the relationship and depth of relationship [7–9], where trust factor is computed based on the social relationship. In [10], the authors divided trust into two categories: trust among friends and trust based on similarity. A trust recommendation method based on a reliable path in the social network was presented in [11]. A recommendation-based trust chain model was developed in [12]. This model could inhibit the behavior of dishonest recommendation nodes effectively. However, their work did not rely on the information propagation process that is exhibited across social networks with different trust factors during critical and normal incidents.

The work in this paper intends to address the above limitations. We jointly consider information propagation data during critical and normal incidents, and use a trust-based

© ICST Institute for Computer Sciences, Social Informatics and Telecommunications Engineering 2018
I. Romdhani et al. (Eds.): CollaborateCom 2017, LNICST 252, pp. 416–424, 2018.
https://doi.org/10.1007/978-3-030-00916-8_39

information propagation model to indicate the difference in information propagation with varying trust factor in critical and normal incidents.

2 Data Sets

Data from two typical real-world networks (Sina micro blog and QQ Zone) are selected as the data sets for simulations. Sina micro blog has become one of China's most used micro blogs. We collected information propagation records from 576 volunteers through QQ Zone and Sina micro blog during crisis and normal incidents that occurred between Jan. 1, 2008 and Mar. 31, 2013 [13]. Data time stamps are accurate to within a second. For the sake of experiment, posts from public accounts are removed to simplify the data. The Baidu local news service (news.baidu.com) is used to search for news across the country for the time of data sets in critical incidents. Incidents include emergencies like "explosion", "earthquake", and "group incidents", and ordinary incidents like "BRT is put in operation", "festival shows", and "concerts". These words are used as keywords to extract the data. Table 1 shows the information propagation for the two data sets.

Table 1. Data sources

Source	Nodes	Side	Diameter	Clustering coefficient	Density	Weighted degree
Micro blog Sina	958006	6156091	4	0.022	0.001	20.63
QQ zone	820484	16044572	5	0.107	0.01	34.629

3 Modeling

The trust-based SEIR model is used to study information propagation across different social networks during critical and normal incidents. Data from QQ Zone and Weibo constitutes an information propagation network, where each node represents a user in the network, the degree of a node refers to the number of users for the node, and the edge denotes communication between a pair of nodes. We define all nodes to have four states: susceptible (S), infected (I), immune to the propagated message (R), and unknown after infection (E). Depending on the trust factor g, state E is likely to change to R or S [14].

Consider a network with $N(t)$ nodes at time t. Then, we have:

$$S(t) + E(t) + I(t) + R(t) = N(t) \tag{1}$$

Assume that node j is at state E at time t. Let P_{es}^j denote the probability that node j turns from E to S at time $[t, t + \Delta t]$, and P_{er}^j denote the probability that node j turns from E to R at time $[t, t + \Delta t]$. Then, we have $P_{ss}^j + P_{se}^j = 1$.

According to the definition, a node turns from E to S at a probability P. Then, we have:

$$P_{se}^{j} = \Delta t p(t) \tag{2}$$

where $P(t) = g\beta\frac{I(t)}{N(t)}$, g denotes the trust factor that a node turns from E to S or R, β denotes the node degree, $\frac{I(t)}{N(t)}$ denotes the ratio of infected nodes to the total number of nodes in the network at time t, and P(t) is in the range [0, 1].

Similarly, we can obtain node expressions for state E at time $[t, t + \Delta t]$.

$$E(t+\Delta t) = E(t) + Gs(t)p_{se} - E(t)p_{ei} - E(t)p_{es}$$
$$= E(t) + gS(t)\Delta\beta\frac{I(t)}{N(t)} - gE(t)\Delta t\varepsilon - gE(t)\Delta t\gamma \tag{3}$$

Since unknown node E(t) is likely to turn into I(t) or R(t) under the influence of propagation time and trust among friends, we define a function as follows.

The trust factor of node a in its social network L is computed as:

$$g(a,L) = \frac{1}{\sum_{\substack{b \in V(L) \\ b \neq a}} g(b,L)} \sum_{\substack{b \in V(L) \\ b \neq a}} (g(b,L) \times e_{ba}) \tag{4}$$

where g(a, L) denotes the trust factor of node a in social network L, V(L) denotes the set of all nodes in L, and e_{ba} denotes the direct trust factor of b for a. If there is no direct interaction between b and a, then $e_{ba} = 0$.

In a social network with n nodes, g(a, L) can be computed through iterations. The steps are as follows [15]:

Step 1:   The trust factor g(a, L) for each node in the social network is set to 0.5.

Step 2:   Update g(a, L) of node a in the social network via e_{ba} in $\overline{g(i,R)}$ using Eq. (4):

$$\overline{g(a,L)} = \frac{1}{\sum_{\substack{b \in V(L) \\ b \neq a}} g(b,L)} \sum_{\substack{b \in V(L) \\ b \neq a}} (g(b,L) \times e_{ba}) \tag{5}$$

Step 3:   All nodes in the social network can be updated iteratively. The value of g(a, L) converges to $\overline{g(a,L)}$. Hence, $g(a,L) = \overline{g(a,L)}$, which yields the trust factor g:

$$g = s(a,L)|a \in V(r) \tag{6}$$

Based on the above equations, when $\Delta t \to 0$, we have:

$$E' = \{s(a, L) | a \in V(r)\} \left(\beta \frac{I(t)}{N(t)} S(t) - \varepsilon E(t) - \gamma E(t) \right) \tag{7}$$

where $g \in [0, 1]$. The higher the value of g, the higher the probability that a message is sent to other individuals. This means that the message is spread more quickly to more nodes.

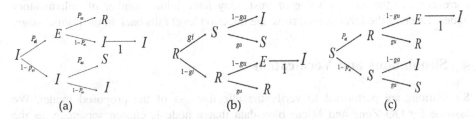

(a)   (b)   (c)

Fig. 1. The probability tree on the graph describes the states of dynamics in different trust networks, i.e. susceptible (S), infected (I), immune to the propagated message (R), and unknown after infection (E). gi is the probability of node infection in the case of high trust degree, ga is the probability of node infection in the case of low trust, and gu is the probability of infected node turning to R due to the influence of the trust degree.

Based on this selected scheme, a person can have four different states, i.e., susceptible (S), infected (I), immune to the propagated message (R), and unknown after infection (E). We suggest using the probability tree, as shown on Fig. 1, to reveal the possible states of the nodes and their changes based on trust. According to the total probabilities of different states given on Fig. 1, the MMCA equation of coupling dynamics in multiplexing can be derived.

$$ga(t) = \prod_j (1 - a_{ji} p_j^I(t) p_{is})$$

$$gu(t) = \prod_j (1 - a_{ji} p_j^I(t) p_{ir}) \tag{8}$$

Using Eq. 7 we can develop the Microscopic Markov Chains for the coupled processes for each node i as following:

$$p_i^R(t+1) = p_i^I(t) p_{ei}\mu + p_i^R(t) gi(t) gu(t) + p_i^S(t) p_{ei} gu(t)$$
$$p_i^S(t+1) = p_i^I(t)(1 - p_{ei}) p_{es} + p_i^R(1 - gi(t)) ga(t) + p_i^S(t)(1 - p_{ei}) ga(t)$$
$$p_i^I(t+1) = p_i^I(t)(1 - p_{es}) + p_i^R[(1 - gi(t))(1 - ga(t)) + gi(t)(1 - gu(t))]$$
$$+ p_i^S(t)[p_{ei}(1 - gu(t)) + (1 - \delta)(1 - ga(t))] \tag{9}$$

The MMCA can be extended near the critical point, assuming that the probability of the node is the same in the Sina Weibo and QQ zones. Using stationarity we are now in the position of computing the on set of the epidemic β_c Near the critical point the MMCA can be expanded assuming that the probability of nodes to be infected is $p_i^I = \varepsilon_I \leq 1$. Inserting this in Eq. 8 and we obtain:

$$\sum_j \left[(1 - (1 - \gamma)i)g_{ji} - \frac{p_{es}}{\beta^{p_{es}}}p_{ei}\right]\varepsilon_j = 0 \tag{10}$$

Even if there are only two different phases in the steady state, for those nodes who correspond to the specific value of trust, they have initial number of inflammatory nodes. Later, as the level of trust rises, the infection level falls back to the normal stage.

4 Simulations and Verification

Simulations are performed to verify the effectiveness of the proposed model. We assume for QQ Zone and Micro blog data that a node is chosen separately as the promulgator to initiate information propagation and that all remaining nodes are unknown nodes.

4.1 Analysis of Time on Information Propagation

The trust factor of the model, g, is set to 0.5 in order to observe the number of the four types of nodes as a function of time. As shown in Fig. 2, due to widespread publicity, the number of susceptible nodes S(t) dwindles quickly in the initial stage for Weibo and QQ Zone. This means that information is spread very quickly across the social network, and that the number of immune nodes R(t) increases quickly in the initial stage until it approaches 1, indicating that all users receive this information. As shown in Fig. 2, a peak occurs earlier in QQ Zone than in Weibo. But a message in Weibo is spread to more nodes than in QQ Zone because QQ Zone relies more so on a circle of acquaintances than Weibo. Most nodes in QQ Zone are friends, family members, or colleagues. Hence, QQ Zone users can spread information more quickly or be immune to the information.

4.2 Influence of Trust Factor on the Promulgating Node

Simulations are conducted on critical and normal incidents across different data sets to explore the influence of trust factor on the promulgating node. The trust parameter is determined by analyzing simulation results obtained with varying trust factors. In order to discuss the influence of trust factor on information propagation, a node is randomly chosen as the source of information propagation. We set the number of people as N = 10,000, ε = 0.5, γ = 0.5, and p = 0.5. We observe the variation in the number of promulgating nodes with time in each data set. Based on Eqs. (4–9), we analyze the simulation results during critical and normal incidents when the trust factor is 0.2, 0.4, 0.6, and 0.8.

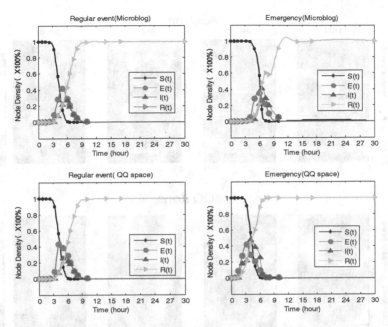

Fig. 2. Black, red, blue, and green lines represent the susceptible node, unknown node, infected node, and immune node, respectively. The number of nodes as a function of time within 30 h, given a trust factor of 0.5 for each node, are shown. (Color figure online)

From Fig. 3, we can see that the propagation range of activities is relatively small when the trust threshold $g = 0.4$, which indicates that the current activity has no reliable or unreliable nodes. However, when we increase the influence of reliable neighbors, the proportion of active nodes rises rapidly when the threshold of trust equals to 0.8, which indicates that the nodes easily cover the entire propagation area.

Simulations conducted with a trust factor of 0.8 show that, during critical incidents, information propagation via QQ Zone matches the simulation model well, but information propagation via Macro-blog only partially matches the simulation model. This agrees with reality, because during crisis incidents people tend to send a message to old acquaintances and accept a message from whom they trust. An exception is the case of group incidents, when the model matches the two data sets well. This means that after a group incident, if the trust factor reaches a threshold, people tend to follow the herd or put too much trust in who they think is reliable, rather than making their own decision based on information they have. As a result, individuals may be influenced or incited during group incidents. But at some time after the crisis incident, the two data sets show almost the same response and match the simulation well. This is consistent with reality because at some time after the crisis happens, the truth comes out and thus only the true message is accepted. An exception is with communication censorship, where the amount of information propagation in Macro-blog and QQ Zone slumps during crisis incidents.

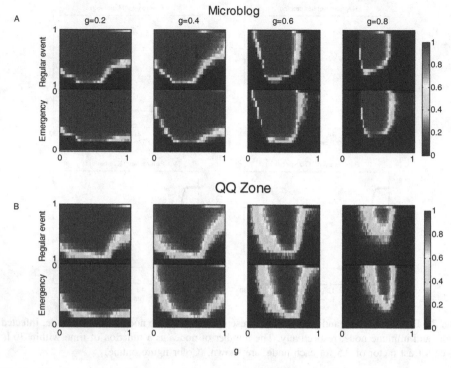

Fig. 3. The figure shows the results of the model SEIR based on the influence of trust factor g in two different social networks of QQ Zone and Micro-blog, when the trust factor is 0.2, 0.4, 0.6, and 0.8. The first line presents the results of simulating routine events in monte carlo, and the second one presents the results of emergency events by the monte carlo simulation.

The simulation model is more consistent with real-world data from the old acquaintance-based QQ Zone. This agrees with reality because during critical incidents, people tend to trust friends rather than strangers.

4.3   Comparison of Trust-Based SEIR and Traditional SEIR

In this subsection, we compare trust-based SEIR and traditional SEIR models. Figure 4 shows a comparison of the two models during critical incidents for a trust factor of 0.8 and also during normal incidents for a trust factor of 0.6. Due to the existence of trust factor in the trust-based SEIR model, information propagation varies in terms of propagation speed and scope with trust factor. Hence, the trust-based SEIR model takes more time to reach stability. In fact, information propagation behavior among people varies with trust factor during critical and normal incidents.

Figure 4 shows information propagation in QQ Zone with the trust-based SEIR model. The promulgating nodes reach the peak earlier than Weibo with a smaller trust factor. This agrees with reality because users of QQ Zone trust information from one another more than users of Weibo. Also, QQ Zone users are more prone to be

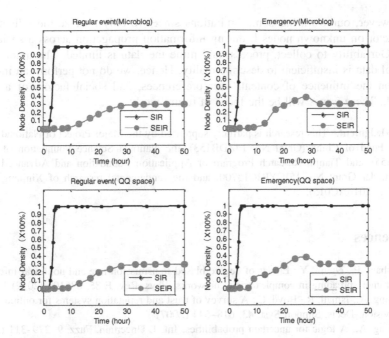

Fig. 4. Black lines represent the variation of promulgating nodes in the SEIR model as a function of time, and red lines represent the variation of promulgating nodes in the trust-based SEIR model as a function of time. (Color figure online)

influenced by other users in the social network. As a result, if one user posts inaccurate information, other friends may respond and comment. In other words, the false information fabricated by one user of the social network may be accepted by many other users in the same network. But, the SEIR model assumes that most nodes accept a certain message without taking trust factor into account. This disagrees with reality. As shown in Fig. 4, the curve of the SEIR model for QQ Zone is similar to that of Weibo for both critical and normal incidents; the promulgating nodes stabilize at the peak level soon. Hence, SEIR is an ideal model, while trust-based SEIR is more consistent with reality.

5   Conclusions and Future Work

A trust-based model of information propagation across a social network is proposed using data sets from QQ Zone and Sina Weibo. The proposed model is helpful for understanding information propagation mechanisms of social networks, exploring key factors that influence information propagation, and ascertaining propagation patterns of social network user relationships during different incidents given different trust factors. Moreover, our work offers guidance on prediction and direction development for diverse real-world incidents, and provides insight into crisis management and public opinion guidance for decision makers.

However, our work has some limitations since we only analyze the influence of trust factor on unknown nodes E during information propagation across a social network. Our ability to collect, process, and mine the data is limited. The amount and scope of data is insufficient to describe reality. Hence, we do not perform an in-depth study on the influence of content, user preferences, and social factors of a social network. These issues will be the focus of future work.

Acknowledgment. This research is partially supported by the Major Project of National Social Science Fund of China (Grant No. 14ZDB153), the National Science Foundation of China (61572355), and Tianjin Research Program of Application Foundation and Advanced Technology under Grant No. 15JCYBJC15700, and the fundamental research of Xinjiang Corps (Grant No. 2016AC015).

References

1. Roshani, F., Naimi, Y.: Effects of degree-biased transmission rate and nonlinear infectivity on rumor spreading in complex social networks. Phys. Rev. E **85**, 036109 (2012)
2. Jøsang, A., Ismail, R., Boyd, C.: A survey of trust and reputation systems for online service provision. Decis. Support Syst. **43**, 618–644 (2007)
3. Jøsang, A.: A logic for uncertain probabilities. Int. J. Uncertain. Fuzz. **9**, 279–311 (2001)
4. Yu, B., Singh, M.P.: An evidential model of distributed reputation management. In: Proceedings of the First International Joint Conference on Autonomous Agents and Multiagent Systems, Bologna, Italy, July 15–19, 2002, pp. 294–301 (2002)
5. Resnick, P., Kuwabara, K., Zeckhauser, R., Friedman, E.: Reputation systems. Commun. ACM **43**, 45–48 (2000)
6. Wang, Y., Vassileva, J.: Bayesian network-based trust model. In: Proceedings of IEEE/WIC International Conference on Web Intelligence, Halifax, NS, Canada, Canada, 27 October 2003, pp. 372–378 (2003)
7. Alves, L.G., Ribeiro, H.V., Lenzi, E.K., Mendes, R.S.: Distance to the scaling law: a useful approach for unveiling relationships between crime and urban metrics. PLoS ONE **8**, e69580 (2013)
8. Song, X., Yan, X.: Influencing factors of emergency information spreading in online social networks: a simulation approach. J. Homel. Secur. Emerg. Manag. **9**, 1–14 (2012)
9. Kenett, D.Y., Portugali, J.: Population movement under extreme events. Proc. Natl. Acad. Sci. USA **109**, 11472–11473 (2012)
10. Lu, X., Bengtsson, L., Holme, P.: Predictability of population displacement after the 2010 Haiti earthquake. Proc. Natl. Acad. Sci. USA **109**, 11576–11581 (2012)
11. Wesolowski, A., et al.: Quantifying the impact of human mobility on malaria. Science **338**, 267–270 (2012)
12. Clauset, A., Gleditsch, K.S.: The developmental dynamics of terrorist organizations. PLoS ONE **7**, e48633 (2012)
13. Fu, Z., Ren, K., Shu, J., Sun, X., Huang, F.: Enabling personalized search over encrypted outsourced data with efficiency improvement. IEEE Trans. Parallel Distr. **27**, 2546–2559 (2016)
14. Ma, T., et al.: Social network and tag sources based augmenting collaborative recommender system. IEICE Trans. Inf. Syst. **98**, 902–910 (2015)
15. Xie, S., Wang, Y.: Construction of tree network with limited delivery latency in homogeneous wireless sensor networks. Wirel. Pers. Commun. **78**, 231–246 (2014)

Impact of the Important Users on Social Recommendation System

Zehua Zhao[1,2], Min Gao[1,2(✉)], Junliang Yu[1,2], Yuqi Song[1,2], Xinyi Wang[1,2], and Min Zhang[3]

[1] Key Laboratory of Dependable Service Computing in Cyber Physical Society, Chongqing University, Ministry of Education, Chongqing 400044, China
{zhzhao,gaomin,yu.jl,songyq,xywang}@cqu.edu.cn
[2] School of Software Engineering, Chongqing University, Chongqing 400044, China
[3] Changle Bowen School, Dezhou 262400, Shandong, China
zhangliuyiming@163.com

Abstract. Recommendation methods have attracted extensive attention recently because they intent to alleviate the information overload problem. Among them, the social recommendation methods have become one of the popular research fields because they are benefit to solve the cold start problem. In social recommendation systems, some users are of great significance, because they usually have decisive impacts on the recommendation results. However, it is still lack of research on how the important users make influence to recommendation methods. This paper presents three types of important users and utilizes three social frequently-used recommendation methods to analyze the influence from multiple perspectives. The experiments demonstrate that all the recommendation methods achieve better performance with important users, and the important neighbor users have the greatest impact on the recommendation methods.

Keywords: Recommendation systems · Social network
Important users

1 Introduction

Nowadays, people have entered an era of information overload [1,2]. To help users find the information they want, researchers have designed and developed the search engines and the recommender system. Unlike the search engine which has specific requirements for its input, the recommender system has become an inseparable part of people's daily life because of its automation, convenience and high efficiency.

The common recommender systems are divided into three categories: content based recommender systems, collaborative filtering [3] based recommender systems and hybrid recommender systems [4]. Existing collaborative filtering methods can be categorized into memory-based methods and model-based

I. Romdhani et al. (Eds.): CollaborateCom 2017, LNICST 252, pp. 425–434, 2018.
https://doi.org/10.1007/978-3-030-00916-8_40

methods [5–7]. Model-based methods are very fast once the parameters of the model are learnt. The bottleneck for model-based methods is the training phase, while in memory-based methods there is no training, but the prediction (test) phase is slower [8]. So model based algorithm is more suitable for big data. In order to improve the efficiency of the experiment, the three recommendation methods used in this paper are the model-based method.

Although the recommendation methods have been greatly supplemented and improved, there are still a few serious problems. For example, when a user's rating vector is extremely sparse, it is difficult to recommend the product to the user accurately. This is "cold start problem". To alleviate this problem, researchers try to integrate social information into recommender algorithms that form social recommender algorithms such as SoRec [9] and TrustMF [3].

In social recommendation, an important step is to filter important users. The so-called "important users" means those who play a crucial role in the recommender system and have a decisive impact on the sales of certain products. It can be seen that understanding the impact of important users on the social recommendation system will help us make better use of the important users and produce better recommendation results. But so far, there is little research in this area, so we choose comparative experiments to analyze the impact of important users on social recommender systems scientifically.

The contributions of this paper are as follows. (1) We propose three types of important users based on the reality of online social networks. (2) Compared the impact of different types of important users through different recommendation methods, and found that the important neighbor users have the greatest impact on the methods.

The rest of the paper is organized as follows: Some related work is discussed in Sect. 2. We introduce the methods of filtering important users in Sect. 3. Then, the experiments are reported in Sect. 4. Finally, we conclude the paper and present some directions for future work in Sect. 5.

2   Related Work

In this section, we will introduce the recommendation methods and the filtering methods for important users, especially three social recommendation methods which will be used in the experiments.

2.1   Recommendation Methods

Normally, the input of the social recommendation method includes a social network (as shown in Fig. 1) and a user-item rating matrix (as shown in Fig. 2). In the social network, it contains a set of nodes $u_i \in U$ which represent the users and a set of edges $s_{ik} \in (0, 1]$ which represent the trust weight from user i to user k (in this paper, we use the adjacency matrix of social trust graph to represents the social network, and called this adjacency matrix as user-user trust matrix). In the user-item rating matrix, it contains a set of users $u_i \in U$, a set of items

$v_j \in V$ and a set of rating records $r_{ij} \in R$ (r_{ij} shows how much the user i prefers the item j, in this paper, $r_{ij} \in [1,6]$, where "1" represents the least preferred and "6" indicates the preference. If the user i has no rated on the item j, then r_{ij} is "?").

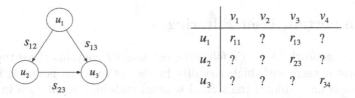

	v_1	v_2	v_3	v_4
u_1	r_{11}	?	r_{13}	?
u_2	?	?	r_{23}	?
u_3	?	?	?	r_{34}

Fig. 1. Social trust graph   **Fig. 2.** User-item rating matrix

RSTE: Recommend with Social Trust Ensemble [10]. It is a probabilistic factor analysis framework, which naturally fuses the user's tastes and their trusted friends' favor together.

SocialMF: A Matrix Factorization Based Model for Recommendation in Social Rating Networks [8]. It is a model-based method which employing matrix factorization techniques. To improve previous work, they incorporate the mechanism of trust propagation into the model.

SoReg: Recommender Systems with Social Regularization [11]. SoReg coined the term Social Regularization to represent the social constraints on recommender systems. When recommending a product to the target user, it gives different weights to other users according to the similarity between the other users and the target users to distinguish the influence of different users on the target users.

2.2 Research Status of Important Users

As for the filtering methods of important users, new solutions have been put forward in recent years.

Shen [12] proposed a collaborative filtering method, incorporating both user-based method and item-based method. In their research, users' relationships are divided into two main categorizes: well-known people, institutions or other users of higher visibility, and their own friends and those who have low popularity.

Zhang [13] used the Bayesian network [14] model to compute user influence. Based on the location of nodes in the network and the number of edges connected by nodes, Wang [15] used the degree and betweenness to filter the important user. And Fang [16] used the degree centrality and the betweenness centrality to filter the center node and tested its effect on the recommendation system, which shows the center node plays a particularly important role in the recommendation methods.

On the basis of the above work, considering the role of users in the social network and the relationship between them, we proposed three new filtering methods of important user.

3 Important User Filtering

In social network, A user's following list usually contains three types of users: The first is users with high visibility in the entire social network, such as Sina V users in micro-blog[1]; the second is users with high reputation in the Interest tribe, such as music blogger; the last one is users who are less well-known but have a offline relationship with target user, such as target user's classmates and colleagues. Based on this phenomenon, we proposed three types of important users to analysis which kind of important users have the greatest impact on recommendation results. Some users may be considered as more than one types of important users when filtering important users.

The important users of these three types of users are listed as the important overall users, the important community users and the important neighbor users.

3.1 The Important Overall Users

One of the obvious features of the important overall users is that a lot of users follow them while they only follow few users. In social network graph, the ratio of the in degree to the out degree of these users will be high.

Based on this intuition, we proposed Algorithm 1 to filter the important overall users.

Algorithm 1. Filter the important overall users

Input: user-user trust matrix.
Output: the top-k important overall users.
1: **for** $u_i \in U$ **do**
2:    Count the in degree in_i of user u_i.
3:    Count the out degree out_i of user u_i.
4:    Calculate the ratio r_i of in_i to out_i of user u_i.
5: **end for**
6: Sort users in descending order according to r
7: Select the top-k users as the important overall users

In lines 1–5, the algorithm calculates the ratio of the in degree to the out degree for each user; then we sort users in descending order according to their ratio and select the top-k as the important overall users.

---

[1] http://www.weibo.com.

3.2   The Important Community Users

The important community users usually play an important role in an interest tribe, which means their preferences have a higher similarity with others.

Based on this intuition, we proposed Algorithm 2 to filter the important community users.

In lines 2–5, we calculate two users' preference similarity $sim_{i,k}$ by their user-item rating vector. The similarity is calculated by cosine similarity (Eq. (1)). After that, we set a threshold θ_2 according to the specific situation of the dataset. If $sim_{i,k} > \theta_2$, we will add both of the users into the nearest neighbor [17] list l. Then we count the number of occurrences of each user in the list, sort users in descending order, and select the top-k users as the important community users [18].

$$sim_{i,k} = \frac{\sum_{j=1}^{m}(R_{u_i j} \times R_{u_k j})}{\sqrt{\sum_{j=1}^{m} R_{u_i j}^2} \times \sqrt{\sum_{j=1}^{m} R_{u_k j}^2}} \tag{1}$$

Algorithm 2. Filter the important community users

Input: user-item rating matrix.
Output: the top-k important community users.
    Initialize the similarity list l
2: **for** $< u_i, u_k > (i \neq k, u_i \in U, u_k \in U)$ **do**
        Calculate the preference similarity $sim_{i,k}$ between u_i and u_k according to their rating vectors
4:     **if** $sim_{i,k} > \theta_2$ **then** add $< u_i, u_k >$ to list l
    end for
6: Count the number of occurences o of each user in the list l
    Sort users in descending order according to o
8: Select the top-k users as the important community users

3.3   The Important Neighbor Users

The important neighbor users usually have offline relationships with the target user and have more common friends with the target user. In the social trust graph, their friends lists have a higher similarity with others.

Based on this intuition, we proposed Algorithm 3 to filter the important neighbor users for the target user.

Algorithm 3 is similar with Algorithm 2. The difference is the input. In Algorithm 2, the input is the user-item rating matrix while in Algorithm 3 it is the user-user trust matrix.

Algorithm 3. Filter the important neighbor users

Input: user-user trust matrix.
Output: the top-k important neighbor users.
    Initialize the similarity list l
    for $< u_i, u_k > (i \neq k, u_i \in U, u_k \in U)$ **do**
3:     Calculate the friends lists similarity $sim_{i,k}$ between u_i and u_k according to their trust vectors
       if $sim_{i,k} > \theta_3$ then add $< u_i, u_k >$ to list l
    end for
6: Count the number of occurences o of each user in the list l
    Sort users in descending order according to o
    Select the top-k users as the important community users

---

4 Experiments

4.1 Dataset

The data used in our experiments is Ciao [19]. Ciao is a product review website, with ratings ranging from 1 to 6. This dataset is extremely sparse and imbalanced containing 3951 users and 60552 items. The total number of trust relations between users is 40133, the number of ratings is 327120, and the average rating is 4.777. The densities of relations and ratings are 0.257% and 0.137%, respectively.

4.2 Experimental Setup

The recommendation methods used in this paper are RSTE, SocialMF, and SoReg. We used a 10-fold cross-validation for learning and testing. In each time we randomly selected 90% of data as training set and the rest 10% as test set.

We set $\alpha = 0.1$ in RSTE method, the parameter α controls how much do users trust themselves or their trusted friends; In Algorithm 2, $\theta_2 = 0.5$, it is a threshold, if the preference similarity $sim_{i,k}$ is greater than θ_2, it means user u_i and user u_k have higher preference similarity and they are important community user for each other; Similar to θ_2, θ_3 is the threshold in Algorithm 3, and $\theta_3 = 0.5$, if the friends lists similarity $sim_{i,k}$ is greater than θ_3, it means user u_i and user u_k are important neighbor user for each other.

First we filter the top-0, top-200, top-400, top-600, top-800 and top-1000 important users of the overall users, the community users and the neighbor users, respectively. Thus we get 18 different sets of important users. After that, one important users set is deleted from the original dataset each time, so we obtain 18 new datasets. Finally, we input these new datasets into the three algorithms and reevaluate the recommendation results.

4.3 Metrics

The evaluation metrics used in our experiments are mean absolute error (MAE) and root mean square error (RMSE) [20], which are defined as Eq. (2) and Eq. (3).

$$MAE = \frac{\sum_{t=1}^{N} |(predicted_t - observed_t)|}{N} \tag{2}$$

$$RMSE = \sqrt{\frac{1}{N} \sum_{t=1}^{N} (predicted_t - observed_t)^2} \tag{3}$$

In addition, we define a metric the rate of change (Δ) to evaluate the impact of important users on the MAE and RMSE of different methods. As shown in Eq. (4).

$$\Delta = \frac{delete_{1000} - delete_0}{delete_0} \tag{4}$$

$delete_{1000}$ is the MAE/RMSE value after deleting the top-1000 important users, and $delete_0$ is the MAE/RMSE value without deleting important users.

4.4 Experimental Results

The experimental results are shown in Fig. 3 and Table 1. Figure 3 shows the MAE and RMSE of three kinds of recommendation methods without important overall users, important community users and important neighbor users, respectively. Table 1 shows the rate of change of MAE and RMSE.

Table 1. The rate of change of MAE and RMSE of different recommendation methods for different kinds of important user

		#overall user	#community user	#neighbor user
RSTE	MAE	0.1295196	0.1258491	0.4498069
	RMSE	0.1238030	0.1146042	0.3450586
SocialMF	MAE	0.1444981	0.1057310	0.3822633
	RMSE	0.1000046	0.0834284	0.3178401
SoReg	MAE	0.1290263	0.1116101	0.2788628
	RMSE	0.1107464	0.0866980	0.2262674

We will analyze the results from two perspectives.

From Metrics Perspective

– MAE
   As can be seen from Eq. (2), MAE is sensitive to the accumulation of small errors. In Fig. 3, with the reduction of important users, MAE shows an upward trend, indicating that the reduction of important users increases the number of minor errors.

– RMSE

It can be seen from Eq. (3) that RMSE has higher sensitivity to large errors. In Fig. 3, with the reduction of important users, RMSE is also showing an upward trend, indicating that the reduction of important users will increase the error of hot items.

– The rate of change

All those recommendation methods will be affected by the deletion of the important users, among which RSTE usually has the largest rate of change as can be seen in Table 1.

Among the three kinds of important users, the important neighbor users have the greatest impact on the rate of change, and the largest rate of change of MAE and RMSE are 0.4498 and 0.3451, respectively.

From Important User Perspective. Table 1 shows that the important neighbor users have the greatest impact on the methods compared to the important overall users and the important community users, which can be seen visually from Fig. 3.

In addition, in Fig. 3, as more and more important overall users and important neighbor users are deleted, RMSE and MAE are increasing gradually: the top600 users have obvious influence on the recommendation result, and then the influence of the important users is waning. This is in contrast to the important community users: the top600 users almost have no effect on the recommendation result or even to make a small decline in MAE and RMSE, and after that the effect of important users increased gradually. That may due to the noise in the data: there are some noise in the top600 important community users, causing

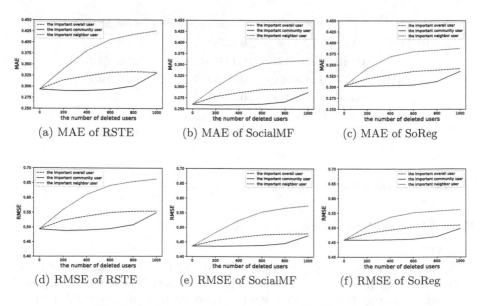

(a) MAE of RSTE   (b) MAE of SocialMF   (c) MAE of SoReg

(d) RMSE of RSTE   (e) RMSE of SocialMF   (f) RMSE of SoReg

Fig. 3. Analysis results for rating data in Ciao dataset

the MAE and RMSE to stay almost unchanged before top 600 important users are deleted.

As can be seen in Fig. 3, the effect of each type of important users on different recommendation methods is almost the same, which demonstrates that the important user filtering methods have good universality in different recommendation methods.

5 Conclusions and Future Work

This paper focuses on the impact of important users on recommendation results in social recommender systems. First, we classify users who are in the target user's following lists, and propose three types of users that are usually followed by others: the overall users, the community users and the neighbor users. Then, based on the characteristics of these three types of users, we design the filtering methods of important users. Finally, we analyze the impact of different types of important users on three social recommendation algorithms. The experimental results show that both the RMSE and MAE of the social recommendation methods show a downward trend after adding important users, which indicates that the recommended results are more accurate with the addition of important users. In addition, the important neighbor users have the greatest impact on recommender systems among the three important users.

In the future work, we will focus on the impact of the important users on the long tail items, to help businesses promote items better and users to find the more attractive items in the long tail to improve the diversity of recommendation results.

Acknowledgements. The work is supported by the Basic and Advanced Research Projects in Chongqing under Grant No. cstc2015jcyjA40049, and the Guangxi Science and Technology Major Project under Grant No. GKAA17129002.

References

1. Levitin, D.J.: The organized mind: thinking straight in the age of information overload. Dutton (2014)
2. Lee, A.R., Son, S.M., Kim, K.K.: Information and communication technology overload and social networking service fatigue: a stress perspective. Comput. Hum. Behav. **55**, 51–61 (2016)
3. Yang, B., Lei, Y., Liu, J., Li, W.: Social collaborative filtering by trust. IEEE Trans. Pattern Anal. Mach. Intell. **39**(8), 1633–1647 (2017)
4. Tang, J., Xia, H., Liu, H.: Social recommendation: a review. Soc. Netw. Anal. Min. **3**(4), 1113–1133 (2013)
5. Goldberg, D., et al.: Using collaborative filtering to weave an information tapestry. Comm. ACM **35**(12), 61–70 (1992)
6. Breese, J.S., Heckerman, D., Kadie C.: Empirical analysis of predictive algorithms for collaborative filtering. In: Fourteenth Conference on Uncertainty in Artificial Intelligence, pp. 43–52 (1998)

7. Su, X., Khoshgoftaar, T.M.: A survey of collaborative filtering techniques. Adv. Artif. Intell. **2009**(12), 4 (2009)
8. Jamali, M., Ester, M.: A matrix factorization technique with trust propagation for recommendation in social networks. In: ACM Conference on Recommender Systems, pp. 135–142 (2010)
9. Ma, H., Yang, H., Lyu, M.R., King, I.: SoRec: social recommendation using probabilistic matrix factorization. In: ACM Conference on Information and Knowledge Management, pp. 931–940 (2008)
10. Ma, H., King, I., Lyu, M.R.: Learning to recommend with social trust ensemble. In: International ACM SIGIR Conference on Research and Development in Information Retrieval, pp. 203–210 (2009)
11. Ma, H., Zhou, D., Liu, C., Lyu, M.R., King, I.: Recommender systems with social regularization. In: Forth International Conference on Web Search & Web Data Mining, pp. 287–296 (2011)
12. Shen, C.W.: Research and analysis on the influence of micro blogging users based on micro blogging data. Ph.D. thesis, Beijing University of Posts and Telecommunications (2013)
13. Song, C., Zhang, X.K., Jia, J., et al.: Ranking importance of user node in microblog social network. Comput. Eng. Des. **37**(8), 2050–2056 (2016)
14. Chickering, D.M.: Learning equivalence classes of Bayesian network structures. In: Twelfth International Conference on Uncertainty in Artificial Intelligence, pp. 150–157 (1996)
15. Wang, H.X., Shan, Z., Liu, H.Y.: An importance analytical approach for online social network. J. Shanghai Jiaotong Univ. **47**(7), 1055–1059 (2013)
16. Wen, J.H., Fang, Q.Q., Liu, L., et al.: Impact of social relationship on model-based social recommender system. J. Front. Comput. Sci. Technol. (2017)
17. Weinberger, K.Q., Saul, L.K.: Distance metric learning for large margin nearest neighbor classification. J. Mach. Learn. Res. **10**(1), 207–244 (2009)
18. Cao, G., Kuang, L.: Identifying core users based on trust relationships and interest similarity in recommender system. In: IEEE International Conference on Web Services, pp. 284–291 (2016)
19. Lo, Y.Y., Liao, W., Chang, C.S.: Temporal matrix factorization for tracking concept drift in individual user preferences. Comput. Sci. (2015)
20. Chai, T., Draxler, R.R.: Root mean square error (RMSE) or mean absolute error (MAE)? Geosci. Model. Dev. **7**(1), 1525–1534 (2014)

Analysis on Communication Cost and Team Performance in Team Formation Problem

Weijun Chen, Jing Yang, and Yang Yu[(⊠)]

School of Data and Computer Science, Sun Yat-Sen University,
Guangzhou, People's Republic of China
{chenwj96,yangj357}@mail2.sysu.edu.cn,
yuy@mail.sysu.edu.cn

Abstract. Team formation problem refers to finding a set of skillful individuals to accomplish given tasks as a team. A growing interest of recent researches on team formation is to concern the collaboration factor, following the general idea that effective communication among team members may contribute to better team performance. Previous studies have introduced a variety of ways to model the collaboration factor applying the concept communication cost, yet few have investigated the effectiveness of the proposed metrics. In this paper, an empirical study is conducted to evaluate the effectiveness of existing communication cost metrics in terms of the influence on team performance. We select real data from IMDb as an example for the study and apply statistical analysis. Based on the result of evaluation, we further propose modification for the communication cost metrics and demonstrate the feasibility. This empirical study is expected to provide suggestion and inspiration for both researchers and practitioners, while design or select models to solve team formation problem in different application scenarios.

Keywords: Team formation · Collaboration · Communication cost
Social network metrics

1 Introduction

Team formation problem refers to finding a team of actors (i.e. human resources) to accomplish a project with certain constraints such as skill qualification, business roles, etc. The problem of team formation origins from the Operations Research. One may find various real-life scenarios for the application of team formation, such as software development, task distribution in workflow management, partner selection in virtual enterprises, etc.

There is a growing interest on the study of the collaboration among individuals in group work and its potential impact on team performance [1, 2]. Lappas et al. addresses the problem of team formation concerning the collaboration of team members [3], which states that effective cooperation contributes to better team performance and should therefore be considered besides the requirements for skills. The concept of communication cost is used to measure the effectiveness of cooperation within a team, and may be calculated using techniques from social network analysis, based on the

© ICST Institute for Computer Sciences, Social Informatics and Telecommunications Engineering 2018
I. Romdhani et al. (Eds.): CollaborateCom 2017, LNICST 252, pp. 435–443, 2018.
https://doi.org/10.1007/978-3-030-00916-8_41

social network model that captures the interactions of the individuals. Later researches in the same stream have proposed different network-based metrics for measuring communication cost, depending on the application scenarios of group work. Despite the well-recognized existence of social network in real-life, these scenarios may vary in terms of the interaction patterns. For example, in a team that requires every team member cooperating smoothly with one another during group activity, such as surgical teams in health care [4], the Sum of Distance metric [5] may be used for modelling the communication; while for a leader-centric team on the other hand, the interactions between ordinary team members and team leader may be more important, thus Leader Distance metric [5, 6] is more appropriate for capturing the pattern. The selection of metrics for measuring communication cost of members within teams would require domain knowledge in practical use.

However, while most of the researches focus on modeling the diversity of application scenarios, few have evaluated the effectiveness of these metrics. Although the concept of higher communication cost bringing adverse effect is well-accepted, it remains unclear how much communication cost would influence the performance of a team. On the other hand, most of the existing researches recognize different communication structures of teams as abstract graph patterns, while practitioners face more complex structures and may use more specific suggestion during the modeling phase. There is need for methods of evaluating the effectiveness of these communication cost metrics.

In this paper, we seek to achieve better understanding on the influence of communication cost in team formation problem through an empirical study. We select the IMDb movie data [7] commonly adopted in previous researches as one real example for case study. Statistical analysis is used to discover the potential correlation between four typical communication cost metrics and the performance of teams. By leveraging the results of analysis, we also provide suggestion on designing more effective metrics for measuring team communication cost. The presented research is expected to serve as a supplement to the current study on team formation problem concerning the collaboration factor, and may contributes to team formation in practical use.

The rest of this paper is organized as follows. Section 2 introduces related work on team formation problem, and from which four typical types of communication cost metrics are selected for later analysis. Section 3 reports the results of the empirical study that aims to investigate the correlation between communication cost and team performance. The suggested improvements on the metrics are demonstrated in Sect. 4. Section 5 givens a brief conclusion of the presented study.

2 Related Work and Preliminaries

Cooperative behaviors in teamwork affect service quality and performance [1, 8]. Related researches on team formation have taken into account communication cost among team members [3, 5, 6, 9–13]. Reference [3] first considered communication as one important factor affecting the effectiveness of a team, and formulated team formation problem based on communication cost functions on diameter distance and minimum spanning tree distance. [5, 6] further extended previous researches and proposed team formation algorithms based on communication cost functions on the sum of distances and leader distance. [9] considered both communication cost and personnel cost of team members. [11] proposed an algorithm to optimize both individual expertise and handover relations to form a required team of high performance. [12, 13] proposed algorithms to ensure the balanced workload of team members. [10] introduced the concept of capacity of actors, adding the constraint of capacity as the maximum workload allowed. [14–16] argued that team members would cooperate better if they have closer relations and tried mining social relations from historic data. [17] summarized recent team formation researches and developed a platform called Unified System for Team Formation to show the performance of different team formation algorithms.

The collaboration among potential members in team formation can be modeled as a social network graph $G(V, E)$, where V represents the set of all individuals and E is the set of direct association between two different individuals v_i and v_j, denoted as $e(v_i, v_j)$. Assign weights to the associated edges with social distance value, then the communication cost of v_i and v_j in G is therefore determined by the shortest path distance between v_i and v_j, denoted as $sp(v_i, v_j)$. In the following chapter, we study to investigate and compare the following metrics [3, 5, 6] commonly adopted for measuring communication cost of a team X, which is a subset of V and form subgraph G':

$Cc - R(X)$: The communication cost of a team X on diameter distance is defined as the diameter of G', which is the longest shortest path length between any pair of members in X.

$Cc - MST(X)$: The communication cost of a team X on minimal spanning tree (MST) distance is defined as the cost of the minimum spanning tree on G'.

$Cc - SD(X)$: The communication cost of a team X on the sum of distances is defined as the sum of all $sp(v_i, v_j)$ for all pairs of members (v_i, v_j) in X.

$Cc - LD(X)$: The communication cost of a team X on leader distance is defined as the sum of all $sp(v_i, v_L)$ in X, where v_L is the team leader and v_i is any other member.

3 Correlational Analysis

The movie data from Internet Movie Database (IMDb) are commonly adopted by previous researches for evaluating the feasibility of the proposed algorithms [5, 9, 12, 13]. We choose it for case study and apply statistical analysis to discover about the potential correlation between communication cost and the performance of the team.

3.1 The IMDb Dataset

IMDb dataset provides massive records about movie information. Each of the record contains information including *year, title, directors, actors* and *ratings* of a movie. Specifically, the *ratings* of a movie are given by the users of the IMDb website, ranged from 0 to 10. Movie data from 2010 to 2016 are selected, containing a total of 132936 movies.

We follow the similar experimental setup [5, 9], and take directors and actors as individuals in the group work (of producing movies), and pick only the "skillful" individuals who have participated in at least 5 movies. Given a team, the ratings of the produced movies may serve as the result of a relative objective evaluation of the team's performance. The extracted dataset for analysis includes 89800 skillful individuals, who combined and produced 79669 movies. Examples of the dataset are shown in Table 1, where numerical ids are used to replace titles and names of persons.

Table 1. Examples of the experimental dataset.

Movie ID	Year	Ratings	Team members
4027597	2016	7	[578448, 208647, 44352, 82602, 546937, 273875, 781837, 624307, 338718]
4028026	2016	6.5	[702169, 132988, 826693, 306446, 4444, 89452]
4028061	2016	7.8	[276204, 415364, 29396, 51812, 151432, 799030, 224061, 20734, 331220, 465837, 126350, 3434, 622141]
4028295	2016	4.7	[183758, 507130, 219560, 128275, 298734]
4027597	2016	7	[578448, 208647, 44352, 82602, 546937, 273875, 781837, 624307, 338718]

We use the history of cooperation in producing movies (i.e. simultaneous appearance in the cast) to construct the collaboration network $G(V, E)$ of the directors and actors. Accordingly, the social distance value $e(v_i, v_j)$ could be determined by utilizing the movie ratings:

$$e(v_i, v_j) = 10 - avg\_ratings(v_i, v_j),$$ (1)

where $avg\_ratings(v_i, v_j)$ represents the average of ratings of all movies in which v_i and v_j cooperate. The definition of $e(v_i, v_j)$ can be interpreted as: with past experiences of cooperating as team members and performing well, two individuals are expected to have shorter distance and thus communicate better.

3.2   Analysis of Correlation

To perform the analysis, split the dataset into two parts and pick the earlier one (ranged from year 2000 to 2009) for constructing the collaboration network of individuals, while the other (2010–2016) is left for observation. The four selected communication cost metrics are calculated respectively for each of the teams in the observation data. For teams in the observation data, we calculate the communication cost measured by each of the four selected metrics. Depending the definition of these graph-based metrics, it requires that the subgraph network G' of a team being connected. Thus we omit the records of unqualified teams during calculation and keep only those on which all four metrics could be applied.

The obtained results along with the corresponding movie ratings are used for correlational study. Pearson correlation coefficient (PCC) is adopted for analysis, which is a measure of the linear correlation between two variables. It also applies to a sample: Given two sets of sampling data of size n, $\{x_1, \ldots, x_n\}$ and $\{y_1, \ldots, y_n\}$, the sample PCC denoted by r can be calculated as follows.

$$r = \frac{\sum_{i=1}^{n}(x_i - \bar{x})(y_i - \bar{y})}{\sqrt{\sum_{i=1}^{n}(x_i - \bar{x})^2}\sqrt{\sum_{i=1}^{n}(y_i - \bar{y})^2}}, \tag{2}$$

where x_i, y_i are the single samples while $\bar{x}$, $\bar{y}$ being the sample means respectively. The value of r lies between $+1$ and -1, where $+1$ indicates total positive linear correlation between the two sets of data, and -1 for total negative correlation, and 0 for no linear correlation.

Table 2 demonstrates the results of correlational analysis using Pearson correlation coefficient. For all four metrics, negative PCC values were obtained, which imply negative correlation between the measured communication cost and the performance of the teams in observation data. In terms of the size of correlation, we found the PCC values relatively low. This is expected since the movie ratings are adopted to evaluate team performance, while there may be various other complicating factors other than the communication cost among team members. Nevertheless, the PCC value still vary to certain extent for these four metrics. By comparison the absolute value of PCC of $Cc - R$ is greater than that of $Cc - SD$, indicating that communication cost on *diameter distance* has stronger negative linear correlation with the team performance in this specific context. The result of comparison suggests that we may choose $Cc - R$ over $Cc - SD$ while modeling team formation problem in this case, since it is more confident that communication cost measured by $Cc - R$ would follow the tendency "as communication cost increases, the performance of team decreases".

Table 2. PCC between four communication cost metrics and team performance for observation data with 3623 records.

Communication cost metric	Pearson correlation coefficient
$Cc - R$	-0.34293
$Cc - MST$	-0.27914
$Cc - SD$	-0.10675
$Cc - LD$	-0.24793

The above analysis could be applied as a part of the solution to team formation problem in different contexts. After modeling the collaboration, one may leverage the historical results of group work by the focused individuals, and then determine whether the current modeling approach needs improvement or not. The results of group work are assessed through the use of Key Performance Indicators (KPI), which is a common practice in many fields and applications. Analysis should be done from case to case, and consider the specific characteristics of cases that may influence the analysis process.

In the following chapter, we continue the study on the movie production case, and introduce the modification on the existing metrics that may contribute to more effective measuring of communication cost.

4 Design of More Effective Metrics

4.1 Modifying the Original Definitions

Recall that at the end of chapter 2, the communication cost between any two individuals v_i and v_j in G is defined as the shortest path distance $sp(v_i, v_j)$. We further consider the transitive characteristic of social relationships, and make the following assumption on the communication pattern among individuals: if v_i and v_j communicate and collaborate well, and so do v_j and v_k, then it is likely that v_i and v_k may also achieve smooth communication and well collaborate as team members; and the transitivity applies as long as there exists a path between the pair of two individuals in G.

Based on the assumption above, we replace shortest path distance $sp(v_i, v_j)$ with the following definition, to define the communication cost between two individuals v_i and v_j as

$$d(v_i, v_j) = \frac{sp(v_i, v_j)}{length(v_i, v_j)}, \tag{3}$$

where $length(v_i, v_j)$ defines the number of edges involved in the path. For measuring the communication cost of a team X which forms subgraph G', we referred to the concept of average path length and made the modification on the four selected communication cost metrics as follows:

- $Cc - R'(X)$ is defined as the maximum $d(v_i, v_j)$ of any pair of members in X.
- $Cc - MST'(X)$ is defined as the cost of the minimum spanning tree on G' divided by $(|X| - 1)$ where $|X|$ stands for the size of team X.
- $Cc - SD'(X)$ is defined as the sum of all $d(v_i, v_j)$ for all pairs of members in X, divided by $(|X| * (|X| - 1)/2)$.
- $Cc - LD'(X)$ is defined as the sum of all $d(v_i, v_L)$ in X divided by $(|X| - 1)$, where v_L is the team leader and v_i is any other member.

4.2 Verifying the Improvement

Correlational analysis was performed under the same setup as chapter 3 to verify the feasibility of the modification. Results are shown in Table 3. While being negative for PCC of all four new metrics, the absolute value also increases. Following the conclusion drawn in chapter 3, we consider the new metrics more effective in measuring communication cost in the movie production case.

We have conducted a regression analysis between communication cost measured by new metrics and team performance to further support the verification.

Table 3. PCC between four modified communication cost metrics and team performance for observation data with 3623 records.

Communication cost metric	Pearson correlation coefficient
$Cc - R'$	−0.50132
$Cc - MST'$	−0.46810
$Cc - SD'$	−0.51658
$Cc - LD'$	−0.46006

Communication cost measured by each of the new metrics is picked as the independent variable x (the predictor) while the corresponding team performance (assessed by movie ratings) is taken as the dependent variable y (the response) respectively. The results of correlational analysis using PCC suggest certain linear dependence of team performance on communication cost, therefore we built the following model from observation data, using the least square method:

$$y = \beta_0 + \beta_1 \cdot x + \varepsilon, \tag{4}$$

where $\beta_0 + \beta_1 \cdot x$ is the deterministic part and ε is the residual (random error assumed normally distributed and independent of x). The statistics in Table 4 show the result of four groups of regression analysis.

Table 4. Statistics of regression analysis on modified communication cost metrics and team performance.

Communication cost metric	R Square	Significance F	Standard Error	Coefficient β_1	Intercept β_0
$Cc - R'$	0.251322	6.8E−230	1.388732	−0.51518	8.846803
$Cc - MST'$	0.219118	9.5E−197	1.418290	−0.69157	8.785556
$Cc - SD'$	0.266855	2.2E−246	1.374257	−0.74434	9.131815
$Cc - LD'$	0.211655	2.9E−189	1.425046	−0.68587	8.675663

Notice that for all four groups, the *p-value* (Significance F) < 0.0001, so we conclude that the regression model (Eq. 4) is a good fit at significant level 0.0001. More importantly, the *R Square* shows the percentage of variance in team performance explained by the linear model. By comparing the *R Square* among these four metrics, we noticed the results in statistical analysis being consistent with those shown in Table 3, which indicate that $Cc - SD'$ may work better in measuring communication cost. The lower value of *Standard Error* (1.374257) also corresponds with the above result of comparison.

We may now conclude that our modified definitions of communication metrics are more effective comparing to the original design. Moreover, the new metric $Cc - SD'$ may be a better choice in terms of modeling team formation problem in the current case.

5 Conclusion

The presented study focuses on the team formation problem with concern of the collaboration factor. The general idea that effective collaboration would help achieve better team performance applies to group work in various domains. However, while related researches have contributed a variety of metrics and methods to model different communication structures within teams, there is a lack of investigation on the effectiveness of the proposed metrics. In this paper we conducted an empirical study to obtain better understanding to the problem, in which we referred to representative studies in the stream and selected four metrics for analysis. We used the real example of movie production teams, and utilized statistical analysis methods to reveal the potential correlation between communication cost and team performance. Results of analysis demonstrated that communication cost does have an adverse effect on team performance. Furthermore, we made improvements on the design of communication cost metrics based on the existed ones and verified the effectiveness in the same context of movie production teams.

Nevertheless, it is necessary to state that the results of analysis on those metrics may not apply to other cases and we do not intend to draw generalization from one single empirical study. There exist a lot of factors that may influence team performance other than collaboration, and they may vary in different domains. Still we expect the insights gained from the current empirical study would inspire researches on team formation problem to account for the effectiveness of modeling collaboration.

Further extension to the presented work may consider including more real-life examples for case study, such as DBLP, BibSonomy, etc. Comparative study among different cases might result in more valuable and solid conclusion. Also, in-depth statistical analysis methods could be applied to give more comprehensive understanding.

Acknowledgments. This work is supported by the National Natural Science Foundation of China under Grant No. 61572539; the Research Foundation of Science and Technology Major Project in Guangdong Province under Grant Nos. 2015B010106007, 2016B010110003; the Research Foundation of Science and Technology Plan Project in Guangdong Province under Grant No. 2016B050502006; the Research Foundation of Science and Technology Plan Project in Guangzhou City under Grant Nos. 2016201604030001, 201704020092. Information courtesy of IMDb (http://www.imdb.com). Used with permission.

References

1. Kumar, A., Dijkman, R., Song, M.: Optimal resource assignment in workflows for maximizing cooperation. In: Daniel, F., Wang, J., Weber, B. (eds.) BPM 2013. LNCS, vol. 8094, pp. 235–250. Springer, Heidelberg (2013). https://doi.org/10.1007/978-3-642-40176-3_20
2. Liu, R., Kumar, A.: Impact of socio-technical network on process performance. In: 2014 International Conference on Collaborative Computing: Networking, Applications and Worksharing (CollaborateCom), pp. 243–252. IEEE (2014)

3. Lappas, T., Liu, K., Terzi, E.: Finding a team of experts in social networks. In: Proceedings of the 15th ACM SIGKDD International Conference on Knowledge Discovery and Data Mining, pp. 467–476. ACM (2009)
4. Turrentine, B., Calland, J.F., Adams, R., Shin, T., Guerlain, S.: Studying communication patterns during surgery. In: Proceedings of the Human Factors and Ergonomics Society Annual Meeting, vol. 47, no. 12, pp. 1488–1492. SAGE Publications, Los Angeles (2003)
5. Kargar, M., An, A.: Discovering top-k teams of experts with/without a leader in social networks. In: Proceedings of the 20th ACM International Conference on Information and Knowledge Management, pp. 985–994. ACM (2011)
6. Juang, M.C., Huang, C.C., Huang, J.L.: Efficient algorithms for team formation with a leader in social networks. J. Supercomput. 66(2), 721–737 (2013)
7. Internet Movie Database. http://www.imdb.com/interfaces
8. Tjosvold, D., Moy, J., Sasaki, S.: Co-operative teamwork for service quality in East Asia. Manag. Serv. Qual. Int. J. 9(3), 209–216 (1999)
9. Kargar, M., An, A., Zihayat, M.: Efficient bi-objective team formation in social networks. In: Flach, P.A., De Bie, T., Cristianini, N. (eds.) ECML PKDD 2012, Part II. LNCS (LNAI), vol. 7524, pp. 483–498. Springer, Heidelberg (2012). https://doi.org/10.1007/978-3-642-33486-3_31
10. Majumder, A., Datta, S., Naidu, K.V.M.: Capacitated team formation problem on social networks. In: Proceedings of the 18th ACM SIGKDD International Conference on Knowledge Discovery and Data Mining, pp. 1005–1013. ACM (2012)
11. Lin, S., Luo, Z., Yu, Y., Pan, M.: Effective team formation in workflow process context. In: 2013 Third International Conference on Cloud and Green Computing (CGC), pp. 508–513. IEEE (2013)
12. Anagnostopoulos, A., Becchetti, L., Castillo, C., Gionis, A., Leonardi, S.: Online team formation in social networks. In: Proceedings of the 21st International Conference on World Wide Web, pp. 839–848. ACM (2012)
13. Anagnostopoulos, A., Becchetti, L., Castillo, C., Gionis, A., Leonardi, S.: Power in unity: forming teams in large-scale community systems. In: Proceedings of the 19th ACM International Conference on Information and Knowledge Management, pp. 599–608. ACM (2010)
14. McDonald, D.W.: Recommending collaboration with social networks: a comparative evaluation. In: Proceedings of the SIGCHI Conference on Human Factors in Computing Systems, pp. 593–600. ACM (2003)
15. Wolf, T., Schröter, A., Damian, D., Panjer, L.D., Nguyen, T.H.: Mining task-based social networks to explore collaboration in software teams. IEEE Softw. 26(1), 58–66 (2009)
16. Van Der Aalst, W.M., Reijers, H.A., Song, M.: Discovering social networks from event logs. Comput. Support. Coop. Work (CSCW) 14(6), 549–593 (2005)
17. Wang, X., Zhao, Z., Ng, W.: USTF: a unified system of team formation. IEEE Trans. Big Data 2(1), 70–84 (2016)

An Efficient Black-Box Vulnerability Scanning Method for Web Application

Haoxia Jin[1], Ming Xu[1(✉)], Xue Yang[1], Ting Wu[1], Ning Zheng[1], and Tao Yang[2(✉)]

[1] Internet and Network Security Laboratory,
Hangzhou Dianzi University, Hangzhou, China
{151050013,mxu,153050004,wuting,nzheng}@hdu.edu.cn
[2] Key Lab of the Third Research Institute of the Ministry
of Public Security, Shanghai, China
yangtao@stars.org.cn

Abstract. To discover web vulnerabilities before they are exploited by malicious attackers, black-box vulnerability scanners scan all the web pages of a web application. However, a web application implemented by several server-side programs with a backend database can generate a massive number of web pages, and may raise an unaffordable time consuming. The root cause of vulnerabilities is the mal-implemented server-side program, instead of any certain web pages that generated by the server-side program. In this paper, an efficient black-box web vulnerability scanning method – handler-ready – is proposed, which highlights the scanning on the server-side programs – *handlers* – rather than concrete web pages. Handler-ready reduces the HTTP requests of massive web pages to a small number of *handlers*, and gives the *handlers* an even chance of being scanned. Therefore, the handler-ready can avoid being stuck with massive web pages that generated by the same *handler* when scanning. The experimental result shows that the proposed scanning method can discover more vulnerabilities than traditional methods in a limited amount of time.

Keywords: Web application · Black-box vulnerability scanner

1 Introduction

Web applications are the most popular way of delivering services via the Internet. The complexity of modern web application has caused massive vulnerabilities in web applications, and, in fact, the number of reported web applications is growing sharply [1].

Web vulnerabilities threaten the security and privacy for both citizens and enterprises. For example, an attacker exploited a vulnerability of CSDN's (China Software Developer Network) website in Apr. 2010, and published the database in Dec. 2011, which contains over 6 million user informations [2].

© ICST Institute for Computer Sciences, Social Informatics and Telecommunications Engineering 2018
I. Romdhani et al. (Eds.): CollaborateCom 2017, LNICST 252, pp. 444–455, 2018.
https://doi.org/10.1007/978-3-030-00916-8_42

An approach for fighting security vulnerabilities is to discover defects before malicious attackers find and exploit them by conducting automated black-box vulnerability scanning. Black-box vulnerability scanners observe the application's output in response to a specific input, and verify whether a vulnerability exists.

However, virtually any website that serves content from a database use one or more server-side programs to generate pages on the website, leading to a site considering of several clusters of pages, each generated by the same server-side program [3]. Taking stackoverflow.com for example, which has over 13 million web pages. A thorough black-box scanning against 13 million web pages is impossible and unnecessary. A pre-defined maximum pages to be crawled may neglect some of the functionalities of web application not being scanned. Alternatively, the impact of the massive server-side generated web pages on efficiency can be mitigated by our method.

In addition, web applications are released or updated with new features all the time, which may also introduce new vulnerabilities. It is necessary to discover their vulnerabilities with a rapid reaction.

In this paper, we propose the method – handler-ready – to improve the efficiency of black-box web vulnerability scanning against the massive automatically generated web pages under the time-restrict situation. Handler-ready is based on the motivation that the web pages generated from the same server-side program have similar patterns of their HTTP requests, and scanning on a small number of web pages could find vulnerabilities as much as scanning on all the web pages.

In summary, the main contributions of this paper are following:

- An efficient scanning method. It avoids being stuck in massive pages that related to the same server-side handler.
- Proposing the *sharing-the-same-handler problem* and the relevant concepts.
- A method of the handler learning along with the method of request sampling.
- An evaluation of both efficiency and effectiveness of the proposed method under the time-restrict situation. The experimental result promisingly shows that the efficiency is improved with no decrease in effectiveness.

The rest of the paper is organized as follows. We discuss related work in Sect. 2. In Sect. 3, we describe proposed handler-ready method along with its important formulations for *request* and *handler*. The evaluation of various scanning methods for effectively discovering web vulnerabilities are presented in Sect. 4.

2   Related Work

Another approach for fighting web application vulnerabilities is using white-box vulnerability scanners, which requires a web application's source code or target code. However, white-box scanners are commonly programming-language-specified, which reduce the scope of target web applications. In addition, there is the problem of substantial false positives [4]. Finally, the source code or target code of the applications itself may be unavailable. In contrast, black-box vulnerability scanners observe the application's output in response to a specific input to verify the existence of vulnerabilities.

Automated black-box web application vulnerability scanning has been a hot topic in research for many years. A number of tools have been developed to automatically discover vulnerabilities in web applications, produced as academic prototypes [5,6], and open-source projects, such as skipfish, w3af, and OWASP Zed Attack Proxy.

The evaluation of [7] acknowledges challenges of web application vulnerability scanning in depth. [8] makes a comparison of the efficiency and effectiveness of vulnerability discovery techniques. A common theme of web vulnerability scanning is to improve effectiveness. [9,10] emphasizes the importance of crawling and application's internal states, and introduces a state-aware scanning method, which captures the web application's state changing, to find more vulnerabilities under different states. Different with these works, our aim is improving the efficiency, while not downgrading the effectiveness.

3   Method: Handler-Ready

Traditional scanning method takes following steps to scan a web application:

1. **Crawling.** The crawling process collects the target application's web pages automatically or manually. The automatic crawling often fails to trigger the AJAX requests which dominated by the client-side dynamic codes. Therefore, a common practice is manually browsing the target application first, then launching the automatic crawling.
2. **Scanning.** The scanning process constructs and sends some sophisticated HTTP requests to a collected web page's every injection point (such as a text input box, a parameter inside the URL) for every type of vulnerabilities. After the HTTP request received and processed by the target application, the scanning process receives the HTTP response of its constructed HTTP request, verifies whether a certain type of vulnerability has been found.
3. **Reporting.** The discovered vulnerabilities along with the relevant information are represented to the user.

The challenge is that the scanning processes often costs unaffordable time consuming, due to the massive number of web pages collected in the crawling process. These pages are generated by the very same server-side programs [3]. However, the number of web application's handlers is limited despite the massive number of server-side generated web pages. In addition, the duplicated web pages may reports spurious vulnerabilities that related to the same root cause [10]. Therefore, we introduce our efficient scanning method, handler-ready, which does two extra steps before scanning launched:

1. **Handler-Learning.** It reduces the HTTP requests of a massive number of web pages to a small number of *handlers* by utilizing the state-of-art frequent pattern mining algorithm.

2. **Request-Sampling.** It generates a partial sequence of HTTP requests for scanning such that the *handlers* have even chance of being scanned and avoid being stuck.

The steps of the proposed handler-ready method are shown in Fig. 3. Only two steps are inserted into the traditional steps. Therefore, handler-ready is ready to plug into existing scanners (Fig. 1).

Fig. 1. Handler-ready steps for vulnerabilities scanning.

The traditional method can also be interpreted by the proposed method, whose "handler-learning" treats every web page come from the same handler, and whose "request-sampling" just sample every web pages for scanning. The commonly used setting of "maximum children to crawl", which modifies the behavior of the crawling process, can also be a special "request-sampling" that samples a web page unless the number of its siblings sampled in the same directory not exceeds the threshold of "maximum children to crawl". Therefore, in our evaluation, we treat all traditional methods as different "request-sampling" methods, and compared them with the proposed method.

3.1 Modeling: The *Request* and *Handler*

In this section, we define the *request* and the *handler*, along with their *relations*.

Definition (Request). A *request* u is a map $u : K \to V$ from the key-set K to the value-set V. The set of all possible *requests* is denoted by U.

Where K is the set of keys $\{k_{\text{method}}, k_{\text{scheme}}, k_{\text{port}}\} \cup \{k_{\text{host},1}, ..., k_{\text{host},h}\} \cup \{k_{\text{path},1}, ..., k_{\text{path},p}\} \cup \{k_{\text{qs},*}\}$. V is the set of all values of any possible HTTP requests, augmented with token $\perp$ that denotes the empty value. In describing any request u, u maps the keys of K to the corresponding values occurred in the original HTTP request, or the default empty value $\perp$ unless the corresponding values are not exist.

Example 1. Given a request

$$u_1 = \text{GET http://example.com/foo/bar?hello=world,}$$

it has following mapping:

·	k_{method}	k_{scheme}	k_{port}	$k_{\text{host},2}$	$k_{\text{host},1}$	$k_{\text{path},1}$	$k_{\text{path},2}$	$k_{\text{qs,hello}}$	·
u_1	GET	http	$\perp$	example	com	foo	bar	world	$\perp$

Notice that the *keys* $\{k_{host,1}, ..., k_{host,h}\}$ are encoded reversely to the domain name's segments of a web application's for the alignment of the multiple sub-domains that the web application may employ.

Definition (Handler). A *handler* r is a map $r : K \to W$, mapping each key in K to a value in W. Let R be the set of all possible *handlers*. Where W is the set of values V extended with regular expression characters. For simplicity, in this paper, we only consider $W = V \cup \{\star\}$, where $\star$ represents the wildcard character that can match any non-empty value in V. We define the *match* relation between *handlers* and *requests*, the *handler partial ordering* relation between *handlers*, and the *supports* of *handlers* as follows:

- **Match.** A *handler* r matches *request* u, written as $r \oplus u$, if for every *key* k, either $r(k) = \star$ or $r(k) = u(k)$.
- **Handler Partial Ordering.** A *handler* r' is less general than r, written as $r' \leq r$, if for every *key* k, $r'(k) \neq r(k) \Rightarrow r(k) = \star$. This is saying that a *handler*, which is more specific, is less general than other *handlers*.
- **Supports.** The support of r in U, denoted $supp(r)$, is the set of *requests* $\{u|\forall u(r \oplus u) \wedge \neg \exists r'(r' \neq r \wedge r' \leq r \wedge r' \oplus u)\}$. This is saying that a *request* u belongs and only belongs to $supp(r)$, if r is most preceding one of the *handlers* that *match* the *request* u.

Given sets of *handlers* R' and R'' that match all the *requests*, the sets $\{supp(r)|\forall r \in R'\}$ and $\{supp(r)|\forall r \in R''\}$ are partitions(i.e. equivalence classes) on U. Therefore, the *similarity* $\Theta(R', R'')$ is calculated by Jaccard Similarity: $\Theta(R', R'') = \frac{sum(min(M_{R'}, M_{R''}))}{sum(max(M_{R'}, M_{R''}))}$, where $M_{R'}, M_{R''}$ are the upper triangular matrixes of R', R'''s relation matrixes.

Our definition of *handler* coincides with the definition "pattern" or "script" of works about URL classification, such as [3,11]. In addition, our definition of *handler partial ordering* relation enables the ordering between *handlers*, which is not defined in the previous works. As show in Example 2, the *handler partial ordering* is useful when modeling *handlers* which seems very similar.

Example 2. Given following instances:

·	k_{method}	k_{scheme}	k_{port}	$k_{host,2}$	$k_{host,1}$	$k_{path,1}$	$k_{path,2}$	$k_{path,3}$	$k_\star$
u_1	GET	http	$\perp$	stackoverflow	com	questions	666	subrasi	$\perp$
u_2	GET	http	$\perp$	stackoverflow	com	questions	233	lol	$\perp$
u_3	GET	http	$\perp$	stackoverflow	com	questions	tagged	java	$\perp$
u_4	GET	http	$\perp$	stackoverflow	com	questions	ask	$\perp$	$\perp$
r_1	GET	http	$\perp$	stackoverflow	com	questions	ask	$\perp$	$\perp$
r_2	GET	http	$\perp$	stackoverflow	com	questions	tagged	$\star$	$\perp$
r_3	GET	http	$\perp$	stackoverflow	com	questions	$\star$	$\star$	$\perp$

On the stackoverflow.com, r_1 represents a web page for asking a new question; r_2 represents the web pages about questions tagged with the value indicated by $k_{\text{path},3}$; and r_3 represents a question specified by $k_{\text{path},2}$ and $k_{\text{path},3}$. They have similar URL formats, but represent totally different functionalities.

There are $r_1 \le r_3, r_2 \le r_3, r_1 \ne r_2 \ne r_3$, $r_1 \oplus u_4$, $r_2 \oplus u_3$, and $r_3 \oplus u_i, i = 1, 2, 3, 4$. Although r_3 *matches* $u_{1,2,3,4}$, $u_{3,4}$ are not *supports* of r_3. The *supports* of r_1, r_2, and r_3 are $supp(r_1) = \{u_4\}$, $supp(r_2) = \{u_3\}$, and $supp(r_3) = \{u_1, u_2\}$.

The definitions of *handler partial ordering* and *supports* provide the ability to model multiple *handlers* that very similar to each other.

Assumption. We assume the web application is a *handler-dispatcher machine* that a *request* u is dispatched to the *handler* r if $u \in supp(r)$.

It should be note that our assumption *handler-dispatcher machine* meets the implementations of popular web servers, such as Microsoft IIS, Apache HTTPD, Nginx, as well as web application frameworks, such as SpringMVC, Struts, and Django. These implementations employ a regular expression rule based mechanism for request matching, and support the ordering between rules in the configuration file. All these features can be interpreted by our model. For web applications implemented by dynamic web pages and even static websites, the *handler-dispatcher machine* can still work.

Problem. The proposed problem is called *sharing the same handler problem*. Given a subset of *requests* U', find the a subset of *handlers* R', such that $\Theta(R, R') \to 1.0$.

Where R is the true set of *handlers* decided by the server-side programs or web server's configuration. Solving the *sharing the same handler problem* is the very aim of the handler-learning process of the proposed handler-ready method.

3.2   Handler Learning

As shown in Example 1 and Example 2, a bundle of *requests* is literally encoded into a multi-dimensional database. Therefore, a frequent closed itemset mining algorithm can be used to learn the patterns of *requests*. The handler-learning process follows the following steps:

1. **Itemset Encoding.** Transform a *request* u to itemset u' by Eq. (1).
2. **Frequent Pattern Mining.** Mine frequent itemsets $\{u'', ...\}$ from $\{u', ...\}$.
3. **Handler Constructing.** A frequent pattern u'' can be converted to a handler $r_{u''}$ by Eq. (2).

$$u' = \{e_k, v_{k,u(k)} | \forall k \in K, u(k) \ne \bot\} \tag{1}$$

$$r_{u''}(k) = \begin{cases} u(k), & \text{if } e_k \in u'' \wedge v_{k,u(k)} \in u''. \\ \star, & \text{if } e_k \in u'' \wedge v_{k,u(k)} \notin u''. \\ \bot, & \text{otherwise.} \end{cases} \tag{2}$$

In the Eq. (1), e_k represents the existence of *key* k, and $v_{k,u(k)}$ represents that the *value* of *key* k is $u(k)$. The choosing algorithm for frequent pattern mining is FPClose [12], which is a state-of-art algorithm, and its output is so called "closed itemset pattern". The closed itemset pattern is not included in another pattern having exactly the same occurrence. This feature make sure that the learned *handlers* are representative.

FPClose needs a parameter `minsup`, which is the minimum occurrence of a pattern. In our problem, FPClose with `minsup` = 5% produces patterns that not trivial. For large web application that have many functionalities, the `minsup` may be smaller to preserve more details. The *requests* that not matched by the FPClose produced patterns, are grouped together, and form a special *handler*, which is also used as a *handler* in the hereafter request-sampling process.

3.3   Request Sampling

In this section, we introduce our sampling method, which generates the sequence of *requests* for vulnerabilities scanning. Our sampling method needs following principles to do sampling:

- The chances of all *handlers* being sampled should be equivalent, as we don't know whether a given *handler* is more vulnerable than another.
- The chances of all *requests* of a *handler*'s *support* being sampled should be even. As we are agnostic with the values' meaning of *requests* even when their sets of keys are same, the only thing we can do is giving them the equivalent chance of being sampled.

To meet the above principles, the request-sampling take a sampling threshold p, a given set of *requests* U' and the learned *handlers* R' as input, and follows the following steps:

1. Shuffle the order of the *requests* in the set $supp(r)$ for all $r \in R'$.
2. Traverse every $r \in R'$ in turn, and sample a $u \in supp(r)$ for scanning.
3. Stop when the ratio p of *requests* of U' are sampled.

4   Evaluation

The purpose of the proposed method is to detect vulnerabilities of web applications. In this section, we evaluate the effectiveness of our handler-ready method in terms of the following questions:

- Whether efficiency improved by employing handler-ready?
- Whether more vulnerabilities discovered by handler-ready when scanning same number of objects that scanned by the traditional method?

Table 1. Evaluated applications.

Application	Description	Version	Lines
Gallery3	A photo hosting	3.0.2	26,622
Vanilla Forum v2.0	A discussion forum	2.0.17.10	43,880
WackoPicko	An intentionally vulnerable web application	2.0	900
WackoRESTful	WackoPicko's URL rewrite version	2.0	941
WordPress v3	A Blog hosting platform	3.2.1	71.698

4.1   Preparations

Table 1 provides an overview of the evaluated web applications. Most of them are evaluated in [10]. WackoRESTful is WackoPicko's URL rewrite version modified by us. All of them are varied in size, complexity, and functionality.

In order to collect the data sets, OWASP Zed Attack Proxy 2.6.0 is used to crawl and to scan pages on the web applications listed in Table 1. The sequence of *requests* scanned by the OWASP Zed Attack Proxy is the input of our handler-ready method, and is also the other sampling-methods' input. After the sequence of *requests* being scanned is collected, the handler learning process is started to extract handler information.

The statistics of handler learning against evaluated applications are shown in Table 2, and the labeling is made by us manually to calculate the *similarity*. The column "Similarity" shows the *similarities*, which are not very close to 1.0. These *similarities* is actually saying the ratios of the relations of the *requests* that dispatched to the same *handler* with 100% confidence. A bigger *similarity* may potentially introduce a higher scanning efficiency. Therefore, the proposed handler-ready can still improve the scanning efficiency against Vanilla Forum v2.0 despite its small *similarity*.

The column "Distribution" shows the distribution of $||supp(r)||/||U'||$ of the evaluated applications, and suggests that a minority of *handlers* could matches the largest portions of *requests*. The processes handler-learning and request-sampling of handler-ready are necessary to give all *handlers* even chance of

Table 2. The statistics of the evaluated applications after handler-learning.

Application	Requests	Handlers	Similarity	Distribution
Gallery3	1,710	38	0.5536	
Vanilla Forum v2.0	1,353	42	0.1988	
WackoPicko	144	19	0.4120	
WackoRESTful	276	22	0.4166	
WordPress v3	253	24	0.7884	
Total	3,736	145	N/A	0% 5% 10% 15% 20% 25% 30%

being scanned rather than the chances positively correlated to the number of matched *requests*.

4.2 Sampling Methods

To simulate the time-restrict situation, the following are evaluated sampling methods:

- **handler-ready$_p$.** The proposed method. The first ratio p of request-sampling's result are used for scanning.
- **DFS$_p$.** The first ratio p of the lexicographical order of *requests*.
- **owasp-zap$_p$.** The first ratio p of original sequence of *requests* scanned by OWASP Zed Attack Proxy.
- **max-children$_m$.** The sequence of *requests* scanned by OWASP Zed Attack Proxy when setting the parameter "maximum children to crawl" to m.

where p is the ratio of *requests* being scanned, and m is the maximum children to crawl under a certain directory.

4.3 Vulnerabilities Scanning Results

To evaluate the performance of the handler-ready for vulnerabilities scanning under the p and m, we conduct two sets of comparison experiments:

- Comparisons between handler-ready$_p$, DFS$_p$, and owasp-zap$_p$. The threshold p is ranging from 0.1 to 1.0.
- Comparisons between handler-ready$_{p_m}$ and max-children$_m$. Where p_m is the threshold related to m, such that $\|\text{handler-ready}_{p_m}\| = \|\text{max-children}_m\|$. Without loss of generality, the parameter m is ranging from 0 to 20.

handler-ready$_p$ vs. DFS$_p$ vs. owasp-zap$_p$. The vulnerabilities reported by three sampling methods under different threshold p are shown in Fig. 2. In most cases, the proposed handler-ready$_p$ performs better than other methods.

For Gallery3 and WordPress v3, the true positives are omitted, because they have no true positives found in this experiment. It is interesting that Vanilla Forum v2.0 has two reflected XSS vulnerabilities and three external redirect vulnerabilities discovered during our experiment. As all of these vulnerabilities are placed in the management module of the application, the damage of these vulnerabilities being exploited will be very harmful. The reflected XSS vulnerabilities can be exploited by a malicious user to collect another user's(web master's) credential.

The sampling method owasp-zap$_p$ is actually a breadth first traversing of *requests*. owasp-zap$_p$ and DFS$_p$ are often being stuck, for they often enter a directory with massive web pages derived by the same server-side handler. In contrast, the proposed handler-ready$_p$ does not.

Comparing with the traditional scanning methods, handler-ready has a 40% efficiency improvement against the evaluated web applications with no decrease in effectiveness.

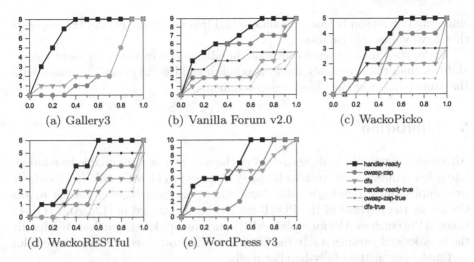

Fig. 2. Vulnerabilities reported under different threshold p. Handler-ready-true, owasp-zap-true, and dfs-true are three methods' true positives respectively.

handler-ready$_{p_m}$ vs. max-children$_m$. The vulnerabilities reported by two methods under different parameter m and m's related p_m are shown in Fig. 3.

The proposed handler-ready$_p$ performs better than "maximum children to crawl" method, i.e. max-children$_m$. As shown in Fig. 3(a), max-children$_m$ still neglects vulnerabilities that should be discovered when $m = 20$, which is quite large. Although handler-ready seems not superior than max-children against Vanilla Forum v2.0, the former can still find true positives earlier than max-

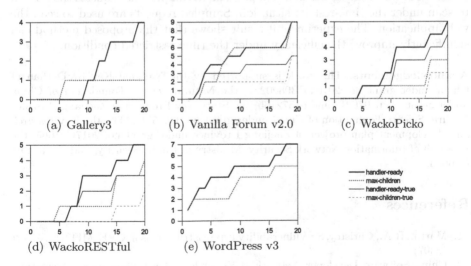

Fig. 3. Vulnerabilities reported under different parameter m and p_m. Handler-ready-true and max-children-true are two methods' true positives respectively.

children. The reason is that "maximum children to crawl" prunes the *requests* that have vulnerable children.

Under the time-restricted condition, handler-ready can discover more vulnerabilities than the commonly used "maximum children to crawl" approach with the same number of the object being scanned.

5   Limitation

Although the web applications nested in the web browser are unable to manipulate other request fields (such as Request Headers) to identify different handlers, web applications' developers still have chance to hide handler tokens in the Cookie or the payload of the POST request as mentioned in [13]. And HTTP-based APIs (such as API for mobile APP) may manipulate these fields to identify the handler and parameters. In the future, we will study how to model these fields and make our method fully-handler-ready.

6   Conclusion

New web vulnerabilities emerge quickly and threaten the security and privacy for both citizens and enterprises. Web applications update all the time to import new features, which may also introduce new vulnerabilities in the meanwhile. It is necessary to discover web vulnerabilities with a rapid reaction. However, traditional scanning methods do not scan quickly against web applications, which utilize server-side programs to generate massive web pages from a backend database.

The proposed method, handler-ready, learns the pattern of requests for the massive automatically generated web pages, and samples the requests that worth to scan under the time-restrict situation. Sampled requests are used to scan the web application. The experimental result shows that the proposed method can significantly improve the efficiency under the time-restricted condition.

Acknowledgements. This work is supported by the National Key R&D Plan of China under grant no. 2016YFB0800201, the Natural Science Foundation of China under grant no. 61070212 and 61572165, the State Key Program of Zhejiang Province Natural Science Foundation of China under grant no. LZ15F020003, the Key research and development plan project of Zhejiang Province under grant no. 2017C01065, the Key Lab of Information Network Security, Ministry of Public Security, under grant no C16603.

References

1. Martin, R.A., Christey, S.: Vulnerability type distributions in CVE. MITRE Report (2007)
2. China Software Developer Network (CSDN) leaked 6 million user information. http://www.williamlong.info/archives/2933.html

3. Blanco, L., Dalvi, N., Machanavajjhala, A.: Highly efficient algorithms for structural clustering of large websites. In: WWW, pp. 437–446 (2011)
4. Medeiros, I., Neves, N.F., Correia, M.: DEKANT: a static analysis tool that learns to detect web application vulnerabilities. In: ISSTA, pp. 1–11 (2016)
5. Felmetsger, V., Cavedon, L., Kruegel, C., Vigna, G.: Toward automated detection of logic vulnerabilities in web applications. In: USS, pp. 143–160 (2010)
6. Halfond, W.G.J., Choudhary, S.R., Orso, A.: Penetration testing with improved input vector identification. In: ICST, pp. 346–355 (2009)
7. McAllister, S., Kirda, E., Kruegel, C.: Leveraging user interactions for in-depth testing of web applications. In: RAID, pp. 191–210 (2008)
8. Austin, A., Holmgreen, C., Williams, L.: A comparison of the efficiency and effectiveness of vulnerability discovery techniques. IST **55**(7), 1279–1288 (2013)
9. Doupé, A., Cova, M., Vigna, G.: Why Johnny can't pentest: an analysis of black-box web vulnerability scanners. In: DIMVA, pp. 111–131 (2010)
10. Doupé, A., Cavedon, L., Kruegel, C., Vigna, G.: Enemy of the state: a state-aware black-box web vulnerability scanner. In: USS, pp. 523–538 (2012)
11. Hernndez, I., Rivero, C.R., Ruiz, D., Corchuelo, R.: CALA: classifying links automatically based on their URL. JSS **115**, 130–143 (2016)
12. Grahne, G., Zhu, J.: Fast algorithms for frequent itemset mining using FP-trees. TKDE **17**(10), 1347–1362 (2005). https://doi.org/10.1109/TKDE.2005.166
13. Shezaf, O.: Rest assessment cheat sheet. http://tinyurl.com/mkqd8br

Collaboration with Artificial Intelligence

Collaborative Shilling Detection Bridging Factorization and User Embedding

Tong Dou[1,2], Junliang Yu[1,2], Qingyu Xiong[1,2(✉)], Min Gao[1,2], Yuqi Song[1,2], and Qianqi Fang[1,2]

[1] Key Laboratory of Dependable Service Computing in Cyber Physical Society, Chongqing University, Ministry of Education, Chongqing 400044, China
{doutong,yu.jl,xiong03,gaomin,songyq,fqq}@cqu.edu.cn
[2] School of Software Engineering, Chongqing University, Chongqing 400044, China

Abstract. The recommender system based on collaborative filtering is vulnerable to shilling attacks due to its open nature. With the wide employment of recommender systems, an increasing number of attackers are disordering the system in order to benefit from the manipulated recommendation results. Therefore, how to effectively detect shilling attacks now becomes more and more crucial. Most existing detection models recognize attackers in statistics-based manners. However, they failed in capturing the fine-grained interactions between users and items, leading to a degradation in detection accuracy. In this paper, inspired by the success of word embedding models, we propose a collaborative shilling detection model, CoDetector, which jointly decomposes the user-item interaction matrix and the user-user co-occurrence matrix with shared user latent factors. Then, the learned user latent factors containing network embedding information are used as features to detect attackers. Experiments conducted on simulated and real-world datasets show that CoDetector has a good performance and generalization capacity and outperforms state-of-the-art methods.

Keywords: Collaborative filtering · Shilling attack · User embedding Matrix factorization

1 Introduction

Nowadays recommender systems play an important role in dealing with the problem of information overload. In recommender systems, collaborative filtering (CF) is a widely used technique which recommends items according to the assumption that users who have the similar preferences would like to choose similar items. CF model has been proven to be effective but is vulnerable to shilling attacks due to its open nature [1,2]. In shilling attacks, attackers inject user profiles to increase or decrease the recommended frequency of the targeted items, which will reduce the accuracy of recommendation and robustness of a recommender system. As a consequence, they can benefit from the manipulated

© ICST Institute for Computer Sciences, Social Informatics and Telecommunications Engineering 2018
I. Romdhani et al. (Eds.): CollaborateCom 2017, LNICST 252, pp. 459–469, 2018.
https://doi.org/10.1007/978-3-030-00916-8_43

results whereas normal users may not trust the system anymore. Therefore, how to detect shilling attacks is a big challenge in the studies of recommender systems.

Generally, shilling attacks can be seen as a binary classification problem, that is, for each user profile, the classified result can only be a normal user or an attacker. Therefore, the key point for this problem is to appropriately design the user features [17]. Most existing detection models recognize attackers in statistics-based manners [5,7]. However, they failed in revealing the fine-grained interactions between users and items, leading to a degradation in detection accuracy when attackers are disguised elaborately.

Matrix factorization (MF) characterizes both items and users by decomposing the user-item rating matrix. Latent factors derived from MF capture the implicit features underlying the interactions between users and items. In this paper, we propose a detection model named **CoDetector** based on MF. However, to further include more information, we bridge basic MF and the word embedding model [4] which can uncover the context structure of users. Inspired by [3], our model jointly factorizes the rating matrix and the user-user co-occurrence matrix with shared user latent factors. For each pair of users, the user-user co-occurrence matrix encodes the number of items they both consumed, which is similar to the word co-occurrence matrix in word-embedding models. The main idea of our model is that attackers tend to promote the target item in group so as to enhance the attack effect [16]. Therefore, factorizing these two matrices can fuse rating preferences and structural information in the user-item bipartite network into the user latent factors, which are the input of the classifier. The experimental results show that CoDetector has a good performance and generalization capacity and significantly outperforms state-of-the-art methods in real scenarios.

The rest of this paper is organized as follows: Sect. 2 reviews the related work of shilling detection. Section 3 focus on the proposed method. In Sect. 4, experimental results of CoDetector on both simulated and real-life dataset are reported. Finally, Sect. 5 concludes our work.

2   Related Work

2.1   Shilling Attack Models

In CF, users who have the similar preferences would like to choose the similar items. Based on this idea and the open nature of recommender systems, attackers can inject biased profiles to manipulate the recommendations [1,2].

In order to behave like a normal user without being detected, malicious users use attack models to generate attacker profiles based on knowledge of recommender systems. The general profile of an attacker can be divided into four segments [1] and is depicted in Fig. 1. I^T denotes target item set which is just what attackers want to promote (push attack) or demote (nuke attack), I^S denotes the selected items based on specific needs of the spam user, I^F denotes filler item set which is used to disguise attackers, and $I^\emptyset$ denotes unrated item set which forms the majority of the profile and are always empty.

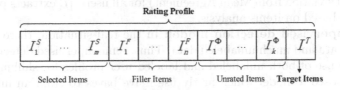

Fig. 1. General framework of attack profile

In accordance with the different chosen items and given ratings in the user profile, attack models are categorized into five types [5]. Table 1 describes these attack strategies.

- **Average attack:** Filler items are assigned the corresponding average ratings of items.
- **Random attack:** Filler items are assigned random values.
- **Bandwagon attack:** Selected items are the frequently rated items and assigned the maximum rating.
- **Segment attack:** Segment attacks choose items similar to target items as selected items.
- **Sampling attack:** The user profile is a copy of that of a normal user.

Table 1. The features of the attack models

Attack model	I^S	I^F	I^T
Random	$\emptyset$	$\beta(i) \sim N(u; \sigma)$, selected randomly	$push : \gamma(i) = r_{max}$ $nuke : \gamma(i) = r_{min}$
Average	$\emptyset$	$\beta(i) \sim N(u; \sigma)$ selected randomly	$push : \gamma(i) = r_{max}$ $nuke : \gamma(i) = r_{min}$
Bandwagon	Widely popular items $\alpha(i) = r_{max}, \forall_i \in I^S$	$\beta(i) \sim N(u; \sigma)$, selected randomly	$push : \gamma(i) = r_{max}$ $nuke : \gamma(i) = r_{min}$
Segment	Similar items to target items $\alpha(i) = r_{max}, \forall_i \in I^S$	$\beta(i) = r_{max}/r_{min}$, selected randomly	$push : \gamma(i) = r_{max}$ $nuke : \gamma(i) = r_{min}$
Sampling	A copy of a exiting users profile		

2.2   Shilling Attacks Detection Methods

According to whether training labels are needed, shilling detection methods can be divided into three categories.

– **Supervised detection model:** This type of detection methods usually recognize attackers by elaborately designing user features. [6] computes rating indicators like DegSim (Degree of Similarity with Top Neighbors) and RDMA (Rating Deviation from Mean Agreement) for all users. [7] extracts popularity patterns based on items analysis.

– **Semi-supervised detection model:** In the real situation, there exist few labeled data and much unlabeled data. Thus, semi-supervised detection models make use of both unlabeled and labeled user profiles for shilling attacks. [10] proposed a model which firstly use naive bayes to train an initial classifier and then improve it with unlabeled data. In [18], a model based on PU-Learning [19] which relies on a few positive labels and much unlabeled data to construct a classifier iteratively was introduced.

– **Unsupervised detaction model:** Compared with supervised detection algorithms, unsupervised ones are more applicable to real scenarios because of less labeled data set. [11] proposed a graph-based detection approach which finds most associated sub-matrices in a user-user similarity matrix for shilling attacks. In [15], the authors exploited the similarity structure in shilling user profiles to separate them from normal user profiles using principal components analysis.

3   Proposed Method

In this section, we propose our model, **CoDetector**, which bridges MF and user embedding to exploit the implicit interactions between users and items.

3.1   Preliminaries

MF and word embedding are pillars of CoDetector. First, we will briefly retrospect these two models.

Matrix Factorization. MF is a basic method in collaborative filtering which uncovers the latent features underlying the interactions between users and items by mapping both users and items into a low-dimensional latent-factor space [12]. The objective function of MF is:

$$L = \sum_{u,i}(y_{ui} - p_u^T q_i)^2 + \lambda(\sum_u \|p_u\|^2 + \sum_i \|q_i\|^2), \tag{1}$$

where user and item latent factors are denoted by $p_u \in \mathbb{R}^d$ and $q_i \in \mathbb{R}^d$ respectively, y_{ui} denotes the observed rating expressed by user u on item i and the algorithmic parameter λ controls the magnitudes of the latent factors.

Word Embedding. Word embedding represents a set of successful models in natural language processing. Using these methods, each word in a sequence of words can be embedded into a continuous vector space. SGNS (the skip-gram neural embedding model) in word2vec [13] is a neural model which trained with the negative-sampling procedure. [3] proved that SGNS is equivalent to factorizing a word-context matrix, whose cells are the pointwise mutual information (PMI) of the respective word and context pairs. PMI between a word w and a context c is an information-theoretic measure, can be empirically estimated as:

$$PMI(i,j) = \log \frac{\#(i,j) \cdot |D|}{\#(i) \cdot \#(j)} \tag{2}$$

where $\#(i,j)$ is the number of times word j appears in the context of word i, $\#(i) = \sum_j \#(i,j)$ and $\#(j) = \sum_i \#(i,j)$, and $|D|$ is the total number of word-context pairs in the corpora. Then [3] proposed SPPMI (Shifted Positive PMI) based on PMI with different negative samples count k to improve the resulting embedding.

$$SPPMI(i,j) = \max\{PMI(i,j) - \log k, 0\} \tag{3}$$

3.2 CoDetector

Attackers manipulate recommendation results by injecting biased user profiles in a large scale, causing abnormalities not only in the given ratings but also in the local clusters in the user-item bipartite graph. Therefore, to further capture the fine-grained characteristics of attackers, both rating and structural information are supposed to be fused into the user features. In CoDetector, we adopt user embedding to discover the anomalies.

User Embedding. In word2vec [13], given a center word, the sequence of words surrounding it are defined as the context of the center word. Likewise, in the user-item bipartite graph of the recommender system, we can define the context of a user u as other users who consumed or rated same items. For example, both u_1 and u_2 consumed i_1 and i_2, therefore, u_1 and u_2 are contexts of each other. Then, the user-user co-occurrence SPPMI matrix $M \in \mathbb{R}^{m \times m}$ is constructed by computing $\#(i,j)$ that denotes the number of items which both user i and user j consumed. After that, we can obtain user embedding by factorizing M. As attackers tend to promote/demote target items in group, factorizing SPPMI matrix can reveal the implicit interactions among attackers in the user-item bipartite graph and embed structural information into user latent factors. In addition, by tuning the value of negative samples, noises in the bipartite can be neglected whereas available connections are preserved.

Training Procedure. To fuse both rating and structural information into user latent factors, CoDetector jointly decomposes the rating matrix R and the SPPMI matrix M with shared user latent factors. The overall process is shown in Algorithm 1. The objective function of CoDetector is stated as:

$$L = \sum_{u,i} (y_{ui} - p_u^T q_i)^2 + \sum_{u,j} (m_{uj} - p_u^T g_j - w_u - c_j)^2$$
$$+ \lambda(\sum_u \|p_u\|^2 + \sum_i \|q_i\|^2 + \sum_j \|g_j\|^2) \tag{4}$$

Algorithm 1. The process of CoDetector
___
Input: User labels U; user−item ratings matrix R, which include attack profiles.
Output: Labels of users to be recognized.
1: Constructing SPPMI matrix M
2: **for** user i in U **do**
3:     **for** user j in U **do**
4:         Count the number of items both user i and user j consumed.
5:         Compute the shifted positive point-wise mutual information.
6:     **end for**
7: **end for**
8: **while** notConverged **do**
9:     Jointly decompose R and M with shared user latent factors P;
10:     update latent vectors.
11: **end while**
12: Use P to predict user labels.

---

where p_u is the shared user latent factors which embeds rating and structure information, m_{uj} denotes the shifted positive point-wise mutual information between user u and user j, g_j is the context of user u, and w_u and c_j are the biases of the user and context. The model parameters are updated by using stochastic gradient descent method. The update rules are as follows:

$$\frac{\partial L}{\partial p_u} = \lambda p_u - (y_{ui} - p_u^T q_i)q_i - (m_{uj} - p_u^T g_j - w_u - c_j)g_j$$

$$\frac{\partial L}{\partial q_i} = \lambda q_i - (y_{ui} - p_u^T q_i)p_u \qquad \frac{\partial L}{\partial g_j} = \lambda g_j - (m_{uj} - p_u^T g_j)p_u \qquad (5)$$

$$\frac{\partial L}{\partial w_u} = m_{uj} - p_u^T g_j - w_u - c_j \qquad \frac{\partial L}{\partial c_j} = m_{uj} - p_u^T g_j - w_u - c_j$$

It should be noted that constructing SPPMI matrix is time-consuming due to its $O(n^2)$ complexity. This part should be computed off-line. Fortunately, updates for elements in this matrix is not computationally expensive. For each update, only the cells related to this consumption or click need to be modified.

4 Experimental Results

To evaluate the performance of the proposed algorithm, we conduct experiments on MovieLens and Amazon datesets. Here we show the results of CoDetector in comparison with four state-of-the-art shilling attack detectors and analyze the effect of model parameters.

Datasets including MovieLens and Amazon, are used in our experiments. MovieLens contains 100,000 ratings rated by 943 users on 1,682 movies, and Amazon dataset released by [20] contains 60,000 ratings rated by 4,902 users on 21,394 items. Precision, recall and F1-score were used to measure the performance.

To tune the methods included, we use 80% of the data as the training set, from which we randomly select 10% as the validation set. For the remaining 20% of the data, we consider the users and items that appear in the training and validation sets to obtain the test set. We record the best parameters of these methods according to their performance on the validation set. Afterwards, all the experiments are performed with 5-fold cross validation. The dimensionality d of latent factors in CoDetetor is 10, and negative samples count k is 25 in Sect. 4.1. After 200 iterations, the CoDetector reached a stable result.

Table 2. Detection results on three typical shilling attacks on MovieLens

Attack Size		Filler Size	%3	%5	%7	%10	%15
average	%3	Precision	0.5000	0.7500	0.8000	0.8182	0.8889
		Recall	0.2500	1.0000	1.0000	1.0000	1.0000
		F1	0.3333	0.8571	0.8889	0.9000	0.9412
	%5	Precision	0.6667	0.9091	1.0000	1.0000	0.9600
		Recall	1.0000	1.0000	0.8333	0.7778	0.9917
		F1	0.8000	0.9254	0.9091	0.8750	0.9756
	%7	Precision	0.7857	0.8939	0.8333	0.8889	0.9880
		Recall	1.0000	0.9158	1.0000	1.0000	0.9832
		F1	0.8800	0.9023	0.9091	0.9412	0.9845
random	%3	Precision	0.2500	0.8000	0.9300	0.9057	0.8268
		Recall	1.0000	1.0000	0.9588	0.9023	0.9478
		F1	0.4000	0.8889	0.9442	0.9030	0.8832
	%5	Precision	0.7778	1.0000	0.9550	0.9600	0.9917
		Recall	1.0000	0.8750	1.0000	0.9917	0.9835
		F1	0.8750	0.9333	0.9770	0.9756	0.9876
	%7	Precision	0.9416	0.6667	0.9300	0.7143	0.8182
		Recall	0.9453	1.0000	0.9588	1.0000	1.0000
		F1	0.9421	0.9017	0.9442	0.8333	0.9000
bandwagon	%3	Precision	0.6667	0.8442	0.8000	0.9057	0.8430
		Recall	1.0000	0.9145	1.0000	0.9023	0.9158
		F1	0.8000	0.8779	0.8889	0.9030	0.8779
	%5	Precision	0.8000	1.0000	0.9000	0.8268	0.9565
		Recall	1.0000	0.8571	0.9000	0.9479	0.9483
		F1	0.8889	0.9231	0.9000	0.8832	0.9524
	%7	Precision	0.9426	0.9915	1.0000	0.9416	0.9750
		Recall	0.8928	1.0000	0.8750	0.9453	0.9832
		F1	0.9017	0.9957	0.9333	0.9421	0.9791

4.1   Performance for Detecting Profile Injection Attacks

In this section we firstly evaluate the performance of CoDetector on three different attack models: random attack, average attack, and bandwagon attack, respectively. Then we compare CoDetector with other four methods on the hybrid attack model which contains simulated attackers generated by three attack models and real-world dataset, Amazon, to show the excellent generalization capacity of CoDetector. In MovieLens, we assume that the original users are normal user, and inject simulated attackers manually according to the definition of attack models. In Amazon, normal users and genuine spammers have been labeled by the authors of [20]. In addition. as the principle of push attacks and nuke attacks is almost the same, we only inject attackers to promote the target items.

As can be seen in Table 2, CoDetector is very successful at detecting spam users generated from specific attack models mentioned in Sect. 2. In most cases, with the rise of the filler size and attack size, the values of the measures gradually increase. All of the attackers can be detected. The results confirm the robustness of CoDetector.

Table 3. Comparison of multiple methods

Method		DegreeSAD	FAP	PCASelectUsers	SemiSAD	CoDetector
MovieLens	Precision	**0.9565**	0.9631	0.9062	0.9415	0.9500
	Recall	1.0000	0.9539	0.9667	0.9181	**1.0000**
	F1	**0.9825**	0.9564	0.9355	0.9255	0.9744
Amazon	Precision	0.6880	**0.8943**	0.5465	0.6035	0.8812
	Recall	0.5850	0.7320	0.8852	0.6208	**0.8915**
	F1	0.6324	0.8050	0.6757	0.6120	**0.8863**

Table 3 shows the results of DegreeSAD [7], FAP [14], PCASelectUsers [15], SemiSAD [10] and CoDetector on MovieLens and Amazon. Simulated attacker here are generated with attack size at %15 and filler size at 10%. We can see that CoDetector and other methods have the comparable performance on MovieLens. However, on the real-world dataset, Amazon, CoDetector beats other methods by a fairly large margin. Specifically, the improvements on $F1$ are 40.14%, 10.09%, 31.16%, and 44.82% respectively. It should be noted that DegreeSAD is based on statistical features. By contrast, underlying features fusing rating and structure information in CoDetector can significantly improve the performance.

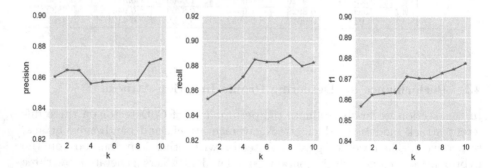

Fig. 2. Impact of the count of negative samples

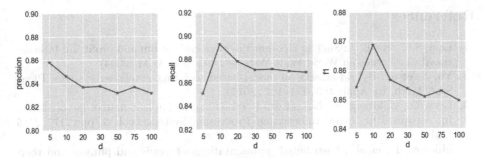

Fig. 3. Impact of parameter d

4.2   Impact of Model Parameters

Two parameters are introduced in CoDetector. One is the dimensionality d of latent factors, the other is the count of negative samples k considered in the construction of SPPMI matrix. Experiments in this part investigate the sensitivity of these two parameters on Amazon. First we fix d at 10 to tune negative samples count ranging from 2^1 to 2^{10}. Figure 2 shows that precision, recall and F1 rise with the increase of negative samples count. We can see in Eq. 3, a larger negative samples count means a more sparse SPPMI matrix. As attackers tend to launch attacks in group, larger co-occurrences between two users means that they may be accomplices. Giving a larger negative count can help to filter noises generated by coincidences.

Then, we fix negative samples count at 25, to see the influence of d ranging from 5 to 100. In Fig. 3, we can see CoDetector obtains best recall and F1 when d=10. However, results on other d values are also acceptable, which validates the stability of our model.

5   Conclusion

In this paper, we present a collaborative shilling detection model called CoDetector bridging factorization and user embedding. It integrates rating and structure information into shared user latent factors to recognize shilling attackers in recommender systems. Experiments conducted on common datasets show that our model significantly outperforms state-of-the-art methods.

Shilling attacks in this paper disorder recommender systems by injecting biased ratings. However, hybrid attacks based on both fake ratings and social connections were proposed [2]. In the future, we will extend our model to detect spammers in the social network.

Acknowledgment. This research is supported by the National Key Basic Research Program of China (973) (2013CB328903), and the Graduate Scientific Research and Innovation Foundation of Chongqing (cys17035).

References

1. Lam, S.K., Riedl, J.: Shilling recommender systems for fun and profit. In: International Conference on World Wide Web, pp. 393–402. ACM (2004)
2. Yu, J., et al.: Hybrid attacks on model-based social recommender systems. Phys. Stat. Mech. Its Appl. **483**, 171–181 (2017)
3. Levy, O., Goldberg, Y.: Neural word embedding as implicit matrix factorization. In: Advances in Neural Information Processing Systems, vol. 3, pp. 2177–2185 (2014)
4. Mikolov, T., et al. : Distributed representations of words and phrases and their compositionality. In: Advances in Neural Information Processing Systems, vol. 26, pp. 3111–3119 (2013)
5. Burke, R., et al.: Classification features for attack detection in collaborative recommender systems. In: ACM SIGKDD International Conference on Knowledge Discovery and Data Mining, pp. 542–547. ACM (2006)
6. Chirita, P.-A., Nejdl, W., Zamfir, C.: Preventing shilling attacks in online recommender systems. In: Proceedings of the 7th Annual ACM International Workshop on Web Information and Data Management. ACM (2005)
7. Li, W., et al.: Shilling attack detection in recommender systems via selecting patterns analysis. IEICE Trans. Inf. Syst. **99**(10), 2600–2611 (2016)
8. Mobasher, B., Burke, R., Williams, C., Bhaumik, R.: Analysis and detection of segment-focused attacks against collaborative recommendation. In: Nasraoui, O., Zaïane, O., Spiliopoulou, M., Mobasher, B., Masand, B., Yu, P.S. (eds.) WebKDD 2005. LNCS (LNAI), vol. 4198, pp. 96–118. Springer, Heidelberg (2006). https://doi.org/10.1007/11891321_6
9. Burke, R., et al.: Segment-based injection attacks against collaborative filtering recommender systems. In: Fifth IEEE International Conference on Data Mining. IEEE (2005)
10. Cao, J., et al.: Shilling attack detection utilizing semi-supervised learning method for collaborative recommender system. World Wide Web **16**(5–6), 729–748 (2013)
11. Zhang, Z., Kulkarni, S.R.: Graph-based detection of shilling attacks in recommender systems. In: 2013 IEEE International Workshop on Machine Learning for Signal Processing (MLSP). IEEE (2013)
12. Koren, Y., Bell, R., Volinsky, C.: Matrix factorization techniques for recommender systems. Computer **42**(8), 30–37 (2009)
13. Mikolov, T., et al.: Efficient estimation of word representations in vector space. arXiv preprint arXiv:1301.3781 (2013)
14. Zhang, Y., et al.: Catch the black sheep: unified framework for shilling attack detection based on fraudulent action propagation. In: IJCAI (2015)
15. Mehta, B., Nejdl, W.: Unsupervised strategies for shilling detection and robust collaborative filtering. User Model. User Adapt. Interact. **19**(1), 65–97 (2009)
16. Jiang, M., Cui, P., Faloutsos, C.: Suspicious behavior detection: current trends and future directions. IEEE Intell. Syst. **31**(1), 31–39 (2016)
17. Wu, Z.A., Wang, Y.Q., Cao, J.: A survey on shilling attack models and detection techniques for recommender systems. Chin. Sci. Bull. **59**(7), 551–560 (2014)
18. Wu, Z., et al.: Spammers detection from product reviews: a hybrid model. In: 2015 IEEE International Conference on Data Mining (ICDM). IEEE (2015)

19. Li, X.-L., et al.: Positive unlabeled learning for data stream classification. In: Proceedings of the 2009 SIAM International Conference on Data Mining. Society for Industrial and Applied Mathematics (2009)
20. Xu, C., et al.: Uncovering collusive spammers in Chinese review websites. In: ACM International Conference on Conference on Information and Knowledge Management, pp. 979–988. ACM (2013)

Integrating User Embedding
and Collaborative Filtering for Social
Recommendations

Junliang Yu[1,2], Min Gao[1,2(✉)], Yuqi Song[1,2], Qianqi Fang[1,2],
Wenge Rong[3], and Qingyu Xiong[1,2]

[1] School of Software Engineering, Chongqing University, Chongqing 400044, China
{yu.jl,gaomin,songyq,fqq0429,xiong03}@cqu.edu.cn
[2] Key Laboratory of Dependable Service Computing in Cyber Physical Society,
Chongqing University, Ministry of Education, Chongqing 400044, China
[3] School of Computer Science and Engineering, Beihang University,
Beijing 100191, China
w.rong@buaa.edu.cn

Abstract. Social recommendation has attracted increasing attention over the years due to the potential value of social relations, which can be harnessed to mitigate the dilemma of data sparsity in traditional recommender systems. However, recent studies show that social recommenders fail in the practical use in industry for the reason that some problems in social relations, such as the noise, lead to a degradation in recommendation quality. To solve the problem, in this paper, a social recommender, SocialEM, which integrates the neural user embedding and collaborative filtering is proposed. Enlightened by the factorization of the word co-occurrence matrix which is equivalent to the skip-gram model in word2vec, SocialEM will jointly decomposes the user-item rating matrix and the user-user co-occurrence matrix with shared user latent factors. For each pair of users, the co-occurrence matrix encodes the number of being trusted together by other users in the social relation network. Experiments conducted on the real-world datasets have shown that the side effect of social relations can be diminished by tuning parameters for SocialEM. And compared with previous studies, our method significantly improves the quality of recommendations.

Keywords: Social recommendations · User embedding
Collaborative filtering · Matrix factorization

1 Introduction

Nowadays, the recommender system is playing an important role in information filtering. The basic technique of recommender systems is collaborative filtering, which depends on the collective historical ratings to predict items that will be positively rated by the active user [10]. However, traditional rating-based only

© ICST Institute for Computer Sciences, Social Informatics and Telecommunications Engineering 2018
I. Romdhani et al. (Eds.): CollaborateCom 2017, LNICST 252, pp. 470–479, 2018.
https://doi.org/10.1007/978-3-030-00916-8_44

recommenders may suffer from the problem of data sparsity since most users rate few of the millions of available items. With the prosperity of social platforms, abundant social information can be harnessed to mitigate the problem, for the reason that the users' preferences can be inferred from those of their friends [18]. Based on this startup idea, social recommender systems [15] emerged and have attracted increasing attention over the years. Nevertheless, recent reports [1,2] show that social recommenders fail in the practical use in industry. Key findings from negative experiences in applying social recommender systems include: (1) social relations are too noisy and may have a negative impact; (2) social relations have different interpretations in different contexts [20]. Therefore, utilizing the explicit social relations without further processing will lead to a degradation in recommendation quality.

To diminish the aforementioned negative influence, the ways which can reveal the implicit nature of the social relations should be explored. Most existing social recommenders are based on matrix factorization [7], a CF model which usually decomposes the observed user-item rating matrix into user and item latent factors. But almost all of them utilize the explicit social relations directly. Enlightened by the recent success of word embedding models such as word2vec [16], we consider that users in recommender systems can be embedded likewise. The prior work [8] proves that the skip-gram model of word2vec is equivalent to the implicit factorization for the word co-occurrence matrix. Based on this work and CF, our model, SocialEM is proposed.

In the model of SocialEM, the user-item rating matrix and the user-user co-occurrence matrix are jointly decomposed with shared user latent factors. For each pair of users, the co-occurrence matrix encodes the number of being trusted together by other users in the social relation network. With the help of the user co-occurrence embedding, the recommender can further expand its model capacity and eliminate the side effect of explicit social relations. Firstly, learned with a context, the embeddings of users can uncover more interactions among users. Secondly, by tuning the minimal co-occurrence counts, users with few attention will be regarded as the anomalies which should be filtered. The experiments conducted on real-world datasets show that SocialEM is superior to state-of-the-art methods in terms of recommendation accuracy. At last, we also provide exploratory analysis to better understand the effectiveness of SocialEM.

The remainder of this paper is organised as follows. In Sect. 2, the preliminaries are briefly introduced. Section 3 will focus on the proposed method - SocialEM. Section 4 reports the experimental results. In Sect. 5, the related studies are introduced. Finally, in Sect. 6 we conclude this paper and point out some potential future work.

2   Preliminaries

In this section, we will briefly introduce matrix factorization and word embedding, which are the pillars of the SocialEM model.

Matrix Factorization. Generally, most model-based CF methods are based on matrix factorization [7], which maps both users and items into a low-dimensional latent-factor space such that user-item interactions are modeled as inner products in that space and user and item latent factors are denoted by $p_u \in \mathbb{R}^k$ and $q_i \in \mathbb{R}^k$, respectively. The resulting dot product, $p_u^T q_i$, can capture the interaction between user u and item i, which is used to predict the missing ratings.

Let I_{ui} be an indicator of whether a rating has been observed in the user-item rating matrix R,

$$I_{ui} = \begin{cases} 1 \; if \; r_{ui} \text{ is observed} \\ 0 \; if \; r_{ui} \text{ is missing} \end{cases} \tag{1}$$

Matrix factorization optimizes the following objective:

$$\mathcal{L} = \frac{1}{2} \sum_{u,i} I_{ui}(r_{ui} - p_u^T q_i)^2 + \lambda(\|p_u\|^2 + \|q_i\|^2), \tag{2}$$

where r_{ui} denotes the rating expressed by user u on item i and the algorithmic parameter λ controls the magnitudes of the latent factors.

Word Embedding. Word embedding models [5,6,16] have caught much attention in a variety of NLP tasks recently for its extraordinary performance. The skip-gram model trained with negative sampling value of k in word2vec [16] has been proven to be equivalent to the implicit factorization for the point-wise mutual information (PMI) matrix shifted by k [8]. PMI between a word w and its context word c can be empirically estimated as:

$$PMI(i,j) = \log \frac{\#(w,c) \cdot |D|}{\#(w) \cdot \#(c)}, \tag{3}$$

where $\#(w,c)$ is the number of times word w appears in the context of word c, $\#(w) = \sum_c \#(w,c)$, $\#(c) = \sum_w \#(w,c)$, and $|D|$ is the total number of the pairs in the corpora.

When PMI has been constructed, the distributed representation of word w is obtained by factorizing the shifted positive point-wise mutual information matrix (SPPMI) which is defined as:

$$SPPMI_k(w,c) = \max(PMI(w,c) - \log k, 0), \tag{4}$$

where k is the number of the negative sampling that controls the sparsity of the SPPMI matrix here.

3   SocialEM: Integrating User Embedding and CF for Social Recommendations

In this section, we propose a Social recommender that combines user Embedding and Matrix factorization, called **SocialEM**.

User Embedding. In word2vec, given a center word, the sequence of words surrounded are defined as the context of the center word. Likewise, in social recommender systems we can define the context of a user u as other users who are trusted together with u by a same user. For example, both u_1 and u_2 are trusted by u_3, therefore, u_1 and u_2 are contexts of each other. Then, the user co-occurrence SPPMI matrix $T \in \mathbb{R}^{m \times m}$ is constructed by computing $\#(i,j)$ that denotes the number of times both user i and user j are trusted by other users. After that, we can obtain user embedding by factorizing T. In contrast to the explicit trust or relation, co-occurrences can express the trust degree or affection in a finer grained view. Factorizing SPPMI matrix further reveals the implicit interactions among users in the social network. In addition, by tuning the value of k, noises in the social relations can be neglected whereas available connections are preserved.

Training Procedure. SocialEM has two main components: factorization for the user-item rating matrix and the user-user co-occurrence matrix. To fusing both the rating and social information into the latent factors, we jointly decompose the two matrices with a shared user latent space. Factorizing the rating matrix encodes users' preferences and items' characteristics; factorizing the co-occurrence matrix can extract the implicit connection pattern among the user network. Sharing a same user latent space ensures that both preferences and the pattern are included in the user latent factors. After training, low dimensional shared user latent factors $P \in \mathbb{R}^{m \times d}$, item latent factors $Q \in \mathbb{R}^{n \times d}$, and the context embedding $G \in \mathbb{R}^{m \times d}$ are obtained. Then, missing ratings can be predicted by the dot products of shared user latent factors and item latent factors.

Model Formulation. The objective function of SocialEM is stated as:

$$
\mathcal{L} = \overbrace{\frac{1}{2} \sum_{u,i} I_{ui}(r_{ui} - P_u^T Q_i - b_u - b_i)^2}^{\text{Factorization for the rating matrix}} + \overbrace{\frac{\alpha}{2} \sum_{t_{uj} \neq 0} (t_{uj} - P_u^T G_j - w_u - c_j)^2}^{\text{Social user embedding}}
$$
$$
+ \overbrace{\frac{\lambda}{2}(\sum_u (P_u^2 + G_u^2 + b_u^2 + w_u^2 + c_u^2) + \sum_i (Q_i^2 + b_i^2))}^{\text{Regularization}}. \tag{5}
$$

As can be seen in Eq. 5, the objective function has three parts. In the part of factorization for the rating matrix, the errors between observed ratings and predicted ratings are quadratically cumulated. b_u and b_i indicate the deviations of user u and item i. In the part of social user embedding, the user co-occurrence matrix is factorized. The user latent factors connect these two parts and account for both user-item interactions and user-user co-occurrence. w_u and c_j are the biases of the user and context. In the last part, all model parameters are regularized. Besides, to balance the effect of the rating information and social information, we introduce a hyper-parameter α. The impact of α will be investigated in Sect. 4.

In [8], several optimizers are available to identify good solutions for factorizing the word co-occurrence matrix. In our work, we use stochastic gradient descent because it works very efficiently in the case of redundant data. A local minimum of the objective function given by Eq. 5 can be found by performing gradient descent in all model parameters:

$$\frac{\partial \mathcal{L}}{\partial b_u} = \lambda b_u - e_{ui} \qquad\qquad \frac{\partial \mathcal{L}}{\partial b_i} = \lambda b_i - e_{ui}$$

$$\frac{\partial \mathcal{L}}{\partial b_u} = \lambda w_u - e_{uj} \qquad\qquad \frac{\partial \mathcal{L}}{\partial c_j} = \lambda c_j - e_{uj}$$

$$\frac{\partial \mathcal{L}}{\partial Q_i} = \lambda Q_i - e_{ui} P_u \qquad\qquad \frac{\partial \mathcal{L}}{\partial G_j} = \lambda G_j - e_{uj} P_u \qquad (6)$$

$$\frac{\partial \mathcal{L}}{\partial P_u} = \lambda P_u - e_{ui} Q_i - \alpha e_{uj} g_j$$

where e_{ui} denotes the error between the observed rating and the predicted rating, e_{uj} denotes the error between co-occurrences and the dot products of user latent factors and context embedding, coupled with biases.

Complexity. With regard to complexity, compared with matrix factorization, SocialEM needs to learn only an additional context embedding matrix with $m \times d$ elements. Since d is a small number, which is consistent with the dimensionality of the latent factors of users and items, the cost is not be computationally expensive. However, SocialEM computes the user-user co-occurrence with a $O(n^2)$ complexity at the beginning, which is time-consuming. To save time, the user-user co-occurrence should be computed off-line. Fortunately, the computation for co-occurrence is new-user-friendly. When a new user enters, SPPMI merely has few entries which are related to the new user need to be updated.

4 Experimental Results

In this section, we present the experimental results. Two types of experiments are conducted: (1) the recommendation quality of the previous models and SocialEM is compared; (2) the impact of the parameters α and k is investigated.

Two common real-world datasets, Ciao and Epinions, are used in our experiments. The statistics of the datasets released by [15, 19] are shown in Table 1. The mean absolute error (MAE) and root mean square error (RMSE) are chosen to measure the prediction error for all methods. A lower MAE or RMSE indicates that missing ratings are predicted more precisely.

Table 1. Dataset statistics

Dataset	#Users	#Items	#Ratings	#Relations	Rating scale
Ciao	7,375	105,114	284,086	111,781	1.0 – 5.0
Epinions	40,163	139,738	664,823	487,182	1.0 – 5.0

To demonstrate the performance improvement of SocialEM, we compare our method with the following methods: PMF [17], SoRec [13], SocialMF [4], and RSTE [11].

To tune the methods, we use 80% of the data as the training set, from which we randomly select 10% as the validation set. For the remaining 20% of the data, we consider the users and items that appear in the training and validation sets to obtain the test set. We record the best parameters of these methods according to their performance. Afterwards, all the experiments are performed with 5-fold cross validation (Table 2).

Table 2. The MAE and RMSE for all methods

	Ciao						
Metric	UserMean	ItemMean	PMF	SoRec	SocialMF	RSTE	**SocialEM**
MAE	0.780	0.767	0.772	0.760	0.753	0.757	**0.736**
Improve	5.64%	4.04%	4.66%	3.15%	2.25%	2.77%	
RMSE	1.030	1.034	1.029	1.020	1.013	1.022	**0.975**
Improve	5.33%	5.70%	5.24%	4.41%	3.75%	4.60%	
	Epinions						
Metric	UserMean	ItemMean	PMF	SoRec	SocialMF	RSTE	**SocialEM**
MAE	0.927	0.856	0.839	0.834	0.822	0.831	**0.811**
Improve	12.51%	5.25%	3.33%	2.75%	1.33%	2.40%	
RMSE	1.198	1.152	1.135	1.127	1.091	1.117	**1.077**
Improve	10.18%	6.41%	5.11%	4.44%	1.28%	3.58%	

4.1 Performance for Predicting Missing Ratings

In this section, we compare the performance of SocialEM with that of the baselines. We set the step size $\gamma = 0.05$, $\alpha = 0.5$ on Ciao and 1 on Epinions, and $k = 5$ for SocialEM. The dimensionality d of the latent factors is set to 20, and the regularization parameter λ is set to 0.01 for all the methods.

As can be seen in Table 1, SocialEM is superior to the corresponding methods which utilize explicit social relations directly, along with two baselines. The main findings are summarized as follows: (1) SocialEM beats PMF by a convincing margin, demonstrating the effectiveness of incorporating social relations; (2) SocialEM outperforms social-related methods by an average improvement of 2.44% on MAE, and 3.84% on RMSE, which proves that adopting user embeddings to reveal the implicit interactions among users is promising. In particular, both SocialEM and SoRec jointly decompose the user-item rating matrix and the relation matrix with a shared user latent space. The difference on performance further validates the positive effect of user embeddings.

4.2 Impact of Parameters α and k

In SocialEM, two hyper-parameters, α and k, are introduced. α is the trade-off used to balance the effect of ratings and relations; k controls the sparsity of the user co-occurrence matrix. First, we fix $k = 5$ and increase the value of η from 0 to 10 with different intervals to observe the variation in the performance. Then, we fix $\alpha = 0.1$ to observe the influence of changing k. The experiments are conducted on both datasets, and the other settings are the same as those in Sect. 4.2.

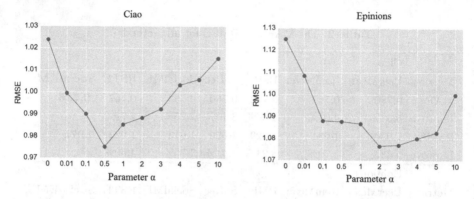

Fig. 1. Impact of parameter α

From Fig. 1, we can witness the fluctuation. Initially, SocialEM has poor performances when $\alpha = 0$, which illustrates the importance of considering social relations. Then the curves decline until that $\alpha = 0.5$ on Ciao and 2 on Epinions where the best performance is reached. And then the curves climb back to a poor level with the increase of α. The observed changes once again emphasize the effectiveness of social relations and also exhibit a proper range of the trade-off on different datasets.

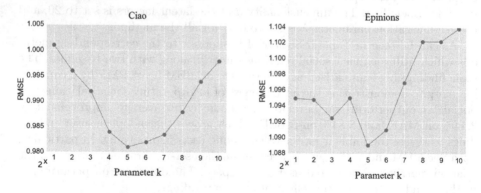

Fig. 2. Impact of parameter α

As can be seen in Fig. 2, SocialEM reaches its best performance when $k = 2^5$. Neither larger values nor smaller values lead to a performance degradation.

Specifically, larger k value means a more sparse SPPMI matrix, otherwise a more dense one. The result demonstrates that user pairs with few co-occurrence times can be the noises which negatively impact the accuracy. Because the few co-occurrences are likely to derive from the coincidence, they can not uncover the real interactions among users. In addition, a more sparse SPPMI matrix leaves out finer grained interactions and only considers user pairs with many co-occurrence times. Therefore, the predictions for users with few relations may fail. According to the result, we can draw a conclusion that finding a proper k helps to relieve the problem of noises in social relations.

5   Related Work

Complementing matrix factorization with further data, e.g., implicit feedback, temporal information or predefined metadata, has widely been accepted to increase algorithmic accuracy. Because of the convenience of matrix factorization for incorporating social information, several social recommenders based on matrix factorization have been proposed recently [3, 4, 11–14, 21].

In [11], the authors proposed an ensemble method that considers the preference of users to be determined by their own tastes and their friends' tastes. Therefore, the missing ratings of a given user are predicted as a linear combination of the ratings of the user and his friends. [13] proposed a model to co-factorize the rating matrix and the relation matrix into three low-rank matrices. In this model, social information and rating information are connected through the shared user latent feature space. In [21], two trust models were proposed. In contrast to other social recommenders, this work considers that both the trustors and trustees can affect users' preferences. The authors of [4] proposed a method named SocialMF. The idea behind SocialMF is that a user's preferences should be similar to those of his friends. Thus, for a given user, the method forces the latent factors to be close to that of his friends. In [12], a method was proposed that takes both trust and distrust into consideration. The authors deemed that each user's latent factors should be similar to those of his friends and differ widely from those of distrusted users. However, all these methods use social relations directly, which makes these methods less reliable.

Among the existing research, the principle of [9, 22] is similar to that of our method. In [9], the authors investigated the interactions among items. It is the earliest work which combines word embeddings with CF, but it ignores the potential value in social relations. [22] adopts the skip-gram model of word2vec to embeds the social network structure. Then it forces the user latent factors to approximate the top-k friends embedding. This model has been prove to be effective, however, it is time-consuming for the construction of network embeddings.

6   Conclusion

This paper is motivated by the recent success of the word embedding model, word2vec, which can be interpreted as the implicit factorization for the word co-occurrence matrix. Based on this work, we proposed a novel social recommender called SocialEM that combines user embedding and CF. For each pair of users, the user co-occurrence matrix encodes the number of being trusted together by other users in the social relation network. Then SocialEM jointly decomposes the user-item rating matrix and the user co-occurrence matrix with shared latent user factors, and next uses the dot products of user latent factors and item latent factors to predict missing ratings. Experiments conducted on real-word datasets show that SocialEM outperforms state-of-the-art methods in terms of recommendation accuracy.

In contrast to general CF-based recommenders, models which integrates user embeddings can further reveal implicit interactions among users. Therefore, the extensions of our model can be applied to other fields related to recommender systems. For instance, spammers who are known as shilling attackers can insert malicious ratings to manipulate the recommendations, which results in different user profiles. User embeddings can uncover the nuance between normal users and spammers, which will contribute to the spammer detection.

Acknowledgment. This research is supported by the National Key Basic Research Program of China (973) (2013CB328903), the National Natural Science Foundation of China (61472021), and the Graduate Scientific Research and Innovation Foundation of Chongqing (cys17035).

References

1. Ibm: Ibm's black friday report says twitter delivered 0 percent of referral traffic and facebook sent just 0.68 percent (2012). http://t.cn/ROA8BeQ
2. Quora: Why does the startup idea of social recommendations consistently fail? (2012). http://t.cn/ROA8gPS
3. Guo, G., Zhang, J., Yorkesmith, N.: TrustSVD: collaborative filtering with both the explicit and implicit influence of user trust and of item ratings, pp. 123–129 (2015)
4. Jamali, M., Ester, M.: A matrix factorization technique with trust propagation for recommendation in social networks, pp. 135–142 (2010)
5. Ji, S., Yun, H., Yanardag, P., Matsushima, S., Vishwanathan, S.V.N.: WordRank: learning word embeddings via robust ranking. In: Conference on Empirical Methods in Natural Language Processing, pp. 658–668 (2016)
6. Joulin, A., Grave, E., Bojanowski, P., Mikolov, T.: Bag of tricks for efficient text classification (2016)
7. Koren, Y., Bell, R.M., Volinsky, C.: Matrix factorization techniques for recommender systems. IEEE Comput. **42**(8), 30–37 (2009)
8. Levy, O., Goldberg, Y.: Neural word embedding as implicit matrix factorization. In: Advances in Neural Information Processing Systems, vol. 3, pp. 2177–2185 (2014)
9. Liang, D., Altosaar, J., Charlin, L., Blei, D.M.: Factorization meets the item embedding: regularizing matrix factorization with item co-occurrence. In: ACM Conference on Recommender Systems, pp. 59–66 (2016)
10. Lu, J., Wu, D., Mao, M., Wang, W., Zhang, G.: Recommender system application developments: a survey. Decis. Support Syst. **74**, 12–32 (2015)

11. Ma, H., King, I., Lyu, M.R.: Learning to recommend with social trust ensemble, pp. 203–210 (2009)
12. Ma, H., Lyu, M.R., King, I.: Learning to recommend with trust and distrust relationships, pp. 189–196 (2009)
13. Ma, H., Yang, H., Lyu, M.R., King, I.: SoRec: social recommendation using probabilistic matrix factorization. In: Proceedings of the 17th ACM Conference on Information and Knowledge Management, pp. 931–940. ACM (2008)
14. Ma, H., Zhou, D., Liu, C., Lyu, M.R., King, I.: Recommender systems with social regularization. In: Proceedings of the Fourth ACM International Conference on Web Search and Data Mining, pp. 287–296. ACM (2011)
15. Massa, P., Avesani, P.: Trust-aware recommender systems. In: Proceedings of the 2007 ACM Conference on Recommender Systems, pp. 17–24. ACM (2007)
16. Mikolov, T., Chen, K., Corrado, G., Dean, J.: Efficient estimation of word representations in vector space. Computer Science (2013)
17. Salakhutdinov, R., Mnih, A.: Probabilistic matrix factorization, pp. 1257–1264 (2007)
18. Sinha, R., Swearingen, K.: Comparing recommendations made by online systems and friends. In: Proceedings of the DELOS-NSF Workshop on Personalization and Recommender Systems in Digital Libraries (2001)
19. Tang, J., Gao, H., Liu, H.: mTrust: discerning multi-faceted trust in a connected world. In: International Conference on Web Search and Web Data Mining, WSDM 2012, Seattle, WA, USA, pp. 93–102, February 2012
20. Tang, J., Hu, X., Liu, H.: Social recommendation: a review. Soc. Netw. Anal. Min. 3(4), 1113–1133 (2013)
21. Yang, B., Lei, Y., Liu, J., Li, W.: Social collaborative filtering by trust. IEEE Trans. Pattern Anal. Mach. Intell. 39(8), 1633–1647 (2017)
22. Zhang, C., Yu, L., Wang, Y., Shah, C., Zhang, X.: Collaborative user network embedding for social recommender systems (2017)

CORB-SLAM: A Collaborative Visual SLAM System for Multiple Robots

Fu Li[1,2], Shaowu Yang[1,2(✉)], Xiaodong Yi[1,2], and Xuejun Yang[1,2]

[1] State Key Laboratory of High Performance Computing (HPCL),
National University of Defense Technology, Changsha, China
shaowu.yang@nudt.edu.cn

[2] College of Computer, National University of Defense Technology, Changsha, China

Abstract. With the single-robot visual SLAM method reaching maturity, the issue of collaboratively exploring unknown environments by multiple robots attracts increasing attention. In this paper, we present CORB-SLAM, a novel collaborative multi-robot visual SLAM system providing map fusing and map sharing capabilities. Experimental results on popular public datasets demonstrate the performance of the CORB-SLAM. Furthermore, we make the source code of CORB-SLAM to be publicly available (https://github.com/lifunudt/CORB-SLAM.git).

Keywords: Collaborative visual SLAM · Map fusing · Map sharing

1 Introduction

Simultaneous localization and mapping (SLAM) is originally proposed to locate a robot while simultaneously building a consistent map of an unknown environment. It has been a fundamental technology for autonomous navigation of robots in the past decades. Researchers have proposed a number of SLAM methods using different types of sensors, e.g. cameras or 2D/3D laser scanners. Specifically, the visual SLAM systems that utilize cameras to obtain sensor-data have become an attractive research focus in robotics.

Some milestone visual SLAM systems have been proposed, such as PTAM [1], and ORB-SLAM2 [2]. Most of these visual SLAM methods focus on the single-robot applications. However, because of the increasing demands for robotic applications in large-scale environments, multi-robot systems are expected to work collaboratively to resolve complex tasks that cannot be handled by a single robot. For instance, some emergency situations, e.g. earthquakes and conflagrations, would require a team of rescue robots to work in a cooperative way to efficiently and robustly explore damaged scenes. In those cases, collaborative visual SLAM can significantly improve the capability of multi-robot explorations.

Project 91648204 supported by NSFC, project ZDYYJCYJ20140601 supported by NUDT, and project 201602-01 supported by HPCL.

© ICST Institute for Computer Sciences, Social Informatics and Telecommunications Engineering 2018
I. Romdhani et al. (Eds.): CollaborateCom 2017, LNICST 252, pp. 480–490, 2018.
https://doi.org/10.1007/978-3-030-00916-8_45

Existing works on collaborative visual SLAM methods for multi-robots have generally fallen into the centralized and decentralized types. The centralized method tries to process and fuse all the local maps from the individual robots in a central server. For example, [3] proposes the visual C^2SLAM framework that provides the services of map optimization and storage in the cloud infrastructure. However, the clients cannot process the essential tasks of environmental mapping and highly rely on the central server. [4] proposes the Team SLAM method that aggregates local pose graphs from multiple robots into a global pose graph and feeds it back to the robots. However, it lacks global map optimization and may cause larger drifting errors. [5] proposes a monocular SLAM system employed on multiple unmanned aerial vehicles (UAVs). Its server manages the maps of all UAVs, and handles map fusing. The monocular cameras utilized in the system may cause larger errors due to the lack of scale information. On the other hand, decentralized methods reach global map consensus by sharing the local map of each individual robot via communication. [6] proposes the D-RPGO algorithm (distributed riemannian pose graph optimization) to perform collaborative localization by fusing the inter-time and inter-robot relative measurements to obtain an estimate of the absolute pose of each robot. [7] presents DDF-SAM, a decentralized data fusing approach for multi-robot SLAM by performing local SLAM and sharing a subset of map variables with neighbors in the form of summarized maps. [8] presents a frontier-based approach that uses a utility function to guide explorations, which takes the information gain and the distance costs of the robots into consideration. [9,10] use a distributed Gauss-Seidel (DGS) algorithm to reduce the information exchange among robots without a reliable communication infrastructure. Comparing to decentralized methods, centralized methods can support more complex operation in the central server.

In this paper, we present CORB-SLAM (collaborative ORB-SLAM), a centralized multi-robot visual SLAM system based on ORB-SLAM2 [2]. The ORB-SLAM2 is a versatile visual SLAM method that has been popularly applied in single-robot applications. However, this method cannot provide support to multi-robot cooperation in environmental mapping. The CORB-SLAM system consists of multiple ORB-SLAM2 clients for local mapping and a central server for global map fusing. Specifically, we extend each of the ORB-SLAM2 clients with a memory management module that organizes the local map and communicates with the central server. In the central server, we detect the overlaps of multiple local maps by the DBoW method [11], and fuse these maps by utilizing the Perspective-n-Point (PnP) [12] method and global optimization through bundle adjustment. We have evaluated the performance of the CORB-SLAM system with several systematic experiments on a public dataset KITTI [13].

2   The CORB-SLAM System

Considering scenarios of multiple robots collaboratively exploring an unknown environment, each robot agent in the CORB-SLAM system is designated to explore parts of the environment and build the local map.

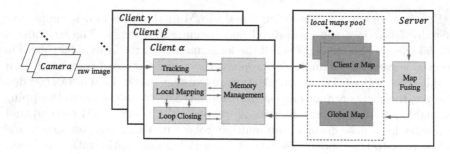

Fig. 1. The framework of CORB-SLAM system.

Figure 1 presents the framework of the CORB-SLAM system which consists of multiple ORB-SLAM2 clients and a server. Each robot is deployed with one SLAM client instance that builds a local map independently as the robot explores. The ORB-SLAM2 client is performs pose tracking, local mapping, and loop closing. We extend the original ORB-SLAM2 system by incorporating a novel memory management module for local map organization. All the modules in the SLAM client run in separate threads.

The central server receives the local maps from multiple clients and put them into the local-map pool. Global map fusing is achieved by three steps in a separate thread. Firstly, overlaps between two local maps are detected by the DBoW method to establish the spatial connections of all the local maps, when overlaps become available. Secondly, the local maps are merged into a global map through PnP and global BA. After the map fusing, the global map can be shared to each individual robot for further explorations.

2.1 The Robot-End SLAM Client

The robot-end SLAM client extends the ORB-SLAM2 to independently build the map of the environment around the robot, and thus, to facilitate autonomous exploration of the robot.

Tracking: The tracking module processes each raw image frame for pose tracking, and decides which frame should be inserted into the local map as a keyframe. ORB features [16] in raw images are used to match to existing map points to achieve pose tracking. When a new keyframe should be added, it will be transferred to the memory management module which schedules all map data.

Local Mapping: The local mapping module triangulates new map points from ORB features in keyframes. Moreover, it refines keyframe and map points in the local map, which is a sub-map of the client global map that affects current pose tracking and mapping, by using local bundle adjustment (BA).

Loop Closing: The loop closing module detects loop closures among keyframes, and refines the client global map using BA whenever a loop closure is found. All keyframes sharing similar ORB features with the new keyframe are used to compute similarity scores to the new keyframe. Several keyframes with the highest scores are selected as loop candidates. The candidates whose similarity transformations are supported by enough inliers will be accepted as loop closures.

Memory Management: The memory management module stores local map and transfers the map data between the SLAM clients and the server in a bi-direction way. Specifically, when new keyframes and map points are created, this module transfers the new map data to the local-map pool within the server. When the poses in the local map are updated, all updated pose data will be transferred to the server in the forms of light keyframe and light map point, which only store the pose and identity data to reduce the communication bandwidth. The memory management module also receives the global map data that shared by the server. The global map is built in the server-end as will be described in Sect. 2.2. The SLAM client can use these map data to better facilitate exploring unknown environments, but is not allowed to update them in case of causing data inconsistency in other clients.

2.2   Map fusing in the server end

In the server, the map fusing module fuses local maps received from the SLAM clients, achieving an optimized global map. The map fusing algorithm is shown in the Fig. 2. It includes two main parts: map overlap detection and local-map fusion.

Initializing Global Map. Initially, the global map is set empty as the server system starts. The SLAM clients build the local maps independently without any initial information from other clients and the server. The local maps from different clients have the different reference coordinate system. When the server receives local maps from the SLAM clients, the first local map will be directly inserted into the global map, and thus, the global reference coordinate system can be decided.

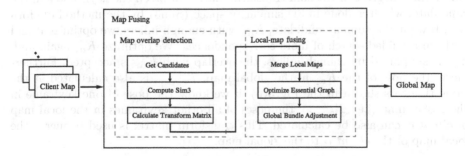

Fig. 2. The flowchart of Map Fusing module.

Map Overlap Detection. To determine the spatial connections among local maps in the server, we detect the overlaps among the local maps and further calculate the transform matrices using PnP method.

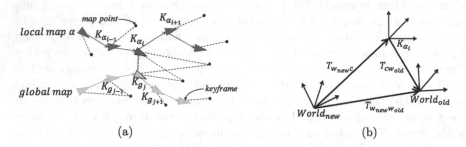

Fig. 3. In (a), the server detects the overlap between the *local map* α and the *global map*. (b) shows the transform relationships among the keyframe pose, the original and new world coordinate systems.

This module employs a bags of binary words (DBoW) approach [11] for map overlaps detection. The vocabulary is created offline with the ORB descriptors extracted from a large set of images and is loaded while system initializing [18]. The server incrementally builds a keyframe database for each local map and the global map. The keyframe database contains an invert index, which stores the ID of the keyframe in which each visual word in the vocabulary has been seen. Thus, querying the keyframe database can be done very efficiently. The keyframe database is updated when a keyframe is inserted or deleted from the map.

This module detects overlaps between local maps and the global map. It obtains a list of keyframes from the keyframe database of the global map according to the ORB features of the traversed keyframe in the operated local map. The keyframes in the list which have enough ORB feature matches will be accepted as rough candidates, as shown in the Fig. 3(a).

Then, it performs RANSAC iterations with all the rough candidates to calculate the 7 degrees-of-freedom transform matrix between the keyframe and the candidate, which is done in 3D similarity space (Sim3) by the method of Horn [14]. If we find a similar candidate, K_{α_i}, with enough inliers, we optimize it and perform a guided search of more correspondences. We optimize K_{α_i} again and, if it is supported by enough inliers, the overlap with K_{α_i} is accepted. Furthermore, the pose of the K_{α_i} in the global map, $T_{w_{new}c}$, is also calculated at the same time. As shown in the Fig. 3(b), if we know the pose of one keyframe in the global map (i.e., $T_{w_{new}c}$), the poses of all other keyframes in the local map of *client* α can also be calculated. This transform matrix is used to merge the local map of the *client* α to the global map.

Local-Map Fusing. To fuse local maps into a consistent global map, we optimize the essential graph in the server, and further optimize the global map by bundle adjustment (BA).

The local maps are merged into the global map by applying the previously calculated transformations to the keyframes and map points. Then, we perform a global 7 DoF optimization using BA to reduce map errors caused by different SLAM clients. Since global BA is time consuming, the optimization process only optimizes essential graph in the main thread, and performs global BA in a separate thread. Optimizing essential graph optimizes the poses of the keyframes in the global map and adds constraints by merging the duplicate map points in the overlapped maps. Global BA optimizes a graph by minimizing the re-projection error for all keyframes and map points that have been taken into account for the optimization. The implementation of the global BA uses the Levenberg-Marquardt implementation of g^2o [15].

2.3 Sharing the Globally Consistent Map

In the CORB-SLAM, the local maps built by the SLAM clients can be shared with the server and other clients. The map data, including keyframes and map points, will be transferred between clients and the central sever module when new map data is inserted or old map data is updated. Each keyframe mainly stores the camera pose, ORB features of the image frame, the IDs of all map points it observes and IDs of its co-related keyframes in the map. Each map point mainly stores its 3D position, its representative ORB feature, the IDs of keyframes that able to observe this map point. When new keyframes and map points are transferred, all the data in the keyframe and map point is packaged and transferred to the server or other clients. Furthermore, to reduce the band-width of updating poses in the map, we only transfer the light keyframe and light map point data which only stores the ID of the keyframe or map point and the pose or position of it.

When sharing map data among multiple robots, map data consistency, i.e. data values being consistent among robots, is taken into consideration. In this paper, we keep data consistency in all SLAM clients and the server by the following rules: (1) The SLAM clients share the newly created and updated data in local maps to the server in a particular rate. (2) The server share the newly created and updated data in the global map to all SLAM clients in a particular rate. (3) The SLAM clients can only update the map data created by themselves and keep the map data from the server and other clients fixed.

3   Experimental Results

The CORB-SLAM system is implemented in the Robot Operating System (ROS) [17]. The ROS provides a run-time environment that facilitates the client-server communication. Experiments are conducted to evaluate the performance of our CORB-SLAM system on the KITTI dataset in two different robot setup, i.e., two robots and three robots. The KITTI dataset contains stereo data sequences recorded from a car in different urban environments. The computer that runs the experiments is deployed an Ubuntu 14.04 64-bit operating system, an Intel core i7-4790 (8 cores @ 3.6 GHZ) CPU and 8GB RAM. Although in the experiments of this paper all SLAM clients and the server run on one computer, each SLAM client is free to run on an individual robot, owing to the distributed communication mechanism of ROS. On the other hand, running all those processes on one computer can prove the real-time performance of the proposed system.

3.1   Customized Datasets

Without popular public datasets specially designed for multi-robot SLAM being available, we build our multi-robot datasets based on the single-robot KITTI dataset. We select the sequences 00 and 05 of the KITTI dataset and divide them into several sub-sequences according to the number of the robots involved in our CORB-SLAM system. Each SLAM client runs with a sub-sequence, and each sub-sequence should have overlaps with at least one other sub-sequence to support the map fusing algorithm.

We use the following method to produce the sub-sequences. We assume the time period of a KITTI sequence is $Seq.[0, t]$. For the two-robot case, we set $Seq.[0, \frac{t}{2} + \delta t]$, and $Seq.[\frac{t}{2} - \delta t, t]$ as two sub-sequences. For the three-robot case, we set $Seq.[0, \frac{t}{3} + \delta t]$, $Seq.[\frac{t}{3} - \delta t, \frac{2t}{3} + \delta t]$, and $Seq.[\frac{2t}{3} - \delta t, t]$ as three sub-sequences. The δt ensures the overlaps among the sub-sequences.

3.2   Experiments with Two Robots

In this experiment, the sequence 00 of the KITTI dataset is used for two-robot collaborative visual SLAM, after being divided into two sub-sequences. Figure 4 shows the procedures of exploring the sequence 00 on two SLAM clients.

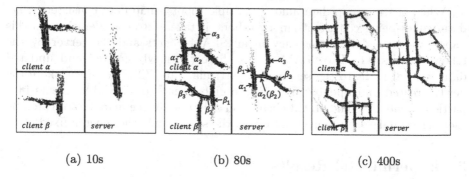

(a) 10s   (b) 80s   (c) 400s

Fig. 4. The running snapshots of CORB-SLAM at different timestamp. In (a), (b), and (c), the green lines mark the poses of keyframes built by the clients themselves, and the blue lines mark the poses of keyframes from other clients. The black points are the map points. (Color figure online)

Figure 4(a) shows initial map status of CORB-SLAM at $t = 10s$. *Client* α and *client* β initialize their local maps independently in their own local coordinate

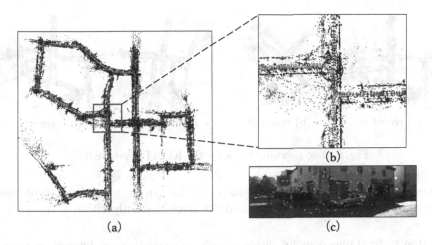

(b)

(a)   (c)

Fig. 5. (a) is the global map in *client* β. (b) is the detailed local zoom-in of the global map. In the street corner (the red circle area of (b)), *client* β builds the local map (green lines) and detects the loop closure in the map from the server (blue lines). (c) is the street-corner image from the camera in the red circle area of (b). (Color figure online)

system. The server has not detected an overlap between the two local maps, and thus, the two clients explore the environment independently.

In Fig. 4(b), the server has detected the overlap at $t = 80s$. *client* α has built the local map $\alpha_1\alpha_2\alpha_3$, and *client* β has built $\beta_1\beta_2\beta_3$. The server detects the overlap $\alpha_2 \cong \beta_2$, and fuses the local maps $\alpha_1\alpha_2\alpha_3$ and $\beta_1\beta_2\beta_3$ to global map $\alpha_1\beta_1\alpha_2(\beta_2)\alpha_3\beta_3$. Then, the server shares the global map with *client* α and *client* β. *client* α transforms the new map data $\beta_1\beta_2\beta_3$ to its own reference coordinate system and inserts $\beta_1\beta_2\beta_3$ to its local map as shown in the blue lines of *client* α, so does *client* β. Figure 4(c) shows the resulting map at $t = 400s$, and we present the detailed global map of *client* β in Fig. 5 as an example.

3.3   Experiment with Three Robots

In this experiment, the sequence 05 of the KITTI dataset is used for three-robot collaborative visual SLAM, after being divided into three sub-sequences.

The resulting maps in Fig. 6 show that, in the three SLAM clients case, each client can build its own local map and the local maps from the three different clients can be fused in the server and be shared back to different clients. The experiments with different numbers of robots also prove that the CORB-SLAM system is extendable for different scales of robot clients.

3.4   System Performance

There are some factors that can limit the scalability and the performance of the CORB-SLAM system, such as the communication, algorithm complexity in the

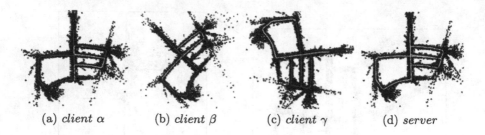

(a) *client α*   (b) *client β*   (c) *client γ*   (d) *server*

Fig. 6. The resulting maps on the KITTI sequence 05.

server end, and robot hardware resource. In this paper, we evaluate time costs of the client-server communication and the map-fusion algorithm.

Table 1. Total time costs for clients-server communications on different datasets.

	Full Keyframe		Full Map Point		Light Keyframe		Light Map Point	
	Num.	Time	Num.	Time	Num.	Time	Num.	Time
Seq. 00	937	98.15 s	499681	14.02 s	1083	2.570 s	139418	6.045 s
Seq. 05	818	89.97 s	429938	12.10 s	1375	2.889 s	156466	7.969 s

Table 2. Time costs on merging local map and global BA

	Keyframes in map	Merging local map	Global bundle adjustment
Seq. 00	136	0.5346 s	1.955 s
Seq. 05	456	2.835 s	4.535 s

As shown in Table 1, the total time cost for transferring full keyframes is about 35 times more than that of the light keyframes, although the number of light keyframes is much larger than that of full keyframes. The average transferring time cost for one full keyframe is about 45 times more than that of the light keyframe. The reason behind these is that the ORB features in the full keyframe occupy most of the keyframe storage. We find that the average time cost of transferring the light map point is more than that of the full map point, which is resulted from the fact that the updating operation is more complex than the inserting operation.

As shown in Table 2, the time cost of map fusing in the server is mainly spent on the map merging operation and the global BA. The global BA costs much more time than the merging operation which can be indicated from Table 2.

4   Conclusions

This paper proposes the CORB-SLAM system, a collaborative multiple-robot visual SLAM for unknown environment explorations. Experimental results with public KITTI dataset demonstrate that the CORB-SLAM system can perform SLAM collaboratively with multiple clients and a server end. The experiments are also shown in a video online[1].

References

1. Klein, G., Murray, D.: Parallel tracking and mapping for small AR workspaces. In: 6th IEEE and ACM International Symposium on Mixed and Augmented Reality, ISMAR 2007, pp. 225–234. IEEE (2007)
2. Mur-Artal, R., Tardos, J.D.: ORB-SLAM2: an open-source SLAM system for monocular, stereo and RGB-D cameras. arXiv preprint arXiv:1610.06475 (2016)
3. Riazuelo, L., Civera, J., Montiel, J.: C2TAM: a cloud framework for cooperative tracking and mapping. Robot. Auton. Syst. **62**(4), 401–413 (2014)
4. Deutsch, I., Liu, M., Siegwart, R.: A framework for multi-robot pose graph SLAM. In: IEEE International Conference on Real-time Computing and Robotics (RCAR), pp. 567–572. IEEE (2016)
5. Schmuck, P., Chli, M.: Multi-UAV Collaborative Monocular SLAM (2017)
6. Knuth, J., Barooah, P.: Collaborative localization with heterogeneous inter-robot measurements by Riemannian optimization. In: 2013 IEEE International Conference on Robotics and Automation (ICRA), pp. 1534–1539. IEEE (2013)
7. Cunningham, A., Paluri, M., Dellaert, F.: DDF-SAM: Fully distributed SLAM using constrained factor graphs. In: 2010 IEEE/RSJ International Conference on Intelligent Robots and Systems (IROS), pp. 3025–3030. IEEE (2010)
8. Colares, R.G., Chaimowicz, L.: The next frontier: combining information gain and distance cost for decentralized multi-robot exploration. In: Proceedings of the 31st Annual ACM Symposium on Applied Computing, pp. 268–274. ACM (2016)
9. Choudhary, S., Carlone, L., Nieto, C., Rogers, J., Christensen, H.I., Dellaert, F.: Distributed trajectory estimation with privacy and communication constraints: a two-stage distributed Gauss-Seidel approach. In: 2016 IEEE International Conference on Robotics and Automation (ICRA), pp. 5261–5268. IEEE (2016)
10. Choudhary, S., Carlone, L., Nieto, C., Rogers, J., Christensen, H.I., Dellaert, F.: Distributed mapping with privacy and communication constraints: lightweight algorithms and object-based models. arXiv preprint arXiv:1702.03435 (2017)
11. Gálvez-López, D., Tardos, J.D.: Bags of binary words for fast place recognition in image sequences. IEEE Trans. Robot. **28**(5), 1188–1197 (2012)
12. Moreno-Noguer, F., Lepetit, V., Fua, P.: Accurate non-iterative o (n) solution to the PnP problem. In: IEEE 11th International Conference on Computer vision, ICCV 2007, pp. 1–8. IEEE (2007)
13. Geiger, A., Lenz, P., Stiller, C., Urtasun, R.: Vision meets robotics: the KITTI dataset. Int. J. Robot. Res. **32**(11), 1231–1237 (2013)
14. Horn, B.K.P.: Closed-form solution of absolute orientation using unit quaternions. JOSA A **4**(4), 629–642 (1987)
15. Kümmerle, R., Grisetti, G., Strasdat, H., Konolige, K., Burgard, W.: g2o: a general framework for graph optimization. In: 2011 IEEE International Conference on Robotics and Automation (ICRA), pp. 3607–3613. IEEE (2011)
16. Rublee, E., Rabaud, V., Konolige, K., Bradski, G.: ORB: an efficient alternative to SIFT or SURF. In: 2011 IEEE International Conference on Computer Vision (ICCV), pp. 2564–2571. IEEE (2011)

---

[1] http://v.youku.com/v_show/id_XMjg5MTkyMzY3Ng.

17. Quigley, M., et al.:. ROS: an open-source robot operating system. In: ICRA Workshop on Open Source Software, vol. 3, p. 5. Kobe (2009)
18. Mur-Artal, R., Montiel, J.M.M., Tardos, J.D.: ORB-SLAM: a versatile and accurate monocular SLAM system. IEEE Trans. Robot. **31**(5), 1147–1163 (2015)

Security and Trustworthy

An Efficient and Privacy Preserving CP-ABE Scheme for Internet-Based Collaboration

Jinmiao Wang[✉] and Bo Lang

State Key Laboratory of Software Development Environment,
Beihang University, Beijing 100191, China
{wangjinmiao,langbo}@buaa.edu.cn

Abstract. The development of Internet applications facilitates enterprises and individuals to share information and work together across physical barriers. In such environment, flexible and efficient data-protection methods are required because data are out of the control domain of its owners. By encrypting with an access policy, ciphertext-policy attribute-based encryption (CP-ABE) can simultaneously achieve data encryption and access control, making it an ideal mechanism for data protection in Internet-based environments. However, the existing CP-ABE schemes usually have limitations regarding efficiency and privacy leakage from the access policy. In this paper, we propose a CP-ABE scheme with hidden access policy and fast decryption that improves the decryption efficiency and preserves the privacy of the access policy. In addition, by adopting dual-system encryption methodology, our scheme achieves full security, which is a higher security level in CP-ABE. The performance analysis revealed that the comprehensive capability of our scheme outperforms the existing CP-ABE schemes.

Keywords: Data protection · Attribute-based encryption
Hidden policy · Fast decryption · Fully secure

1 Introduction

With the development of Internet applications and smart devices, people can interact, share information and work together across physical barriers typically exploiting Internet-based environments. Thus, the cooperation among enterprises, public institutions and user communities is evolving into self-organizing and open pattern. For instance, using online social networks to form a collaborative group is very popular at present. During the collaboration, users and institutions tend to outsource their data to an external server on Internet to accomplish data sharing and enable cooperation. In this case, the data objects are out of the control domain of data owners and stored in the untrusted servers, which causes the prominent data security problem. Furthermore, data owners

© ICST Institute for Computer Sciences, Social Informatics and Telecommunications Engineering 2018
I. Romdhani et al. (Eds.): CollaborateCom 2017, LNICST 252, pp. 493–507, 2018.
https://doi.org/10.1007/978-3-030-00916-8_46

usually want to share data to some specific users. For example, in e-Health environment patients usually want to share their physical data to doctors in a specific hospital, which can be ensured by access control. Hence, building an effective data protection and access control mechanism for Internet-based collaboration has become a major challenge.

Currently, encryption is the primary mechanism used to ensure data confidentiality. However, traditional public-key encryption cannot achieve efficient and fine-grained access control. Fortunately, the introduction of ciphertext-policy attribute-based encryption (CP-ABE) [1] has made important steps toward solving these problems. In CP-ABE, data are encrypted under an access policy that is specified by the data owner, and a user's private key is generated based on a set of user attributes. If and only if a user's attributes satisfy the access policy can the user decrypt the corresponding ciphertext. Hence, CP-ABE integrates encryption and access control. The access policy in CP-ABE can be expressed based on AND-gate, Tree or Linear Secret-Sharing Scheme (LSSS) matrix. The tree and LSSS structures can express any monotone access policy; hence, both of them are more expressive than the AND-gate. Using its hierarchy, the tree structure allows the data owner to specify a complex access policy in intuitionistic form, thereby delivering a better user experience than LSSS.

In CP-ABE mechanism, not just the data are sensitive but also the access policy, because the access policy may directly contain private information about the protected data and users. For example, through the access policy of a patient's physical data, one can obtain some personal information about the patient, such as the age, the diseases, etc. However, in the original CP-ABE schemes, the access policy is published together with the ciphertext, and anyone who receives the ciphertext can obtain the policy. CP-ABE with hidden access policy presents a good solution to this problem [2–11]. In these schemes, the attributes in the access policy are hidden such that even the legitimate recipient cannot obtain any information about the access policy more than the fact that he can decrypt the ciphertext, which ensures anyone cannot obtain attribute information about the data owner and recipients. However, some existing policy hiding schemes [2–8,10] are based on AND-gate which has limited policy expression ability, and some are proven *selectively* secure [4–9], a weaker security model in which part of the challenged ciphertext description must be declared before the attacker receives the public parameters [12].

In addition, CP-ABE is usually characterized by problems with efficiency. In most existing CP-ABE schemes, the number of pairing operations in decryption, which consumes substantially more CPU time and memory than other operations, increases linearly with the number of attributes involved, which makes the decryption of CP-ABE schemes expensive. To improve the decryption efficiency, many researchers focused on fast decryption [2–5,13,14], i.e., reducing the number of pairing operations in decryption to a constant. However, some of them are based on expressive-ability limited AND-gate, some reveals the access policy, and some are just proven selectively secure. In other words, none of the existing

CP-ABE schemes can achieve fast decryption and policy hiding while remaining policy-expressive and *fully* secure[1].

To address the above limitations, we propose a tree-based CP-ABE with hidden access policy and fast decryption (CP-ABE-HF) in this paper. In the decryption of CP-ABE-HF, the number of pairing operations is reduced to three, which greatly improves the decryption efficiency. To the best of our knowledge, this is the first tree-based CP-ABE scheme that can achieve fast decryption. To preserve the privacy of the access policy, we compute a ciphertext element and record a path in the access tree for each attribute in the system. Thus, no one can obtain what attributes are used in the *real* access policy, even if they are authorized to access the data object. Regarding security, by adopting the dual-system encryption methodology [12], CP-ABE-HF is proven fully secure, thereby overcoming the weakness of the selectively secure model and reaching a higher security level.

The paper is organized as follows. We review the related work in Sect. 2. The preliminaries and background knowledge of our scheme are introduced in Sect. 3. In Sect. 4, we describe the method of policy hiding and propose the CP-ABE scheme with hidden access policy and fast decryption. In Sect. 5, we analysis the security and efficiency of our scheme and compare it with some existing CP-ABE schemes. The paper is concluded in Sect. 6.

2 Related Work

To preserve the access-policy privacy, several CP-ABE schemes with hidden access policy have been proposed. Nishide et al. [6] first constructed an anonymous CP-ABE based on AND-gate, which has limited policy-expression ability. Subsequently, several policy-hiding schemes were proposed with the same access structure [2–5, 7, 8, 10]. Hur [9] proposed a CP-ABE with hidden policies based on the tree structure. However, the access policy can be determined by comparing the index of a user's attributes with the attributes in the ciphertext. Regarding security, the aforementioned schemes are all proven selectively secure. To improve the security, some additional schemes constructed over composite-order groups are proven fully secure. Lai et al. [10] proposed a fully secure and policy-hiding CP-ABE scheme, which is also based on AND-gate. Lai et al. [11] proposed a partially policy-hidden scheme (i.e., the attribute name is revealed while the attribute value is hidden) based on LSSS structure. However, this scheme is inefficient because it adds some redundant components to the ciphertext.

To improve the decryption efficiency of CP-ABE, some researchers focused on reducing the number of pairing operations to a constant. Emura et al. [13] proposed a CP-ABE in which both the ciphertext length and the number of pairing operations are constant. Miyaji et al. [14] proposed a dual-policy ABE that requires four pairing operations to decrypt. Both schemes are based on AND-gate and proven selectively secure.

---

[1] Full security overcomes the weakness of selective security; i.e., it does not require the attacker to declare the challenged access policy in advance.

There are also some schemes achieved both of policy hidden and fast decryption. The selectively secure schemes proposed in [4,5] reduced the pairing operations to two and four times, respectively, while preserving the policy privacy. Rao and Dutta [2] proposed a fully secure CP-ABE with hidden policy and constant decryption costs. The fully secure scheme proposed by Li et al. [3] also preserved the policy privacy and reduced the number of pairing operations to a constant. However, the aforementioned schemes can only express restricted-access policies; thus, their expression abilities need to be improved.

3 Background Knowledge

3.1 Preliminaries

Composite-Order Bilinear Group. Let $\mathcal{G}$ denote an algorithm that takes as input a security parameter γ and outputs a tuple $(N = p_1 p_2 p_3 p_4, \mathbb{G}, \mathbb{G}_T, e)$, where p_1, p_2, p_3, p_4 are distinct primes, $\mathbb{G}$ and $\mathbb{G}_T$ are cyclic groups of order N, and $e : \mathbb{G} \times \mathbb{G} \to \mathbb{G}_T$ is a bilinear map such that:

- (Bilinear) $\forall g, h \in \mathbb{G}$ and $x, y \in \mathbb{Z}_N$, it satisfies $e(g^x, h^y) = e(g, h)^{xy}$.
- (Non-degenerate) $\exists g \in \mathbb{G}$ such that $e(g, g)$ has order N in $\mathbb{G}_T$.

We require that the group operations in $\mathbb{G}$ and $\mathbb{G}_T$ and the bilinear map e are all computable in polynomial time. Let $\mathbb{G}_{p_1}, \mathbb{G}_{p_2}, \mathbb{G}_{p_3}$ and $\mathbb{G}_{p_4}$ denote the subgroups of $\mathbb{G}$ with orders p_1, p_2, p_3 and p_4, respectively. Note that if $g_i \in \mathbb{G}_{p_i}$ and $g_j \in \mathbb{G}_{p_j}$ for $i \neq j$, then $e(g_i, g_j) = 1$. If the generator of $\mathbb{G}_{p_i}$ is $g_i (i \in \{1, 2, 3, 4\})$, then every element $h \in \mathbb{G}$ can be expressed as $g_1^{a_1} g_2^{a_2} g_3^{a_3} g_4^{a_4}$ for some values $a_1, a_2, a_3, a_4 \in \mathbb{Z}_N$.

Complexity Assumption. We now present the complexity assumptions that will be used in our scheme. These assumptions are the same as those in [12], and we use them in the group whose order is a product of four primes.

Assumption 1. *Given a group generator $\mathcal{G}$, we define the following distribution:*

$$(N = p_1 p_2 p_3 p_4, \mathbb{G}, \mathbb{G}_T, e) \xleftarrow{R} \mathcal{G}(\gamma),$$

$$g_1 \xleftarrow{R} \mathbb{G}_{p_1}, X_3 \xleftarrow{R} \mathbb{G}_{p_3}, X_4 \xleftarrow{R} \mathbb{G}_{p_4},$$

$$D = (\mathbb{G}, g_1, X_3, X_4), \tag{1}$$

$$T_1 \xleftarrow{R} \mathbb{G}_{p_1 p_2}, T_2 \xleftarrow{R} \mathbb{G}_{p_1}.$$

The advantage of algorithm $\mathcal{A}$ in breaking this assumption is defined as

$$Adv_{\mathcal{G},\mathcal{A}}^1(\gamma) = |Pr[\mathcal{A}(D, T_1) = 1] - Pr[\mathcal{A}(D, T_2) = 1]|. \tag{2}$$

Definition 1. *If for any probabilistic polynomial time (PPT) algorithm $\mathcal{A}$, $Adv_{\mathcal{G},\mathcal{A}}^1(\gamma)$ is negligible, then we say $\mathcal{G}$ satisfies Assumption 1.*

Assumption 2. *Given a group generator $\mathcal{G}$, we define the following distribution:*

$$(N = p_1p_2p_3p_4, \mathbb{G}, \mathbb{G}_T, e) \xleftarrow{R} \mathcal{G}(\gamma),$$

$$g_1, X_1 \xleftarrow{R} \mathbb{G}_{p_1}, X_2, Y_2 \xleftarrow{R} \mathbb{G}_{p_2},$$

$$X_3, Y_3 \xleftarrow{R} \mathbb{G}_{p_3}, X_4 \xleftarrow{R} \mathbb{G}_{p_4}, \tag{3}$$

$$D = (\mathbb{G}, g_1, X_1X_2, Y_2Y_3, X_3, X_4),$$

$$T_1 \xleftarrow{R} \mathbb{G}_{p_1p_2p_3}, T_2 \xleftarrow{R} \mathbb{G}_{p_1p_3}.$$

The advantage of algorithm $\mathcal{A}$ in breaking this assumption is defined as

$$Adv^2_{\mathcal{G},\mathcal{A}}(\gamma) = |Pr[\mathcal{A}(D, T_1) = 1] - Pr[\mathcal{A}(D, T_2) = 1]|. \tag{4}$$

Definition 2. *If for any PPT algorithm $\mathcal{A}$, $Adv^2_{\mathcal{G},\mathcal{A}}(\gamma)$ is negligible, then we say $\mathcal{G}$ satisfies Assumption 2.*

Assumption 3. *Given a group generator $\mathcal{G}$, we define the following distribution:*

$$(N = p_1p_2p_3p_4, \mathbb{G}, \mathbb{G}_T, e) \xleftarrow{R} \mathcal{G}(\gamma),$$

$$g_1 \xleftarrow{R} \mathbb{G}_{p_1}, g_2, X_2, Y_2 \xleftarrow{R} \mathbb{G}_{p_2},$$

$$X_3 \xleftarrow{R} \mathbb{G}_{p_3}, X_4 \xleftarrow{R} \mathbb{G}_{p_4}, \alpha, s \xleftarrow{R} \mathbb{Z}_N, \tag{5}$$

$$D = (\mathbb{G}, g_1, g_2, g_1^{\alpha}X_2, g_1^sY_2, X_3, X_4),$$

$$T_1 = e(g_1, g_1)^{\alpha s}, T_2 \xleftarrow{R} \mathbb{G}_T.$$

The advantage of algorithm $\mathcal{A}$ in breaking this assumption is defined as

$$Adv^3_{\mathcal{G},\mathcal{A}}(\gamma) = |Pr[\mathcal{A}(D, T_1) = 1] - Pr[\mathcal{A}(D, T_2) = 1]|. \tag{6}$$

Definition 3. *If for any PPT algorithm $\mathcal{A}$, $Adv^3_{\mathcal{G},\mathcal{A}}(\gamma)$ is negligible, then we say $\mathcal{G}$ satisfies Assumption 3.*

3.2   Background of CP-ABE

Access Tree. Let $\mathcal{T}$ be a tree representing an access structure. Each non-leaf node of the tree represents a threshold operator, which is described by its children and a threshold value. If num_x is the number of children of node x, and k_x is its threshold value, then $1 \le k_x \le num_x$. When $k_x = 1$, the threshold is an OR operator, and when $k_x = num_x$, it is an AND operator. Each leaf node x of the tree is described by an attribute and a threshold value $k_x = 1$ [1].

Let $\mathcal{T}$ be an access tree with root r. The subtree of $\mathcal{T}$ rooted at node x is denoted by $\mathcal{T}_x$. Thus, $\mathcal{T}$ is the same as $\mathcal{T}_r$. If a set of attributes ω satisfies the access tree $\mathcal{T}_x$, we denote it as $\mathcal{T}_x(\omega) = 1$. We compute $\mathcal{T}_x(\omega)$ recursively as follows. If x is a non-leaf node, we evaluate $\mathcal{T}_{x'}(\omega)$ for each child x' of node x. $\mathcal{T}_x(\omega)$ returns 1 if and only if at least k_x children return 1. If x is a leaf node, then $\mathcal{T}_x(\omega)$ returns 1 if and only if $att(x) \in \omega$, where $att(x)$ denotes the attribute associated with node x [1].

CP-ABE Algorithms. The CP-ABE consists of the following algorithms [1]:

- **Setup** (U). This algorithm takes as input an attribute universe U. It will initialize the system and generate the master key mk and the public key pk.
- **KeyGen** (pk, mk, ω). This algorithm takes as input the public key pk, the master key mk and a user's attribute set ω. It will output a private key sk_ω.
- **Encryption** $(pk, M, \mathcal{T})$. This algorithm takes as input the public key pk, a message M and an access-policy tree $\mathcal{T}$. It will produce a ciphertext $C_\mathcal{T}$.
- **Decryption** $(sk_\omega, C_\mathcal{T})$. The decryption algorithm takes as input a private key sk_ω and a ciphertext $C_\mathcal{T}$. It will output the plaintext M if ω satisfies $\mathcal{T}$.

Security Model. In our scheme, the security under chosen-plaintext attack (CPA) is modeled as a game between a challenger and an adversary. It includes five phases, which are detailed as follows:

- **Setup.** The challenger initializes the system to generate pk and mk. Then, he sends pk to the adversary.
- **Phase 1.** The adversary is allowed to make private key requests for any attribute set ω. The challenger returns sk_ω to the adversary.
- **Challenge.** The adversary sends two equal-length message M_0 and M_1 and two access trees $\mathcal{T}_0^*$ and $\mathcal{T}_1^*$ to the challenger, with the restriction that $\mathcal{T}_0^*$ and $\mathcal{T}_1^*$ cannot be satisfied by any requested attribute set in Phase 1 or contain repeated attributes. The challenger chooses random $\theta \in \{0, 1\}$ and encrypts M_θ with $\mathcal{T}_\theta^*$. Then, the ciphertext $C_{\mathcal{T}_\theta^*}$ is returned to the adversary.
- **Phase 2. Phase 1** is repeated with the restriction that none of the requested attribute sets can satisfy $\mathcal{T}_0^*$ or $\mathcal{T}_1^*$ or contain repeated attributes.
- **Guess.** The adversary outputs a guess $\theta' \in \{0, 1\}$.

Definition 4. *A CP-ABE scheme with hidden policy is said to be fully secure against CPA if any polynomial-time adversaries have at most a negligible advantage in this security game. The advantage of an adversary is defined as $\varepsilon = |Pr[\theta' = \theta] - 1/2|$.*

Selective security is defined by adding an initialization phase in which the adversary must declare $\mathcal{T}_0^*$ and $\mathcal{T}_1^*$ before receiving pk. In our scheme, we do not impose this restriction on the adversary.

4   Our Constructions

4.1   Hiding the Access Policy

In our construction, the access policy is expressed by an access tree $\mathcal{T}$. To achieve the goal of policy hiding, we randomly choose $index(x) \in \mathbb{Z}_N^*$ for each node x, where $index(x)$ denotes the index of node x in $\mathcal{T}$. Next, for each leaf node x, let $att(x) = A_i$ and record a node path $path_i$ which consists of the index $index(x')$ of each node x' on the path from the root node r to x. For example, the path record of the leaf node associated with attribute A_1 in Fig. 1(a) is $path_1 = \{1, 3, 4\}$.

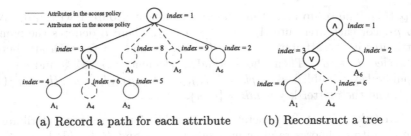

(a) Record a path for each attribute   (b) Reconstruct a tree

Fig. 1. The hiding of access policy

For each attribute that is not in $\mathcal{T}$, we also need to record a node path. The $path_i$ for attribute A_i can be obtained by randomly choosing a non-leaf node z in the tree and implicitly setting A_i to be a dummy child node of z, such as the attributes A_3, A_4 and A_5 which are illustrated as dotted lines in Fig. 1(a). Thus, each of the attributes in the attribute universe has a path record associated with the access tree $\mathcal{T}$. Finally, the path records are sent along with the ciphertext while the access tree $\mathcal{T}$ is discarded, thereby the access policy is hidden. Note that each attribute can only be used once in the access policy because the reuse of an attribute will introduce another path. Thus one can determine that the attributes with more than one path must have appeared in the access policy, which means such attribute is leaked.

In our scheme, the index i for each attribute in the attribute universe is fixed. Hence, with the index i of attributes A_i in the user's attribute set, the decryption algorithm can extract the corresponding $path_i$ from the ciphertext. Then a tree $\mathcal{T}'$ is reconstructed with the records in these paths, and the decryption operation is performed over $\mathcal{T}'$. For example, suppose a user's attribute set is $\omega = \{A_1, A_4, A_6\}$, then the paths $path_1, path_4$ and $path_6$ will be extracted to construct a tree $\mathcal{T}'$, as shown in Fig. 1(b). We can notice that A_4 is not in the access policy, yet it still takes part in the decryption because the user does not know the fact. By performing the decryption algorithm in Sect. 4.2, the ciphertext and private key elements associated with A_4 will be cancelled. Hence, if the user's attributes satisfy the access policy, the user can decrypt successfully without knowing the access policy.

4.2   The CP-ABE-HF Scheme

We construct the fully secure CP-ABE-HF scheme in composite-order groups with order $N = p_1 p_2 p_3 p_4$. Let $\mathbb{G}_{p_i}$ denote the subgroup whose order is prime p_i. The normal operations of the scheme essentially occur in the subgroup $\mathbb{G}_{p_1}$. Private keys are additionally randomized in $\mathbb{G}_{p_3}$, and ciphertexts are additionally randomized in $\mathbb{G}_{p_4}$. The subgroup $\mathbb{G}_{p_2}$ is not used in the real scheme but serves as the semi-functional space in the security proof. We also define the Lagrange coefficient $\ell_{i,V}$ for $i \in \mathbb{Z}_N^*$ and a set, V, of elements in $\mathbb{Z}_N^*$: $\ell_{i,V}(x) = \prod_{j \in V, j \neq i} \frac{x-j}{i-j}$. The CP-ABE-HF scheme includes the following algorithms:

Setup (U). The setup algorithm chooses a bilinear group $\mathbb{G}$ with order $N = p_1 p_2 p_3 p_4$. For each attribute $A_i \in U$ $(1 \leq i \leq n$, where n denotes the number of attributes in the attribute universe U, and the index i for each attribute is fixed), select $h_i \in \mathbb{Z}_N^*$. Then, choose random elements $\alpha, \kappa \in \mathbb{Z}_N^*$ and $g \in \mathbb{G}_{p_1}$. The public key is published as $pk = \{N, g, y = e(g,g)^\alpha, L = g^\kappa, H_i = g^{h_i} (1 \leq i \leq n)\}$, and the master key is $mk = \{\alpha, \kappa\}$.

KeyGen (pk, mk, ω). To generate a private key for a user with attribute set ω, the algorithm chooses random elements $t \in \mathbb{Z}_N^*$ and $R, R_0, \{R_i\}_{A_i \in \omega} \in \mathbb{G}_{p_3}$ and returns the following private key to the user:

$$
\begin{aligned}
sk_\omega = \{D = g^{\alpha - \kappa t} R, D_0 = g^t R_0 \\
\forall A_i \in \omega : D_i = H_i^t R_i\}.
\end{aligned}
\tag{7}
$$

Encryption $(pk, M, \mathcal{T})$. To output the ciphertext of message M encrypted under the access tree $\mathcal{T}$, the algorithm first chooses a polynomial f_x for each node x in $\mathcal{T}$ in the following way, starting with the root node and then proceeding in a top-down manner.

For each node x in the tree, set the degree d_x of the polynomial f_x to be one less than the threshold value k_x; i.e., set $d_x = k_x - 1$. For the root node r, the algorithm chooses a random element s and sets $f_r(0) = s$. Then, it chooses d_r other points of the polynomial f_r randomly to define it. For any other node x, it sets $f_x(0) = f_{parent(x)}(index(x))$ and chooses d_x other points randomly to completely define f_x, where $parent(x)$ indicates the parent of node x. After all of the polynomials are defined, set $\lambda_x = f_x(0)$ for each node x in the tree.

Next, for each attribute A_i in the attribute universe, the node path $path_i$ is recorded using the method detailed in Sect. 4.1. Finally, choose random elements $Z_0, \{Z_i\}_{A_i \in U} \in \mathbb{G}_{p_4}$, and let $att(x) = A_i$, the ciphertext is generated as follows.

$$
\begin{aligned}
C_\mathcal{T} = \{E = My^s, E_0 = g^s Z_0, \\
\forall A_i \in \mathcal{T} : E_i = L^{\lambda_x} H_i^s Z_i, path_i, \\
\forall A_i \notin \mathcal{T} : E_i = H_i^s Z_i, path_i\}.
\end{aligned}
\tag{8}
$$

We note that for $A_i \in \mathcal{T}$ and $A_i \notin \mathcal{T}$, E_i is properly distributed as a random element of $\mathbb{G}_{p_1 p_4}$. Thus, the recipient cannot distinguish E_i of $A_i \in \mathcal{T}$ from E_i of $A_i \notin \mathcal{T}$, indicating that the access policy is fully hidden.

Decryption $(sk_\omega, C_\mathcal{T})$. To decrypt the ciphertext $C_\mathcal{T}$ with sk_ω, the ciphertext component E_i that corresponds to $A_i \in \omega$ should be extracted according to the index i in the attribute universe. Then, an access tree $\mathcal{T}'$ can be reconstructed with the path record $path_i$ in E_i. Next, the decryption algorithm will be executed with tree $\mathcal{T}'$.

First, we define two recursive functions: $DecryptNode\_CT(C_\mathcal{T}, x)$, which takes as inputs the ciphertext $C_\mathcal{T}$ and node x from tree $\mathcal{T}'$, and $DecryptNode\_SK(sk_\omega, x)$, which takes as inputs the private key sk_ω and node x from tree $\mathcal{T}'$, as follows.

If node x is a leaf node, let $att(x) = A_i$ and set:

$$DecryptNode\_CT(C_T, x) = E_i = \begin{cases} L^{\lambda_x} H_i^s Z_i & \text{if } A_i \in T \\ H_i^s Z_i & \text{if } A_i \notin T \end{cases} \tag{9}$$

$$DecryptNode\_SK(sk_\omega, x) = D_i = H_i^t R_i.$$

Next, we consider the recursive case when x is an internal node. The functions $DecryptNode\_CT(C_T, x)$ and $DecryptNode\_SK(sk_\omega, x)$ will proceed as follows: For any node y that is the child of x, $DecryptNode\_CT(C_T, y)$ and $DecryptNode\_SK(sk_\omega, y)$ are invoked, and the outputs are stored as F_y and K_y, respectively. Let Q_x be a set of child nodes y that is in T and Q'_x be a set of y that is not in T. Note that the set $Q_x \cup Q'_x$ denotes all child nodes of x in the reconstructed tree T'. If node y is a leaf node, we compute

$$
\begin{aligned}
F_x &= \prod_{y \in (Q_x \cup Q'_x)} F_y^{\ell_y, V_x (0)} \\
&= \prod_{y \in Q_x} (L^{\lambda_y} H_i^s Z_i)^{\ell_y, V_x (0)} \cdot \prod_{y \in Q'_x} (H_i^s Z_i)^{\ell_y, V_x (0)} \\
&= \prod_{y \in Q_x} g^{\kappa \lambda_y \cdot \ell_y, V_x (0)} \cdot \prod_{y \in (Q_x \cup Q'_x)} H_i^{s \cdot \ell_y, V_x (0)} \cdot \prod_{y \in (Q_x \cup Q'_x)} Z_i^{\ell_y, V_x (0)} \\
&= g^{\kappa \lambda_x} \cdot \widetilde{F}_{x,1} \cdot \widetilde{F}_{x,2}
\end{aligned}
\tag{10}
$$

and

$$
\begin{aligned}
K_x &= \prod_{y \in (Q_x \cup Q'_x)} K_y^{\ell_y, V_x (0)} \\
&= \prod_{y \in (Q_x \cup Q'_x)} H_i^{t \cdot \ell_y, V_x (0)} \cdot \prod_{y \in (Q_x \cup Q'_x)} R_i^{\ell_y, V_x (0)} \\
&= \widetilde{K}_{x,1} \cdot \widetilde{K}_{x,2}.
\end{aligned}
\tag{11}
$$

If node y is a non-leaf node, we compute:

$$
\begin{aligned}
F_x &= \prod_{y \in (Q_x \cup Q'_x)} F_y^{\ell_y, V_x (0)} \\
&= \prod_{y \in (Q_x \cup Q'_x)} (g^{\kappa \lambda_y} \cdot \widetilde{F}_{y,1} \cdot \widetilde{F}_{y,2})^{\ell_y, V_x (0)} \\
&= \prod_{y \in Q_x} (g^{\kappa \lambda_y})^{\ell_y, V_x (0)} \cdot \prod_{y \in (Q_x \cup Q'_x)} \widetilde{F}_{y,1}^{\ell_y, V_x (0)} \cdot \prod_{y \in (Q_x \cup Q'_x)} \widetilde{F}_{y,2}^{\ell_y, V_x (0)} \\
&= g^{\kappa \lambda_x} \cdot \widetilde{F}_{x,1} \cdot \widetilde{F}_{x,2}
\end{aligned}
\tag{12}
$$

and

$$
\begin{aligned}
K_x &= \prod_{y \in (Q_x \cup Q'_x)} K_y^{\ell_y, V_x (0)} \\
&= \prod_{y \in (Q_x \cup Q'_x)} \widetilde{K}_{y,1}^{\ell_y, V_x (0)} \cdot \prod_{y \in (Q_x \cup Q'_x)} \widetilde{K}_{y,2}^{\ell_y, V_x (0)} \\
&= \widetilde{K}_{x,1} \cdot \widetilde{K}_{x,2}.
\end{aligned}
\tag{13}
$$

In the above equations, we have $\widetilde{F}_{x,1}^t = \widetilde{K}_{x,1}^s$. The parameter $V_x = \{index(y)|y \in (Q_x \cup Q'_x)\}$, and $\ell_{y,V_x}(0)$ is a Lagrange coefficient which can be computed by everyone who knows the index of attributes in T'.

Now that we have defined the functions $DecryptNode\_CT$ and $DecryptNode\_SK$, the decryption algorithm should first call the functions on the root r of T'. Thus, we obtain

$$A = DecryptNode\_CT(C_T, r) = g^{\kappa s} \cdot \widetilde{F}_{r,1} \cdot \widetilde{F}_{r,2} \tag{14}$$

and

$$B = DecryptNode\_SK(sk_\omega, r) = \widetilde{K}_{r,1} \cdot \widetilde{K}_{r,2}. \tag{15}$$

Then, we compute

$$
\begin{aligned}
C &= e(A, D_0)/e(E_0, B) \\
&= e(g^{\kappa s} \cdot \widetilde{F}_{r,1} \cdot \widetilde{F}_{r,2}, g^t R_0)/e(g^s Z_0, \widetilde{K}_{r,1} \cdot \widetilde{K}_{r,2}) \\
&= e(g^{\kappa s}, g^t) \cdot e(\widetilde{F}_{r,1}, g^t) \cdot e(\widetilde{F}_{r,2}, g^t) \cdot e(g^{\kappa s} \cdot \widetilde{F}_{r,1} \cdot \widetilde{F}_{r,2}, R_0) \\
&\quad /(e(g^s, \widetilde{K}_{r,1}) \cdot e(g^s, \widetilde{K}_{r,2}) \cdot e(Z_0, \widetilde{K}_{r,1} \cdot \widetilde{K}_{r,2})) \\
&= e(g,g)^{\kappa t s}.
\end{aligned} \tag{16}
$$

Finally, the algorithm returns the plaintext M', where

$$M' = \frac{E}{e(E_0, D) \cdot C} = \frac{Me(g,g)^{\alpha s}}{e(g^s Z_0, g^{\alpha - \kappa t} R) \cdot e(g,g)^{\kappa t s}} = M. \tag{17}$$

If the attributes in ω satisfy the hidden access policy, the recipient can decrypt the ciphertext successfully. To inform the recipient whether the decryption is successful, we use a hybrid encryption method in practice [15]. First, the encryptor picks a random $\varphi \in \mathbb{G}_T$ and derives two uniform and independent b-bit symmetric keys (φ_0, φ_1) from φ. Next, it encrypts the message M using a symmetric encryption scheme under key φ_0 to obtain ciphertext C_0. Our encryption algorithm **Encryption** is used to encrypt φ under access tree T to obtain ciphertext C_T. The final ciphertext consists of (φ_1, C_0, C_T). In the decryption phase, the recipient first recovers φ' from C_T using our **Decryption** algorithm. Then, it derives (φ'_0, φ'_1) from φ'. If $\varphi'_1 = \varphi_1$, it decrypts C_0 under φ'_0 using the symmetric encryption scheme and outputs the plaintext of message M. Otherwise, it outputs $\perp$. According to [15], the false error probability is approximately $1/2^b$. Thus, the recipient can use φ'_1 to check whether the decryption was successful. Furthermore, the hybrid encryption also greatly improves the efficiency because the message is encrypted using symmetric encryption, which is the most efficient encryption mechanism currently available.

5   Security and Performance Analysis

5.1   Security Analysis

Theorem 1. *If Assumptions 1, 2 and 3 hold, then the proposed CP-ABE-HF scheme is fully secure.*

To prove the security of our scheme, we apply the dual-system encryption methodology in [12]. We first define two structures—the semi-functional ciphertext and semi-functional key—which are not used in the real system, but will be used in our proof. A normal private key can decrypt normal or semi-functional ciphertexts, and a normal ciphertext can be decrypted by normal or semi-functional private keys. However, when decrypting a semi-functional ciphertext with a semi-functional private key, an additional pairing under elements in $\mathbb{G}_{p_2}$ will cause decryption to fail.

Semi-functional Ciphertext. Let g_2 denote a generator of $\mathbb{G}_{p_2}$. To produce a semi-functional ciphertext associated with an access tree $\mathcal{T}$, we first produce a normal ciphertext $C_{\mathcal{T}} = (E, E_0, \{E_i, path_i\})$ with the encryption algorithm. Then, we choose random elements $\kappa', s' \in \mathbb{Z}_N^*$ and a random exponent h_i' for each attribute in the attribute universe. Next, we share the secret s' in the manner detailed in the encryption algorithm and obtain a piece of share λ_x' for each attribute in the access tree. The ciphertext is created as follows:

$$E' = E, E_0' = E_0 \cdot g_2^{s'},$$
$$\forall A_i \in \mathcal{T} : E_i' = E_i \cdot g_2^{\kappa' \lambda_x'} g_2^{s' h_i'}, path_i, \qquad (18)$$
$$\forall A_i \notin \mathcal{T} : E_i' = E_i \cdot g_2^{s' h_i'}, path_i.$$

Semi-functional Key. A semi-functional key will take one of two forms. To produce the semi-functional key, we first produce a normal key $sk = (D, D_0, \{D_i\}_{\forall A_i \in \omega})$. Then, we choose random elements $\delta, t' \in \mathbb{Z}_N^*$. The semi-functional key of type 1 is set as follows:

$$D' = D \cdot g_2^{\delta}, D_0' = D_0, \{D_i' = D_i\}_{\forall A_i \in \omega}. \qquad (19)$$

The semi-functional key of type 2 is set as follows:

$$D' = D \cdot g_2^{\delta}, D_0' = D_0 \cdot g_2^{t'}, \{D_i' = D_i \cdot g_2^{t' h_i'}\}_{\forall A_i \in \omega}. \qquad (20)$$

We will prove the security of our scheme using a hybrid argument over a sequence of games. The first game, $Game_{Real}$, is the real security game (i.e., the ciphertext and all keys are normal). In the next game, $Game_0$, all of the keys will be normal, but the ciphertext will be semi-functional. We let q denote the number of key queries made by the adversary. For k from 1 to q, we define:

$Game_{k,1}$. In this game, the challenge ciphertext is semi-functional, the first $k-1$ keys are semi-functional of type 1, the kth key is semi-functional of type 2, and the remaining keys are normal.

$Game_{k,2}$. In this game, the challenge ciphertext is semi-functional, the first k keys are semi-functional of type 1, and the remaining keys are normal.

For notational purposes, we think of $Game_{0,2}$ as another way of denoting $Game_0$. Note that in $Game_{q,2}$, all keys are semi-functional of type 1. The final game, $Game_{Final}$, is defined to be similar to $Game_{q,2}$, except that the ciphertext is a semi-functional encryption of a random message. Hence, in Game_{Final} the adversary's advantage is 0. To prove Theorem 1, we have the following lemmas:

Lemma 1. *Under Assumption 1, any PPT adversary has at most a negligible advantage in distinguishing between Game_{Real} and Game_0.*

Lemma 2. *Under Assumption 2, any PPT adversary has at most a negligible advantage in distinguishing between $\text{Game}_{k-1,2}$ and $\text{Game}_{k,1}$.*

Lemma 3. *Under Assumption 2, any PPT adversary has at most a negligible advantage in distinguishing between $\text{Game}_{k,1}$ and $\text{Game}_{k,2}$.*

Lemma 4. *Under Assumption 3, any PPT adversary has at most a negligible advantage in distinguishing between $\text{Game}_{q,2}$ and Game_{Final}.*

Due to the space limitation, we omit the formal proofs of Lemmas 1–4, which will be given in the full version of the paper. Through Lemmas 1–4, we can prove that Game_{Real} is indistinguishable from Game_{Final}. Therefore, we can conclude that the adversary's advantage in breaking the CP-ABE-HF scheme (i.e., Game_{Real}) is negligible, which completes the proof of Theorem 1.

5.2 Efficiency Analysis

An overview comparison of our scheme with some existing CP-ABE schemes is presented in Table 1. Our scheme achieves policy hiding and fast decryption simultaneously. The access policy is specified based on the tree structure, which is as expressive as LSSS and more expressive than AND-gate. Regarding security, our scheme is proven *fully* secure in the standard model. The comparison

Table 1. An overview comparison of our scheme with other CP-ABE schemes.

Scheme	Access structure	Policy hidden	Fast decryption	Security
EMN+09 [13]	AND-gate	No	Yes	Selective
MT12 [14]	AND-gate	No	Yes	Selective
NYO08 [6]	AND-gate	Yes	No	Selective
ZHW15 [7]	AND-gate	Yes	No	Selective
LWZ+16 [8]	AND-gate	Yes	No	Selective
H13 [9]	Tree	Yes	No	Selective
DJ12 [4]	AND-gate	Yes	Yes	Selective
PJ14 [5]	AND-gate	Yes	Yes	Selective
LDL12 [11]	LSSS	Yes	No	Full
LDL11 [10]	AND-gate	Yes	No	Full
RD13 [2]	AND-gate	Yes	Yes	Full
LGR+12 [3]	AND-gate	Yes	Yes	Full
CP-ABE-HF (ours)	Tree	Yes	Yes	Full

Table 2. Efficiency comparison of CP-ABE schemes with hidden access policy and full security.

Scheme	Structure	Encryption	KeyGen	Decryption
LGR+12 [3]	AND	$2\mathbb{G} + \mathbb{G}_T$	$4\mathbb{G}$	$2C_e$
RD13 [2]	AND	$2\mathbb{G} + \mathbb{G}_T$	$3\mathbb{G}$	$2C_e$
LDL11 [10]	AND	$(\hat{n} + 1)\mathbb{G} + \mathbb{G}_T$	$(\hat{n} + 1)\mathbb{G}$	$(\hat{n} + 1)C_e$
LDL12 [11]	LSSS	$(8\hat{t} + 2)\mathbb{G} + 2\mathbb{G}_T$	$(2\hat{n} + 3)\mathbb{G}$	$(4\hat{t} + 2)C_e + 2\hat{t}\mathbb{G}_T$
CP-ABE-HF (ours)	Tree	$(n + \hat{t} + 1)\mathbb{G} + \mathbb{G}_T$	$(|\omega| + 2)\mathbb{G}$	$3C_e + 2|\omega|\mathbb{G}_T$

Note: $\mathbb{G}$ and $\mathbb{G}_T$ represent the exponentiations on groups of $\mathbb{G}$ and $\mathbb{G}_T$, respectively. C_e denotes the pairing operation. n denotes the number of attributes in the attribute universe. $\hat{n}$ denotes the number of attribute categories in the AND-gate based schemes. $\hat{t}$ denotes the number of attribute in an access structure. $|\omega|$ is the number of attributes associated with a user.

indicates that our scheme is superior to the existing CP-ABE schemes because it is the first CP-ABE scheme that has all of the following features: hidden policy, fast decryption, expressivity and full security.

The performance comparisons of our scheme with other policy-hiding and fully secure CP-ABE schemes are shown in Table 2. Although LGR+12 and RD13 are more efficient than our scheme, their access policy is expressed by AND-gate which has restricted expression ability. Based on the comparisons, we can conclude that our scheme is more suitable for the Internet-based collaboration environments, where data protection and fine-grained access control are required, and the access policy contains sensitive information.

6 Conclusions

In this paper, focusing on the data-protection problem in Internet-based collaboration, we propose an efficient and privacy-preserving scheme based on CP-ABE, i.e., CP-ABE-HF. CP-ABE-HF improves the efficiency of decryption by reducing the number of pairing operations to three, regardless of how complex the access policy is. The privacy of the access policy is also preserved so that no one can obtain the access policy after encryption, which ensures the attribute information of data owners and recipients will not be leaked. By adopting the dual-system encryption methodology, CP-ABE-HF is proven fully secure. The performance analysis indicates that CP-ABE-HF outperforms the existing CP-ABE schemes in terms of its comprehensive capability, because it is the first CP-ABE to simultaneously achieve policy hidden, fast decryption, expressivity and full security. In the future, it would be interesting to construct a fully secure CP-ABE with policy hidden and fast decryption over prime-order groups of which efficiency is higher than the composite-order groups.

Acknowledgements. This work was supported by the National Natural Science Foundation of China (Grant No. 61170088) and the Foundation of the State Key Laboratory of Software Development Environment (Grant No. SKLSDE-2015ZX-05).

References

1. Bethencourt, J., Sahai, A., Waters, B.: Ciphertext-policy attribute-based encryption. In: IEEE Symposium on Security and Privacy, pp. 321–334. IEEE, Washington, DC (2007)
2. Rao, Y.S., Dutta, R.: Recipient anonymous ciphertext-policy attribute based encryption. In: Bagchi, A., Ray, I. (eds.) ICISS 2013. LNCS, vol. 8303, pp. 329–344. Springer, Heidelberg (2013). https://doi.org/10.1007/978-3-642-45204-8_25
3. Li, X., Gu, D., Ren, Y., Ding, N., Yuan, K.: Efficient ciphertext-policy attribute based encryption with hidden policy. In: Xiang, Y., Pathan, M., Tao, X., Wang, H. (eds.) IDCS 2012. LNCS, vol. 7646, pp. 146–159. Springer, Heidelberg (2012). https://doi.org/10.1007/978-3-642-34883-9_12
4. Doshi, N., Jinwala, D.: Hidden access structure ciphertext policy attribute based encryption with constant length ciphertext. In: Thilagam, P.S., Pais, A.R., Chandrasekaran, K., Balakrishnan, N. (eds.) ADCONS 2011. LNCS, vol. 7135, pp. 515–523. Springer, Heidelberg (2012). https://doi.org/10.1007/978-3-642-29280-4_60
5. Padhya, M., Jinwala, D.: A novel approach for searchable CP-ABE with hidden ciphertext-policy. In: Prakash, A., Shyamasundar, R. (eds.) ICISS 2014. LNCS, vol. 8880, pp. 167–184. Springer, Cham (2014). https://doi.org/10.1007/978-3-319-13841-1_10
6. Nishide, T., Yoneyama, K., Ohta, K.: Attribute-based encryption with partially hidden encryptor-specified access structures. In: Bellovin, S.M., Gennaro, R., Keromytis, A., Yung, M. (eds.) ACNS 2008. LNCS, vol. 5037, pp. 111–129. Springer, Heidelberg (2008). https://doi.org/10.1007/978-3-540-68914-0_7
7. Zhou, Z., Huang, D., Wang, Z.: Efficient privacy-preserving ciphertext-policy attribute based-encryption and broadcast encryption. IEEE Trans. Comput. **64**(1), 126–138 (2015)
8. Li, J., Wang, H., Zhang, Y., Shen, J.: Ciphertext-policy attribute-based encryption with hidden access policy and testing. KSII Trans. Internet Inf. Syst. **10**(7), 3339–3352 (2016)
9. Hur, J.: Attribute-based secure data sharing with hidden policies in smart grid. IEEE Trans. Parallel Distrib. Syst. **24**(11), 2171–2180 (2013)
10. Lai, J., Deng, R.H., Li, Y.: Fully secure cipertext-policy hiding CP-ABE. In: Bao, F., Weng, J. (eds.) ISPEC 2011. LNCS, vol. 6672, pp. 24–39. Springer, Heidelberg (2011). https://doi.org/10.1007/978-3-642-21031-0_3
11. Lai, J., Deng, R.H., Li, Y.: Expressive CP-ABE with partially hidden access structures. In: 7th ACM Symposium on Information, Computer and Communications Security, pp. 18–19. ACM, New York (2012)
12. Lewko, A., Waters, B.: New proof methods for attribute-based encryption: achieving full security through selective techniques. In: Safavi-Naini, R., Canetti, R. (eds.) CRYPTO 2012. LNCS, vol. 7417, pp. 180–198. Springer, Heidelberg (2012). https://doi.org/10.1007/978-3-642-32009-5_12
13. Emura, K., Miyaji, A., Nomura, A., Omote, K., Soshi, M.: A ciphertext-policy attribute-based encryption scheme with constant ciphertext length. In: Bao, F., Li, H., Wang, G. (eds.) ISPEC 2009. LNCS, vol. 5451, pp. 13–23. Springer, Heidelberg (2009). https://doi.org/10.1007/978-3-642-00843-6_2

14. Miyaji, A., Tran, P.V.X.: Constant-ciphertext-size dual policy attribute based encryption. In: Xiang, Y., Lopez, J., Kuo, C.-C.J., Zhou, W. (eds.) CSS 2012. LNCS, vol. 7672, pp. 400–413. Springer, Heidelberg (2012). https://doi.org/10.1007/978-3-642-35362-8_30
15. Boneh, D., Waters, B.: Conjunctive, subset, and range queries on encrypted data. In: Vadhan, S.P. (ed.) TCC 2007. LNCS, vol. 4392, pp. 535–554. Springer, Heidelberg (2007). https://doi.org/10.1007/978-3-540-70936-7_29

An Efficient Identity-Based Privacy-Preserving Authentication Scheme for VANETs

Jie Cui[1], Wenyu Xu[1], Kewei Sha[2], and Hong Zhong[1(✉)]

[1] School of Computer Science and Technology, Anhui University, Hefei 230039, China
cujie@mail.ustc.edu.cn, zhongh@ahu.edu.cn
[2] Department of Computing Sciences, University of Houston - Clear Lake, Houston, TX 77058, USA

Abstract. Vehicular ad hoc networks (VANETs) are proposed to improve the traffic safety and efficiency through communications among vehicles and between vehicle and roadside units (RSUs). When a vehicle broadcasts messages to nearby vehicles and roadside units (RSUs), it needs to resist attacks and to preserve the privacy of the message senders. Therefore, security and privacy issues are of great interests and remain challenging. Many authentication schemes are proposed to tackle above challenges while most of them are heavy in computation and communication. In this paper, we propose a novel authentication scheme that utilizes the double pseudonym method to hide the real identity of vehicle and adopts the dynamic update technology to periodically update the information (such as member secret, authentication key, internal pseudo-identity) stored in the tamper-proof device (TPD) to prevent the side-channel attack. Because of not using bilinear pairing, our scheme yields a better performance in terms of computation overhead and communication overhead and is more suitable to be applied in VANETs.

Keywords: Batch verification · VANETs · TPD · Bilinear pairing

1 Introduction

In recent years, the proposal of VANET [1–4] aims to enhance driving safety through inter-vehicle communications and communications between vehicles and roadside infrastructure. Both academia and industry show great interests in developing a secure and efficient VANET. A typical VANET consists of a trusted third party (TA), a set of RSUs distributed along the roads, and many vehicles driving on the road. When the RSUs and vehicles receive the information from vehicle, they need to verify the integrity of the message to ensure that it is not modified by the attacker during the transmission. Moreover, for security concerns, the real identity of vehicle should not be known by a malicious attacker during the transmission to preserve the identity privacy of the sender.

© ICST Institute for Computer Sciences, Social Informatics and Telecommunications Engineering 2018
I. Romdhani et al. (Eds.): CollaborateCom 2017, LNICST 252, pp. 508–518, 2018.
https://doi.org/10.1007/978-3-030-00916-8_47

Many efforts have been made to tackle the above challenge, and many authentication schemes have been proposed. Most of them are heavy in computation and communication.

In 2008, Zhang et al. [5] first proposed an identity-based batch authentication scheme using a bilinear mapping. Firstly, in Zhang's scheme [5], they use the batch authentication method to verify the many messages at the same time which can reduce the computation overhead. Secondly, because a vehicle uses a pseudonym identity attached to the message during the transmission process, some untrustworthy parties and malicious attackers could not know the real identity of the vehicle. However, in 2013, Lee and Lai [6] pointed out that Zhang's scheme [5] had some flaws. First of all, Zhang's scheme [5] cannot resist replay attack. In the absence of the corresponding inspection device, the receiver maybe receive a valid signature that has been verified before. Secondly, Zhang's scheme [5] could not achieve non-repudiation. Although a trusted third party (TA) could recover the real identity of false message which is sent by an adversary, the attacker also could deny that sending the corresponding message. Hence, Lee and Lai [6] proposed an improved scheme to achieve better privacy preserving.

Recently, Zhang et al. [7] and Bayat et al. [8] found that Lee and Lai's scheme [6] was not able to resist impersonation attacks, that is, malicious attackers could simulate a legal vehicle to send false messages. Therefore, Zhang et al. [7] and Bayat et al. [8] proposed two improved schemes to address the problem in Lee and Lai's [6] scheme. However, as pointed out in He et al.'s scheme [9], the above two schemes have flaws that they cannot prevent the modification attack, in which the signature of message could be modified by the malicious attacker. Therefore, He et al. [9] proposed a conditional privacy protection scheme that does not use bilinear paring.

In He et al.'s scheme [9], because the system's master private key is stored in a tamper-proof device (TPD) which is a device that no attacker can extract any stored data. However, because of side-channel attack, the assumption of TPD is shown to be too strong in practice. In side-channel attack, the adversary collects side channel information leak from some cryptographic operations. Once the TPD is compromised, the attacker could acquire the system's master private key so that the whole system will be compromised. In order to prevent side-channel attacks, Zhang et al. [10] proposed a novel privacy-preserving authentication scheme. Instead of storing the mast private key in the TPD that cannot be updated, their scheme store security-related information in the TPD, which can be periodically updated. This approach can get rid of the ideal TPD, so it is more practical. However, this scheme uses bilinear mapping and multiple Map-To-Point operations, thus leads to a heavy computational overhead.

To reduce the computation and communication overhead of the existing authentication scheme, in this paper, we propose an efficient identity-based privacy-preserving authentication scheme for VANETs. Our scheme makes use of the double pseudonym method and dynamic update technology. The computation and communication overhead are reduced because no bilinear paring is needed in the signature generation and verification. In addition, we show that the proposed scheme is secure via comprehensive security analysis. Finally, we periodically update the informations (e.g., member secret, authentication key, IPID) stored in the tamper-proof device, therefore, our scheme can resist the side-channel attack.

2   System Model and Design Goals

In this chapter, we briefly introduce the network model, security requirements. Some notations are defined as shown in Table 1.

Table 1. List of notations and definitions

Notation	Definitions
TA	A trusted authority
s, P_{pub}	The private key and public key of TA
$cert_{R_j}$	A certificate of R_j issued by TA
$ID_{\{R_j, V_i\}}$	The real identity of R_j or V_i
VP_i	The validity period of $IPID_{V_i}$
$IPID_{V_i}$	An internal pseudonym identity of V_i, generated by the TA
$PPID_{i,t}$	The public pseudonym identity of V_i, generated from $IPID_{V_i}$ of V_i
$h_{\{R_j, TA\}}$	A hash-based message authentication code generated by R_j or the TA
$E_\pi(.)/D_\pi(.)$	A symmetric encryption scheme, where π is the key

2.1   Network Model

As shown in Fig. 1, a VANET consists of a third-party trusted authority (TA), some RSUs distributed on the roadside and multiple vehicles.

- **TA:** TA is a trusted third party in VANET, with sufficient storage and computing power, and is considered impossible to compromise with an adversary. When an attacker simulates a legal vehicle sends a false message, the TA can resume the true identity of the sent message.
- **RSUs:** The RSU is an infrastructure that is distributed on the roadside and communicates with the TA via a wired connection, and communicates with vehicles over a wireless connection to verify the validity of the received message.
- **Vehicles:** Each vehicle is equipped with TPD, and communicates with other vehicles and RSUs through wireless connections. The vehicle periodically broadcasts security-related messages to nearby vehicles and RSUs through the Dedicated Short Range Communications (DSRC) [11] protocol.

2.2   Security Requirements

A security scheme for VANETs should meet some of the following features.

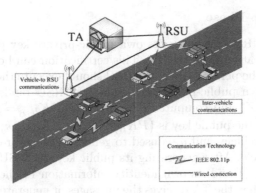

Fig. 1. System model.

1. Message integrity: In VANETs, we need to ensure that the recipient received the message from the sender, and the message during the sending process has not been modified by the attacker to maintain integrity.
2. Non-forgery: The attacker should not generate a valid signature on behalf of any vehicle under the randomly selected message attack in the random oracle model.
3. Resistance against side-channel attack: The attacker should not be able to obtain any informations stored in the TPD through the side-channel attack.

3   The Proposed Scheme

In this section, we proposed an efficient identity-based privacy-preserving authentication scheme that does not use bilinear paring to address the security problem existing in VANET. They are some initialization parameters that pre-load into the vehicles and RSUs generated by the TA using the following steps.

1. TA selects a random number $s \in Z_q^*$ as the secret key of the TA and calculates $P_{pub} = s \cdot P$ as the public key of the TA, where the P is the generator of G.
2. TA selects $E_\pi(\cdot)/D_\pi(\cdot)$ and some hash functions: $h_1 : G \to Z_q, h_2 : \{0,1\}^* \to Z_q, H_{1_{key}}(\cdot) : \{0,1\}^* \to \{0,1\}^l, H_2(\cdot) : \{0,1\}^* \to \Gamma, H_3(\cdot) : \{0,1\}^* \to \{0,1\}^{l'}$, where $H_{1_{key}}(\cdot)$ as a keyed hash.
3. The system parameters $\psi = (P, P_{pub}, h_1, h_2, H_{1_{key}}(\cdot), H_2(\cdot), H_3(\cdot), E_\pi(.)/D_\pi(.))$. Pre-load the system parameters ψ into the vehicles and RSUs.

This scheme consists of six phases: RSU setup phase, vehicle setup phase, member key generation phase, vehicle signature phase, message verification phase, IPID and authentication key update phase.

3.1 RSU Setup Phase

In this phase, the RSU generates its own public-private key pairs and the corresponding certification from the TA. This certification can be used only in the short time. Once the period is over, the RSU should execute the step once again. To generate its own public-private key pairs, the RSU randomly chooses two numbers $k_j, \eta_j \in Z_q^*$ and computes $PK_{R_{j1}} = k_j P, PK_{R_{j2}} = \eta_j P$. The private key is (k_j, η_j) and the public key is $\left(PK_{R_{j1}}, PK_{R_{j2}}\right)$, where k_j is used to generate the shares of vehicle, and η_j is used to generate the secure channel between the RSU and vehicle. After generating its public key, the RSU sends the public key $\left(PK_{R_{j1}}, PK_{R_{j2}}\right)$ and its own identity information to the TA through the secure channel. When the TA receives the messages, it generates the certification of RSU. Then the $cert_{R_j}$ is broadcasted within RSU range.

3.2 Vehicle Setup Phase

In this phase, when the vehicle joins the range of the VANETs, the information stored in the TPD should be initialized. Assuming the real identity of vehicle is RID, the TA can compute the inter-pseudonym identity $IPID_{V_i} = H_{1_\Lambda}(RID\|VP_i)$, where the VP_i is the valid period of the inter-pseudonym identity like 02.03.2017–03.04.2017. The vehicle chooses the authentication key λ_i, putting the $\psi, IPID_{V_i}, \lambda_i$ into the TPD. (RID, $VP_i, IPID_{V_i}, \lambda_i$) is stored into the member list ML in the TA.

3.3 Member Key Generation Phase

In this phase, when the vehicle enters the communication range of RSU, it will receive the certification from RSU and first check the validity of the $cert_{R_j}$. If the certification is valid under the public key of system, extracting the public key and identity of RSU from the certification $cert_{R_j}$. Then, the vehicle chooses a random number $r \in Z_q^*$, and computes $f = rP$, $\pi_{i1} = H_2(f, PK_{R_{j2}}, rPK_{R_{j2}}, ID_{R_j}, T_i)$, $\pi_{i2} = H_2\left(f, P_{pub}, rP_{pub}, ID_{R_j}, T_i\right)$. Where T_i is a timestamp, π_{i1}, π_{i2} are used as the keys of the symmetric encryption scheme $(E_\pi\left(.\right)/D_\pi\left(.\right))$. Finally the vehicle computes $p_j = E_{\pi_{i2}}\left(\lambda_i, T_i\right)$ and sends s $= \left(f, ID_{R_j}, p_j, T_i\right)$ to RSU.

After receiving s from vehicle, the RSU checks the validity of T_i, if it is invalid, then it aborts; otherwise it sends s to the TA through the secure channel. When TA receives s and computes $\pi_{i2} = H_2\left(f, P_{pub}, sf, ID_{R_j}, T_i\right)$, $D_{\pi_{i2}}\left(p_j\right)$ to get (λ_i', T_i'). If it does not appear the equation $\lambda_i' \neq \lambda_i$ in a tuple of member list (RID, $VP_i, IPID_{V_i}, \lambda_i$) of the TA or $T_i \neq T_i'$ or VP_i is invalid, it aborts; otherwise TA authenticates the vehicle and sends authenticated message to RSU.

Upon the RSU receives the authenticated message from the TA, it means the vehicle is legal. RSU first computes $\pi_{i1} = H_2\left(f, PK_{R_{j2}}, f\eta_j, ID_{R_j}, T_i\right)$; and chooses an authenticated period τ_p and member secret (β_j, γ_j), where β_j and γ_j satisfy $k_j = \beta_j \cdot \gamma_j$; it computes $h_{R_j} = H_{1_{\pi_{i1}}}\left(\beta_j, \gamma_j, \tau_p\right)$, and $p_j' = E_{\pi_{i1}}\left(\beta_j, \gamma_j, \tau_p, h_{R_j}\right)$; and sends t $= \left(H_3\left(f\right), p_j'\right)$ to the vehicle.

When the vehicle receives the t and $D_{\pi i1}\left(p'_j\right)$ to get $\left(\beta_j, \gamma_j, \tau_p, h_{R_j}\right)$, it verifies whether the equation $h_{R_j} = H_{1_{\pi i1}}\left(\beta_j, \gamma_j, \tau_p\right)$ holds. If so, it lets the member secret and authenticated period in the TPD; otherwise, it aborts. This member key can only be used under the authenticated period, and once it expires, the member key stored in the TPD is deleted.

3.4 Vehicle Signature Phase

In this phase, when a vehicle obtains the member secret (β_j, γ_j) and the corresponding validity period from the RSU, the vehicle first computes the external pseudonym identity $PPID_i = H_3\left(IPID_{V_i}, T_i\right)$ and the one time signature key $sk_i = (\beta_j \cdot \gamma_j) \cdot h_1\left(PPID_i\right) \bmod n$. Then, the vehicle chooses a random number $r_i \in Z_q^*$, and computes $R_i = r_i \cdot P$, $\beta_i = h_2\left(PPID_i \| R_i \| M_i\right)$, $S_i = sk_i + \beta_i \cdot r_i$. Finally, it sends $(M_i, PPID_i, R_i, S_i)$ to nearby vehicles and RSUs.

The member secret (β_j, γ_j) stored in the TPD needs to be periodically updated. Choose a random number $r \in Z_q^*$, and set the $\beta_j = r \cdot \beta_j$, $\gamma_j = r \cdot \gamma_j$ as the new member secret.

3.5 Message Verification Phase

In this phase, after receiving multiple message $(M_1, PPID_1, R_1, S_1)$, $(M_2, PPID_2, R_2, S_2), ..., (M_n, PPID_n, R_n, S_n)$ from the vehicle, verifier first checks the validity of T_i, where $i = 1, 2, \ldots, n$. If T_i is invalid, the verifier rejects the messages; otherwise, it chooses a random vector $\mathrm{v} = \{v_1, v_2, \ldots, v_n\}$, where v_i is a small random integer in $[1, 2^t]$ and t is a small integer with low overhead. Then, the verifier checks the correctness of the equation $(\sum_{i=1}^{n} v_i \cdot S_i) \cdot P = \sum_{i=1}^{n} (V_i \cdot h_1\left(PPID_i\right)) \cdot PK_{R_{j1}} + \sum_{i=1}^{n} (v_i \cdot \beta_i \cdot R_i)$. If it does not hold, the verifier rejects the messages; otherwise, the verifier receives the messages.

Since $sk_i = (\alpha_j \cdot \beta_j) \cdot h_1\left(PPID_i\right) \bmod n$, $\beta_j \cdot \gamma_j = k_j$, $PK_{R_{j1}} = k_j \cdot P$, $R_i = r_i \cdot P$, $\beta_i = h_2\left(PPID_i \| R_i \| M_i\right)$ and $S_i = sk_i + \beta_i \cdot r_i$, we can get the equation hold. Hence, the correctness of the multiple messages verification is verified.

3.6 IPID and Authentication Key Update Phase

At this phase, when a vehicle wants to update the internal pseudo-identity and authentication key, it first chooses a random number $t \in Z_q^*$, and computes $g = t \cdot P$, $\pi_i = H_2\left(g, P_{pub}, tP_{pub}, T_i\right)$, $p_i = E_{\pi_i}\left(\lambda_i, T_i\right)$. Then, it sends $\mathrm{z} = (g, T_i, p_i)$ to the TA through the nearby RSU.

After the TA receives z, if T_i is invalid, it aborts; otherwise, it first computes $\pi_i = H_2(g, P_{pub}, s \cdot g, T_i)$, $D_{\pi_i}\left(p_i\right)$ to get (λ'_i, T'_i) and checks the validity of T'_i. If T'_i is invalid, it aborts; otherwise, it searches the member list for a tuple $(RID, VP_i, IPID_{V_i}, \lambda_i)$ such as $\lambda_i = \lambda'_i$. If such a tuple does not exist, it aborts; otherwise, TA checks the validity of VP_i. If it is invalid, choose a new valid period VP_i'. Then, it computes $IPID_{V_i}' = H_{1_A}(RID\|VP_i')$ and chooses a new authentication key $\widehat{\lambda}_i$; otherwise, it aborts. Finally, TA computes $p_i = E_{\pi_i}(IPID_{V_i}', \widehat{\lambda}_i, T_i', h_{TA})$. If $h_{TA} = H_{1_{\lambda_i'}}\left(IPID_{V_i}', \widehat{\lambda}_i, T_i\right)$ is an $HAMC$, sends $(H_3(g), p_i')$ to the vehicle and put $(RID, VP_i', IPID_{V_i}', \widehat{\lambda}_i)$ into ML.

Upon receiving $(H_3(g), p_i')$, the vehicle first computes $D_{\pi_i}\left(p_i'\right)$ to get $(IPID_{V_i}', \lambda_i', T_i', h_{TA}'$. Then, it checks the validity of T_i' and h_{TA}'. If it is invalid, set the $\left(IPID_{V_i}', \lambda_i'\right)$ as the new internal pseudo-identity and authentication key.

4   Security Proof and Analysis

Because the computational Elliptic Curve Discrete Logarithm (ECDL) problem is hard to address, so any attacker could not generate a valid signature on behalf of any vehicle through the game that is made up of a challenger C and an adversary A.

Theorem 1: Our scheme for VANETs is secure existential forgery under the randomly selected message attack in the random oracle model.

Proof: Assuming there is an adversary could forge message $(M_i, PPID_i, R_i, S_i)$, then we construct a challenger C, which could address the ECDL problem through running A as a subroutine. The details are as the following steps:

Setup stage: Challenger C first sets $Q = PK_{R_{j1}}$, then it sends the system parameters ψ to an adversary A.

$h_1 - oracle$: Challenger C first initializes the list L_{h_1} with the form of $(\langle PPID_i, \tau_{h_1}\rangle)$. When receiving the query of the message with the form of $<PPID_i>$ from the adversary A, the challenger C checks a tuple of the $<PPID_i>$ to find out whether it appears in the list L_{h_1}. If the tuple exists in the list L_{h_1}, then send $\tau_{h_1} = h_1(PPID_i)$ to the adversary A; otherwise, C chooses a random number $\tau_{h_1} \in Z_q^*$ and sets the tuple $\langle PPID_i, \tau_{h_1}\rangle$ into the L_{h_1}, finally sends the $\tau_{h_1} = h_1(PPID_i)$ to A.

$h_2 - oracle$: Challenger C first initializes the list L_{h_2} with the form of L_{h_2} $(\langle PPID_i, R_i, M_i, \tau_{h_2}\rangle)$. When receiving the query of the message with the form of $\langle PPID_i, R_i, M_i\rangle$ from the adversary A, the challenger C checks a tuple of the $\langle PPID_i, R_i, M_i\rangle$ whether it appears in the list L_{h_2}. If the tuple exists in in the list L_{h_2}, then send $\tau_{h_2} = h_2(PPID_i\|R_i\|M_i)$ to the adversary A; otherwise, C chooses a random number $\tau_{h_2} \in Z_q^*$ and sets the tuple $(\langle PPID_i, R_i, M_i, \tau_{h_2}\rangle)$ into the L_{h_2}, finally sends the $\tau_{h_2} = h_2(PPID_i\|R_i\|M_i)$ to A.

$sign - oracle$: Upon receiving the message M_i from adversary A, challenger C generates random numbers $S_i, h_{i,1}, \beta_i \in Z_q^*$ and $PPID_i$. Challenger C puts $\langle PPID_i, h_{i,1}\rangle$ and $(M_i, PPID_i, R_i, S_i)$ to adversary A, which is easy to verify equation $S_i \cdot P = h_1(PPID_i) \cdot PK_{R_{j1}} + \beta_i \cdot R_i$ hold. thus, the message and signature $(M_i, PPID_i, R_i, S_i)$, which A acquired from the inquiry from C, is valid.

Output: Finally, A outputs the message $(M_i, PPID_i, R_i, S_i)$. C checks whether the equation holds.

$$S_i \cdot P = h_1(PPID_i) \cdot PK_{R_{j1}} + \beta_i \cdot R_i \tag{1}$$

If it does not hold, C aborts the process; otherwise, because of the forged lemma, if A executes $h_1 - oracle$ once again, a valid message $(M_i, PPID_i, R_i, S_i')$ will be generated. It can also conclude the similar equation.

$$S_i' \cdot P = (h_1(PPID_i))' \cdot PK_{R_{j1}} + \beta_i \cdot R_i \tag{2}$$

According to the Eqs. (1) and (2), we could get

$$\left(S_i - S_i'\right) = \left(h_1(PPID_i) - (h_1(PPID_i))'\right) \cdot k_j \tag{3}$$

Therefore, C output the $\left(h_1(PPID_i) - (h_1(PPID_i))'\right)^{-1} \cdot \left(S_i - S_i'\right)$. However, it is difficult to address the ECDL problem, so our scheme is secure against forgery under the randomly selected message attack in the random oracle model. We will introduce the security requirement as described in Subsect. 2.2.

1. **Message integrity:** According to the Theorem 1, because it is difficult to address the ECDL problem, the signature used in our scheme is not forged under the random oracle model. Therefore, no adversary can simulate a legal vehicle to generate a valid signature or modify a legal signature. We can verify the equation that $S_i \cdot P = h_1(PPID_i) \cdot PK_{R_{j1}} + \beta_i \cdot R_i$ holds to check the validity and integrity of the message $(M_i, PPID_i, R_i, S_i)$. Thus, the proposed scheme can achieve message integrity.
2. **Non-forgery:** Because it is difficult to address the ECDL problem, so the attacker could not generate a valid signature on behalf of any vehicle under the randomly selected message attack in the random oracle model. Thus, the proposed scheme can achieve non-forgery.
3. **Resistance side channel attack:** Due to the IPID is often used, if the vehicle does not periodically update this information, it will give the attacker a chance to recover the real identity of vehicle. In our scheme, before the attacker can probe the related information to recover the IPID through the side channel attack, the IPIP has already been updated. Secondly, the authenticated key can only be used during the authentication of vehicle. It is much harder for the attacker to resume the authenticated key than recover the IPID. In addition, as for the member secret, even if the adversary could recover the member secret, only vehicle in the nearby RSU can be influenced. Furthermore, because the RSU can periodically update its public-private key pairs, hence, the attacker could not acquire enough information through the side channel to resume the member key stored in the TPD.

5 Performance Analysis and Comparison

5.1 Computation Overhead Analysis

Table 2 shows some time-consuming cryptographic operations [12] need to be executed in each scheme. The processing time for the bilinear pairing operation T_p is 4.211 ms, the time for small scale multiplication operation T_{mp-p} is 1.709 ms and the Map-To-Point operation T_{mtp} is 4.406 ms. The time for small scale multiplication operation based on the Elliptic Curve T_{mp-ECC} is 0.442 ms [9]. Figure 2 shows the total execution time of the batch verification as the amount of the vehicle increasing in each scheme. When the authenticated vehicle is increased to 100, in our scheme, the total execution time is less than 50 ms. Hence, our scheme is more suitable for the scene of multiple vehicles in VANETs.

5.2 Communication Overhead Analysis

In the group G_1 based on bilinear mapping, the size of the elements in G_1 is $64 \times 2 = 128$ byte [13]. However, in the group G based on the Elliptic Curve, the size of the elements in G is $20 \times 2 = 40$ byte [9]. Furthermore, we assume that the size of result of the general hash function is 20 byte and the size of the timestamp is 4 byte [14]. In addition, we do not consider the size of the message which is transmitted by the vehicle in this phase [15]. Table 3 lists the

Table 2. The computation overhead of each scheme

Scheme	Pseudonym and signature generation phase	Multiple messages verification phase
Zhang et al. [7]	$6T_{mp-tp} + T_{mtp}$	$(n+1)\,T_{mp-bp} + 3T_{bp}$
Bayat et al. [8]	$5T_{mp-bp} + T_{mtp}$	$3T_{bp} + nT_{mp-bp} + nT_{mtp}$
Zhang et al. [10]	$2T_{mtp}$	$2T_{bp} + 2nT_{mtp}$
He et al. [9]	$3T_{mp-ECC}$	$(n+2)\,T_{mp-ECC}$
Our Scheme	T_{mp-ECC}	$(n+2)\,T_{mp-ECC}$

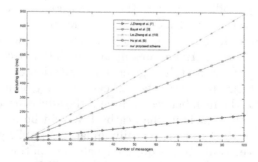

Fig. 2. Computation overhead comparison of verifying multiple message.

Table 3. THE communication overhead of each scheme

Scheme	Sending a single message	Sending n messages
Zhang et al. [7]	388 bytes	388n bytes
Bayat et al. [8]	388 bytes	388n bytes
Zhang et al. [10]	148 bytes	148n bytes
He et al. [9]	144 bytes	144n bytes
Our Scheme	80 bytes	80n bytes

communication overhead of our scheme compared with the schemes of Zhang et al. [7], Bayat et al. [8], Zhang et al. [10] and He et al. [9].

6   Conclusion

In this paper, we propose an efficient identity-based privacy-preserving authentication scheme supports both V2V communication and V2I communication in VANETs. Firstly, unlike other schemes, which stores the system master secret (that cannot be updated) in the TPD, in our scheme, the informations stored in the TPD are regularly updated. Therefore, the proposed scheme can resist side-channel attacks and hence is more practical. Secondly, the security analysis shows that our scheme can satisfy the security requirements for VANETs. Furthermore, performance analysis and comparison shows that our scheme is better than other schemes in terms of computation overhead and communication overhead. This shows our scheme is more suitable used in the VANETs.

References

1. Sha, K., Xi, Y., Shi, W., Schwiebert, L., Zhang, T.: Adaptive privacy-preserving authentication in vehicular networks. In: First International Conference on Communications and Networking in China, ChinaCom 2006, pp. 1–8. IEEE (2006)
2. Xi, Y., Sha, K., Shi, W., Schwiebert, L., Zhang, T.: Enforcing privacy using symmetric random key-set in vehicular networks. In: Eighth International Symposium on Autonomous Decentralized Systems, ISADS 2007, pp. 344–351. IEEE (2007)
3. Qu, F., Wu, Z., Wang, F.-Y., Cho, W.: A security and privacy review of VANETs. IEEE Trans. Intell. Transp. Syst. **16**(6), 2985–2996 (2015)
4. Wen, X., Shao, L., Xue, Y., Fang, W.: A rapid learning algorithm for vehicle classification. Inf. Sci. **295**, 395–406 (2015)
5. Zhang, C., Lu, R., Lin, X., Ho, P.-H., Shen, X.: An efficient identity-based batch verification scheme for vehicular sensor networks. In: The 27th Conference on Computer Communications, INFOCOM 2008, pp. 246–250. IEEE (2008)
6. Lee, C.-C., Lai, Y.-M.: Toward a secure batch verification with group testing for VANET. Wirel. Netw. **19**(6), 1441 (2013)
7. Zhang, J., Xu, M., Liu, L.: On the security of a secure batch verification with group testing for VANET. Int. J. Netw. Secur. **16**(5), 351–358 (2014)

8. Bayat, M., Barmshoory, M., Rahimi, M., Aref, M.R.: A secure authentication scheme for VANETs with batch verification. Wirel. Netw. **21**(5), 1733 (2015)

9. He, D., Zeadally, S., Xu, B., Huang, X.: An efficient identity-based conditional privacy-preserving authentication scheme for vehicular ad hoc networks. IEEE Trans. Inf. Forensics Secur. **10**(12), 2681–2691 (2015)

10. Zhang, L., Wu, Q., Domingo-Ferrer, J., Qin, B., Hu, C.: Distributed aggregate privacy-preserving authentication in VANETs. IEEE Trans. Intell. Transp. Syst. **18**(3), 516–526 (2017)

11. Oh, H., Yae, C., Ahn, D., Cho, H.: 5.8 GHz DSRC packet communication system for its services. In: IEEE VTS 50th Vehicular Technology Conference, VTC 1999-Fall, vol. 4, pp. 2223–2227. IEEE (1999)

12. He, D., Kumar, N., Shen, H., Lee, J.-H.: One-to-many authentication for access control in mobile pay-TV systems. Sci. China Inf. Sci. **5**(59), 1–14 (2016)

13. Boyen, X., Martin, L.: Identity-based cryptography standard (IBCS) 1: supersingular curve implementations of the BF and BB1 cryptosystems. Technical report (2007)

14. Adams, C., Pinkas, D.: Internet X.509 public key infrastructure time stamp protocol (TSP) (2001)

15. Lo, N.-W., Tsai, J.-L.: An efficient conditional privacy-preserving authentication scheme for vehicular sensor networks without pairings. IEEE Trans. Intell. Transp. Syst. **17**(5), 1319–1328 (2016)

ProNet: Toward Payload-Driven Protocol Fingerprinting via Convolutions and Embeddings

Yafei Sang[1,2], Yongzheng Zhang[1,2(✉)], and Chengwei Peng[2,3]

[1] Institute of Information Engineering, Chinese Academy of Sciences,
Beijing, China
{sangyafei,zhangyongzheng}@iie.ac.cn
[2] School of Cyber Security, University of Chinese Academy of Sciences,
Beijing, China
pengchengwei@iie.ac.cn
[3] Institute of Computing Technology, Chinese Academy of Sciences, Beijing, China

Abstract. Protocol fingerprinting (PF) focuses on the capability to derive a series of distinguishable features for recognizing which protocol or application generated the network traffic. Unfortunately, deep packet inspection (DPI), a widely adopted method for PF, requires significant expert effort to develop and maintain protocol signatures. Additionally, the new solution paradigm, deep flow inspection (DFI) using machine learning for PF, also relies on hand-designed features. In this paper, we present *ProNet*, a payload based approach to protocol fingerprinting, which overcomes the limitation of artificial feature engineering. The key novelty of *ProNet* is two-fold: *(i)* it takes generic, raw short packet payloads as input, instead of the typical flow-statistical-features (*e.g.*, port, packet size, packet-interval); *(ii)* it learns to simultaneously extract features via convolutional operations on the *byte-level* embeddings and *ngram-level* embeddings. We implement and evaluate *ProNet* on real-world traces, including DNS, QQLive, PPLive, PPStream, SopCast, DHCP, NBNS, HTTP, SMTP and SMB. Our experiment results show that *ProNet* achieves over 99% precision and recall with low false-positives (less than 1%) and nearly no false-negatives.

Keywords: Protocol fingerprinting · Convolutions · Embedding

1 Introduction

Motivation: Last years witnessed a very fast-paced deployment of new Internet applications, ignited by the introduction of the successful Peer-to-Peer (P2P) paradigm and fueled by the growth of Internet access rates. This undermined the reliability of the L7-layer protocol identification mechanisms. Protocol identification (PI for short in this paper), *associating traffic flows/packets with the applications/protocols*, is a fundamental and crucial component for network monitoring, traffic billing, Quality of Service (QoS), security services (such as IDS/IPS),

© ICST Institute for Computer Sciences, Social Informatics and Telecommunications Engineering 2018
I. Romdhani et al. (Eds.): CollaborateCom 2017, LNICST 252, pp. 519–529, 2018.
https://doi.org/10.1007/978-3-030-00916-8_48

and so on. The existing PI methods can roughly be divided into two categories: DPI and DFI. The core of DPI is to match the content of the traffic payload with the pre-constructed literal fingerprints, also called signatures, typically in form of regular expression. DFI is to define common flow statistical fingerprints (features) such as per-flow duration and volume, mean packet size, inter-packet times of a flow. Note that the key of both DPI and DFI is the protocol fingerprints for PI task. Thus, how to systematically and efficiently automated extract these fingerprints from network payloads remains a challenging issue. We refer to *Protocol Fingerprinting* (PF for short in this paper) as the process that a distinguishable unique pattern is extracted in the absence of the formal protocol specification (including parameters, format, and semantics).

Limitations of Prior Art: The problem PF has received wide research interests in the past decades. However, existing studies including DPI and DFI fingerprints rely heavily on hand-designed features by artificial experience and prior knowledge. The manual feature engineering is a laborious, time-consuming process. Specifically, DPI fingerprints inference falls into some drawbacks. *(i)* A majority of proprietary protocols lack publicly available documentations, although there are standard RFCs for the public-domain protocols. *(ii)* The labor-intensive manual protocol fingerprints extraction process has to be repeated from time to time so as to maintain the latest signature repository. DFI statistical fingerprints also face some limitations. *(i)* They require an in-depth exploration of the feature representation of a given traffic flow type, and an exploration of what machine learning detection approaches yield the best accuracy given those representations. *(ii)* These features were proposed based on intuition and heuristic arguments on why these features are supposed to identify a protocol category. Therefore, The key challenge we address is that protocol fingerprints cannot be automatically generated for traffic identification. Deep learning, a subfield of machine learning, promises to change this by operating on raw input signals and automating the process of feature design and extraction.

Our Research: We present *ProNet*, a deep learning approach to extract protocol fingerprints and perform PI task. Our goal is to directly work on raw traffic payload inputs, which does not require the syntactical understanding of the protocol message, such as field boundaries and delimiters. Specifically, *ProNet* first directly models raw traffic payload data with *byte-level* and *ngram-level* embeddings; then automatically learns fingerprints (signatures/features) by convolution and pool operations on these embeddings; last *ProNet* resorts to a dense softmax neural network to assign a protocol class to every traffic payload.

ProNet has several advantages over classical DPI and DFI fingerprints (signatures/features):

- It considers the process of protocol fingerprinting as part of a holistic optimization objective of protocol identification task; (Typically PF is based on local optimization, *i.e*, protocol feature extraction and identification are two separate parts.)
- It automatically derives protocol fingerprints i.e., no cumbersome and tedious reverse engineering is required;

– The fingerprints learned from traffic payloads are fine-grained comparing with DFI statistical features; (This is helpful for improving classification accuracy.)

Our results show that this approach can achieve the desired performance results, which proves that deep learning is a novel applicable technique to protocol fingerprinting that does not require the explicit definition of the features. Through experiments over a real network trace for protocol identification task, we obtain over 99% precision and recall with low false-positives (less than 1%) and nearly no false-negatives. The rest of this paper is organized as follows: Sect. 3 describes the design and implementation of our proposal. In Sect. 4, we provide experimental results to evaluate the designed approache. Section 2 reviews related work. Finally, conclusions are drawn in Sect. 5.

2 Related Work

Several network security and management tasks require automatic PF technology or fine-grained traffic classification. Here we review selected work related to payload-based PF. Park *et al.* proposed LASER [8] approach which tries to find the longest common subsequence (LCS) among given packet payloads under three constraints: number of packets per flow, minimum substring length and packet size. The LASER is susceptive to the noises and the comparison of the order in the packet payload samples. Ye *et al.* presented a system with a certain tolerance for noises, AutoSig [11], which extracts multiple common substring sequences from sample flows as protocol fingerprints. Some ngram-based proposals [2,9,10,12] try to extract fields by parsing keywords by utilizing a series of stages such as payload segmentation, payload clustering, payload sequence alignment. For example, keywords such as "GET" and "POST" in HTTP have specific delimiters or a similar interval. Notably, keyword parsing methods from the kind of textual protocol analysis, and clearly ineffective for binary protocols since they ignore the fine-grained fingerprints (less than one byte and even multiple bytes). This situation calls for a new paradigm using statistical features to PF problem.

In contrast, the statistical fingerprint methods usually employ machine learning algorithms on the protocol fingerprints (a feature vector with real values). Haffner *et al.* provided the first statistical fingerprint based work called ACAS [4] that explores automatically extracting protocol signatures from packet payload content. And they directly take the values of the first payload content bytes as features for three machine learning classifiers. Different from the ACAS, Finamore *et al.* proposed a system named KISS [3] for UDP traffic, which first extracted the randomness of the first payload bytes, in form of a 24-dimensional feature vector, by using Chi-Square test, then created and evaluated geometric-distance-based and SVM-based traffic classifier in a conventional manner. The KISS leverages the observation that application-layer protocols running over UDP must carry a protocol-specific information header. Afterwards, they extended this idea to support TCP traffic classification [6]. Alas, the limitation of KISS is its high dependency on the number of packet payloads for the online PI task. A more detailed survey of PI and PF studies may be found in [7,9].

3   ProNet

In this section, we describe how we architected our neural network to operate directly on raw payload input, and the intuition behind our decisions. Figure 1 gives an intuitive overview of our approach, showing that our neural network is divided into three notional components: *Byte/Ngram embedding, feature detection, and an identifier.* It is important to note, however, that the entire model is simultaneously optimized, end-to-end, and thus all components are optimized for the singular classification task. The *byte embedding* component embeds the alphabet of single-byte values into a multi-dimensional feature space; Additionally, the *ngram embedding* component embeds the alphabet of ngrams into a multi-dimensional feature space; Thus encoding an input payload's sequence of bytes/ngrams as two two-dimensional tensors from different views. Using the two tensors, the *feature detection* component respectively detects important local sequence patterns within the full byte sequence and ngram sequence, and then aggregates this information into a fixed-length feature vector. Finally, the *identification* component classifies the detected features using a dense neural network. All of these components are optimized jointly using stochastic gradient descent. After we construct a neural network model for the given target protocols from *ProNet*, we can use it to classify traffic.

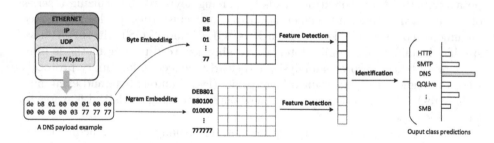

Fig. 1. The architecture of ProNet

3.1   Embedding: A Multi-view Representation of Payload

The input of *ProNet* includes multi-view feature maps of a considered packet payload, each is a matrix initialized by a different embedding version. We use two different payload chunkings and the corresponding embeddings (i.e., views), *Byte Embedding* and *Ngram Embedding*. Let s be payload length, m_s dimension of byte embeddings, m_g dimension of n-gram embeddings. Hence, the whole initialized input of ProNet consists of a two-dimensional array of size $s \times m_s$ and a two-dimensional array of size $(s - n + 1) \times m_g$. In implementation, payloads in a mini-batch will be padded to the same length, and unknown chunks for the corresponding channel are randomly initialized or can acquire good initialization from the mutual-learning phase described in next section. Multi-view initialization brings two advantages: *(i)* a payload (different payload chunking tactics) can have multiple representations in the beginning (instead of only one), which means it has more available information to leverage; *(ii)* different granularity chunk captures are helpful for handling the variant-length message fields, which enhance the robustness of *ProNet* targeting textual and binary protocols.

View 1: Byte Embedding. The first input view of our model is the raw length s sequence of bytes and embeds them into an $s \times m_s$ floating point matrix. This operation is a simple dictionary lookup, where each byte, irrespective of the bytes that came before it or after it, is mapped to its corresponding vector, and then these vectors are concatenated into this matrix. The matrix's rows represent the sequence of bytes in the original payload, and the matrix's columns represent the dimensions of the embedding space.

Formally, we denote $x_i \in \mathbb{R}^{m_s}$ as the m_s-dimensional byte representation for the i-th byte in a payload. A payload with s bytes is denoted as

$$X_{1:s} = x_1 \oplus x_2 \oplus \cdots \oplus x_s \tag{1}$$

where $\oplus$ is the concatenation operator. By this, each input payload (a sequence of bytes) is represented as a $s \times m_s$ matrix. In practice, short payload sequences are padded with zeros to the same length, such that, each matrix shares the same size. In our implementation we set $s = 16$ and $m_s = 50$.

View 2: Ngram Embedding. The another input view of *ProNet* is the length g sequence of ngrams and embeds them into a $g \times m_g$ floating point matrix. Note that different n will produce different ngram sequences and ngram vocabulary. Hence, each special ngram by varying n value, we will obtain an input view. In our implementation we only use 3-grams and $m_g = 50$ (*i.e.*, 3-gram embedding). Notice that for a given n value and s bytes, we have $g = s - n + 1$.

Formally, we denote $z_j \in \mathbb{R}^{m_g}$ as the m_g-dimensional ngram representation for the j-th ngram in a payload with g ngrams. A payload with g ngrams is denoted as

$$Z_{1:g} = z_1 \oplus z_2 \oplus \cdots \oplus z_g \tag{2}$$

where $\oplus$ is the concatenation operator. By this, each input payload (a sequence of ngrams) is represented as a $g \times m_g$ matrix. In practice, short sentences are padded with zeros to same length, such that, each matrix shares the same size.

3.2   Feature Detection

Once we embed our payload input into an $s \times m_s$ matrix and an $g \times m_g$ matrix, the next step is extracting and aggregating locally detected features. This is done in three stages: ① *ByteConv(t, h) and NgramConv(t, h)* - we detect local features by applying multiple kernel convolutions (t) with h-length; ② *ByteMax-Pool and NgramMaxPool* - we aggregate the results across the entire sequence by maximizing the kernels' activations; ③ *AggreateView* - we aggregate the extracted features from two different embedding views by means of convolution and pool operations. Notice that the first two steps are done separately for each $h \in \{3, 4, 5\}$. For example, we empirically set $t = 30$, the three results for each h tower are then concatenated together into a 90 length vector. The t filters in our *ProNet* spans the entire length of the byte embedding m_s, and can be thought of as sliding of convolution kernels (or masks) over the sequence of byte embeddings. More details about these feature learning operations as follows.

ByteConv(t, h): A convolution filter $w \in \mathbb{R}^{h \times m_s}$, which is applied to a window of h bytes of m_s-dimensional embeddings, produces a new feature. For instance, given a window of bytes $X_{i:i+h-1}$ and a bias term $b \in \mathbb{R}$, a new feature c_i is generated by

$$c_i = f(w \cdot X_{i:i+h-1} + b), \tag{3}$$

where f is a non-linear function. In our case, we apply the element-wise function Rectified Linear Unit (ReLU) to the input matrices:

$$ReLU(x) = \begin{cases} x, & if \quad x > 0 \\ 0, & otherwise \end{cases} \tag{4}$$

Each filter produces a feature map $c = [c_1, c_2, \cdots, c_{s-h+1}]$ from every possible window $X_{1:h}, X_{2:h+1}, \cdots, X_{s-h+1:s}$ of a sentence of length s.

ByteMaxPool(t): There are several pooling (sub-sampling) methods, such as average pooling, median pooling and max pooling. In this case, we apply max pooling over each feature map produced by the convolution layer and take the maximum element $\hat{c} = \max\{c\}$. Let's denote features generated by this max pooling layer as

$$\hat{c} = \hat{c}_1 \oplus \hat{c}_2 \oplus \cdots \oplus \hat{c}_t \tag{5}$$

where t is the number of feature maps.

NgramConv($\cdot$) and NgramMaxPool($\cdot$). For ngram embedding, we also execute the similar two operations to extract and aggregate locally detected features. Formally, for a given payload p, we will obtain the convolved and pooled features

$$\hat{d} = \hat{d}_1 \oplus \hat{d}_2 \oplus \cdots \oplus \hat{d}_t. \tag{6}$$

After convolution and pools operations, we focus on the problem of learning to aggregate multiple views in order to synthesize the information from all views into a single payload features. In our implementation, we simply concatenate the extracted features from two different embedding versions.

AggreateView: In this case, we simply concatenate the extracted features from two different embedding views. Let's denote features generated by this view pooling layer as

$$\hat{e} = \hat{c} \oplus \hat{d}. \tag{7}$$

3.3 Identification Algorithm

Once we extract the features from packet payload, we use a standard dense neural network to predict the protocol class of the packet. The neural network only has one layers with $l = 10$ units (10 classes). Formally, given $\hat{e}$ as the input, the fully connected layer produces

$$P(Y = j | \hat{e}, \theta) = softmax_j(W \cdot (\hat{e} \circ r) + b), \tag{8}$$

where Y is the prediction, θ denotes parameters $\{W, b\}$, W denotes weights, $\circ$ denotes the element-wise multiplication operator and $r \in \mathbb{R}$ is a dropout mask vector of Bernoulli variables with probability ρ of being zero. The fully softmax layer output provides the probability that the input payload belongs to the class label given the convolution based features. We measure our detector's prediction loss using cross entropy,

$$L(\hat{y}, y) = -\frac{1}{N} \sum_i^N [y_i \log \hat{y}_i + (1 - y_i) \log(1 - \hat{y}_i)] \tag{9}$$

where $\hat{y}$ is our model's prediction probability vector for all the packet samples and y is the vector of true label. We use Adam [5] method to minimize Eq. 9.

4 Experiments

4.1 Data Set

We collect real-world IP traffic traces from a edge router of a local area network (LAN) in mainland China. We evaluate *ProNet* on ten typical application-layer protocols: DNS, SopCast, PPStream, NBNS, DHCP, QQLive, PPLive, HTTP, SMTP and SMB. Notice that the ten target protocols involve both connection oriented protocols (such as TCP) and connection less protocols (such as UDP). Simultaneously, the ten target protocols also contain both textual and binary protocols. Note that DNS, SMTP, HTTP and SMB are representatives of well-known protocols, and they are both textual and connection-oriented protocols. QQLive, PPLive and PPStream are popular peer-to-peer video streaming protocols, and they are representatives of proprietary and new protocols. All of the above protocols offer a great amount of Internet traffic. Our evaluations only consider the first 16 bytes of the payload of an IP packet, which suffice for traffic classification. We do not examine the remaining payload and ensure that the privacy is preserved and for early flow identification. In this work, we obtain ground-truth by combining port-based method and a rather frequently used open tool nDPI [1].

4.2   Performance Metrics

To quantitatively evaluate the effectiveness of our proposal: given a packet trace of one application protocol, we are interested in the following three metrics.

- *Precision:* The Precision is the ratio of the number of true positives to the total number of packets that identified as the target protocol (including true positives and false positives) by *ProNet*.
- *Recall:* The Recall is the ratio of the number of true positives to the total number of packets that actually belong to the target protocol (including true positives and false negatives).
- *F-Measure:* The F-measure is a compromise between recall and precision. It is defined as $2 * \frac{Precision * Recall}{Precison + Recall}$.

4.3   Parameter Configuration

In this section, we'll discuss how to select parameters in our approach. In fact, many different combinations of parameters can give similarly good results. We choose some parameters empirically in our experiment. Before training, we randomize the weights using Gaussian distributions, in which the mean and standard deviation is (0, 0.05). In each convolution layer, the stride is set to 1. In max-pooling layers, the stride is equal to the number of units, as the units are non-overlapping. To speed up model training and prevent overfitting, we use layer-wise batch normalization and dropout (0.5) between layers. The main parameters that we tune in our work are as follows:

The embedding size (m): Recall that in Sect. 3, we introduced two embedding strategies for descripting payload. For a given payload example, we converted it into a $s \times m_s$ matrix, and a $s-n+1 \times m_g$ matrix. The byte embedding size (m_s) and the ngram embedding size (m_g). For parameter simplify, we empirically set $m_s = m_g = m = 30$, $s = 16$.

The number of convolution filters (t): We use filter windows (h) of 3, 4, 5 with t feature maps each. The number of filters impact the ability of feature detection of *ProNet*. In the following evaluations, we carry out our experiments for $t \in \{10, 30, 50\}$.

Mini-batch size of SGD (batch): SGD is used in the *ProNet* model to optimize the loss function. We choose $batch \in \{32, 64, 128\}$.

Steps in *ProNet* training phase (step): In one step, the *ProNet* will update the weights once. We need to select the appropriate number of steps, so that the *ProNet* model can converge. The loss function is used to evaluate whether it is convergence or not.

Figure 2 shows the results of selecting above parameters for PI-task. We can observe that the training loss generally converges after 500 steps. The bigger the batch size the faster the loss can converge, and the value of loss is also smaller. Also, when the batch size is set to a larger value, the loss declines more smoothly.

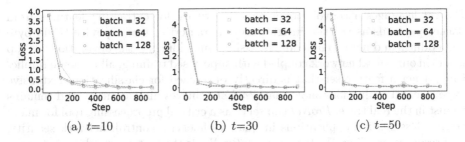

(a) $t=10$ (b) $t=30$ (c) $t=50$

Fig. 2. Parameter tuning with embedding size $m = 50$

4.4 Performance Results

We conducted five separate 5-fold cross-validation experiments, where for each experiment we randomly split our data into five equally sized partitions. For each of the five partitions, we trained against four partitions and tested against the fifth. The results of performance metrics are shown in Table 1. We can observe that our approach can achieve above 99% in precision and recall.

Our experiments were carried out on a single machine with 8 G RAM and a quad-core Intel processor of 3.6 GHz. In the training phase, it takes about 3 min to train 2000 steps for one protocol class with about 200K samples. The larger the data set the longer the time it takes to train. In the evaluation phase, it takes about 5 ms to predict on a packet on average.

Table 1. The results of 5-folds cross validation of *ProNet* on PI-task

	Precision	Recall	F-Measure
DNS	0.9989 ± 0.00084	1.0 ± 0.0	0.9994 ± 0.00042
SopCast	0.9961 ± 0.00209	0.9959 ± 0.00142	0.9961 ± 0.00090
PPStream	0.9976 ± 0.00065	0.9828 ± 0.00116	0.9902 ± 0.00063
NBNS	0.9971 ± 0.00158	0.9995 ± 0.00037	0.9983 ± 0.00083
DHCP	1.0 ± 0.0	0.9979 ± 0.00030	0.9989 ± 0.00015
QQLive	0.9898 ± 0.00185	0.9993 ± 0.00043	0.9945 ± 0.00080
PPLive	1.0 ± 0.0	0.9930 ± 0.00108	0.9964 ± 0.00054
HTTP	1.0 ± 0.0	1.0 ± 0.0	1.0 ± 0.0
SMTP	0.9936 ± 0.00161	0.9979 ± 0.00065	0.9957 ± 0.00065
SMB	0.9998 ± 0.00024	0.9987 ± 0.00127	0.9992 ± 0.00070

5 Conclusion

We present *ProNet*, a robust automatic protocol fingerprint learning approach that can operate on raw packet payloads, for accurately traffic identification.

ProNet leverages a convolutional neural network for extracting features from packet payloads as the key insight, and characterizes traffic payloads via byte embeddings and ngram embeddings. Using embeddings with convolutions as top layers in our neural network coupled with supervised training, allows us to implicitly extract a feature set that is directly optimized for classification. Extensive experimental evaluations show that *ProNet* achieves high accuracy and remains robust in the real trace. *ProNet* can serve as a critical preprocessing tool for many traffic classification applications in quality-of-service control, network security, and resource profiling. We believe that *ProNet* is the first approach that demonstrates how top to bottom deep-learning method can be adapted to the traffic identification problem, where payload data are purposely obfuscated to prevent obvious feature extraction.

Acknowledgment. This work was supported by the National Natural Science Foundation of China (No. 61572496), and National Key Research and Development Program of China (No. 2016YFB0801502).

References

1. Open and extensible lgplv3 deep packet inspection library. http://www.ntop.org/products/deep-packet-inspection/ndpi/
2. Cui, W., Kannan, J., Wang, H.J.: Discoverer: automatic protocol reverse engineering from network traces. In: USENIX Security, vol. 158 (2007)
3. Finamore, A., Mellia, M., Meo, M., Rossi, D.: KISS: stochastic packet inspection classifier for UDP traffic. IEEE/ACM Trans. Netw. **18**(5), 1505–1515 (2010)
4. Haffner, P., Sen, S., Spatscheck, O., Wang, D.: ACAS: automated construction of application signatures. In: Proceedings of the 2005 ACM SIGCOMM Workshop on Mining Network Data, MineNet 2005, pp. 197–202. ACM, New York (2005). http://doi.acm.org/10.1145/1080173.1080183
5. Kingma, D., Ba, J.: Adam: a method for stochastic optimization. arXiv preprint arXiv:1412.6980 (2014)
6. La Mantia, G., Rossi, D., Finamore, A., Mellia, M., Meo, M.: Stochastic packet inspection for TCP traffic. In: 2010 IEEE International Conference on Communications (ICC), pp. 1–6, May 2010
7. Nguyen, T.T., Armitage, G.: A survey of techniques for internet traffic classification using machine learning. IEEE Commun. Surv. Tutor. **10**(4), 56–76 (2008)
8. Park, B.C., Won, Y., Kim, M.S., Hong, J.: Towards automated application signature generation for traffic identification. In: Network Operations and Management Symposium, NOMS 2008, pp. 160–167. IEEE, April 2008
9. Sang, Y., Li, S., Zhang, Y., Xu, T.: ProDigger: towards robust automatic network protocol fingerprint learning via byte embedding. In: 2016 IEEE Trustcom/BigDataSE/ISPA, pp. 284–291. IEEE (2016)
10. Tongaonkar, A., Keralapura, R., Nucci, A.: SANTaClass: a self adaptive network traffic classification system. In: IFIP Networking Conference, pp. 1–9. IEEE (2013)

11. Ye, M., Xu, K., Wu, J., Po, H.: AutoSig-automatically generating signatures for applications. In: Ninth IEEE International Conference on Computer and Information Technology, CIT 2009, vol. 2, pp. 104–109, October 2009
12. Zhang, Z., Zhang, Z., Lee, P., Liu, Y., Xie, G.: ProWord: an unsupervised approach to protocol feature word extraction. In: 2014 Proceedings IEEE INFOCOM, pp. 1393–1401, April 2014

Formal Verification of Authorization Policies for Enterprise Social Networks Using PlusCal-2

Sabina Akhtar[1](✉), Ehtesham Zahoor[2], and Olivier Perrin[3]

[1] Bahria University, Islamabad, Pakistan
sabina.buic@bahria.edu.pk
[2] Secure Networks and Distributed Systems Lab (SENDS), National University of Computer and Emerging Sciences, Islamabad, Pakistan
ehtesham.zahoor@nu.edu.pk
[3] Université de Lorraine, LORIA, BP 239, 54506 Vandoeuvre-lès-Nancy Cedex, France
olivier.perrin@loria.fr

Abstract. Information security research has been a highly active and widely studied research direction. In the domain of Enterprise Social Networks (ESNs), the security challenges are amplified as they aim to incorporate the social technologies in an enterprise setup and thus asserting greater control on information security. Further, the security challenges may not be limited to the boundaries of a single enterprise and need to be catered for a federated environment where users from different ESNs can collaborate. In this paper, we address the problem of federated authorization for the ESNs and present an approach for combining user level policies with the enterprise policies. We present the formal verification technique for ESNs and how it can be used to identify the conflicts in the policies. It allows us to bridge the gap between user-centric or enterprise-centric approaches as required by the domain of ESN. We apply our specification of ESNs on a scenario and discuss the model checking results.

Keywords: Enterprise social network · Formal verification
Model checking · PLUSCAL-2, TLA⁺, TLC

1 Introduction

Information security research has been a highly active and widely studied research direction. In the last decade, the widespread usage of social networks has further amplified the need to protect user information. Recently, a number of organizations have started to use social networks as a tool for enhancing collaboration amongst their employees. Social network in an enterprise setting is termed as Enterprise Social Network (ESN). Implementations can be either homegrown systems built internally or tailoring existing social network implementations for

© ICST Institute for Computer Sciences, Social Informatics and Telecommunications Engineering 2018
I. Romdhani et al. (Eds.): CollaborateCom 2017, LNICST 252, pp. 530–540, 2018.
https://doi.org/10.1007/978-3-030-00916-8_49

an enterprise setting. One such implementation is Yammer[1] and one example of ESN usage for increase in productivity is Yammer usage within Boral Limited, a building and construction materials company. One important aspect to emphasize here is that an ESN is not just deployment of a social network in an enterprise environment. It may not be limited to the boundaries of a single enterprise and users from different ESNs can collaborate in a federated environment. For instance, Yammer has a concept of external groups, where external partners can collaborate with members of an organization. Addressing ESN security and privacy issues is a challenging domain as it requires to consider the perspective of both federated enterprises and the ESN users.

The security policy of an organization helps to better prepare for and address these security challenges. It specifies a high level specification of how to implement security principles and technologies. For instance, the Authentication policy of an organization specifies which users are allowed to use its services. Once a user has been authenticated, the authorization process allows to determine who can access what resources, under what conditions, and for what purpose. The authorization process can be based on temporal aspects and may involve delegation. An authorization policy is a high level description of access rules that will determine what rights an authenticated user has. While the federated authentication has been an active area of research with approaches such as SAML providing SSO for federated environments, the authorization capabilities, challenges and solutions are not thoroughly explored. The challenges are amplified in the case of ESN as authorization policies are not limited to the case of a single enterprise. We need to cater for authorization policies for each enterprise within the federation as well as user policies, as and ESN is essentially a social network allowing users to share and collaborate.

In this paper we address the challenges related to one important class of security policies, called the access control or authorization policies in a federated ESN setting. From an enterprise point of view, authorization policies are very important to express the access on resources. Their need is even more evident in the context of enterprise federation, where different enterprises trust each other. With the advent of Web 2.0, information sharing allowed users to collaborate more easily, thanks for the use of the social technologies. In this context, approaches such as OAuth and Lockr are based on the user perspective, rather than the classical enterprise point of view. In an ESN, the users share and access resources and at the same time, the enterprise imposes some polices to be taken care of. We address the problem of federated authorization for the ESNs and present an approach for combining user level policies with the enterprise policies. We present the formal verification approach for ESNs and detail how it can be used to identify the conflicts in the policies. It allows us to bridge the gap between user-centric or enterprise-centric approaches as required by the domain of ESN. We use PLUSCAL-2 [1,12] as a formal modeling language for specifying the authorization policies. Formal methods are being used extensively at large scale distributed systems, for instance Amazon uses TLA$^+$ and PLUSCAL to

---

[1] https://www.yammer.com.

model and verify AWS services such as *S3*, *DynamoDB* and *EBS*. The proposed specification approach is generic and expressive and is also based on TLA$^+$.

2   Related Work

In this work, we address the challenges associated with authorization policies in the context of enterprise federation within an Enterprise Social Network [17]. Two major research directions in this domain have been to investigate the authorization from the enterprise or federation point of view, using approaches such as XACML, and the other is to address the challenge from a user point of view, with approaches such as OAuth and Lockr. Authorization issues in ESN is a relatively unexplored domain.

Access control and authorization in general has been an active research areas since decades. In this context, the focus of traditional research approaches has been the RBAC model [15] and its variations. Task based access control (TBAC) considers task based contextual information [18]. Team based access control [8,19] introduces the concept of team to accomplish collaborative activities. Even though RBAC is a well defined model, it suffers from *role explosion* as too many rules (may even surpass the number of users) may need to be managed. In distributed environment (more precisely in an enterprise federation), RBAC may also introduce interoperability concerns as the semantics of different roles may be inconsistent across domains. Some approaches have investigated the use and challenges for RBAC in a distributed environment [6,16]. One such approach is D-Role [14] in which authors propose extensions to XACML for distributed roles. In contrast to RBAC models, the Attribute based access control (ABAC) model is based on the attributes [10]. The resources, subjects and environment have attributes, and the policy rule is a boolean function on these attributes. ABAC provide more flexibility and expressiveness than RBAC in term of rules definition as a role itself can be an attribute in an ABAC model. For ESN authorization decisions, ABAC is thus the preferred model and it subsumes RBAC model.

XACML (eXtensible Access Control Markup Language) is a declarative, XML-based access control policy language for managing access to resources, based on ABAC model. As XACML is verbose and based on XML, a number of approaches to provide formal semantics of XACML using formal logic have been proposed [7,11]. Further, a number of approaches have been proposed that build upon XACML for its usage in collaborative and distributed environments [23]. These include [5] in which the authors propose a distributed device access control architecture called *MPABAC*. In [21] authors have developed a formal policy language BelLog that can express both delegation and composition operators.

The second class of authorization policies specification is when the user determines the access for their resources. The most prominent approach being the OAuth [9] which allows users to share their personal resources, such as images, hosted on one Website with other sites without giving them their username and password. User-Managed Access (UMA)[2] is another user centric and it provides

---

[2] http://docs.kantarainitiative.org/uma/draft-uma-core.html.

services for authorization, monitoring and changing data sharing. Lockr [20] is an access control system based on social relationships. Users can base ACLs for applications based on social relationships as defined in some social network. When it comes to specifying authorization policies within a social network, in [2] authors presented Persona, a system that promotes data privacy by allowing users to use attribute encryption for specifying policies themselves and not relying on the social network.

In the context of ESN, neither XACML nor User centric authorization mechanisms are sufficient on their own. Using XACML, an enterprise can easily define a set of policies for subjects within the enterprise, but it is more difficult for a user to define its own policy for managing access to its own data. User centric authorization mechanisms are well adapted for user defined access controls. However, in the context of ESN, it is not just about users, it is also about enterprises, and even more complex, enterprises federation. In this context, it is mandatory to allow the users to define their own policies, and to combine them with the enterprise ones, and to be able to decide if an access is granted or not. Our work builds upon our previous work in handling temporal, trust and delegation aspects in distributed environments [3,24]. In this work we provide an approach that combines user level policies with the enterprise policies to bridge the gap between traditional federated authorization approaches.

3 Motivating Example

For the motivating example, we consider the case of a large municipality (we will call it a *commune* as in France) that is willing to take benefit from the rise of ESNs[3]. We consider a situation such as child protection case, where the relevant information could be scattered across different departments such as social services, education, healthcare, and police agencies. The information sharing between these different departments in an ESN would allow timely decisions to be made but comes with the challenge for managing such collaboration in a secure manner. We consider that each department has its own associated security policy and belong to a federation where they trust each other.

We further consider that a new child protection case has been forwarded to an employee at the commune, Alice, and she needs to create a case file and gather information from different departments to reach a decision about the case. As a standard practice she wants to give permissions to another person in her team, Genny, working on the case in another department. We assume that the case requires access to some database, thus Alice would grant permission to access it. However, there might be another policy already in the enterprise policies or user defined policies that doesn't allow Genny to access that particular database. These conflicts effect the overall performance and reliability of an enterprise social network where it is a major concern for the users. Our idea is to formally

---

[3] Idea is based on real world example as briefly discussed in Social Networking In The Enterprise: Benefits And Inhibitors, a commissioned study conducted by Forrester Consulting on behalf of Cisco Systems.

verify the set of policies before actually deploying the ESNs or anytime during
the scheduled update of the network. This would reduce the need for the decision
making algorithms to be invoked at the time of the request.

4   Proposed Approach

Our approach combines the two major classes of authorization policies; user
level and enterprise level, in a federated environment and provides a federation-
level authorization process. We use finite-state model checking [4] technique,
used for formal verification of distributed systems, to address the challenges
raised by the different enterprises in a federation. It allows to decide automatically whether the invariants and properties hold for the specified system or not.
They are verified for finite instances of systems, described in a formal modeling language. We use PLUSCAL-2 [1,12] as a formal modeling language for the
formally specifying the enterprises in a federated environment. It is intended to
provide the programmers the platform where they can specify their systems and
generate the TLA$^+$ specifications. TLA$^+$ is a formal specification designed by
Leslie Lamport provides a method for specifying the systems. It is supported
by the model checker TLC [22] that verifies the system for the specified set of
properties and invariants. PLUSCAL-2 features non-determinism, mathematical
abstractions, and user-specified grain of atomicity. It emphasizes on the abstract
model of the system instead of focusing on its efficient execution. Compared to
PLUSCAL algorithm language [13] by Leslie Lamport, it introduces several other
statements and flexibility for the programmer and reduces the dependency on
TLA$^+$. They will be used in the specification of enterprise social networks to
demonstrate their need in system specification. In the proposed architecture,
policies are specified using ABAC model. As an ESN builds upon the notion of
sharing and collaboration, the users can access authorization policies with the
resources they are in control of (such as the ones they have created or the control has been delegated to them). This user level policy specification approach is
consistent with the user-controlled authorization schemes that aim to put user
in the control of authorization process.

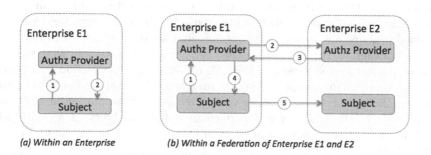

(a) Within an Enterprise   (b) Within a Federation of Enterprise E1 and E2

Fig. 1. Policies evaluation

However in an ESN setting, the collaboration is under the control of an enterprise and it has its own policies about the access to resources, for instance the enterprise policy that some critical resources can be accessed within some time frame. Thus the proposed approach allows to specify the policies also at the enterprise level. Indeed the two set of policies may be inconsistent and a set of decision algorithms can decide the resolution scheme in case of conflict. The policy evaluation at an enterprise level is shown in the Fig. 1-a. Inside an enterprise, when a user, *user*, tries to access a resource, *res*, its request, R, along with, its attributes and the attributes of the resource, composed formally as *(user, res)*, is sent to the Authorization Provider (AzP). The task of Authorization Provider (AzP) is to gather the user defined policies, UP and the enterprise policies, EP for the resource in order to process the request. Formally, we define a policy, P, as

$$P \triangleq (user,\ res,\ action)$$

where an *action* can be to allow or deny the resource, *res*, for the user. Once, the Authorization Provider (AzP) has gathered all the policies, it filters out a subset of policies, SP, concerning the request, R, *(user, res, X)* from the set of policies for user defined policies, UP and enterprise policies, EP

$$SP \triangleq R \cap (UP \cup EP)$$

X in the request R allows to ignore all the actions in the set of policies and selects only the policies from entire set of policies related to the user and the resource. If the set SP is empty this means their is no policy written for that specific user and resource in the set of policies. In this case the request will be denied by the Authorization Provider (AzP). If there is only a single policy in the set SP, then in that case Authorization Provider (AzP) can take a decision immediately by applying the action mentioned in the policy. However, if there are more than one policies in the set then there might be conflict and the AzP will have to resolve it. AzP will deny the request if one of the policies in the set denies the resource formally written as

$$\exists\, p \in SP : p.action = \text{``deny''} \rightarrow Deny\ request$$

The Authorization Provider (AzP) will allow the resource access if all of policies allow the resource for the user. It can be formally specified as

$$\forall\, p \in SP : p.action = \text{``allow''} \rightarrow Allow\ access$$

When a user wants to access a resource that is not within the enterprise but belongs to another enterprise within the same federation, the request is first validated by the local AzP of the enterprise to which the user belongs. The enterprise checks if the request conforms to the enterprise policy, for instance to enforce that the request might be not allowed for the users with a specific set of attributes. The request is then forwarded to the AzP of the enterprise to which the resource belongs and the AzP checks if the request conforms to the user specified resource policies and the enterprise policies, Fig. 1b.

5   ESNs Specification in PlusCal-2

Our specification[4] of enterprises in a federation allows us to identify the
inter enterprise or intra enterprise level conflicts in the policies. Figure 2 shows
the specification of a federation with two ESNs. The specification can be used
for one or more than one enterprises. It only requires to add the information
about the new enterprise along with the set of policies for each one added in the
federation. In PLUSCAL-2, the specification starts with the keyword **algorithm**
followed by the name of the specification. Then we have standard modules for
specific constructs used from TLA$^+$ that are required by the TLC model checker.

```
1   algorithm ESNSpec
2   extends Naturals, Sequences , TLC, FiniteSets
3   variable EP1Users = {"Alice", "Tim"}, EP2Users = {"Bob", "Genny"},
4           AllUsers = EP1Users ∪ EP2Users,
5           EP1Res = {"R1", "R2"}, EP2Res = {"R3", "R4"},
6           AllRes = EP1Res ∪ EP2Res,
7           ReqPool = [u ∈ AllUsers, r ∈ AllRes ↦ [status ↦ {}]]
8   process Enterprise1[1]
9   variable  rules = 0, status = 0, statusRecord = 0,
10          Policies = [u ∈ AllUsers ↦
11              CASE (u = "Alice") →  {[res ↦ "R2", act ↦ "deny"], [res ↦ "R3", act ↦ "allow"]}
12                 □ (u = "Tim") →  {[res ↦ "R4", act ↦ "deny"], [res ↦ "R3", act ↦ "allow"]}
13                 □ (u = "Bob") →  {[res ↦ "R3", act ↦ "allow"], [res ↦ "R2", act ↦ "deny"]}
14                 □ (u = "Genny") →  {[res ↦ "R4", act ↦ "deny"], [res ↦ "R4", act ↦ "deny"]} ]
15  begin
16      atomic
17      for u ∈ AllUsers  for r ∈ AllRes
18          rules := Policies[u];
19          for rule ∈ rules
20              if rule.res = r then
21                  statusRecord := ReqPool[u,r];
22                  statusRecord.status := statusRecord.status ∪ {rule.act};
23                  ReqPool[u,r] := statusRecord;
24              end if; end for; end for; end for;
25      end atomic;
26  end process
27  process Enterprise2[1]
28  variable  rules = 0, status = 0, statusRecord = 0,
29          Policies = [u ∈ AllUsers ↦
30              CASE (u = "Alice") →  {[res ↦ "R2", act ↦ "deny"], [res ↦ "R1", act ↦ "allow"]}
31                 □ (u = "Tim") →  {[res ↦ "R1", act ↦ "deny"], [res ↦ "R2", act ↦ "allow"]}
32                 □ (u = "Bob") →  {[res ↦ "R1", act ↦ "deny"], [res ↦ "R4", act ↦ "deny"]}
33                 □ (u = "Genny") →  {[res ↦ "R1", act ↦ "deny"], [res ↦ "R4", act ↦ "allow"]} ]
34  begin
35      atomic
36      for u ∈ AllUsers  for r ∈ AllRes
37          rules := Policies[u];
38          for rule ∈ rules
39              if rule.res = r then
40                  statusRecord := ReqPool[u,r];
41                  statusRecord.status := statusRecord.status ∪ {rule.act};
42                  ReqPool[u,r] := statusRecord;
43              end if; end for; end for; end for;
44      end atomic;
45  end process end algorithm
46  invariant ∀ u, ∈ AllUsers, r ∈ AllRes : (ReqPool[u,r].status ∩ {"allow", "deny"}) ≠ {"allow", "deny"}
```

Fig. 2. Specification of a federation with two enterprises in PLUSCAL-2.

---

[4] Available at https://github.com/sabinaakhtar/ESNSpecs.

The global variables are defined at line 3. In our specifications, we assume that we have two enterprises *Enterprise1*, *Enterprise2* representing Alice's and Genny's departments respectively. Then we specify their users globally as *EP1Users* and *EP2Users*. *AllUsers* is the union of all the users in all the enterprises. Each enterprise owns its own set of resources, specified in our specification as *EP1Res* and *EP2Res*. Similarly, we have *AllRes* as a union of all the resources. The two processes *Enterprise1* and *Enterprise2* will represent Authorization providers in our specifications. To keep the specification at an abstract level, we removed the role of a user that sends the request for the resources and replaced it with a pool of requests that includes all possible requests that can be made by any user in a federation. At line 7, we define *ReqPool* as function whose domain is in *AllUsers* and *AllRes* specifies the pool of requests that can be made by the users. Its range is represented by a record with a field *status* that is initially an empty set. Its purpose is to contain all the actions that can be applied to a request by any policy in an enterprise/federation. The functionality of the enterprises remains same except for the policies that they have defined at their own level. The policies are specified at line 10 for *Enterprise1* as a function whose domain is in *AllUsers* and range represents a set of rules for each users corresponding to the resources. For example, user *Tim* has an access to some resource *R3* but does not have an access to resource *R4* specified a line 12.

The specification of the enterprise is at line 15 till line 25. For each possible request, it consults its own set of policies and if it finds a policy it updates the field *status* of the *ReqPool* with action specified in the policy. This role of an enterprise is enclosed in a construct **atomic** to avoid the interleavings with the other process. This makes our specification more coarse grained to avoid the state space explosion problem. The specification ends with an invariant at line 46 of Fig. 2. The TLC model checker verifies the invariant at each state and if the invariant is violated, it stops the execution and shows the counter example. The invariant specifies that for each user, $u \in AllUsers$, and for each resource, $r \in AllRes$, the specified formula must hold and the intra or inter enterprise policies must never allow and deny the access at the same time.

As per our motivating example introduced a scenario where an employee, Alice, was working on a case from a department, in collaboration with another employee, Genny, of another department. They had to access a database, lets call it *R4*, to complete the processing of the case. Now, even if Alice grants access of this resource to Genny, there might be a possibility that she cannot access this resource. We can formally verify this scenario through our specifications and identify the policies with the conflict using the counter example. In Fig. 2, we have modeled such a scenario to find out that counter example. PlusCal-2 compiler translates our specifications to TLA⁺ specifications. Then we model checked those specifications using TLC model checker and it stops with the following message

```
Error: Invariant Inv0 is violated. The behavior up to this point is:...
```

Inv0 is the name of the invariant used in the TLA⁺ specifications for the invariant at line 46 of Fig. 2. The TLC model checker gives a counter example that clearly shows where it was voilated. In the last state of the counter example, it shows the state of the variable *ReqPool*.

```
... /\ ReqPool = ( <<"Alice", "R1">> :> [status |-> {"allow"}] @@ ...
  <<"Tim", "R1">> :> [status |-> {"deny"}] @@ ...
  <<"Bob", "R1">> :> [status |-> {"deny"}] @@ ...
  <<"Genny", "R4">> :> [status |-> {"deny", "allow"}] ) ...
```

The output clearly show that the policies had conflict for request by user *Genny* for the resource *R4*. However, if there will be no such conflict in the policies, then this specific invariant will never be violated. Similarly, we can use formal verification techniques for identifying various other issues in the federated environment as well. The PLUSCAL-2 compiler has not been released yet as it is in testing phase and it will be released in few months time. The current version of PLUSCAL-2 compiler along with the TLC model checker are also available at InriaForge[5].

6   Conclusion

In this paper, we have presented a formal specification of federated environment and how formal verification can be used for the authorization challenges associated with Enterprise Social Networks (ESNs). The traditional approaches for authorization are either user-centric or enterprise-centric and we have advocated to bridge the gap between them. In contrast to traditional XML based authorization policy specification languages, our approach is formal and provides a precise, expressive, flexible and non-ambiguous representation. It also allows for reasoning about authorization policies (e.g. to find inconsistencies or hard constraints). We have also presented the model checking results for our specifications and discussed how these tools can be used to identify conflicts by stating invariants and properties. In future, we plan to automate the translation of actual user defined and enterprise level policies to PLUSCAL-2 so that we can formally verify them and identify conflicts in the policies. We also plan to investigate other challenges and issues in Enterprise Social Networks from the perspective of formal verification techniques.

References

1. Akhtar, S., Merz, S., Quinson, M.: A high-level language for modeling algorithms and their properties. In: Davies, J., Silva, L., Simao, A. (eds.) SBMF 2010. LNCS, vol. 6527, pp. 49–63. Springer, Heidelberg (2011). https://doi.org/10.1007/978-3-642-19829-8_4
2. Baden, R., Bender, A., Spring, N., Bhattacharjee, B., Starin, D.: Persona: an online social network with user-defined privacy. In: SIGCOMM (2009)

---

[5] https://gforge.inria.fr/projects/pcal2-0/.

3. Bouchami, A., Perrin, O., Zahoor, E.: Trust-based formal delegation framework for enterprise social networks. In: 2015 IEEE Trust-Com/BigDataSE/ISPA, Helsinki, Finland (2015)
4. Clarke, E.M., Grumberg, O., Peled, D.: Model Checking. MIT Press, Cambridge (1999)
5. Liang, F., Guo, H., Yi, S., Zhang, X., Ma, S.: An attributes-based access control architecture within large-scale device collaboration systems using XACML. In: Yang Y., Ma M. (eds.) Green Communications and Networks. LNEE, vol 113. Springer, Dordrecht (2012). https://doi.org/10.1007/978-94-007-2169-2_124
6. Wu, T.: A distributed collaborative product design environment based on semantic norm model and role-based access control. J. Netw. Comput. Appl. **36**(6), 1431–1440 (2013)
7. Nguyen, T.N., et al.: Towards a flexible framework to support a generalized extension of xacml for spatio-temporal rbac model with reasoning ability. In: ICCSA, no. (5) (2013)
8. Georgiadis, C. K., Mavridis, I., Pangalos, G., Thomas, R.K.: Flexible team-based access control using contexts, In: SACMAT (2001)
9. Hardt, D.: The OAuth 2.0 authorization framework (2012)
10. Hu, V.C., et al.: Guide to attribute based access control (ABAC) definition and considerations. NIST Special Publication, 800:162 (2014)
11. Kolovski, V., Hendler, J., Parsia, B.: Analyzing web access control policies. In: WWW, pp. 677–686 (2007)
12. Lamport, L.: Specifying Systems, The TLA+ Language and Tools for Hardware and Software Engineers. Addison-Wesley (2002)
13. Lamport, L.: The PlusCal algorithm language. In: Leucker, M., Morgan, C. (eds.) ICTAC 2009. LNCS, vol. 5684, pp. 36–60. Springer, Heidelberg (2009). https://doi.org/10.1007/978-3-642-03466-4_2
14. Lee, H.K., Luedemann, H.: Lightweight decentralized authorization model for inter-domain collaborations. In: SWS (2007)
15. Park, J.S., Sandhu, R.S., Ahn, G.-J.: Role-based access control on the web. ACM Trans. Inf. Syst. Secur. 4(1), 37–71 (2001)
16. Ruan, C., Varadharajan, V.: Dynamic delegation framework for role based access control in distributed data management systems. Distrib. Parallel Databases **32**, 245–269 (2014)
17. Stei, G., Sprenger, S., Rossmann, A.: Enterprise social networks: status quo of current research and future research directions. In: Abramowicz, W., Alt, R., Franczyk, B. (eds.) BIS 2016. LNBIP, vol. 255, pp. 371–382. Springer, Cham (2016). https://doi.org/10.1007/978-3-319-39426-8_29
18. Thomas, R.K., Sandhu, R.S.: Task-based authorization controls (TBAC): a family of models for active and enterprise-oriented authorization management. In: Lin, T.Y., Qian, S. (eds.) Database Security XI. IFIP Advances in Information and Communication Technology, pp. 166–181. Springer, Boston (1998). https://doi.org/10.1007/978-0-387-35285-5_10
19. Thomas, R.K.: Team-based access control (TMAC): a primitive for applying role-based access controls in collaborative environments. In: ACM Workshop on Role-Based Access Control, pp. 13–19 (1997)
20. Tootoonchian, A., Saroiu, S., Ganjali, Y., Wolman, A.: Lockr: better privacy for social networks. In: CoNEXT (2009)
21. Tsankov, P., Marinovic, S., Dashti, M.T., Basin, D.A.: Decentralized composite access control. In: POST (2014)

22. Yu, Y., Manolios, P., Lamport, L.: Model checking TLA$^+$ specifications. In: Pierre, L., Kropf, T. (eds.) CHARME 1999. LNCS, vol. 1703, pp. 54–66. Springer, Heidelberg (1999). https://doi.org/10.1007/3-540-48153-2_6
23. Zahoor, E., Asma, Z., Perrin, O.: A formal approach for the verification of AWS IAM access control policies. In: De Paoli, F., Schulte, S., Broch Johnsen, E. (eds.) ESOCC 2017. LNCS, vol. 10465, pp. 59–74. Springer, Cham (2017). https://doi.org/10.1007/978-3-319-67262-5_5
24. Zahoor, E., Perrin, O., Bouchami, A.: CATT: a cloud based authorization framework with trust and temporal aspects. In: CollaborateCom 2014, Miami, Florida, USA (2014)

High Performance Regular Expression Matching on FPGA

Jiajia Yang, Lei Jiang(✉), Xu Bai, and Qiong Dai

School of Cyber Security, Institute of Information Engineering,
University of Chinese Academy of Sciences, UCAS,
Beijing, People's Republic of China
{yangjiajia,jianglei,baixu,daiqiong}@iie.ac.cn

Abstract. Deep Packet Inspection (DPI) technology has been widely deployed in Network Intrusion Detection System (NIDS) to detect attacks and viruses. State-of-the-art NIDS uses Deterministic Finite Automata (DFA) to perform regular expression matching for its stable matching speed. However, traditional DFA algorithm's throughput is limited by the input character's width (usually one character per time). In this paper, we present an architecture named Parallel-DFA to accelerate regular expression matching by scanning multiple characters per time. Experimental results show that, our architecture can achieve as high as 1200 Gbps (1.17 Tbps) rate on current single Field-Programmable Gate Array (FPGA) chip. This makes it a very practical solution for NIDS in 100G Ethernet standard network, which is currently the fastest approved standard of Ethernet. To the best of our knowledge, this is the fastest matching performance architecture on a single FPGA chip. Besides, the throughput is nearly 3 orders of magnitude (916×) than that of original DFA implemented on software. Our architecture is about 183.2× efficiency than that of original DFA.

Keywords: Deep Packet Inspection · Regular expression matching
DFA · FPGA · Network security

1 Introduction

Networking security in collaborative networks is becoming crucial with the various attacks networks are being exposed to [1]. In order to protect networking devices and computer systems from such attacks, Signature-based DPI technologies have taken root as a dominant security mechanism to detect and neutralize potential threats by discarding malicious traffic. Most of the attacks are described by regular expressions (REs) for its powerful and flexible expressive ability. There has been a lot of recent works on implementing REs for use in high-speed networking environment, particularly with representations based on DFA [2]. However, DFA suffers from huge memory consumption. Moreover, matching network traffic against a DFA is inherently a serial activity. These existing

© ICST Institute for Computer Sciences, Social Informatics and Telecommunications Engineering 2018
I. Romdhani et al. (Eds.): CollaborateCom 2017, LNICST 252, pp. 541–553, 2018.
https://doi.org/10.1007/978-3-030-00916-8_50

problems make DFA a challenge to be implemented in current limited resources network devices.

In order to accelerate DFA matching, many accelerated methods on different platforms have been proposed. These methods have already achieved high throughput theoretically but still suffer their drawbacks respectively. Some schemes achieve high throughput at the expense of consuming huge memory, making them impractical in current dedicated hardware with limited resources. Thus, satisfying low memory consumption and high throughput requirement in high-speed network environment simultaneously is difficult and challenging.

In this paper, we present Parallel-DFA, a high-throughput DFA accelerated architecture. Using tight integration of logic resources available on-chip on FPGA, we can achieve a throughput as high as 1200 Gbps. With the requirements of high performance in high-speed network and the advancements in memory technology, coping with the acceleration problem has become a firstly concern while the memory efficiency is a secondly concern. Thus, Parallel-DFA mainly focuses on the acceleration of DFA. We summarize our contributions as follows:

(1) A high-speed DFA accelerated architecture on a single chip. It's throughput can achieve as high as 1200 Gbps.
(2) Theoretical analysis of time and space consumption of our proposed architecture. We also compare the time and space consumption of our architecture with that of original DFA and multi-stride DFA.
(3) Detailed performance analysis wrt throughput, resource usage and the number of supported rules under various configurations.

The rest of this paper is organized as follows. Section 2 discusses the previous work related to RE matching. Section 3 describes the detail of Parallel-DFA architecture. Section 4 describes the performance evaluation. Finally, Sect. 5 concludes this paper.

2   Related Work

With the widespread use of REs, RE matching has become research interests and a hot topic in academic and industries area. Many works have been extensively studied to promote RE matching, especially DFA algorithms' practical application in NIDS. Currently, researches on RE matching mainly focus on two aspects: One is to reduce the memory consumption of RE automaton, the other is to improve the throughput of RE matching.

Many compression strategies have been proposed to reduce the memory consumption of RE transition tables. Most of the strategies relate to compress techniques based on the characteristic of RE transition tables. Kumar et al. [3] propose D^2FA based on observing the similarity of transitions between two states and applying default transitions to compress DFA transition table. At the expense of accessing memory multiple times per input character, D^2FA achieves more than 95% compression ratio than the original DFA transition table. Motivated by the idea of D^2FA, Becchi et al. in [4] propose A-DFA, which is also a novel DFA compression algorithm. A-DFA quantifies a state's distance from the initial state, and results in at most $2N$ state traversals when processing an input string of length N. In comparison with the D^2FA method, A-DFA yields a comparable compression ratio and has lower complexity. Jiang et al. [5] use the clustering algorithms to cluster the similar states together. In this way, they achieves memory consumption by more than 95%.

Besides, some strategies focus on improving the performance of RE matching. For example, Brodie et al. [6] use multi-stride DFAs to increase the throughput. Specially, a stride-k DFA consumes k characters per state transition, thus yielding a k-fold performance increase. However, multi-stride DFAs lead to an exponentially increased memory requirement. Jan et al. [7] present a pattern-matching engine built on an extended version of the B-FSM scheme that provides a substantially more compact data structure on DFA. Experimental results show the B-FSM implemented on FPGA can achieve scan rates on $16\,Gb/s$ per B-FSM. Chad [8] et al. use dedicated TCAM to accelerate RE matching. In order to reduce TCAM space and improve matching speed, three novel techniques are proposed: transition sharing, table consolidation, and variable striding. Their method can achieve potential matching throughput of 10 to $19\,Gbps$ using only a single $2.36\,Mb$ TCAM chip. But it is challenging to implement RE on TCAM for its expensive and not scalable with respect to clock rates and power consumption.

3 The Detail of Our Architecture

This section includes 3 subsections. Subsection 3.1 introduces original DFA and multi-stride DFA. Subsection 3.2 gives the description of our algorithm. In Subsect. 3.3, we design and analyze our hardware architecture.

3.1 The Introduction of Original DFA and Multi-stride DFA

We introduce the basic original DFA by an example. Figure 1 (I) shows a standard DFA defined on the alphabet a, b. In this DFA, state 0, 1 (in white cycle) are normal states, while state 2 (in grey cycle) is match state. We define a graph $G = <V, E>$, where V is a set of vertices (states) and E is a set of edges (transitions). In this example, $V = \{v_0, v_1, v_1\} = \{0, 1, 2\}$, where v_i is a vertex. $E = \{e_0, e_1, e_2, e_3, e_4, e_5\}$, where e_i denotes a transition (edge). A transition denotes a state (vertex) jumps to another state. Its additional information is an alphabet, such as a, b. If the initial state is state 0 and a input string is 'abab', the traversal path will be: $(0) \xrightarrow{a} (1) \xrightarrow{b} (2) \xrightarrow{a} (0) \xrightarrow{b} (0)$.

Suppose the length of *input string* is n and the number of DFA states is S. As the number of ASCII characters is 256, original DFA graph's space consumption is: $256 \times S \times \lceil log_2 S \rceil$, where $\lceil log_2 S \rceil$ denotes the bit-width of an edge (transition). The processing time of original DFA is $O(n)$.

Because the processing time is too large for DFA, Becchi et al. [9] introduce classical multi-striding technique, which is used to increase throughput of a system for matching strings against a set of REs. An example is given in Fig. 1 (II).

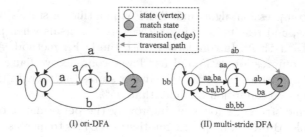

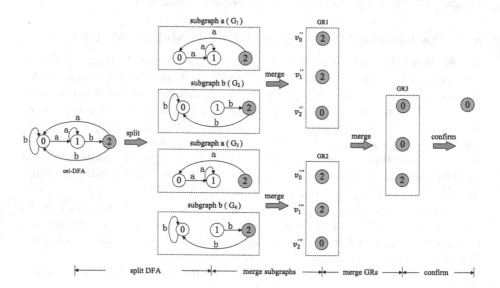

Fig. 1. The DFA algorithms. (I) the original DFA. (II) a multi-stride DFA that consumes 2 characters per time.

In this 2-DFA, it can consume 2 characters per time. If processing n characters, it just consumes $\frac{n}{2}$ times. In another words, it can achieve $2\times$ speedup of original DFA. The traversal path is: $(0) \xrightarrow{ab} (2) \xrightarrow{ab} (0)$.

As for multi-stride DFA, its space consumption is about $S \times \lceil log_2 S \rceil \times 256^n$. This is a huge memory consumption. Although the time complexity is only $\frac{1}{2}$ of original DFA's, the space consumption is too huge to make it practical on current limited resource device.

3.2 The Description of Our Algorithm

Now, we give an example to show the process of our algorithm in Fig. 2. In Fig. 2, our algorithm can be divided into four stages: **(1)** we split original DFA into 4 subgraphs based on the input string 'abab'. The additional information of

Fig. 2. An example to show the whole process.

Algorithm 1. MergeSubGraph(G_j, G_k)

Input: G_j, G_k
Output: G
Procedures:
1: $G.V \leftarrow \varnothing$, $G.E \leftarrow \varnothing$
2: **for all** v, v', ($v \in G_j.V$, $v' \in G_k.V$) **do in parallel**
3:    **if** $\exists v_{mid}$, satisfy $<v,v_{mid}> \in G_j.E$, $<v_{mid},v'> \in G_k.E$ **then**
4:       **if** these states v,v_{mid},v' has one in grey **then**
5:          v' is in grey
6:       **end if**
7:       $G.V \leftarrow v'$
8:    **end if**
9: **end for**

Algorithm 2. MergeNodeGroup(GR_x, GR_y)

Input: GR_x, GR_y
Output: GR_z
Procedures:
1: $GR_z.V \leftarrow \varnothing$, $GR_z.E \leftarrow \varnothing$
2: **for all** v_i'', v_j''', ($v_i'' \in GR_x.V$, $v_j''' \in GR_y.V$) **do in parallel**
3:    **if** $\exists i,j$, satisfy $j == v_i''$ **then**
4:       $GR_z \leftarrow v_j'''$
5:    **end if**
6: **end for**

---

transitions of each subgraphs is only an alphabet. **(2)** We merge these subgraphs to GRs (i.e. a group of state nodes). **(3)** We merge GRs into the last GR. **(4)** If given the *current state*, we confirm the *next state*, and justify whether the input string 'abab' is accepted by this DFA.

The pseudo-code of stage (2) is shown in Algorithm 1. By Algorithm 1, we can merge two subgraphs G_j, G_k into a GR, which only contains state nodes. The pseudo-code of stage (3) is shown in Algorithm 2. By Algorithm 2, we can merge two GRs into one GR.

We give an example to explain the Algorithm 2. In Fig. 2, $GR_1 = \{v_0'', v_1'', v_2''\} = (2, 2, 0)$, where $v_0'' = 2$, $v_1'' = 2$, $v_2'' = 0$. $GR_2 = \{v_0''', v_1''', v_2'''\} = (2, 2, 0)$, where $v_0''' = 2$, $v_1''' = 2$, $v_2''' = 0$. Because $v_0'' = 2$, then $GR_3.V \leftarrow v_2'''$; $v_1'' = 2$, then $GR_3.V \leftarrow v_2'''$; $v_2'' = 0$, then $GR_3.V \leftarrow v_0'''$. In summary, $GR_3 = \{v_2''', v_2''', v_0'''\} = (0, 0, 2)$.

The pseudo-code of the whole process is shown in Algorithm 3. Line 1–11 show how to split original DFA. The ori-DFA is split into several subgraphs based on input string *str*. $\{G\}$ denotes a set of subgraphs. Line 6–8 show all the edges that their additional information equals to the input character will be extracted to form a subgraph. Line 12–17 show how to merge these subgraphs. Each two adjacent subgraphs are merged into a GR. All the GR's will be put into the set $\{GR\}$. Line 18–26 show how to merge these GRs. Line 21–23 show

---

Algorithm 3. The whole process

Input: G, str, the *current state*
Output: *accepted*
Procedures:
1: // 1.split DFA based on input string str
2: $i \leftarrow 0$
3: $\{G\} \leftarrow \varnothing$
4: **for all** character $ch \in str$ **do in parallel**
5:    $\forall e \in$ DFA //e := edge
6:    **if** ($e.character == ch$) **then**
7:       Copy e and its vertices to G_i // form the ith subgraph
8:    **end if**
9:    $\{G\} \leftarrow \{G\} \bigcup G_i$
10:    $i++$
11: **end for**
12: // 2.merge subgraphs
13: $\{GR\} \leftarrow \varnothing$
14: **for all** G_{2i}, G_{2i+1} ($G_{2i}, G_{2i+1} \in \{G\}$) **do in parallel**
15:    $GR' \leftarrow$ MergeSubGraph(G_{2i}, G_{2i+1})
16:    $\{GR\} \leftarrow \{GR\} \bigcup GR'$
17: **end for**
18: // 3.merge GRs
19: **while** ($\{GR\}$ only has a group) **do**
20:    **for all** GR_{2i}, GR_{2i+1} ($GR_{2i}, GR_{2i+1} \in \{GR\}$) **do**
21:       $GR_{new} \leftarrow$ MergeNodeGroup(GR_{2i}, GR_{2i+1})
22:       $\{ \} \leftarrow \{ \} \bigcup GR_{new}$
23:    **end for**
24:    $\{GR\} \leftarrow \varnothing$
25:    $\{GR\} \leftarrow \{ \}$
26: **end while**
27: // 4. justify whether the input string is accepted
28: $GR_{last} \leftarrow \{GR\}$
29: **if** *current state* $== i$ **then**
30:    *next state* $= GR_{last}.v_i$
31:    **if** ($GR_{last}.v_i$ is in grey) **then**
32:       accepted $=$ Y // Y := yes
33:    **else**
34:       accepted $=$ N // N := no
35:    **end if**
36: **end if**

---

we merge each two adjacent GRs into a GR, then put it into a new set $\{ \}$. After merging, all the GR_{new}s in $\{ \}$ are put into previous $\{GR\}$, which has been clear out (Line 24–25). Finally, we only has a GR in $\{GR\}$ (line 19). Line 27–36 show whether the input string str is accepted. As $\{GR\}$ only has a group (i.e. GR), we set $GR_{last} = GR$. If $GR_{last}.v_i$ is in grey cycle, then str is accepted (line 32). Otherwise, it's not accepted (line 34).

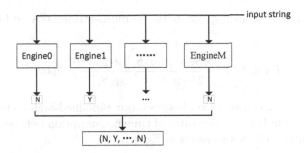

Fig. 3. Each rule is compiled into an engine. Our architecture consists of multiple engines.

The space consumption of these subgraphs is: $n \times S \times \lceil log_2 S \rceil$. The space consumption of GRs is: $S \times \lceil log_2 S \rceil \times (n-1)$. Space consumption mainly includes the consumption of DFA, subgraphs and GRs. So our algorithm's total memory consumption is: $(2n - 1 + 256) \times S \times \lceil log_2 S \rceil$. In general, S is a constant, so the space complexity of algorithm 3 is $O(n)$. If algorithm 3 is implemented by non-pipelined technique, it takes $(\lceil log_2(n) \rceil + 1)$ clock cycles to process n characters. If accelerated by the pipelined technique, it only takes 1 clock cycles to process n characters.

3.3   Hardware Architecture

(1) *design our hardware architecture*

Suppose each rule is compiled into an engine, which performs RE matching by Algorithm 3. Since a ruleset may include many rules, we make these engines in parallel. An example is given in Fig. 3. In Fig. 3, the $Engine_i$ denotes the ith engine. The lookup process is fairly simple. The *input string* is sent into these engines. At last, each engine shows whether the *input string* is accepted.

(2) *the analysis of space and time consumption*

Suppose there are m rules. The ith rule is compiled into S_i states. The length of input string is n. So the total space consumption of our architecture is: $\sum_{i=1}^{m}[(2n - 1) + 256] \times S_i \times \lceil log_2 S_i \rceil$. If we use original DFA as baseline, the ratio of space consumption between our architecture and original DFA is shown in Eq. (1):

$$MA = \frac{\sum_{i=1}^{m}[(2n - 1) + 256] \times S_i \times \lceil log_2 S_i \rceil}{\sum_{i=1}^{m} 256 \times S_i \times \lceil log_2 S_i \rceil} = \frac{2n + 255}{256} \qquad (1)$$

Suppose $m = 4$, $S_i = 16$, $n = 8$, then $MA = 1.06$. That means we only consume additional 6% space consumption than the original DFA's, while we can achieve 8× speedup acceleration than that of original DFA.

The ratio of space consumption between multi-stride DFA and original DFA is shown in Eq. (2):

$$MA \approx \frac{\sum_{i=1}^{m} \times S_i \times \lceil log_2 S_i \rceil \times 256^n}{\sum_{i=1}^{m} 256 \times S_i \times \lceil log_2 S_i \rceil} = 256^{n-1} \qquad (2)$$

The ratio of time consumption between our pipelined architecture and original DFA is shown in Eq. (3). The ratio of time consumption between multi-stride DFA and original DFA is also same as Eq. (3):

$$TA = \frac{1}{n} \qquad (3)$$

From Eq. (3), our architecture's time consumption is equal to the multi-stride DFA. However, the multi-stride DFA's space consumption is too huge to be implemented practically. Suppose $n = 8$, the $MA = 256^7 = 2^{56} \gg 1.06$.

Theoretically, we have the following inequation (4), where C denotes the available resource and k denotes coefficient of utilization.

$$\sum_{i=1}^{m} [(2n - 1) + 256] \times S_i \times \lceil log_2 S_i \rceil \leq k \times C. \qquad (4)$$

We change the expression form of inequation (4)–(5).

$$n \leq \frac{1}{2} \times (\frac{k \times C}{\sum_{i=1}^{m} S_i \times \lceil log_2 S_i \rceil} - 255) \qquad (5)$$

We use $freq$ to denote the evaluated frequency of FPGA. As for pipelined architecture, the throughput is shown in Eq. (6), while the throughput of non-pipelined architecture is shown in Eq. (7).

$$TH_{pipelined} = freq \times n \times 8 \qquad (6)$$

$$TH_{non-pipelined} = \frac{freq \times n \times 8}{\lceil log_2(n) \rceil + 1} \qquad (7)$$

We plug Eqs. (5)–(6) and get Eq. (8). Meanwhile, we plug Eqs. (5)–(7) and get Eq. (9).

$$TH_{pipelined} \leq 4 \times freq \times (\frac{k \times C}{\sum_{i=1}^{m} S_i \times \lceil log_2 S_i \rceil} - 255) \qquad (8)$$

$$TH_{non-pipelined} \leq 4 \times freq \times (\frac{k \times C}{\sum_{i=1}^{m} S_i \times \lceil log_2 S_i \rceil} - 255) \times \frac{1}{\lceil log_2(n) \rceil + 1} \qquad (9)$$

Now, we set $k = 0.7$, which is the (maximum) average value of Fig. 5 calculated by inequation (4). Also, we set $freq = 300$ MHz depended on our experimental synthetical frequency. We set $C = 712000$, which equals to the total available resource of our experimental FPGA chip.

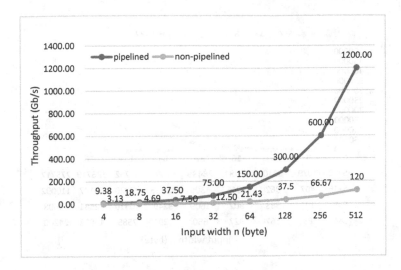

Fig. 4. The throughput of pipelined and non-pipelined architecture.

Suppose each S_i is the same. In the case of $m = 1$, $S_i = 32$, we get $n \leq$ 1430 (byte). The $TH_{pipelined} \leq 3.27$ (Tb/s), $TH_{non-pipelined} \leq 272.75$ (Gb/s). In another words, we can get the maximum throughout $MAX(TH_{pipelined}) \approx$ 3.27 (Tb/s), $MAX(TH_{non-pipelined}) \approx 272.75$ (Gb/s). However, the throughput of 3.27 Tb/s is hard to achieve by the place-and-route of Xilinx tool.

4   Performance Evaluation

In this section, we provide a detailed analysis of our architecture on a state-of-the-art Xilinx chip XC7VX1140t. This considered chip has 712000 LUTs. The RE rules are all publicly available in real-life rulesets, such as Bro [11], Snort [12]. The performance is measured in throughput, resource consumption and efficiency. However, since these rules are finally compiled into DFA states, we use states as a measurement standard but not the rules themselves.

4.1   Throughput

Synthesis was performed by using the Xilinx tool. From the synthetical result, we use 300 MHz to evaluate the throughput. We can deduce the throughput based on the considered frequency. The input widths (i.e. the lengths of input string) are rounded up to be a power of two.

Our architecture can be implemented on two forms: pipelined-architecture and non-pipelined-architecture. Figure 4 shows the throughput variation with the size for various input width. n denotes the input width. It can be observed that our proposed pipelined-architecture can sustains 1200 Gbps, while the non-pipelined-architecture only sustains 120 Gbps at the best case. It can be seen

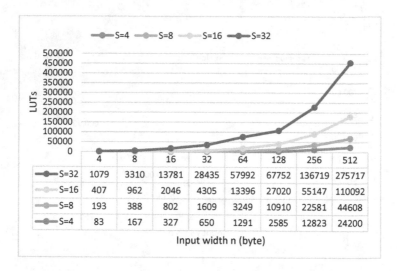

Fig. 5. Under the conditions of different number of states Ss, the LUT's consumption vs. the input width n.

that on the average, using a larger input width size if desirable from a throughput point of view. With the increasing of input width, the throughput is also increasing. Apparently, our architecture is practical for 100G Ethernet standard that is currently the fastest approved standard of Ethernet. Noted that because of stable performance, the throughput is independent of tested data.

4.2   Resource Consumption

The resource consumptions of pipelined and non-pipelined architecture are almost the same. In this work, only logic resources are utilized. Figure 5 illustrates the LUT's consumption of each rule. Suppose S denotes the number of states each rule generated. We can observer that: (1) under the conditions of the same number of states, with the increasing of input width, the consumption of LUT is increasing. (2) under the conditions of the same input widths, with the increasing of the number of states, the consumption of LUT is also increasing. (3) the larger value of the number of states S and input width n, the much more consumption of LUTs. In the case of $n = 512$ and $S = 32$, almost $275717/712000 = 38.72\%$ of the logic resources available on this considered FPGA are consumed.

Besides, that how many rules can be implemented in parallel is shown in Fig. 6. In the best case of $n = 4$ and $S = 4$, our single chip can support 8578 rules. In the case of $n = 512$ and $S = 32$, this chip only supports 2 rules.

4.3   Comparison with Existing Approaches

In order to make a fair comparison, we set $S = 32$. The evaluated frequency of FPGA is 300 MHz. We compare throughput and space consumption between

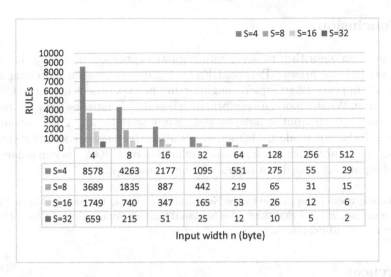

Fig. 6. The number of rules supported by our current chip under the conditions of various Ss and ns.

Table 1. Comparison between different algorithms and platforms.

Approach	Throughput (Gbps)	Space consumption (byte/trans.)	Efficiency (Gbps * trans./byte)	Platform	Stable
Software DFA	1.31	1.63	0.80	Intel CPU	No
TCAM [8]	10–19	N/A	N/A	TCAM	No
B-FSM [7]	18.4	1.38	13.33	PowerEn	No
GregEx [13]	25.6	1.63	15.71	GPU	No
Multi-DFA	4.69	417.28	0.01	FPGA	Yes
Ours	1200	8.80	136.36	FPGA	Yes

*Software-based DFA was carried out on a dual core, 2.93 GHz Intel(R) Core(TM) matchine with 8 GB of RAM and running Ubuntu Linux 12.4.

different DFA algorithms or platforms. Multi-stride DFA's *stride* is equal to 2 for resource of this chip is limited. Although compression algorithms lead to memory efficiency, they result in low throughput. So we doesn't implement compression algorithms on it.

We compare space consumption between different platforms. Table 1 summarizes these comparisons. The throughput of our architecture is about 1200 Gbps, which is 916 times than that of original software-based DFA. Though space consumption is not the best, our architecture's efficiency can achieve as high as 136.36.

5 Conclusion

We propose an algorithm to accelerate regular expression matching. Based on this algorithm, we present Parallel-DFA, a regular expression matching architecture. It supports 1200 Gbps throughput in our experiment on current Xilinx Virtex-7 chip. What's more, its performance is stable. It must be pointed that our architecture's throughput is independent of any tested data. These advantages make it suitable for modern high-speed collaborative network security environment. In the future, with more resources available on FPGA, we can enlarge the value of input width easily to support higher throughput.

Acknowledgment. Supported by the National Science and Technology Major Project under Grant No. 2017YFB0803003, the National Science Foundation of China (NSFC) under grant No. 61402475.

References

1. Dubrawsky, I.: Firewall evolution-deep packet inspection. In: Security Focus, vol. 29 (2003)
2. Hopcroft, J.E.: Introduction to Automata Theory, Languages, and Computation. Pearson Education India (1979)
3. Kumar, S., Dharmapurikar, S., Yu, F., Crowley, P., Turner, J.: Algorithms to accelerate multiple regular expressions matching for deep packet inspection. ACM SIGCOMM Comput. Commun. Rev. **36**(4), 339–350 (2006)
4. Becchi, M., Crowley, P.: A-DFA: a time-and space-efficient DFA compression algorithm for fast regular expression evaluation. ACM Trans. Arch. Code Optim. (TACO) **10**(1), 4 (2013)
5. Jiang, L., Dai, Q., Tang, Q., Tan, J., Fang, B.: A fast regular expression matching engine for NIDS applying prediction scheme. In: IEEE Symposium on Computers and Communication (ISCC), pp. 1–7. IEEE (2014)
6. Brodie, B.C., Taylor, D.E., Cytron, R.K.: A scalable architecture for high-throughput regular-expression pattern matching. ACM SIGARCH Comput. Arch. News **34**(2), 191–202 (2006)
7. Van Lunteren, J., Rohrer, J., Atasu, K., Hagleitner, C.: Regular expression acceleration at multiple tens of Gb/s. In: 1st Workshop on Accelerators for High-performance Architectures in conjunction with ICS 2009 (2009)
8. Meiners, C.R., Patel, J., Norige, E., Liu, A.X., Torng, E.: Fast regular expression matching using small TCAM. IEEE/ACM Trans. Netw. (TON) **22**(1), 94–109 (2014)
9. Becchi, M., Crowley, P.: Efficient regular expression evaluation: theory to practice. In: Proceedings of the 4th ACM/IEEE Symposium on Architectures for Networking and Communications Systems, pp. 50–59. ACM (2008)
10. Prithi, S.. Sumathi, S.: Review on grouping algorithms for finite state automata (2016)
11. The Bro Network Security Monitor. http://www.bro.org

12. Roesch, M.: Snort: lightweight intrusion detection for networks. LISA **99**(1), 229–238 (1999)
13. Wang, L., Chen, S., Tang, Y., Su, J.: Gregex: GPU based high speed regular expression matching engine. In: 2011 Fifth International Conference on Innovative Mobile and Internet Services in Ubiquitous Computing (IMIS), pp. 366–370. IEEE (2011)

Adaptive Carving Method for Live FLV Streaming

Haidong Ge[1], Ning Zheng[1], Lin Cai[1], Ming Xu[1(✉)], Tong Qiao[2],
Tao Yang[3(✉)], Jinkai Sun[1], and Sudeng Hu[4]

[1] Internet and Network Security Laboratory, School of Computer Science
and Technology, Hangzhou Dianzi University, Hangzhou, China
{151050149,nzheng,mxu,152050160}@hdu.edu.cn, cail@zj.gov.cn
[2] School of Cyberspace, Hangzhou Dianzi University, Hangzhou, China
tong.qiao@hdu.edu.cn
[3] Key Lab of the Third Research Institute of the Ministry
of Public Security, Shanghai, China
yangtao@stars.org.cn
[4] Ming Hsieh Department of Electrical Engineering,
University of Southern California, Los Angeles, CA, USA
sudenghu@usc.edu

Abstract. Currently, most video carving methods are to recover video files from disk file system, but these methods often do not work well for video form network streams, especially for live streaming video. In this paper, an adaptive video carving method is proposed to recover the live FLV (Flash Video) streaming video from network traffic. Firstly, to recover videos when there is no packet loss during data capture, a method based on network data structure is proposed. Secondly, to solve the problem of packet loss or corruption during data capture, another video carving method is proposed based on both the FLV structure and network data structure. Finally, to achieve good balance between computational complexity and recovery accuracy, an adaptive method based above two methods is proposed. The experimental results show that the proposed methods achieve good performance both in consuming time and recovery rate.

Keywords: Live streaming video · Recovery · Forensic
Network traffic

1 Introduction

Digital forensics is the process of preserving, acquiring, checking, analyzing and presenting digital evidence from any digital devices. Recovering videos from digital data fragments is an important work in digital forensics. With the rapid development of computer network, live streaming videos have been popular in our daily life. Meanwhile live video related crimes have occurred more and more frequently and it has aroused great concerns in society [1–4]. In addition, since

© ICST Institute for Computer Sciences, Social Informatics and Telecommunications Engineering 2018
I. Romdhani et al. (Eds.): CollaborateCom 2017, LNICST 252, pp. 554–566, 2018.
https://doi.org/10.1007/978-3-030-00916-8_51

criminal evidence in storage media can be easily accessed by criminals and suffer irreversible damages, the traditional digital forensics based on storage media becomes less reliable in the case of providing direct and effective evidence in criminal investigations [5–7]. Criminal evidence [8] sent to networks with live streaming video could be hardly damaged by criminals. Therefore live streaming video is safer to store criminal scenes and evidence, and carving methods for live streaming videos are highly desired.

In the literature, most video carving methods use file structures to restore video files from disk file system, but such methods do not perform well for videos from network packet data. A few number of carving methods can restore videos from network streams, like the open source FLV download tool FLVCD, which downloads the FLV video from servers. However FLVCD does not work for live streaming videos, because it requires source's IP addresses, which are often encrypted or hidden to prevent video stealing. Wireshark [9] is one of the excellent network security and monitoring tools, which can extract parts of the video in the network stream. The Flash Video (FLV) format is widely used in live streaming video and usually transmitted with Hypertext Transfer Protocol (HTTP)[10] chunked transfer encoding method. Inspired by the working principle of Wireshark and structure of FLV, the HTTP chunk based carving (HCBC) is proposed to extract video data.

Furthermore, network data used for live streaming video recovering is usually captured at certain gateways, where video data flows through with large volume of other data. Sometimes we cannot capture all the needed video data, but inevitably have some video packets lost, corrupted or disordered during capture process [11,12]. Recovering from partial live streaming data is quite challenge work. For example, HCBC does not perform well in such cases. To solve this problem, we propose the FLV tag based carving (FTBC) method, which is based on both FLV tag structure and network data structure, rather than network data structure only. Since FLV data is only the subset of network data, we can recover videos in the absence of some irrelevant network data. Moreover, the redundancy in FLV data can be used to further recover videos precisely.

FTBC is better than HCBC in terms of video recovery rate, however it consumes much more time than HCBC due to the complicated retrieving scheme it adopts. In the case of losing no packet or a few packet, HCBC could also achieves good performance in recovery rate. To make a good balance between consuming time and recovery rate, an adaptive method based on FTBC and HCBC is finally proposed in this paper.

The remainder of the paper is structured as follows: In Sect. 2, related video carving work is described; In Sect. 3, the adaptive video carving method is introduced; in Sect. 4, the experimental results are given to compare the performance of the proposed methods and other benchmarks. Finally, Sect. 5 concludes this paper.

2 Related Work

The traditional recovery technique recover the video files from the storage device, we recover video from the captured network traffic based on the network data structures and video structure. Basic video recovery technique for video file restoration use the meta-information [13] of the file system to recover a video file stored in a storage medium. New attempts have been made to recover the files depending on the file structure or file content instead of the file system information. The Scalpel [14] is one of the file carving tools which do not rely on the file system meta-information to restore a video file. This carver uses header and footer of video files to restore the video file in a whole disc. Pal and Memon proposed [15] a general framework to restore a file. This method identifies fragments and reorders the fragments by uses three main steps: preprocessing, collation and reassembly. These files in the storage medium which was not allocated. Park and Lee proposed a procedure for use on video data fragments forensics related to DVRs [16]. They present a way to sort the extracted video frames based on the above properties. These frames will be converted to images and these images is used to construct a playable video file. Yang et al. [17] proposed a technique in their paper is an AVI carving method based on frame size and index. This method extracts video data from a storage medium using signatures and statistic information rather than file system information. However, to the best of our knowledge, there is only a little research of network flow solution that is available for video craving.

Most of the previous works focused on MPEG4 or some other formats and not much work has been proposed in video carving for network flows. With the consideration of wide use of the FLV format in live streaming videos, recovering FLV data in network flows remains important.

3 The Proposed Methods

In this section, two carving methods based on network data structure and FLV structure are developed to handle different packet loss rate. In order to handle various network situations, an adaptive carving method is proposed based on these two methods. These proposed carving methods mainly include three stage:

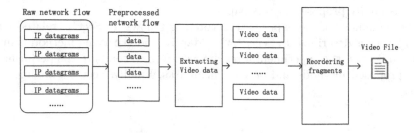

Fig. 1. Processing steps of the proposed video file restoration technique

preprocessing, extraction and connection, as shown in Fig. 1. Due to the huge amount of data flowing on the network, directly recovering video files this data may not be efficient. In the preprocessing stage, network work data is screened based on the source IP, destination IP and port and playloads of selected TCP packets are extracted. In the extraction stage, the FLV header data and the video data is extracted in the data blocks based on the characteristics of the network flow or the structural features of the FLV file. Finally, in the reordering stage, extracted data is sorted and merged into video files.

3.1   FLV File Structure

The FLV file consists of a file header and a number of tags that could be classified into three categories including audio tags, video tags and script tags based on the types of streams they represent. The overview structure of a FLV file is shown in Fig. 2. The FLV file starts with a file header consisting of 9 bytes, while the first three bytes are the signature of the FLV file "46 4C 56". 4 bytes followed by the 9 bytes are the first tag size which is always 0. After that, the FLV file is splitted into different tags. The first eleven bytes of a tag is tag header, where first byte indicates tag types, followed by three bytes indicating playload size of a tag. Other information like timestamp is indicated in the remaining bytes. Since we are only interested in video and audio files in this work, our discussion on FLV tags is limited to these two types. Table 1 shows typical values of different types of FLV tags, where we can see each type of FLV tag has a unique value in the first byte. For example, '0x08' represent audio, '0x09' for video, '0x12' for metadata which contains codec specifications. Furthermore, the first byte of tag playload, which indicates its type, should be restricted to certain values according to tag types. For instance, as shown in Table 2, inside a 'video' tag, the first byte of tag playload is either'0x17' denoting a keyframe of video data or '0x27' denoting interframe of video data. Other values are invalid.

3.2   Video Carving with HCBC

In China, the technique of HTTP-FLV is widely used in live video streaming. Due to the real-time nature of live video, the size of the transmitted content

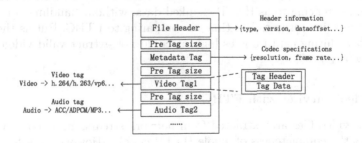

Fig. 2. The structure of video file

Table 1. FLV tag type. 'x' is hexadecimal data.

Tag code	Name	Description
0x08xxxxxxxxxxxxxxxxxxxxxx	Audio	Contains a audio packet similar to a SWF SoundStreamBlock plus codec information
0x09xxxxxxxxxxxxxxxxxxxxxx	Video	Contains a video packet similar to a SWF VideoFrame plus codec information
0x12xxxxxxxxxxxxxxxxxxxxxx	Meta	Contains two AMF packet, the name of the event and the data to gowith it

could not be determined when HTTP is used to transmit video data. Therefore most websites adopt HTTP chunked transfer encoding. HCBC is developed to recover video data from such network data.

Table 2. Tag data type.

Tag type	First byte of playload	Description
Meta	0x02	Metadata
Audio	0xAF	Audio data
Video	0x17	Keyframe data
	0x27	Interframe data

Firstly, HTTP chunks is scanned byte by byte to search for the FLV file signature "46 4C 56". When the signature is identified, the data after it is extracted. Secondly, the header and data portion of the HTTP chunks are extracted. Finally, we stop scanning when meeting the end tag. In the reordering process, the fragments are merged into videos based on the extraction order of the chunk data.

In our experiments, it was found that the performance of HCBC is close to that of the file-based transfer method when no packet is missing or corrupted during the capture at gateways. This method can be realized on network data structure, referencing to as HTTP chunked data, without handling complicated file structures, it consumes less time as comparing to FTBC. But as the packet missing rate during capture goes high, it could not extract valid video data as effectively as FTBC.

3.3   Video Carving with FTBC

In HCBC, video files are extracted from network streams in a coarse way that it requires the completeness of whole HTTP chunks. However due to the huge mount of data passing through gateways, sometimes it is impossible to capture all the related packets. When captured IP datagrams are incomplete or corrupted [11], HTTP chunks are more likely to become incomplete, and thus the possibility of successfully extracting data will be reduced significantly. Therefore instead of extracting at HTTP chunk level, we extract video at a lower and finer level: FLV file level.

Firstly, video or audio tags are detected and verified in the captured network data. We obtain data parts of HTTP chucks by removing headers. In this way, no header information from HTTP chunks is utilized. Then FLV header is located in the data parts of HTTP chunks by searching for the FLV signature. Video and audio FLV tags could be identified by searching for tag signatures in Table 1 after the FLV header. For instance, if a tag starts with '08', it is audio tag and the following bit stream is audio stream; if it starts with '09', it is a video tag; if it starts with '12', it is a metadata tag. Moreover, according to the FLV structure described in Sect. 3.1, we could access the first byte of tag playload and use it to validate the detected tags. As discussed in Sect. 3.1 and shown in Table 2, for a video tag, the first byte should be either '0x17' or '0x27', for a audio tag, it should be 'AF' and for a metadata tag, it should be '02', otherwise the detected tags are invalid. For clarity, an example of video tag is given in Fig. 3, which is highlighted in the red box. It starts with video tag signature '09' and the first eleven bytes within the red box is the tag header. The first byte following the tag header is '17', which confirms the validity of the video tag.

Secondly, video and audio file information is extracted from tag header. It is straightforward to access the size of tag playload once tag is found. For example, as shown in Fig. 3, the three bytes right after the tag signature, $i.e.,$ "00 00 1E" indicates the size of tag playload, which is 30 in decimal. Timestamps, which is another important information that will be used in the reordering stage, could be extracted from the four bytes after size bytes of tag data. It is "6F 8D A8 01" in this example.

Finally, the size of tag data is verified. The last four bytes before the next tag denotes the size of whole tag, denoted by LH. At the same time, the size of tag is recorded. Sometimes, video tags could cross multiple network packets as shown in Fig. 4, where block X is the first network packet that a new tag comes up, and block X+n is the last packet it ends with. L_1 and L_n are the bytes that the tag takes in the first block and the last block, respectively. Li,

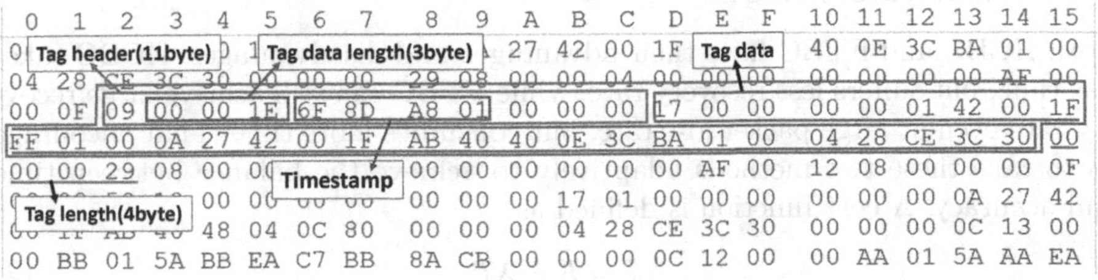

Fig. 3. The structure of video tag

$i = 2, \cdots, n - 1$ is the size of block i between the first and last blocks. if $\sum L_i$ equals LH, the detected tag data is correct. Otherwise, the data is corrupted and should be dropped.

When a network packet containing a tag header is lost, two nearby tag data streams could be incorrectly concatenate into a single tag in FTBC. To deal with that case, M is set as the maximum size of a tag. If the size of the inspected tags exceed M, we will drop them. M is critical to the performance of our algorithm. If M is too small, it could falsely drop valid tags. If M is too large, it could be ineffective in detecting invalid tags. Through intensive experiments, our algorithm FTBC could achieve the optimal results when it is set as

$$M = 19 \times \bar{L}_{TCP} \tag{1}$$

where $\bar{L}_{TCP}$ is the average size of TCP packets.

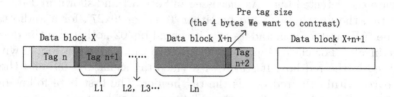

Fig. 4. Calculate the length of tag

In the extraction phase, timestamp is extracted for each video and audio tag. Since according to the timestamp format in FLV file, the first three bytes are low, the fourth byte is high, the correct timestamp could be calculated by recording these four bytes. In the case of Fig. 3, the right order of the timestamp information is "01 6E 8D A8". A packet may contains multiple tags and these tags within the same packet is in sequential order. Therefore instead of sorting tags, it is convenient to sort packets. For the packets containing multiple tags, only the timestamp from the first tag is used for sorting. Finally, tags and the fragments that contain these tags could be sorted according to the value of converted timestamp.

3.4 Adaptive Carving

Both HCBC and FTBC have their advantages and disadvantages. HCBC takes less time, but suffers less recovery rate, while FTBC can still achieve large recovery rate even at large packet loss rate, but consumes more time. That encourage us to take these two methods adaptively to achieve the balance between time and accuracy. A cost function is defined as

$$J = F + \lambda T \tag{2}$$

where F is failure rate that indicates the percentage of tags with failing to recover; T denotes the average time to process a packet. The algorithm that gives the lowest cost in Eq. (2), is the optimal solution we want to adopt. λ is a balance parameter to set the priority between accuracy and time. If λ is 0, accuracy is the only factor we care about when choosing between HCBC and FTBC. Based on our experimental results in Sect. 4, we assume failure rate of both method could be approximated by a linear model to packet loss rate as

$$F_H = \alpha R, \quad F_F = \beta R \tag{3}$$

where F_H and F_F is failure rate of HCBC and FTBC, respectively; R is the loss rate of the packets captured at gateways; α and β are the slopes of the linear models and $\alpha > \beta$.

Decision is made based on the cost of each method, and HCBC should be adopted when its cost is less than that of FTBC as

$$F_H + \lambda T_H < F_F + \lambda T_F \tag{4}$$

where T_H and T_F are the average processing time of a packet in HCBC and FTBC, respectively. By substituting Eq. (3) into Eq. (4), decision could be made based on

$$R < \phi(T_H - T_F) \tag{5}$$

where $\phi = \frac{\lambda}{\alpha - \beta}$ is a pre-setting parameter that sets preference between accuracy and consuming time. When Eq. (5) occurs, HCBC is adopted, otherwise FTBC is adopted. To calculate Eq. (5), R needs to be estimated. TCP packet could be sorted according to their sequence number and then a sliding window with size of n can be used to estimate R.

4   Experimental Results

4.1   Experimental Settings

To evaluate the performance of the proposed methods, an experimental network is set up to simulate the real environment as shown in Fig. 5, 10 virtual machines as users are linked to the Internet via the same gateway. The user machines are running on Microsoft Windows 10 (64-Bit) with IPs from 192.168.1.1 to 192.168.1.10 and the gateway is on Linux (CentOS 6.7) with IP 192.168.1.254. FengYunlive, which is one of the most popular live streaming video website in China, is used as our dataset source and video files from Google Chrome cache is used as original data. The network bandwidth at the gateway is set to 10 Mbps. The network packets use for video carving are captured at the gateway with open source software tcpdump while 3 user machines are watching live videos from FengYunlive, and the rest are browsing random websites. To simulate the packet loss during data capture, the captured network data are randomly deleted in 0%, 10%, 30% and 50% for different experiments. In order to estimate R in this paper, n is set to 1000. By extracting the sequence numbers of the first and the last TCP packets in the window, we are able to calculate the total number of TCP packets m between them if no packet is missing. Finally, the R is calculated

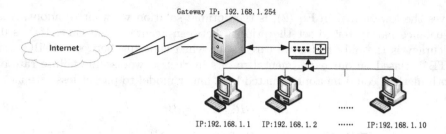

Gateway IP: 192.168.1.254

IP:192.168.1.1   IP:192.168.1.2   ......   IP:192.168.1.10

Fig. 5. The environment of experiment

as $\frac{m-n}{m}$. In our experiments, we found T_H and T_F are very stable and thus right side of Eq. (5), *i.e.*, $\phi(T_H - T_F)$ is set as a constant value, 0.07 in our experiments.

The performance of proposed methods was compared with one of similar video carving tools: Wireshark. It extracts video data in a way similar to HCBC. However when a IP datagram is lost or corrupted, it could only recover video data before the lost or corrupted network data and is unable to extract data after that.

4.2   Evaluation Metrics

The performance of the proposed methods are evaluated in three metrics: precision, recall and F-Measure calculate as

$$P(Precision) = \frac{A}{A + B} * 100\% \tag{6}$$

$$R(Recall) = \frac{A}{A + C} * 100\% \tag{7}$$

$$F - value = \frac{2 * P * R}{P + R} * 100\% \tag{8}$$

where A represents the number of true recovered FLV tags, B is the number of false recovered FLV tags, and C is the number of unrecovered FLV tags. F-value is the weighted average of precision and recall. To check if the tag data is restored, the hash values of the restored video tags and the original video tags is compared through the MD5 function.

4.3   Performance Comparison

Three FLV files are tested in our experiments, where each file contains 63991, 23678 and 31231 tags, respectively. Table 3 shows the recall of different methods when there is no packet missing or corrupted in the captured data. HCBC consumes less time than FTBC as expected and they achieves similar performance in recall, 93.73% and 95.66% on average by HCBC and FTBC, respectively. The performance of adaptive carving is exactly the same as HCBC, because HCBC is

Table 3. Experiment results of no packet losing or corrupted

Method	Recovered tags count						Average recall (%)	Time taken (hh:mm:ss)
	test1.flv (63991)	Recall	test2.flv (23678)	Recall (%)	test3.flv (31231)	Recall (%)		
Wireshark	63991	100.00	23678	100.00	31231	100.00	**100.00**	00:13:25
HCBC	61021	95.36	22054	93.14	28971	92.76	**93.75**	00:19:24
FTBC	61821	96.61	22354	94.41	29971	95.97	**95.66**	00:49:48
Adaptive	61021	95.36	22054	93.14	28971	92.76	**93.75**	00:19:24

Table 4. Experiment results of deleting 10% related IP datagrams

Method (Del-10%)	Recovered tags count						Average recall (%)	Time taken (hh:mm:ss)
	test1.flv (60191)	Recall (%)	test2.flv (21308)	Recall (%)	test3.flv (27893)	Recall (%)		
Wireshark	33915	56.35	16131	75.70	19231	68.95	**67.00**	00:13:25
HCBC	54637	90.77	18904	88.72	24601	88.20	**89.23**	00:18:34
FTBC	58318	96.89	20138	94.51	26971	96.69	**96.03**	00:48:18
Adaptive	57492	95.52	19904	93.41	26108	93.60	**94.18**	00:22:59

always preferred in the adaptive method when there is no packet loss. Wireshark achieves the highest recall 100% and consumes the least time.

However when parts of the captured packets are missing, as shown in Tables 4, 5 and 6, the performance of Wireshark decreases dramatically. It only achieves 67.00%, 39.95% and 22.16% on average in recall when packet loss rate is 10%, 30%, 50%, respectively. HCBC also suffers less recovery rate, but its performance

Table 5. Experiment results of deleting 30% related IP datagrams

Method (Del-30%)	Recovered tags count						Average recall (%)	Time taken (hh:mm:ss)
	test1.flv (46703)	Recall (%)	test2.flv (18537)	Recall (%)	test3.flv (22501)	Recall (%)		
Wireshark	13815	29.58	9131	49.26	19231	41.02	**39.95**	00:13:25
HCBC	36021	77.13	12054	65.03	17083	75.92	**72.69**	00:16:43
FTBC	45802	98.07	17913	96.63	21285	94.60	**96.43**	00:42:57
Adaptive	42827	91.70	17231	92.95	20231	89.91	**91.52**	00:33:43

Table 6. Experiment results of deleting 50% related IP datagrams

Method (Del-50%)	Recovered tags count						Average recall (%)	Time taken (hh:mm:ss)
	test1.flv (38095)	Recall (%)	test2.flv (13349)	Recall (%)	test3.flv (17839)	Recall (%)		
Wireshark	5917	15.53	5131	38.44	2231	12.51	**22.16**	00:13:25
HCBC	25917	68.03	8019	60.07	10971	61.50	**63.20**	00:15:02
FTBC	37021	97.18	13054	97.79	17202	96.43	**97.13**	00:38:08
Adaptive	36561	95.97	12563	94.11	16941	94.97	**95.02**	00:28:54

in recall is still better than that of Wireshark. Even though FTBC consumes the most time among all the methods, it could achieve recall higher than 95% in all conditions, because FTBC has traversed all the data as much as possible to extract the video data based on network data structure and FLV structure. As for the adaptive carving, benefiting from adaptively switching between HCBC and FTBC, it could always achieve comparable performance to FTBC in term of recall, but consumes less time, especially at low packet loss rate, *e.g.* 10%.

As measured in precision P in Eq. (6), all methods in all cases achieve 100%, which means there is no false recovery. This is because the redundant information in both network packet header and FLV tag header could effectively prevent false recovery.

Figure 6 shows the curves of recall and F-value versus packet loss rate for all methods, where we can see both FTBC and adaptive methods could maintain high recall and F-value in various the packet loss rates, while recall and F-value of HCBC and Wireshark sharply decrease as packet loss rate increases. In addition,

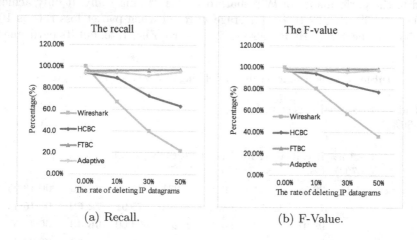

(a) Recall.   (b) F-Value.

Fig. 6. Recall and F-Value of different methods in various packet loss rate.

in Fig. 6(a), the relation between packet loss and recall of HCBC and FTBC can be both modeled linearly, which verifies our assumption of linear model on the failure rate in Eq. (3).

5   Conclusion

This paper presents a recovery technology for live streaming videos. FLV is a popular video container widely used in live streaming videos and the proposed carving methods target at recovering data from FLV based video network data. First, two different carving approaches are proposed to process network data captured at gateways in different situations. When captured data is complete or with a small scale of data loss, HCBC is able to recover video quickly and accurately. When captured data suffers severe packet loss, FTBC could obtain high recovery rate at cost of high consuming time. To achieve the balance between recovery rate and consuming time, an adaptive method is proposed based FTBC and HCBC. The experimental results verify the effectiveness of the proposed methods as comparing with the prior such as Wireshark.

Acknowledgment. This work is supported by the National Key R&D Plan of China under grant no. 2016YFB0800201, the Natural Science Foundation of China under grant no. 61070212, 61572165 and 61702150, the State Key Program of Zhejiang Province Natural Science Foundation of China under grant no. LZ15F020003, the Key research and development plan project of Zhejiang Province under grant no. 2017C01065, the Key Lab of Information Network Security, Ministry of Public Security, under grant no C16603.

References

1. Zhu, X., Chen, C.W.: A joint source-channel adaptive scheme for wireless H.264 video authentication. In: IEEE International Conference on Multimedia and Expo, pp. 13–18 (2010)
2. Dong, Y.N., Zhao, J.J., Jin, J.: Novel feature selection and classification of internet video traffic based on a hierarchical scheme. Comput. Netw. **119**, 102–111 (2017)
3. Li, J., Bhattacharyya, R., Paul, S., Shakkottai, S.: Incentivizing sharing in realtime D2D streaming networks: a mean field game perspective. In: Computer Communications, pp. 2119–2127 (2016)
4. Espina, F., Morato, D., Izal, M., Magaña, E.: Analytical model for MPEG video frame loss rates and playback interruptions on packet networks. Multimed. Tools Appl. **72**(1), 361–383 (2014)
5. Na, G.H., Shim, K.S., Moon, K.W., Kong, S.G., Kim, E.S., Lee, J.: Frame-based recovery of corrupted video files using video codec specifications. IEEE Trans. Image Process. Publ. IEEE Signal Process. Soc. **23**(2), 517–26 (2014)
6. Zheng, X., Liu, Y., Mei, L., Chuanping, H., Chen, L.: Semantic based representing and organizing surveillance big data using video structural description technology. J. Syst. Softw. **102**(C), 217–225 (2015)
7. Uzun, E., Sencar, H.T.: Carving orphaned JPEG file fragments. IEEE Trans. Inf. Forensics Secur. **10**(8), 1549–1563 (2015)

8. Chen, S., Pande, A., Zeng, K., Mohapatra, P.: Live video forensics: source identification in lossy wireless networks. IEEE Trans. Inf. Forensics Secur. **10**(1), 28–39 (2015)
9. Laing, S., Locasto, M.E., Aycock, J.: An experience report on extracting and viewing memory events via Wireshark. In: USENIX Conference on Offensive Technologies (2014)
10. Wu, T., Petrangeli, S., Huysegems, R., Bostoen, T., De Turck, F.: Network-based video freeze detection and prediction in HTTP adaptive streaming. Comput. Commun. **99**, 37–47 (2016)
11. Matoušek, P., et al.: Advanced techniques for reconstruction of incomplete network data. In: James, J.I., Breitinger, F. (eds.) ICDF2C 2015. LNICST, vol. 157, pp. 69–84. Springer, Cham (2015). https://doi.org/10.1007/978-3-319-25512-5_6
12. Ning, J., Singh, S., Pelechrinis, K., Liu, B., Krishnamurthy, S.V., Govindan, R.: Forensic analysis of packet losses in wireless networks. IEEE/ACM Trans. Netw. **24**(4), 1975–1988 (2016)
13. Sommer, P.: File system forensic analysis, B. carrier. Addison Wesley, ISBN 0-321-26817-2. Digit. Investig. **3**(2), 103 (2006)
14. Richard III, G.G., Roussev, V.: Scalpel: a frugal, high performance file carver. In: Refereed Proceedings of the Digital Forensic Research Workshop, DFRWS 2005, Astor Crowne Plaza, New Orleans, Louisiana, USA, August 2005
15. Pal, A., Memon, N.: The evolution of file carving. IEEE Signal Process. Mag. **26**(2), 59–71 (2009)
16. Park, J., Lee, S.: Data fragment forensics for embedded DVR systems. Digit. Investig. **11**(3), 187–200 (2014)
17. Yang, Y., Zheng, X., Liu, L., Sun, G.: A security carving approach for AVI video based on frame size and index. Multimedia Tools Appl. **76**, 3293–3312 (2016)

Android App Classification
and Permission Usage Risk Assessment

Yidong Shen[1(✉)], Ming Xu[1], Ning Zheng[1], Jian Xu[1], Wenjing Xia[1],
Yiming Wu[2], Tong Qiao[2], and Tao Yang[3]

[1] Internet and Network Security Laboratory of Hangzhou
Dianzi University, Hangzhou, China
{151050043,mxu,nzheng,jian.xu,161050051}@hdu.edu.cn
[2] School of Cyberspace, Hangzhou Dianzi University, Hangzhou, China
{ymwu,tong.qiao}@hdu.edu.cn
[3] Key Lab of the Third Research Institute of the Ministry of Public Security,
Shanghai, China
yangtao@stars.org.cn

Abstract. With Android6.0, users can decide whether to grant an app runtime permission. However, users may not understand the potential negative consequences of granting app permissions. In this paper, we investigate the feasibility of using an app's requested permissions and the intent-filters, app's category and permissions requested by other apps in the same category to better inform users about whether to install a given app and the risk scores associated with granting each of the app's required permissions. In an evaluation with 10,979 benign and 3,205 malicious apps, we demonstrate the effectiveness of the proposal approach.

Keywords: Android · Runtime permission · Risk score · Category

1 Introduction

More than seven million malicious mobile apps were identified in 2016 [10]. However, smartphones remain vulnerable to malware. Nevertheless, there is an increasing number of advanced benign apps that provide intelligent and person-alised services, such as location-based services and social sharing services, even though such apps may have potential security and privacy risks. For instance, users may not expect their locations (e.g. home locations, workplaces) and other privacy information (e.g. contact lists, SMS records) to be spied by the third party apps [19].

The Android platform provides several security measures such as the Android permission system, that reduce security and privacy risks. The Android operating system requires apps to request permissions before they can use certain system data and features [7]. Users must decide whether to grant such permissions. However, this approach has been proven ineffective. Studies have shown that

© ICST Institute for Computer Sciences, Social Informatics and Telecommunications Engineering 2018
I. Romdhani et al. (Eds.): CollaborateCom 2017, LNICST 252, pp. 567–577, 2018.
https://doi.org/10.1007/978-3-030-00916-8_52

more than 70% of smartphone apps request permission to collect data that is not directly required by the app's primary functionality. However, typically, users rush through the installation process and tend to grant all permissions [6]. In addition, even if users pay attention to the permission request, most do not have sufficient knowledge to understand permissions and their possible harm. Effective permission recommendations can provide additional information that can help users grant permissions appropriately to prevent privacy breaches [14].

Recent studies about Android permission recommendations can be found in the literature. Several studies have focused on expert recommendations based on crowdsourcing [9,13,14], utilising an app's runtime behaviour to evaluate the risks associated with granting permissions [12] and learning user behaviour to propose rules with different levels of abstractions [11]. Prior to Android 6.0, all permissions had to be accepted in order to install an app; therefore, these studies proposed modifying an Android source code to modify its permission system. They also could not consider the permission group mechanism in Android6.0.

With Android 6.0, the system permissions in Android are divided into two categories, normal and dangerous (runtime). Normal permissions do not directly risk the user's privacy. If an app lists a normal permission in its manifest, the system grants the permission automatically. Apps request runtime permissions as required at runtime. Android 6.0 has nine runtime permission groups with 24 runtime permissions related to personal user information and critical system resources. If a permission associated with a permission group has been granted, future permission requests in the same group are granted automatically for the given app. For example, if an app had previously requested and been granted the READ_CONTACTS permission, the WRITE_CONTACTS permission will be granted automatically because they are both in the Contacts permission group.

In this study, we consider the intended functionality of the app, i.e. what the app is expected to do, and which runtime permissions are requested by apps with a similar functionality to create an effective permission risk score. Currently, Google Play divides apps into 49 categories. Apps in the same category provide similar functionalities. The risk score measures whether a risk is commensurate with the benefit when granting runtime permission to an app in a given category. The higher the risk score, the greater the risk. Conversely, a low risk score indicates that granting permission would be beneficial and the associated risk is not significant.

We also utilise intent-filter to assess the risks with installing an app. Intent is a complex messaging system in the Android platform, and is considered as a security mechanism to hinder apps from gaining access to other apps directly. To receive intents, apps must define what type of intent they accept in the AndroidManifest.xml file, as intent-filter.

Therefore, we have designed an automatic analysis framework that does not require modifying the Android permission system to provide users with additional information prior to installation of an app. The proposed framework consists of malicious app detection and permission recommendation. Malicious app detection assesses the risks associated with installing an app, and permission recommendation assesses the risk score of each requested permission. First, we collect permissions and intent-filters from AndroidManifest.xml and then feed this extracted data to a Random-Forest-based classifier [8]. After the classifier has been trained using a training set, it can classify apps as benign or malicious. Utilising the frequency of occurrence of a runtime permission in different categories, the framework provides risk scores for the requested runtime permissions of benign apps relative to the app's category.

The contributions of this study can be summarised as follows.

1. To provide users with additional information prior to installing an app, we propose an automatic framework that combines Android malware detection and permission recommendations.
2. We introduce an effective risk score for each requested app permission relative to the given app's category.
3. For efficiency, we utilise lightweight features that enable extracting features in reasonable time.

The remainder of this paper is organised as follows. Related work is discussed in Sect. 2. Section 3 describes the datasets, and our methodology is presented in Sect. 4. We describe experiments in Sect. 5, and conclusions are presented in Sect. 6.

2   Related Work

In this section, we outline the state-of-the-art studies that focus on Android malware detection, Android app recommendation and Android permission recommendation.

2.1   Android Malware Detection

DREBIN [5] is notable among early machine-learning-based malware detection approaches. It performs a broad static analysis, gathering features including permissions, intent-filters, API calls, strings, etc., and then utilises support vector machines to classify apps. It also provides explainable detection. However, DREBIN does not consider the benefit of granting a permission to an app in a specific category. For example, the permission SENS_SMS has the same risk value in the Communication and Sport app categories.

Sokolova et al. [16] modelled permission-based decision support systems to classify apps. They modelled permission requests by different categories using graphs, obtained patterns for each category and verified the performance of different patterns in order to select the most descriptive patterns. Their results demonstrate that they could detect 80% of the malware with a low false-positive rate (FPR).

Sarma et al. [15] proposed a risk warning system based on the occurrence of 24 overall permissions (manually identified as dangerous) in each app category. A risk signal is triggered if an app requires critical permissions that are used by less than a given percentage of apps in the corresponding category. Understanding the reason for a risk signal helps the user determine whether to install an app.

2.2 Android Permission Recommendation

DroidNet [14], Rashidi et al. [13] and Jha et al. [9] utilised crowdsourcing technology to recommend whether to grant permissions. An evaluation of DroidNet demonstrated that, given a sufficient number of experts in the network, it can provide accurate recommendations and cover most app requests given a small coverage from a small set of initial experts.

Oglaza et al. [11] learned user behaviours to propose rules with different levels of abstractions. Such rules can help users protect their privacy more easily.

Rashidi et al. [12] proposed XDroid, an Android app resource access risk estimation framework that employs a hidden Markov model. XDroid utilises an app's runtime behaviors to evaluate risks associated with granting an app's permissions. However, XDroid cannot provide additional information about requested permissions prior to app installation.

2.3 Android App Recommendation

Taylor et al. [17] proposed SecuRank, a contextual permission analysis framework, to recommend functionally-similar alternative apps that require less sensitive access to the device. They discovered that up to 50% of apps can be replaced by a preferable alternative. They noted that alternatives are more likely to be available for free and popular apps.

Zhu et al. [19] proposed a recommendation system that considers app ratings and app-related privacy issues, such as required permissions. They developed an app risk score based on the number of required permissions and the occurrence of such permissions in a given app category, i.e. a lower penalty is incurred if a permission is used more frequently in a given category, and as more permissions are required by an app, its associated risks increase.

3 Datasets

In this section, we describe the datasets used in our study. In our experiments, we used two datasets consisting of 14,184 and 6,400 apps. The number of app categories in each dataset was 32. The former dataset included 10,979 benign and 3,205 malicious apps. The latter dataset contained 6,400 benign apps (200 apps per category). All apps in the datasets were from Androzoo [4], which is a growing collection of Android apps collected from several sources, including the official Google Play app market. We determined the app categories in our datasets from Google Play. To prepare reliable ground truth data, each app was uploaded to VirusTotal [3] and scanned by tens of different Antivirus product. If no malicious content was detected, the app was considered benign. If more than four VirusTotal scanners detected a malicious content, the app was considered malicious. This procedure ensures that our data is (almost) correctly split into benign and malicious apps, even if several scanners falsely labels a benign app as malicious.

4 Methodology

The proposed framework involves three main steps: (1) extracting features from apps, (2) classifying apps using machine learning and (3) assessing the risk score of runtime permissions requested by apps classified as benign and recommending permissions by providing the risk score. Here, the overall objective is to provide users with additional information to help them make decisions.

4.1 Feature Extraction

Every Android app must include a manifest file called AndroidManifest.xml which contains information of package, including requested permissions and components of the app such as activities, services, intents, intent-filters, content providers etc.

To obtain permissions and intent-filters, we first used Androgurad [1], which is an open-source project for the static analysis of Android apps, to obtain the AndroidManifest.xml file. Then, we utilised the Python Beautiful Soup [2] library to extract features from the obtained file. In this study, we use permissions and broadcast receivers, a type of intent-filter, as features. A broadcast receiver is used to receive broadcast intent sent by an Android system. Finally, the extracted features including normal permissions, runtime permissions and broadcast receivers are embedded in feature vectors that are used to classify the apps, and runtime permissions are used to assess the permission risk scores.

4.2 App Classification Using Machine Learning

We used a machine learning method to automatically train a model to distinguish between benign and malicious apps. The feature vectors were used to train a classifier. Thus, manual analysis was not required to construct corresponding malware detection rules. We selected a Random-Forest-based [8] classifier to classify apps.

4.3 Permission Risk Assessment

In this section, we present our methodology for assessing the risk score of runtime permissions requested by a given app that is classified as benign. We focus on creating an effective risk score. An effective risk score should have a simple semantic meaning that is easy to understand. Understanding the risk score will help users determine whether to grant each requested permission. Most malware might be simply repackaged versions of official apps. Evidence of the widespread use of repackaging by malware writers is provided in MalGenome [18], a dataset in the Android security community, where 80% of the malicious samples are known to be built via repackaging other apps. If the malicious code interacts with more sensitive resources than the original app, new permissions must be requested in the Manifest file. Therefore, malicious apps request more permissions with high risk scores than benign apps. When a user sets a threshold to filter out permissions with high risk scores (e.g. greater than 0.75), a small percentage of permissions requested by benign apps will be denied, and many permissions requested by malicious apps will be denied.

We are inspired by the observation described in the literature [15,19]. The observation states that, if a permission is used more frequently in a given category, the penalty incurred by this permission in this category will be lower. [15] use this observation to detect malware, a risk signal is triggered by an app if it requests critical permissions used by less than a certain percentage of apps in the given app category. [19] employ this observation to calculate the risk score of an app and recommend apps by considering both an app's popularity and the user's security preferences. [15,19] prove the validity of this observation in malicious and benign apps, respectively.

We calculate a permission's risk score for apps that belong to different categories according to the frequency of occurrence of the permission in these categories. A smaller permission risk score indicates that the permission is likely required and the risks associated with allowing the app are smaller. We used a dataset that contains 6,400 benign apps (200 apps in each category) to calculate the risk score. $RiskScore_{ij}$ denotes the risk score of granting permission j to an app in category i. $RiskScore_{ij}$ is defined as follows.

$$RiskScore_{ij} = \frac{\sum_{c \in C_i} f_{cj}}{\sum_{c \in C} f_{cj}}$$

Here, f_{cj} is the number of apps in category c that request permission j. C is the category set (32 categories), and C_i is a subset of C. All the categories that the number of apps request permission j greater than f_{ij} are in C_i. Note that a permission's risk score decreases as it is used more frequently in the apps of a given category. $RiskScore_{ij}$ has a simple semantic meaning, i.e. the risk score of permission j requested by apps in category i is less than or equal to $1 - RiskScore_{ij}$ percent of risk scores of permission j requested by apps that request this permission in the category balance dataset.

In terms of the permission group mechanism in Android 6.0, we show users all of the risk scores of an app's permissions requests and use the highest risk score of requested permissions in a permissions group to represent the risk score of the given group.

5   Experiments

Here, we evaluate the performance of the proposed approach. All experiments were conducted on a 4.2-GHZ four-core CPU, 32 GB main memory personal computer. These experiments were conducted to evaluate the performance of the malware detection and permission recommendation system in the proposed approach.

5.1   Evaluation of Malware Detection

In our first experiment, we evaluated malware detection performance. A dataset with 10,979 benign and 3,205 malicious apps was used in this experiment. We used 10-fold cross validation, which randomly selects parts of the data for training and the rest for testing. This was repeated 10 times to obtain a reasonable result. The two criteria utilised in our experiments were the true-positive rate (TPR) and FPR. The TPR is the proportion of actual positives correctly identified as such, and the FPR is the proportion of actual negatives falsely identified as positive. Here, positive indicates a malicious app, and negative indicates a benign app. The TPR and FPR values of the proposed approach were 86.8% and 0.99%, respectively. The results demonstrate that our machine-learning-based malware detection can detect 86.8% of the malicious apps with only a few false detections.

All the features we used in our experiments are lightweight features that can extracted from AndroidManifest.xml. It took 127 min to extract permissions and intent-filters from 14,184 apps. The average time required to extract features was 0.5 s. From this evaluation, we conclude that the proposed framework is capable of performing this task in practical time.

5.2   Evaluation of Permission Recommendation

In our second experiment, we evaluated the performance of permission recommendation based on the risk score. Note that apps classified as benign are used in the proposed approach's permission recommendation system. Here, 10,870 benign and 422 malicious apps were considered. We focus on the following permission groups: Phone, SMS, Location and Contacts. Permissions in the Location group are used to obtain the user's location information. Permissions in the Phone group are used to obtain the state of the device, IMEI, the call log and the ability to initiate a phone call. Permissions in the Contacts group are used to access the list of accounts in the Accounts Service and read/write contact information. Permissions in the SMS group are used to receive, read and send text messages.

We evaluated the performance of the risk score by setting a threshold range from 0.05 to 0.9. If the risk score of a permission group is greater than $1 - threshold$, the permissions in this group will be denied. This evaluation was configured as follows. The deny ratio of a permission group is defined as the number of permissions denied in the given permission group divided by the number of permission requests by apps in the same group. The overall deny ratio is defined as the number of permissions denied in the four permission groups divided by the number of permission requests by apps in these groups.

The performance of the proposed approach is shown in Table 1. We list the performance of the four permission groups and overall performance. Here, 'B' denotes benign, and 'M' denotes malicious. For example, Contacts B indicates the deny ratio of the Contacts group for benign apps. The results show that the deny ratio of each permission group for benign apps was less than the deny ratio for malicious apps. When the threshold for each permission group is less than or equal to 0.25, the deny ratio shown an obvious distinction. We recommend that users deny a permission if the risk score of the permission group it belongs to is greater than 0.75. If the user denies permissions for which the risk scores of the corresponding permission groups are greater than 0.75, the overall deny ratio for benign and malicious apps are 27.3% and 56.7%, respectively. The results show that the risk score we provide is effectiveness.

On the basis of user preferences, users can also deny a permission according to the risk score of the corresponding permission group, and users can set different threshold values to filter out permissions in different permission groups. For example, a user is very concerned about leaking their location information; thus, they can deny permissions in the LOCATION group for which the Location risk score is greater than θ (e.g., 0.3).

Table 1. Deny ratio of the proposed approach

Threshold	Contacts B	Contacts M	Location B	Location M	Phone B	Phone M	SMS B	SMS M	Overall B	Overall M
0.05	3.5%	9.3%	1.9%	14.2%	7.9%	16.7%	8.4%	35.5%	4.2%	16.3%
0.1	11.0%	26%	5.5%	24.6%	13.5%	17.7%	16.9%	45.5%	9.8%	25.1%
0.15	16.7%	34.9%	7.5%	35.8%	24.6%	29.2%	25.6%	56.4%	15.6%	35.8%
0.2	18.3%	42.8%	18.2%	45.8%	28.8%	40.7%	37.1%	74.5%	22.0%	46.8%
0.25	23.6%	55.3%	24.1%	59.2%	32.7%	46.9%	43.8%	78.2%	27.3%	56.7%
0.3	28%	60.5%	30.6%	64.2%	41.1%	55.7%	48.1%	78.2%	33.4%	62.3%
0.4	42.3%	68.4%	44.3%	80.2%	50.3%	64.3%	56.9%	82.7%	45.9%	72.9%
0.5	52.3%	79.1%	48.8%	81%	54.7%	71.8%	63%	84.5%	52.2%	78.1%
0.6	65.5%	83.3%	64.5%	88.8%	54.7%	71.8%	69.3%	85.5%	62.7%	82.0%
0.7	70.1%	85.1%	72.5%	89.4%	75.6%	80.7%	82.3%	91.8%	73.2%	86.0%
0.8	81.8%	90.7%	78.3%	93.6%	80.6%	83%	84.2%	91.8%	80.3%	89.5%
0.9	93.2%	96.3%	80.8%	96.1%	90.5%	93.8%	84.2%	91.8%	87.1%	94.9%

To the best of our knowledge, no related study has examined permission recommendation in order to automatically provide a risk score relative to granting an app's permission prior to installation of the app. We compared the proposed approach to a previously reported approach [15] that related to malware detection. For each app category, the existing approach refers to any critical permission (i.e. a runtime permission in Android 6.0) requested by less than θ% of the apps in this category as a θ-Rare Critical Permission ($\theta - RCP$) for this category. Here, CRCP (θ) denotes the Category-based Rare Critical Permission signal. Any app that requests one of the $\theta - RCP$'s in its category triggers $CRCP(\theta)$. On the basis of the permission group mechanism, we set the θ range from 5% to 30% to evaluate the performance of denying permissions that trigger $CRCP(\theta)$. The CRCP performance is shown in Table 2.

The frequency of occurrence of permissions shown an obvious difference for benign apps. For example, the average frequency of occurrence of

Table 2. Deny ratio of CRCP

θ	Contacts B	Contacts M	Location B	Location M	Phone B	Phone M	SMS B	SMS M	Overall B	Overall M
5%	12.4%	19.5%	1%	8.4%	12.8%	22%	66.7%	84.5%	11.5%	23.5%
10%	26.9%	35.8%	2.4%	19.0%	16.2%	26.6%	86.2%	95.5%	18.5%	33.5%
15%	31.6%	46%	7.5%	35.8%	26.0%	28.5%	87.1%	95.5%	24.3%	42.4%
20%	39.8%	58.6%	8.0%	36.9%	43.0%	34.4%	95.8%	100%	31.6%	47.9%
25%	48.4%	74.4%	21.8%	57.3%	49.4%	42.0%	98.7%	100%	41.4%	61%
30%	63.5%	86.0%	34.1%	70.1%	63.0%	66.2%	100%	100%	54.1%	75.7%

ACCESS_FINE_LOCATION in all categories is 26.4%; however, the frequency of occurrence of READ_SMS in Communication is 18%, and the frequency of occurrence of READ_SMS in Communication is greatest in all categories. Therefore, when setting θ to deny permissions, it may perform well for some permission groups and not perform well for other permission groups. For example, when θ is 10%, the deny ratios of the Location group for benign and malicious apps are 2.4% and 19.0%, respectively; however, the deny ratios of the SMS group for benign and malicious apps are 86.2% and 95.5%, respectively. Even though the frequency of occurrence of permissions has an obvious difference in a permission group. As a result, this may not perform well for some permission groups. For example, when θ is 25%, the deny ratios of Phone for benign and malicious apps are 49.4% and 42.0%, respectively. There are two permissions in the Location group, and the average frequencies of occurrence are 26.4% and 27.6%. Therefore, in the Location group, the CPCR performance is comparable to the proposed approach. Thus, owing to the obvious difference relative to the frequency of occurrence of different permissions, the user cannot understand the risk of granting a permission using the frequency of occurrence of this permission for the given app category. The results show that the CRCP perform not well in permission recommendation.

6 Conclusion

We have proposed a method that combines Android malware detection and Android permission recommendation to provide users with additional information about apps to help make appropriate decisions about app installation and usage. We investigated the feasibility of using app permission requests, the intent-filters, the app's category and which permissions are requested by other apps in the same category to better inform users about whether to install a given app and the risk scores of granting each required permission. This risk score has a simple semantic meaning that is easily understood. The results of a malware detection experiment indicate that the proposed approach can extract features that we used from an Android app in 1 s and that our malware detection can detect 86.8% of malicious apps with only a few alarms (less than 1%). The results of a permission recommendation experiment show that, when a user denies a permission for which the risk score of the corresponding permission group is greater than 0.75, 27.3% and 56.7% of permissions for benign and malicious apps will be denied, respectively.

Acknowledgment. This work is supported by the National Key R&D Plan of China under grant no. 2016YFB0800201, the Natural Science Foundation of China under grant no. 61070212 and 61572165, the State Key Program of Zhejiang Province Natural Science Foundation of China under grant no. LZ15F020003, the Key research and development plan project of Zhejiang Province under grant no. 2017C01065, the Key Lab of Information Network Security, Ministry of Public Security, under grant no. C16603.

References

1. Androgurad. https://github.com/androguard
2. Beautifulsoup. https://pypi.python.org/pypi/beautifulsoup4
3. Virustotal. https://www.virustotal.com/zh-cn/
4. Allix, K., Bissyandé, T.F., Klein, J., Le Traon, Y.: AndroZoo: collecting millions of android apps for the research community. In: 2016 IEEE/ACM 13th Working Conference on Mining Software Repositories (MSR), pp. 468–471. IEEE (2016)
5. Arp, D., Spreitzenbarth, M., Hubner, M., Gascon, H., Rieck, K., Siemens, C.: DREBIN: effective and explainable detection of android malware in your pocket. In: NDSS (2014)
6. Felt, A.P., Ha, E., Egelman, S., Haney, A., Chin, E., Wagner, D.: Android permissions: user attention, comprehension, and behavior. In: Proceedings of the Eighth Symposium on Usable Privacy and Security, p. 3. ACM (2012)
7. Google: Android system permission 2015 (2015). https://developer.android.com/guide/topics/permissions/index.html
8. Ho, T.K.: Random decision forests. In: Proceedings of the Third International Conference on Document Analysis and Recognition, vol. 1, pp. 278–282. IEEE (1995)
9. Jha, A.K., Lee, W.J.: Analysis of permission-based security in android through policy expert, developer, and end user perspectives. J. UCS **22**(4), 459–474 (2016)
10. McAfee: Mcafee labs threats report April 2017 (2017). https://www.mcafee.com/us/resources/reports/rp-quarterly-threats-mar-2017.pdf
11. Oglaza, A., Laborde, R., Benzekri, A., Barrère, F.: A recommender-based system for assisting non-technical users in managing android permissions. In: 2016 11th International Conference on Availability, Reliability and Security (ARES), pp. 1–9. IEEE (2016)
12. Rashidi, B., Fung, C., Bertino, E.: Android resource usage risk assessment using hidden Markov model and online learning. Comput. Secur. **65**, 90–107 (2017)
13. Rashidi, B., Fung, C., Vu, T.: Dude, ask the experts!: Android resource access permission recommendation with recdroid. In: IFIP/IEEE International Symposium on Integrated Network Management, pp. 296–304. IEEE (2015)
14. Rashidi, B., Fung, C., Nguyen, A., Vu, T.: Android permission recommendation using transitive Bayesian inference model. In: Askoxylakis, I., Ioannidis, S., Katsikas, S., Meadows, C. (eds.) ESORICS 2016, Part I. LNCS, vol. 9878, pp. 477–497. Springer, Cham (2016). https://doi.org/10.1007/978-3-319-45744-4_24

15. Sarma, B.P., Li, N., Gates, C., Potharaju, R., Nita-Rotaru, C., Molloy, I.: Android permissions: a perspective combining risks and benefits. In: Proceedings of the 17th ACM symposium on Access Control Models and Technologies, pp. 13–22. ACM (2012)
16. Sokolova, K., Perez, C., Lemercier, M.: Android application classification and anomaly detection with graph-based permission patterns. Decis. Support. Syst. **93**, 62–76 (2017)
17. Taylor, V.F., Martinovic, I.: Starving permission-hungry android apps using Secu-Rank. In: Proceedings of the 2016 ACM SIGSAC Conference on Computer and Communications Security, pp. 1850–1852. ACM (2016)
18. Zhou, Y., Jiang, X.: Dissecting android malware: characterization and evolution. In: IEEE Symposium on Security and Privacy, pp. 95–109 (2012)
19. Zhu, H., Xiong, H., Ge, Y., Chen, E.: Mobile app recommendations with security and privacy awareness. In: Proceedings of the 20th ACM SIGKDD International Conference on Knowledge Discovery and Data Mining, pp. 951–960. ACM (2014)

A Privacy Settings Prediction Model for Textual Posts on Social Networks

Lijun Chen[1], Ming Xu[1(✉)], Xue Yang[1], Ning Zheng[1], Yiming Wu[2], Jian Xu[1], Tong Qiao[2], and Hongbin Liu[1]

[1] Internet and Network Security Laboratory, School of Computer Science and Technology, Hangzhou Dianzi University, Hangzhou, China
{151050053,mxu,153050004,nzheng,jian.xu,162050127}@hdu.edu.cn
[2] School of Cyberspace, Hangzhou Dianzi University, Hangzhou, China
{ymwu,tong.qiao}@hdu.edu.cn

Abstract. Privacy issues of social media are getting tricky due to the increasing volume of social media users sharing through online social networks (OSNs). Existing privacy policy mechanisms of OSNs may not protect personal privacy effectively since users are struggle to set up the privacy settings. In this paper, we propose a privacy policy prediction model to help users to specify privacy policies for their textual posts. We investigate the semantic of posts, social context, and keywords associated with users' privacy preferences as possible indicators of decision making, and build a multi-class classifier based on their historical posts and decisions. During the cold-start periods, the proposed model integrates crowdsourcing and machine learning to recommend privacy policies for new users. Experimental results shows that the overall match rate for all the data with random forest classifier is over 70%, with more than 50% correct prediction rate for new users.

Keywords: Social networks · Privacy · Policy recommendation

1 Introduction

Wide spread of online social networks (OSNs) make the volume of personal resources publicly available on OSNs has drastically increased. The public shared content often contains sensitive information (e.g., likes, friendships, education and work experience) about people, which may be threats to one's privacy. Most OSNs allows users to manage the audiences of their posts by specifying privacy settings [12]. However, existing access control of OSNs mostly require users to manually setting their privacy policies for each post. Recent studies show that users frequently mis-configure the privacy settings [8] of their posts.

Many researchers have acknowledged the need for policy recommendation systems which can assist users to easily and properly configure privacy policies [6,7,16,18]. However, these works focus on privacy preferences of photo, location and profile etc, few have focused on predicting the privacy policies of text-based post. Text-based information contains users' behavior or personal opinions is

© ICST Institute for Computer Sciences, Social Informatics and Telecommunications Engineering 2018
I. Romdhani et al. (Eds.): CollaborateCom 2017, LNICST 252, pp. 578–588, 2018.
https://doi.org/10.1007/978-3-030-00916-8_53

considered to be particularly risky from the privacy perspective. Previous works about predicting the policies of text-based posts focused on predicting whether a post is high or low privacy [9] rather than predicting a fine-grained privacy policy. Furthermore, [1, 9] did not deal with the cold start problem.

In this paper, we present a random forest based privacy policy prediction model, which aims to recommend fine-grained privacy policies to users. We define privacy policy inference as a multi-class classification problem. The model takes user's past decisions and text-based content as input and output appropriate privacy policies to them. In order to build the classifier, we utilize factors in the following criteria that influence one's privacy settings of posts:

- Social context of posts. Such as users' emotion, timestamps of publish, location semantics.
- The semantics of posts' content. Generally, users with similar tend to have similar privacy preferences.
- Keywords associated with corresponding privacy policy. For instance, Alice publishes a post: {How vexing! Boss gets me overtime every day! }, she may specify that her colleague members are not allowed to see this post. Hence keywords may be "Boss", "overtime".

As for new users, our model blends crowdsourcing and machine learning techniques, and predicts a new user's privacy policies by training the data of other users. Our contributions in this paper are twofold: (1) We propose a privacy policy recommendation model aims at helping OSNs users to configure privacy settings for text-based posts. (2) Our model can predict privacy policies for new users to protecting their privacy.

The rest of the paper is organized as follows. Section 2 reviews related works. Section 3 presents the methodology of privacy recommendation model. Evaluation and user study are described in Sect. 4. Section 5 outlines some future works and summaries the paper.

2   Related Work

Several works have studied how to assist users with privacy policy configuration. [4] proposed a privacy wizard based on supervised learning to help users grant privileges to their friends whether profile attributes allow someone to see or not. Similarly, an semantics-based privacy configuration system is proposed to configure the users' privacy settings on Facebook profile [6]. To protect the privacy of location on social networks, methods of machine learning and recommendation systems are used to refine user's location privacy settings [2, 14, 18]. There also exist large body of work on photo sharing preferences [7, 15, 17], including build a binary-class classifier [17], consider social context, image content, and meta data as possible indicators of user's privacy preferences [7].

Aforementioned approaches focus on deriving policy settings for profiles, images or locations, and they mainly consider social context such as one's friend list, image content and then using recommendation system or machine learning technology to help users to specify policies for corresponding social media. While interesting, these methods may not be sufficient to address challenges brought by text-based posts. For the reason of the privacy preference may vary substantially not only influenced by social context but also due to the semantic of texts. Textual posts contain users' social interaction and background knowledge which are considered to be particularly risky from the privacy perspective. Previous works about predicting privacy policies of textual posts were focused on judging the post is high privacy or low privacy [9] rather than a fine-grained privacy policy. [1] propose a policy recommendation system to assist users with privacy policy configuration. The authors built a classifier based on users' historical policies and posts. Nevertheless, their system may not perform well for new users during the cold-start periods. In our work, we attempt to investigate the feasibility of deploying both social context and semantics of posts, and provides users a personalized privacy policies (even during the cold-start period).

3 Methodology

Users can manage their sharing content's privacy via privacy policies. For ease of description, some basic concepts are given:

- Audience: The one who can access the user's sharing content.
- Social Groups: Subset of a user's socially connected users.

The privacy settings in most OSNs regarding the audience of a post can be one of the following four main alternatives: {everyone, allfriends, custom, self}. With setting *custom*, user deliberately specifies a customized privacy settings that includes or excludes specific social groups. For example, Alice publishes a textual post and selects two social groups(e.g., friends, colleagues) visible. Anybody other than friends and colleagues can not access this post.

3.1 Model Overview

Privacy policy prediction based on users' historical decision is suitable for our work. We focus on users who assign multiple privacy settings rather than just one to their past posts. As shown in Fig. 1, the proposed model process two types of users (New users and others). When a user publishes a post, the model builds keyword repository based on user's historical posts. After that, five features are constructed and fed into multi-class classifier to predict the privacy policy. Note that, the keyword feature is extracted based on this user's keyword repository.

In order to alleviate the cold start problem (new users on OSNs), our model integrates cowdsourcing [11] and machine learning to recommend privacy policies for new users relies on the other users' past decisions. New users include users that don't aware or understand the privacy setting mechanism for existing OSNs (their historical decisions are all *everyone*) and users that just register on the site. In this case, machine learning model may not perform well because the training data are insufficient or the historical decisions are default privacy policy.

Predictions based on crowdsourcing, which uses opinions from a group of users, are also used to provide privacy preference recommendations.

For a new user, the process of generating keyword repository is not the same as before since new user does not have enough posts and policies stored. The model transforming crowd users' policies into four labels (*everyone, all friends, custom, self*) and building global keyword repository based on their past posts and policies. Afterwards, extracting features and building a global classifier. On a separate note, the train set is crows users' data for predicting new user's policies.

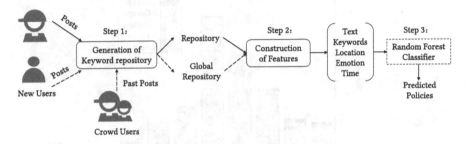

Fig. 1. Overview of the proposed model.

3.2 Feature Extraction

Word Features. Similar pieces of user-generated content have similar privacy policies. we apply short text classification technology to extract word features. All users' historical posts are considered as corpus $\Omega = \{p_1, p_2, \ldots, p_n\}$. For each post p_i in corpus Ω, tokenizing (transform the corpus Ω into small units) it to individual words. After that, we removing stop words and useless characters (e.g., special symbols) from Ω and building a term vocabulary V. Finally, we vectorizing Ω, each post p_i is represented as a m-dimensional (m represented V's dimension) vector $\mathbf{c_i} = \langle f_{i1}, f_{i2}, f_{i3}, \ldots, f_{im} \rangle$ in a vector space. TF-IDF [13] is used for calculating each word's term-weighting (f_{ik}). After above steps, each post is transformed to a row feature vector $\mathbf{c_i} = \langle f_{i1}, f_{i2}, f_{i3}, \ldots, f_{im} \rangle$.

Context Features. The sharing content always contain personal information in corresponding contexts (e.g., time, location, emotion). We consider three values (weekday, weekend, night [14]) for time, since privacy preferences are found to be time sensitive in many scenarios. Finally the time vector $\mathbf{t_i}$ has three attributes.

For location, 20 location semantics [14] are considered in our work. These location semantics are supported by Google Places: Airport, Art Gallery, Bank, Bar, Bus Station, Casino, Cemetery, Church, Company Building, Convention Center, Hospital, Hotel, Law Firm, Library, Movie Theater, Police Station, Restaurant, Shopping Mall, Spa, Workplace. $\mathbf{loc_i}$ represent the location vector.

For emotion, most of previous works obtain users' emotions by guiding users to choose one from several emotion dimensions they assume. For a deeper insight, we investigate how does emotion affect users make their privacy decisions? We randomly sample 385 posts from our data set which cover 86 participants, then utilize the lexicon-based sentiment analysis [10] technology to compute the sentiment score of each post.

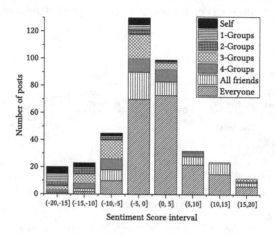

Fig. 2. The relationship between sentiment and sharing policies.

Figure 2 summarizes the relationship between sentiment score and sharing policies. The x-axis represents the sentiment score interval, ranging from −20 to 20 in our samples. The y-axis is the number of posts with selected privacy policy. To aid interpretation, privacy policies are categorized into several groups: 1-Group, 2-Group, 3-Group, 4-Group, Self, Everyone, All friends. The $x − Group$ indicates that x (x = 1, 2, 3, 4) social groups (defined in Sect. 3) are selected in the privacy settings. For instance, policy $[families, friends]$ and $[friends, colleagues]$ belong to 2-Group. From our observation, the general trend is the lower sentiment score of a post, the less visible the audiences. For example, in the interval $[−5, 5]$, more than half of the users selected *everyone* policy. But there also exists posts with low sentiment score but with *everyone* policy. This is due to different users may have different privacy preferences, yet the general trend is mostly identical.

We extract emotion features (positive, negative) e_i based on sentiment scores. It should be note that, normally, the score ≥ 0 represents positive emotion, vice vise. However, the dividing value of positive and negative is not zero. This is consistent with ground truth that users usually publish negative posts to vent their emotions. Hence, the threshold δ that used for deciding whether the emotion is positive or negative is −5 in our work. And this has been validated in our experiments.

Generation of Keyword Repository. The author in [9] considered the keyword feature to captures whether a post includes a keyword that might be related to certain concept like family, friends, work, etc. Their manually complied 20 representative words for all the users. Nevertheless, different users may have different privacy preferences and the keywords related to each user is different. For instance, Alice may not grant permission on her parents when she publishes a post about she is sick. Therefore, "hospital", "doctor" may be the keywords that related to the Alice's privacy preference. The process of extracting keyword features consists three steps. First, we build a keyword repository for each user. Different users have different keyword (associated with privacy preferences) repositories. We set the rule as equation Eq. (1)

$$Dict = \{\langle P_1, Kw_1 \rangle, \ldots, \langle P_n, Kw_n \rangle\},$$
$$where \ Kw_i = [k_1, \ldots, k_m] \ and \ 0 \le i \le n \tag{1}$$

Kw_i is a list of keywords belongs to policy P_i. The process of building keywords dictionary is as follows: scan all posts that have been assigned policy *custom* or *self*, because of posts with fewer audiences may contain sensitive terms (keyword). Then adapting keyword extraction technology to extract keywords of each post and adding to Kw_i. Each P_i belongs to policy *custom* or *self* in historical policies will maintain a keyword list Kw_i (there are no duplicate elements in this list). Finally, update the list if the next private post contains new terms.

The keyword feature vector $\mathbf{K_i} = \langle f_{k1}, f_{k2}, \ldots, f_{kn} \rangle$ of a post is built based on keyword repositories. $\mathbf{K_i}$'s dimensions is the total number of different policies (except for *everyone* and *all friends*) the ith user has used in his/her historical posts. Different people may have various policies usage, thus the number of dimensions of $\mathbf{K_i}$'s for i^{th} user is different from other each users'. For instance, Alice has used the following policies: $\langle friends, colleagues \rangle$, $\langle everyone \rangle$ and $\langle families \rangle$ in her past decisions. $\mathbf{K_i}$'s dimensions: $n = 2$ (except policy *everyone*).

$$w_j = \begin{cases} n & \text{if } Pst \text{ has } n \text{ words that in } Kw_i \\ n \times 0.5 & \text{else } Pst \text{ has } n \text{ synonyms that in } Kw_i \end{cases} \tag{2}$$

According to Eq.(2), if a post Pst contains n words and n synonyms that exist in the Kw_i, then the value of f_{ki} is $\sum w_j$, where j=1, 2.

For example, assume Bob has a post Pst: {Today, I go to the **college!**} with policy P_1. There also exists a dictionary built from Bob's historical posts: $Dict = \{\langle P_1, [Sad, \ university] \rangle, \langle P_2, [happy] \rangle\}$, thus the Pst has one synonym: "university" in $Kw_1 = [Sad, \ university]$ and no word completely matched in Kw_1, then f_{ki} is 0.5. Note that, Chinese Open Wordnet[1] is utilized here to extract words'synonyms.

The main process of building global repository is similar to the process described above. However, the keywords in global $Dict$ is the most representative words and reflect the privacy preferences of most users. The keyword extraction

---

[1] Chinese Open Wordnet http://compling.hss.ntu.edu.sg/cow/.

technology is adapt to extract keywords from the crowd users' historical posts. In order to prevent keyword list Kw_i from being to long, we keep top -1000 most words with the highest TF-IDF scores among all keywords.

4   Evaluation

4.1   Data Collection

In this section, we collected actual user-specified policies to be used as ground truth for our evaluation. The process of data collection is similar to the author in [7]. We recruited 160 volunteers to accomplish our online survey during December 2016 to March 2017. Volunteers are required to be Chinese-speaking and have created at least 60 text-based posts over the past eight months. The survey contains two parts. The first part contains users demographic questions, usage frequency, privacy concerns, etc. The second part is to acquire user's privacy policies. Each user will receive distinct set of posts (crawled from OSNs: QQ Zone and Facebook) according to volunteers' choices (publish frequency) in the first part. The larger the publish frequency of a volunteer, the more posts he/she received. For each post, we asked the user to choose the privacy settings by assuming these posts as their own posts. In addition, assuming volunteers have four Social Groups (SGs): friends, colleagues, families, classmates. For each question, the volunteer may choose one among the following options: *everyone*, *all friends*, *custom*, *self*. Note that *custom* policy is a combination of one or more social groups. For instance, [friends, colleagues] and [classmates] belong to policy *custom*. If the participants choose policy *custom*, the options of *everyone*, *all firends*, *self* will be invalided, vice versa. This constraint is implemented in our online survey [3] to prevent participants from inputting noisy data. Out of 160 volunteers, we just keep data for 94 of them, as the remaining ones (56) generated poor quality data (e.g., data was incomplete, policies for all posts are the same).

4.2   Experimental Settings

We conduct three sets of experiments based on the data collected from Sect. 4.1. The privacy policies in our data set were regarded as labels and we transform policies into numbers (e.g., *everyone*: 0, *all friends*: 1, *self*: 2, *custom*: 3). Note that our method can be easily adapted to different social media platforms, because the privacy policy mechanism is compatible with the existing OSNs. Three representative classification methods are considered: Random Forest (RF), Support Vector Machine (SVM), K-Nearest Neighbor (KNN).

To evaluate the accuracy of our recommended policies, the following metrics are used:

- Correct prediction rate (CPR). The proportion of correctly predicted policies.
- Overall match rate. The proportion of predicted policies among all policies in our data set.

4.3   Evaluation and Analysis

The first experiment focus on evaluate the performance of the proposed model with respect to each user. We select different proportions (from 40% to 90%) of each user's data to train a classifier, and evaluate the classifier on the rest of the data (test set). The value of neighbors K for KNN we set $K = 2$, $K = 3$ and $K = 4$. Among the three values, best results can be gained when $k = 3$. Therefore, we keep using $k = 3$ for the rest of our experiments.

As shown in Fig. 3(a), (b) and (c), KNN and RF outperform SVM. KNN keeps stable performance even in the case of 40% training set, while RF outperform KNN when obtain sufficient training set. We observes that the highest median CPR reachs 0.85 at a training set of 80% with RF classifier. Above the training set of 50%, most users obtain the CPR higher than 80% with RF. Moreover, with the change of the training set size, the median of RF and KNN's CPR is similar, but KNN has more anomalous points than RF. e.g., the minimum value of CPR is lower than RF. Therefore, we take random forest classifier as our core predictive engine. Even at a training set of 40%, the median CPR is over 65%. This means we could already build an acceptable model using a very small number of posts and their past policies.

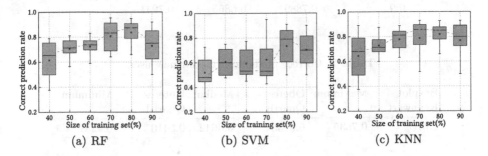

Fig. 3. Correct prediction rate at different sizes of training sets with RF, SVM and KNN.

Table 1 presents the overall prediction performance of our model. We calculate the proportion of correct matched policies among all policies in our data set (all users') at different training ratio. As can be seen, even we only use 40% as training data and 60% as test data, our model can still correctly predict 60.98% policies among all users with random forest and 63.41% policies with K-Nearest Neighbor.

The second experiment is to evaluate the global classifier described in Sect. 3.2. For each user u, we train a classifier with random forest on the data of the remaining users, which is then evaluated on the data of user u. New users will get one of the following four privacy policies: *everyone*, *all_friends*, *custom*, *self*. The policies of selected users (random select 50 from 94 users) in our data set are transformed into these four privacy policy. Table 2 illustrates the results of correct prediction rate for recommending privacy polices to the 50 new users. The median correct prediction rate of all selected new users is above 68.42%. The prediction performance of our model for new users is not as good as the personalized classifier built on each user's own data. Because users may have different behaviors and privacy attitudes towards sharing content. However, such a crowdsourcing-based classifier could already provide a more acceptable performance better than a random guess.

Table 1. Correct match rate

Ratio of Training Data (from 40% to 90%)	RF Correct match rate	SVM Correct match rate	KNN (K = 3) Correct match rate
0.4	0.6098	0.4927	0.6341
0.5	0.6576	0.4971	0.7193
0.6	0.7080	0.5912	0.7591
0.7	0.7467	0.6214	0.7573
0.8	0.7941	0.6912	0.7647
0.9	0.7889	0.6865	0.7941

Table 2. Correct prediction rate for new users

Boxplot Kennwert	Maximum	Oberes Quartil	Median	Unteres Quartil	Minimum
CPR	0.7536	0.6953	0.6642	0.5410	0.4281

At the end, we evaluate the performance of decision making on different combinations of different features. As mentioned before, we use Random Forest classifier as the core prediction method and set training set ratio at 70%. The correct prediction rates of 94 users are shown in Fig. 4, the prediction rate increases along with the features. The combination of text, sentiment, keyword features achieves the highest median correct prediction rate, which is larger than 73%. It proves that combining these features together can achieve a better performance. We also found that, the median correct prediction rate will not significantly change or be improved by adding time feature and location feature. This implies that the time or location has very weak or even negative influences on decision making. The reason is that some users are unaware of location privacy and time privacy when publishing a post. However, this is not always the case for every user.

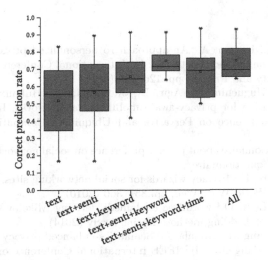

Fig. 4. Feature combination.

5   Conclusion and Future Work

In this paper, we discussed a prediction model for privacy management within text-based social media. The proposed model utilizes content and contextual information of posts to recommend fine-grained privacy policy to users. The experimental results show that our model can achieve 79.41% overall match rate with random forest (ratio of training data is 0.8). As for cold start problem, the proposed model integrates crowdsourcing and machine learning to recommend privacy policies for new users. Results show that our model can reducing the risk of being overexposed for new users.

Regarding the future work, we will try to obtain more social context information(e.g., user's social groups, photos) because users with a similar background tend to have similar privacy concerns (as been in previous research studies). The proposed model adopt TF-IDF (based on bag-of-words model) to compute the weight of each word, however, it does not capture position in text semantics, co-occurrences in different posts. Therefore, extracting word features by utilizing neural networks (e.g.,Word2Vec [5]) is a part of our future work.

Acknowledgments. This work is supported by the National Key R&D Plan of China under grant no. 2016YFB0800201, the Natural Science Foundation of China under grant no. 61070212 and 61572165, the State Key Program of Zhejiang Province Natural Science Foundation of China under grant no. LZ15F020003, the Key research and development plan project of Zhejiang Province under grant no. 2017C01065, the Key Lab of Information Network Security, Ministry of Public Security, under grant no C16603.

References

1. Abuelgasim, A., Kayem, A.: An approach to personalized privacy policy recommendations on online social networks. In: International Conference on Information Systems Security and Privacy, pp. 126–137 (2016)
2. Bilogrevic, I., Huguenin, K., Agir, B., Jadliwala, M., Hubaux, J.P.: Adaptive information-sharing for privacy-aware mobile social networks. In: ACM International Joint Conference on Pervasive and Ubiquitous Computing, pp. 657–666 (2013)
3. Chen, L.: Questionnaire about privacy preference on social networks (2016). http://sec.hdu.edu.cn/questionnaire/
4. Fang, L., Lefevre, K.: Privacy wizards for social networking sites. In: International Conference on World Wide Web, pp. 351–360 (2010)
5. Goldberg, Y., Levy, O.: word2vec explained: deriving Mikolov et al'.s negative-sampling word-embedding method. Eprint Arxiv (2014)
6. Li, Q., Li, J., Wang, H., Ginjala, A.: Semantics-enhanced privacy recommendation for social networking sites. In: IEEE International Conference on Trust, Security and Privacy in Computing and Communications, pp. 226–233 (2011)
7. Lin, D., Wede, J., Sundareswaran, S.: Privacy policy inference of user-uploaded images on content sharing sites. IEEE Trans. Knowl. Data Eng. 27(1), 193–206 (2015)
8. Madejski, M., Johnson, M., Bellovin, S.M.: A study of privacy settings errors in an online social network. In: IEEE International Conference on Pervasive Computing and Communications Workshops, pp. 340–345 (2012)
9. Naini, K.D., Altingovde, I.S., Kawase, R., Herder, E., Niederée, C.: Analyzing and predicting privacy settings in the social web. In: Ricci, F., Bontcheva, K., Conlan, O., Lawless, S. (eds.) UMAP 2015. LNCS, vol. 9146, pp. 104–117. Springer, Cham (2015). https://doi.org/10.1007/978-3-319-20267-9_9
10. Taboada, M., Brooke, J., Tofiloski, M., Voll, K., Stede, M.: Lexicon-based methods for sentiment analysis. Comput. Linguist. 37(2), 267–307 (2011)
11. Toch, E.: Crowdsourcing privacy preferences in context-aware applications. Pers. Ubiquitous Comput. 18(1), 129–141 (2014)
12. Watson, J., Besmer, A., Lipford, H.R.: +your circles: sharing behavior on Google+. In: Eighth Symposium on Usable Privacy and Security, p. 12 (2012)
13. Wu, H.C., Luk, R.W.P., Wong, K.F., Kwok, K.L.: Interpreting TF-IDF term weights as making relevance decisions. ACM Trans. Inf. Syst. 26(3), 55–59 (2008)
14. Xie, J., Knijnenburg, B.P., Jin, H.: Location sharing privacy preference: analysis and personalized recommendation. In: International Conference on Intelligent User Interfaces, pp. 189–198 (2014)
15. Yeung, C.M.A., Kagal, L., Gibbins, N., Shadbolt, N.: Providing access control to online photo albums based on tags and linked data. In: AAAI-SSS: Social Semantic Web (2011)
16. Yuan, L., Theytaz, J., Ebrahimi, T.: Context-dependent privacy-aware photo sharing based on machine learning. In: IFIP International Conference on ICT Systems Security and Privacy Protection, pp. 93–107 (2017)
17. Zerr, S., Siersdorfer, S., Hare, J., Demidova, E.: Privacy-aware image classification and search. In: International ACM SIGIR Conference on Research & Development on Information Retrieval, Portland, Oregon, pp. 35–44 (2012)
18. Zhao, Y., Ye, J., Henderson, T.: Privacy-aware location privacy preference recommendations. In: International Conference on Mobile and Ubiquitous Systems: Computing, NETWORKING and Services, pp. 120–129 (2014)

Collaboration Techniques in Data-intensive Cloud Computing

HSAStore: A Hierarchical Storage Architecture for Computing Systems Containing Large-Scale Intermediate Data

Zhoujie Zhang[1,2], Limin Xiao[1,2(✉)], Shubin Su[1,2], Li Ruan[1,2],
Bing Wei[1,2], Nan Zhou[1,2], Xi Liu[1,2], Haitao Wang[3], and Zipeng Wei[3]

[1] State Key Laboratory of Software Development Environment,
Beihang University, Beijing 100191, China
{jokerzhang, xiaolm, dreamsu}@buaa.edu.cn
[2] School of Computer Science and Engineering,
Beihang University, Beijing 100191, China
[3] Space Star Technology Co., Ltd, Beijing 100086, China
wanghaitao@spacestar.com.cn, wei.zipeng@outlook.com

Abstract. This paper introduces HSAStore, a newly designed storage system whose goal goes to build an efficient storage system for computing systems that containing large-scale intermediate data. HSAStore involves three sub-systems to work together, a distributed file system which is in charge of the intermediate data, a centralized Network Attached Storage (NAS) which stores the raw input data and the results data, and a local file system that serves for the local data. The HSAStore takes full advantage of the network bandwidth of the computing cluster. Moreover, HSAStore adopts the distributed file system, so it is helpful for efficient execution of parallel programs. Experiments show that HSAStore has a significant improvement on efficiency in the computing systems that containing large-scale intermediate data.

Keywords: Hierarchical storage architecture · Bandwidth bottleneck
Large-scale intermediate data · Distributed file system

1 Introduction

Large-scale computer systems play an important role in scientific computing. A completely scientific computing task can be divided into three sub-steps: Input, Compute and Output [1, 2]. It has been a consensus that the development of storage devices is not as fast as the computing devices. As suggested by the "Bucket Effect", Input & Output component of the system, as know as storage system, deserves a special attention.

When the topic comes to storage system, the distributed solution has become a consensus. Google's distributed file system GFS (Google File System) [3] is a wonderful practice of this distributed idea. The core concept of Distributed File System (DFS) is constructing robust storage system with cheap disks. DFS has been widely applied by many companies. Three advantages make DFS to be an alternative to the conventional system. First, the distributed system is elastic, and system managers can

I. Romdhani et al. (Eds.): CollaborateCom 2017, LNICST 252, pp. 591–601, 2018.
https://doi.org/10.1007/978-3-030-00916-8_54

easily introduce a new storage node and need not to interrupt any of the running nodes. Second, DFS has a congenital advantage for parallel programs [4], such a feature can improve the performance of the scientific computing that can be parallelized. The last characteristic is that DFS is designed to be inexpensive and this goal is finally achieved by the engineers, users can adopt cheap hard disks and nodes to build it [5]. However, DFS is a complicated software system that just offers the necessary interface to accomplish its task, which makes the management job inflexible. On the other hand, the Centralized Storage System (CSS) is a traditional solution which can be tracked back down a very early age [6]. It is a straightforward thought to accomplish I/O requests in one place. The devices of a centralized system are always reliable. Unlike DFS, there is no extra steps are needed to maintain consistency [7], so the read and write requests are more efficient on the CSS. Furthermore, the CSS is better manageable than DFS.

This paper shows the design and implementation of HSAStore, a hierarchical storage system that is well designed for the computing systems containing large-scale intermediate data. Now, due to explosive growth of data, the data processing applications become more and more complex. These applications often involve multiple steps, many intermediate steps will produce a large amount of intermediate data. For example, the depth learning, each level of neural network will produce a lot of intermediate data. Another example is the seismic data processing application, general seismic data processing applications often read raw data from the storage system first, and then perform multiple iterations to complete the computing task. The whole task involves several procedures. Except the last procedure, each of them has its input and output. The output of the iterations is only useful for the next one or two steps, we call these output "intermediate data". These intermediate data are often several times as large as the raw data. While thousands of nodes coordinate to complete a task, those frequently read and write requests of intermediate data can result in considerable bandwidth consumption and competition.

The previous storage system deploys Network Attached Storage (NAS) devices to serve those huge I/O traffic from the compute component. However, the NAS is very expensive device, and its performance is limited by hardware manufacturing technology. Simply replace the centralized system with a distributed one is not a wise choice. We will introduce more details in Sect. 2 to explain this point. In this context, we designed HSAStore.

The rest of the paper is organized as follows. Section 2 introduces the traditional system and its problems. Section 3 shows how and why HSAStore performs well. We do evaluation jobs to verify our new system in Sect. 4. Section 5 displays some related works and the Sect. 6 is the conclusion of this paper.

2   The Previous System

In this section, we will make a brief description of NAS-based CSS. HSAStore is an improve version based on the NAS-based CSS, a general understanding of the CSS is necessary.

2.1   Background

When a computing task comes to the system, the cluster will distribute it to the available compute nodes. Every read/write request from those nodes will finally distribute to the storage system. Restricted by the performance of the hardware, if there are too many requests, the storage system cannot respond timely to each of them, especially when nodes come up to hundreds and thousands.

The CSS often employs Network Attached Storage (NAS) as the storage system. As Fig. 1 shows, since the bandwidth determines the maximum amount of data transmission per unit time, the bandwidth between the NAS and other components is much more important. In the CSS, data transmission bandwidth will be overloaded if a large number of nodes request the storage system at the same time. Here is a classic example, consider there is a cluster with 256 nodes, each of the nodes owns 2 CPU, and each CPU has 8 process cores and another 2096 GPU cores. Therefore, we have 4096 CPU cores (256 * 2 * 8) in our system. Suppose that the bandwidth of the storage system is 5 GB/s (1 GB = 1024 MB), the average bandwidth of each core (GPU cores and CPU cores) is just 0.83 MB/S. This figure will be even lower if we add more nodes in the cluster. As the Table 1 shows, the third row shows the average read bandwidth of applications, the fourth row tells us about the write bandwidth. Obviously, 0.83 MB/s is not a satisfactory count. Unfortunately, more nodes just make more traffic jams.

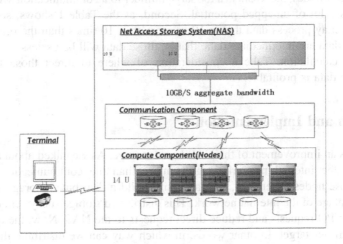

Fig. 1. NAS-based system

In other hand, there are two reasons that we cannot simply replace this NAS with a DFS to finish the optimization work of these computing systems. The first reason is about reliability. DFS has turned out to be a stable solution, but there is no sophisticated scheme for a scientific data processing system to work on DFS. Besides that, the original data should have flexibility to substitute. An example is that when doing geological exploration, we may replace an old storage device with a new one that has loaded new seismic data that collected from the field, the DFS cannot meet this demand.

Table 1. Typical features of a real-world computing system

Applications	Serial applications	Parallel application
Data size*	20	6~7
Storage space*	10	3
Read bandwidth /CPU core	12 MB/S	100 KB/S (with intermediate data) 750 KB/S (without intermediate data)
Write bandwidth/CPU core	4 MB/S	20 KB/S (with intermediate data) 450 KB/s (without intermediate data)

*Assume that the size of the raw input data is 1

2.2   Discussion

We have discussed about the advantages of the NAS-based version. In fact, NAS is a more efficient choice for some applications, especially under lightly loaded conditions. Due to those reasons we mentioned above, we cannot just simply displace the CSS by Distributed File System.

A wise man's question contains half the answer. We find two things deserve our attention. First is about the network of the cluster. The network's bandwidth can always reach 5.6 GB/s. But in the NAS-based storage system, it serves only the communication between nodes. 5.6 GB/s is a too large number to a communication service. This network has a lot of untapped potential. Second, as the Table 1 shows, some of the applications may process data that is 10 or more than 10 times than the original data, most of the data are intermediate data, that is, those data will be useless after the next step of the calculation. Take a consideration of where to direct those large-scale intermediate data is profitable.

3   Design and Implementation

HSAStore is an improvement of the NAS-based storage. As we talked about above, the capacity of the internal network is great more than the communication demands between those nodes. Therefore, we can easily build a distributed storage subsystem taking advantage of the internal network. This distributed storage subsystem can shares part of those I/O requests and reduce direct requests to the NAS. Now, the question is how to reach our target. In other words, in which way can we distribute the requests efficiently? Recall that those computing applications always generate large intermediate and very short-lived data. Obviously, any requests of these data, including read and write operations would be better not to direct to NAS. In this work, we put all of this data into the DFS. Thus, the DFS is just like a very huge cache for intermediate data, greatly relieve the load of NAS.

3.1   Overview

As the Fig. 2 shows, the architecture of HSAStore consists of three parts: the original storage component, the DFS which is used to be an intermediate data Cache, and the

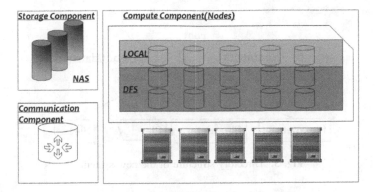

Fig. 2. HSAStore storage system

local storage. In addition, we have built a handy interface to make it more easily for applications programmers. The main idea is to provide a uniform access interface for the three subsystems of the storage system: the original storage component, the local storage, the DFS storage.

The DFS is the core component of HSAStore. Every node is equipped with one or more hard disks to make up this system. Besides requests of the intermediate data, other data can use the DFS if it is necessary. The interface will offer functions to tag useful data and these data will be transmitted to the NAS storage by a daemon process. The NAS subsystem offers the raw data and stores the result of the applications. Like the DFS, other data can be stored on this system, too. We build the local storage subsystem to store local data. Such as configuration information, it will be better to keep these data locally and this local storage system is responsible for handling these data. Local storage requires only another hard disk for each node.

3.2 Implementation

In this part, we will show more details about the interface of our new system. We employ HDFS [8] (Hadoop Distributed File System) as an instance of our DFS, and a unix-like file system as an instance of the local storage system. We will introduce the word "metadata" first. Metadata is a special data structure to store important information for a file [9, 10]. After that, we will explain basic file operations: read, write and delete.

Metadata
When a read/wirte request comes to the HSAStore, the first reaction is to read/write information from/to the metadata file. For example, if it is a request to write a new file on the DFS, the first is to record its location. This location string is a parameter of the requests. By recording this information into metadata file, a file can be accessed correctly in the future. In addition, metadata also includes some useful information such as the expiration time of a file.

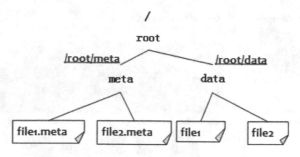

Fig. 3. Directory structure of the new system

As the Fig. 3 shows, we create a metadata directory on each subsystem. Here is an instance to specify how it works. Suppose that we create a new file named "file1", a complete representation of file1 is hdfs://ip:port/root/data/file1, and the path of its metadata has the same form like hdfs://ip:port/root/meta/file1.meta, they are quite the same except a extra "meta" directory of the meta file's path.

Write and Read

Write operations begin with a preparation process. To write a new file, the interface should find the boot file first. A boot file records all available location paths of the three subsystems, the interface knows how to find this boot file. Then, according to the parameter of the request, the interface chooses a valid path and saves all of the necessary information into the metafile. Finally, act just like a common write call. To write an existing file, sometimes we call this operation "append", we will search metadata file inside the metadata directory which we mentioned above. Once get the metafile, we know the path of the file we want to write, call native write interface of HDFS to do the remaining jobs. The read operation is similar to the write, the only difference is that the last step of read will call the native "read" interface.

Delete

Most of the data are intermediate data and it is short-lived. We recommend the users of our interface to delete files which are no longer useful by themselves. In these kinds of scenarios, our delete interfaces act like the native delete interface. Actually, such a delete operation is not a necessity. Interface users probably never care about if the useless files have been deleted. Sometimes the users are not sure whether this file will be useful for other users, and sometimes they just forget to delete that file. Thus, our write operation offers a parameter to make sure that a file will be expired after an exact time. The metafile of that data file will record this number. We set a default time of 15 days. Then we run an independent process accomplish the deletion work. This process checks each of the metafile inside the metadata directory, figure out how long it take since the file was created. Compare the result with the number we record in the metafile, if the result is greater than the recording time, then delete the metafile and its data file.

4   Evaluation

We performed several experiments to evaluate the performance of our new system. The environment of our experiments is shown in Table 2. The test cluster consists of 64 nodes, each node has 20 cores. Besides that, we equipped this cluster with a 10 Gb/s-ethernet. The storage system of our test cluster has a storage space of over 600 TB, including a Distributed File System whose space over 216 TB and a 400 TB NAS storage system.

Table 2. Test environment

CPU	64 nodes * 20 cores/node
Network	10 GB full wire-speed ehternet
Net access storage	4* Isilon X400 (over 400 TB SATA)
Distribute storage	Hadoop Distribute File Sytem (54 nodes/216 TB SATA)

We run seismic applications as typical scientific data processing applications on HSAStore and the NAS-based platform to finish the experiments. We use a custom test framework to generate real seismic application I/O requests. We concerned about three important performance characteristics in our experiment: the utilization of CPU, the latency of interactive applications and the efficiency of the critical steps.

Firstly, it is better to introduce the conception of "load level". As is shown in Table 3, the test framework submits tasks to the cluster. There are two typical tasks, one is compute intensive applications and another is I/O intensive applications. Compute intensive application won't burden the storage system. On the contrary, I/O intensive applications often launch lots of requests to the storage system, so it will cause an additional burden on the storage system. For example, the second column which we call "Low Load", there are 4 nodes run I/O intensive applications with 20 CPU cores each node, and 60 nodes run CPU-intensive applications. Contrast with 10 nodes run I/O intensive applications and 54 nodes run CPU-intensive applications, the former lead to fewer requests to the storage system. Thus, the former is "Low Load" and the latter is "Heavy Load".

Table 3. Load level of the experiments

Features	Low load	Medium load	Heavy load
Compute intensive	4 nodes * 20 cores	7 nodes * 20 cores	10 nodes * 20 cores
I/O intensive	60 nodes * 20 cores	57 nodes * 20 cores	54 nodes * 20 cores

Figure 4 shows the CPU efficiency of the HSAStore and the CSS under the different work load. Obviously, the utilization of CPU on HSAStore is relatively high. Especially in high load conditions, the result of HSAStore is over twice as much as the CSS. In other words, the "storage bottleneck" occurs in the high load situation has been broken. The performance improvement under light load is not that significant as the

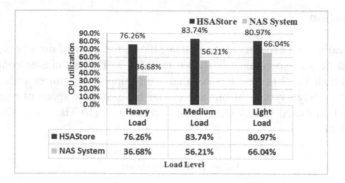

Fig. 4. CPU utilization at different loads under different platform

performance improvement under high load condition because that the bottleneck effect is not so obvious at low load condition. The result of this experiment shows that HSAStore can really help to improve the throughput of the system.

Figure 5 shows the latency of the interactive applications under different work load. We find that when the storage system is lightly loaded, there is about 60% performance improvement of our new system. The same as the previous experiments, high load leads to a marked decrease of the latency time. As the figure shows, there are almost 6 or 7 times of latency reduced under high load situation. The decrease is quite remarkable because that on the CSS the bottleneck occurs when I/O traffic gets busy. This is another proof that the HSAStore is more efficient than the CSS.

In a seismic data processing application, accomplish its critical steps as soon as possible is the ultimate goal. We insert code before and after those critical steps to record its execution time. Figure 6 shows that the critical steps of HSAStore always cost less time than the CSS regardless of the load level. Under heavy load situation, the execution time of HSAStore reduces to one fourth of the CSS. This is further evidence that our new system achieves our performance goal.

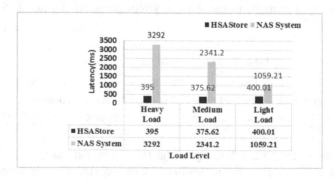

Fig. 5. Application latency at different loads under different platform

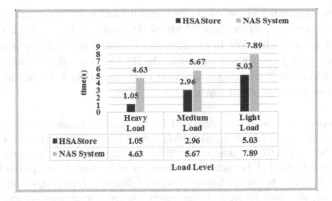

Fig. 6. Execution time of critical steps in seismic data processing application

5 Related Work

Our project is inspired by the research on hierarchical storage and metadata management. Hierarchical storage is a topic focus on how to use different storage subsystems for different working sets. Early works on this can be dated back to HP AutoRAID [11], a storage system which is divided into two levels. One with replications and another with RAID5. The system transfers data according to its status automatically. Facebook's storage system f4 [12], build such a hierarchical storage on a larger scale, and make choices in a more complicated strategy. Besides that, it takes a more simple model to distinguish different work load. Yang et al. [13] propose an I/O scheduler works on three layers: block, system call and page cache, such a multi-layer framework can make decisions with a more comprehensive information. And their split-I/O framework can be easily deployed to traditional operating system and databases. As a storage system for scientific applications, we construct our system with three parts, the system distributes requests of every special stage of the application to different storage subsystems.

Metadata management plays an important role in file systems. Beaver et al. [10] propose a design to minimize the size of metafile and thus the system can cache more metafiles into memory. More metafiles in memory can greatly reduce disk I/O. Zhang et al. [14] proposes several ways to group related metafiles, and they address an algorithm to accomplish this job intelligently. Patil et al. [15] use a sophisticated algorithm to manage millions of metafiles of a system. In our system, we just use a straight-forward way to manage metafiles, a more efficient method can be a further exploration of our future work.

6 Conclusion

In this paper, we proposed a new design of the storage architecture for computing systems containing large-scale intermediate data. The main idea of HSAStore is to avoid distributing all of the I/O requests to the NAS. In HSAStore, DFS will process most of the requests of the intermediate data, and it takes full advantage of the cluster's communication network, so the bandwidth of HSAStore is the network's bandwidth plus the NAS's bandwidth. We have increased the bandwidth of the storage system with a very low cost. Experiments show that the HSAStore is effective and efficient for the computing systems containing large-scale intermediate data. In the future, we will apply HSAStore to the depth of learning.

Acknowledgments. This work was supported by the National Science Foundation of China (Grant Nos. 61370059, 61772053 and 61232009 (key project)), Beijing Natural Science Foundation (Grant No. 4152030), the fund of the State Key Laboratory of Computer Architecture (CARCH201507), the fund of the State Key Laboratory of Software Development Environment (SKLSDE-2017ZX-10), the State Administration of Science Technology and Industry for National Defense, the major projects of high resolution earth observation system under Grant No. Y20A-E03, and the National Key R&D Program of China under Grant NO. 2017YFB1010000.

References

1. Zhou, A.C., He, B., Ibrahim, S.: A taxonomy and survey of scientific computing in the cloud (2016)
2. Maheshwari, K., Wozniak, J.M., Yang, H., et al.: Evaluating storage systems for scientific data in the cloud. In: Proceedings of the 5th ACM Workshop on Scientific Cloud Computing, pp. 33–40. ACM (2014)
3. Ghemawat, S., Gobioff, H., Leung, S.T.: The Google file system. ACM SIGOPS Oper. Syst. Rev. ACM **37**(5), 29–43 (2003)
4. Dean, J., Ghemawat, S.: MapReduce: simplified data processing on large clusters. Commun. ACM **51**(1), 107–113 (2008)
5. Gibson, G.A., Nagle, D.F., Amiri, K., et al.: A cost-effective, high-bandwidth storage architecture. ACM SIGOPS Oper. Syst. Rev. ACM **32**(5), 92–103 (1998)
6. Gibson, G.A., Van Meter, R.: Network attached storage architecture. Commun. ACM **43**(11), 37–45 (2000)
7. Bai, S., Wu, H.: The performance study on several distributed file systems. In: 2011 International Conference on Cyber-Enabled Distributed Computing and Knowledge Discovery (CyberC), pp. 226–229. IEEE (2011)
8. Shvachko, K., Kuang, H., Radia, S., et al.: The hadoop distributed file system. In: 2010 IEEE 26th Symposium on Mass Storage Systems and Technologies (MSST), pp. 1–10. IEEE (2010)
9. Deng, K., Song, J., Ren, K., et al.: Exploring portfolio scheduling for long-term execution of scientific workloads in IaaS clouds. In: Proceedings of the International Conference on High Performance Computing, Networking, Storage and Analysis, p. 55. ACM (2013)
10. Beaver, D., Kumar, S., Li, H.C., et al.: Finding a needle in haystack: Facebook's photo storage. OSDI **10**, 1–8 (2010)
11. Wilkes, J., Golding, R., Staelin, C., et al.: The HP AutoRAID hierarchical storage system. ACM Trans. Comput. Syst. (TOCS) **14**(1), 108–136 (1996)
12. Muralidhar, S., Lloyd, W., Roy, S., et al.: f4: Facebook's warm blob storage system. In: Proceedings of the 11th USENIX conference on Operating Systems Design and Implementation, pp. 383–398. USENIX Association (2014)

13. Yang, S., Harter, T., Agrawal, N., et al.: Split-level I/O scheduling. In: Proceedings of the 25th Symposium on Operating Systems Principles, pp. 474–489. ACM (2015)
14. Zhang, Z., Ghose, K.: hFS: A hybrid file system prototype for improving small file and metadata performance. ACM SIGOPS Oper. Syst. Rev. **41**(3), 175–187 (2007)
15. Patil, S.V., Gibson, G.A., Lang, S., et al.: Giga+: scalable directories for shared file systems. In: Proceedings of the 2nd International Workshop on Petascale Data Storage: Held in Conjunction with Supercomputing'07, pp. 26–29. ACM (2007)

Early Notification and Dynamic Routing: An Improved SDN-Based Optimization Mechanism for VM Migration

Xuanlong Qin[1], Dagang Li[1(✉)], Ching-Hsuan Chen[2], and Nen-Fu Huang[2]

[1] Peking University Shenzhen Graduate School, Shenzhen, China
xuanlong@pku.edu.cn, dgli@pkusz.edu.cn
[2] National Tsing Hua University, Hsinchu, Taiwan
napolenon0sam@gmail.com

Abstract. Virtual Machine (VM) live migration is a crucial practice commonly applied in data centers, which can help users and enterprises manage network services more flexibly and economically. In general, large enterprises always require uninterrupted network service in VM migration, but the VM's own behavior and limited link resources often result in increased transmission times. We found that VMs may have two types of problems in live migration: bursty traffic and packet loss in the tail of the migration round, both of which tend to cause performance loss in the process of iterative migration. Thus, we propose an early notification (E-N) algorithm that can deal with these two problems. Simultaneously, considering more flexible software-defined networks, we put forward a dynamic routing (D-R) algorithm to ensure the link performance of VM live migration. Finally, we present experiments prove that VM migration performance can be improved by combining E-N algorithm and D-R algorithm.

Keywords: Live migration · Software-defined network
Transport layer · Migration performance

1 Introduction

With the development of network techniques, virtualization technology has been widely used on modern computing platforms. VM technology allows a customer with multiple parallel tasks to replace multiple servers with a single server. In addition, VM migration can reallocate and schedule resources. VM migration technology has attracted considerable interest for data center management and cluster computing in recent years. Representative products include XenMotion and Vmotion, which were implemented as built-in tools for virtualization platforms. In data centers, VM migration is often combined with software-defined

This work was supported by Science, Technology and Innovation Commission of Shenzhen Municipality (JCYJ20160525154348175, ZDSYS201603311739428).

© ICST Institute for Computer Sciences, Social Informatics and Telecommunications Engineering 2018
I. Romdhani et al. (Eds.): CollaborateCom 2017, LNICST 252, pp. 602–612, 2018.
https://doi.org/10.1007/978-3-030-00916-8_55

networks (SDNs), because SDN characteristics can separate network into control plane and data plane, making traffic more transparent and easier to distinguish. This improves the load balance of system, increases the fault tolerance of the system, and provides various other benefits.

1.1 Background

Live VM migration is one of the key enabling technologies for fault tolerance and load balancing, they use the migration time in exchange for a lower downtime. For some services, a downtime of one second may result in approximately 1100 dollars of lost revenue [5]. So How to minimize the total migration time and downtime is a crucial research topic.

At present, numerous well-known practices focus on hosts for VM live migration; such practices include compressing memory [4], removing memory redundancies, establishing a Writing Work Set, establishing a path with a routing algorithm, dynamic resource assignment, and managing the order of VM transfers. However, few people have precisely optimized the resource consumption of the transport layer and link layer. In this paper we put forward a method combining SDNs and transport layer optimization to improve the performance of VM migration.

Currently, VM migrations are usually executed at data centers, using connections with high bandwidth and low latency. A typical network is fat tree structure with shared links. Any congestion that occurs during data transmission causes extremely serious link congestion and incurs an exorbitant cost. Because SDNs are flexible enough to guarantee excellent performance, the trend of VM migration involves SDN technology in data centers has become ubiquitous.

1.2 Our Contribution

This paper presents a Transmission Control Protocol (TCP) approach to optimize VM migration from the perspective of data transmission. The proposed approach solves the problem of traffic bursts and packet loss during the tails of the migration rounds (Packet lost at the memory iteration copy phase). This paper puts forward a method of SDN-based link optimization and proposes a routing strategy to reduce link congestion and total migration time.

The remainder of this paper is structured as follows. Section 2 presents precopy live migration and SDN dynamic resource assignment. In Sect. 3, we analyze the problems that arise in live migration. In Sect. 4, we propose an algorithm to solve these problems and list its pseudocode. In Sect. 5, we test the correctness of our VM and SDN models; then evaluate the performance of our proposed algorithm in Sect. 6. Finally, we conclude our work in Sect. 7.

2   Related Work

To clarify the optimization mechanism for VM live migration, we introduce precopy migration and SDN dynamic resource assignment in this section.

2.1 Precopy Live Migration

The precopy algorithm proposed by Clark [1], have proven to be remarkably effective tools for enabling data center management in a non-disruptive manner. Xen, KVM, and VMware all use precopy algorithms for live migration; they all use a memory-to-memory approach as depicted in Fig. 1.

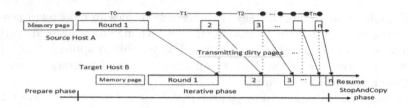

Fig. 1. Precopy timeline

Different hypervisors implement precopy migration differently, but most hypervisors use the same basic pattern of three phases: the preparation phase, the iterative phase, and the stop-and-copy phase. During the preparation phase, the main responsibility of the application is the preparation of relevant resources before the migration starts. During the first round of the iteration phase, the host transfers all the memory pages, at this time the VM is still working, thus some memory pages must be overwritten (the overwritten pages are usually called dirty pages). The dirty pages must be retransferred to the destination in the next round. After several rounds of synchronization, VM arrives stop-and-copy condition and enters the stop-and-copy phase. When the VM resumes service on the destination host, indicates the migration is complete. Unlike static replication algorithms, a precopy method optimizes downtime to avoid unforeseen overhead and errors caused by long VM downtimes.

The preparation phase generally requires a fixed amount of time to execute procedures and to allocate resources. The stop-and-copy phase typically requires approximately 200 ms of downtime. We focus on optimizing the iteration stage.

Xen hypervisor requires four conditions before it enters the stop-and-copy phase: (1) The speed at which memory pages are dirtied exceed the memory transfer speed. (2) The dirty page to be transferred next round reach a certain threshold. (3) The number of rounds executed within the iteration phase exceed a given value. (4) The total migrated data must be larger than three times the VM memory size.

When the stop-and-copy conditions have been satisfied, the VM is shut down on the source host and the remaining dirty pages are transferred to the destination host.

2.2 SDN Dynamic Resource Assignment

SDNs technology is mainly used in traffic engineering and it can also benefit VM migration. When multiple VMs must be migrated at the same time, with a centralized view of the network, it is possible to compute the bandwidth required for each migration [6]. By minimizing the correlations between the migration schemes of different VMs, we can maximize the migration bandwidth and thus we can minimize the total migration time and the downtime [7]. Furthermore, topology-aware live migration can reduce the communication costs of pairwise VMs [8] and increase the overall throughput.

An SDNs controller can obtain various types of network information and control that information to optimize the flexibility of the data center network in response to traffic challenges.

3   Problem Statement

3.1   Bursty Traffic in the Migration Rounds

In the previous section, we described the precopy algorithm of VM live migration. Precopy migration captures dirty pages through a shadow page table and marks these dirty pages with a bitmap. In each round of the iteration phase, the bitmap determines what data must be transmitted in the current round, what data must be transmitted during next round, and what data must be transmitted in the last round. After all data of one round has been sent, the bitmap is flushed. After bitmap designates data to be transmitted this round, Xen transmits the designated dirty pages batch by batch; these dirty pages are copied to the TCP buffer in the kernel through socket functions, then transmitted by TCP services. At the same time, the socket functions record the amount of data; when data transmission is completed this round, Xen evaluates whether the stop-and-copy condition has been reached. If the iteration phase continues, then the bitmap starts a new round, scans the data, and transfers the next set of dirty pages. This process produces a short round interval; it is almost negligible, but Xen cannot see the behavior of TCP after the data has been copied to the TCP buffer.

In general, the interval between one round and the previous round is so short that the TCP receiver does not send a window update message to the sender when a round finished. Therefore, at any given round, the TCP sending window usually maintains the status of the previous round. Because the previous migration data has already been transferred, no data packets are in the sending window for transmission. Thus, when the next round's data is ready to be transferred, the TCP sender usually sends all the packets of data that the sending window can hold to the network at once. Network congestion is probable.

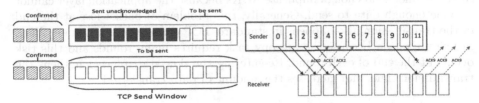

Fig. 2. Change of cwnd in live migration   **Fig. 3.** Packet loss in the tail

Figure 2 illustrates the state of the standard TCP sending window. The data packets of the TCP sending window are divided into two categories: those that have been sent but remain unacknowledged and those that remain to be sent. To achieve flow control, the sender can use the notification window passed by receiver to adjust the size of the sending window. During the iteration phase, when the previous round has been transferred, the TCP sending window is empty. When the next round of transmission starts, all packets that can be contained within the sending window are usually sent to the network at the same time.

Considering the business value and cost of performance, most commercial switches are shallow buffer switches. The sudden flows of traffic required for VM migration can easily cause a switch's cache to overflow, resulting in a loss of packets and network congestion. With the number of lost packets increased, the TCP congestion algorithm enters its congestion avoidance phase even slow-start phase, thus increases both the total migration time and the amount of data transferred. Once congestion occurs, especially in the stop-and-copy phase, system downtime increases, and the cost is unacceptable.

3.2   Packet Loss in the Tail of the Migration Rounds

TCP congestion control is divided into four segments: slow start, congestion avoidance, fast retransmission, and fast recovery. When TCP in congestion avoidance phase and the TCP sender is continuously receiving three duplicate ACKs for one packet, TCP executes its fast retransmission algorithm and retransmit this packet immediately without waiting for the retransmission counter to expire.

In live VM migration, the data packets are transmitted round by round; if the last packet for a round is transmitted successfully and confirmed by receiver's ACK, then the data of that round has been completely transmitted. But if the system is transmitting the last three packets, and if one of the data packets is lost, this round has no data packet can be used to send ACK. The result is TCP can only wait for the retransmission counter to run out.

This case as shown in Fig. 3, the TCP receiver thinks that the network congestion is serious and need re-entering the slow-start phase. The initial window value of the slow start was default set to be 1, which means that at least two rounds of transmission are required for the final three packets.

However, the actual situation may be that the network traffic is not sufficiently heavy to cause the TCP system to enter its slow-start phase. The TCP sender cannot send enough duplicate ACKs because the application layer cannot provide enough data to send. Generally, this problem of packet loss at the end of the transmission also happens in standard TCP connections, but is amplified in live migration because the precopy task requires many rounds and this risk occurs at the end of each round. Re-entering the slow-start phase lengthens the transmission time, and increases the amount of data transferred.

3.3 Link Contention Problem

In data centers, the network topology usually contains redundant links to provide fault tolerance. In the present work, redundant links provide extra bandwidth in addition to their failover function [3]. We chose not to implement a spanning tree protocol because it could have blocked several ports.

Consider a fat tree topology as shown in Fig. 4. Assume each link in the topology has the same capacity. Three VMs migrate simultaneously; three source hosts are paired with three destination hosts. Without load balancing, all migration pairs would choose one of the upper switches as a route. For example, they might pass through switches (5, 1, 4) at the same time, resulting in link contention, as shown in Fig. 4. In this scenario, some of the links have noteworthy collisions whereas other links are idle. With load balancing, such contention can be avoided, as shown in Fig. 5. Ideally, the transfer speed would be three times higher since the migration pairs are not required to share a single link, and two redundant links are fully utilized.

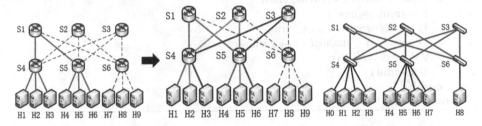

Fig. 4. Multiflow single path   **Fig. 5.** Multiflow multipath   **Fig. 6.** Experiment topology

The difference between the existing load balancing mechanisms of legacy networks and our SDN dynamic routing is that the traditional mechanisms do not consider the characteristics of VM migration, and VM migrations cannot retrieve usage information from the underlying network. Also, VM migrations do not occur evenly among hosts so different link loads typically occur.

4 Algorithm

4.1 E-N Algorithm

For the precopy task, we propose an early notification (E-N) algorithm to optimize the performance of VM live migration.

The algorithm counts how many packets have been sent. When this round of data has been completely sent, the E-N algorithm notifies the application layer to prepare the next round's data immediately, instead of waiting for all the packets that have been sent to be acknowledged at this round. This algorithm is equivalent to eliminate the interconnection between the rounds.

Because the time required to scan the dirty page bitmap is short, when the next round of data is ready to be sent, the data in the TCP sending window has not yet been sent. At that moment, TCP has sufficient data waiting to be sent that TCP can avoid the problem caused by packet loss in the tail of the migration round. Thus TCP can avoid entering its slow-start mode. Our E-N algorithm also solves bursty traffic problems in the migration rounds. When two rounds of data have been generated without any pause, TCP can use the standard sliding window protocol to expand or shrink its windows, and thus can avoid the aforementioned bursty traffic problem. The pseudocode for the E-N algorithm is as follows:

Algorithm 1. Early Notification Algorithm

1: **Input:** V_{mem}, **Output:** T_i, V_i
2: Connect(); sending a SYN packet
3: Last_turn_seq := iss; T_last_turn := now();
4: **if** idle() **then**
5:     **if** seqno + datalen < curseq **then**
6:         T_current := now()
7:         Ti := T_current - T_last_turn;
8:         Vi := seqno + datalen - last_turn_seq;
9:         VM_model(Ti, Vi);
10:        Senddata()
11:    **end if**
12: **end if**

V_{mem} represents the size of a memory page, T_i is the time of transmission for one iteration, V_i is the amount of data in that iteration, *iss* is the current sequence number, *curseq* is the sequence number of the last byte provided by the application.

Our E-N algorithm was executed when the TCP connection is established; VM record initial sequence number. If the sum of the sequence number and the length of the data is greater than curseq, which means that this round's data has been sent.

In addition, the proposed approach is more feasible and compatible than standard TCP. For ordinary TCP flows, the application layer does nothing and the transport behavior is as same as standard TCP. No hardware support is required; a simple interaction between TCP and host improve the performance of VMs live migration.

4.2   Dynamic Routing Algorithm

We implemented a dynamic routing mechanism using Ryu as the Openflow controller. Ryu is a component-based SDN framework that is concise and agile.

The controller constructs a graph using the detected network topology. Every time new communication pair enters the system, no matching happens in the flow table; a packet-in is required. Then the controller obtains the source IP and the destination IP and maps them to the nodes in the graph. With a source, a destination, and a graph, the controller is capable of computing the shortest path using Dijkstra's algorithm. After choosing a best route, its weight will be set to a maximum value to avoid multiple connection selecting the same optimal route in an update period.

The controller queries the statistics of each port for all switches every five seconds. We define the weight of each edge as the sum of the statistics over five seconds for the two ports connected by the edge. Because every new communication pair is routed along the least busy links, the total VM migration time can be minimized.

5   Test Model

We built a VM live migration model, implemented our algorithms in that model, validated the correctness of the model, and verified the performance of the algorithms.

5.1   VM-Based Model

We selected a VM performance and energy prediction model as proposed in [2] as our experimental model, and output the value of the congestion window to verify the behavior of the VM for the problem we proposed.

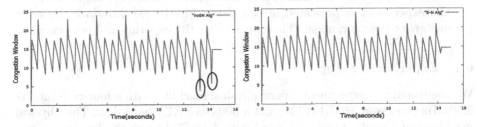

Fig. 7. Size of the congestion window   **Fig. 8.** Congestion Window after E-N algorithm

Figure 7 displays a horizontal axis to represent the time of migration, and displays a vertical axis to represent the size of the congestion window. For a system without our algorithm, the congestion window suddenly become smaller as indicated by dotted black ellipses. We examined the time at which the window fluctuated and found that the windows shrank during a round with bursty traffic and packet loss in the tail. The result of a system with our algorithm is illustrated in Fig. 8; the bursty traffic and packet loss were eliminated.

5.2   SDN Test Model

We used Mininet, a famous network emulation tool, to test the link contention problem. The topology is shown in Fig. 6. Three transmissions occurred in parallel: 4 to 1, 5 to 2, and 6 to 3. Without dynamic routing, the transmissions experienced severe link contention. As Fig. 9 shows, all transmissions were influenced. We implemented our dynamic routing mechanism, and Fig. 10 shows that it was notably effective. All transmissions were able to proceed at full speed.

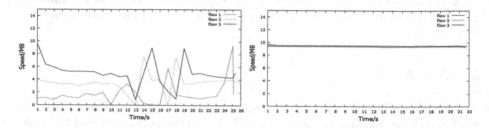

Fig. 9. Without dynamic routing   **Fig. 10.** With dynamic routing

6   Experiment Environment

In this section, we evaluate our E-N algorithm and D-R algorithm through a comparison experiment; the main performance indicator is total migration time.

The experiment is presented in two parts. Firstly, we introduce the basic parameters of the experiment. Then we analyze the experimental performance.

6.1   Experiment Setup

We conducted the experiment on one physical machine, with a four-core Intel i7 3.50 GHz processor, 16 GB RAM, and a 500 GB SATA hard disk. The physical machine ran Ubuntu 14.04 with the Linux 4.4.0-79 kernel; the hypervisor was virtualbox. The guest OSes were Ubuntu 14.04 with the Linux 4.4.0-31 kernel.

We use Mininet to construct network topology. The experiment topology was a simple fat tree that shown in Fig. 6. The bandwidth was set to 500 Mbps, link delay was set to 25 s, and the size of the VM was set to 128 MB, 256 MB, 512 MB, and 1024 MB for different trials. The dirty pages rate was set to 5000 and 10000 dirty pages (4 KB/page) to represent high and low rates of dirty pages.

NS3 is a famous network simulator used in some scientific papers; we implemented the VM's base model in NS3 as an individual host. With our setup, NS3 was able to send packets to a real network through the real network interface of its host and was identified by the Ryu controller. We set the VM stop-and-copy conditions by using the default parameters of Xen. The iteration round was 30. The stop-and-copy threshold was set as 200 KB. The transmitted data was not permitted to exceed three times the VM memory size.

6.2   Performance of Algorithm

Our experiment was divided into two parts, without and with background flow. The first part of this experiment verified the effectiveness of our algorithms for VM migration at different dirty page rates without background flow.

Because no background flow occurred, the probability of packet loss was reduced. In this condition, our total migration time was still reduced 0.5–2 s as Fig. 11 indicates.

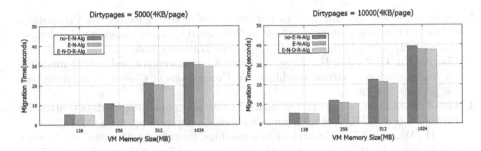

Fig. 11. No background flow

The second part used the same configuration with background flow and the result is illustrated in Fig. 12.

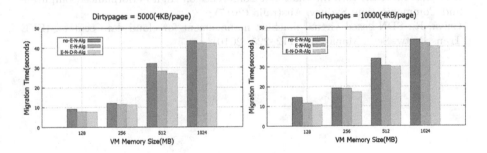

Fig. 12. With background flow

A high dirty page rate and the presence of background flow tend to enlarge the problem we explained in Sects. 3.1 and 3.2. A high dirty page rate and the presence of background flow tend to increase the benefits of using our algorithms.

With background flow, the total migration time is reduced about 2–3 s or more. If hundreds of migrations were done simultaneously, the optimization results would be more significant. The experimental results indicate that our algorithms are effective.

7   Conclusion

This paper uses the D-R and E-N algorithms to optimize the performance of VM live migration. It solves two problems: bursty traffic and packet loss at the tail. These problems often occur during VM migration. Our algorithms can minimize the total time for VM migration and improve performance.

References

1. Clark, C., Fraser, K., Hand, S.: Live migration of virtual machines. In: Proceedings of the 2nd conference on Symposium on Networked Systems Design and Implementation, NSDI 2005, Berkeley, USA, vol. 2, pp. 273–286 (2005)
2. Liu, H., Xu, C. Z., Jin, H., Gong, J., Liao, X.: Performance and energy modeling for live migration of virtual machines. In: Proceedings of Cluster Computing, vol. 16, pp. 249–264 (2013)
3. Liu, J., Su, L., Jin, Y., Li, Y.: Optimal VM migration planning for data centers. In: Proceedings of IEEE Global Communications Conference, pp. 2332–2337 (2014)
4. Jin, H., Wu, S., Shi, X.H.: Live virtual machine migration with adaptive, memory compression. In: IEEE International Conference on Cluster Computing and Workshops, Louisiana, USA (2009)
5. Salfner, F., Troger, P.: Downtime analysis of virtual machine live migration. In: 4th International Conference on Dependability, France, August 2011
6. Wang, H., Li, Y., Zhang, Y.: Virtual machine migration planning in software-defined networks. IEEE Trans. Cloud Comput. **PP**(99) (2017)
7. Yao, X., Wang, H., Gao, C.: VM migration planning in software-defined data center networks. In: IEEE 18th International Conference on High Performance Computing and Communication, Sydney, Australia (2017)
8. Cziva, R.: SDN-based virtual machine management for cloud data centers. IEEE Trans. Netw. Serv. Manag. **13**, 212–225 (2016)

Cloud Data Assured Deletion Based on Information Hiding and Secondary Encryption with Chaos Sequence

Yijie Chen and Wenbin Yao[✉]

Beijing Key Laboratory of Intelligent Telecommunications Software
and Multimedia, Beijing University of Posts and Telecommunications,
Beijing 100876, China
yaowenbin_cdc@163.com

Abstract. The strategic point of data assured deletion in cloud storage is how to avoid unauthorized users accessing or backing up data. The main choice for this issue is how to improve the data access strategy or how to manage the encryption keys better. However, these methods are still put whole encrypted data in the cloud. In case that the encryption key is pick up by an attacker, the data is not secure. A new scheme named AD-IHSE is proposed in this paper. In this method, the bit stream of encrypted data will be divided into two parts. Big part of encrypted data is uploaded to the cloud directly, while the small part of encrypted data is embedded in the carrier and then uploaded to the cloud after secondary encryption with logistic chaotic sequence encryption. This method can even guarantee the security of the data when the encryption key is lost. In addition, the scheme does not bring other third parties to lessen the risk of data leakage. Both safety certificates and experimental results show that it not only realizes the certainty of the cloud data assured deletion but also has good security.

Keywords: Data assured deletion · Bit stream extraction
Data hiding · Secondary encryption · Logistic chaotic mapping

1 Introduction

In recent years, cloud storage has brought opportunities in improving information technology efficiency costs and green computing, as well as some security challenges. In cloud storage mode, data is stored in a third-party cloud storage platform. Data owners lose direct control of their personal data. The security of data highly depends on the cloud service provider (CSP). Data assured deletion is one of those security issues. CSP can not guarantee faithful deletion of data user's data when he received this request. When a data owner intends to delete the data, he wants his data can not be accessed forever once the request is sent out. Considering that CSP is not credible, the most direct way to protect the confidentiality of data is to encrypt the data first, and then outsource the encrypted data to the cloud. The encryption key will be protected by data owner itself. Due to the unreliability of CSP, the data stored in the cloud is at risk of being leaked. For example, for the sake of improve the dependability of the service,

© ICST Institute for Computer Sciences, Social Informatics and Telecommunications Engineering 2018
I. Romdhani et al. (Eds.): CollaborateCom 2017, LNICST 252, pp. 613–623, 2018.
https://doi.org/10.1007/978-3-030-00916-8_56

CSP may have a lot of data backups and store them onto several servers. In this case, once the data is expired and the data owner commands CSP to make its data deleted, CSP may not completely delete all of the data and the backup. In the case that an attacker uses an encrypted key and encrypted data that is not deleted from CSP through a brute force attack, the security of the data will be influenced. While the data owner wants to delete the data, if CSP does not execute the actual data deletions, he is not sure that the deleted data will not appear in the future. This is what this article will discuss.

2 Related Works

In this section, we have proposed several proposed solutions to solve the issue of data assured deletion.

The previous work [1] completed a file assured delete system that can restore encrypted data at the appropriate time to destroy the encryption key. But they only bring up a conceptual method that has not been implemented, and their theoretical models are not very convincing. In a cloud environment, the ownership and management of the data are separated. For the sake of the security of data, it must be encrypted before it is outsourced to the cloud. To some extent, this method makes the issue of data assured deletion into another issue, that is, how to delete the encryption key. However, this is a risk that an attacker may get an encryption key through cryptanalysis or brute force. The scheme in [2] points out a kind of strategy based on the approach. The key idea is that the data is encrypted with the data encryption key at the very beginning, and then encrypts the data encryption key with the control key related to the policy. The last but not the least, deleting the control key in the file is equal to the deletion of the data. Although, the control key used in [2] is managed by third party, namely centralized management. There is a security risk. The untrusted key manager may delete or abandon the control key. Distributed management obtains higher security than key centralized management [3].

In addition, document [4] points out that if the scheme destroys the encryption key only without encrypting data, there will be potential security risks, which may cause encrypted data to be attacked by cryptanalysis or brute force attack. In its scheme, they distribute encryption keys and partially encrypted data into the DHT. Although this method has prevented some attacks mentioned above, if someone has already obtained the key and has some backup, someone can also decode encrypted data. Moreover, [5] improves the Shamir secret sharing algorithm and the length of the key is extended to resist the presence of jump attacks in the Vanish system. Resistance to sniffing attacks, [5] uses public-private key encryption and decryption. However, the cloud stores complete encrypted data, the scheme can not resist brute force attacks and cryptographic attacks.

Next, [6] points out a kind of solution that divides the very beginning encrypted data into the sampling data and the remaining data. Then, they deliver the remaining data to the cloud, which makes it impossible for the unreliable CSP to get all the encrypted data. The drawback in document [6] is that it introduces the third party that should be trusted to save the sampled data. But, this premise is too idealized. As mentioned in [7], if we can't totally trust the cloud service provider, should not we have the same doubt to the other third parties? When the government has a court order to force the cloud and third parties to hand over the data and key of the investigated company, no matter how hard the data owner tries to delete the data, it will be useless [8, 9].

In order to reduce the risk of data leakage, we propose AD-IHSE, which not only allows the encryption key to be stolen, but also does not need any other third party's management or storage. In AD-IHSE, we firstly do some data extraction for the encrypted data at the bit stream level. The algorithm of extraction guarantees the randomness of data extraction position. When data owner needs to delete data, the only thing to do for him is to delete the random sequence that is used as the location number of the extraction. This can guarantee the security even if CSP does not delete the encrypted data as normal. Without the location information, the extraction can not be recovered by anybody. After data extraction, the encrypted data is divided into two parts. The big part of encrypted data will be sent to the cloud service provider directly. The small one is embedded into default carrier by using information hiding technology. After being hidden, the Stego is encrypted for the second time. Finally, the encrypted Stego is also uploaded to the cloud. Moreover, this method does not need any other third party. The content stored in the cloud is not the entire encrypted data, but the two parts of the encrypted data. The above process ensures that even if the cloud data and encryption keys are stolen by an attacker, the deleted data will not be accessed again.

3 Security Assumptions and Threat Model

3.1 Security Assumptions

Our security intention is to complete reliable data deletion when the encryption key has been stolen by an attacker. This method has three hypotheses. First, the encryption operation is safe, in the situation that an attacker can not recover encrypted data without a decryption key. Secondly, although attackers can decrypt the encrypted data of cloud into corresponding data, they cannot recover and merge encrypted data without random sequence. Third, because of the high cost of storage, data users will not backup the original data after access.

In this article, we consider an idea which has three main entities: the data owner, the cloud service provider (CSP) and the data user.

Data owners are responsible for data encryption, data extraction, information hiding, and two level encryption.

The cloud service provider is responsible for storing the uploaded data. But CSP is not trusted. It works faithfully to data storage, but it is also curious about sensitive information and wants to get sensitive data.

Data users are responsible for data decryption and data recovery.

The data access process is shown in Fig. 1. The red line is used to represent the process for data owner uploading the data. The blue line is used to represent the process for data user visiting the data.

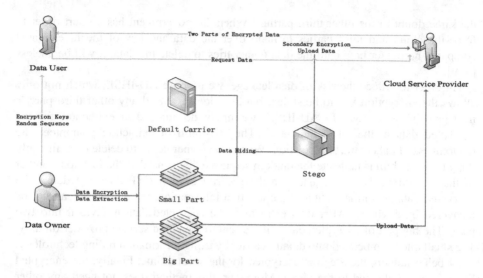

Fig. 1. Data access (Color figure online)

3.2   Threat Model

According to the above security hypothesis, several conditions are defined as follows:
CSP is not trusted. It will divulge encrypted data to other people or some malicious
users. The contents stored in CSP are not safe. The attacker's behavior is not real, but a
subsequent act. Therefore, an attacker will not know what useful data is available
before the data is accessed. Data users are trusted. It does not retain the original data or
use for transmission.

4   Design and Security Analysis

In this method, it is not the original complete encrypted data that is retained on the
cloud. It is based on the following conditions: if an attacker leaks the encryption key in
the active and passive case, the data can also be secure. In addition, this method has
only data owners and data users, without any other third parties performing some
transmission or storage work, which improves safety.

In this design, the chaotic system generates a random sequence as the location
information for the next step in the preparation of information extraction. Besides, the
random sequences are just stored by the data owner. Choosing the appropriate
parameter values, the logical mapping can enter the chaotic state. When you need to
delete data, the only thing to do is to delete a random information that is used as the
number of the transformation positions. If there is no position numbers, the extraction
for encrypted data can not be recovered by anyone. Then, data is split into two fragments according to the logistic chaotic sequences. The small part is hidden into a
default gray image by using the modified LSB algorithm. The image with the small
fragment of the encryption data is encrypted by logistic algorithm for the second time.

Both the big part cipher text and the encrypted image containing the small fragment of encrypted data are uploaded to CSP. For formalization, we now modify our symbols as follows. Let {M} be the original data. Let q be the bit number of extracting bits. Let {K} be the small part of encrypted data. Let $\{S_i\}(1 \leq S_i \leq q)$ be the position number. Let $\{C_i\}$ be the encrypted data. Let k be the encryption key. Let *Extract*() be the function of bit stream extraction. The detail will be explained in the following parts.

4.1 Data Extraction

If the hiding position is selected in order, it will cause the image of the various parts of the statistical characteristics of inconsistencies leading to serious security problems. The modified part of carrier and the unmodified part have different statistical characteristics, which increases the possibility that the attacker has doubts the secret communication.

For the sake of solving this issue, the random sequences are used to select the sequence of pixel by logistic chaotic mapping to product chaos sequences. It is the random sequence that makes the conversion safer. According to the traditional definition, the expression of logistic chaotic mapping is (1):

$$X_{i+1} = f(X_i) = \mu X_i(1 - X_i) \tag{1}$$

In this formula: $X_i \in [0, 1]$ is a logistic mapping state. From the Chaotic Sequence definition, logical mapping parameter $\mu \in [3.5699456, 4]$, the logistic mapping will enter into chaotic state [10]. There are n irregular numbers generated by logistic mapping. In order to ensure data security without bringing additional third party management operations, the encrypted data will be extracted. The random sequence is generated by using the logistic chaotic system as the data extraction position, and the cipher text is divided into two parts.

$$K_i = Extract(M, S_i) \tag{2}$$

The small portion of the extracted data is called the extraction of data, and the other is called the change of data. After extracting, the location information extracted from the extracted data and data will be saved only by the data owner and not sent to anyone else. The sketches extracted by the bitstream are shown in Fig. 2.

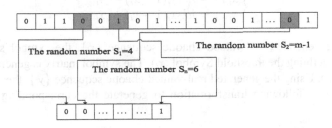

Fig. 2. Data extraction

4.2   Extracted Data Hiding and Secondary Encryption

After extracting the cipher text, the small fragment is hidden as secret information into the vector image by using LSB algorithm. This hidden algorithm is generally in the BMP format images, with a good concealment, hidden capacity, low computational complexity. However, we need to make some improvements to strengthen its security.

Firstly, select the encrypted information rather than the plaintext as a secret to hide into vector image. Secondly, choose the random position rather than a sequential position to be the hidden location. Data owner uses logistic chaotic sequence to generate an random index sequence $\{j_1, j_2, \ldots, j_{L(m)}\}$. The k_{th} secret extracted cipher text bit is hidden in the lowest bit of the index carrier element j_k. Moreover, in order to prevent the random sequence from colliding, the generated index values are recorded. If a collision occurs, the currently used value is discarded and the next index value will be used. From a mathematical point of view, the grayscale image is a matrix whose mathematical expression is as follows:

$$I = \begin{bmatrix} g_{11} & g_{12} & \cdots & g_{1N} \\ g_{21} & g_{22} & \cdots & g_{2N} \\ \vdots & \vdots & & \vdots \\ g_{M1} & g_{M2} & \cdots & g_{MN} \end{bmatrix} \tag{3}$$

$$I = \{g_{xy} | 1 \leq x \leq M; 1 \leq y \leq N\} \tag{4}$$

M and N denote the image samples as M rows and N columns, g_{ij} is the image after sampling and quantization of the pixel position of the gray value. In order to improve the anti-privacy performance of dense images, it is necessary to change the gray value of the pixel that hides the bit when embedding the secret information.

$$T = \sum_{u=i-1}^{i+1} \sum_{v=j-1}^{j+1} g(u, v) - 9g(i, j) \tag{5}$$

The secret information has been hidden into the vector image in the previous section. For higher security, this paper uses two-dimensional logistic mapping for image encryption processing. The dynamic equations of the two-dimensional logistic mapping are as follows:

$$\begin{cases} x_{i+1} = \mu\lambda_1 x_i(1 - x_i) + \gamma y_i \\ y_{i+1} = \mu\lambda_2 x_i(1 - y_i) + \gamma x_i \end{cases} \tag{6}$$

Using the generated real-valued chaotic sequence $\{x_i\}$, the symbol sequence is generated by defining the threshold Symbol (x_i). The symbol matrix is generated in row by Symbol (x_i). Using the generated real-valued chaotic sequence $\{y_i\}$, the sequence is generated by the following transformation to generate the corresponding gray-scale matrix G.

$$\text{Symbol}(x_i) = \begin{cases} -1, & -1 \leq x_i < 0 \\ 1, & 0 \leq x_i \leq 1 \end{cases} \qquad (7)$$

$$\text{Gray}(y_i) = \text{Round}\left(y_i \times \frac{225}{2} + \frac{225}{2}\right) \qquad (8)$$

$$I_{encrypt} = I \oplus G \cdot S \qquad (9)$$

4.3   Data Decryption and Recovery

While the data owner wants to access the data, its request is firstly sent to CSP. After checking data user's legal identity, CSP will send both big part of cipher text and the encrypted image with small part of cipher text to data user. Besides, data owner will send the encryption key and the chaotic sequence of this file to data user. Next, the encrypted image is decrypted by encryption key and a small cipher text is extracted from the image. The cipher text is synthesized according to the extracted position of the chaotic sequence.

4.4   Data Assured Deletion

While the data owner expects to delete the data, the only thing that he need to do is to delete the location sequences of the bit stream extraction process. This information is saved by the data owner after the data is extracted. If CSP deletes the encrypted data, it will be more secure. However, as CSP is trustless, it is not guaranteed to operate as expected. When the location has been deleted, the attacker can not restore the data even if the encryption key and any cloud encrypted data have been extracted at the same time, changed and encrypted for the second time. The way to delete data is to delete it in real time. And the data can be guaranteed to be deleted. Without deleting the request, the location part extracted from the data will be saved by the data owner.

4.5   Security Analysis

In this paper, information hiding is used to encrypt the part of cipher text for the second time. This solution does not need other third parties, nor does it put the original cipher text directly up to the cloud. In this case, for the sake of getting the original data, an attacker needs to not only get two encryption keys for both first and second encryption, but also has to combine the two parts of cipher text into the original one. Or, if he only gets the encryption key, the cloud does not have a complete cipher text ready for the attacker to decrypt.

Theorem: in the condition of the same data length, when attackers acquire the encryption key, it is more difficult for attackers to get encrypted data by AD-IHSE than to recover raw data in traditional way.

Proof: From the above mentioned procedure, it is not hard to see that the key process is to obtain the function of extracting bit stream. This scheme has better security compared with the scheme that an attacker has no encrypted key to get the complete encrypted data. Though attackers already have encryption keys, it is more difficult for him to know the real raw data instead of converting the functions of bit streams, rather than using complete encrypted data and encryption keys to guess the original data. The security of the method is determined on the security of the conversion code flow algorithm. Let D_t become a difficult problem for an attacker to guess the original data in the scenario described in this article. Let D become an attacker's difficulty in guessing original data with complete encrypted data without encryption keys. That is. $D = 2^P$, p is the length of the encryption key of the symmetric encryption algorithm. When each data block length is l bits, then $D_t = (2l)^n$, n is the number of data blocks. That is $p \approx l \cdot n$. Supposed, the length of encryption key is equal to the length of data block, that is. $p = n$.

$$\frac{D_t}{D} = l^n \tag{10}$$

As shown by (10), AD-IHSE has at least a higher security than a traditional attacker having encrypted data without encryption keys. The sequences generated by the chaotic system is irregular, the more the number of iterations, the more intense the chaos will be. However, the pseudorandom sequences have inherent regularity because of the system seeds. The last but not the least, the encryption key and the encrypted data are stolen by an attacker, as long as the data owner has deleted the chaotic sequence, the

Table 1. Comparison of security with other schemes

Comparison item	Deletion content	Whether the cipher text is destructed	
FADE in [2]	Decryption key	NO	
Vanish in [3]	Decryption key	NO	
SSDD in [4]	Decryption key and extracted cipher text	YES	
Safe Vanish in [5]	Decryption key	NO	
Two-party in [7]	Decryption key	NO	
ADCSS in [6]	Extracted cipher text	YES	
Our scheme	Information of extracted cipher text	YES	
Comparison item	Whether introduces a third party	Whether can resist brute force attack	Whether can resist cryptography analysis
FADE in [2]	YES	NO	NO
Vanish in [3]	NO	NO	NO
SSDD in [4]	NO	YES	YES
Safe Vanish in [5]	NO	NO	NO
Two-party in [7]	NO	NO	NO
ADCSS in [6]	YES	YES	YES
Our scheme	NO	YES	YES

attacker will only affect the current file. Because of the chaotic characteristics of the logical chaotic mapping, the attacker can not obtain any useful information about the former or the post files. Therefore, the AD-IHSE guarantees the forward secrecy and the backward secrecy.

Table 1 compares our scheme with other security related guaranteed deleting schemes.

5 Implementation and Experimental Analysis

We have done experiments as follows to show both the security of our scheme and the time costs of this process. We have implemented a prototype system of our scheme using JAVA and the experiments are conducted on a PC with Mac OS, Intel Core i5 2.7 GHz Processor and 8 GB Memory.

5.1 Performance of Information Hiding

The Mean Square Error (MSE) and Peak Signal to Noise Ratio (PSNR) are two objective evaluation method. The MSE represents the cumulative squared error between the original image and dense image whereas PSNR represents a measure of the peak error. Suppose $r = n/L$ is the ratio of the length of the secret information to the total number of carrier pixels.

When r is becoming higher, the image quality will be lower. However, the greater the amount of information embedded in the image, the more difficult for the attacker to recover the original data. The PSNR is often expressed on a logarithmic scale in decibels (dB). PSNR values falling below 30 dB indicate a fairly low quality. A high quality Stego should strive for 40 dB and above [11]. Considering the above two factors, this paper chose that 40 dB is more appropriate. As is shown in Fig. 3, the Guides line means that PSNR is 35 dB. r = 2.5.

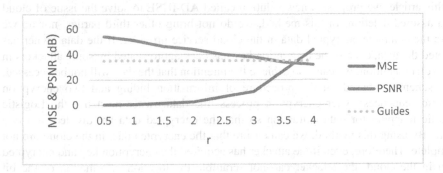

Fig. 3. PSNR changes with the embedding rate

When the carrier image is selected, the number of embedded bits can be determined according to the r calculation formula.

5.2 Time Costs for Data Extraction

This section analyzes the time performance of the cipher text extraction, according to the relationship between the size of the encrypted file and the time consumption. The trend is shown in Table 2.

Table 2. Time costs

File size (M)	1	8	16	32	64	128	256	512	1024
Time for encryption (ms)	24	102	195	380	734	1505	2912	5735	11445
Time for extraction and hiding (ms)	8534	9019	10010	9716	10514	11218	17325	23542	39439
Time for decryption (ms)	16	96	254	366	722	1416	2805	5919	12533
Time for recovery (ms)	8620	9090	10102	11542	11403	11753	17924	24012	40137
Total time (ms)	17194	18307	20561	22004	23373	25892	40966	59208	103554

From Table 2, we can see that the time of extraction and hiding for 1024 M file is less than one minute. The time it takes for the steps we introduce is consumed within a reasonable range. This scheme has a little more time costs, but it gains more security as we had proved in security analysis.

6 Conclusion and Future Works

In this article, we propose a new solution called AD-IHSE to solve the issue of cloud data assured deletion. In this method, we do not bring other third parties, nor do we store the complete encrypted data in the cloud service provider. If the data owner has deleted the data, even if the encryption key has been appropriated by some attackers in the worst condition, we can also achieve the intention that the data will not be accessed. The scheme is based on the procedure of information hiding and two encryption chaotic sequences. After encryption process, the data owner must use the Logistic chaotic mapping for data extraction so that the encrypted data are divided into two parts. By using this method, we can ensure that the encrypted data in the cloud are not complete. Therefore, even if the attacker has acquired the encryption key and encrypted data in the cloud, the attacker can not scramble the location information of the bit stream of the raw data and encrypted data, but can not decrypt the encrypted data in the cloud. So, if the data is determined to be deleted, what we really delete is information about the change location. Finally, security analysis and experimental results show that our method can satisfy the desire of data owners to make sure that deleted data will not be accessed by illegal users. The next work is to consider the optimization of vectors in information hiding.

Acknowledgment. This work was partly supported by the NSFC-Guangdong Joint Found (U1501254) and the Co-construction Program with the Beijing Municipal Commission of Education and the Ministry of Science and Technology of China (2012BAH45B01) and the Fundamental Research Funds for the Central Universities (BUPT2011RCZJ16, 2014ZD03-03) and China Information Security Special Fund (NDRC).

References

1. Perlman, R.: File system design with assured deletion. In: The 14th Annual Network & Distributed System Security, pp. 1–7. IEEE (2007)
2. Tang, Y., Lee, P.P.C., Lui, J.C.S., Perlman, R.: FADE: secure overlay cloud storage with file assured deletion. In: Jajodia, S., Zhou, J. (eds.) SecureComm 2010. LNICST, vol. 50, pp. 380–397. Springer, Heidelberg (2010). https://doi.org/10.1007/978-3-642-16161-2_22
3. Xiong, J., Yao, Z., Ma, J.: A secure document self-destruction scheme with identity based encryption. In: The 5th International Conference on Intelligent Networking and Collaborative Systems, pp. 239–243. IEEE, Xi'an (2013)
4. Wang, G., Yue, F., Liu, Q.: A secure self-destructing scheme for electronic data. J. Comput. Syst. Sci. **79**(2), 279–290 (2013)
5. Zeng, L., Shi, Z., Xu, S., Feng, D.: Safevanish: an improved data self-destruction for protecting data privacy. In: Proceedings of CloudCom, pp. 521–528. IEEE (2010)
6. Zhang, K., Yang, C., Ma, J.F., Zhang, J.W.: Novel cloud data assured deletion approach based on cipher text sample slice. J. Commun. **36**(11), 108–111 (2015)
7. Mo, Z., Qiao, Y., Chen, S.: Two-party fine-grained assured deletion of outsourced data in cloud systems. In: International Conference on Distributed Computing Systems, pp. 308–317. IEEE (2014)
8. Li, C., Chen, Y., Zhou, Y.: A data assured deletion scheme in cloud storage in China. Communications **11**(4), 98–110 (2014)
9. Shahzad, F.: Safe haven in the cloud: secure access controlled file encryption (SAFE) system. In: Science and Information Conference, pp. 1329–1334. IEEE (2015)
10. Patidar, V., Pareek, N.K., Purohit, G., et al.: A robust and secure chaotic standard map based pseudorandom permutation-substitution scheme for image encryption. Opt. Commun. 4331–4339. IEEE (2011)
11. Deshmukh, P.U., Pattewar, T.M.: A novel approach for edge adaptive steganography on LSB insertion technique. In: International Conference on Information Communication and Embedded Systems, pp. 1–5. IEEE (2015)

Performance Analysis of Storm in a Real-World Big Data Stream Computing Environment

Hongbin Yan[1], Dawei Sun[1(✉)], Shang Gao[2], and Zhangbing Zhou[1]

[1] School of Information Engineering, China University of Geosciences,
Beijing 100083, People's Republic of China
{yanhongbin, sundaweicn}@cugb.edu.cn,
zhangbing.zhou@gmail.com
[2] School of Information Technology, Deakin University,
Geelong, Victoria 3216, Australia
shang.gao@deakin.edu.au

Abstract. As an important distributed real-time computation system, Storm has been widely used in a number of applications such as online machine learning, continuous computation, distributed RPC, and more. Storm is designed to process massive data streams in real time. However, there have been few studies conducted to evaluate the performance characteristics clusters in Storm. In this paper, we analyze the performance of a Storm cluster mainly from two aspects, hardware configuration and parallelism setting. Key factors that affect the throughput and latency of the Storm cluster are identified, and the performance of Storm's fault-tolerant mechanism is evaluated, which help users use the computation system more efficiently.

Keywords: Storm · Performance analysis · Stream computing
Big data computing · Big data

1 Introduction

1.1 Background

With the rapid development of the Internet, the amount of data generated by various industries is growing exponentially. It is expected that the amount of data generated worldwide will exceed 80 ZB by 2020, which shows that we have entered the era of big data [1]. Big data contains a lot of useful information; therefore, data analysis and calculation becomes more and more important [2]. In recent years, there have been some data processing systems developed such as Hadoop and Spark which made it possible for us to handle much more data, However, they are not real-time systems, and cannot handle data in real time. Large-scale real-time data processing has become a business need, and the appearance of Storm fills the gap.

As one of the most popular distributed data processing systems, Hadoop has been successfully applied to various industries. It uses a simple programming model for distributed processing of large datasets [3, 4]. While Storm is more like a real-time

I. Romdhani et al. (Eds.): CollaborateCom 2017, LNICST 252, pp. 624–634, 2018.
https://doi.org/10.1007/978-3-030-00916-8_57

Hadoop computing system. It has its own master node and work node that are connected by external resources and submitted with application code to complete calculation tasks like Hadoop. As stated in paper [5, 6], in terms of data processing, especially for batch computing and streaming computing [7], their data processing methods are very different. Hadoop stores the data first, then processes the static data. Hard disk, as the intermediate media of data exchange, needs to read and write data during processing [8]. However, the data of Storm is always stored in memory. The data is read through the network into memory directly. In terms of computing speed, Storm is much faster than Hadoop because of this feature. Storm is therefore being applied in various industries more and more widely.

1.2 Purposes

We have been developing real-time big data processing applications using Storm for years, and understand how important it is to improve the processing efficiency. After investigating all kind of features and mechanisms of Storm, we identify the key factors which affect system throughput capacity and latency. In this paper, we examine the performance of a Storm cluster from two aspects, hardware configuration and parallelism setting, and analyze the influencing factors for throughput capacity and latency. These factors will help users design and implement more efficient applications based on Storm platform.

1.3 Paper Organization

The rest of this paper is organized as follows. Section 2 introduces the components, features and working mechanism of Storm system. Section 3 describes the experimental environment, experimental procedure and experimental results. Section 4 analyzes the factors affecting Storm throughput and latency. Finally, this paper is concluded in Sect. 5.

2 Storm System

2.1 Cluster Composition

Apache Storm is a free and open sourced distributed realtime computation system. The design of Storm makes it easy to process massive streams of data in real time and can be used with any programming language. Storm is mainly used for data stream processing and real-time search [9, 10].

The various components of Storm are shown in Fig. 1:

Nimbus: The master node in a Storm cluster, responsible for sending code in the cluster, assigning tasks, and monitoring the entire cluster state.
Supervisor: The work node in a Storm cluster, responsible for accepting nimbus assigned tasks, starting and stopping their own management of the worker process.
Worker: Worker is a process that runs specific processing component logic.
Executor: Executor is a concrete physical thread in the Worker process.

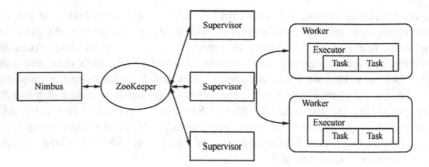

Fig. 1. Structure of a Storm cluster

Task: Task is the work that each component does.

Zookeeper: Zookeeper is an external resource that Storm relies heavily on, connecting the master node and the work node, coordinating the operation of the entire cluster.

Topology: Topology is a real-time application running in Storm, similar to a job in Hadoop, but it will run until it is explicitly killed [11].

As shown in Fig. 2. There are two components in a topology, Spout and Bolt. Spout is a component that generates the source data stream in the topology. Normally a spout pulls data from the outside and then sends it to the Bolt component for its consumption. Bolt is a component that accepts the data sent from Spout and processes it. It can perform filtering, merging, writing database and other operations.

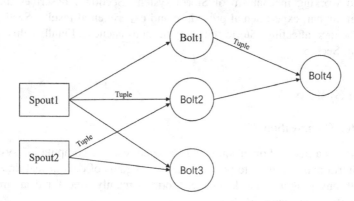

Fig. 2. Structure of a topology in Storm

Tuple is a basic unit of message passing between Spout and Bolt, and the constant Tuple will form a Stream. These data streams can be grouped between two components according to mission requirements [12]. The most common grouping methods are the following four:

- Shuffle Grouping: Randomly distributed tuple to the bolt and each bolt at the same level accepts the same number of Tuples.
- Fields Grouping: Grouped based on the value of the specified one or more fields.
- All Grouping: Copy all tuples to all bolt tasks and use them carefully.
- Global Grouping: Route all tuples to a single task, Storm select the task of receiving data by the latest task ID.

2.2 Work Mechanism

When a client submits a task topology to the master node Nimbus, Nimbus first establishes a local directory based on the configuration information of the topology, instructing zookeeper to assign the task to each work node, finally starts the topology. Supervisors get assigned tasks from Zookeeper and start multiple worker processes, and establish the connection between tasks according to the configuration information of the topology. Now the topology is running. The Storm system provides a UI monitoring interface in master node, through which the client can monitor the running status of the entire cluster in real time. The whole process is shown in the Fig. 3.

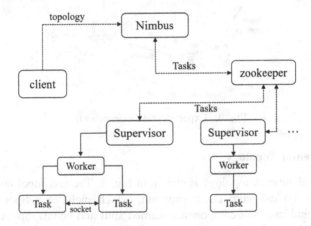

Fig. 3. Workflow of a Storm cluster

The configuration information of the topology and grouping methods might affect the system throughput and latency. We thoroughly examine the Storm features and mechanisms, design and conduct series experiments to investigate the potential factors which might affect the system processing efficiency.

3 Experiment

3.1 Experimental Environment

In this experiment, Storm parallelism and fault tolerance are tested using the following hardware configuration: intel Core i5-2400CPU @ 3.10 GHz × 4, memory 4G, and the operating system is 64-bit ubuntu 16.04 LTS. Twelve (12) machines are used to test parallelism, and ten (10) machines are used to test fault tolerance. For hardware performance test, the following hardware configurations are used: the first group is a Dell desktop computer, with processor intel Core i5-2400CPU @ 3.10 GHz × 4, memory 4G, and 64-bit operating system ubuntu 16.04 LTS; second group is a DELL laptop, with processor Intel (R) Core (TM) i5-2430 M CPU @ 2.4 GHz × 4, memory 8G, and 64-bit ubuntu 16.04 LTS; the third group is a HP laptop, with processor Intel (R) Core (TM) i7-7700HQ CPU @ 2.80 GHz 2.81 GHz, 8G memory, and 64-bit ubuntu 16.04 LTS.

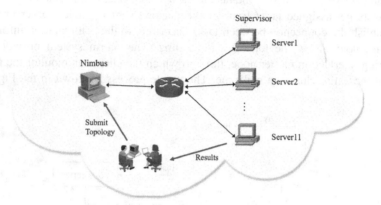

Fig. 4. Experimental environment.

3.2 Experimental Topology

The experimental network topology is shown in Fig. 4. The task topology used in this experiment is a typical word count program, which includes a Spout component (named spout) and two Bolt components (named split and count). Spout components are used to randomly launch English sentences. The split component receives the sentences sent from the spout component and divides it into words, and finally sends it to the count component for word counting. The topology structure is shown in Fig. 5.

3.3 Experimental Process

(1) Parallelism Test

In Storm settings, the degree of parallelism is generally addressed in three areas: a topology specifies how many worker processes run in parallel; a worker process specifies how many executor threads run in parallel; and an executor thread specifies how many tasks run in parallel. In parallelism tests, the first two areas are mainly considered, with each executor assigned one task by default.

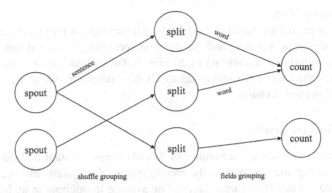

Fig. 5. Structure of the wordcount topology

Firstly, the number of threads assigned to three components spout, split, and count is (5, 8, 12) unchanged, and the number of Workers is set to 1, 3, 6, 12, and 24 respectively.

Secondly, the number of workers for each topology is not changed, and the number of threads increases in turn. The first test sets the number of Worker to 3, the numbers of threads are (5, 8, 12), (10, 16, 24), (15, 24, 36), (20, 34, 48), (25, 40, 60), (50, 80, 120), (100, 160, 240), (150, 240, 360), (200, 320, 480), (250, 400, 600). The second test sets the number of Worker to 12, and the number of threads is the same as the first.

Finally, the number of processes set by the topologies is the same, the total number of threads of all components is unchanged, but the number of threads of each component is adjusted. The number of Worker is set to 3, and the number of threads in the three components is (5, 8, 12), (5, 10, 10), (5, 12, 8), (3, 10, 12) (7, 10, 8), (7, 8, 10), (9, 7, 9), (12, 5, 8), respectively.

(2) Hardware Performance Test

The number of Workers set by the topology and the number of threads for each component are unchanged. The configuration of the three machines is shown in Fig. 6.

PC	CPU	Memory	operating system
DELL Desktop	Intel Core i5-2400 CPU @ 3.10GHz×4	4G	ubuntu 16.04 LTS
DELL Notebook	Intel(R) Core(TM) i5-2430M CPU @ 2.4GHz×4	8G	ubuntu 16.04 LTS
HP Notebook	Intel(R) Core(TM) i7-7700HQ CPU @ 2.80GHz 2.81GHz	8G	ubuntu 16.04 LTS

Fig. 6. Hardware configuration

(3) Robustness Test

We test Storm on fault handling and analyze its impact on throughput and latency. Two special scenarios are designed. In the first scenario, we shut down two of the nodes when the cluster is running up to 20 min. In the second scenario, we shut down one node when the cluster is running up to 20 min. After the two tests, we compare them with the normal scenario.

3.4   Experimental Results

In the parallelism test, when the number of threads keeps constant and the number of Workers in the topology increases, the throughput of the system and the latency of processing data are essentially unchanged. The average throughput in an hour is about 366 Tuple/s. In terms of processing latency, when the number of threads assigned to each component keeps constant and the system becomes stable, as the number of Worker increases, the processing latency does not change much as shown in Fig. 7. It basically remains between 3 and 4 ms.

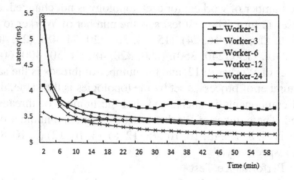

Fig. 7. Latency test results of worker

When the number of Worker in the topology is 3, as the number of threads assigned to each component increases, the average throughput over an hour also increase. Also, if the number of Workers is set to 12, when the number of threads assigned to each component increases, the throughput also increases in a positive correlation. In terms of system latency, as shown in Fig. 8, if the number of Worker in the topology is 3, when the number of threads assigned to each component increase, the processing delay of the system decreases first but then increases. When the number of threads assigned to each component is (50, 80, 120), the processing delay of the system is minimized and then gradually increases. The same result applies when the number of Worker is set to 12, when the delay achieves minimum, the number of threads assigned to each component is (100, 60, 240).

Given the number of processes in topologies keeps the same, the total number of threads of all components unchanged, if the number of threads in the three components is set to (5, 8, 12), (5, 10, 10), (5, 12, 8), (3, 10, 12) (7, 10, 8), (7, 8, 10), (9, 7, 9), (12, 5, 8) respectively, the average throughput and latency during the one-hour testing

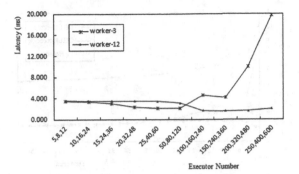

Fig. 8. Latency test results of executor

period are shown in Fig. 9. It is observed that the system throughput is only related to the number of threads assigned to the delivery component spout; when the number of threads assigned to Spout component increases, the system throughput also increases; when the number of threads assigned to Spout component decreases, the system throughput also decreases. In terms of system latency, no matter how the threads are allocated to the three components, the system latency is unchanged, although the delay is mainly caused by the Bolt component (named split), but adding threads to it does not decrease the delay at all.

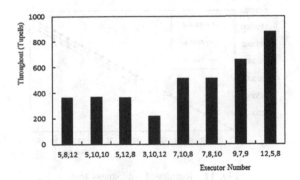

Fig. 9. Throughout test results of thread allocation

In the hardware performance test, when using three different performance computers to run the same topology, the amount of data processed within one hour is basically the same. The average throughput is 366 Tuple/s. But in terms of data processing latency, the DELL laptop with poorer performance has obviously higher latency than the other two as shown in Fig. 10. The average delay of DELL notebook with lowest CPU performance is much higher than the other two during the one-hour testing period. CPU performance has a greater impact on data processing latency than memory.

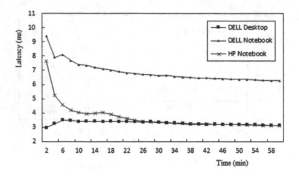

Fig. 10. Results of hardware performance test

In the robustness test, as shown in Fig. 11. In the first test, when two nodes are shut down after 20 min, the system reduces the speed of data processing, because the system has to redistribute the task from the down node. The data processing speed resumes to normal 10 min later. In the second test, we shut down a node after 20 min, the outcome observed is almost the same as the first. There is slight reduction in the number of data processed within one hour in the second test. The average throughput is 361,351,350 Tuple/s. But in terms of system latency, task redistribution does not affect it.

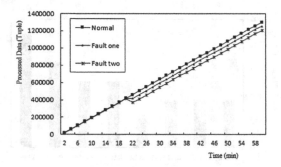

Fig. 11. Results of robustness test

4 Result Analysis

After analyzing the test results, we can conclude that:

- Increasing the number of Worker in a topology alone does not improve system throughput. The throughput of the system has positive correlation to the number of threads assigned to each component and mainly related to the number of threads of components that emit data.
- The latency in data processing is related to Worker number and the number of threads that assigned to each component. However, the impact is limited. Larger

numbers of worker and threads do not lead to a significant low latency. Therefore, a reasonable value is to be set according to different computing tasks. The processing latency is also affected by hardware performance.

- Storm handles faulty nodes quickly. Task redistribution has little impact on the data processing speed and does not increase the data processing latency.

5 Conclusion

In this paper, we test the Storm cluster from three aspects: the parallelism, hardware performance and fault handling. The results observed show that Storm has strong scalability and robustness. For users who use Storm to develop real-time big data processing applications and want to improve the speed of processing, it is recommended that: besides of increasing the number of Worker or threads that assigned to components, the number of the Worker and the threads of individual components should also be set appropriately. To improve the degree of parallelism, both of the CPU performance and system memory should be considered. What's more, each node should leave out memory to accommodate redistributed tasks from failed nodes.

In future work, we are interested in investigating the impact on Storm performance caused by the topology and algorithm complexity. Moreover, we plan to examine the behavior of Storm on receiving data from the cloud and its impact on performance.

Acknowledgment. This work is supported by the National Natural Science Foundation of China under Grant No. 61602428; the Fundamental Research Funds for the Central Universities under Grant No. 2652015338.

References

1. Václav, S., Jana, N., Fatos, X., Leonard, B.: Geometrical and topological approaches to Big Data. Future Gener. Comput. Syst. **67**, 286–296 (2017)
2. Chen, D.Q., et al.: Real-time or near real-time persisting daily healthcare data into HDFS and ElasticSearch Index inside a Big Data platform. IEEE Trans. Ind. Inform. **13**(2), 595–606 (2017)
3. Mavridis, L., Karatza, H.: Performance evaluation of cloud-based log file analysis with Apache Hadoop and Apache Spark. J. Syst. Softw. **125**, 133–151 (2017)
4. Lv, Z.H., Song, H.B., Basanta-Val, P., Steed, A., Jo, M.: Next-generation Big Data analytics: state of the art, challenges, and future research topics. IEEE Trans. Ind. Inform. **13**(4), 1891–1899 (2017)
5. Zhang, J., Li, C.L., Zhu, L.Y., Liu, Y.P.: The real-time scheduling strategy based on traffic and load balancing in storm. In: Proceedings of the 18th International Conference on High Performance Computing and Communications, pp. 372–379. IEEE Press (2016)
6. Xu, J.F., Miao, D.Q., Zhang, Y.J., Zhang, Z.F.: A three-way decisions model with probabilistic rough sets for stream computing. Int. J. Approx. Reason. **88**, 1–22 (2017)
7. Zhang, W.S., Xu, L., Li, Z.W., Lu, Q.H., Liu, Y.: A deep-intelligence framework for online video processing. IEEE Softw. **33**(2), 44–51 (2016)

8. Rahman, M.W., Islam, N.S., Lu, X.Y., Panda, D.K.: A comprehensive study of MapReduce over lustre for intermediate data placement and shuffle strategies on HPC clusters. IEEE Trans. Parallel Distrib. Syst. **28**(3), 633–646 (2017)

9. Karunaratne, P., Karunasekera, S., Harwood, A.: Distributed stream clustering using micro-clusters on Apache Storm. J. Parallel Distrib. Comput. **108**, 74–84 (2017)

10. Cardellini, V., Nardelli, M., Luzi, D.: Elastic stateful stream processing in storm. In: Proceedings of the 14th International Conference on High Performance Computing & Simulation, pp. 583–590. IEEE Press (2016)

11. Shieh, C.K., Huang, S.W., Sun, L.D., Tsai, M.F., Chilamkurti, N.: A topology-based scaling mechanism for Apache Storm. Int. J. Netw. Manag. **27**(3), 1–12 (2017)

12. Li, C.L., Zhang, J., Luo, Y.L.: Real-time scheduling based on optimized topology and communication traffic in distributed real-time computation platform of storm. J. Netw. Comput. Appl. **87**, 100–115 (2017)

Collaborative Next Generation Networking

Shortest Path Discovery in Consideration of Obstacle in Mobile Social Network Environments

Dawei Sun[1(✉)], Wentian Qu[1], Shang Gao[2], and Li Liu[3]

[1] School of Information Engineering, China University of Geosciences,
Beijing 100083, People's Republic of China
`sundaweicn@cugb.edu.cn, qunty496047796@163.com`
[2] School of Information Technology, Deakin University,
Geelong, VIC 3216, Australia
`shang.gao@deakin.edu.au`
[3] School of Automation and Engineering, University of Science
and Technology Beijing, Beijing 100083, People's Republic of China
`liuli@ustb.edu.cn`

Abstract. The issue of shortest path discovery in consideration of obstacle is one of the problems for location-based services in mobile social network environments. Currently, most research focuses on quickly discovering the shortest path in obstacle free area with reasonable latency, while the obstacle issue, especially the obstacles that enter temporarily is not fully considered. This creates the need for investigation on shortest path discovery at the same time avoiding detected obstacles. In this paper, a shortest path discovery approach is proposed. The following contributions are made: (1) Modeling the shortest path discovery problem in consideration of obstacle. (2) Discovering the shortest path using an improved A-star algorithm with reasonable latency. (3) Evaluating the accuracy rate of shortest path discovery with acceptable latency for a location-based service in a mobile social network. Experimental results conclusively demonstrate the efficiency and effectiveness of the proposed approach.

Keywords: Mobile social network · Location-based service
Shortest path discovery · A-star algorithm

1 Introduction

1.1 Background and Motivation

In the era of big data, mobile social network, as one of the major application scenes, is playing a more and more important role in our daily lives. It is advised that nearly all services in a mobile social network are location-based. If a mobile social network scene can be abstracted as a large-scale graph, composed of vertex set and edge set, location-based services can be achieved by manipulating the large-scale graph. For example, the shortest path discovery is alway one of the most important search queries for large-scale graph, and has received intense attention owing to its broad applications, such as

© ICST Institute for Computer Sciences, Social Informatics and Telecommunications Engineering 2018
I. Romdhani et al. (Eds.): CollaborateCom 2017, LNICST 252, pp. 637–646, 2018.
https://doi.org/10.1007/978-3-030-00916-8_58

path planning in mobile social network, vehicle routing in traffic network, and package routing in computing network [1, 2].

It is common that obstacles exist between locations in location-based in application scenarios. For example, part of an optimal path is under construction or there are road work on the path, so this "shortest path" is no longer an ideal shortest path. The shortest path only considering physical distance is not alway work well, and needs to take into account the actual obstacles, especially these temporary ones. The issue of shortest path discovery in consideration of obstacle is realistic and one to-be-resolved problem for location-based service. Currently, most research only considers quickly discovering the shortest path with reasonable latency, while the obstacle is not fully considered [3, 4]. It is necessary to consider the avoidance of existing and temporary obstacles while discovering the shortest path.

1.2 Contributions

Motivated by the above discussion, and our previous work [5], we propose the shortest path discovery approach in consideration of obstacle (ASPO) for location-based services in a mobile social network environment. In this paper, we move one step further to a real world application scenario in a large-scale graph based experimental environment. Three aspects of ASPO are covered and summarized as follows: (1) Modeling the shortest path discovery problem in consideration of obstacle. (2) Discovering the shortest path using an improved A-star algorithm with a reasonable latency. (3) Evaluating accuracy rate of the shortest path discovery approach with acceptable latency. Experimental results conclusively demonstrate the efficiency and effectiveness of the proposed approach.

1.3 Paper Organization

The remainder of this paper is organized as follows. In Sect. 2, the modeling of the shortest path discovery problem in consideration of obstacle is presented. Section 3 focuses on the detailed discussion of the ASPO. Section 4 addresses the experimental environment, parameter setup and performance evaluation of the ASPO. Conclusions are given in Sect. 5.

2 Problem Statement

This section focuses on modeling the shortest path discovery problem in consideration of obstacle in a mobile social network environment [6, 7].

The mobile social network environment can be described as a grid, and the location-based service can be represented as a connected graph G, as shown in Fig. 1. The graph G is composed of a vertex set and a directed edge set, denoted as $G = (V, E)$, where $V = \{v_1, v_2, \cdots, v_n\}$ is a finite set that contains n vertices. Each vertex represents a location of service or user. $E = \{e_{1,2}, e_{1,3}, \cdots, e_{n-i,n}\} \subset V \times V$ is a

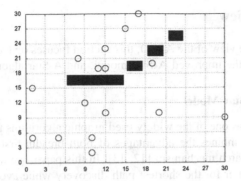

Fig. 1. Location-based services and obstacles in a grid (points of hollow circle are the location of service/user, and points of black squares are the location of existing or temporary obstacles)

finite set of directed edges, which represents reachable paths between two related vertices. If $\exists e_{i,j} \in E$, then $v_i, v_j \in V$, $v_i \neq v_j$, the weight $w_{i,j}$ associated with an edge $e_{i,j}$ represents the distance from v_i to v_j. If an obstacle is on $e_{i,j}$, then $e_{i,j}$ is a reachable path from v_i and v_j, and $e_{i,j}$ should be discovery immediately, and removed or avoided from the directed edge set E.

Let v_s and v_d be a source and destination vertex, respectively, and $P_{s,d} = \{p_{s,d}^1,$ $p_{s,d}^2, \cdots, p_{s,d}^m\}$ be a set of available path set between v_s and v_d in the grid. Length $L_{s,d}^i$ of the ith path $p_{s,d}^i$ can be calculated by (1).

$$L_{s,d}^i = \sum_{e_k \in E^i(v_s, v_d)} l_{e_k}, \tag{1}$$

where $E^i(v_s, v_d)$ is the edge set of the ith path $p_{s,d}^i$, and l_{e_k} is the length of edge e_k.

The shortest path length between v_i and v_j in consideration of obstacle is defined as the average number of steps along the shortest paths for all available path set P between v_i and v_j. Updating the obstacle information in grid, if an obstacle is on a path between v_i and v_j, the path is removed from available path set.

The shortest path discovery problem [8, 9] is to discover the shortest path length $SL_{s,d}$ connecting two specified vertices v_s and v_d with reasonable latency, can be described as (2).

$$SL_{s,d} = \min(P_{s,d}), s.t. L_{s,d}^i < rs - lat. \tag{2}$$

where rs-lat is a pre-set acceptable latency threshold for one specific location-based service.

If the grid has millions of vertices or edges, millions of available paths can be selected, resulting in unbearable latency.

3 ASPO Overview

To provide a bird-eye view of the ASPO, this section focuses on the detailed discussion of ASPO, including the improved A-Star model, and A-Star algorithm [10, 11].

3.1 Improved A-Star Model

A-Star is considered as one of the widely used graphic algorithms for its simplicity and performance, as it combines the advantages of both breadth-first graphic search and depth-first graphic search mechanism [12, 13]. In this paper, we modify the algorithm and make it work better for the shortest path discovery while avoiding obstacle.

Evaluation function $f(n)$, described as (3), is the sum of function $g(n)$ and $h(n)$, used to guide the visiting order of vertices in the search space.

$$f(n) = g(n) + h(n), \tag{3}$$

where $g(n)$ can be calculated by Dijkstra's algorithm [14], described as (4), is the distance of the optimal path from the source vertex v_s to the current vertex v_n, and $h(n)$, calculated by (5), is the heuristic estimated distance of the optimal path from the current vertex v_n to the destination vertex v_d.

$$g(n) = g(n') + 1, \tag{4}$$

where $v_{n'}$ is direct predecessor vertex on the path from the source vertex v_s to the current vertex v_n.

$$h(n) = d(v_c, v_d, \alpha, \beta) + d'(V_c, v_d, \alpha, \beta), \tag{5}$$

where $d(v_c, v_d, \alpha, \beta)$ is a Manhattan distance [15] with adjustment parameter α and β. It can be calculated by (6). V_c is the set vertices of the vertices on the path from v_s to v_c, and $d'(V_c, v_d, \alpha, \beta)$ can be calculated by (7)

$$d(v_s, v_c, \alpha, \beta) = \alpha \cdot |x_{v_s} - x_{v_c}| + \beta \cdot |y_{v_s} - y_{v_c}|, \tag{6}$$

where $\alpha \in [0, 1]$, $\beta \in [0, 1]$, and $\alpha + \beta = 1$.

$$d'(V_c, v_d, \alpha, \beta) = \frac{1}{m} \sum_{i=1}^{m} d(v_{c(i)}, v_d, \alpha, \beta) \tag{7}$$

where $v_{c(i)} \in V_c$, and m is the number of vertices on the path from v_s to v_c.

3.2 Improved A-Star Algorithm

The improved A-Star model can be further described by an improve A-Star algorithm. The improved A-Star algorithm maintains two tables [16], an OPEN table and a CLOSE table. The OPEN table is used to keep the vertices to be searched with least evaluation function $f(n)$ to select next optimal vertex based on priority. The CLOSE table is used to keep the vertices that have already been searched and examined [17, 18].

The improved A-Star algorithm is described in Algorithm 1.

Algorithm 1: improved A-Star algorithm.

Input: location-based service in a grid environment, the source vertex v_s, and the destination vertex v_d of the service.

Output: the shortest path in consideration of obstacle from source vertex v_s to destination vertex v_d in the grid.

1.   Initialize OPEN table, CLOSE table.
2.   Add source vertex v_s to OPEN table. Set CLOSE table is NULL.
3.   **while** OPEN table is not NULL **then**
4.   Delete the highest priority vertex v_h from OPEN table
5.   Add the vertex v_h to CLOSE table.
6.   **if** vertex v_h is the destination vertex v_d **then**
7.   **break.**
8.   **end if**
9.   **if** vertex v_h can be spreading **then**
10.   **for** each spreader vertex v_i of vertex v_h **do**
11.   Check whether vertex v_i is in OPEN table or CLOSE table.
12.   **if** vertex v_i is not in the OPEN table and CLOSE table and not a obstacle **then**
13.   Add the vertex v_i to the OPEN table.
14.   Calculate priority by evaluation function $f(n)$.
15.   **else**
16.   **if** vertex v_i is the on the path from source vertex v_s to vertex v_h **then**
17.   Delete vertex v_i.
18.   **else**
19.   Spread vertex v_i and calculate priority by evaluation function $f(n)$.
20.   **end if**
21.   **end if**
22.   **end for**
23.   Sort all vertices in OPEN table by priority in ascending order.
24.   **end if**
25. **end while**
26. return the shortest path in consideration of obstacle from source vertex v_s to destination vertex v_d in the grid.

The inputs of the improved A-Star algorithm are location-based service in a grid environment, the source vertex v_s, and the destination vertex v_d of the service. The output is the shortest path in consideration of obstacle from source vertex v_s to destination vertex v_d in the grid. Step 3 to step 25 are to discover the shortest path from source vertex v_s to destination vertex v_d.

4   Experiments and Performance Evaluation

Experiments are conducted to evaluate the performance of the proposed ASPO. Experimental environment and parameter settings are firstly discussed in this section, followed by performance evaluation results.

4.1   Environment and Parameter Setup

In the experimental environment, one machine is employed. The machine runs Windows 10 with dual 4-core, Intel Core i5-4200, 2.5 GHz, 8 GB Memory, and a 100 Mbps network interface card. The mobile social network environment is simulated as a 1000 × 1000 grid environment.

4.2   Performance Evaluation

The experiment evaluates the impact of search time and search depth.

(1) Search time

The search time is the time to discover the shortest path in consideration of obstacle in a grid environment.

Relationship of search depth and search time with different distances between source vertex v_s and obstacle is shown in Fig. 2. The distance between destination vertex v_d and obstacle is 300 units, and the length of obstacle is 1600 units. When varying the distance between source vertex v_s and obstacle from 50 to 300 units, the corresponding average search time is 1.1 s, 1.2 s, and 1.3 s, respectively. The shortest path is discovered within 5 depths.

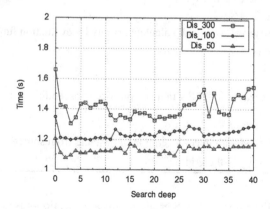

Fig. 2. Relationship of search depth and search time with different distances between source vertex v_s and obstacle

Relationship of search depth and search time with different distances between destination vertex v_d and obstacle is shown in Fig. 3. The distance between source vertex v_s and obstacle is 300 units, and the length of obstacle is 1600 units. When varying the distance between destination vertex v_d and obstacle from 50 to 300 units, the corresponding average search time is 2.3 s, 2.2 s, and 1.4 s, respectively. The shortest path is discovered within 5 depths.

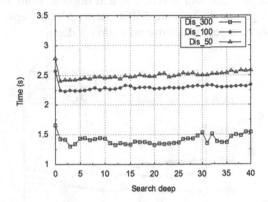

Fig. 3. Relationship of search depth and search time with different distances between destination vertex v_d and obstacle

Relationship of search depth and search time with different length of the obstacle is shown in Fig. 4. The distance between source vertex v_s and obstacle is 300 units, and the distance between the destination vertex v_d and obstacle is also 300 units. When varying the length of the obstacle from 1500 to 1800 units, the corresponding average search time is 1.8 s, 1.4 s, 3.4 s, and 4.3 s, respectively. The shortest path is discovered within 5 depths.

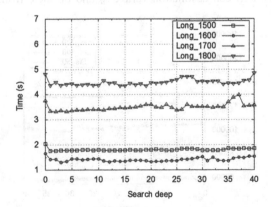

Fig. 4. Relationship of search depth and search time with different long of the obstacle

(2) Search depth

The search depth is the level of search depth to discover the shortest path in consideration of obstacle in a grid environment.

Relationship of search depth and search time with different distances between source vertex v_s and obstacle is shown in Fig. 5. The distance between destination vertex v_d and obstacle is 300 units, and the length of obstacle is 1600 units. When varying the distance between source vertex v_s and obstacle from 50 to 300 units, the corresponding average search steps are 55000 steps, 57000 steps, and 59000 steps, respectively. The shortest path is discovered within 3 depths.

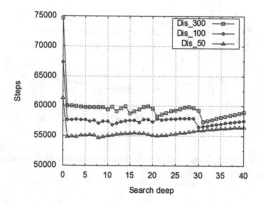

Fig. 5. Relationship of search depth and search steps with different distances between source vertex v_s and obstacle

Relationship of search depth and search time with different distances between destination vertex v_d and obstacle is shown in Fig. 6. The distance between source vertex v_s and obstacle is 300 units, and the length of obstacle is 1600 units. When varying the distance between destination vertex v_d and obstacle from 50 to 300 units,

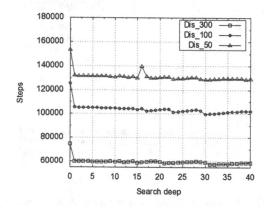

Fig. 6. Relationship of search depth and search steps with different distances between destination vertex v_d and obstacle

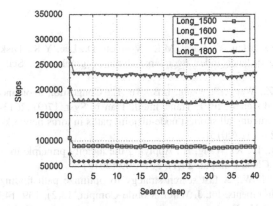

Fig. 7. Relationship of search depth and search steps with different length of the obstacle

the corresponding average search steps are 130000 steps, 110000 steps, and 59000 steps, respectively. The shortest path is discovered within 2 depths.

Relationship of search depth and search time with different lengths of the obstacle is shown in Fig. 7. The distance between source vertex v_s and obstacle is 300 units, the destination vertex v_d and obstacle is also 300 units. When varying the length of the obstacle from 1500 to 1800 units, the corresponding average search steps are 89000 steps, 59000 steps, 170000 steps, and 220000 steps, respectively. The shortest path is discovered within 2 deeps.

5 Conclusions

In this paper, the shortest path discovery approach ASPO in consideration of obstacle for location-based services in a mobile social network environment is proposed. Our work and contributions are summarized as follows: (1) Modeling the shortest path discovery problem in consideration of obstacle. (2) Discovering the shortest path in a location-based mobile social network via an improved A-star algorithm with reasonable latency. (3) Evaluating accuracy rate of shortest path discovery with acceptable latency for a location-based service.

Acknowledgment. This work is supported by the National Natural Science Foundation of China under Grant No. 61602428 and 61370132; the Fundamental Research Funds for the Central Universities under Grant No. 2652015338.

References

1. Hong, J., Park, K., Han, Y., Rasel, M.K., Vonvou, D., Lee, Y.K.: Disk-basedshortest path discovery using distance index over large dynamic graphs. Inf. Sci. **382–383**, 201–215 (2017)
2. He, K., Xu, Z.Z., Wang, P., Deng, L.B., Tu, L.: Congestion avoidance routing based on large-scale social signals. IEEE Trans. Intell. Transp. Syst. **17**(9), 2613–2626 (2016)
3. Lai, C.N.: Constructing all shortest node-disjoint paths in torus networks. J. Parallel Distrib. Comput. **75**, 123–132 (2015)
4. Wang, X., Li, J., Li, X., Wang, H.: Applying the locality principle to improve the shortest path algorithm. Clust. Comput. **20**(1), 301–309 (2017)
5. Qu, W.T., Sun, D.W.: A fast search strategy to optimize path finding in big data graph computing environments. Int. J. Wirel. Mobile Comput. **13**(2), 139–143 (2017)
6. Mao, G., Zhang, N.: Fast approximation of average shortest path length of directed BA networks. Phys. A Stat. Mech. Appl. **466**, 243–248 (2017)
7. Huang, W., Wang, J.: The shortest path problem on a time-dependent network with mixed uncertainty of randomness and fuzziness. IEEE Trans. Intell. Transp. Syst. **17**(11), 3194–3204 (2016)
8. Feng, G., Korkmaz, T.: Finding multi-constrained multiple shortest paths. IEEE Trans. Comput. **64**(9), 2559–2572 (2015)
9. Sang, Y., Lv, J., Qu, H., Yi, Z.: Shortest path computation using pulse-coupled neural networks with restricted autowave. Knowl. Based Syst. **114**, 1–11 (2016)
10. AlShawi, I.S., Yan, L., Luo, W., Pan, W., Luo, B.: Lifetime enhancement in wireless sensor networks using fuzzy approach and A-star algorithm. IEEE Sens. J. **12**(10), 3010–3018 (2012)
11. Wei, Q., Liang, X., Fang, J.: A new star identification algorithm based on improved hausdorff distance for star sensors. IEEE Trans. Aerosp. Electron. Syst. **49**(3), 2101–2109 (2013)
12. Li, B., Sun, Q., Zhang, T.: A star pattern recognition algorithm for the double-FOV star sensor. IEEE Aerosp. Electron. Syst. Mag. **30**(8), 24–31 (2015)
13. Huang, J., Sun, L., Du, F., Wan, H., Zhao, X.: Genetic adaptive A-star approach for ttrain trip profile optimization problems. In: Proceedings of the 2014 IEEE Symposium on Computational Intelligence in Vehicles and Transportation Systems, CIVTS 2014, pp. 1–6. IEEE Press (2014)
14. Zhang, X.G., Chan, F.T.S., Yang, H., Deng, Y.: An adaptive amoeba algorithm for shortest path tree computation in dynamic graphs. Inf. Sci. **405**, 123–140 (2017)
15. Chiu, W.Y., Yen, G.G., Juan, T.K.: Minimum manhattan distance approach to multiple criteria decision making in multiobjective optimization problems. IEEE Trans. Evolut. Comput. **20**(6), 972–985 (2016)
16. Ghaffari, A.: An energy efficient routing protocol for wireless sensor networks using A-star algorithm. J. Appl. Res. Technol. **12**(4), 815–822 (2014)
17. Cui, X., Shi, H.: A*-based pathfinding in modern computer games. Int. J. Comput. Sci. Netw. Secur. **11**(1), 125–130 (2011)
18. Ducho, F., et al.: Path planning with modified a Star algorithm for a mobile robot. Procedia Eng. **96**, 59–69 (2014)

Minimize Residual Energy of the 3-D Underwater Sensor Networks with Non-uniform Node Distribution to Prolong the Network Lifetime

Gaotao Shi[1,2]($\boxtimes$), Jia Zeng[1,2], Chunfeng Liu[1,2], and Keqiu Li[1,2]

[1] School of Computer Science and Technology, Tianjin University, Tianjin, China
[2] Tianjin Key Laboratory of Advanced Networking (TANK), Tianjin, China
{shgt,jiazeng,cfliu}@tju.edu.cn, likeqiu@gmail.com

Abstract. Underwater sensor networks (UWSNs) have caused widespread concern of academia due to their wide range of applications. Efficient energy depletion and avoiding energy holes are the important issues. In this paper, we study on the theoretical aspects of the non-uniform node distribution strategy in the 3-D underwater environment, which aim to mitigate the energy holes and balance energy depletion of nodes in the 3-D underwater sensor networks. Based on extensive analysis and theoretical proofs, the absolute balanced energy depletion in the whole underwater sensor networks is not achievable, while the maximized balanced energy depletion except for the nodes in the outermost *AGR* (Annular Globular Region) is possible. Furthermore, we propose a non-uniform distribution routing algorithm based the minimum energy consumption called MEC to address the energy hole problems and prolong the network lifetime. Extensive simulations show that the network achieves a high energy efficiency, less than 5% of total initial energy is wasted and the network lifetime is prolonged more than 400% compared with the uniform node distribution strategy.

Keywords: Underwater sensor networks · Energy holes
Minimize residual energy · Non-uniform node distribution
Load balancing

1 Introduction

As the application extension of the traditional terrestrial wireless sensor networks, the underwater sensor networks (UWSNs) enable application for underwater data collection, ocean sampling and assisted navigation. Due to the complicated underwater environment and node energy constraint, it is difficult to obtain a perfect deployment strategy which ensures high energy efficiency, long network lifetime, strong connectivity and low costs of whole networks.

In the UWSNs, energy constraint is a big challenge. The traffic scheme is many-to-one, and the nodes nearer to the sink will forward more data than

© ICST Institute for Computer Sciences, Social Informatics and Telecommunications Engineering 2018
I. Romdhani et al. (Eds.): CollaborateCom 2017, LNICST 252, pp. 647–659, 2018.
https://doi.org/10.1007/978-3-030-00916-8_59

the nodes far away from the sink. Therefore, the nodes near to the sink will consume more energy, even die because of using up their initial energy. At the same time, an energy hole occurs around the sink. Many existing works focus on planar networks [1–4], while those deployment schemes and algorithms are very difficult to directly apply to 3-D underwater situations [5–8]. Intuitively, the 3-D networks are more suitable for real-life situations.

Olariu et al. [4] first prove that the energy hole is unavoidable under some situations in traditional circular terrestrial region WSNs. In a circular area, Wu et al. [1,2] prove completely balanced energy consumption among all nodes is impossible. Akbar et al. [5] use a mobile sink node i.e., AUV, in each sub rectangular cuboid region. Although they can achieve energy efficiency and avoid energy hole in some cases, however, the AUVs will spend much extra money and deplete much energy on controlling the moving trajectory.

In this paper, we explore the energy hole problem by means of theoretical analysis and mathematical models in the UWSNs with the non-uniform node distribution strategy. Firstly, we divide the spherical region into different annular globular regions ($AGRs$, as shown in Fig. 1). Secondly, we analyze and prove that the absolute balanced energy depletion (ABED) is not achievable among all nodes which are equipped the same initial energy. Then, the maximum balanced energy depletion (MBED) is possible among all nodes with non-uniform deployment in the UWSNs through theoretical analysis. Finally, we carry out extensive simulations to evaluate the performance of the proposed non-uniform distribution strategy and the proposed routing algorithm.

The main contributions of this paper can be summarized as follows. We theoretically prove that the absolute balanced energy depletion in the whole UWSN is not achievable, while the maximized balanced energy depletion except for the nodes in the outermost AGR_K is possible. The proposed the non-uniform node distribution strategy of the 3-D UWSNs can achieve high energy efficiency and prolong the network lifetime. We carry out extensive simulation experiments to evaluate the performance of the proposed schema. The simulation results show that the proposed schema achieve a high energy efficiency and less than 5% of total initial energy is wasted. Moreover, the network lifetime can be prolonged more than 400% compared with the uniform node distribution strategy.

The remainder of this paper is organized as follows. In Sect. 2, related work will be presented. Assumptions and network models will be introduced in Sect. 3. Theoretical analysis and the proposed routing algorithm are illustrated in Sect. 4. Section 5 presents the simulation results of the proposed non-uniform node distribution strategy. Finally, we conclude this paper in Sect. 6.

2   Related Work

Pal et al. [10] propose a centralized cluster head selection scheme based on genetic algorithm. The proposed scheme aims at selecting an optimal cluster head in different clusters according to their residual energy and taking trade-off of inter- and intra-cluster communication distance into account. Different from [9], the proposed scheme in [10] takes trade-off of inter- and intra-cluster communication distance into account for optimizing cluster heads instead of just considering the Eulerian distance between each nodes like in [9]. Therefore, they can achieve better balanced energy depletion in the WSNs. The proposed method in [11] addresses the energy depletion problem via introducing various states of a node such as sleep, idle, start-up and busy for conserving energy as much as possible. They utilize a randomized N-policy queuing model to derive the probabilities of various states, not similar to [12], in which the switch of different states just depends on a fixed time threshold, i.e., when a specific time is used up, the state of the node will change immediately.

Wang et al. [13] take node mobility and density of water into account and proposed EGRCs scheme that can select optimal cluster heads considering residual energy and locations of sensor nodes. The proposed algorithm also decides the next-hop by combining residual energy, locations and end-to-end delay.

Khan et al. [14] utilize an AUV as a mobile sink to collect data from cluster heads and propose a distributed data-gathering scheme. The proposed scheme can control the topological changes in a small range. Hence, it can avoid energy hole phenomenon and balance energy depletion to some extent. Chen et al. [12] propose a mobile geocast routing to tackle the energy unbalanced problem in the underwater environment by introducing the sleep/active modes, thus the proposed protocol minimizes the energy depletion of the sensor nodes.

3   Assumptions, Definitions and Network Model

We assume that all nodes are distributed in a spherical region with spherical center O and radius R. The unique special relay node (SRN) is located at the center of the spherical region, which is shown in Figs. 1 and 2. All sensors have an unique ID number used to identify them and its transmission radius is $r(r \ll R)$. Note that we ignore the size of nodes. We divide the spherical region into K adjacent annular globular regions $(AGRs)$ with the same width of $\frac{R}{K}$, where K is the number of $AGRs$. We denote the $i-th$ annular globular region as AGR_i and nodes are uniformly deployed in AGR_i with the density $\rho_i(\rho_{i-1} \neq \rho_i, 2 \leq i \leq K)$. As shown in Fig. 1, the darker AGR shows a higher node density. The upper radius R_U and lower radius R_L are $\frac{R}{K}i$ and $\frac{R}{K}(i+1)$, respectively. We assume that each node sends data at a certain rate H which means a sensor node generates and sends H bits of data per unit time. We assume that ε energy will be depleted when a node transmits or receives a bit of data. Similar to [1,2], we assume that there is no data aggregation at any forwarding nodes and the initial energy of each node is E_{init}. Due to the need to forward data collected by other nodes to the sink on surface of the water, we assume the SRN has no energy limitation. Furthermore, we assume that a node consumes different energy when sending and receiving a bit of data. For simplicity, e_t and e_r units of energy will be depleted respectively when sending and receiving a bit of data. We assume that e_t, e_r are constant and satisfy the limitation $e_t > e_r > 0$.

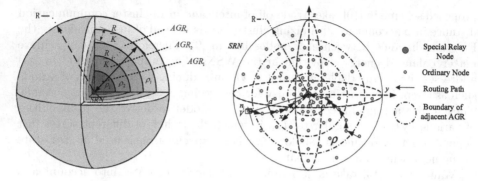

Fig. 1. A spherical region consisting with multiple annular globular
regions (*AGRs*).

Fig. 2. Network model in a spherical region
with non-uniform node distribution strategy.

4 Theoretical Analysis and Routing Strategy of Non-uniform Node Distribution

A. The Energy Depletion Model of Non-uniform Node Distribution

We define the load of node n as $load_n$ which presents the energy that node n consumes because of sending and receiving data. The average load of node n is $\overline{load}_n$ which presents an average load over both a time period and a subset of nodes within the transmission range of n. Obviously, the $\overline{load}_n$ is distance-variant.

Motivated by [3], we discuss the energy load of a node. Given a node n_i that is at distance d from the SRN, as shown in Fig. 1. The geographic average load taken by this node is in proportion to $\frac{V_1\rho_i+V_2\rho^*}{V_1\rho_i}$.

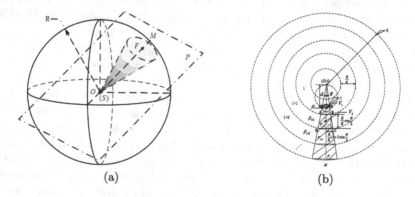

(a)   (b)

Fig. 3. Non-uniform node distribution in a spherical region. (b) is sectional view of (a) by plane P.

Intuitively, all the traffic routing from both region V_1 and V_2 have to through nodes in region V_1 shown in Fig. 3(b). The average energy that a node in region V_2 consumes to forward the data to the SRN can be calculated as the intensity pressure:

$$\overline{load}_{in_i} = \frac{V_1\rho_i + V_2\rho^*}{V_1\rho_i}H\varepsilon \tag{1}$$

where $V_1\rho_i = \frac{1}{2} \cdot \frac{4}{3}\pi r^3 \rho_i = \frac{2}{3}\pi r^3 \rho_i$, $V_2 = V_{i+1} + V_{i+2} + \cdots + V_K + V_{ABFE}$, $\rho^* = \{\rho_j\}, j = i+1, \ldots, K$. For the sake of simplicity, we approximately regard the region V_i as a circular truncated cone. The simple calculation process of $\overline{load}_{in_i}$ as follows, when $d > r$:

$$V_2\rho^* \approx \frac{1}{3}\pi\frac{R}{K}cos\frac{\theta}{2}\left(\left(\frac{R}{K}\right)^2 sin^2\frac{\theta}{2} \cdot \sum_{j=i+1}^{K}[(j-1)^2 + j^2 + (j-1)j]\rho_j \right.$$
$$\left. + [(\frac{R}{K}isin\frac{\theta}{2})^2 + r^2 + \frac{R}{K}ir sin\frac{\theta}{2}]\rho_i\right) \tag{2}$$

Applying Eq. (2), the Eq. (1) can be rewritten as:

$$\overline{load}_{in_i}$$
$$\approx \begin{cases} \frac{\frac{R}{K}cos\frac{\theta}{2}((\frac{R}{K})^2 sin^2\frac{\theta}{2}\cdot\sum_{j=i+1}^{K}[(j-1)^2+j^2+(j-1)j]\rho_j+[(\frac{R}{K}isin\frac{\theta}{2})^2+r^2+\frac{R}{K}ir sin\frac{\theta}{2}]\rho_i)H\varepsilon}{2r^3\rho_i} + 1, & d > r, \\ (\frac{R}{K})^3 \cdot \sum_{i=1}^{K}[i^3 - (i-1)^3]\rho_i H\varepsilon, & d \leq r \end{cases} \tag{3}$$

where $\theta = 2arcsin(r/d)$. Figure 4(a) presents the average load of a sensor node. With the distance increasing between the node and the SRN, the average of load of a node decreases sharply. It illustrates that the nodes near to the SRN will use up their initial energy quickly.

Figure 4(b) illustrates that the load of nodes in the outermost AGR_K is never equal to the load of nodes in the inner $AGRs$, even though there are different densities in different $AGRs$. However, we can observe that there exist different

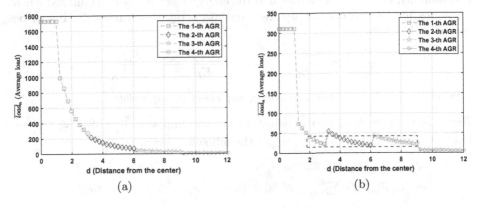

(a)   (b)

Fig. 4. (a) Load distribution with a stationary SRN at the place of the center of sphere. We assume $R = 12$, $K = 4$, $r = 1$, $H = 1$, $\varepsilon = 1$ and $\rho_1 = \rho_2 = \rho_3 = \rho_4$; (b) Except for $\rho_1 \neq \rho_2 \neq \rho_3 \neq \rho_4$, the other parameters are same to (a).

densities in inner $AGRs$ except for the outermost AGR_K that make their load balanced (see the dotted area in Fig. 4(b)). In other words, the ABED is not achievable and the MBED is possible.

B. Energy Depletion Analysis of Non-uniform Node Distribution

Let N_i present the number of nodes in the AGR_i and E_i present the energy consumed per unit time by the nodes in the AGR_i. $H[e_t + (bw)^2]$ presents the consumed energy per unit time with the distance bw, where b is coefficient of energy depletion; w is the width of two adjacent $AGRs$. The parameters K, e_t and e_r are defined in Sect. 3.

According to the above assumptions, the energy of the outermost AGR_K consumed per unit time can be computed as:

$$E_K = N_K H[e_t + (bw)^2]$$

Note that the nodes in the outermost only need to forward data collected by themselves. The nodes in other $AGRs$ have to forward both the data generated by themselves and the data generated by nodes near to them. The energy consumed in the AGR_i can be computed as:

$$E_i = H\Big(\sum_{j=i+1}^{K} N_j(e_t + (bw)^2 + e_r) + N_i[e_t + (bw)^2])\Big) \tag{4}$$

Thus, we can merge E_i as follows:

$$E_i = \begin{cases} N_K H[e_t + (bw)^2], & i = K, \\ H\Big(\sum_{j=i+1}^{K} N_j(e_t + (bw)^2 + e_r) + N_i[e_t + (bw)^2])\Big), & 1 \leq i \leq K-1 \end{cases} \tag{5}$$

C. Impossibility of the Absolute Balanced Energy Depletion

Intuitionally, the network lifetime and the energy efficiency are maximized when all nodes in the network use up their initial energy simultaneously. It can be formalized as follows:

$$\frac{N_1 E_{init}}{E_1} = \frac{N_2 E_{init}}{E_2} = \cdots = \frac{N_{K-1} E_{init}}{E_{K-1}} = \frac{N_K E_{init}}{E_K} \tag{6}$$

Claim 1: *An absolute balanced energy depletion is impossible.*

Proof. Similar to [3,6], we use rebuttal to prove. Suppose $\frac{N_{K-1} E_{init}}{E_{K-1}} = \frac{N_K E_{init}}{E_K}$ holds. Combining Eq. (5), we can get the following formula:

$$N_{K-1} E_{init} N_K H[e_t + (bw)^2]$$
$$= N_K E_{init} H\Big(\sum_{j=i+1}^{K} N_j[e_t + (bw)^2 + e_r] + N_{K-1}[e_t + (bw)^2]\Big) \tag{7}$$

After simplifying Eq. (7), we can get the following equation:

$$N_K[e_t + (bw)^2 + e_r] = 0 \tag{8}$$

Obviously, the Eq. (8) is impossible, i.e., the assumption is impossible, thus the Eq. (6) is impossible. The ABED is never achieved.   □

D. The Maximized Balanced Energy Depletion

In the last part, we have proved the impossibility of ABED, but except for nodes in the outermost AGR_K, there exists a maximized balanced energy depletion in other $AGRs$, in which nodes can use up their initial energy at the same time.

Claim 2: *The Maximized Balanced Energy Depletion is achievable, i.e., the system can achieve a maximum energy efficiency among all AGRs except for the outermost AGR_K.*

Proof. Suppose the following equation holds.

$$\frac{N_i E_{init}}{E_i} = \frac{N_{i+1} E_{init}}{E_i}, 1 \leq i \leq K - 2 \tag{9}$$

Combining Eq. (5) and after simplification and basic transformations, we can rewrite Eq. (9) as:

$$\frac{N_i}{N_{i+1}} = \frac{\sum_{j=i+1}^{K} N_j}{\sum_{j=i+2}^{K} N_j}, 1 \leq i \leq K - 2 \tag{10}$$

We denote N as the total number of nodes in the whole network, i.e., $N = \sum_{j=1}^{K} N_j$. By *Equal Ratios Theorem*, we get the following equation:

$$\frac{N_i}{N_{i+1}} = \frac{N_{i-1}}{N_i}, 2 \leq i \leq K - 2 \tag{11}$$

Thus, if we satisfy the Eq. (11), the Eq. (9) can hold. In other words, if we make $\frac{N_i}{N_{i+1}} = q, 1 \leq i \leq K - 2$ satisfied, the Maximized Balanced Energy Depletion is achieved. Where q is a proportional constant.   □

E. Routing Strategy With Non-uniform Node Distribution

In this part, we introduce the non-uniform distribution routing algorithm called MEC (Minimum Energy Consumption). Different from [1,2], the proposed MEC not only considers the distance between two nodes but also considers the all neighbor nodes near to the node, which can allow each node to make full use of their initial energy.

The proposed MEC is based on the previous sections. Before the all nodes are deployed, we first calculate the coordinate of each node according to the proportional constant q and ensure that any node has at least q relay nodes in its upstream AGR. Thus, we can derive a set of upstream neighbor nodes (upList) and a set of neighbor nodes (neiList). To reduce energy consumption, a node should select one optimal relay node in upList or neiList according to the maximum residual energy and the distance between them. The pseudo-code of the proposed routing algorithm is presented in Algorithm 1.

Algorithm 1. Routing strategy with non-uniform node distribution

---

1: The function of the proposed algorithm: Data are forwarded by node i

Input: Net: consists of many nodes marked with unique ID

2: N = Net[i] // N represents the i-th node in the Net

3: **if** IsNotEmpty(N.upList) **then**

4:     K = SelectNextNodeWithMinConsumedEnergy (N, N.upList)

5: **else if** IsNotEmpty(N.neiList) **then**

6:     K = SelectNextNodeWithMinConsumedEnergy (N, N.neiList)

7: **else**

8:     DiscardMsg

9: **end if**

10: SendDataTo(K)

11: UpdateResidualEnergy (N, K)

12: UpdateNetWork (Net)

---

5   Simulations Evaluation

In this Section, we evaluate the performance of the non-uniform node distribution with the proposed routing algorithm. We assume a perfect MAC layer to ensure wireless channel communication, as in [2,15,16]. The experimental parameters are listed in Table 1. Note that all the simulation results of our simulation experiments are averaged over 1000 independent runs.

Table 1. Experimental parameters

Parameter	Value
Initial energy of each node (E_{init})	500 units
System constant (e_t)	7.510^3 unit
Receiving energy cost (e_r)	510^3 unit
Energy depletion coefficient (b)	1
Unit time	60 s
The amount of data sent per second (H)	10 units
Proportional constant (q)	2, 3
Transmission range (r)	1, 2
Radius of the spherical region R	5–12

A. Residual Energy of Each Node

We deploy 2000 nodes in a spherical region with a radius 8. The transmission range of each node is 2, and the proportional constant is 3. There are 50, 150, 450, 1350 nodes in AGR_4, AGR_3, AGR_2 and AGR_1 respectively. Figure 5 shows the residual energy of each node when the network lifetime ends. Nodes with a smaller ID numbers means near to the SRN while those with large ID number belong to the outer AGR_4. The four fragments of lines are not straight lines but have tiny fluctuations.

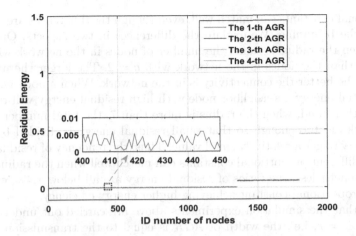

Fig. 5. Residual energy of each node when the network lifetime ends, where $N = 2000$, $q = 3$ and $K = 4$.

We notice that the nodes near to the SRN nearly use up their initial energy while the nodes in outermost AGR_K have much residual energy. This phenomenon is in line with our previous analysis. The reason for this phenomenon is that the nodes near to the SRN need to transmit both the data collected by themselves and the data forwarded by nodes in downstream, which makes their energy burn up quickly. Whereas, the nodes in the outermost AGR_K only need to transmit the data collected by themselves.

B. Residual Energy Ratio

When the network lifetime ends, the residual energy can be computed as:

$$E_{res} = \sum_{i=1}^{K} \sum_{j=1}^{N_i} (E_{init} - E_{ij}) \tag{12}$$

where E_{init} presents the initial energy of each node, and E_{ij} donates the $j-th$ node in the $i-th$ AGR. The total number of the network is given as:

$$N = \frac{N_K(q^K - 1)}{q - 1}, q > 1 \tag{13}$$

Thus, the residual energy ratio is

$$\lambda = \frac{E_{res}}{N E_{init}} = \frac{(q - 1) \sum_{i=1}^{K} \sum_{j=1}^{N_i} (E_{init} - E_{ij})}{N_K E_{init}(q^K - 1)} \tag{14}$$

As shown in Fig. 6, the residual energy ratio decreases rapidly when the radius is less than 6, but there is slow change when the radius exceeds 7. With the growth of the network radius, the tendency of residual energy ratios in different proportional constants can match well, even though the differences are relatively large at the beginning. We explain the differences in two aspects. On the one hand, when the radius is same, the number of nodes in the network with $q = 3$ are more than the nodes in the network with $q = 2$. The larger the number of nodes is, the better the connectivity is in the network. When a node nearly uses up its initial energy, its neighbor node with high residual energy will replace it. On the other hand, when the radius is more than 7, the total number of nodes in network are too enough so that small residual energy is divided by a large total energy to get a relatively small value. Thus, the tendency of residual energy ratios in different proportional constants can match well when the radius is more than 7. Nonetheless, the ratios of residual energy are all below 1.4%, even with a small proportional constant achieving higher energy efficiency.

Note that the simulation experiments above are carried out under the condition of $w = r$, i.e., the width of AGR is equal to the transmission range of a node. The next simulation, we relax this constraint. Figure 7 illustrates the residual energy ratio under different widths of AGR and different proportional constants. We obverse that the ratios of residual energy decrease greatly at the beginning but decrease slowly (for example, $K = 3$, $q = 3$; $K = 4$, $q = 3$) or increase slowly (for example, $K = 3$, $q = 2$) when the radius of network exceeds a threshold. Comparing with Fig. 6, under the premise of same radius, the residual energy ratios in Fig. 6 are all less than those in Fig. 7. Thus, we can draw the conclusion that the best strategy is to design all the $AGRs$ to be of the same width and the best width of AGR is equal to r. We explain why the residual energy ratios will increase slowly when the radius of network exceeds a threshold under the premise of $K = 3$, $q = 2$. On the one hand, when the radius exceeds a threshold (9 or 10), the volume of the outermost AGR_K becomes larger and larger with the radius increasing. On the other hand, the number of nodes in the outermost AGR_K is fixed, and the connectivity of the outermost AGR_K begins to decrease. Those eventually leads to an increase in residual energy ratio.

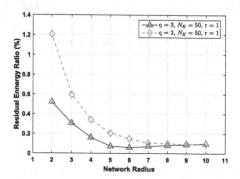
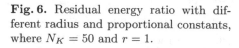
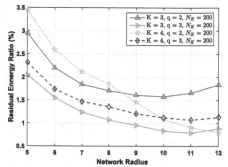

Fig. 6. Residual energy ratio with different radius and proportional constants, where $N_K = 50$ and $r = 1$.

Fig. 7. Residual energy ratio under different widths of AGR, where $K = 3, 4$, $q = 2, 3$, $N_K = 200$ and $r = 1$.

C. Comparison with Uniform Node Distribution

In this part, we perform simulations to compare the proposed strategy with the uniform node distribution strategy in the two aspects: (1) the residual energy ratios and (2) the network lifetime. *Uniform Node Distribution*, where nodes are deployed at any place with equal probability, and different from non-uniform node distribution strategy, the number of nodes in each AGR is linearly related to the volume of the AGR. Figure 8 shows the simulation results of different node distribution strategies. We observe that the residual energy ratios of network with uniform node distribution are greatly higher than that of network with non-uniform node distribution. The residual energy ratios remain related stable when the radius exceeds a threshold (7, approximately) and increase greatly at the beginning with the uniform node distribution strategy. While the network with non-uniform node distribution strategy performs well. This also illustrates the effectiveness of the proposed node distribution strategy.

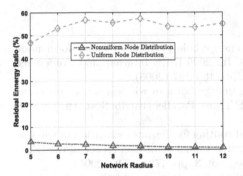
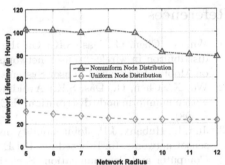

Fig. 8. Residual energy ratios of different node distribution, where $K = 4, q = 2, r = 1, N_K = 200$ under non-uniform node distribution; and $r = 1$ under uniform node distribution.

Fig. 9. Network lifetime of different node distributions, where $K = 4, q = 2, r = 1, N_K = 200$ under non-uniform node distribution simulations; and $r = 1$ under uniform node distribution.

Figure 9 shows the network lifetime (the duration till the death of the first node in the whole network) using the two strategies: (1) the uniform node distribution and (2) the non-uniform node distribution. We obverse that the network lifetime of the network with non-uniform node distribution are more than four times greater than those of the network with uniform node distribution. There is a downward trend when the radius is greater than 9. We explain this phenomenon as follows. On the one hand, with the increasing of the radius exceeding a threshold, the number of nodes in the network is more and more (exceed a threshold), and the load in the innermost AGR is greater and greater, thus, the nodes in the innermost AGR use up their energy relatively fast. On the other hand, when the radius exceeds a threshold, the number of relay nodes around a node is very close to $q(q = 3)$, and the number of optional relay nodes for a node is reduced and its load increases, thus, those nodes will die early.

6   Conclusions

In this paper, we propose a non-uniform node distribution strategy to address the energy hole issue in the 3-D underwater sensor networks consisting of a static SRN and other ordinary sensor nodes. We also propose a new routing algorithm that the distance between two adjacent nodes is considered in the non-uniform node distribution strategy. In our extensive simulations, the network achieves a high energy efficiency, less than 5% of total initial energy is wasted and the network lifetime is prolonged more than 400% compared with the uniform node distribution strategy.

Acknowledgments. This work was supported in part by the National Natural Science Foundation of China (NSFC) under Grant No. 60903193, No. 61402327, and the Tianjin Research Program of Application Foundation and Advanced Technology under Grant No. 12JCQNJC00200.

References

1. Wu, X., Chen, G., Das, S.K.: On the energy hole problem of nonuniform node distribution in wireless sensor networks. In: 2006 IEEE International Conference on Mobile Ad Hoc and Sensor Systems, pp. 180–187 (2006)
2. Wu, X., Chen, G., Das, S.K.: Avoiding energy holes in wireless sensor networks with nonuniform node distribution. IEEE Trans. Parallel Distrib. Syst. **19**, 710–720 (2008)
3. Jun, L., Hubaux, J.P.: Joint mobility and routing for lifetime elongation in wireless sensor networks. In: Proceedings IEEE 24th Annual Joint Conference of the IEEE Computer and Communications Societies, vol. 3, pp. 1735–1746 (2005)
4. Olariu, S., Stojmenovic, I.: Design guidelines for maximizing lifetime and avoiding energy holes in sensor networks with uniform distribution and uniform reporting. In: Proceedings 25th IEEE International Conference on Computer Communications, IEEE INFOCOM 2006, pp. 1–12 (2006)
5. Akbar, M., Javaid, N., Khan, A., Imran, M., Shoaib, M., Vasilakos, A.: Efficient data gathering in 3D linear underwater wireless sensor using sink mobility. Sensors **16**, 404 (2016)
6. Wang, Z., Wang, B.: A novel node sinking algorithm for 3D coverage and connectivity in underwater sensor networks. Ad Hoc Netw. **56**, 43–55 (2017)
7. Jiang, P., Liu, J., Wu, F., Wang, J., Xue, A.: Node deployment algorithm for underwater sensor networks based on connected dominating set. Sensors **16**, 388 (2016)
8. Abbasi, J.S., Javaid, N., Gull, S., Islam, S., Imran, M., Hassan, N.: Balanced energy efficient rectangular routing protocol for underwater wireless sensor networks. In: 2017 13th International Wireless Communications and Mobile Computing Conference (IWCMC 2017), pp. 1634–1640 (2017)
9. Chunawale, A., Sirsikar, S.: Minimization of average energy consumption to prolong lifetime of Wireless Sensor Network. In 2014 IEEE Global Conference on Wireless Computing and Networking (GCWCN), pp. 244–248 (2014)
10. Pal, V., Yogita, G.S., Yadav, R.P.: Cluster head selection optimization based on genetic algorithm to prolong lifetime of wireless sensor networks. Procedia Comput. Sci. **57**, 1417–1423 (2015)

11. Nidhi, M., Goswami, V.: A randomized N-policy queueing method to prolong lifetime of wireless sensor networks. In: Proceedings of 3rd International Conference on Advanced Computing, Networking and Informatics, vol. 1, pp. 347–357 (2016)
12. Chen, Y.S., Lin, Y.W.: Mobicast routing protocol for underwater sensor networks. IEEE Sens. J. **13**, 737–749 (2013)
13. Wang, K., Gao, H., Xu, X., Jiang, J., Yue, D.: An energy-efficient reliable data transmission scheme for complex environmental monitoring in underwater acoustic sensor networks. IEEE Sens. J. **16**, 4051–4062 (2016)
14. Khan, J., Cho, H.-S.: A distributed data-gathering protocol using AUV in underwater sensor networks. Sensors **15**, 19331 (2015)
15. Ramos, H.S., Boukerche, A., Oliveira, A.L.C., Frery, A.C., Oliveira, E.M.R., Loureiro, A.A.F.: On the deployment of large-scale wireless sensor networks considering the energy hole problem. Comput. Netw. **110**, 154–167 (2016)
16. Kumar, V., Kumar, S.: Energy balanced position-based routing for lifetime maximization of wireless sensor networks. Ad Hoc Netw. **52**, 117–129 (2016)

Combinational Meta-paths Mining
for Correlation Relationship Evaluation
in Bibliographic Networks

Qinchen Wu, Peng Wu, and Li Pan[✉]

National Engineering Laboratory for Information Content Analysis Technology,
School of Electric Information and Electrical Engineering,
Shanghai Jiao Tong University, 800 Dong Chuan Rd, Shanghai, China
panli@sjtu.edu.cn

Abstract. Correlation relationships between objects are pervasive in heterogeneous information networks such as bibliographic networks, which made it possible to evaluate proximity between nodes from different perspectives. To explain these semantically rich correlations, meta-paths formed by interconnected node types and edge types have been widely used. This means, using meta-paths and their combinations we can explicitly evaluate relationships between nodes, and thus made it possible to search for proximate nodes according to specific correlations they carried. In this paper, we propose a combinational meta-paths mining algorithm to evaluate correlation relationships between nodes in bibliographic networks. Experiments with bibliographic networks have proved its effectiveness with respect to prior knowledge based results.

Keywords: Heterogeneous information networks · Meta-paths
Correlation relationships · Node-pairs proximity

1 Introduction

Heterogeneous Information Networks (HIN) are graph structures containing multiple typed nodes and edges, where diversities in node and edge types make them carry rich semantics [1, 2]. To explain these semantics, meta-paths that formed by sequence of node and edge types have been widely used [3–5]. Due to diversity of correlations between nodes in HIN, it is preferred to explain them with combinational meta-paths to ensure their semantical completeness. For example, in bibliographic networks that contain node types Paper (P), conference (C), Author (A) and Topic (T), we can describe correlations carried by example pair (Jiawei Han, Philip S. Yu) using combinational meta-path <A-P-A, A-P-T-P-A, A-P-C-P-A> to explain their correlations. These meta-paths have been widely used in recommendation system, information retrieval, link prediction [6–9] in HINs.

Combinational meta-paths provide us solution to describe correlations between nodes in HINs, but we can't greedily include infinite paths. To tackle this problem, we propose combinational meta-path mining (CMPM) algorithm to describe inter-nodes

© ICST Institute for Computer Sciences, Social Informatics and Telecommunications Engineering 2018
I. Romdhani et al. (Eds.): CollaborateCom 2017, LNICST 252, pp. 660–669, 2018.
https://doi.org/10.1007/978-3-030-00916-8_60

correlations in HINs. This algorithm only requires single example pair as input, and it begins with top-k shortest path searching algorithm to find candidate meta-path that connects source and target nodes. Then, weighting the meta-paths with path instances distribution information, and refining candidate meta-paths by maximizing their correlation semantics. Extensive experiments on two bibliographic networks (ACM and DBLP) have proved its effectiveness. Moreover, CMPM detects new meta-paths that are not able to be given by domain knowledge.

The rest of the paper is organized as follows. Section 2 reviews existing methods in meta-paths mining. Section 3 explains basic concepts and definitions in this paper. Then, implementation details of CMPA algorithm are given in Sect. 4. Section 5 evaluates CMPM's effectiveness by detecting proximate nodes. Finally, we conclude this paper in Sect. 6.

2 Related Work

Meta-path has been widely used in HIN related studies to explain their rich semantics, but dependences on prior knowledge have limited their usages in practical applications. Early research by Yizhou Sun et al. [1] summarize meta-paths mining methods into domain knowledge based methods [9, 10], exhaustive trail-selection methods and statistical learning methods [11, 12]. The first category can give concise meta-paths by domain experts when correlation relationships and HINs are simple enough, but they are fragile to outside interference. The trail-selection methods require exhaustive greedy search for meaningful paths, such operation is time consuming when the given heterogeneous information network is large. The third learning algorithm based category relies more on high quality training data. Specific algorithm such as Path Ranking [11] aims at using pre-provided single path as input to obtain optimal path weighting coefficients. AMIE [13] tries to mining meta-paths based on association rules in data, but suffers from global solution. FSPG [12] iteratively selects currently the most relevant meta-path by using step selection but requires highly quality positive/negative example pairs.

Traditional meta-paths mining algorithms as mentioned previously heavily relies on prior knowledge, which limited their usage in large scale heterogeneous information networks. Other automatic path mining algorithms such as Path Ranking, AMIE are either constrained by uncertain hyper-parameter or high computational expenses. In facing with these facts, our CMPM algorithm only takes single example pair as input. Except for this, CMPM also avoids greedy path searching with YenKSP.

3 Problem Definition

In this section, we introduce basic concepts and definitions in combinational meta-paths mining for correlation relationships description.

Heterogeneous Information Network (HIN) is the core concept in this paper. It contains multiple type of nodes and edges [1]. Bibliographic network is typical HIN.

Definition 1. Heterogeneous Information Network is directed graph structure $G = (V, E, \Phi, \Psi)$ with nodes from V interconnected with each other by edge from E. Functions $\Phi : v \rightarrow A$ and $\Psi : E \rightarrow R$ in the network specifies mapping relationships from node $v \in V$ to node type $\Phi(v) \in A$ and from edge $e \in E$ to edge type $\Psi(e) \in R$.

Compared with traditional homogeneous network, HINs generally carry richer semantics because of $|A| > 1$ or $|R| > 1$. To describe the rich semantics, we use meta-paths [1, 3, 15].

Definition 2. Meta-Path carries correlation semantics between interconnected nodes in HINs. Meta-path is defined as $\Pi^{1,2,\dots,l} = A_1 \xrightarrow{R_1} A_2 \xrightarrow{R_2} \dots \xrightarrow{R_{l-1}} A_l$, where l is the path length, A_i and R_i with $i \in [1, l]$ are node type and edge type respectively.

Definition 3. Combinational meta-paths $F_{(s,t)} = \{(\Pi_i, w_i), 1 \le i \le P\}$ carry correlation semantics within the sample, where $\Pi_i, 1 \le i \le P$ are P single meta-path, w_i are weights for Πi as a measure of importance, which subject to $\sum_{i=1}^{P} w_i = 1$ and is solved according to path instances distributions.

Using $F_{(s,t)}$ given by (s, t), the correlation semantics intensity vector associated with it is $f_{(s,t)} = \{\omega_i \sigma((x, y)|\Pi_i), 1 \le i \le P\}$, where $\sigma((s,t)|\Pi_i)$ is semantic intensity score measured with nodes similarity function. One fact should be strengthened here; we quantify semantics intensity as similarity score because classical node similarity measures such as PathSim [1], HeteSim [10], Path Constrained Random Walk [11] are all meta-paths based, and node-similarity relationship is exception of more general concept of nodes correlations. To find proximate node pair (x, y) that sharing similar correlations as (s, t), we calculate $f_{(x,y)} = \{w_i \sigma(x, y)|\Pi_i, 1 \le i \le P\}$.

Then, the proximity between node pair (s, t) and (x, y) by their correlation semantics is given as,

$$Rsim((x, y)|(s, t)) = 1/Euc(f_{(x,y)}, f_{(x,t)}) \tag{1}$$

where $Euc(a, b)$ is Euclidean distance between vector a and b. We will use the formula to achieve proximate node pairs searching in experiments and evaluate CMPM's effectiveness.

4 Combinational Meta-paths Mining

The implementation of Combinational Meta-Path Mining Algorithm (CMPM) is based on two basic assumptions: (1) shorter meta-paths generally carry more significant semantics, and longer meta-paths are good at ensuring semantic completeness; (2) path instance distribution in network is relevant to path importance, it can be used to weight meta-paths. Rational behind the first assumption is intuitive, long path can bring remote weak-connected neighboring nodes into path searching steps, which undermines the discriminative ability between node pairs [1]. For the second assumption, distribution of path instance is implicitly influenced by path length, using it as path weighting reference can balance semantics carried by meta-paths of different length. Follow the basic assumptions, we implement combinational meta-path mining algorithm in two steps: candidate meta-paths preliminary screening step and path refinement step, as showed by flow chart in Fig. 1.

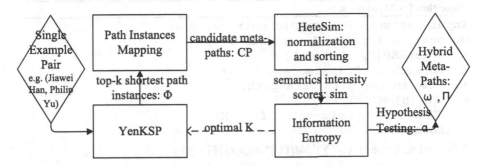

Fig. 1. Flow chart of CMPM implementation steps.

In candidate meta-paths preliminary screening step, CMPM uses YenKSP algorithm [16] to obtain representative path instances that connect nodes in example pair. YenKSP starts with shortest path algorithms to find path instance P^1 connects (s,t). Then, setting node in $P^{t-1}(2 \leq t \leq K)$ one after another as deviation point, and defining sub-path from source to deviation node as root path R_i^t. Subsequently, starting from deviation point to find another shortest path to target and define as spur path S_i^t. Finally, merge them as $P_i^t = R_i^t + S_i^t$ and push into a priority queue to pop the shortest one as P^t. Repeat the process until all top-k shortest path instances in Φ are found. We map paths in Φ to candidate meta-paths $CP=\{\Pi_i, 1 \leq i \leq Q\}$, where Q is the number of candidate meta-paths. During the path mapping step, we also record number of path instances included with respect to each unique meta-path as $M = \{\Pi_1 : n_1, \Pi_2 : n_2, \ldots, \Pi_Q : n_Q\}$.

Path refinement is the main step of this paper. Number of path instances mapped to each meta-path is defined as $n_i = M[\Pi_i]$, it implicitly reflects significance of specific path by their degree of prevalence in HINs. We weight Π_i by $w_i = n_i / \sum_{i=1}^{Q} M[\Pi_i]$ to show relative meta-path importance. Now, weighted candidate meta-paths still contain redundancies. We can remove them by calculating their semantical significance. Using HeteSim, the semantic intensity score corresponds to $\omega_i \Pi_i$ is $\omega_i * \sigma(s,t|\Pi_i, G)$ as defined in Sect. 3, and we store them in vector sim. Next, scores in sim are normalized and sorted in descend order, and paths in CP are also updated accordingly to maintain one-by-one matching relationship between meta-path and corresponding semantic score. Semantic intensity scores in sim actually describe the likelihood that given example pair carries semantics specified by meta-paths in CP. This made it reasonable to use information entropy [17] to measure the expected semantics carried by combinational meta-paths. Define global entropy for candidate meta-paths CP as H, we use statistical hypothesis test to remove redundant meta-paths. Because each time we add meta-path from CP into combinational meta-paths, corresponding entropy will increase step by step until it covers $1 - \alpha$ of H, where α (5%–10%) is the significance level. As a result, there exists P genuinely selected single meta-paths from CP, and we update their weights again using $\omega_i = n_i / \sum_{i=1}^{P} M[\Pi_i]$.

Algorithm 1: CMPM (G, s, t)

Input: network G, example pair (s, t)
Output: meta paths Π, weights ω
1: Φ←**YenKSP**(G, s, t, k);
2: **foreach** path instance φ in Φ:
3:     π←mapping φ to meta-path;
4:     M [π]←M [π] +1;
5: CP←candiate meta-paths from M;
6: **foreach** (π, n) in M:
7:     sim.insert($n / \sum_{i=1}^{Q} M[\Pi_i] * \sigma((s,t)|\Pi,G)$);
8: sim=sim/ $\sum_{i=1}^{Q} sim[i]$;
9: sim.sort();
10: CP←update candidate paths accordingly;
11: H = sim.entropy()
12: **foreach** similarity score s in sim:
13:    area←area-s*log(s);
14:    if area/H<1-α:
15:       Π.insert(CP[sim.index(s)]);
16: **foreach** π in Π:
17:    ω.insert($M[\Pi]/\sum_{k\in\Pi} M[k]$);
18: **return** Π, ω

According to description above, Algorithm 1 gives the detailed implementation of CMPM. The most time consuming part of CMPM is YenKSP, which occupies $O(KV(E + V \log V))$ if search for shortest path using Fibonacci heap [16], where K, E, V are path instance numbers, edge and node numbers. In path refinement step, the time complexity is $O(QL^2)$ if using dynamic programming based HeteSim [10] to measure semantic intensity scores, where Q is candidate meta-paths numbers and L is maximum meta-paths length among all meta-paths.

5   Experiments and Analysis

In this section, we perform proximate node pairs detection in HINs to validate the effectiveness of CMPM algorithm. In experiments, we use bibliographic networks ACM and DBLP from Artminer [14] archived in 2016. In preprocessing step, we remove data before 2006, and only reserve papers published in top conference related to data mining, information retrieval, database system and AI, finally only 16310 and 24332 papers are remained. In algorithm evaluation step, we use CMPM to mine author-similarity correlations and author-publication correlations between given example pairs. Equation (1) is used to detect proximate node pairs carrying similar correlation semantics as that defined by combinational meta-paths given previously. Because there has no benchmark for author-similarity correlation comparison, we collect paper-citations, h-index, i10-index and scholar-closeness data from Google Scholar as $\lambda = (citations, h\_index, i10\_index, ranking)$, and ranking benchmarks by calculating Euclidean distance with respect to $\lambda_{JiaweiHan}$,

$$\Delta = \|\lambda_{others} - \lambda_{JiaweiHan}\| \tag{2}$$

the smaller Δ is the researcher will be more similar with Jiawei Han.

In meta-paths mining step for author-similarity correlations, we choose (Jiawei Han, Philip S. Yu) as example pair, because they have high publication and citation index in data mining area, and their work also have been recognized by peers. Most importantly, they share no extra close correlation like teacher-student, colleges, classmates. Path mining results given by CMPM in our experiment shows that single meta-path A-P-T-P-A has the largest weight among combinational meta-paths, and A-P-A-P-A, A-P-C-P-A follows. This phenomenon suggests us that research interests, co-authorships and conferences are vital to describe researcher's similarity in academic capability.

Then, we detect proximate node pairs similar to (Jiawei Han, Philip S. Yu) using Eq. (1), and Jiawei Han is set as source node for simplicity. Nodes detection results constrained under CMPM based combinational meta-paths and prior knowledge based meta-paths (controlled groups have meta-paths APA, APTPA, APCPA and their simple combinations PriorComb) are listed in Table 1. It shows node pairs searching results under CMPM in both datasets are more likely to find top researchers such as Jian Pei, Xifeng Yan, Charu Aggarwal and Christos Faloutsos than that of controlled groups. This means, meta-paths given by CMPM do capture meaningful correlation semantics carried by example pair, and they also outperform prior knowledge based ones.

Table 1. Top 5 node pair proximity searching results for author-similarity correlation relationships with ACM and DBLP datasets.

Rank	CMPM	APA	APTPA	APCPA	PriorComb
	ACM datasets				
1	PhilipS.Yu	JiaweiHan	Jiawei Han	JiaweiHan	PhilipS.Yu
2	JianPei	XifengYan	PhilipS.Yu	PhilipS.Yu	Jia Pei
3	XifengYana	PhilipS.Yu	ChrisFaloutsos	MarianneWinslett	XifengYan
4	CharuAggarwal	JianPei	CharuAggarwal	ChrisFaloutsos	YizhouSun
5	ChrisFaloutsos	YizhouSun	JianPei	CharuAggarwal	ChiWang
	DBLP datasets				
1	PhilipS.Yu	JiaweiHan	PhilipS.Yu	JiaweiHan	PhilipS.Yu
2	CharuAggarwal	XifengYan	Jiawei Han	PhilipS.Yu	YizhouSun
3	JeffreyXuYu	YizhouSun	CharuAggarwal	CharuAggarwal	Dong Xin
4	ChristosFalouts	PhilipS.Yu	MarianneWinsle	JeffreyXuYu	XifengYan
5	XifengYan	Dong Xin	ChristosFalouts	ChristosFaloutsos	XiaoleiLi

Table 1 only shows a general profile of performance advance by CMPM, so we introduce normalized degree of disorder [18] as a measure,

$$D(\Phi, \Phi') = \begin{cases} 2/N^2 \sum_{k=t_1}^{t_n} |\Phi'[k] - \Phi[k]|, & n \in even \\ 2/(N^2 - 1) \sum_{k=t_1}^{t_n} |\Phi'[k] - \Phi[k]|, & n \in odd \end{cases} \tag{3}$$

where $\Phi = \{t_1 : 1, t_2 : 2, \ldots, t_n : n\}$ contains rankings in google benchmarks and Table 1.

It calculates normalized deviation between Φ and Φ', smaller deviation means better searching results. Precision, recall and F1-score are also used in experiments. Results under the four measuring schemas with ACM datasets are showed in Fig. 2. In (a), it shows degree of disorder for node pair searching results using meta-paths CMPM, APA and PrioriComb, where disorder value for CMPM constrained results consistently smaller than the prior knowledge based results, this means searching

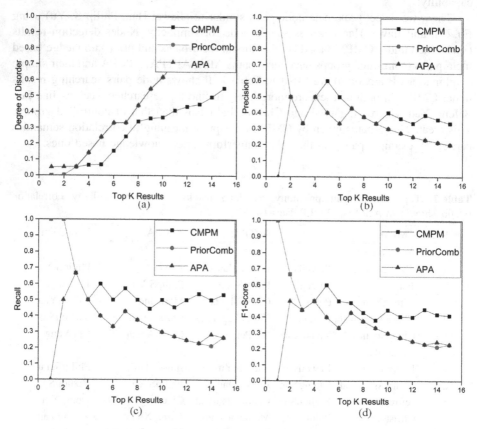

Fig. 2. Normalized degree of disorder, precision, recall, and F1-score measuring results for proximate node pairs detection results under ACM datasets.

results under CMPM will be closer to google benchmarks we proposed previously. Except for low degree of disorder using CMPM, we also find that the performance boost for CMPM will be enlarged when we request for more top K node pairs. This means, the overall searching results measured by degree of disorder will be better than that showed in (a). In (b) and (c), we use precision and recall as a measure. Results from precision and recall showed us that CMPM based searching results outperform both PriorComb and APA, and CMPM seems to have pretty good performance when measured with recall. To compromise the measures given by precision and recall, (d) is measured with F1-score, which prefers higher precision and recall. It's obvious to observe that CMPM has higher F1-score than the other two prior knowledge based meta-paths. Moreover, one common phenomenon under the four measures is that results for PriorComb and A-P-A are very close to each other, this signaling us that if meta-paths are not genuinely weighted, correlation semantics may at the risk of being covered by their their counterparts. On the other hand, top 3 searching results by PriorComb are close to CMPM based results, but their gaps gradually enlarged. This means prior knowledge based meta-paths do carry vital correlation semantics, but their depth is weaker than CMPM based combinational meta-paths. To validate scalability of CMPM, we use example pair (Jiawei Han, SIGKDD) to reveal author-publication correlation relationships. After similar experiment procedure, results are showed in Table 2. We rate the ranking result with scores between 0–2, represent irreverent, some-relevant and complete-relevant. Then nDCG [19] is used to measure ranking accuracy based on ranking positions in the list with scores between 0–1, the higher the better. It shows, in both datasets, CMPM still outperforms prior knowledge based PriorComb.

Table 2. Top 10 node pairs proximity searching results for author-publication correlation relationships, where nDCG scores are given below.

Rank	ACM		DBLP	
	CMPM	PriorComb	CMPM	PriorComb
1	SIGKDD	SIGKDD	SIGKDD	SIGKDD
2	SIGMOD	SIGMOD	TKDD	TKDD
3	VLDB	VLDB	TWEB	TWEB
4	SIGIR	SIGIR	DKE	EDBT
5	TKDD	TKDD	IPM	DKE
6	TODS	AI	EDBT	IPM
7	TOIS	CVPR	SIGMOD	SIGIR
8	TWEB	TODS	SIGIR	SIGMOD
9	SDM	ACL	VLDB	ICDE
10	WWW	TOIS	ICDE	WWW
nDCG	0.74	0.61	0.57	0.50

We also studied the influence of path instance numbers to YenKSP based preliminary screening, it shows entropy carried by candidate meta-paths increase steadily at beginning, but it slows down immediately when path instance numbers exceed some thresholds. This hints us to choose optimal K for YenKSP. All experiments are performed on Dell XPS 8900 with eight 3.4 GHz Intel i7-6700 CPUs and 16 GB of memory, the time consumed in CMPM based meta-paths mining for the author-similarity example pair are 132.9 s under ACM datasets and 153.1 s under DBLP datasets (initial path instance numbers are all set to 500).

In summary, author-similarity and author-publication based correlation relationships mining experiments in this section have proved the effectiveness of CMPM algorithm in combinational meta-paths mining. Experiment results showed us that meta-paths mined by CMPM carry more complete correlation semantics than prior knowledge based meta-paths, and it also captures subtler semantics. Additionally, path weighting schema in CMPM also balance semantics carried by each single meta-path, which prevents global semantics from being covered by single semantically significant meta-path.

6 Conclusion

In this paper, we propose a new algorithm CMPM to mine combinational meta-paths that describe correlation relationships between nodes in HINs. The algorithm is based on two assumptions: (1) shorter meta-paths generally carry more significant semantics, but longer meta-path is helpful to guarantee semantic completeness; (2) path instance distributions in networks is relevant to path importance, we can use them to weight meta-paths. Then a preliminary screening step and a path refinement step are included in its implementation. In experiment, author-similarity and author-publication correlation relationships in bibliographic networks are evaluated. Corresponding nodes proximity detection results measured by average degree of disorder, accuracy, recall, F1-score and nDCG proved the effectiveness of CMPM algorithm. In the future, we will further improve the algorithm by propose better path weighting methods, and extend the algorithm to other HINs also deserve efforts.

Acknowledgements. This work is supported by National Key Research and Development Plan in China (2017YFB0803300), National Natural Science Foundation of China (U1636105).

References

1. Sun, Y., Han, J., Yan, X., Yu, P.S., Wu, T.: Pathsim: meta path-based top-k similarity search in heterogeneous information networks. Proc. VLDB Endow. **4**, 992–1003 (2011)
2. Cao, B., Kong, X., Philip, S.Y.: Collective prediction of multiple types of links in heterogeneous information networks. In: 2014 IEEE International Conference on Data Mining, pp. 50–59. IEEE (2014)
3. Cao, X., Zheng, Y., Shi, C., Li, J., Wu, B.: Meta-path-based link prediction in schema-rich heterogeneous information network. Int. J. Data Sci. Anal. **3**(4), 285–296 (2017)

4. Vahedian, F., Burke, R., Mobasher, B.: Meta-path selection for extended multi-relational matrix factorization. In: The Twenty-Ninth International Flairs Conference (2016)
5. Shi, C., Li, Y., Philip, S.Y., Wu, B.: Constrained-meta-path-based ranking in heterogeneous information network. Knowl. Inf. Syst. **49**(2), 719–747 (2016)
6. Vahedian, F., Burke, R., Mobasher, B.: Weighted meta-path generation, multi-relational recommender system, heterogeneous information network, weighted random walk sampling (2017). ArXiv preprint arXiv:1703.00034
7. Liang, T., Chen, L., Wu, J., Dong, H., Bouguettaya, A.: Meta-path based service recommendation in heterogeneous information networks. In: International Conference on Service-Oriented Computing, pp. 371–386. Springer (2016)
8. Shi, C., Zhou, C., Kong, X., Yu, P.S., Liu, G., Wang, B.: Heterecom: a semantic-based recommendation system in heterogeneous networks. In: Proceedings of the 18th ACM SIGKDD International Conference on Knowledge Discovery and Data Mining, pp. 1552–1555. ACM (2012)
9. Gupta, M., Kumar, P., Bhasker, B.: HeteClass: a meta-path based framework for transductive classification of objects in heterogeneous information networks. Expert Syst. Appl. **68**, 106–122 (2017)
10. Shi, C., Kong, X., Huang, Y., Philip, S.Y., Wu, B.: Hetesim: a general framework for relevance measure in heterogeneous networks. IEEE Trans. Knowl. Data Eng. **26**, 2479–2492 (2014)
11. Lao, N., Cohen, W.W.: Relational retrieval using a combination of path-constrained random walks. Mach. Learn. **81**, 53–67 (2010)
12. Meng, C., Cheng, R., Maniu, S., Senellart, P., Zhang, W.: Discovering meta-paths in large heterogeneous information networks. In: Proceedings of the 24th International Conference on World Wide Web, pp. 754–764. ACM (2015)
13. Galárraga, L.A., Teflioudi, C., Hose, K., Suchanek, F.: AMIE: association rule mining under incomplete evidence in ontological knowledge bases. In: Proceedings of the 22nd International Conference on World Wide Web, pp. 413–422. ACM (2013)
14. Tang, J., Zhang, J., Yao, L., Li, J., Zhang, L., Su, Z.: Arnetminer: extraction and mining of academic social networks. In: Proceedings of the 14th ACM SIGKDD International Conference on Knowledge Discovery and Data Mining, pp. 990–998. ACM (2008)
15. Zhang, J., Yu, P.S., Zhou, Z.-H.: Meta-path based multi-network collective link prediction. In: Proceedings of the 20th ACM SIGKDD International Conference on Knowledge Discovery and Data Mining, pp. 1286–1295. ACM (2014)
16. Yen, J.Y.: Finding the k shortest loopless paths in a network. Manag. Sci. **17**, 712–716 (1971)
17. Shannon, C.E.: A mathematical theory of communication. ACM SIGMOBILE Mobile Comput. Commun. Rev. **5**, 3–55 (2001)
18. Gunetti, D., Picardi, C.: Keystroke analysis of free text. ACM Trans. Inf. Syst. Secur. (TISSEC) **8**, 312–347 (2005)
19. Järvelin, K., Kekäläinen, J.: Cumulated gain-based evaluation of IR techniques. ACM Trans. Inf. Syst. (TOIS) **20**, 422–446 (2002)

Detecting Spammer Communities Using Network Structural Features

Wen Zhou, Meng Liu$^{(\boxtimes)}$, and Yajun Zhang

School of Computer Engineering and Science,
Shanghai University, Shanghai 200444, China
zhouwen@shu.edu.cn, saraliu1994@gmail.com, zyj1985email@163.com

Abstract. Spammers generate fake reviews to influence the reputation of products. By grouping together, spammers can dramatically alter how products are perceived. Different from previous research, which has mostly used behavioral indicators and structural indicators, we propose a new perspective on spammer detection. In our approach, we portray reviewers as a comment-based reviewer network through a new collusion similarity measure, divide reviewers into different communities using an effective community detection method and separate spammer communities from normal reviewer communities through network structure. We find that spammer communities have different network structural features from normal reviewer communities, a high clustering coefficient and high self-similarity. In our experiments, we show that our method achieves a detection accuracy of 94.59% - substantially higher than the current state-of-the-art methods which achieve an 80.00% accuracy.

Keywords: Fake reviews · Spammer community
The comment-based reviewer network · Network structural features

1 Introduction

With the rapid development of social networks, the fake information of the platform can bring great harm [12]. Spammers on e-commerce platforms such as Amazon, Yelp or the large Chinese website Dianping, are paid to boost or libel products by generating a large number of fake reviews. In 2015, Amazon sued 1,114 spammers who were paid $5 each to provide fake 5 stars reviews for products. Fake reviews make review data lack authenticity and create barriers for follow-up research. This problem must be solved effectively.

The first technique for spammer detection was proposed by Jindal et al. [2]. Many papers e.g. [1,3,4], identify spam or individual spammers by content analysis. Mukherjee et al. [6] were the first use behavioral indicators of fake reviews to detect spammers. Since then, behavioral indicators have become an important basis for spammer detection. Besides this work, few papers, e.g. [7], [10], identify spammer communities. The problem of spammer community detection was first proposed by Mukherjee et al. [7]. They ranked the "spamicity" of each community using several behavioral indicators (BIs). Generally, spammer community

© ICST Institute for Computer Sciences, Social Informatics and Telecommunications Engineering 2018
I. Romdhani et al. (Eds.): CollaborateCom 2017, LNICST 252, pp. 670–679, 2018.
https://doi.org/10.1007/978-3-030-00916-8_61

detection is largely based on BIs. However, the method proposed by Want et al. [10] constructs the reviewer network as a bipartite graph, and discovers spammer communities by structural indicators (SIs).

Unfortunately, spammers have become extremely sophisticated. The behavior of spammers has become more hidden and it is more difficult to identify spammers only by using BIs or SIs. To make matters worse, there are more spammers working together in spammer communities. Compared with individual spammers or spam, a spammer community is more harmful because of the use of clever technology. At this point, a single index can't effectively detect spammer communities, and previous spammer detection methods encounter unprecedented challenges.

Coincidentally, review data can be represented as a comment-based reviewer network. Hence, spammer community detection can be solved by using the theories and methods developed in the research on complex networks [13]. In order to effectively distinguish spammer communities from normal reviewer communities, this paper applies a community detection method to spammer community detection. We find that previous research ignores the network structure of spammer communities. To identify spammer communities, this paper uses self-similarity (SS) and clustering coefficient (CC) as network structural features (NSFs). In terms of NSFs, the internal links of a spammer community are dense and different from a normal reviewer community, and the similarity among spammers in a spammer community is extremely high. For the case of Dianping (a popular website in China), this paper shows that CC has the best performance in detecting spammer communities. Therefore, spammer community detection based on NSFs is worth studying.

The method proposed in this paper as follows: based on how the reviews were made, the reviewers form a comment-based reviewer network. Thereafter, reviewers can be formed into communities through community detection. We check the structural features of detected spammer communities and find that:

- Different from normal reviewers who tend to have little contact, spammers in spammer communities tightly group together.
- Spammers in the same spammer community behave in a highly similar way.
- Spammer communities have very different network structure compared with normal reviewer communities, due to the different behavior of spammers and normal reviewers. The network structures of spammer communities are characterized by a high clustering coefficient and high self-similarity.

2   Related Work

Early spammers detection mainly concentrated in E-mail [8]. In a wide field, the most investigated spam activities have been in the field of social networks. The first technique in fake review detection was proposed by Jindal et al. [2], who treated duplicate reviews as fake reviews and non-duplicate reviews as truthful reviews. What's more, a rule-based method was proposed [3] to find unusual review patterns by mining unexpected rules as review behavior.

Similarly, behavioral features were used to detect individual spammers. Lim et al. [5] exploited four types of suspicious behavior to detect spammers from the content and rating of a review. Mukherjee et al. [6] treated the concentricity, burstiness and extreme rating of reviews as spammer behavior features, and established a Bayes model to detect spammers. Another approach used the relationship between reviewers [11], calculating the similarity between a spammer and its neighbors, and correcting its label with the votes of neighbors. There also exists a graph-based method [9] computing the trustworthiness of reviewers, the honesty of a review and the reliability of stores, finally creating a ranking list of suspicious reviews and reviewers.

Few studies have focused on spammer community detection. Mukherjee et al. [7] initially proposed the review spammer community detection problem. They used the FIM method to find candidate spammer communities, and ranked the "spamicity" for each community using several behavioral indicators (BIs) derived from the collusion phenomenon of reviewers. The BIs contain the following six indicators: community rating deviation (CRD), community review timestamp gap (CRTG), community reviewed store proportion (CRSP), community size (CS), community early time frame (CETF), and community size ratio (CSR).

Another approach [10] proposed a loose spammer community detection based on the bipartite graph. The method constructed a reviewer network represented as a bipartite graph, and proposed structural indicators (SIs) to evaluate the "spamicity" of detected communities and ranked loose spammer communities. SIs contain the following four indicators: review tightness (RT), neighbor tightness (NT), product tightness (PT), and product reviewer ratio (RR).

3   Methodology

An NSFs-based spammer community detection method is presented in this section. A diagram of the method's architecture is shown in Fig. 1. The first step is creating a comment-based reviewer network based on the review data. The second step is detecting communities in the comment-based reviewer network. The third step is extracting community features of spammer communities. The final step is identifying spammer communities by communities' NSFs.

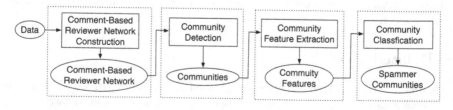

Fig. 1. The architecture of spammer community detection

3.1   Comment-Based Reviewer Network Construction

The comment-based reviewer network is an undirected weighted graph $G = (V, E, W)$. V is a node set, E is an edge set, $v_i \in V$ is a node, $(v_i, v_j) \in E$ is an edge between v_i and v_j, and each edge has a weight $w_{v_i,v_j} \in [0, 1]$ which presents the similarity between two nodes. Reviewers of online-review sites are mapped onto nodes in the comment-based reviewer network. Each reviewer has a review set $\{u, (s, c, t, r)\}$ including a series of reviews, s is store_id, c is the comprehensive rating of a store, u is the reviewer_id, r is the rating of the review, and t is the post time of the review. For reviewers A and B, the review sets are as follows:

$$R(A) = \{u_A, (s_i, c_i, t_i, r_i)\} \quad i = [1, n];$$
$$R(B) = \{u_B, (s_j', c_j', t_j', r_j')\} \quad j = [1, m].$$

Generally, if two reviewers are neighbors, they have published some collusive reviews [11]. $C_{A,B}(k)$ measures whether a review of A is similar to a review of B. For any two reviewers A and B, $C_{A,B}(k) = 1$, if $(u_A, s_k, c_k, t_k, r_k) \in R(A)$ and $\exists\ (u_B, s_l', c_l', t_l', r_l') \in R(B)$, where:

(a) $s_k = s_l'$, which means the two reviews are posted at the same store;
(b) $|t_k - t_l'| < \Delta t$, which means the two reviews are posted within a certain time interval;
(c) $r_k = r_l' = 1$ star or $r_k = r_l' = 5$ stars, which shows the two reviews are posted with an extreme rating.

Different from previous research [10] using Jaccard similarity to measure neighbor tightness between two reviewers, a new similarity measure, Collusion Similarity, is proposed here. The new similarity measure not only depends on the store_id of collusive reviews, but also considers the concentricity and extreme rating of collusive reviews. The collusion similarity between two reviewers A and B is defined as follows:

$$S(A, B) = \frac{\sum_{k=1}^{n} C_{A,B}(k) + \sum_{l=1}^{m} C_{B,A}(l)}{|R(A)| + |R(B)|} \tag{1}$$

where, $|R(A)|$ is the total number of reviews for A. The larger the similarity, the more collusive reviews two reviewers share. If the similarity between two reviewers exceeds the threshold, the pairwise reviewers are considered to be neighbors. The collusion similarity $S(A, B)$ is defined as the weight of edges $w_{A,B}$, so the edge between A and B is $(A, B, w_{A,B})$.

3.2   Community Detection

Community is a structural feature of complex networks. Specifically, the whole network is composed of some "groups" and the internal links of communities are dense, and the links between communities are sparse. Likewise, the comment-based reviewer network consists of some communities.

Despite its role as a normal reviewer or a spammer, a node only belongs to one community. Therefore, non-overlapping community detection can perform well. We use a fast unfolding method to detect communities on large undirected weighted networks, as shown below:

Algorithm 1. Community detection on undirected weighted networks

---

Input: the comment-based reviewer network $G = (V, E, W)$
Output: communities, optimal modularity Q
1: initialize each node as a community;
2: calculate the modularity Q of the initial network;
3: **repeat**
4:     calculate the number of communities n;
5:     **for** each $i \in [1, n]$ **do**
6:         calculate the number of neighbors m for i;
7:         **for** each $j \in [1, m]$ **do**
8:             calculate the change of modularity ΔQ if assign i to a the community where j is located;
9:         **end for**
10:        assign i to the community with j where $\Delta Q\ != 0$ and ΔQ is highest
11:    **end for**
12:    compress G into G': compressing one community into one new node; compressing the weights of all links between two communities into one weight of the link between two new nodes; and compressing the weights of all links within the community into one weight of the ring of a new node;
13:    calculate the modularity Q of G';
14: **until** the modularity Q no longer changes;

3.3   Network Structural Features

Most previous research has put forward a series of behavioral indicators to detect spammer communities. These indicators, however, do not apply to the current situation. Further, certain structural indicators were used to improve the effect of classification, but their performance was found to be poor [1].

However, the network structure of spammer communities provides a novel idea for spammer community detection. NSFs can identify some spammer communities, in which the behavior of spammers tends to normal reviewers. As shown in Fig. 2, the links between reviewers of a normal reviewer community are sparse, but the links between reviewers of a spammer community are dense. This example suggests that the network structure within the normal reviewer community and the spammer community is different. Therefore, NSFs can be used as an important basis for spammer community detection. The NSFs of a community are defined in the following:

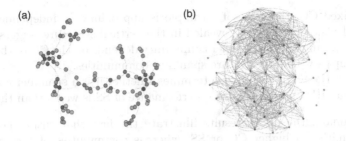

Fig. 2. Comparison between normal community an spammer community. (a) An example of normal community. (b) An example of spammer community.

Self-Similarity (SS).

$$SS = \frac{\sum_{(v_i,v_j)\in E} w_{v_i,v_j}}{|E|} \tag{2}$$

where $|E|$ is the number of edges in a community and w_{v_i,v_j} is the similarity between pairwise nodes v_i and v_j. A spammer community is an organized group with high self-similarity. In order to efficiently complete tasks, spammers post more collusive reviews, the similarity between two spammers is extremely high. And, the local structure is similar with the global structure.

Clustering Coefficient (CC).

$$CC = \frac{\sum_{v_i \in V} \frac{2n}{k(k-1)}}{|V|} \tag{3}$$

where $|V|$ is the number of community members, k is the degree of v_i, n is the number of edges between the neighbors of v_i. The clustering coefficient reflects the tightness of community structure. Most pairwise members in a spammer community post collusive reviews, the link density of nodes in the spammer community is very large. The higher the clustering coefficient, the greater the suspiciousness of that community.

To quantify the importance of network structure in detecting spammer communities, this paper studies a series of samples (a manual annotated data set from Dianping) including spammer communities and normal reviewer communities. Analysis of these samples in the comment-based reviewer network reveals three results (As shown in Fig. 3):

– For fixed BIs or SIs, there is a wide difference between the state of samples. The larger the CC of a sample, the greater the probability that the sample is a spammer community. In particular, there are many samples (large BIs, low CC or large SIs, low CC) that are normal reviewer communities.

- For a fixed CC, the state of a sample is approximately independent of the BIs and SIs. This result is revealed in the vertical structure, suggesting that whether a sample is a spammer community depends on the CC of the sample, and samples with large CC are spammer communities.
- Similarly, the SS of a sample determines whether it is a spammer community more than BIs and SIs. But, the performance of SS is worse than that of CC.

In summary, the above results illustrate the fact that suspicion is larger for communities of higher CC or SS, whereas communities of a given BIs or SIs value can result in either small or large suspicion, depending on the value of NSFs. Therefore, spammer communities in the comment-based reviewer network are not necessarily related to the BIs and the SIs. Instead, NSFs are a better predictor of spammer communities and CC has the best performance.

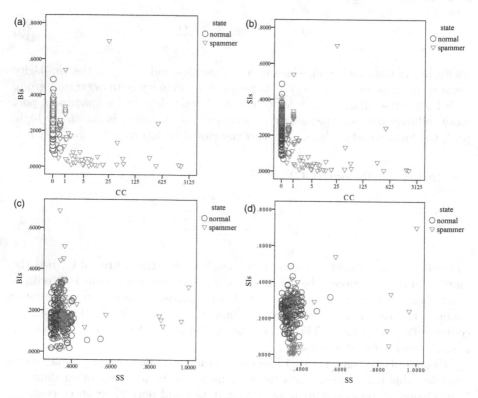

Fig. 3. Analysis of samples from different dimensions. (a) The CC of samples is compared with the BIs of samples. (b) The CC of samples is compared with the SIs of samples. (c) The SS of samples is compared with the BIs of samples. (d) The SS of samples is compared with the SIs of samples. The circles denote the samples of normal reviewer communities; the triangles denote the samples of spammer communities.

4 Experiment and Analysis

4.1 Dataset and Community Detection

In this section, we apply spammer community detection through NSFs to a large-scale data set including 5,427 stores, 1,669,060 reviewers and 2,920,122 reviews collected from January 2014 to December 2016 from the online-review website Dianping (https://raw.githubusercontent.com/SaraLiu1994/Dianping-Dataset/master/review.txt). The sample of dataset is shown in Fig. 4. Each line is a review set of one reviewer. A review set contains one or more reviews published by the reviewer. For example, the last reviewer in Fig. 4 has two reviews and other reviewers have only one review respectively. In a line, the first field is reviewer_ id. The rest are its reviews. Each review contains 4 fields including s - store id, c - the comprehensive rating of s, t - the post time of the review, and r - the rating of the review.

```
75221271,5584128,5.0,16-02-29,4.0
37722206,4199561,4.5,14-09-17,5.0
137883821,12592243,5.0,14-11-19,5.0
892285261,23737947,4.0,16-04-17,5.0
31904504,8011561,3.5,15-05-31,5.0
89370,2564851,5.0,15-09-11,4.0,4684802,5.0,15-09-11,4.0
```

Fig. 4. Extract from main dataset.

In order to reduce the impact of noise, some reviewers who write few reviews are removed. The final review set contains 89,006 reviewers and 709,220 reviews. Thereafter, we create the comment-based reviewer network by using the collusion similarity measure described in Sect. 3.1. Next, we divide the comment-based reviewer network into communities by using a non-overlapping community detection algorithm. At this point, the optimal modularity is 0.806, and the comment-based reviewer network consists of 289 communities (communities in which the number of members is less than three are removed). After manual evaluation, 289 communities are labeled into 89 spammers communities and 200 normal reviewer communities. The training set contains 50 spammer communities and 105 normal reviewer communities, and the test set contains 39 spammer communities and 95 normal reviewer communities.

4.2 Evaluation

Spammer community classification is a binary classification problem. The evaluation indexes of binary classification include precision, recall, F1 and AUC. Precision refers to how many real positive samples in all positive samples are predicted by the classifier. Recall refers to how many real positive samples are predicted as positive samples. F1 can be regarded as a weighted average of precision and recall, used when precision clashes with recall. AUC is the area under the ROC curve commonly being used to measure classification performance. The larger the AUC, the better the classification performance.

As shown in Table 1, we compare the classification performance of each indicator using different evaluation indices. We find:

- In terms of precision, CC performs the best, CRD preforms the worst which reveals that spammers reduce the deviation by publishing little truthful reviews.
- In terms of recall, CC performs the best, CETF preforms the worst which confirms that the time interval of fake reviews is not concentrated in the early days.
- In terms of F1, CC performs the best, CETF preforms the worst.
- In terms of AUC, CRD, CETF and CSR perform poorly, which proves spammer communities weaken their behavioral features to hide their true identity. But, CC does best with 0.969 AUC which confirms that it is a good indicator for spammer community detection.
- Although NSFs contain only two indicators (SS, CC) which is fewer than SIs (PT, NT, RT, RR), the NSFs perform the best with 83.72% precision, 92.31% recall, 87.80% F1 and 0.959 AUC.

Table 1. The performance of each indicator

	SS	CC	CRD	CRTG	CRSP	CS	CETF	CSR	NT	PT	RT	RR	NSFs	BIs	SIs
P(%)	71.88	**94.59**	21.43	45.71	32.88	29.33	28.57	35.48	80.00	43.38	63.16	73.91	**83.72**	37.93	72.41
R(%)	58.97	**89.74**	15.38	41.03	61.54	56.41	5.13	28.21	51.28	76.92	30.77	43.59	**92.31**	28.21	53.85
F1(%)	64.79	**92.11**	17.91	43.24	42.86	38.60	8.70	31.43	62.50	55.56	41.38	54.84	**87.80**	32.35	61.76
AUC	0.692	**0.969**	0.441	0.605	0.652	0.632	0.500	0.544	0.612	0.698	0.619	0.652	**0.959**	0.599	0.735

The above results illustrate the fact that SIs can improve the accuracy of spammer community detection, but have limited effectiveness. Thus, spammer community detection is not necessarily related to the BIs or SIs. Instead, NSFs can contribute to spammer community detection, with CC being the best predictor of spammer communities.

5 Conclusion

In this paper, reviewers form a comment-based reviewer network based on their reviews. Reviewers can be formed into communities through community detection and we check the structural characteristics of spammer communities. Our findings include: (a) the behavior of spammers has become more hidden and it is more difficult to identify spammers using only BIs or SIs. (b) Compared with normal reviewer communities, spammer communities have different network structural features, a high clustering coefficient and high self-similarity. (c) Compared with BIs, SIs can improve the accuracy of spammer community detection, but their effectiveness is limited. Instead, CC is the best predictor of spammer communities.

This work aims to use NSFs to identify spammer communities in comment-based reviewer networks, and has achieved good performance on real-world review data. However, many different types of community structure have been proposed. Whether these community structure types can further distinguish spammer communities from normal reviewer communities should be evaluated in future research.

Acknowledgments. This research is supported by the National Natural Science Foundation of China (Grant No. 71203135). Thank Nikita Koptyug for proofreading our manuscript.

References

1. Heydari, A., ali Tavakoli, M., Salim, N., Heydari, Z.: Detection of review spam: a survey. Expert Syst. Appl. **42**, 3634–3642 (2015)
2. Jindal, N., Liu, B.: Opinion spam and analysis. In: Proceedings of the 2008 International Conference on Web Search and Data Mining, pp. 219–230. ACM
3. Jindal, N., Liu, B., Lim, E.P.: Finding unusual review patterns using unexpected rules. In: Proceedings of the 19th ACM International Conference on Information and Knowledge Management, pp. 1549–1552. ACM (2010)
4. Li, H., Liu, B., Mukherjee, A., Shao, J.: Spotting fake reviews using positive-unlabeled learning. Computación y Sistemas **18**, 467–475 (2014)
5. Lim, E.P., Nguyen, V.A., Jindal, N., Liu, B., Lauw, H.W.: Detecting product review spammers using rating behaviors. In: Proceedings of the 19th ACM International Conference on Information and Knowledge Management, pp. 939–948. ACM (2010)
6. Mukherjee, A., Kumar, A., Liu, B., Wang, J., Hsu, M., Castellanos, M., Ghosh, R.: Spotting opinion spammers using behavioral footprints. In: Proceedings of the 19th ACM SIGKDD International Conference on Knowledge Discovery and Data Mining, pp. 632–640. ACM (2013)
7. Mukherjee, A., Liu, B., Glance, N.: Spotting fake reviewer groups in consumer reviews. In: Proceedings of the 21st International Conference on World Wide Web, pp. 191–200. ACM (2012)
8. Wang, D., Irani, D., Pu, C.: A study on evolution of email spam over fifteen years. In: International Conference on Collaborative Computing: Networking, Applications and Worksharing, pp. 1–10. IEEE
9. Wang, G., Xie, S., Liu, B., Philip, S.Y.: Review graph based online store review spammer detection. In: 2011 11th IEEE International Conference on Data Mining, pp. 1242–1247. IEEE (2011)
10. Wang, Z., Hou, T., Song, D., Li, Z., Kong, T.: Detecting review spammer groups via bipartite graph projection. Comput. J. **59**, 861–874 (2016)
11. Xu, C., Zhang, J., Chang, K., Long, C.: Uncovering collusive spammers in Chinese review websites. In: Proceedings of the 22nd ACM International Conference on Information and Knowledge Management, pp. 979–988. ACM (2013)
12. Xu, Y., Li, F., Liu, J., Zhang, R., Yao, Y., Zhang, D.: Detecting false information of social network in big data. In: Wang, S., Zhou, A. (eds.) CollaborateCom 2016. LNICST, vol. 201, pp. 642–651. Springer, Cham (2017). https://doi.org/10.1007/978-3-319-59288-6_65
13. Zhou, T., Bai, W., Wang, B., Liu, Z., Yan, G.: A brief review of complex networks. Physics **34**, 31–36 (2005)

Citation Based Collaborative Summarization of Scientific Publications by a New Sentence Similarity Measure

Chengzhe Yuan, Dingding Li[✉], Jia Zhu, Yong Tang,
Shahbaz Wasti, Chaobo He, Hai Liu, and Ronghua Lin

School of Computer Science, South China Normal University,
Guangzhou 510631, Guangdong, China
dingdingli@m.scnu.edu.cn

Abstract. Next-generation network offers unrestricted access for researchers to all kinds of scientific publications, collaborative summarization systems are now being contemplated as a service that can help researchers gain information when they read scientific articles. One way to develop a collaborative summarization system is to measure semantic similarity between sentences to improve its quality. In this paper, we introduce a new sentence similarity measure for summarizing scientific articles with citation context. Our work is based on recent work in document distance metric called the word mover's distance (WMD). Compared to traditional similarity measures, WMD based sentence similarity measure has better performance by capturing the semantic relation between two sentences. Experiments on 2016 version of ACL Anthology Reference Corpus show that our approach outperforms several other baselines by ROUGE metrics.

Keywords: Collaborative summarization · Sentence similarity measure Citation context

1 Introduction

The next-generation network demands for more collaborative academic services i.e. collaborative text summarizations. The amount of research is being published in different fields of life especially in science has made it more difficult for researchers to up to date their interests. To collaborate their new ideas with existing research, they spend a lot of time in reading scientific articles and making collaborative summaries. These summaries on scientific articles can facilitate researchers to capture the salient ideas of an article more quickly and effortlessly.

There are two types of methods in scientific publications summarization [1]: (1) Abstractive summarization, which attempts to generate novel sentences for summary. A common difficulty with this method is *de novo* meaningful and grammatical summary [2]. (2) Extractive summarization or collaborative summarization extracts key sentences or phrases from source documents and group them into shorter form [3].

© ICST Institute for Computer Sciences, Social Informatics and Telecommunications Engineering 2018
I. Romdhani et al. (Eds.): CollaborateCom 2017, LNICST 252, pp. 680–689, 2018.
https://doi.org/10.1007/978-3-030-00916-8_62

According to Elkiss et al. citation contexts usually cover the cited paper in all scenarios such as the research problem, the proposed method, shortcomings and limitations [4]. So different from general free-text extractive summaries, citation based summarization is the set of citing sentences for a given article and this summary is the collaborative summation of other scholars' viewpoints.

Previous work on citation based summarization mainly focused on how to make citation sentences useful. For example, extracting citation context from cited article instead of original article [5] or summarizing articles by detecting common facts in citations [6]. However, the accurate measure of semantic similarity between citation sentences in the process of summarization has been mostly ignored. The absence of semantic similarity measure from summarization process will group the sentences into wrong clusters, this resulted in poor performance for final summarization.

In this paper, we present a WMD [7] based sentence similarity measure to address the aforementioned shortcomings of existing summarization models. Compare to traditional measure of the similarity between two sentences, i.e. (term frequency- inverse document frequency) TF-IDF, (bag of words) BOW, WMD metric is capable of capturing the semantic relation between two sentences by utilizing the high quality of the *word2vec* embedding. Our model generates citation based collaborative summaries in four steps: preprocessing, classifying sentences according to article's discourse structure, semantic clustering and selecting the sentences for final summarization using Maximal Marginal Relevance (MMR). Evaluation results on ACL2016 corpus show that our proposed model outperforms several baselines methods.

2   Related Work

Summarizing scientific publications on the basis of citations is well researched area. According to Elkiss citation-based summary contains more information than abstracts and main contexts [4].

Qazvinian proposed a clustering approach where communities in the citation summary's lexical network are formed and sentences are extracted from separate clusters [8]. Agarwal described a SciSumm system which summarizes document collections that are composed of fragments extracted from co-cited articles [9]. Another similar approach was presented in [6], this approach aims to summarize scientific documents by detecting common facts in citations. Amjad and Dragomir performed a study on how to produce readable summaries [10]. Ronzano and Saggion proposed a platform to automatically extract, enrich and characterize several structural and semantic aspects of scientific publications [11].

Different approaches for the extraction of citation sentences have also been proposed in the past years. Qazvinian proposed a citation based summarization approach which extract important key phrases from a set of citation sentences and build summary by these key phrases [12]. Cohan and Goharian generated summarization by extracting citation context from reference article. This approach overcomes the problem of inconsistency between the citation summary and the article's content by providing context for each citation. Article's inherent discourse model has also been proved helpful in extracting citation sentences [5].

However, above literature do not measure the semantic similarity between sentences in citation based summarization. By utilizing the high quality of the *word2vec* embedding, results from Kusner's work showed that WMD metric works better than any other document distance metrics [7]. Hence, we apply WMD metric to the process of citation based summarization for improving the summarization quality.

3   The Summarization Approach

The framework of our approach is shown in Fig. 1, we describe it in the following four steps:

(1) The Preprocessing step extracts citation sentences from scientific articles as input, then outputs citation semantic similarity between sentences in matrix form by WMD metric.
(2) In the sentences classification step, we use one-vs-rest SVM model with linear kernel to classify sentences into four categories: Introduction, Methods, Results, and Discussion (IMRAD) [13] which is respect to article's discourse structure.
(3) The semantic clustering step takes classified sentences as input, then performs k-means clustering algorithm to cluster sentences into groups by utilizing semantic similarity matrix obtained in step 1.
(4) In the selection of sentences for summary step, we score every sentences in each cluster by MMR strategy (as described in Sect. 3.3) and top ranked sentences are iteratively selected from each IMARD categories until we reach the summary length threshold. Finally, generate the final summary from the selected sentences.

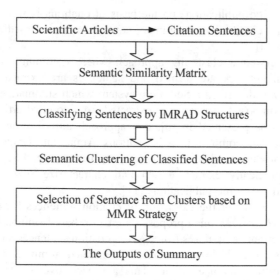

Fig. 1. The framework of proposed approach

3.1 Sentence Similarity Measure

To get the citation sentences, firstly, we need to extract citation context from scientific article and then identify the scope of citation sentence by annotated reference maker, lastly, find fragments of the sentence which are related to given target reference.

There are two main sentence similarity measures: (1) word overlap measure that compute similarity score based on a number of words shared by two sentences. (2) TF-IDF measure that compute sentence similarity based on term frequency-inverse document frequency [14]. The main drawback of these measures is their failure on capturing the semantic relation between sentences. We employ WMD metric to measure semantic similarity between sentences, WMD metric is defined by the distance between sentences in terms of the vector embedding of the words that make up the sentences [7]. Before implementing WMD metric, we get word-vectors that are semantically synonymous in the embedding space by *word2vec* [15], which is a two-layer neural net that are trained to reconstruct linguistic contexts of words. The main idea of WMD-based sentence similarity (WMD-Similarity) measure is to minimize the amount of distance that "transports" from the embedded words of one sentence to another sentence. WMD-Similarity is defined as follows:

$$D(x_i, x_j) = \min_{T \geq 0} \sum_{i,j=1}^{n} T_{ij} \|x_i - x_j\|_2^p, \text{subject to: } \sum_{j=1}^{n} T_{ij} = d_i^a, \sum_{i=1}^{n} T_{ij} = d_i^b, \forall i,j \quad (1)$$

Where $x_i \in R^d$ is the ith word embedding matrix $X \in R^{d \times n} \cdot \mathbf{d^a}$ and $\mathbf{d^b}$ are the n-dimensional normalized bag-of-words vectors for two sentences, where d_i^a represents the number of word i occurs in $\mathbf{d^a} \cdot T_{ij}$ denotes how much of d_i^a "travels" to d_j^b. The minimum cumulative cost of moving d_i^a to d_j^b can be taken as distance between sentences. The smaller the value of WMD-Similarity measure the higher the semantic similarity between two sentences. For example, we have calculated WMD-Similarity measure between sentences (a) and (b) that is 1.15. Our results show that even having very few common words between them still the sentences are semantically similar to each other. Which proves the efficiency of our proposed sentence similarity measure.

(a) *Other work focuses on lexical simplifications and substitutes difficult words by more common WordNet synonyms or paraphrases found in a predefined dictionary.*

(b) *The literature is rife with attempts to simplify text using mostly hand-crafted syntactic rules aimed at splitting long and complicated sentences into several simpler ones.*

3.2 Sentences Classification and Clustering

When researchers writing scientific articles, they generally follow a standardized structure which is known as introduction, methods, results, and discussion (IMRAD). In order to correctly capture all aspects of the article, we include each category of IMARD in the summarization. We use one-vs-rest SVM model with linear kernel to classify citation sentences to their respective category. To train our classification model, we use all the verbs which are lemmatized from 4,685 annotated sentences (1,705 of Introduction, 1,310 of Methods, 1,391 of Results & 279 of Discussion) and they appear at least twice in the same class, besides auxiliary verbs are excluded.

Clustering Model. After classifying each citation sentence. We apply a two-steps cluster method to divide citation sentences that contain similar information into groups of same topic. In first step, hierarchical clustering is assigned for grouping data into subsets. In second step, each formed subsets in first step will be taken as the input data for k-means clustering. Hierarchical clustering is used for better performance of K-means [16]. In two-step cluster method, the measure of distance between two sentences is weighted by semantic similarity matrix obtained from Sect. 3.1.

3.3   Ranking Model

In previous step, we clustered similar citation sentences into groups. But not all sentences in the same cluster are equally important, for example both sentence (c) and (d) mentioned author Søgaard's work, however, sentence (c) is more important, because it contains more useful information.

(c) *For example, recent work by Søgaard explores data set sub-sampling methods.*
(d) *This idea has been previously explored by Zeman and Resnik and recently by Søgaard.*

The goal of this module is to extract the most representative sentences from each classification. There are various ways of ranking sentences based on their importance, we use a well-known method Maximal Marginal Relevance (MMR) [17] for evaluation. MMR is a linear combination of relevance and novelty scores to rank sentences. The MMR-based ranking score for a sentence are defined by following formula:

$$score(S) \overset{def}{=} \lambda Sim_1(S, R) - (1 - \lambda)Sim_2(S, Sum) \qquad (2)$$

Where $Sim_1(S, R)$ represents the linear interpolation of similarity of sentence S with all other sentences, $Sim_2(S, Sum)$ is the similarity between sentence S and the sentences already in the summary. $Sim_1(\bullet)$ and $Sim_2(\bullet)$ are WMD-Similarity from formula (1), and we empirically set $\lambda = 0.7$.

4   Experiments

4.1   Dataset

We use ACL Anthology Reference Corpus[1] (ARC) which is a collection of scholarly publications about computational linguistics. It includes all ACL Anthology files up to December 2015, consisting of 22,878 articles. ARC provides all logical document structure and parsed citation information for each article. We randomly select 556

---

[1] http://acl-arc.comp.nus.edu.sg/.

articles from ARC as our data, each article contains more than 20 citation sentences. After cleaning low-quality sentences (contains less than 5 words) and noise data, we get 17,186 citation sentences in the dataset. We asked two experts in NLP domain read citation sentences and its corresponding cited paper, then they manually create two sets of scientific summary for 10 selected articles, the short summaries of 4 sentences (80–100 words) and longer summaries of 8 sentences (230–250 words).

Evaluation Metrics. We use ROUGE, one of the most popular automatic evaluation metric for evaluation. It automatically measures the quality of a summary by comparing overlapping units such as n-gram, word sequences, and word pairs with ideal summaries created by humans [18]. Specifically, we use ROUGE-N (N-gram Co-Occurrence Statistics) metric for our evaluation. ROUGE-N is defined as follows:

$$\text{ROUGE - N} = \frac{\sum\limits_{S \in \{ReferenceSummaries\}} \sum\limits_{W \in S} f_{match}(W)}{\sum\limits_{S \in \{ReferenceSummaries\}} \sum\limits_{W \in S} f(W)} \tag{3}$$

Where W is the n-gram, $f(\bullet)$ is the count function, $f_{match}(\bullet)$ is the maximum number of n-grams co-occurring in the generated summary and a set of reference summaries, and ROUGE-topic is a novel metric for measuring the topical relation between two documents, this metric is well illustrated in [14].

4.2   Baselines

To evaluate the performance of our approach in citation based summarization, we conducted experiments with 5 widely-used baseline approaches.

- ***KL-Sum.*** KL-Sum greedily adds sentences to a summary as long as it minimizes the Kullback–Leibler Divergence (KLD). Where KLD is a measure of 'closeness' between probability distribution of two documents [19].
- ***LexRank.*** In this approach, it computes sentence importance based on the concept of eigenvector centrality in a graph representation of sentences [20].
- ***LSA.*** By capturing main topics of a document, the sentences with most important topics are selected for the summary [21].

Table 1. ROUGE-1, ROUGE-2 and ROUGE-topic recall scores for different approaches.

Metric	Our System	KL	LexRank	LSA	SumBasic	TextRank
Rouge-1–4	**0.556**	0.456	0.507	0.540	0.359	0.485
Rouge-2–4	**0.447**	0.316	0.363	0.409	0.158	0.342
Rouge-topic-4	**0.463**	0.313	0.387	0.432	0.211	0.366
Rouge-1–8	**0.697**	0.576	0.577	0.625	0.571	0.646
Rouge-2–8	**0.626**	0.454	0.449	0.512	0.407	0.525
Rouge-topic-8	**0.618**	0.454	0.475	0.540	0.454	0.553

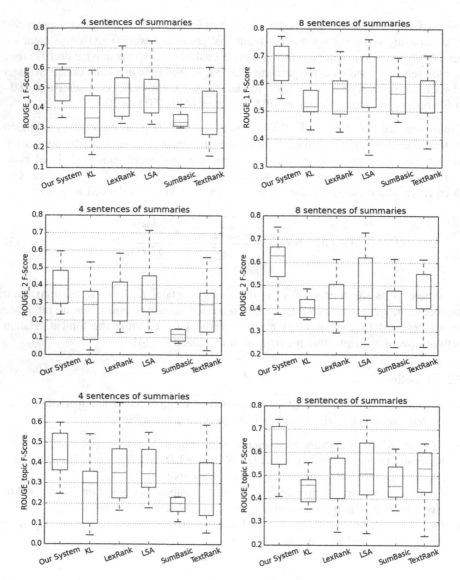

Fig. 2. The comparison of different approaches on Rouge-1, Rouge-2 and Rouge-topic F-scores.

- *TextRank.* It is a graph-based ranking model for sentence extraction and summarization using Levenshtein distance as relation between text units [22].
- *SumBasic.* SumBasic is a generic summarization system that exploits frequency information exclusively [23].

5   Results and Discussion

In this section, we present the results of our method with other baselines in ROUGE scores. The citation context for all the methods were removed numeric values, stop words and citation markers. We compute the ROUGE scores based on 2 * 10 gold standard summaries.

Table 1 shows the average ROUGE recall scores for all summarization approaches of 10 articles in dataset, metric "Rouge-*-4" and "Rouge-*-8" mean ROUGE scores on short summaries (4 sentences) and long summaries (8 sentences).

From Table 1 and Fig. 2, it is clear that semantic similarity measure based models (System & LSA) performed better than TF-IDF based models. With WMD based sentence similarity model, our system achieves better results on all the ROUGE metrics in both short and long summaries and has improved the performance in summarizing scientific articles. In longer summaries, the performance gap is even wider between our approach and others.

Among baseline approaches, KL and SumBasic performed below average, due to their failure on selecting optimal sentences for summarization. However, LSA performed slightly better than baseliners. LexRank and TextRank showed almost similar performance. The main idea behind these two unsupervised approaches is to find sentences which are very similar to each other therefore diversity in summarization is not considered in both approaches. Our approach can address this problem by selecting important sentences from IMARD category of the article. We attribute the competitive performance of our approach to its accurate measure of semantic similarity between sentences which improve the quality of clustering and ranking model in the process of summarization.

6   Conclusion

In this paper, we proposed a four steps approach based on WMD-similarity to measure semantic similarity between sentences for scientific article summarization. This will generate a semantically collaborative summary. The first step pre-processes citation sentences and obtain semantic similarity between sentences by WMD-similarity metric. In the second step, we classify the clusters based on article's discourse structure: IMARD. In the third step, we employ a two-step clustering algorithm by semantic similarity matrix obtained in step 1. In the last step, we rank citation sentences within four categories by MMR strategy. Our experiments show that our proposed approach effectively achieved improvement over several baselines. In future, we will expand the application of our approach to other types of publications.

Acknowledgements. This work was funded by the National Natural Science Foundation of China under grant number 61772211 and 61502180, by the Natural Science Foundation of Guangdong Province, China under grant number 2014A030310238, 2015B010129009, 2016A030313441 and 2017A030303074, by the Special Fund for Key Program of Science and Technology of Guangdong Province, China under grant number 2014B010116002, by the Pearl River S&T Nova Program of Guangzhou under grant number 201710010189 and 201604016007.

References

1. Nenkova, A., McKeown, K.: Automatic summarization. Found Trends® Inf. Retr. **5**(2–3), 103–233 (2011)
2. Khan, A., Salim, N.: A review on abstractive summarization methods. J. Theor. Appl. Inf. Technol. **59**(1), 64–72 (2014)
3. Gupta, V., Lehal, G.S.: A survey of text summarization extractive techniques. J. Emerg. Technol. Web Intell. **2**(3), 258–268 (2010)
4. Elkiss, A., et al.: Blind men and elephants: what do citation summaries tell us about a research article? J. Assoc. Inf. Sci. Technol. **59**(1), 51–62 (2008)
5. Cohan, A., Goharian, N.: Scientific article summarization using citation-context and article's discourse structure (2017). ArXiv preprint arXiv:1704.06619
6. Chen, J., Zhuge, H.: Summarization of scientific documents by detecting common facts in citations. Future Gener. Comput. Syst. **32**, 246–252 (2014)
7. Kusner, M., et al.: From word embeddings to document distances. In: International Conference on Machine Learning (2015)
8. Qazvinian, V., Radev, D.R.: Scientific paper summarization using citation summary networks. In: Proceedings of the 22nd International Conference on Computational Linguistics, vol. 1. Association for Computational Linguistics (2008)
9. Agarwal, N., et al.: Towards multi-document summarization of scientific articles: making interesting comparisons with SciSumm. In: Proceedings of the Workshop on Automatic Summarization for Different Genres, Media, and Languages. Association for Computational Linguistics (2011)
10. Abu-Jbara, A., Radev, D.: Coherent citation-based summarization of scientific papers. In: Proceedings of the 49th Annual Meeting of the Association for Computational Linguistics: Human Language Technologies, vol. 1. Association for Computational Linguistics (2011)
11. Ronzano, F., Saggion, H.: Knowledge extraction and modeling from scientific publications. In: González-Beltrán, A., Osborne, F., Peroni, S. (eds.) SAVE-SD 2016. LNCS, vol. 9792, pp. 11–25. Springer, Cham (2016). https://doi.org/10.1007/978-3-319-53637-8_2
12. Qazvinian, V., Radev, D.R., Özgür, A.: Citation summarization through keyphrase extraction. In: Proceedings of the 23rd International Conference on Computational Linguistics. Association for Computational Linguistics (2010)
13. Sollaci, L.B., Pereira, M.G.: The introduction, methods, results, and discussion (IMRAD) structure: a fifty-year survey. J. Med. Library Assoc. **92**(3), 364 (2004)
14. Achananuparp, P., Hu, X., Shen, X.: The evaluation of sentence similarity measures. In: Song, I.-Y., Eder, J., Nguyen, T.M. (eds.) DaWaK 2008. LNCS, vol. 5182, pp. 305–316. Springer, Heidelberg (2008). https://doi.org/10.1007/978-3-540-85836-2_29
15. Goldberg, Y., Levy, O.: word2vec explained: deriving Mikolov et al.'s negative-sampling word-embedding method (2014). ArXiv preprint arXiv:1402.3722
16. Lu, J.-F., et al.: Hierarchical initialization approach for K-Means clustering. Pattern Recognit. Lett. **29**(6), 787–795 (2008)
17. Carbonell, J., Goldstein, J.: The use of MMR, diversity-based reranking for reordering documents and producing summaries. In: Proceedings of the 21st Annual International ACM SIGIR Conference on Research and Development in Information Retrieval. ACM (1998)
18. Lin, C.-Y., Och, F.: Looking for a few good metrics: ROUGE and its evaluation. In: NTCIR Workshop (2004)

19. Haghighi, A., Vanderwende, L.: Exploring content models for multi-document summarization. In: Proceedings of Human Language Technologies: The 2009 Annual Conference of the North American Chapter of the Association for Computational Linguistics. Association for Computational Linguistics (2009)
20. Erkan, G., Radev, D.R.: Lexrank: graph-based lexical centrality as salience in text summarization. J. Artif. Intell. Res. 22, 457–479 (2004)
21. Steinberger, J., Křišťan, M.: LSA-based multi-document summarization. In: Proceedings of 8th International Workshop on Systems and Control (2007)
22. Mihalcea, R., Tarau, P.: TextRank: bringing order into text. In: EMNLP (2004)
23. Nenkova, A., Vanderwende, L.: The impact of frequency on summarization. Technical report MSR-TR-2005-101. Microsoft Research, Redmond, Washington (2005)

Collaborative Manufacturing System and Machinery Fault Diagnosis

Exploiting User Activities for Answer Ranking in Q&A Forums

Chenyang Zhao$^{(\boxtimes)}$, Liutong Xu, and Hai Huang

School of Computer Science, Beijing University of Posts
and Telecommunications, Beijing, China
chyzhao@bupt.edu.cn

Abstract. Many Q&A forums suffer high variance in the quality of their contents because of their loose edit control. To solve this problem, many methods are proposed to rank answers based on their quality. Most existing works in this domain focus on using variable features or employing machine learning techniques to automatically assess the quality of answers. Few of these works noticed that the relationship formed by user's activities can be helpful in capture the expertise of users in a specific topic. In this paper, we consider the relationship between users's activities in answer ranking task, create three new topic-aware features based on user profile information and the network formed by user's question-answering and comment activities, then we combine new created features with texture, user, comment features together and adopt a pairwise L2R approach SVMRank to rank answers. Experiments on a dataset extracted from Stack Overflow show that, (a) the new created features can better capture the expertise of users than other user features in answer ranking task. (b) the answer ranking approach get better performance when adding our new created features to the features used in previous works.

Keywords: Q&A forums · Answer ranking · Learning to rank

1 Introduction

Question and Answer Forums(Q&A Forums), such as Stack Overflow[1], Yahoo! Answers[2] and Quora[3] are characterized by loose edit control, which allows anyone to freely publish and edit almost everything, the varying quality of their contents has raised much concern.

To extract high quality contents from these forums, Q&A forums adopt voting mechanism, where users can indicate the quality of contents and even the reputation of the editors, or give the asker the right to select one of the answers as the best answer. While voting mechanism is effective in deemphasizing the low

---

[1] https://stackoverflow.com/.
[2] https://answers.yahoo.com/.
[3] https://www.quora.com/.

© ICST Institute for Computer Sciences, Social Informatics and Telecommunications Engineering 2018
I. Romdhani et al. (Eds.): CollaborateCom 2017, LNICST 252, pp. 693–703, 2018.
https://doi.org/10.1007/978-3-030-00916-8_63

quality answers, it is dependent on the users's votes to the high quality answers. As a consequence, for many questions in Q&A forums, a high quality ranking of the answers is not provided. Our preliminary study on a dataset extracted from Stack Overflow shows that more than 60% of the questions without selected best answer, and more than 50% of questions the sum votes quantity of its answers is less than 200, which is not enough to get reliable ranking results.

Since such questions would largely benefit from ranking algorithms based on automated quality assessment strategies, in this paper, we propose a learning to rank approach (L2R) to rank answers in Q&A forums according to their quality. Unlike previous works, instead of directly estimating answer quality, we try to use the information of the answerer and the relationship between their activities to get better ranking results.

We first use the combination of up and down votes users got in a specific topic to create a new feature, then we combine the new feature with the question-answering network and comment network of user's activities to create other two features. At last, we combine the new created features with some other features we studied to get better ranking performance. Zhou et al. [7] found that almost all users are experts on only one or two topics, so all the methods to create new features and answer-ranking approaches in this paper are topic-aware. Experiments on a Stack Overflow dataset show that our new created features are significantly helpful in ranking answers in Q&A forums. Combining our new created features with features used in previous works, we get the best ranking performance.

2   Related Works

Answer ranking task attracts more and more attention in recent years along with the explosive growth with Q&A forums. Answer ranking is different from traditional Q&A system which is to generate an answer automatically, but to find a set of best answers among a list of answer candidates with various features.

Some researchers exploited a number of features to predict answer quality for ranking. Jeon et al. [3] built a framework to predict answer quality with non-textual features on maximum entropy approach and kernel density estimation. They also incorporated the quality scores into language modeling-based model and achieved significant improvements. Bian et al. [1] defined question-answer pair features to find high quality information in social media environment. They combined these features into Perceptron ranking model and achieved considerable improvements in accuracy.

User profile information attracts more and more attention as effective features in answer ranking task. Zhou et al. [7] extracted three groups of features from user profile information and tested their performance. Dalip et al. [2] summarized 97 features used in previous works and proposed 89 new features, devided them into eight groups, then applied them into Random Forest method to rank answers. They compared the performance of eight groups of features, found that user features is most helpful in answer ranking task.

Few of these works noticed that the relationship of user's activities can be helpful to capture the expertise of users in a specific topic. In this paper, we consider user profile information and the network formed by user's activities to create new topic-aware features and apply them into answer ranking task.

3   Create New Features

To create new features that can accurately represent user's expertise in a specific topic, we do an experiment to compare the performance of some commonly used user features in this domain, we use them individually as the basis to rank answers. The experiment results in Table 1 show that the quantity of up votes user's answers got in a specific topic is better than other information of the user in ranking answers. Besides the up votes, the down votes are also useful to capture the expertise of users. So we have Eq. (1) as the new feature and reffered it to as $F1$:

Table 1. The ranking performance of some user features. The meaning of features in the table are shown in Sect. 4.4. The meaning of metrics are shown in Sect. 5.2.

Feature	MRR	P@1	P@2
uf_{repu}	0.3487	0.2345	0.3976
uf_{uvac}	0.3767	0.2921	0.4293
uf_{ac}	0.3513	0.1932	0.3190
uf_{qc}	0.2830	0.1691	0.2883

In this equation $UpVotes(u_i)$ is the amount of up votes user u_i got and $DownVotes(u_i)$ is the amount of down votes user u_i got. All these values are topic-aware, which means they are calculated in a specific topic. Then we change the α to get the best ranking performance, it is shown that when α is 4.5, we get the best ranking accuracy.

$$F1(u_i) = UpVotes(u_i) - \alpha * DownVotes(u_i) \qquad (1)$$

It also shows that the ranking performance when we only use the $F1$ feature is not good enough, so we combine it with the question-answering network and the comment network of user's activities to create another two features.

The question-answering network is a network that describes the relationship of user's question-answering activities. As shown in Fig. 1(a), we use $q_j \leftarrow u_i$ to represent u_i answering q_j.

With this network, a question can be seen as a hub of users and it is given a hub value to indicate its quality. And also we give every user an authority value to indicate his expertise. Then we have the following assumptions: (a) a good question will attract many expert users to answer it, (b) a expert user is the one

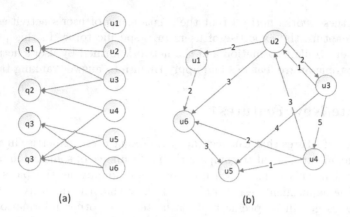

Fig. 1. The graphical representation of question-answering network and comment network.

whose answers are contained in many good questions. Then we use the HITS [5] algorithm to create a new user feature and refer it as to $F2$.

The other network we use in this work is the comment network between users. In Q&A forums, users can publish their comments to questions, answers and other comments. Because we only care the quality of answers, we only use the comments that posted to answers. As shown in Fig. 1(b), we use $u_i \rightarrow u_j$ to represent that user u_i commented the answer published by u_j and the integer in the arrow is the quantity of comments. The PageRank [6] algorithm is used to combine $F1$ with the comment network, then we get a new feature reffered to $F3$.

The three new created features are comprehensive combination of user's up votes, down votes and the relationship of their activities such as question-answering and comment, they are all topic-aware and they can well capture the expertise of users in a specific topic.

4   Other Features

In this section, we present other features used to represent the answer quality. These features try to capture the quality of the answer either directly, through texture features, as well as indirectly, through non-texture features, such as author profile information and comments to the answer. Totally, we study 43 features and organize them into groups according to the characteristics they try to capture. Thus, the features are devided into texture features, user features and comment features.

4.1   Texture Features

Texture features are one of the most successful and commonly used indicators of the answer quality in Q&A forums. Some of them are features about the length of text, the general intuition behind them is that a mature and good quality text is probably neither too short, which could indicate an incomplete topic coverage, nor excessively long, which could indicate a verbose content. Some other texture features try to capture the structure of the answer text, they try to describe the answer quality directly through, analyzing the use of images, separation into sections, links and HTML format tags. A good answer should have the following attributes: (a) relevant to the question. (b) organized into sections, contains images and quoted blocks to improve understanding. (c) link to additional information for further study. Because the dataset we use is extracted from Stack Overflow, which is a Q&A forum serves for programmers, we use tf_csc to capture the use of code snippets in the answers. All texture features used in this work are listed in Table 2.

Table 2. Texture Features

Symbol	Description
tf_wc	n. of words in the text
tf_sc	n. of sentences in the text
tf_cc	n. of characters in the text
tf_avgpl	Average paragraph length
tf_cl	n. code lines
tf_avgcl	Average n. of code lines per code snippet
tf_pc	n. of paragraphs in the text
tf_ic	n. of images in the text
tf_lc	n. of links in the text
tf_outlc	n. of links to external sources
tf_inlc	n. of links to other questions/answers in the same forum
tf_lic	n. of lists in the text
tf_liic	n. of list items in the text
tf_qbc	n. of quoted blocks in the text
tf_stc	n. of $< strong >$ tags
tf_csc	n. of code snippets
tf_bm25	BM25 ranking function, based on a probabilistic retrieval framework
tf_ssc	n. of sentences shared by question and answer
tf_swc	n. of words shared by question and answer
tf_wciso	n. of words which appear in question and answer in the same order
tf_ldbw	Largest distance between two words that appear in answer and question

4.2 User Features

User features are frequently used in this domain in recent years and get very good performance in answer ranking task. The intuition behind user features is to indirectly infer the answer quality by examing the user who post it. More specifically, we are interested in features related to the user profile or its behavior, captured from events such as (a) posting questions and answers, (b) posting comments to questions and answers, (c) gain of merit votes and badges for questions and answers. In Table 3, we present all the user features computed for each answer.

4.3 Comment Features

Comment features try to capture the point of view of others to the answers, it is an important sign to show the answers are in high quality or not. All comment features used in this work are listed in Table 4.

Table 3. User features

Symbol	Description
uf_ac	n. of posted answers
uf_qc	n. of posted questions
uf_cac	n. of comments posted to answers
uf_cqc	n. of comments posted to questions
uf_uvac	n. of up votes to posted answers got from other users
uf_dvac	n. of down votes to posted answers got from other users
uf_avgcac	avg n. of comments per posted answer
uf_avgcqc	avg n. of comments per posted question
uf_avgac	avg n. of answers per posted question
$uf\_avguvac$	avg n. of up votes per posted answer
$uf\_avgdvac$	avg n. of down votes per posted answer
uf_bac	n. of posted answers selected as the best answer
uf_avgrp	avg rank position for posted answers
uf_tcq	n. of topics in which user post questions
uf_tca	n. of topics in which user post answers
uf_tcc	n. of topics in which user post comments

These three groups of features are used in previous works and get good performance in answer ranking task, so we build three baselines use the three different groups of features.

Table 4. Comment features

Symbol	Description
cf_cc	n. of comments posted to the answer
cf_maxccs	max n. of comments in one comment session
cf_uc	n. of users who commented the answer
cf_sumcl	sum of comment text length of all comments posted to the answer
cf_avgcl	avg length of comments posted to the answer
cf_cla	n. of comments posted by the answerer

5 Experiments

In this section, we first describe the dataset used in our experiments, then we introduce the metrics we use to represent the ranking performance, at last we explain our experiments in detail.

5.1 Dataset

The dataset used in our experiments consists of contents extracted from Stack Overflow, a Q&A forum for programmers. It consists of two parts, one part is about questions, answers and comments. Our methods to create new features and the approach to rank answers are topic-aware and in this work and we take the first tag of the question as its topic. We extract six different topics of questions and related answers and comments as our dataset. The detail of it is shown in Table 5.

The other part of the dataset is about users and their activities. To create the question-answering network and the comment network, we consider the Stack Overflow users who interacted with the users posted questions, answers and comments in the first part of the dataset. This part of dataset consists of 1356745 users, 13457828 question-answering pairs and 7112213 comments between these users.

Table 5. The detail of the dataset of questions, answers, comments and votes.

Statistics	Value					
	Topic-1	Topic-2	Topic-3	Topic-4	Topic-5	Topic-6
N. of questions	2045	2221	2079	2105	2160	1985
N. of answers	33569	38990	37653	35584	36535	30783
N. of comments	43420	50893	48540	44328	39893	36783
N. of upvotes	1229250	1233284	1185430	1256348	1283356	1055638
N. of down votes	84285	104782	82023	78876	103593	67328

As the same as some previous works, We use the ranking results based on quantity of up votes received by answers as the ground truth.

5.2 Metrics

Two standard information retrieval metrics are adopted in this work to evaluate the ranking performance as follows:

Precision@K(P@K): The K stands for the position of the correct answer. The precision at K reports the proportion of answers of the answer results set that has the corrent answer in position K.

Mean Reciprocal Rank (MRR): The reciprocal rank of a query response is the multiplicative inverse of the rank of the first correct answer. The mean reciprocal rank is the average of the reciprocal ranks of the results for a sample of queries. For a given query set Q, we calculate the MRR from below formula:

$$MRR = \frac{1}{|Q|} \sum_{i=1}^{|Q|} \frac{1}{rank_i}$$

where $|Q|$ is the number of test questions and $rank_i$ is the position of the best answer in the ground truth.

5.3 Experiments and Results

To prove that the new created features can better represent the expertise of users in a specific topic, we first rank answers use the created features and other common used features like uf_ac, uf_uvac and uf_repu introduced in Sect. 4 as basis individually. Results are shown in Fig. 2.

The results show that the three new created features are all get better ranking results than other commonly used features in previous works, and the $F2$ feature get the best ranking performance in all the tested features. This indicates the effectiveness of the relationship of user's question-answering activities and comment activities in answer ranking task.

To compare the ranking performance of different groups of features described in Sect. 4 and the performance when the new created features are added, we adopt SVMRank [4] as the ranking algorithm to evaluate the performance of different combinations of feature groups. Table 6 shows all the combinations of features and experiment results. The SVMRank algorithm is also used in the work published by Zhou *et al.* [7] and achieved good results.

From the experiment results, we can see that in our three baselines user features get the best performance in ranking answers, that means user profile information is most helpful in answer ranking task. Most importantly, we get better ranking results when adding three new created features to any group of features used by previous works, for example, the accuracy is increased by 12.4% when $3F$ is added to user features. In particular, the combination of user features, structure features, length features, relevance features, comment

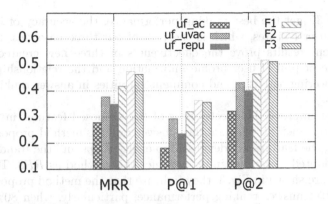

Fig. 2. The graphical representation of the performance of new created and user features when used individually in answer ranking task.

Table 6. The ranking performance of different combinations of feature groups. For simplicity, we use the combinations of capitalized first letter of every feature group to represent it, the three new created features are represented by $3F$ and $All = \{TF + UF + CF + 3F\}$.

No.	Comb.	Training Data						Metric.
		30%	40%	50%	60%	70%	80%	
1	TF	0.6521	0.663	0.675	0.6875	0.6983	0.7021	MRR
2	UF	0.6933	0.7021	0.7145	0.7188	0.722	0.7311	
3	CF	0.62	0.6399	0.6549	0.6675	0.6689	0.6731	
4	TF+3F	0.7156	0.7349	0.7499	0.7589	0.7691	0.7634	
5	CF+3F	0.6539	0.6678	0.6784	0.6875	0.6954	0.7022	
6	UF+3F	0.7265	0.7356	0.7523	0.7642	0.7751	0.7765	
7	TF+CF+3F	0.7431	0.759	0.7689	0.7742	0.779	0.785	
8	TF+UF+3F	0.7763	0.7869	0.798	0.8021	0.8093	0.8132	
9	**All**	**0.798**	**0.8005**	**0.8154**	**0.8245**	**0.8287**	**0.8396**	
1	TF	0.4231	0.4266	0.4336	0.4428	0.45	0.4579	P@1
2	UF	0.4758	0.4803	0.4889	0.496	0.49	0.5	
3	CF	0.3564	0.3598	0.365	0.369	0.3875	0.3986	
4	TF+3F	0.4657	0.4735	0.4806	0.5032	0.511	0.5198	
5	CF+3F	0.3975	0.4065	0.4135	0.4245	0.432	0.442	
6	UF+3F	0.5064	0.5138	0.5237	0.54	0.555	0.562	
7	TF+CF+3F	0.4981	0.5064	0.5123	0.519	0.5288	0.5372	
8	TF+UF+3F	0.5342	0.5451	0.5576	0.5673	0.569	0.573	
9	**All**	**0.5532**	**0.5669**	**0.578**	**0.582**	**0.592**	**0.6073**	

features and 3F get the best ranking performance, the accuracy of it is 21.4% higher than user features, which is the best of our three baselines. In general, the experiment results prove the effectiveness of three new created features, and show the helpful of user profile information and the relationship of user's question-answering activities and comment activities in answer ranking task in Q&A forums.

To further improve the effectiveness of the proposed features in this work, we compare our method with another answer ranking method proposed by [2]. In that work, the features are devided into eight groups and the Random Forest method is adopted to rank answers, we refer this method as *RF*8. The experiment results are shown in Fig. 3, they indicate that the method proposed in this work get better answer ranking performance, particularly, when 80% training dataset is used, the precision of our method is 6.2% higher than the method proposed by Dalip *et al.* [2] in answer ranking task in Q&A forums.

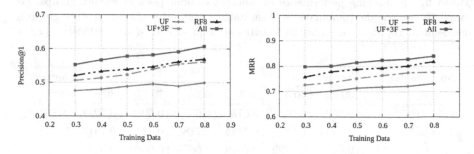

Fig. 3. The graphical representation of ranking performance of different combinations of feature groups and *RF*8.

6   Conclusion

In this paper, we create three new topic-aware features with user profile information and the relationship of user's activities to capture the expertise of users in a specific topic in answer ranking task and studied texture, user and comment features in answer ranking task. Then we compare the ranking performance of three groups of features and combine the new created features with these features to improve the ranking performance. The experiment results on a dataset extracted from Stack Overflow show that the new created features can better represent the expertise of Q&A users in a specific topic, and the new proposed method get better ranking performance than the state of the art method in answer ranking task in Q&A forums.

References

1. Bian, J., Liu, Y., Agichtein, E., Zha, H.: Finding the right facts in the crowd: factoid question answering over social media. In: Proceedings of the 17th International Conference on World Wide Web, pp. 467–476. ACM (2008)
2. Dalip, D.H., Gonçalves, M.A., Cristo, M., Calado, P.: Exploiting user feedback to learn to rank answers in q&a forums: a case study with stack overflow. In: Proceedings of the 36th International ACM SIGIR Conference on Research and Development in Information Retrieval, pp. 543–552. ACM (2013)
3. Jeon, J., Croft, W.B., Lee, J.H., Park, S.: A framework to predict the quality of answers with non-textual features. In: Proceedings of the 29th Annual International ACM SIGIR conference on Research and Development in Information Retrieval, pp. 228–235. ACM (2006)
4. Joachims, T.: Optimizing search engines using click through data. In: Proceedings of the Eighth ACM SIGKDD International Conference on Knowledge Discovery and Data Mining, pp. 133–142. ACM (2002)
5. Kleinberg, J.M.: Hubs, authorities, and communities. ACM Comput. Surv. (CSUR) 31(4es), 5 (1999)
6. Page, L., Brin, S., Motwani, R., Winograd, T.: The page rank citation ranking: Bringing order to the web. Technical report, Stanford InfoLab (1999)
7. Zhou, Z.M., Lan, M., Niu, Z.Y., Lu, Y.: Exploiting user profile information for answer ranking in cQA. In: Proceedings of the 21st International Conference on World Wide Web, pp. 767–774. ACM (2012)

A Two-Level Classifier Model
for Sentiment Analysis

Haidong Hao[1,2], Li Ruan[1,2(✉)], Limin Xiao[1,2], Shubin Su[1,2],
Feng Yuan[3], Haitao Wang[4], and Jianbin Liu[4]

[1] State Key Laboratory of Software Development Environment,
Beihang University, Beijing 100191, China
{haohaidong, ruanli, xiaolm}@buaa.edu.cn
[2] School of Computer Science and Engineering, Beihang University, Beijing
100191, China
[3] Institute of Software Application Technology, Guangzhou and Chinese
Academy of Sciences, Guangzhou 511458, China
yf@gz.iscas.ac.cn
[4] Space Star Technology Co., Ltd., Beijing 100086, China
{wanghaitao, liujianbin}@spacestar.com.cn

Abstract. This paper proposes a fast and high performance classifier model for
sentiment analysis of textual reviews. The key contribution is three fold. First, a
two-level classifier model consists of three base classifiers is proposed, and
theory proves that the model could be better than the strongest classifier among
the base classifiers in both classification performance and time cost of predict.
Second, this paper proposes a lexicon-based classifier as a base classifier using a
new part of speech (POS) which is called "weaken words". Finally, we
implemented several two-level classifiers by combining the lexicon-based
classifier with several machine learning classifiers. Experiments on Chinese
reviews dataset show that the two-level classifier model is effective and efficient.

Keywords: Sentiment analysis · POS · Weaken words
Two-level classifier model · Predict time

1 Introduction

With the further popularization of networks and smart phones, publishing reviews
online on social events, products and service are increasingly common. These reviews
are collectively referred to as IWOM (Internet Word of Mouth), since they contain a lot
of useful information to evaluate the evaluation object from various aspects. Based on
the understanding of these reviews, the government can understand people's attitude
towards a policy, and then make the right decision; the online merchants can find
deficiencies in their products and services according to the user's experience and make
continuous optimization; consumers can make comparison between kinds of products
and service, and ultimately make a reasonable purchase. Therefore, it is very valuable
to mining out these reviews' opinion.

© ICST Institute for Computer Sciences, Social Informatics and Telecommunications Engineering 2018
I. Romdhani et al. (Eds.): CollaborateCom 2017, LNICST 252, pp. 704–717, 2018.
https://doi.org/10.1007/978-3-030-00916-8_64

Online IWOM monitoring system is a kind of real-time system which aims to classify the semantic orientation (positive or negative) of web reviews (or any other speeches), and conducts further analysis. Sentiment analysis is the basic task of the system, and it has to classify massive amounts of data over a limited period of time, so, the system is not only sensitive to classification performance, but also to time cost. Therefore, a fast and high performance classifier is very essential. However, get better classification performance in less time is often a contradictory problem. High performance classifiers are always complicated and need a long time to complete the calculation. On the other hand, more of the existing work is focused on improving the classification performance or reduce the training time, research on the reduction of predict time is relatively little. So, this paper aims to construct a fast and high performance classifier.

Boosting [1] and bagging [2] are two popular methods to improve the classification performance of classifier. The main idea of them is to train a set of classifiers through multiple rounds of sampling on the training set, and then construct a new classifier by combining these base classifiers. Drawing on this kind of combination idea, this paper takes advantage of the classification performance of strong classifiers and the classification speed of weak classifiers, using them as base classifiers to construct a faster and stronger classifier. Compared with boosting and bagging, the main difference is that the two-level classifier model is not through the linear combination of the base classifiers to predict, but through the stratification to predict, so it can significantly reduce the time cost.

In Sect. 3, this paper derives the conditions should these base classifiers meet to achieve the goal, and one condition is the base classifiers are independent from each other, so both lexicon-based and machine learning classifiers are used as the base classifiers. As for the lexicon-based classifier, this paper takes account of two special cases in expression, and proposes a new POS which is called "weaken words" to construct the classifier. And as for machine learning classifiers, this paper uses Naïve Bayesian, Logistic and SVM (support vector machine) classifiers.

The remainder of this paper is organized as follows. In Sect. 2, we present a brief description of existing sentiment analysis approaches. In Sect. 3, we present the definition and proof of the two-level classifier model in detail. In Sect. 4, we present in detail the construction of lexicon-based classifier we applied as a base classifier in the model. In Sect. 5, we present the experiments of the model on Chinese reviews dataset and the results show that the model is efficient and effective. Finally, in Sect. 6 we conclude this work.

2 Related Work

There are two main approaches for sentiment analysis of text. One is machine learning and the other is lexicon-based. In terms of machine learning approach, it can be divided into supervised and unsupervised approaches. Naïve Bayesian, maximum entropy and SVM are the most classic supervised classifiers. Pang and Lee [3] had experimented with these classifiers using kinds of features, like n-gram, term frequency and POS etc. and found SVMs tend to do the best. Turney [4] had presented an unsupervised machine learning algorithm. He firstly proposed PMI (point-wise mutual information) to measure the similarity of given words or phrases with positive or negative reference words. And then, calculate the average semantic orientation of the extracted phrases to assign a classification to the review. Zou et al. [5] had considered the words' syntactic properties in basic words-bag to generate a more accurate solution.

In terms of lexicon-based approach, based on WordNet, Kim and Hovy [6] had proposed a method to constructed semantic dictionary. They assembled a small amount of seed words by hand, and sorted them into positive and negative lists by semantic polarity, and then grow these two lists by adding words obtained from WordNet. Liu et al. [7] had proposed three conjunction rules (intra-sentence conjunction rule, pseudo intra-sentence conjunction rule and inter-sentence conjunction rule) and two word rules (synonym and antonym rule) to determine the polarity of the adjectives in a given domain. In another paper [8], they had extracted attributes of the evaluation object, and proposed a method for feature-level opinion mining. Taboada et al. [9] had analyzed the characteristics of various POS in detail. When calculate the semantic orientation of sentiment-bearing words, they took into account valence shifters (intensifiers, down-toners, negation, and irrealis markers). Their method performs well and is robust across domains and texts.

To reduce the time cost of predict, Wang and Zaniolo [10] proposed a classifier using discretization techniques to limit disk I/O at the cost of accuracy, and they remedied the loss of accuracy by using a simplified version of estimation method proposed in CLOUDS [11]. Based on Chinese web page characteristics, Wu et al. [12] proposed a pre-classification method by giving a keywords list to reduce predict time for Chinese web page classification. Wu et al. [13] proposed a normalized feature weighted KNN (k-Nearest Neighbor) text classifier, their method can reduce the feature dimension thus reduce the time cost of predict.

3 Two-Level Classifier

3.1 Model Definition

Let $C = \{C_1, C_2, C_3\}$ be a set of three two-class classifiers, $P = \{P_1, P_2, P_3\}$ be the average accuracy of each classifier and $T = \{T_1, T_2, T_3\}$ be the time cost of predict of each classifier. Assume that C, P and T satisfy the following three conditions:

- C_1, C_2, and C_3 are independent from each other;
- C_3 is a strong classifier, C_1 and C_2 are two weak classifiers ($P_3 > \max\{P_1, P_2\}$);
- C_3 is more complicated than C_1 and C_2 ($T_3 > \max\{T_1, T_2\}$);

Using C_1 and C_2 as low level base classifiers, C_3 as high level final classifier, and utilize multithreading technology we could construct a faster and stronger classifier. The principle is that for easy to be classified texts be classified by low level fast classifiers, and for texts that difficult to be classified be classified by high level complicated classifier. The workflow of the model is as follows:

Algorithm 1. Work flow of the two-level classifier model

1: **for** each text in buffer
2:     extract the features;
3:     C_1, C_2 and C_3 begin to calculate;
4:     **if** (C_1 and C_2 output the same result)
5:         stop the calculating of C_3;
6:         take the result as the final classification result of this text;
7:     **else**
8:         wait for C_3 to output its result;
9:         take this result as the final classification result of this text;

3.2   Model Proof

Based on the basic three conditions, the next task is to find other necessary or sufficient conditions to improve the classification performance while reduce the time cost of predict. The accuracy and time cost formulas of the model are as follows:

$$dis\_rate = P_2(1 - P_1) + P_1(1 - P_2) \tag{1}$$

$$P = P_1 P_2 + P_3 \times dis\_rate \tag{2}$$

$$T = \max\{T_1, T_2\} + [T_3 - \max\{T_1, T_2\}] \times dis\_rate \tag{3}$$

P is the accuracy of the two-level classifier, T is the time cost, and dis_rate is the ratio of "disagree" of C_1 and C_2 to a certain input text ("disagree" means that C_1 and C_2 output different results).

Conditions that P be Greater than P_1 and P_2: Substituting (1) into (2), we get

$$P = P_1 P_2 + P_3[P_1 + P_2 - 2P_1 P_2)] \tag{4}$$

Without losing generality, assume that $P_2 \geqslant P_1$. If $P > \max \{P_1, P_2\}$, the inequality below should be true:

$$\frac{P}{P_2} = P_1 + P_3 + (\frac{1}{P_2} - 2)P_1 P_3 > 1 \tag{5}$$

It can transform to

$$P_3[1 + (\frac{1}{P_2} - 2)P_1] > 1 - P_1 \tag{6}$$

Since $1 > P_2 > 0$, it can transform to

$$P_3 > \frac{1 - P_1}{1 + (\frac{1}{P_2} - 2)P_1} \tag{7}$$

Regarding P_2 as a constant, and let

$$P_3 > F(P_1) = \frac{1 - P_1}{1 + (\frac{1}{P_2} - 2)P_1} \tag{8}$$

The derivative of $F(P_1)$ is

$$F'(P_1) = \frac{1 - \frac{1}{P_2}}{[1 + (\frac{1}{P_2} - 2)P_1]^2} < 0, (1 > P_2 > 0) \tag{9}$$

Because $F(P_1)$ is a monotonically decreasing function, if P_1 is more closer to P_2, C_3 would be more easier to improve the accuracy of C_1 and C_2, and

$$P_3 > F(P_1 = P_2)_{\min} = \frac{1 - P_2}{1 + \left(\frac{1}{P_2} - 2\right)P_2} = 0.5 \tag{10}$$

So, P would be greater than P_1 and P_2 if inequality (7) is true. Furthermore, P_3 must be greater than 0.5.

Conditions that P be Greater than P_3: If $P > P_3$, the inequality below should be true:

$$\frac{P}{P_3} = \frac{P_1 P_2}{P_3} + P_1 + P_2 - 2P_1 P_2 > 1 \tag{11}$$

It can transform to

$$\frac{1}{P_3} > \frac{1 + 2P_1 P_2 - (P_1 + P_2)}{P_1 P_2} \tag{12}$$

Regarding P_1 as a constant, and let

$$G(P_2) = 1 + 2P_1 P_2 - (P_1 + P_2) \tag{13}$$

The derivative of $G(P_2)$ is

$$G'(P_2) = 2P_1 - 1 \begin{cases} > 0, & 1 > P_1 > 0.5 \\ = 0, & P_1 = 0.5 \\ < 0, & 0 < P_1 < 0.5 \end{cases} \tag{14}$$

Then, the minimum value of $G(P_2)$ is

$$G(P_2)_{min} = \begin{cases} \lim\limits_{p_2 \to 0} 1 + 2P_1P_2 - (P_1 + P_2) = 1 - P_1 > 0, & 1 > P_1 > 0.5 \\ 0.5, & P_1 = 0.5 \\ \lim\limits_{p_2 \to 1} 1 + 2P_1P_2 - (P_1 + P_2) = P_1 > 0, & 0 < P_1 < 0.5 \end{cases} \tag{15}$$

As we can see, $G(P_2) > 0$ is always true, hence, inequality (12) can transform to

$$\frac{P_1P_2}{1 + 2P_1P_2 - (P_1 + P_2)} > P_3 \tag{16}$$

Without losing generality, assume that $P_2 \geqslant P_1$ and take P_1 as a constant, let

$$L(P_2) = \frac{P_1P_2}{1 + 2P_1P_2 - (P_1 + P_2)} > P_3 \tag{17}$$

The derivative of $L(P_2)$ is

$$L'(P_2) = \frac{P_1(1 - P_1)}{[1 + 2P_1P_2 - (P_1 + P_2)]^2} > 0, (1 > P_1 > 0) \tag{18}$$

Because $L(P_2)$ is a monotonically increasing function, if P_3 is more greater, P_1 and P_2 should be more greater either to improve P_3, and

$$L(P_2 = P_1)_{min} = \frac{P_1^2}{1 + 2P_1^2 - 2P_1} > P_3 \tag{19}$$

Then, let

$$K(P_1) = \frac{P_1^2}{1 + 2P_1^2 - 2P_1} > P_3 \tag{20}$$

The derivative of $K(P_1)$ is

$$K'(P_1) = \frac{2P_1(1 - P_1)}{[1 + 2P_1^2 - 2P_1]^2} > 0, (1 > P_1 > 0) \tag{21}$$

$K(P_1)$ is a monotonically increasing function, P_3 is greater than 0.5, and $K(P_1 = 0.5) = 0.5$, so that P_1 should be greater than 0.5, it means P_2 should be greater than 0.5 too.

So, P would be greater than P_3 if inequality (16) is true. Furthermore, P_1 and P_2 must be greater than 0.5.

Conditions that T be Less than T_3: Without losing generality, assume that $T_2 \geqslant T_1$. If $T < T_3$, the inequality below should be true:

$$T = T_2 + (T_3 - T_2) \times dis\_rate < T_3 \tag{22}$$

It can transform to

$$(T_3 - T_2) \times dis\_rate < T_3 - T_2 \tag{23}$$

Because dis_rate is less than 1, if $T_3 > T_2$, inequality (23) would be true and T would be less than T_3.

3.3 Model Conclusions

Based on the basic 3 conditions and model proof, we can get conclusions as below:

- If inequality (16) is true, the classification performance of the model would be better than P_3, and the necessary condition is P_1, P_2 and P_3 are all greater than 0.5;
- The predict time of the model is less than T_3.

In order to ensure the independence of these three base classifiers, this paper used both lexicon-based and machine learning classifiers to construct the two-level classifier.

4 Lexicon-Based Classifier

4.1 Sentence Structure

Lexicon-based classifier needs to extract the words related to sentiment analysis. Except for sentiment-bearing words (we marked the POS as "emo"), this paper takes account negative words (they can reverse the orientation of sentiment-bearing words, and we marked the POS as "non"), degree adverb (they can strengthen or weaken the orientation degree of sentiment-bearing words, and we marked the POS as "dg"), and a new type of words which is called "weaken words" (we marked the POS as "wk"). Why we need weaken words, we would like to show the necessity throng a special case in expression:

> *"这种新药减轻了他的痛苦/This kind of new drug has eased his pain"*.

In this example, if we ignore the word "减轻/eased", the extracted word of this sentence is "痛苦/pain", which expresses negative orientation. However, if we take account the word "减轻/eased", we find it weakened the negativity. It shows that we should consider the role of this new kind of words in sentiment analysis.

4.2 Semantic Dictionary

In Chinese field, HowNet [14] and NTUSD (National Taiwan University Semantic Dictionary) [15] provides the basic semantic dictionary. There are 4,566 positive emotional words and 4,370 negative emotional words in HowNet; 2,810 positive emotional words and 8,276 negative emotional words in NTUSD. HowNet also provides 219 degree adverbs, and these words are subdivided into six types according to the words' tone strength. Because neither HowNet nor NTUSD provides negative words, we concluded 22 negative words from web corpus. By the way, these words should be merged, because each kind of words may be repeated with other kinds of words. The final results are shown in Table 1.

Table 1. The semantic dictionary.

POS	Value	Quantity	
emo	positive emotional word is 1, negative emotional word is –1 "高兴/happy"—1, "难过/sad"— –1 etc.	positive emotional: 6506 negative emotional: 11185	
dg	different "dg" word has different value "极其/extreme"—2, "很/very" — 1.7, "较/more"— 1.4, "稍/-ish"— 1.1, "欠/insufficiently"— 0,8, "超/over"— 0.5	extreme: 61 more: 35 insufficiently: 11	very: 37 -ish: 29 over: 24
non	All are –1 "不/not"— –1, "没有/none"— –1 etc.	22	
wk	All are –0.2 "减轻/ease"— –0.2, "减少/reduce" – –0.2etc.	87	

HowNet is a common-sense knowledge base unveiling inter-conceptual relations and inter-attribute relations of concepts as connoting in lexicons of the Chinese and their English equivalents. The "concept" and "primitive" are two basic concepts in HowNet. In HowNet, one word can be described by several concepts and every concept represents the word's one meaning in different context. Concept is described by primitive, and primitive is the smallest unit in HowNet. We can construct a tree-like semantic hierarchy according to the upper and lower relationship between primitives.

Liu and Li [16] had proposed a method to compute the word similarity based on HowNet. For two Chinese words W_1 and W_2, W_1 has n concepts S_{11}, S_{12}, ..., S_{1n}, W_2 has m concepts S_{21}, S_{22}, ..., S_{2m}, and the similarity of W_1 and W_2 is the max value of each pair of concepts, namely

$$Sim(W_1, W_2) = \max_{i=1...n, j=1...m} Sim(S_{1i}, S_{2j}) \qquad (24)$$

Because concept is described by primitive, $Sim(S_{1i}, S_{2j})$ in (24) can be computed by

$$Sim(P_1, P_2) = \frac{\alpha}{Dis(P_1, P_2) + \alpha} \tag{25}$$

P_1 and P_2 are two primitives, $Dis (P_1, P_2)$ is the distance of P_1 and P_2 in the semantic hierarchy, and α is an adjustable parameter.

Based on the word similarity formula, we chose 20 typical "wk" words as seed words, and took the similarity lower threshold of 0.9 to extend the "wk" words. We got 156 words at the beginning, and after manual selection, 87 words were left (included the 20 seed words).

In the semantic dictionary, every word has two attributes, one is the word's POS tag, and the other is its value. The dictionary looks like below (the last column is the number of this kind of words):

4.3   DFA (Deterministic Finite Automaton) Model of the Algorithm

After extracted the sentiment analysis related words, a sentence's semantic orientation can be analyzed according to the words sequence. The simplest solution is scanning the words sequence from back to front, and for every word update the current emotional value according to its POS tag and value. For example, when scanning to a "dg" word, multiply the current emotional value by the word's value. But there are two special cases should be considered:

- *"non-dg" order words* [17]. *When "non" word's next word is "dg" word. For example, "不是很高兴/not very happy" and "很不高兴/very unhappy", although they all express the feeling unhappy, the strength are not the same;*
- *"dg-wk" order words. When "dg" word's next word is "wk" word. For example, "极大得减轻他的痛苦/greatly eased his pain", the semantic orientation reversed from very negative to very positive;*

Considering these two special cases, we find "non-dg" order words behaves like a "wk" word as a whole, and the "wk" word behaves like a "non" word in "dg-wk" order words. So, "non-dg" order words should be transformed to a "wk" word, and the "wk" word in "dg-wk" words should be transformed to a "non" word (Fig. 1). Add these two transform rules we concluded the DFA model of the algorithm like below:

DFA = {Q, Σ, q0, δ, {F}}
Q = {q0, q1, q2, F}, Σ = {emo, dg, wk, non}
δ(q0, dg) = q1, δ(q0, wk) = q2, δ(q0, {emo, non}) = q0, δ(q1, dg) = q1,
δ(q1, non) = q2, δ(q1,{emo, wk}) = q0, δ(q2, wk) = q2,
δ(q2,{emo, non, dg}) = q0, δ({q0, q1, q2}, ε) = F

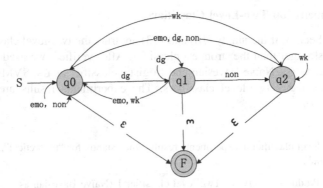

Fig. 1. DFA model of the algorithm

5 Experiments

5.1 Experiments on Base Classifiers

We crawled five different products and service reviews from ctrip.com (http://www.ctrip.com) and jd.com (https://www.jd.com) to test the model. These products and service are clothing, fruit, hotel, PDA (personal digital assistant) and shampoo. For each product or service, we crawled 5,000 positive and negative reviews. The test indicators are average accuracy and time cost of predict (milliseconds per 10,000 pieces of reviews). We used 5 fold cross validation (for lexicon-based classifier, we divided the reviews into 5 groups randomly) and took the average value as the final result. The base classifiers experiments results are as follows (Table 2):

Table 2. The base classifiers experiments results.

Products & service	Test indicators (average accuracy, time cost)			
	Lexicon-based	Naïve Bayesian	Logistic	SVM (Gamma = 0.25, C = 2)
Clothing	(0.87,1032)	(0.89,2520)	(0.90,3180)	(0.94,7280)
Fruit	(0.83,1351)	(0.88,2995)	(0.88,3245)	(0.90,7930)
Hotel	(0.81,3191)	(0.85,9030)	(0.88,9025)	(0.90,22070)
PDA	(0.81,1446)	(0.87,3650)	(0.88,4245)	(0.93,9735)
Shampoo	(0.81,1245)	(0.89,3220)	(0.89,3360)	(0.92,8235)
All	(0.83,1600)	(0.86,4275)	(0.88,4486)	(0.91,11105)

As we can see, in terms of classification performance, the lexicon-based classifier is weaker than other classifiers, Naïve Bayesian and Logistic classifiers are similar, and SVM classifier is the best. And in terms of time cost of predict, SVM classifier takes the longest time, Naïve Bayesian and Logistic classifiers followed, and the lexicon-based classifier takes the shortest time.

5.2   Experiments on Two-Level Classifiers

According to Sect. 3, if inequality (16) and (23) are true, the two-level classifier would be faster and stronger than the strongest classifier. After verified, we used the lexicon-based classifier as C_1, Naïve Bayesian and Logistic classifier as C_2, SVM classifier as C_3 and constructed 2 two-level classifiers. The experiments results are as follows (Tables 3 and 4):

Table 3. Two-level classifier 1 experiments result. "the" stands for "theoretical", "exp" stands for "experimental".

Products & service	Two-level classifier 1 (Naïve Bayesian as C_2)						
	dis_rate (C_1 & C_2)		dis_rate (C_2 & C_3)		P		T
	the	exp	the	exp	the	exp	
Clothing	0.21	0.17	0.16	0.09	0.97	0.94	4840
Fruit	0.25	0.19	0.20	0.07	0.95	0.91	5475
Hotel	0.28	0.22	0.22	0.12	0.94	0.90	11736
PDA	0.27	0.21	0.18	0.09	0.95	0.92	6180
Shampoo	0.26	0.23	0.17	0.08	0.96	0.92	5699
All	0.26	0.21	0.20	0.09	0.95	0.91	6875

Table 4. Two-level classifier 2 experiments result.

Products & service	Two-level classifier 2 (Logistic as C_2)						
	dis_rate (C_1 & C_2)		dis_rate (C_2 & C_3)		P		T
	the	exp	the	exp	the	exp	
Clothing	0.20	0.15	0.15	0.06	0.97	0.94	4691
Fruit	0.25	0.18	0.20	0.07	0.95	0.91	5531
Hotel	0.26	0.20	0.20	0.07	0.94	0.89	11503
PDA	0.26	0.21	0.17	0.07	0.95	0.92	6217
Shampoo	0.27	0.23	0.17	0.07	0.97	0.92	5540
All	0.25	0.20	0.19	0.07	0.96	0.91	6990

As the results show, the two-level classifiers' time cost of predict reduced to about 63% of C_3, but in terms of accuracy, the experimental value had a large gap with the theoretical value. The main reason is C_1, C_2 and C_3 are not independent. In fact, the average dis_rate deviation of C_1 and C_2 is about 21%, C_2 and C_3 is about 51% and 62%, so the independence of C_1, C_2 and C_3 are poor. Thus, as the final classifier, C_3 is the bottleneck of classification performance. Although the accuracy hadn't been improved, at least the same as C_3, it's in line with our needs too.

To maximize have to guarantee the independence of C_1, C_2 and C_3, we divided the "emo" words into two parts and constructed 2 lexicon-based classifiers. Since the semantic dictionaries are almost completely different (other kinds of words are the same), the 2 lexicon-based classifiers are surly almost completely independent. We can take them as C_1 and C_2. In the meanwhile, to meet inequality (16), we constructed a new SVM classifier as C_3. The new base classifiers and two-level classifier experimental results are as follows (Tables 5 and 6):

Table 5. The new base classifiers experiments result.

Products & service	Test indicators (average accuracy, time cost)		
	Lexicon-based (1)	Lexicon-based (2)	SVM(Gamma = 1.5, C = 1)
Clothing	(0.76,1012)	(0.72,952)	(0.83,13495)
Fruit	(0.71,1210)	(0.70,1201)	(0.78,14378)
Hotel	(0.72,3026)	(0.72,3166)	(0.74,30855)
PDA	(0.67,1276)	(0.68,1325)	(0.75,17385)
Shampoo	(0.68,1178)	(0.68,1152)	(0.77,14878)
All	(0.71,1586)	(0.70,1562)	(0.81,18280)

Table 6. Two-level classifier 3 experiments result.

Products & service	Two-level classifier 3						
	dis_rate (C_1 & C_2)		dis_rate (C_1 & C_3)		P		T
	the	exp	the	exp	the	exp	
Clothing	0.38	0.36	0.33	0.28	0.86	0.84	7565
Fruit	0.42	0.40	0.38	0.35	0.82	0.81	8212
Hotel	0.40	0.37	0.39	0.38	0.81	0.80	19258
PDA	0.44	0.40	0.42	0.36	0.78	0.76	11109
Shampoo	0.44	0.37	0.40	0.39	0.80	0.80	8781
All	0.42	0.40	0.37	0.36	0.83	0.83	10360

For this two-level classifier, the average dis_rate deviation of C_1 and C_2 was reduced to about 8%, C_1 and C_3 was reduced to about 8% too, so, C_1, C_2 and C_3 are almost independent from each other. As we can see, the new two-level classifier's time cost reduced to about 59% of C_3, and in terms of accuracy, the experimental value was close to the theoretical value, and higher than C_3. It proved that the model is really effective and efficient.

6 Conclusions

Online IOWM monitoring system is a powerful tool to help people making decisions. A fast and high performance sentiment analyzer is essential for this kind of systems. In order to meet this demand, this paper proposes a two-level classifier model consists of three base classifiers, and derives a theoretical proof, that the classifier could be better than the strongest classifier among the base classifiers in both classification performance and time cost of predict. To ensure the independence of the base classifiers, this paper used both lexicon-based and machine learning classifiers. In addition, this paper constructs a lexicon-based classifiers, and proposes a new POS which is called "weaken word" to improve its accuracy. At last, several two-level classifiers were constructed using the lexicon-based classifier, Naïve Bayesian, Logistic and SVM classifiers, and as the experiments results show, the time cost could be reduced greatly and the accuracy is at least similar to that of the strongest classifier. In short, the two-level classifier model is efficient and effective.

Acknowledgements. This work was supported by the National Science Foundation of China (Grant Nos. 61370059, 61772053 and 61232009 (key project)), Beijing Natural Science Foundation (Grant No. 4152030), the fund of the State Key Laboratory of Computer Architecture (CARCH201507), the fund of the State Key Laboratory of Software Development Environment (SKLSDE-2016ZX-15), the State Administration of Science Technology and Industry for National Defense, the major projects of high resolution earth observation system under Grant No. Y20A-E03, and the National Key R&D Program of China under Grant No. 2017YFB0202004.

References

1. Breiman, L.: Bagging predictors. Mach. Learn. **24**(2), 123–140 (1996)
2. Freund, Y., Schapire, R.E.: A decision-theoretic generalization of on-line learning and an application to boosting. J. Comput. Syst. Sci. **55**(1), 119–139 (1997)
3. Pang, B., Lee, L.: Thumbs up? Sentiment classification using machine learning. In: Proceedings of EMNLP, pp. 79–86 (2002)
4. Turney, P.D.: Thumbs up or thumbs down? Semantic orientation applied to unsupervised classification of reviews. In: Meeting on Association for Computational Linguistics Association for Computational Linguistics, pp. 417–424 (2002)
5. Zou, H., et al.: Sentiment classification using machine learning techniques with syntax features. In: International Conference on Computational Science and Computational Intelligence, pp. 175–179. IEEE (2016)
6. Kim, S.M., Hovy, E.: Determining the sentiment of opinions (2004)
7. Ding, X., Liu, B.: The utility of linguistic rules in opinion mining. In: International ACM SIGIR Conference on Research and Development in Information Retrieval, pp. 811–812. ACM (2007)
8. Ding, X., Liu, B., Yu, P.S.: A holistic lexicon-based approach to opinion mining. In: International Conference on Web Search and Data Mining, pp. 231–240. ACM (2008)
9. Taboada, M., et al.: Lexicon-based methods for sentiment analysis. Comput. Linguist. **37**(2), 267–307 (2011)
10. Wang, H., Zaniolo, C.: CMP: a fast decision tree classifier using multivariate predictions. In: International Conference on Data Engineering, p. 449. IEEE Computer Society (2000)
11. Alsabti, K., Ranka, S., Singh, V.: CLOUDS: a decision tree classifier for large datasets. In: Knowledge Discovery and Data Mining (1998)
12. Shi-Ming, X.U., et al.: Efficient SVM Chinese Web page classifier based on pre-classification. In: Computer Engineering and Applications (2006)

13. Wu, F., Zheng, Y., Cheng, W.: Adaptive normalized weighted KNN text classification based on PSO. Scientific Bulletin of National Mining University (2016)
14. Dong, Z., Dong, Q.: HowNet—a hybrid language and knowledge resource. In: International Conference on Natural Language Processing and Knowledge Engineering Proceedings, pp. 820–824 (2003)
15. http://www.datatang.com/data/44317
16. Liu, Q., Li, S.: Word similarity computing based on how-net. In: Computational Linguistics and Chinese Language Processing (2002)
17. Yang, K., Duan, Q.: Analysis of emotional tendency based on emotional dictionary. Comput. Era **3**, 10–13 (2017)

An Effective Method for Self-driving Car Navigation based on Lidar

Meng Liu[1(✉)], Yu Liu[2], Jianwei Niu[1], Yu Du[3], and Yanchen Wan[2]

[1] State Key Laboratory of Virtual Reality Technology and Systems,
School of Computer Science and Engineering,
Beihang University, Beijing 100191, China
liumeng_scse@buaa.edu.cn

[2] State Key Laboratory of Software Development Environment, School of Computer Science and Engineering, Beihang University, Beijing 100191, China

[3] College of Robotics, Beijing Union University, Beijing, China

Abstract. Existing navigation methods are generally based on GPS or cameras and these methods have limitations in terms of signal strength and brightness. To overcome drawbacks of navigation methods above, we propose a Lidar-based Navigation Approach (LNA) to predict movement trajectory of self-driving vehicles through road edges information, and this approach is a fitting and real-time regression method. By combining regression model with vehicle coordinate system, navigation trajectory is accurately generated. Experiments on common road scenarios demonstrate that our approach is effective to improve navigation techniques.

Keywords: Lidar · Self-driving car · LNA · Navigation
Linear regression

1 Introduction

Navigation plays an important role in autonomous driving scenarios. Currently, navigation methods based on Global Positioning System (GPS) and images are very common. One of popular navigation methods is joint application of global positioning system (GPS) and IMU [1]. [2] shows a vision navigation method. [3,4] use vision technology to extract lane lines for navigation. Modern autopilot systems are commonly equipped with laser scanners. Lidar is very important in unmanned-vehicles areas, and it can provide very accurate environment and road profile information. Therefore, this paper aims at using lidar for navigation. We are not concerned about obstacle detection in complex traffic conditions, positioning and obstacle avoidance problems. Therefore, in this paper, a Lidar-based Navigation Approach (LNA) is proposed for unmaned-vehicles navigation.

Our approach uses linear regression methods, which can fit outline characteristics of road. We use lidar to get real-time point cloud as input. After many preprocessings, we extract clear and effective road sides information. Point cloud of two road edges are linearly fitted to get two linear models. We merge the two

© ICST Institute for Computer Sciences, Social Informatics and Telecommunications Engineering 2018
I. Romdhani et al. (Eds.): CollaborateCom 2017, LNICST 252, pp. 718–727, 2018.
https://doi.org/10.1007/978-3-030-00916-8_65

linear models and translate them into vehicle coordinate system. A series of vehicle motion trajectories are generated. Then, we calculate lateral control data to control the car. Finally, LNA is evaluated in different types of lidars and different cars. Experiment results show that LNA can achieve lidar-based navigation within a general environment on different platforms. The LNA has many advantages, such as large detection range, high accuracy and strong reliability. Except that, it is also applicable to many scenarios which have obvious outline features, such as highway and urban road.

2   Related Work

Existing lidar technologies include maps making, environment detection, real-time positioning and path planning. In this paper, we briefly review previous work on Simultaneous Localization and Mapping(SLAM) and road environment detection.

Over the past years, SLAM develops very fast and there are many applications about SLAM [5]. SLAM can establish a model for spatial environment in process of movement with an absence of prior environment knowledge. [6] shows a SLAM making process. [7] shows a classic method of odometry and mapping using a lidar. [8] describes a method of using lidar for simultaneous localization and mapping. However, all of these SLAM methods mainly focus on environmental modeling and they cannot meet the requirements of realtime navigation.

[9] proposes a road boundary detection and tracking method based on 2d lidar, but this method cannot obtain enough road information. [10] describes a method of detecting road geometric features to identify road shapes. [11] proposes a road surfaces extraction method using a fuzzy cluster. However, these methods based on lidar cannot meet the requirements of realtime navigation. Some researches [12–14] use fusion methods by combing lidar with camera for environment sensing, but these work need complex sensors calibration and fusion algorithms.

Therefore, in this paper, we propose a lidar-based realtime and concise road border modeling method for autonomous driving navigation—Lidar-based Navigation Approach (LNA).

3   The LNA Method

LNA is a lidar-based navigation approach for self-driving cars, which includes lidar data acquisition, data preprocessing, real-time fitting and computing trajectory. It takes lidar point cloud sets as input and clears noises firstly. Then, sparse process can reduce the amount of data and maintain effective data characteristics, which will help to achieve real-time fitting. And a Linear Regression (LR) or Support Vector Regression (SVR) method is followed for linear fitting. Finally, models are transformed into vehicle coordinate system to obtain a trajectory points set, which we use to calculate the lateral control value to reach the goal of navigation.

3.1   Data Preprocessing

This section includes data filtering, interception, classification and sparse processing. In filter stage, we clear noises. In interception stage, we choose point cloud which we have interests in. In classification stage, we get road shoulder and isolation belt information. For sparse processing stage, we reduce the computing load.

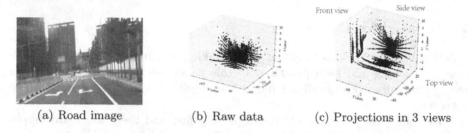

(a) Road image   (b) Raw data   (c) Projections in 3 views

Fig. 1. Road image, point cloud raw data and projections.

Figure 1(b) shows that the collected point cloud has obvious noises. As shown in Fig. 1(a), these noises are mainly from the ground, trees, obstacles and other objects. From Fig. 1, we observe distribution of point cloud in three-dimensional space. Figure 1(c) shows projections of point cloud on top view, front view and side view. We need effectively exploit three views of point cloud distribution. To this issue, we use a meshing method to process point cloud in a three-dimensional spatial grid. Moreover, we use vehicle parameters, lidar placement parameters and some prior knowledge to filter point cloud. Taking HDL-32 lidar as an example, the vehicle height is 1.5 m, which can be defined as h_v. Height of lidar away from vehicle top is 0.3 m, written as h_{l-v}. Height of isolation belt is about 1.5 m, written as h_{ib}. Height of road shoulder is about 0.20 m, written as h_r. Vehicle width is 0.9 m, marked as w_v. Distance from vehicle front to mounting location is 2m, recorded as l_l. Taking lidar scanning distance into account, for HDL-32, we only consider point cloud in range of 20 m, recorded as l_{range}. As we control the highest speed at 20–40 km/h, which equals 5.6–11.1 m/s. And data fitting time is below 0.3 s. These make the forward reaction distance is sufficient. According to conditions above, we design a simple classifier and filter, as expressed by formula 1 and formula 2.

$$\text{Filter}_R = \{[z > -(h_v+h_{l-v})]\&[z < -(h_v+h_{l-v}-h_r)]\}\&\{[y >l_l]\&[y <l_{range}]\}\& \{[x >w_v]\&[x < (x_{sam}+w_{samp})]\}$$

$$(1)$$

$$\text{Filter}_L = \{[z > -(h_v+h_{l-v})]\&[z < -(h_v+h_{l-v}-h_r)]\}\&\{[y >l_l]\&[y <l_{range}]\}\& \{[x < -w_v]\&[x > -(x_{sam}+w_{samp})]\}$$

$$(2)$$

where the x_{sam} is minimum value of samples X set after filtered and classified. w_{samp} is width of samples in x direction, which also is obtained after filtered and classified. This could guarantee the robustness and universality of classifier in different road conditions.

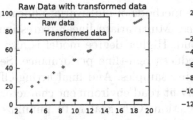 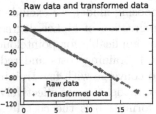

(a) Road shoulder raw data and transformed data (b) Isolation belt raw data and transformed data

Fig. 2. Filter point cloud

The data set before fitting is projected onto the horizontal coordinate system of $x-y$. If the number of points is more than $N(N=50)$, data set will be divided into 10 parts in the X direction, and each part randomly choose samples in proportion of $\lambda(\lambda=90\%)$. Repeatedly sampling in value of λ^n until the number of samples is just below 50. The purpose of dividing set into 10 parts is to keep data descriptive ability for environmental information characteristics. If whole set randomly sampled in ritio of λ^n directly, it is very likely to make data distorted. Also, we make a data transformation by using formula 3 and formula 4 to reduce the fitting cost.

$$
\begin{aligned}
x_{rawData} &\to y', \\
y_{rawData} &\to x'.
\end{aligned}
\tag{3}
$$

The data were originally a set of point cloud datasets approximately parallel to the X axis. This results in training was very difficult to fit, so we did the process.

$$
y_i'' = y_i' \times x_i',
\tag{4}
$$

Eventually, we got the new data set of $D_{New} = (x_1', y_1''), (x_2', y_2''), ..., (x_n', y_n'')$, $n \approx 50$. D_{New} makes data very easy to fit, which greatly improves real-time performance of model training. Figure 2 shows the point cloud data after being preprocessed. Figure 2(a) shows road shoulder raw data after preprocessed and transformed data. Figure 2(b) shows isolation belt raw data after preprocessed and transformed data.

3.2   Real-Time Linear Fitting

In this paper, we use two linear models of LR [15,16] and SVR [17]. Using LR & SVR to fit a series of continuous points is a common sense. Linear regression is relatively simple, it is widely used and has very good effects. In industrial and commercial areas, it has extensive applications.

Linear Regression. Our model can be described as formular 5.

$$f_{LR}(x) = w^T x + b. \tag{5}$$

When choosing model, we exclude methods of multivariate linear regression and linear regression of higher degree. Multivariate linear regression function is proved not applicable for pointcloud. Higher degree model is also excluded. Firstly, it adds training costs and reduces real-time performance. Secondly, it is difficult to converge with few training samples. And final fitting effect shows higher degree model can not effectively fit road environment characteristics. For our model, formula 6 is the cost function. Our goal is to minimize the cost function, which is written as formula 7. And we use a gradient descent method to train it.

$$J_{LR}(\theta) = \frac{1}{2} \sum_{i=1}^{m} (f_\theta(x_i) - y_i)^2. \tag{6}$$

$$\min_\theta J_{LR}(\theta). \tag{7}$$

Support Vector Regression. The SVR regression function is similar to linear regression function, as shown in formula 8. We evaluate the difference between every sample ground truth value and every prediction value to determine whether it is used for cost. This can be seen from formula 9. The final cost function is designed as formula 10.

$$f_{SVR}(x) = w^T x + b \tag{8}$$

$$\max(0, |y_i - f_{SVR}(x)| - \varepsilon) \tag{9}$$

$$J_{SVR}(\theta) = \min_{w,b} \frac{1}{2}||w||^2 + \frac{1}{m} \sum_{i=1}^{m} \max(0, |y_i - f_{SVR}(x_i)| - \varepsilon) \tag{10}$$

In formula 10, if point cloud data is within region from upper fit line to lower fit line, ε makes loss function equal to 0.

3.3   Computing Movement Trajectory

The two models obtained after training need to be merged. There are two methods: predicting two movement trajectories before fusion or fusing two linear models before predicting trajectories. We choose the former way. A concise fusion way is to compute mean of two movement trajectories. We can compute steering angle in real time. As cars are equipped with GPS equipment, we can also transform trajetories lidar predicted into the GPS coordinate system for navigation. The linear fitting models need to be converted into vehicle coordinate system, that is the mounting location of VLP-16. $T(t_x, t_y, t_z)$ is a translation matrix. $R_z(\alpha)$, $R_x(\beta)$, $R_y(\gamma)$ are rotation matrices. Whole coordinate transformation process is denoted by formula 11. After simplified, formula 11 is written as formula 12 . The distance parameters used in translation transformation and angle parameters used in rotation transformation can be measured.

$$
\begin{bmatrix} x_v \\ y_v \\ z_v \\ 1 \end{bmatrix} = \begin{bmatrix} 1 & 0 & 0 & l_x \\ 0 & 1 & 0 & l_y \\ 0 & 0 & 1 & l_z \\ 0 & 0 & 0 & 1 \end{bmatrix} \cdot \begin{bmatrix} \cos\alpha & -\sin\alpha & 0 & 0 \\ \sin\alpha & \cos\alpha & 0 & 0 \\ 0 & 0 & 1 & 0 \\ 0 & 0 & 0 & 1 \end{bmatrix} \cdot \begin{bmatrix} 1 & 0 & 0 & 0 \\ 0 & \cos\beta & -\sin\beta & 0 \\ 0 & \sin\beta & \cos\beta & 0 \\ 0 & 0 & 0 & 1 \end{bmatrix} \cdot \begin{bmatrix} \cos\gamma & 0 & \sin\gamma & 0 \\ 0 & 1 & 0 & 0 \\ -\sin\gamma & 0 & \cos\gamma & 0 \\ 0 & 0 & 0 & 1 \end{bmatrix} \cdot \begin{bmatrix} x \\ y \\ z \\ 1 \end{bmatrix}
\tag{11}
$$

$$
Point_v = T(t_x, t_y, t_z) \cdot R_z(\alpha) \cdot R_x(\beta) \cdot R_y(\gamma) \cdot Point
\tag{12}
$$

The obtained trajectory points need to be processed by formula 13 to get vehicle trajectory set, which is denoted by $T = \{(x_1, f(x_1)'), (x_2, f(x_2)'), (x_3, f(x_3)'), ..., (x_n, f(x_n)')\}$.

$$
f(x)' = f(x)/x.
\tag{13}
$$

Then, we use vehicle trajectory set to compute steering angle. [18] shows a lateral control method, and our work is inspired by it. As shown in following formulas, we makes some changes based on actual situation. Firstly, we respectively compute average Deflection and average Deviation in formula 14. As shown in formula 15, the steering angle can be computed through 4 parameters. $ADef$ is an average Deflection. $ADev$ is an average Deviation. $Kang$ and $Kpos$ are empirical control values which both could be adjusted according to feedback.

$$
ADef = \arctan\left(\frac{(\sum_{i=1}^{m} x_i)/m}{(\sum_{i=1}^{m} y_i)/m} \right) \times 180/\pi, ADev = \frac{\sum_{i=1}^{m} x_i}{m}
\tag{14}
$$

$$
steer = (Kang \times ADef + Kpos \times ADev) \times 2
\tag{15}
$$

This part involves complex vehicle dynamics and control knowledge. In order to ensure safety of experiment, we add some thresholds on speed and steering to ensure that vehicles would not occur some violent driving behavior.

4   Experiments and Results

We evaluate LNA in different vehicles with different lidars. There are three lidars: VLP-16, HDL-32 and HDL-64. They provide different number of points. In this paper, for the typical feature of HDL-32, it is used to introduce the experiments. Previously obtained steering angle can be sent to control node. The control node directly driving an vehicle. Experiments are conducted in an Ubuntu 14.04 + ROS Indigo + tensorlfow environment. In this section, we show fitting effects of different regression methods. The fitting results directly determine final navigation effects.

4.1   Data Acquisition and Correction

To get more reliable data, lidar mounting location should be accurated. Lidars placement structures are shown in Fig. 3. As Velodyne 16-line lidar (VLP16) laser wires are few, which result in sparse point cloud. As shown in Fig. 3(a), we choose to mount VLP16 in a front position. It has been proved that this placement can better collect road information. The HDL32 lidar and HDL64 lidar are mounted on top of cars respectively. As shown in Fig. 4, we can see point cloud collecting effects of three lidars. After preprocessing, we use Linear Regression and Support Vector Regression to fit point cloud respectively.

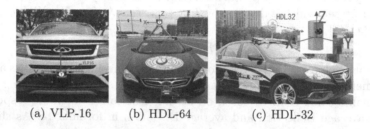

(a) VLP-16   (b) HDL-64   (c) HDL-32

Fig. 3. Lidar placement

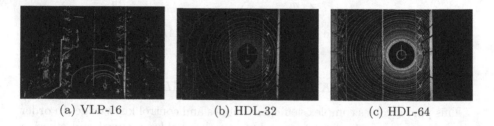

(a) VLP-16   (b) HDL-32   (c) HDL-64

Fig. 4. Point cloud in different lidars

4.2   Linear Regression Results

The parameter w is initialized in a random normal distribution ($mean = -0.2, stddev = 0.01$) and parameter b is initialized as 0. The gradient descent optimizer parameter is set to 0.001.

Road Shoulder Fitting Effects. Figure 5 shows different fitting effects in different iteration times. As shown in Fig. 5(b), line fits data well after 20 iterations. Also, it can be demonstrated in Fig. 5(c) that loss is approximate to zero already at 20th iter or even earlier.

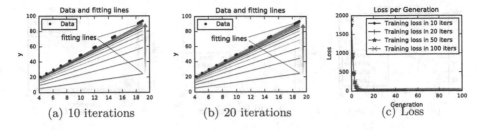

Fig. 5. Road shoulder fitting effects in different training times.

Isolation Belt Fitting Effects. As can be seen from Fig. 6, data is slower to be fitted. After 20 iterations, loss becomes very small. As the number of point cloud is large, which results in a slow convergence. But, it still could reach a good fitting result within 30 iterations. Figure 6(b) shows a fitting effect after 50 iterations. Combining Fig. 6(b) and (c), we can see that, after 30 rather than 50 iterations, model reaches a good fitting effect. All of these features prove our method has better characteristics in the aspects of validity and real-time.

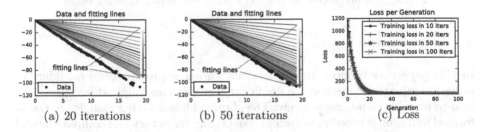

Fig. 6. Isolation belt fitting effects in different training times.

4.3   Support Vector Regression Results

In SVR experiment, we set $\epsilon = 1.0$, $batchsize = 5$ and gradient descent optimizer is set as 0.09. SVR algorithm fitting effects for road shoulders and isolation belt are following.

Road Shoulder Fitting Effects. As shown in Fig. 7, we can see that SVR easily fit data within 20 iterations. After 10 iterations, the model fits the data well and the loss value is very small. After 20 iterations, loss nears to 0.

Isolation Belt Fitting Effects. As shown in Fig. 8, we see that SVR is similar to Linear Regression. SVR is under fitting within 10 iterations. SVR fitting line presents a good fitting effect after 20 iterations. After 50 and 100 iterations, effects are further improved. Before that, loss is approximately reach to zero after 20 iterations.

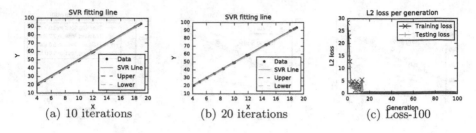

(a) 10 iterations   (b) 20 iterations   (c) Loss-100

Fig. 7. Support Vector Regression Effects in different training times.

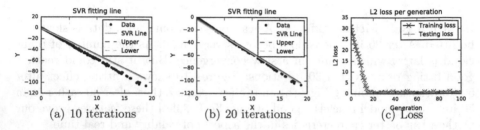

(a) 10 iterations   (b) 20 iterations   (c) Loss

Fig. 8. Support Vector Regression Effects in different training times.

5   Conclusion

In this paper, we propose an effective navigation approach based on lidar. In order to evaluate the method, we use linear regression and support vector regression to fit point cloud, respectively. The obtained linear fitting models are transformed into vehicle coordinate system. We predict trajectory and compute lateral control data to navigate self-driving cars. LNA can fit well of road outlines within 20 iterations. Loss functions of two linear fitting methods converge to 0 quickly. Each calculation cycle is less than 0.3 seconds. LNA does have advanteges of fast convergence and high approximation accuracy. Experiments of different cars with different lidars in general roads get good navigation effects. This real-time navigation method reaches similar effects of RTK locally. In future work, we will exploit other linear regression methods to further improve processing speed and accuracy.

Acknowledgment. This work was supported by the National Natural Science Foundation of China (61572060, 61772060, 61472024, U1433203), CERNET Innovation Project (NGII 20151004, NGII20160316) and the 2016 Technology Project (No. 3) of Fengtai District, Beijing, China (Grant No. KSF201601).

References

1. Sukkarieh, S., Nebot, E.M., Durrant-Whyte, H.F.: A high integrity imu/gps navigation loop for autonomous land vehicle applications. IEEE Trans. Robot. Autom. **15**(3), 572–578 (1999)
2. Bojarski, M. et al.: End to end learning for self-driving cars (2016)
3. Kenue, S.K.: Lanelok: an algorithm for extending the lane sensing operating range to 100-feet. In: Fibers 1991, MA, Boston, pp. 222–233 (1990)
4. Redmill, K.A., Upadhya, S., Krishnamurthy, A., Ozguner, U.: A lane tracking system for intelligent vehicle applications. In: Intelligent Transportation Systems, Proceedings, pp. 273–279 (2001)
5. Cadena, C., Carlone, L., Carrillo, H., Latif, Y., Scaramuzza, D., Neira, J., Reid, I., Leonard, J.J.: Past, present, and future of simultaneous localization and mapping: toward the robust-perception age. IEEE Trans. Robot. **32**(6), 1309–1332 (2016)
6. Engel, J., Schöps, T., Cremers, D.: LSD-SLAM: large-scale direct monocular SLAM. In: Fleet, D., Pajdla, T., Schiele, B., Tuytelaars, T. (eds.) ECCV 2014. LNCS, vol. 8690, pp. 834–849. Springer, Cham (2014). https://doi.org/10.1007/978-3-319-10605-2_54
7. Zhang, J., Singh, S.: LOAM: LiDAR odometry and mapping in real-time (2014)
8. Moosmann, F., Stiller, C.: Velodyne SLAM. In: Intelligent Vehicles Symposium, pp. 393–398 (2011)
9. Wijesoma, W.S., Kodagoda, K.R.S., Balasuriya, A.P.: Road-boundary detection and tracking using ladar sensing. IEEE Trans. Robot. Autom. **20**(3), 456–464 (2004)
10. Peterson, K., Ziglar, J., Rybski, P.E.: Fast feature detection and stochastic parameter estimation of road shape using multiple LiDAR. In: IEEE/RSJ International Conference on Intelligent Robots and Systems, pp. 612–619 (2008)
11. Yuan, X., Zhao, C.X., Zhang, H.F.: Road detection and corner extraction using high definition LiDAR. Inf. Technol. J. **9**(5), 1022–1030 (2010)
12. Bourbakis, N., Andel, R.: Fusing laser and image data for 3D perceived space representations. In: IEEE International Conference on TOOLS with Artificial Intelligence, Proceedings, pp. 50–58 (1997)
13. Castellanos, J.A., Neira, J., Tardos, J.D.: Multisensor fusion for simultaneous localization and map building. IEEE Trans. Robot. Autom. **17**(6), 908–914 (2001)
14. Hong, T.H., Chang, T., Rasmussen, C., Shneier, M.: Feature detection and tracking for mobile robots using a combination of ladar and color images. In: IEEE International Conference on Robotics and Automation, Proceedings, ICRA 2002, vol. 4, pp. 4340–4345 (2002)
15. Explained, P.M.D.: Introduction to linear regression analysis. Am. Stat. **57**(1), 67–67 (2003)
16. Kutner, M.H., Nachtsheim, C.J., Neter, J.: Applied Linear Regression Models, 5th ed. Technometrics, vol. 26, no. 4 (2004)
17. Awad, M., Khanna, R.: Support vector regression. Neural Inf. Process. Lett. Rev. **11**(10), 203–224 (2007)
18. Thrun, S., et al.: The Robot That Won the DARPA Grand Challenge (2006)

Author Index

Printed in the United States
By Bookmasters